AIRPORT AND AVIATION SECURITY

U.S. Policy and Strategy in the Age of Global Terrorism

AIRPORT AND AVIATION SECURITY

U.S. Policy and Strategy in the
Age of Global Terrorism

Bartholomew Elias

CRC Press
Taylor & Francis Group
Boca Raton   London   New York

CRC Press is an imprint of the
Taylor & Francis Group, an **informa** business

Auerbach Publications
Taylor & Francis Group
6000 Broken Sound Parkway NW, Suite 300
Boca Raton, FL 33487-2742

© 2010 by Taylor and Francis Group, LLC
Auerbach Publications is an imprint of Taylor & Francis Group, an Informa business

Printed in the United States of America on acid-free paper
10 9 8 7 6 5 4 3 2 1

International Standard Book Number: 978-1-4200-7029-3 (Hardback)

Library of Congress Cataloging-in-Publication Data

Elias, Bartholomew.
    Airport and aviation security : U.S. policy and strategy in the age of global terrorism / author, Bartholomew Elias.
        p. cm.
    "A CRC title."
    Includes bibliographical references and index.
    ISBN 978-1-4200-7029-3 (hardcover : alk. paper)
    1. Airports--Security measures--United States. 2. Terrorism--United States--Prevention. 3. National security--Government policy--United States. I. Title.

TL725.3.S44.E45 2010
363.28′760973--dc22
                                                                                          2009029825

Visit the Taylor & Francis Web site at
http://www.taylorandfrancis.com

and the Auerbach Web site at
http://www.auerbach-publications.com

This book is dedicated to
the victims of aviation terrorism
and their families

Contents

Preface xvii
Acknowledgments xxiii
Author xxv
Author's Disclaimer xxvii

Chapter 1   Pre-9/11 Threats to Aviation Security and the U.S. Policy Response 1

The Significance of Aviation Terrorism 1
The Late 1960s and Early 1970s: The Dawn of the Age
    of Global Terrorism 2
    Hijackings Tied to Middle Eastern Terrorist Organizations 3
    The Dawson's Field Hijackings 4
    The U.S. Response to Overseas Terrorist Hijackings 4
    The International Response to Terrorist Hijackings 5
    The Period of Hijacking Contagion 6
    Escalating Violence Prompts FAA Action 8
    The Debate over Passenger Screening 10
    The Debate over Aviation Security Roles and Responsibilities 12
The Looming Menace of Aircraft Bombings 15
The 1980s: The Shifting Threat 18
    The TWA Flight 847 Hijacking 21
    Escalating Violence and Terrorist Animosity toward
        the United States 22
    Aerial Suicides and Airplanes as Missiles 22
    U.S. Initiatives to Improve International Aviation Security 23
    The Escalating Threat of Aircraft Bombings 24
    The Bombing of Pan Am Flight 103 25
    The President's Commission on Aviation Security and Terrorism 26
    The Aviation Security Improvements Act of 1990 (P.L. 101-604) 29
The 1990s: The Failure to Imagine and Adequately Prepare 30
    The Gore Commission Recommendations Regarding
        Aviation Security 32
    Aviation Security Provisions in the FAA Reauthorization Act
        of 1996 (P. L. 104-264) 34
    Impact of the Gore Commission on Aviation Security 35
    Lingering Concerns and Persisting Vulnerabilities 35
    The Airport Security and Improvement Act of 2000
        (P.L. 106-528) 37
    Hijackings as a Forgotten Threat 37
References 38

Chapter 2   The 9/11 Attacks and the Ensuing Policy Debate   41

Precursors to 9/11   42
Bojinka Plot   42
Rising Threat of Al Qaeda   43
Buildup to 9/11   45
Preattack Phase: Terrorists in our Midst   48
9/11 Attacks   49
Tactical Response on September 11, 2001   50
DOT Rapid Response Teams   51
   Conclusions and Recommendations of the Airport Security
     Rapid Response Team   52
   Conclusions and Recommendations of the Aircraft Security
     Rapid Response Team   53
Congressional Response to the 9/11 Attacks   55
   Expanding the Federal Role in Aviation Security Operations   56
   Post-9/11 Debate over Federalizing Passenger Screening   57
Aviation and Transportation Security Act (ATSA, P.L. 107-71)   59
Homeland Security Act of 2002 (P.L. 107-296)   62
Vision 100: The Century of Aviation Reauthorization Act (P.L. 108-176)   64
References   66

Chapter 3   Policy Refinement in Response to the Evolving Terrorist Threat   69

The 9/11 Commission and Its Impact on Aviation Security Policy   69
Aviation Security-Related Recommendations of the 9/11 Commission   70
   Enhancing Passenger Prescreening   70
   Improving Measures to Detect Explosives on Passengers   71
   Addressing Human Factor Considerations at Screening Checkpoints   72
   Expediting Deployment of In-Line Baggage Screening Systems   73
   Intensifying Efforts to Identify, Screen, and Track Cargo   73
   Deploying Hardened Cargo Containers   74
   Risk-Based Prioritization as the Basis for Transportation
     Security Policy   74
National Intelligence Reform and Terrorism Prevention Act
   of 2004 (P.L. 108-458)   75
TSA Regulations to Strengthen Air Cargo and the Push for
   100% Cargo Screening   77
Lingering Congressional Policy Concerns   78
Implementing Recommendations of the 9/11 Commission Act
   of 2007 (P.L. 110-53)   80
Continuing Terrorist Threat   82
   Post-9/11 Anthrax Attacks   83
   Attempted Shoe Bombing of American Airlines Flight 63   83
   Al Qaeda's Post-9/11 Ambitions   84
Evolving Terror Threat   86
   The UK Airplanes Bombing Plot   87
Homegrown Terrorist Threats in the United States   88
An Asymmetric Threat Intent on Diminishing Our Resolve   90
Cost of Protecting Aviation   91
References   96

Chapter 4   The U.S. Strategy for Combatting Terror Threats
to the Aviation Domain 99

Pre-9/11 Approaches to Aviation Security 100
Post-9/11 Actions Addressing Aviation Security Policy and Strategy 101
The National Aviation Security Policy 102
Security Threats to Aviation 104
    Aircraft-Related Threats 104
    Threats to Aviation Infrastructure 105
    Threats Involving Exploitation of Air Cargo 106
The Risk-Based Framework 106
Strategic Objectives 109
Strategic Actions 110
    Maximizing Domain Awareness 110
    Deploying Layered Security 110
    Promoting a Safe, Efficient, and Secure Aviation System 112
    Fostering International Cooperation 112
    Assuring Continuity of Operations 112
Strategic Roles and Responsibilities 113
Aviation Mode-Specific Plans 115
    Aviation Transportation System Security Plan 116
        Guiding Principles 116
        Goals and Requirements 117
    The Air Domain Surveillance and Intelligence Integration Plan 120
        Guiding Principles 120
        Considerations and Assumptions 120
    The International Outreach and International Aviation
        Threat Reduction Plans 123
    The Aviation Operational Threat Response Plan 123
        Guiding Principles 124
        Considerations and Assumptions 124
        Concept of Operations 125
    The Domestic Outreach Plan 126
Issues for Consideration 127
    The Validity of Underlying Risk Assumptions 127
    Consideration of System Sustainability 128
    A Proactive or a Reactive Approach? 129
    Consideration of Whether the Strategy Is Comprehensive and Robust 129
    Alignment of Strategic Objectives with Budgetary Planning
        and Resource Allocation Processes 130
References 131

Chapter 5   Evaluating and Managing Security Risks 133

Risk Assessment Methods 133
Using the Risk-Based Framework to Determine a Risk Valuation
    and Assess Costs and Benefits 135
Approaches for Developing Complex Models of Risk in the
    Aviation Security Domain 139
Mitigating Aviation Security Risk 141
The Multilayered Approach to Aviation Security 142

Evaluating the Effectiveness of Mitigation Measures and Security Systems 146
    Applying SDT to Evaluating the Performance of
        Aviation Security Systems 147
    Detection Criteria and System Errors 149
    System Sensitivity 150
Assessing the Impact of Security Measures on Air Transportation
    System Efficiency 153
Mitigating the Consequences of an Attack 155
    Adaptive Systems Approaches to Aviation Security 156
References 158

Chapter 6 Exploiting Intelligence and Counterterrorism Information 159

An Overview of Intelligence Gathering and Analysis 159
Intelligence Reforms in Response to the Global Terror Threat 161
TSA's Role in Transportation Security Intelligence 163
Tracking Terrorist Travel in the Aviation Mode 164
Airline Passenger Prescreening and Terrorist Watch Lists 166
    Pre-9/11 Passenger Prescreening Initiatives 167
    Computer-Assisted Passenger Prescreening System 167
    "No-Fly" and "Automatic Selectee" Lists 169
    The CAPPS II Development Effort 171
    Secure Flight System Development 172
    Operational Implementation of Secure Flight Terrorist
        Watch List Checks 174
    Prescreening of International Passengers 175
    Risk-Based Targeting of International Air Travelers and Shipments 176
    Immigration Controls at International Airports of Entry 177
    Prescreening of Aviation Workers and General Aviation Passengers 179
Policy Issues Related to Passenger Prescreening and Terrorist
    Watch List Checks 180
    Accuracy and Reliability of Underlying Terrorist Databases 180
    False Positive Matches and Potential Failures to Detect
        Terrorist Threats 181
    Passenger Redress Procedures 183
Future Directions for Exploiting Intelligence Information
    to Strengthen Aviation Security 185
Using Intelligence Information to Identify Terrorist Networks 185
Data Fusion in the Aviation Environment 186
    Data Logic and Current Data Fusion Practices 187
    Parametric Data Fusion Networks 188
    Ongoing Initiatives for Improving Data Fusion Practices 189
References 190

Chapter 7 Passenger and Baggage Screening 193

Policy Considerations for Aviation Security Screening 193
    Airline Passenger Traffic Growth 194
    Screening Efficiency and Passenger Wait Times 194
    Space Constraints at Airports 194
    Improving Explosives Detection at Passenger Checkpoints 195

      In-Line EDS Integration 196
      Strategic Planning for Addressing Technology and
          Human Factors Needs 196
      Projected Costs and Funding Issues 196
  Checkpoint Screening Human Performance 197
  Potential Impacts of Respecting Privacy on Screening Performance 198
  Covert Testing 199
  Threat Image Projection 202
  X-Ray Imagery and Carry-On Baggage Screening Performance 203
  Passenger Checkpoint Efficiency 204
      Passenger Wait Times 204
      Potential Security Risks of Checkpoint Inefficiencies 206
      Queuing Practices and Procedures 206
      The Tailored Self-Select Screening Lane Initiative 207
      The RT Program 207
      Options for Further Streamlining Passenger Checkpoint Procedures 209
      Checkpoint Procedures for Liquids 210
      Passenger Education and Informational Materials 211
  The Evolution of Checkpoint Design 211
  Next Generation Checkpoint Technologies 213
      ETD Technologies 215
          ETD Machines 215
          Bottle and Liquid Explosives Scanners 215
          Walk-Through ETD Portals 216
      WBI Technologies 216
          X-Ray Backscatter Imaging Systems 217
          Millimeter Wave Imaging Systems 218
      AT X-Ray Equipment 218
      Other Candidate Technologies and Applications for Aviation
          Security Screening 218
  Screening Airport Workers 219
  Screening and Vetting of Airline Crews 221
  Checked Baggage Screening 222
  Proposed Strategy for Baggage Screening Optimization 223
  Options for Reducing Baggage 224
  Firearms in Checked Baggage 225
  Screener Workforce Issues 226
      Broadening Roles for TSOs 226
  Screener Retention 227
      Screener Hiring Standards 228
      TSA Staffing Needs 229
      Salaries, Benefits, and Career Advancement Initiatives 230
      Reducing Workplace Injuries 230
      Whistleblower Protections 231
  References 232

Chapter 8   Airline In-Flight Security Measures 235

  Hardened Cockpit Doors 236
  Secondary Flight Deck Barriers 237
  Flight Deck Access Procedures 238

Video Surveillance of the Airliner Cabin and Improved
        Cabin–Cockpit Communications 239
Uninterruptable Aircraft Transponders 239
Future Systems for Aircraft Surveillance 240
The Federal Air Marshal Service 241
        Post-9/11 Air Marshal Hiring and Training 241
        Controversies Regarding Air Marshal Force Size and Flight Coverage 242
        Air Marshal Operational and Procedural Issues 245
Armed Pilots and Crew Security Training 246
        Legislative Background 247
        FFDO Program Implementation Issues 248
        Issues Regarding Operational Procedures for Armed Pilots 252
        Special Considerations for FFDOs 254
Consideration of Less-Than-Lethal Weapons for In-Flight Security 254
Security Training for Airline Crews 254
Armed Law Enforcement on Airliners 255
        Historical Context 255
        Federal, State, and Local LEOs Flying Armed 256
        Identity Verification Procedures for Armed LEOs 259
Handling Disruptive Passengers and Other In-Flight Security Incidents 259
Possible Terrorist Probing Incidents 261
Responding to In-Flight Security Threats 263
Mitigating the In-Flight Explosives Threat and Improving
        Aircraft Survivability 265
In-Flight Chemical and Biological Threats 265
References 267

Chapter 9   Commercial Airport Access Controls and Perimeter Security 271

Security Risk in the Airport Environment 271
Commercial Airport Security Program Concepts 274
Airport Security Technology Investment 274
Airport Security Programs 275
Airport Security Terminology 277
        Security Designations within the Passenger Terminal 277
        Security Identification Display Areas 279
        Security of Designated GA Areas 280
        Security of Military Facilities at Commercial Passenger Airports 281
        Security of the AOA 281
        The Airport Perimeter 281
        Airport Contractor and Vendor Security Programs 282
Airport Security Risk Categories 282
Evaluating Airport Compliance with Security Requirements 283
Airport Physical Security and Security Technologies 284
Airport Perimeter Security and Access Control Measures 284
Surveillance Technologies 285
        Infrared Sensors and Thermal Imaging Cameras 286
        Computer Vision Technologies 286
        Ground Surveillance Radar 286
        Ground Vehicle Tracking 286
        Sensor Integration 287

Patrolling the Airfield and the Airport Perimeter 287
Security Awareness Training 288
Law Enforcement Support 288
   Explosives Detection Canine Teams 289
   Law Enforcement Reimbursable Agreements 289
Access Control Measures 290
Background Check Requirements 290
   Transportation Security Clearinghouse 292
   Security Threat Assessments 294
   Regulations Pertaining to Airport Badges and
      Identification Systems 294
Biometric Technologies for Credentialing and Access Controls 295
Planning, Design, and Construction Guidelines for Commercial
   Airport Security 296
   Landside Security Considerations 297
   Crime Prevention Strategies 298
   Countermeasures for Chemical and Biological Threats 298
   Detecting Radiological and Nuclear Threats in
      the Airport Environment 299
Critical Incident Management and Response 299
References 300

Chapter 10   Mitigating the Threat of Shoulder-Fired Missiles and Other
Standoff Weapons 303

The Proliferation of Shoulder-Fired Weapons and the Terrorist
   Threat They Pose 305
   IR-Guided MANPADS 307
   CLOS MANPADS 308
   Laser Beam Rider MANPADS 308
   Terrorist Acquisition and Possession of MANPADS 309
   Other Standoff Weapons 310
The Vulnerability of Commercial Airliners 310
   The Vulnerability of Typical Commercial Flight Operations 311
   The Survivability of Civilian Transport Aircraft 312
   Civilian Aviation Encounters with Shoulder-Fired Missiles 313
Assessing the Potential Consequences of a Standoff Attack 316
U.S. Policy and Strategic Approaches 318
   Nonproliferation and Weapons Reduction Initiatives 319
   Counterterrorism Strategies and Tactics 321
   Airport Security Measures 321
   Flight Operational Procedures 322
   Aircraft-Based Protections and Countermeasures 324
      Homeland Security Counter-MANPADS Systems
         Development and Testing 326
      Policy Considerations for Aircraft-Based Countermeasures
         Deployment 327
   Unmanned Escorts Providing IR-Countermeasure Protection 328
Ground-Based Countermeasures 329
References 330

Chapter 11 Air Cargo Security 333

    Security Risks Posed by Air Cargo 333
        Explosives and Incendiary Devices 335
        Hazardous Materials 336
        Cargo Crime 337
        Aircraft Hijacking and Sabotage 338
        Airmail Consignments 338
    Screening versus Physical Inspection of Cargo Shipments 339
    Security in the All-Cargo Environment 341
        Arming All-Cargo Pilots 342
        Cargo Inspection Methods and Technologies 343
        Known Shipper Approach 344
    Physical Screening and Inspection 346
    Canine Explosives Detection Teams 348
    Cargo Screening Technology 348
        X-Ray Screening 349
        Explosive Detection Systems 350
        Chemical Trace Detection Systems 350
        Neutron Beam Technologies 351
        Millimeter Wave Imaging Systems 351
    Cost of Cargo Screening and Inspection 352
        Potential Impacts on Passenger Airlines and Freight Forwarders 352
        Potential Impacts on Manufacturers and Other Shippers 353
        Hardened Blast-Resistant Cargo Containers 353
    Technologies for Effectively Securing the Supply Chain 355
        Tamper-Evident and Tamper-Resistant Seals 355
        Access Control and Biometric Screening Technology 356
    Physical Security of Air Cargo Facilities 356
    Inspection and Oversight of Air Cargo Facilities 357
    Security Training for Air Cargo Personnel 357
    Increased Control over Access to Aircraft and Cargo Facilities 357
    References 358

Chapter 12 Security for GA Operations and Airports 361

    What Is GA? 362
        GA Flight Operations 362
        GA Aircraft 363
        GA Airports 364
    The Economic Impact of GA 365
    The Security Challenge Posed by GA 365
    Security Vulnerabilities 366
    The Terrorist Threat 368
    Potential Consequences of an Attack Using GA Aircraft 369
        Suicide Attacks and Conventional Explosives 369
        Chemical, Biological, Radiological, and Nuclear Threats 370
        Nuclear Power Facilities as Potential Targets 371
        The Risk Picture for GA Aircraft 372

Options for Mitigating GA Security Risks 372
  Security Risk Assessments 373
  Surveillance and Monitoring 374
  The Airport Watch Program 375
  Applying Behavioral Pattern Recognition Techniques
    in the GA Environment 376
Airport Access Controls 377
Background Checks and Vetting 378
  Vetting of Individuals Seeking Flight Training 379
  Checking FAA Records on Pilots and Others against Criminal
    and Terrorist Databases 379
  Background Check Requirements for Charter Operators 380
  Vetting of Charter and Aircraft Lease Customers 380
  Tracking Aircraft Sales 380
Physical Security Measures for Airports 381
Physical Security Measures for Aircraft 381
Securing Agricultural Aviation Operations 382
Flight School Security 382
Security Practices for Business and Charter Aviation 383
  The TSA Access Certificate Program 383
  Security Measures for Charter Operations 383
  Security Measures for Large Private and Corporate Aircraft 384
Vetting and Tracking GA Flights at the U.S. Borders 385
Airspace Restrictions 386
Airspace Restrictions around Washington, DC 386
  The Flight Restricted Zone 386
  GA Access to DCA 387
  The Maryland Three Airports 387
  The Washington, DC, ADIZ 387
Security-Related Flight Restrictions throughout the United States 389
Airspace Restrictions for Presidential Visits 390
Policy Issues Regarding Airspace Restrictions 390
  Effective Surveillance and Monitoring of Restricted Airspace 391
  Curbing Airspace Violations 391
  Airspace Protection and Homeland Defense 392
References 393

Index 397

Preface

On that fateful day in September, terrorist hijackers targeted four airliners. Following the hijackings, the president and the U.S. Congress faced an immediate challenge to restore public confidence in the security of passenger airline travel. The U.S. government responded swiftly by deploying specially trained armed federal officers on airliners, stepping up security measures at airports, accelerating efforts to develop new security measures for detecting weapons and explosives, working with international partners to combat the menace of air piracy, and imposing sanctions on nations that harbored terrorist hijackers or otherwise interfered with efforts to bring them to justice. Extremists had brought their global campaign of terrorism to the forefront and aviation was a prime target. However, the United States appeared determined to implement effective security measures to protect civil aircraft from these terrorist threats.

Over the years, this core foundation of aviation security evolved in various aspects to address shifting threats, particularly threats posed by explosives. However, many would argue that, in general, U.S. aviation security policy became complacent in its perception and response to the lingering terrorist threat and, in particular, failed to imagine and comprehend the extent to which the threat of terrorist hijackings persisted. Then, 31 years and five days after that fateful day in September 1970, the unthinkable happened. Islamic extremists commandeered four aircraft over the skies of the United States. Unlike the Dawson's Field hijackings of September 6, 1970, which I wrote of above that ended with the release of all hostages taken captive, on September 11, 2001, there were no negotiations with the hijackers. There was no opportunity to gain the release of hostages. The terrorists' mission on September 11, 2001, was to use those hijacked aircraft as weapons to inflict mass civilian casualties. Thousands lost their lives in those attacks. September 11, 2001, was a defining moment in the history of the United States. For many, the collective national tragedy that unfolded that day was also, sadly, a personal tragedy. As noted in the 9/11 Commission's final report, "September 11, 2001, was a day of unprecedented shock and suffering in the history of the United States. The nation was unprepared."[1]

In the aftermath of the terrorist attacks of September 11, 2001, existing policies and strategies for aviation security in the United States were put in the spotlight, focusing on why the United States was so unprepared to defend against such an attack and how to strengthen aviation and homeland security to prevent future terrorist attacks. In many regards, however, the aviation security issues faced by the Bush administration and Congress in 2001 were similar to those faced by the Nixon administration and Congress in the early 1970s in the aftermath of the Dawson's Field hijackings and the scourge of domestic hijacking events that plagued that era. However, the brutality of the 9/11 attacks clearly raised the stakes. The stakes were also raised by the considerable growth in importance of the airline and air cargo industries in the U.S. economy since the early 1970s.

In the days following the 9/11 attacks, the U.S. government was faced with the enormous challenge of restoring the public confidence in the security of air travel. Failure was not an option. For to fail could bring ruin to the airline, air cargo, and aerospace industries in the United States and have lasting effects on the broader economy. Failure could also leave the door open to future terrorist attacks. But there was also a different kind of possible failure. Pursuing policies that could unduly impede the freedom of passenger movement by air or the flow of goods and commerce by air could threaten many of the freedoms and conveniences that have become such an integral part of life in America. Similarly, security measures that may unduly impose upon individual rights to privacy provided for under the U.S. Constitution could also be viewed by many as certain paths to failure by compromising our core values of liberty and freedom.

Frederick the Great offered his generals the following advice, which is particularly apropos to the challenges faced by the United States in protecting the aviation system against terrorist threats: "Little minds try to defend everything at once, but sensible people look at the main point only; they parry the worst blows and stand a little hurt if thereby they avoid a greater one. If you try to hold everything, you hold nothing."[2] Over the years, this has frequently been expressed through the more familiar saying: "To defend everything is to defend nothing." Similarly, former Secretary of Homeland Security Michael Chertoff, discussing his views on U.S. policy for homeland security, asserted that "[i]n a free and open society, we simply cannot protect every person against every risk at every moment in every place. There is no perfect security."[3]

Secretary Chertoff surmised that "... [i]n order to protect our country and defend our freedoms, we must continue to focus resources on the areas that pose the greatest risk ..."[4] This widely held view has given rise to a multilayered risk-based approach to protecting aviation from terrorist threats. Risk is a construct based upon careful evaluation of the nature of various threats posed to the aviation system, the vulnerability of that system to these various threats, and the potential consequences or impacts if such threats are carried out in a successful attack. Accurate estimations of risk, therefore, provide a fundamental basis for establishing aviation security policies, strategies, and resource allocation.

This approach has generated considerable policy debate regarding where the risks lie and how to best defend against these various risks. On one side of the issue, some policymakers and strategists have argued for targeted screening and inspections, to focus limited resources on areas of greatest perceived risk. In contrast, others have argued for comprehensive screening and physical inspection and other elaborate security measures for all persons accessing the aviation system and all items being placed onboard aircraft, arguing that targeting methods and other means of assigning risk to persons and goods are imperfect and could be exploited by terrorists to attack aviation assets. These initiatives, however, are costly and resource intensive. There is concern that, by trying to implement elaborate defenses to protect against all possible threats, security personnel and resources will be spread thin, leaving possible gaps or holes in these security systems that could be detected and exploited by terrorists and criminals. This is exactly the type of scenario that Frederick the Great had warned his generals against.

There is also a considerable concern that elaborate security systems and extensive security regulations and requirements may impede air commerce and air travel by creating undue hassles and other barriers that may restrict free trade and commerce and travel by air, the core elements that these security measures are principally designed to defend. Further, elaborate security measures can be extremely expensive, requiring considerable investment from the government, airports, airlines, the air cargo industry, and other aviation operators. Policymakers on both sides of the debate over risk-based approaches to aviation security generally concede that an appropriate balance is needed to secure aviation in a cost-effective manner without unduly impeding air travel and air commerce. However, there are no simple solutions to finding the right balance.

What is apparent, nonetheless, is that aviation security policies and strategies cannot be static and unchanging, but rather should evolve and respond to changes in perceived threats, changes in technologies and capabilities, as well as changes in the aviation domain and its component industries. It is generally believed that the most formidable terrorist adversaries are constantly shifting their tactics in a continual game of cat and mouse in response to counterterrorism and homeland security efforts and various advances in technologies and practices that effectively reduce vulnerabilities to attack. Consequently, aviation security policies, strategies, and resources need to be designed to both evolve over time and be capable of swiftly shifting focus in response to possible rapid changes in terrorist threats.

In this book, aviation security policy and strategy are examined largely from a systems perspective, relying heavily on the concept of a risk-based, multilayered system that has come to define the essence of post-9/11 aviation security initiatives. A general understanding of these concepts is fundamental to understanding the evolving U.S. policy and strategy for aviation security. Briefly, the systems approach provides for a methodical way to examine complex systems using the tools of scientists and engineers, including various models and constructs that describe the components of the aviation security system, the interaction of these components, and the performance of these individual components and the system as a whole.

The aviation security system can be described as a system of systems in the sense that there are many smaller component systems embedded inside of larger systems that are joined together to make up the entire aviation security system. For example, a screening checkpoint can be viewed as a subsystem that is comprised of many components that themselves can be regarded as systems, such as x-ray scanners, magnetometers, as well as next generation checkpoint technologies like whole-body imagers. These component systems, along with the procedures and training to utilize this equipment, can be regarded collectively as comprising a system for checkpoint screening. Checkpoint screening systems, in combination with other systems (such as baggage screening systems, cargo screening systems, access control systems, intelligence gathering and dissemination systems, passenger watch lists, etc.) make up the web of security at each airport. The network of various airport and airline security systems and the operational control and oversight of these systems provided by the Transportation Security Administration (TSA) and other homeland security agencies, such as the Bureau of Customs and Border Protection (CBP), make up the nationwide aviation security system: a complex system of systems.

The aviation security system is multilayered or multifaceted in the sense that it does not rely on a single layer or system to defend against all threats, but applies a variety of approaches to defend against the numerous threats to aviation. A robust multilayered approach is widely regarded as an essential component of a well-engineered system that is resilient to attacks or failures. That is, by designing engineered systems to have redundant and complementary capabilities to detect and defend against system failures, errors of failures of any particular subsystem or layer are less likely to be catastrophic to the entire system. For example, while terrorist watch lists may be imperfect at detecting all individuals with hostile intent who try to access security checkpoints, screening procedures are in place to detect weapons or other dangerous items that these individuals may use to carry out their hostilities against aircraft or airports. Similarly, while checkpoint screening may not detect every dangerous weapon, behavior detection officers, teams of air marshals, armed pilots, and hardened cockpit doors have all been put it place to serve as additional layers of defense against possible attacks at airports or onboard passenger airliners. These various layers of embedded systems or elements that make up the entire aviation security system are designed to complement each other and make it highly unlikely that an individual or group could successfully carry out an attack against an aviation target. The degree to which the aviation security system that has evolved since the 9/11 terrorist attacks has met this objective of reducing the probability or likelihood of a successful terrorist attack against aviation remains a central issue in the ongoing policy debate over aviation security.

The aviation security system is a complex system of systems, but it is also critical to note that it is fundamentally and most essentially a human system. It is a system designed by humans to defend against threats posed by other humans, principally terrorists, and it is highly dependent on the performance of humans serving in various roles, such as security screeners, air marshals, security directors, intelligence analysts, armed pilots, and airline crews trained to respond to in-flight security threats. Threats must be viewed with regard to terrorist objectives and motives as well as possible terrorist tactics. In addition to the human element associated with the threat, humans performing and managing security functions contribute significantly to the vulnerabilities of the system. Understanding human performance, human error, and the various human factors and organizational aspects of the aviation security system that affect system performance is, therefore, an important consideration in establishing effective policies and strategies and a robust security system, as is understanding and insight regarding the motivations and tactics behind aviation terrorism.

Beyond the human element, understanding the complexity of the aviation security system and the policy and strategy decisions that underlie the system requires a broad, multidisciplinary approach. For example, expertise in physics, chemistry, and engineering is essential to understanding explosives threats and technologies capable of reliably detecting those threats. Reliance on computer science and database applications is necessary to understand how to integrate, fuse, and disseminate a wide array of terrorist watch list information, intelligence data, and security surveillance data in an effective manner. Detailed operations research analyses and human factors studies can help determine optimal screening checkpoint configurations to maximize the capability to detect threats and improve passenger throughput. Policy and legal analyses focusing on individual privacy and constitutional law, as well as international relations, are needed to establish aviation security policies that are accepted by the traveling public and by other countries that the United States wishes to develop and maintain lasting partnerships with to combat terrorism worldwide. What this means simply is that the evolving U.S. policy and strategy for aviation security will likely require a continuing demand for skilled labor, not only on the front lines of security screening and law enforcement but also in the fields of engineering, science, social science, public policy, and law, to address shifting security threats, emerging technical capabilities, and the ever-changing nature of the global aviation industry.

The fact that you are reading this suggests that you either may already be a part of this multidisciplinary team devoted to improving aviation security, or may be considering becoming a part of this team. My sense is that the evolving aviation security policy and strategy will have a continuing need for dedicated men and women willing to contribute their intelligence and skills to the challenge of defeating terrorist threats to aviation. The advances in aviation security policies, strategies, technologies, and human factors that have occurred since the 9/11 attacks provide an indication that these multidisciplinary efforts have arguably made the aviation system, in many regards, more secure.

While significant progress has been made to strengthen aviation security, there is clearly much more work to be done. For example, efforts to develop and manage a government-run system to check passengers against terrorist watch lists remain unfinished despite almost eight years of work to develop the system and establish sound policies for protecting passenger data and providing redress for those falsely targeted by the system. Also, despite significant efforts to screen all bags using explosives detection equipment, few major airports have fully integrated these machines with their baggage handling systems and optimized baggage throughput, an objective that is essential to keeping pace with the anticipated growth in air travel. At checkpoints, technologies to screen passengers for explosives are only now starting to be deployed, and it appears that it will still be quite some time before technologies such as whole-body imagers will routinely screen passengers to check for possible concealed explosives. While considerable policy efforts have been made to strengthen the screening of air cargo operations, the air cargo industry faces daunting challenges to balance new screening and security requirements with customer expectations for efficient, on-time delivery of freight and express packages.

What is more, clear policies and strategies for addressing the security of general aviation operations, which include a wide variety of activities ranging from corporate jets to recreational flying to crop dusting operations, have been slow to emerge. There is growing concern among some policymakers that, as other aspects of aviation and homeland security are addressed, terrorists may increasingly view general aviation aircraft as an option for attacking a city or some other high-profile target using a chemical, biological, radiological, or nuclear weapon. While many are arguing that more needs to be done to secure general aviation, policymakers and aviation security strategists face a dilemma in trying to identify and implement solutions that can effectively protect against these types of threats without unduly impeding general aviation flight activity.

Terrorism has often been described as an asymmetric threat in the sense that vast resources and investment are considered necessary to protect against the threat of attacks that can be carried out by small numbers of individuals, limited resources, and small monetary investments. Take, for example, the threat posed by shoulder-fired missiles, which can be acquired on the black market for a few thousand dollars but could potentially take down an airliner, possibly leading to widespread economic turmoil in the airline industry. The United States is considering missile protection systems for airliners similar to those used on military transport planes, but it would likely cost billions of dollars to deploy and operate these systems on all passenger planes. The policy and strategic decision making to move forward with deploying such systems must compete for budgetary resources along with a wide variety of other aviation threat reduction programs, such as systems to better detect explosives threats, and a broader array of homeland security priorities, such as the detection of nuclear weapons and radiological materials that terrorists may attempt to smuggle into the United States.

This book endeavors to provide a broad overview of U.S. policy and strategy for combatting terrorist attacks in the aviation domain by examining historical threats and the U.S. response to those threats, as well as persisting threats and vulnerabilities and how they have come to shape U.S. policy and strategy. While the book provides a fairly extensive historic background and context, and broadly discusses aviation security strategies and approaches, aviation security in the United States continues to evolve and advance at a rapid pace. Therefore details of various practices and security technologies are constantly changing. Undoubtedly, various policies and approaches discussed in this book will have changed in some aspects, some only in small details while others in much more substantial regards. Nonetheless, the details of these policies, strategies, and programs are often important to discuss in detail to provide a thorough understanding of the context in which policy and strategic decisions have been made.

Various elements impacting aviation security policy including changing threats, changing technologies, and changing political landscapes can result in both evolutionary and rapid changes in the approach to aviation security, or may sometimes contribute to a resistance to change and a favoring of the status quo. Amid the multitude of various factors influencing the general characteristics and direction of the evolving aviation security policy in the United States, there are consistent underlying themes that can be discerned. It is my objective to have readers look for and identify these themes with a critical eye toward determining those policies and strategies that have been effective, those that need further refinement, and those that raise fundamental public policy questions regarding the most appropriate way to establish and maintain security without unduly impacting air commerce, air travel, and individual privacy. As we endeavor to identify and develop aviation security policies that strike an appropriate balance for providing effective protection while maintaining an efficient flow of people and goods through the air transportation system, the memory of September 11, 2001, should serve as a constant reminder of the potentially catastrophic consequences if we fail in our resolve to protect aviation from continuing terrorist threats.

Bartholomew Elias

REFERENCES

1. National Commission on Terrorist Acts Upon the United States, *The 9/11 Commission Report*, p. xv.
2. Frederick the Great, as quoted in Peter G. Tsouras (Ed.), *The Greenhill Dictionary of Military Quotations*, Greenhill Books, London, 2000.
3. Michael Chertoff, Secretary, Department of Homeland Security, "There Is No Perfect Security," *The Wall Street Journal*, February 14, 2006, p. A22.
4. Ibid.

Acknowledgments

I am deeply grateful for the help and advice of the various reviewers who took time out of their busy schedules to provide feedback on drafts of various chapters. I am most especially thankful for the helpful reviews and suggestions provided by John Fischer, Glennon Harrison, Bob Kirk, and Mark Randol. I also wish to gratefully acknowledge two of my colleagues at CRS, Bill Krouse and Christopher Bolkcom, who have worked with me over the past several years on collaborative projects that provided important background research for two of the chapters in this book. I am also extremely grateful to my editor, Mark Listewnik of the Taylor & Francis Group, for his work in making this book a reality, and to all the editorial and technical staff at Taylor & Francis for their efforts. Last, but certainly not least, a special thanks goes to my loving wife and children for their support, patience, and encouragement.

Author

Bartholomew Elias is a specialist in aviation policy for the U.S. Congressional Research Service (CRS) in Washington, DC. The CRS is a component of the Library of Congress and a research arm of the U.S. Congress. Dr. Elias' research at CRS has examined a broad array of civil aviation policy issues including aviation security, aviation safety, air traffic operations, and technology investment for next generation air traffic and airport security systems. Dr. Elias has held a broad array of positions in the federal government related to civil and military aviation. Prior to joining CRS as a specialist in civil aviation policy, Bart served as a senior human performance investigator for the National Transportation Safety Board, where he participated in several major aircraft accident investigations, including the 1999 EgyptAir flight 990 and the 2001 American Airlines flight 587 investigations. Dr. Elias began his career with the U.S. government at the Air Force Research Laboratory at Wright-Patterson Air Force Base, Ohio, where he served as a research psychologist and conducted research on aircraft noise impacts on humans, cockpit auditory displays, human visual target acquisition, and human factors design concepts for Air Force command and control and imagery intelligence applications. He completed his undergraduate training at Franklin and Marshall College in Lancaster, Pennsylvania, and received his master's and doctoral degrees in engineering psychology from the Georgia Institute of Technology. He is an instrument-rated commercial pilot, rated in single-engine aircraft.

Author's Disclaimer

The views and opinions expressed in this book are solely those of the author and do not reflect the views of the CRS, the Library of Congress, or any other entity of the federal government. While extensive efforts have been made to verify the statements of fact presented in this book, any factual errors are to be attributed solely to the author. No position or endorsement by the CRS, the Library of Congress, or any other entity of the federal government regarding the validity of any statements of fact presented in this book is implied or should be inferred. All works of art and graphics contained in this book are original works of the author based on data and concepts from various publicly available federal government sources.

1 Pre-9/11 Threats to Aviation Security and the U.S. Policy Response

A general understanding of historical events and policy decisions over the past 40 years is essential to understanding current aviation security policy in the United States. Therefore, this book begins with an overview of the historical context for current U.S. aviation security policy going back to the late 1960s and early 1970s. This historical examination looks at the key global events impacting aviation security, primarily from a U.S. perspective, and the response of the U.S. government to these events in the years before the terrorist attacks of September 11, 2001. This chapter provides an account of how U.S. policies, strategies, and approaches to aviation security evolved over the past 40 years in the context of significant aviation security incidents and the U.S. government response to those events.

THE SIGNIFICANCE OF AVIATION TERRORISM

Historically, attacks on aviation have been proportionately far more deadly than other forms of terrorist attacks, even though attacks against aviation targets comprise a relatively small percentage of all terrorist attacks targeting U.S. citizens. To illustrate, a 2005 Massachusetts Institute of Technology (MIT) study identified 179 terrorist attacks carried out against U.S. citizens from 1968 up to but not including the terrorist attacks of September 11, 2001.[1] Although only 24 (13.4%) of these attacks were carried out against aviation targets, these attacks on aviation resulted in 294 fatalities, almost 40% of the 740 total fatalities caused by these attacks. Among the attacks against aviation, the average number of American fatalities per event was 12.2. In comparison, among the 155 attacks against nonaviation targets, the average number of American fatalities per attack across all of the other categories of targets was less than 3 per event. Next to aviation, terrorist attacks at the workplace resulted in the highest numbers of fatalities on average (6.5 fatalities per attack). However, this number was heavily influenced by inclusion of the 1995 Oklahoma City bombing (168 fatalities) and American fatalities resulting from the 1999 bombing of the U.S. Embassy in Nairobi, Kenya (12 fatalities). It should also be noted that, because this analysis only considered American fatalities and many terrorist incidents considered occurred in foreign locations, these per event fatality averages significantly understate the deadliness of these attacks. This understatement is especially large for those events involving aviation targets, as illustrated by the study's treatment of the 1985 bombing of an Air India Boeing 747 off the coast of Ireland, the deadliest terrorist attack against aviation prior to the September 11, 2001 attacks. While the attack killed all 329 on board, the study only includes the 19 U.S. citizens killed in the bombing in its tally.

Prior to the 9/11 attacks, aviation terrorism was predominantly an overseas threat with significant events geographically concentrated on international flights originating in Europe and the Middle East. Aerial hijackings and aircraft bombings in the United States were largely the work of lone individuals, or occasionally small bands of criminals, and were not tied to the global terrorist movement. By the mid-1990s, with the World Trade Center (WTC) bombing in 1993 and the Oklahoma City bombing in 1995, there was clear evidence of a growing terror threat within the homeland, both

1

from homegrown antigovernment radicals as well as from Middle Eastern jihadists. However, aviation security strategists and policymakers were slow to recognize the significance of this growing threat to the aviation domain. While the December 21, 1988, in-flight bombing of Pan Am 103, killing all on board the jumbo jet, should have been a wakeup call for U.S. policymakers and aviation security strategists, the Federal Aviation Administration (FAA) was slow to address and implement recommended policy changes and fulfill legislative mandates to improve the implementation and oversight of aviation security and deploy effective technologies to screen baggage for explosives.

The July 1996 accident involving TWA flight 800 off the coast of Long Island, initially thought to be a terrorist bombing, renewed policy interest on aviation security. Inquiry following this tragedy highlighted the FAA's failures to adequately address aviation security needs and the failures of the federal government to provide adequate funding and resources to addresses aviation security needs. This renewed interest in aviation security in the late 1990s provided additional resources and an intensified emphasis on addressing the challenge of effectively and efficiently screening for explosives concealed in checked baggage. These efforts, however, were directed at addressing a single threat: the threat of aircraft bombings. Progress on other initiatives, such as improving the oversight of passenger screening and screener training requirements, were not given any special emphasis or priority.

Domestic hijackings had been completely eradicated by the early 1990s, and the hijacking threat appeared to be minimal. Anti-hijacking measures and passenger screening requirements implemented in the early 1970s appeared to be working just fine, and on the surface there did not appear to be any pressing need for change. However, lurking below, U.S. aviation security policy and practice had left open gaping holes; holes that were easily exploited by suicidal terrorists that carried out the terrorist attacks of September 11, 2001. To understand how and why these gaping holes in the U.S. aviation security system existed, one must consider the history of that aviation security system. The history of this system begins in the early 1970s, with the U.S. policy response to terrorist hijackings in the Middle East and to increasingly violent domestic hijackings involving criminals and mentally deranged individuals.

THE LATE 1960s AND EARLY 1970s: THE DAWN OF THE AGE OF GLOBAL TERRORISM

The global terror threat to aviation can be traced to the late 1960s, and the response to this threat in 1970 marks the beginning of a systematic U.S. policy and strategy for aviation security. Although the first documented hijacking occurred in 1931, when Peruvian rebels attempted to commandeer an airmail plane to drop propaganda leaflets, hijackings were uncommon events until the late 1940s and early 1950s. With the start of the Cold War, defectors from Eastern European countries viewed hijackings as a means of escaping communist oppression. Beginning in 1947, sporadic hijackings of flights in Eastern Europe continued through the 1950s.

Hijackings became commonplace in the United States in the early 1960s amid growing tensions between the United States and Cuba. Initially, Cubans had resorted to hijacking aircraft as a means to escape the Castro regime, but by the early 1960s the flow had reversed, and airplanes in the United States were being hijacked to Cuba by Cuban rebels, radical leftist Americans, and fugitives seeking asylum in Cuba. Somewhat ironically, Raúl Castro—Fidel Castro's brother and his successor as President of Cuba in 2008—may well have planted the idea of hijacking, particularly in the minds of those hijacking Cuban aircraft to the United States. Some have described Raúl Castro as "the father of the modern crime of skyjacking" noting that "there is no doubt that [his actions] provided the seed for the modern skyjacking era."[2] In 1958, rebels led by Raúl Castro carried out hijackings within Cuba as part of an effort to cripple transportation and communications systems and disrupt the Cuban presidential election, flying two aircraft to a landing strip that had been cleared in a rebel-controlled area of northern Cuba. Amid this turmoil, the first hijacking from the United States to Cuba took place on November 1, 1958, when four Cubans aspiring to join Castro's rebel forces hijacked a flight from Miami to Havana. The Cuban-registered airplane crashed over northern Cuba, presumably while attempting to find the rebel-controlled landing strip. After Fidel Castro came to power, there were several hijackings from Cuba to the United States carried out by individuals and groups seeking to escape his oppressive regime. However, the number of these hijackings diminished considerably by the mid-1960s, after Castro deployed his military to provide security at airports and stationed armed guards on Cuban passenger aircraft.[3]

While things quieted down for a while in the mid-1960s, by the late 1960s Cuba-related hijackings intensified considerably and continued into the early 1970s. In addition to Cubans seeking to flee the Castro regime, hijackings from the United States by communist sympathizers, criminals seeking asylum, and those scheming to extort money from the government and the airlines became common occurrences. At the peak in 1969, hijackings between the United States and Cuba were occurring at a rate of more than one every two weeks. By 1973, over 100 fugitive hijackers were believed to be in Cuba.[4] The situation became so bad that the United States and Cuba, countries which otherwise had no diplomatic relations, saw a need to negotiate a bilateral treaty to combat hijackings. Cuba had otherwise not taken part in international conventions to suppress hijackings that established a universality principal regarding the crime of hijacking, meaning that no signatory country would harbor a hijacker, but would either extradite the individual to face trial in the country of jurisdiction or carry out criminal proceedings against the individual under the country's own penal system. The bilateral agreement reached between the United States and Cuba in 1973 was generally framed under this same principal, and undoubtedly, the prospect of being put on trial under the Cuban penal system was a considerable deterrent to would-be hijackers.

HIJACKINGS TIED TO MIDDLE EASTERN TERRORIST ORGANIZATIONS

By the end of the 1960s, terrorist organizations in the Middle East began to view aircraft hijackings as a means of drawing attention to their political causes or to barter for the release of their comrades. Predominantly, these events were closely tied to the terrorist movement to gain recognition of Palestine as a free and independent state, civil unrest and violence in Lebanon, and continued strife between Arabs and Israelis. On July 23, 1968, terrorists belonging to the Popular Front for the Liberation of Palestine (PFLP) hijacked an El Al Boeing 707 flight in Rome, Italy. While the flight was destined for Tel Aviv, Israel the hijackers diverted the plane to Algiers, Algeria, a safe haven for Arab terrorists and hijackers, where the hostages were held until the end of August. Following this hijacking, the Israelis made sweeping changes to their aviation security program, including intensive questioning and profiling of passengers prior to boarding, conducting physical searches of passengers and aircraft, and placing armed guards on board every flight. While hijackings of Israeli aircraft have been attempted since, this incident remains to this day the only successful hijacking of an El Al airplane, a somewhat remarkable feat given terrorist animosities toward Israel. Recognizing the continuing threat, the Israelis have devoted considerable resources to aviation security to protect their relatively small fleet of civilian airliners and small number of airports to prevent aircraft hijackings and bombings.

Effective security measures put in place by the Israelis, and ill feelings toward the United States because of its policies regarding the Middle East and its support of Israel, resulted in Middle Eastern terrorist organizations turning their attention to attacking U.S. air carrier flights operated overseas and international flights bound for the United States, particularly those with a large number of American and Israeli citizens on board. On August 29, 1969, a young Palestinian woman named Leila Khaled became the face of international terrorism when she and an accomplice from the PFLP hijacked a TWA flight from Rome, Italy to Athens, Greece with continuing service to Tel Aviv, Israel, diverting the airplane to Damascus, Syria. The hijackers blew up the nose section of the airplane, and they held two Israeli passengers for more than 40 days. TWA's routes in the Middle East were particularly vulnerable targets for terrorists in the Middle East, and this was to be the first of many acts of aviation terrorism in the region involving TWA aircraft. It was also part of a string of terrorist hijackings and bombings by the PLFP that would compel the United States to take steps to develop an initial policy and strategy for preventing terrorist acts against aviation.

THE DAWSON'S FIELD HIJACKINGS

On Sunday, September 6, 1970, coordinated terrorist hijackings of U.S.-bound flights from Europe began a three-week long ordeal that became embroiled in the Black September conflict in Jordan and set in motion a response from the Nixon Administration that would shape U.S. policy and strategy for aviation security for years to come.

On September 6, 1970, members of the PLFP, armed with pistols and hand grenades, commandeered a TWA Boeing 707 that had departed Frankfurt. Similar hijackings took place on board a Swissair DC-8 that had departed from Zurich and a Pan Am Boeing 747 flight that had originated in Brussels, following a stopover in Amsterdam. While the TWA and Swissair aircraft were flown to Dawson's Field, a remote strip in Jordan, there were concerns over landing the larger Boeing 747 at that site. The Pan Am jet was therefore flown to Beirut, Lebanon, and then on to Cairo, Egypt. Just prior to landing in Cairo, one hijacker lit the fuse of a bomb, leaving precious little time to bring the airplane to a stop and evacuate the passengers and crew. The plane exploded and burned moments after the last passengers and crew got off.[5]

That same day, hijackers also attempted to take over a fourth aircraft, an El Al Boeing 707 that had departed from Amsterdam, but they were thwarted by the actions of the crew, passengers, and an armed guard. The armed Israeli guard on board of the flight shot and killed hijacker Patrick Arguello and subdued his accomplice, notorious PFLP member and veteran hijacker Leila Khaled. The flight was diverted to London Heathrow where Khaled was held. Three days later, a BOAC flight departing Bahrain was hijacked and also brought to Dawson's Field for use in bargaining with the British government for Khaled's release. On September 11th, amid growing violence between Palestinian Fedayeen, including PFLP and Palestine Liberation Organization (PLO) members, and the Jordanian military, most of the hostages were released. The following day, September 12, all three aircraft at Dawson's Field were destroyed by the PFLP terrorists. Although the terrorists had given an ultimatum demanding the release of their comrades, the destruction of the aircraft on this day was apparently carried out more out of fear that an operation against the hijackers was imminent because the deadline they had set had not yet passed. While most of the passengers had been released at this point, the aircrafts' crews, Jewish passengers, and U.S. government and military officials remained hostages and were moved to a secret location after the aircraft were destroyed. All hostages were later released in exchange for the release of Khaled and other PFLP members held captive in Europe for prior terrorist incidents and activity.[6]

While the Dawson's Field hijacking ordeal was still unfolding, the public seemed to take little notice of a domestic incident in which a hijacker was shot and wounded by an armed Brink's security guard on a TWA flight at San Francisco Airport.[7] The relatively limited amount of press coverage devoted to this incident—compared to the headline-grabbing front page coverage of the Dawson's Field hijackings during the three-week ordeal—was not a huge surprise, as Americans had become accustomed to domestic hijackings that were happening, on average, at a rate of more than two per month. While frequent domestic hijackings throughout the late 1960s had failed to move policymakers in Washington to take steps to enhance aviation security, the response in Washington to the Dawson's Field hijackings was swift and would come to shape U.S. aviation security policy for years to come.

THE U.S. RESPONSE TO OVERSEAS TERRORIST HIJACKINGS

On September 11, 1970, while hostages remained captive aboard the aircraft parked at Dawson's Field, President Nixon unveiled a plan to combat air piracy that would lay the groundwork for the U.S. policy and strategy for aviation security. In a press briefing outlining the plan to combat hijackings, President Nixon noted that "[p]iracy is not a new challenge for the community of nations. Most countries, including the United States, found effective means of dealing with piracy on the high seas a century and a half ago. We can—and we will—deal effectively with piracy in the skies today."[8] The plan unveiled by the Nixon Administration centered on establishing a sky marshal program to place armed guards on high-risk flights, inspections and electronic screening of passengers at certain large U.S. airports and overseas stations, and tougher antipiracy laws and international extradition treaties to bring hijackers to justice and prevent countries from providing them with safe harbor.[9]

On September 21, 1970, President Nixon provided further details of his plan, appointing retired Air Force General Benjamin O. Davis, Jr. to serve in the newly created position of Director of Civil Aviation Security within the Department of Transportation (DOT) and pressing Congress to increase airline ticket taxes on domestic flights and increase head taxes of foreign flights to pay, in part, for aviation security enhancements, including the deployment of armed sky marshals and electronic screening technologies for inspecting certain passengers, particularly those traveling on international flights. The biggest cost driver was a plan to deploy 2500 sky marshals on international flights at an initial cost of $28 million for the hiring, training, and initial deployment and $50 million per year thereafter to maintain the force. The airline industry had estimated that it would require a force of 4000 guards to protect all international flights flown by U.S. carriers, so the plan called for strategically placing sky marshals on high-risk flights. A small force of 100 guards was immediately deployed on Pan Am and TWA international flights on routes considered to be high risk. Deployment of additional armed sky marshals, however, would have to await additional funding authority from Congress.

The tax increases to pay for the sky marshals and other aviation security enhancements were not an easy sell. While there was widespread support for enhancing aviation security, domestic ticket taxes had just been raised from 5% to 8% and a new $3 head tax had been established for international flights in July 1970 as part of a trust fund revenue package to pay for expansion of the nation's airports and airways. Nonetheless, Congress swiftly responded with a temporary funding package that went along with the President's request, but set a cutoff date of June 30, 1972.[10] By the late fall of 1970, recruits for the new U.S. Customs Air Security Officers Program, commonly known as the Sky Marshal Program, were completing their initial training at Fort Belvoir, Virginia, and preparing for deployment on high-risk international flights to thwart future hijacking attempts. In all, 1784 recruits completed the training and made up the initial cadre of sky marshals deployed in 1970.[11] While this force was somewhat less than 2500 that President Nixon originally sought, it was still a sizable force. Although the number of air marshals protecting airlines today has not been publicly disclosed, the coverage of flights by the sky marshals during the early 1970s is probably very close to the coverage today, given that there were far fewer commercial passenger flights back then.

Sky marshals made up the primary line of defense to protect against international hijackings of U.S. air carrier flights overseas. Following their deployment, there was a considerable reduction in international hijackings, although it is impossible to determine whether the sky marshals were effective deterrents or to what degree other factors contributed to this trend. It has been noted that the PLFP largely abandoned the use of hijackings tactics as a means to achieve their political objective soon after the Dawson's Field hijackings, although it is difficult to say to what extent the deterrence of armed sky marshals and the impact of meeting armed resistance on the El Al flight may have had in this decision. Although international hijackings decreased after 1970, domestic hijackings remained high, numbering about 25 incidents per year through the late 1960s and into the 1970s.

THE INTERNATIONAL RESPONSE TO TERRORIST HIJACKINGS

At the time of the Dawson's Field hijackings, the International Civil Aviation Organization (ICAO) was already in the process of drafting a multilateral agreement addressing cooperation among nations to bring hijackers to justice. In 1963, ICAO first addressed the issue of hijacking by establishing a general framework under which countries where a hijacked aircraft lands are to take steps to return control of the aircraft to its lawful commander, and permit passengers and crew to continue their journey as soon as practicable. These requirements, which became formally ratified as part of the Tokyo Convention of 1963, were considered a first step in addressing international cooperation in preventing and deterring hijackings, but it did not address protocols or arrangements for dealing with those that committed acts of aerial piracy. The work of ICAO that began in earnest in December 1968 set out to address issues of jurisdiction over and handling of individuals who carry out hijackings. This work culminated in the ratification of the Hague Convention of 1970 for the Suppression of Unlawful Seizure of Aircraft on December 16, 1970, three months after the Dawson's Field hijackings.

The Hague Convention established that either the country where a hijacked aircraft is landed, the nation of aircraft registration, the country of nationality of the alleged aircraft hijackers, or the country where the airline or aircraft lessee is principally based may petition for jurisdiction in the matter. The Convention does not specifically lay out an order of precedence for jurisdictional matters, but provides the framework for each of the described nations to pursue appropriate action to establish its jurisdiction. Under the Convention, the country detaining any alleged hijackers must make a preliminary inquiry into the facts and hold any suspects for the duration of any criminal or extradition proceedings. The Convention stipulates that countries must either present the case against the detained individuals for criminal prosecution or negotiate the extradition of alleged hijackers to stand trial in other countries that establish their jurisdiction in the matter. Work to finalize the Convention was undoubtedly expedited by the Dawson's Field hijackings, and the terms of the Convention were put into force a year later, in October 1971. The following year, ICAO drafted additional terms to cover terrorist acts against aviation that occur prior to flight or otherwise endanger the safety of flight. These terms became formally ratified in September 1971 under the Montreal Convention of 1971.[12] They specifically address various acts of violence that endanger the safety of an aircraft, including acts carried out against aircraft on the ground; destruction or damage to navigation aids and facilities; and disseminating false information that could endanger the safety of an aircraft operations, such as giving false air traffic control instructions.

For the United States, the Hague Convention, along with the additional terms of the Montreal Convention, was a potentially powerful tool to compel other signatory countries to either extradite hijackers of U.S. flag aircraft operating overseas or carry out criminal prosecutions of these individuals under the scrutiny of the international community. However, the continued existence of nations that provided safe haven to international hijackers, which were not signatories to the Convention, limited the scope of its overall effectiveness. The Convention was of limited use in combatting hijackings to Cuba, because Cuba had not been a party to the Convention and was of limited use in the Middle East, where several nations offered safe haven for aircraft hijackers. In addition to the Hague Convention, as the Dawson's Field situation was still unfolding, the U.N. Security Council passed a resolution calling on all nations to take legal actions and cooperate to prevent further aerial hijackings. By itself, this also was of limited effectiveness without effective aviation security measures to thwart would-be hijackers and the capability to impose effective economic and political sanctions to deter nations from aiding or providing safe haven to hijackers.

THE PERIOD OF HIJACKING CONTAGION

While the deployment of sky marshals and various other policy actions seemingly had an impact on reducing hijackings of international flights, hijackings of domestic flights remained at historic high levels in 1971 and 1972, spurred by continued hijackings of domestic flights within the United States to Cuba and a new wave of hijackings aimed at extorting sizeable ransoms from the government and the airlines. Some researchers have aptly referred to the string of hijackings during the late 1960s and early 1970s as an example of a phenomenon known as social contagion.[13] A distinction was made between hijackings strictly for transportation and hijackings for extortion, whether the nature of the extortion involved strictly money or other objectives, such as the release of comrades or demands for policy changes or acceptance of other political concessions. It has generally been shown that widely publicized incidents of successful hijackings spurred copycats to carry out similar crimes, while unsuccessful attempts generally suppressed further hijacking activity.

Particularly among domestic extortion attempts, which were predominantly carried out by those seeking cash ransoms, there was a significant contagion effect, spurred in part by prior successes and by extensive media coverage of these events. Researchers noted, however, that the rise in extortion hijackings in 1972 had the effect of quelling transportation hijackings. In particular, the rate of hijackers demanding transportation to Cuba diminished considerably. Money became a new motivation for hijacking airliners.

The first domestic hijacking for money occurred on June 4, 1970, when a hijacker commandeered an aircraft at Dulles Airport in Virginia demanding $100 million from the government.[14] After a standoff with Federal Bureau of Investigation (FBI) agents and airport police, law enforcement officers (LEOs) shot out the tires of the airplane and subdued the hijacker. After this unsuccessful attempt, there were no additional extortion-style hijackings in the United States for over a year. However, starting in May of 1971, the United States faced a rash of extortion hijackings. While most were ultimately unsuccessful, partial success in at least obtaining a cash ransom prior to being apprehended may have spurred others to follow suit and try their luck at this dangerous game which, to some, seemingly became something of a sport.

The most famous of these incidents was, of course, the November 24, 1971, hijacking of a Northwest Orient Airlines Boeing 727 by a man who called himself Dan Cooper. The hijacker ordered the plane to fly to its intended destination of Seattle, where he demanded $200,000 and four parachutes. After releasing all on board, except for the flight crew and one stewardess, he ordered the airplane to fly at low altitude and low speed to Mexico with planned fuel stops in Reno, Nevada, and Yuma, Arizona. Somewhere near the Washington–Oregon border he apparently parachuted from the aft stairs of the Boeing 727. The hijacker became known in popular culture as D. B. Cooper, a reference to a person of interest living near the jump site, who was questioned early in the investigation but was quickly ruled out as a suspect. Whether the hijacker known as D. B. Cooper survived his escape and was ultimately successful, or perished when he jumped from the airplane, remains a mystery to this day. However, widespread media sensationalism gave this criminal a legend-like status and spurred others to follow suit.

Most notably, just over four months later, on April 7, 1972, Richard Floyd McCoy, Jr., a 29-year-old student and Vietnam veteran hijacked a United Airlines Boeing 727 on a flight from Denver, Colorado to Los Angeles, California. McCoy ordered the pilots to fly to San Francisco and demanded $500,000 dollars and, like D. B. Cooper, four parachutes. Also like D. B. Cooper, McCoy escaped by parachute using the aft stairs of the 727. McCoy made his leap near Provo, Utah. McCoy, who was an experienced parachutist, survived the jump but was apprehended by the FBI two days later. He was convicted of the hijacking and sentenced to 45 years in prison.[15] McCoy, however, escaped from prison in 1974 and was killed when FBI agents attempted to apprehend him after tracking him down at a residence in Virginia Beach, Virginia. Some contend that McCoy was the D. B. Cooper hijacker, a hypothesis that McCoy's widow vehemently denied. Although McCoy was quickly apprehended following the hijacking, news of the incident quickly spurred others to attempt similar hijackings.

Within one month of the McCoy hijacking case, several others followed suit. In one incident, two days after the McCoy hijacking, a lone hijacker—who had similarly requested $500,000 and four parachutes—was overpowered by police in San Diego after leaving the aircraft to fetch navigational charts for the flight crew. In another incident a few days later, a hijacker who threatened to blow up a Continental Airlines Boeing 707 unless he received a ransom of $500,000 gave himself up after an hour-long negotiation with law enforcement. In yet another incident in April 1972, an individual with a history of psychiatric problems hijacked a Frontier Airlines Boeing 737 on a flight from

Albuquerque to Los Angeles, demanding a public forum to voice concerns over injustices to minorities in the United States. After being allowed to conduct on-board television and radio interviews with Spanish-language stations, the hijacker apologized to the pilot and surrendered peaceably.[16]

Then, on May 5, 1972, an extortion hijacking, quite similar to the D.B. Cooper and Richard Floyd McCoy cases, occurred on an Eastern Airlines Boeing 727 en route from Allentown, Pennsylvania to Miami, Florida. The hijacker—later determined to be Frederick Hahneman, a 43-year-old electrical engineer from Pennsylvania—diverted the flight to Dulles Airport in Virginia, where he demanded six parachutes and $303,000 in cash. He then ordered the pilot to fly to Mexico and escaped by parachuting from the aircraft over the Mexican jungle. Like McCoy, Hahneman survived his leap, but was later captured, pled guilty, and was sentenced to life in prison for the hijacking. Immediately following this third incident involving a parachute leap from the aft stairs of a Boeing 727, the FAA moved swiftly to order a modification that would prevent operation of the rear air stairs in flight. The device—a wedge that moves to block the door when air flows over it—became widely known as the Cooper vane, so named for the hijacker known as D. B. Cooper.

A second hijacking occurred later in the day, on May 5, 1972, when 21-year-old Michael Lynn Hansen hijacked a Western Airlines Boeing 737 flight from Salt Lake City to San Francisco. A Vietnam War protester, Hansen initially ordered the plane to fly to North Vietnam, but later elected to fly to Cuba when he was told that the trip across the Pacific exceeded the airplane's range. Hansen was successful in reaching Cuba, but the Cuban government extradited him in 1975 to stand trial in the United States for the hijacking.[17]

ESCALATING VIOLENCE PROMPTS FAA ACTION

Even before the string of incidents in April 1972, the FAA had conceded that more needed to be done to address the persisting problem of domestic hijackings. Beginning in January 1972, the FAA began promulgating new regulations designed to strengthen air carrier security. The regulations required each airline to establish a screening system for passengers and carry-on bags, and take steps to restrict unauthorized access to aircraft. Soon after, on March 18, 1972, the FAA published regulations for airports to establish access control procedures to deter unauthorized access to air operations areas of airports and provide law enforcement support to airline security screening operations. The issues stemming from these regulations set off a lengthy debate over the appropriate role of airlines, airports, and the federal government in carrying out operational aspects of aviation security. The Nixon Administration held the view that the federal government should strictly maintain the role of regulator in the matter and should not be involved in the day-to-day operational aspects of security. The airports, in particular, raised concerns over the burden placed on them, particularly with respect to providing law enforcement support for the airline screening process.

In 1972, the airlines responded to the FAA requirements by adopting a variety of screening systems that used a combination of targeting specific flights and implemented behavioral profiles to select passengers for screening that were in place by the summer of that year. At this point, not all airline passengers were being screened using magnetometers or pat-down searches, and hand searches of their carry-on items, but only those selected by each individual airline's screening program underwent these physical searches. The FAA subsequently instituted expanded use of behavioral profiling techniques, ordering all airlines to implement profiling and deny boarding to any individuals selected through the profile who were not subsequently cleared through metal detector or physical searches of their persons and carry-on items. Amid growing concern in Congress over the string of domestic hijackings in 1972, an alternative plan that sought to implement screening of all passengers and create an armed federal security force that would be deployed to screening checkpoints at airports across the nation won overwhelming approval in the Senate in September 1972. However, the Nixon Administration, which was strongly opposed to the concept of a federal security force, was successful in blocking action on the bill in the House.

While debate over the appropriate role of the federal government and local authorities in providing armed security to protect airports and aircraft continued, the need for effective security and law enforcement was made increasingly clear by the escalating violence of air piracy incidents. Hijackings in the United States during the late 1960s and early 1970s were generally carried out by four general categories of perpetrators: socio-political extremists; criminals seeking to escape prosecution; extortionists seeking ransoms; and the mentally disturbed. In post-9/11 discussion and debate, these earlier hijackings have often been described as being nuisances that were largely nonviolent and generally concluded peaceably through negotiations with hijackers on the ground. This may have been true for many of the transportation hijackings of that era, as well as the D.B. Cooper-style extortion cases and hijackings carried out by socio-political extremists. Many of the hijackings of this era carried out by criminals and mentally disturbed individuals, however, were shockingly violent in nature.

As the hijackings of the early 1970s became more frequent and more brazen, the risk of violence escalated. The risk of violence may have also been intensified by increasing pressure to stop the wave of hijackings that led, in turn, to increasingly heavy-handed law enforcement tactics. For example, airplane tires were often shot out, leaving hijackers with limited options thereby making them more prone to enter into a violent confrontation with law enforcement rather than a peaceable, negotiated surrender. An obvious problem was that it remained simply too easy for hijackers to carry firearms, grenades, makeshift explosives, and other weapons on board, creating a considerable risk that any hijacking would end in a violent showdown with law enforcement.

While passengers had been wounded when gunfire erupted during earlier hijacking incidents, the first domestic hijacking that resulted in a fatality occurred on July 5, 1972. Hijackers commandeered a Pacific Southwest 737 en route from Sacramento to San Francisco, demanding that the jet be flown to the Soviet Union. A gun battle between FBI agents and the hijackers ensued, resulting in the deaths of two hijackers and one passenger. Two other passengers were seriously wounded in the melee.

As the string of hijackings in 1972 continued, more violent incidents followed. Two particularly violent domestic hijacking incidents in the fall of 1972 prompted the FAA to expedite its efforts to implement passenger screening. On October 29, 1972, four fugitives—wanted for a bank robbery and related murder in an Arlington, Virginia heist that had occurred the week prior—shot and killed a ticket agent and wounded a ramp worker as they blasted their way through airport security in Houston, Texas and hijacked an Eastern airlines flight, ordering the pilot to fly to Cuba.

Then on November 10, 1972, three fugitives hijacked a Southern Airways DC-9 in Birmingham, Alabama taking passengers on a harrowing journey including eight stops in the United States and Canada. The hijackers demanded $2 million in cash and 10 parachutes, and threatened to crash the airplane into a nuclear reactor in Oak Ridge, Tennessee unless their demands were met. The ransom was paid by the airline, but the FBI, seeking to put an end to the 28-hour ordeal, shot out the airplane's tires. The hijackers ordered the pilot to take off, despite the tire damage, and fly the airplane to Havana, Cuba, where the airplane landed safely and the hijackers found asylum.

By this point, both Cuba and the United States had had enough, and began to diligently negotiate a bilateral agreement on hijackings that was finalized in February 1973. The treaty, like most international hijacking agreements provided the countries with the option to either extradite or prosecute hijackers. Either option provided a considerable deterrent for hijackers, knowing that they could not get asylum if they made it to Cuba. Soon after, Cuba began returning some hijackers to face trial and punishment in the United States, although Cuba never viewed the agreement as being retroactive in nature, and many hijackers that had commandeered aircraft in the 1960s and 1970s remained in exile in Cuba. Some were able to live comfortable lives in Cuba and benefit from free education and other benefits provided by the Castro regime.[18] For others, however, life was a miserable existence in squalid Cuban prisons or working unskilled manual labor jobs while living in extreme poverty.[19] Some tried to escape their meager existences in Cuba by trying to sneak back into the United States, but were captured and put on trial. For example, three of the four hijackers in the October 29, 1972, incident were able to sneak back into the United States undetected, but were later found in 1975, and put on trial for their crimes and sentenced to consecutive life terms.[20] For most, the crime of hijacking simply did not pay. This realization, along with the additional threat of extradition to the United States or a trial in Cuba, significantly reduced the number of hijackings to Cuba since 1973.

As negotiations with the Cuban government to finalize the bilateral treaty on hijacking were continuing, the FAA turned its attention to developing effective policies, strategies, and procedures for preventing domestic extortion hijackings. Among aviation security policymakers and strategists at the time, debate centered on the limited capability of the sky marshal program and the need for effective preemptive preflight measures to prevent armed hijackers from boarding flights. The FAA had focused its previous efforts related to preflight security on developing methods to pick out would-be hijackers for additional screening measures. Largely in response to the escalation in Cuban hijackings in 1969 and 1970, The FAA had convened a multidisciplinary task force, consisting of specialists in human behavior, security, law, and other fields, to develop a behavioral profile for selecting passengers that would be selected for special examination. The profiles developed by this task force were instrumental in determining which passengers would be subject to preflight screening.

In retrospect, looking at this approach in the context of post-9/11 security debate over passenger prescreening, the behavioral profiling methods of the early 1970s seem extremely forward-looking in their approach. Indeed, Israel has relied on extensive behavioral profiling and extensive interviewing to target passengers for years, and these methods have recently been adopted by the Transportation Security Administration (TSA) to identify elevated risk passengers at security checkpoints and in passenger lounges and other locations throughout airport passenger terminals. However, between 1970 and 1972, the U.S. approach to behavioral profiling was largely born out of necessity, since neither the human resources nor the technology to screen all passengers for weapons or explosives was readily available at that time to address the perceived immediate need to strengthen airline security. It was therefore believed that the best immediate solution was to screen high-risk flights, which were mainly limited to international flights, and those domestic passengers believed to pose a potential hijacking threat based on their profile.

In 1970 and 1971, passenger screening operations targeted high-risk flights at selected airports, predominantly international flights operated by U.S. flag carriers. However, by 1972, continued domestic hijackings and escalating violence associated with hijacking incidents emphasized the need for more effective airline security measures. The FAA responded by requiring air carriers to deny boarding to any passengers selected for screening by behavioral profiling techniques that were not cleared by either metal detectors or physical searches. By that time, the FAA was deploying metal detectors in larger numbers to airports for screening and was sponsoring initiatives to develop and test x-ray equipment for screening passenger carry-on items.

THE DEBATE OVER PASSENGER SCREENING

By 1972, both the Nixon Administration and the Congress had concluded that sweeping changes to improve aviation security were needed to combat the ongoing epidemic of domestic hijackings. However, a disagreement between the Administration and Congress regarding the role of the federal government in aviation law enforcement as well as concerns voiced by the airlines and the airports regarding the impact of new security measures needed to be sorted out. In July 1972, the Administration ordered magnetometer screening of all passengers and searches of all carry-on items prior to boarding all domestic shuttle flights. In August, the FAA issued a requirement that all profile selectees and all accompanying individuals flying with selected individuals be screened and their carry-on items searched prior to boarding. Despite these efforts, hijackings continued and turned more violent. Although all three of the hijackers in the November 10, 1972, hijacking were selected by profiling techniques and underwent handheld wand metal detection screening, they were somehow able to get their weapons past the screening checkpoint. Some have speculated that the handheld wands in use at the time were less able to detect weapons compared to the walk-through magnetometers that were being installed at larger airports, but had not yet been delivered to mid-sized airports like Birmingham, Alabama where the hijackers boarded.[21]

Following the Birmingham incident, there was growing consensus that uniform, consistent, and effective methods for screening both domestic and international passengers were needed to prevent armed hijackings. In December 1972, the FAA issued emergency orders to all air carriers requiring the screening of all passengers and their carry-on items within one month. Under the order, airports were required to station armed guards at the boarding checkpoints by February 1973. Beginning in January 5, 1973, all passengers boarding flights in the United States had to pass through metal detectors and allow inspection of their carry-on items. Despite predictions that airline passengers would not tolerate the hassle and some opposition on the grounds that mandatory screening violated Constitutional privacy rights, passengers fed up with hijackings took the measures largely in stride and recognized the inconvenience as a necessary measure to protect airline flights. Following the FAA's emergency orders that went into effect in early 1973, the number of domestic hijackings dropped precipitously (Figure 1.1).

While the FAA's actions to require screening of all passengers were largely in step with the views of Congress on the matter, 100% passenger screening was not without its critics. One particularly outspoken critic, Senator Vance Hartke of Indiana, led a fight to end airport screening and urged fellow Americans to "smite down a direct threat to the Constitution."[22] Hartke failed to garner mainstream support for his position, perhaps because his tactics centered on arguing that, because of his office, he should be granted special exemption from screening rather than maintaining a consistent argument that all citizens should be exempt from screening. Although Hartke's crusade failed to gain popular support, federal cases were quickly brought against the FAA, arguing that the security screening procedures violated the Fourth Amendment, which guarantees individuals protection against unreasonable searches and seizures. By June 1973, however, the FAA had won a precedent-setting decision, finding that the screening procedures were allowable as part of a general regulatory framework, so long as such searches were conducted reasonably, on a routine and indiscriminate basis, and with the consent of the individual being screened.[23] The 100% passenger screening requirement was seen as not being subject to the Fourth Amendment restrictions because it involved the implicit consent of the passenger, and its intent was to deter hijackings rather than to

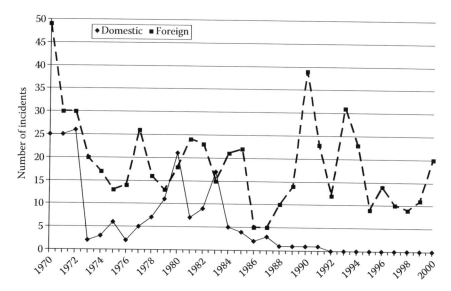

FIGURE 1.1 Domestic and foreign aircraft hijacking incidents (1970–2000). (U.S. Department of Transportation, Bureau of Transportation Statistics.)

obtain evidence for criminal charges against an individual. Also, since the screening was required of all passengers, it could not be viewed as being discriminatory, which arguably put it on more solid legal footing than the prior practice of behavioral profiling.

However, another line of argument against 100% passenger screening centered on the fact that requiring all individuals to undergo screening could be considered unreasonable if the prior method of only screening selected individuals using the profile, or prescreening techniques, was equally effective. In other words, critics of screening all passengers saw no point to doing so if only screening selected passengers based on profiling techniques offered an equivalent level of security. A key advocate for this position was Michael J. Fenello, vice-president for Eastern Airlines who had helped devise and implement the behavioral profiling techniques that were used extensively and favored by Eastern Airlines.[24] Although this line of reasoning was predicated on Fourth Amendment arguments regarding the reasonableness of a search, the real bottom line for the airlines was the impact of 100% passenger screening on the efficiency of their operations, their operating costs, and fear that the hassles could result in delayed flights, fewer passengers, and lost revenues. This argument also failed to gain much support or credibility as there was an immediate and dramatic drop in domestic hijackings after the FAA emergency orders were put into effect, suggesting that the implementation of 100% passenger screening had a positive effect on reducing hijackings. The FAA could point to this drop in hijackings as evidence that 100% screening was arguably more effective than the profiling techniques previously implemented. There was also some consideration of whether screening requirements could be relaxed at certain airports where the hijacking risk was considered to be low. However, after consideration of this option, it was determined that because of the interconnected nature of the air transportation system, a uniform approach to screening at all airports was needed.

Another challenge to screening procedures was levied against the FAA in 1973 by the Aviation Consumer Action Project (ACAP), an advocacy group connected to consumer rights advocate Ralph Nader. The group argued that x-ray screening of carry-on items posed an undue health threat to airline passengers. While this campaign led to improved standards and regulatory processes for certifying x-ray machines used in airport screening, it had no significant impact on the overall approach to screening all passengers and carry-on items, which had the overwhelming support of both Congress and the Administration.[25]

THE DEBATE OVER AVIATION SECURITY ROLES AND RESPONSIBILITIES

As the screening procedures stood up to legal challenges in the courts, the policy debate shifted to consideration of the appropriate aviation security role of the federal government, the airlines, airports, and local law enforcement authorities in carrying out the screening procedures and complying with the regulatory mandates to station arm guards at all airport screening checkpoints. Airlines complained that the 100% screening requirements were costly and overly burdensome, while airlines and airports both complained that the requirement to station armed guards at all air airport checkpoints was particularly onerous, especially at smaller airports. Airlines and airports were united in their position that providing armed guards at airport checkpoints was a federal responsibility, one that would involve a large-scale expansion of the federal role in aviation security.[26]

The interim solution offered by the FAA was to reassign sky marshals to duty at airport screening checkpoints to augment airport security guards, and state and local LEOs assigned to airport checkpoint duties. The sky marshals presence on aircraft were increasingly seen as being limited in their effectiveness because, despite relatively large numbers, they still could only provide coverage on a relatively small percent of flights. About 1700 air marshals were retained and reassigned to airports to serve as federal airport security officers. By June 1974, when x-ray screening equipment was introduced at airport screening checkpoints, the sky marshal program was completely discontinued. The federal government, however, did not view the disbanding of the sky marshals as a signal for a permanent shift in the federal role to one of maintaining an armed security presence at airport checkpoints. Rather, the FAA maintained that law enforcement presence at airport screening checkpoints was fundamentally a local law enforcement responsibility to be shouldered by airport operators. In its emergency order, the FAA mandated a significant expansion of existing requirements for local law enforcement presence at airports, stipulating that at least one armed officer must be posted at each security screening checkpoint and be present continuously throughout the boarding process.[27]

The Senate, however, had unanimously supported a plan to establish a new armed air transportation security force to be housed within the FAA and deployed to all commercial passenger airports throughout the United States.[28] In 1973, Senator Howard Cannon of Nevada, Chairman of the Senate's Subcommittee on Aviation, complained that prior efforts to move Senate-backed legislation to mandate 100% passenger screening and establish a federal airport security force within the FAA were stonewalled in the House by Nixon Administration and DOT officials. Senator Cannon criticized the Administration as having "systematically ignored the hijacking problem throughout 1972 with the naïve view that the federal government really didn't have a major role ...."[29] He characterized the FAA's emergency order requiring airports to supply armed officers at checkpoints as "... a dangerous cop-out ...," and "... a hodge-podge enforcement effort and a continuation of divided responsibility [that] will result in episodes similar to the [November 10, 1972] hijacking incident in which no clearly established, coordinated effort existed."[30] His legislative proposal, which was swiftly acted on and overwhelmingly supported in the Senate, instead called for establishing an armed air transportation security force within the FAA of a sufficient size to provide law enforcement presence at airports throughout the United States.

The Nixon Administration viewed such action as an unnecessary and unwarranted expansion of federal police powers into local jurisdictions and viewed law enforcement presence during the screening and boarding process as a local responsibility.[31] While the Cannon bill that called for an armed federal aviation security force was swiftly passed by the Senate in February 1973, action on the bill languished in the House where lawmakers recognized that a Presidential veto of any measure that included such a provision would stymie other initiatives to strengthen aviation security that had the support of both Congress and the Administration. The Nixon Administration was thus able to ultimately prevail in its view that airport and aviation law enforcement should not be a federal function. To this day, even after federalization of screening forces after the September 11, 2001, terrorist attacks, airport law enforcement presence remains a local responsibility that must be integrated into each airport's security program, much as it was when first required under the FAA's emergency rule issued in December 1972. Regulations, however, have since been relaxed to allow flexibility in law enforcement presence, not requiring continuous presence at checkpoints, so long as LEOs can quickly respond when needed. Whether this arrangement of shared responsibility between airports, airlines, local and state law enforcement, and the federal government is a hodge-podge of divided responsibility, as Senator Cannon contended in 1972, is still a matter of much debate to this day.

With regard to other steps to enhance aviation security and deter acts of aviation piracy, there was general agreement among both the Nixon Administration and the Congress. Despite a few objectors like Senator Hartke, Congress overwhelmingly supported the move to implement 100% screening of passengers and pushed for establishing a federal felony offense for carrying weapons or explosives on aircraft. The Congress also backed a Nixon Administration effort to establish legislation allowing the death penalty to be applied in cases of air piracy, including international incidents that resulted in one or more fatalities.

Congressional debate centered not only on whether there should be a federal law enforcement role at airport checkpoints, but also on whether such a role should involve the creation of a new air transportation security force within the FAA, as provided for in the Senate bill, or whether this responsibility should be given to the FBI. So far as the Nixon Administration was concerned, the entire issue of checkpoint screening and law enforcement presence could be handled through regulation, and a regulatory solution was considered preferable to a legislative solution because it would allow greater flexibility to relax or modify requirements as needed.

In light of the violent domestic hijackings in the fall of 1972, the Administration conceded that the problem of aerial piracy might not be something that would simply go away over time. The Administration, however, remained concerned that the push in Congress to implement a federal aviation police force at airports would significantly expand the federal government's role in a way that could not easily be undone, even if the hijacking threat became a thing of the past. With a price tag of almost $60 million per year, cost was also a significant issue. The Administration was intent on passing the cost along to users of the system, that is, the airline passengers. However, further raising federal ticket taxes, already set at 8%, was an unpopular option. The easiest mechanism for passing the security cost along to passengers was to make the screening and law enforcement functions the responsibility of the airlines and the airports, and have them recover the costs in the form of passenger head taxes and customer surcharges. President Nixon was clear in his resolve to veto any measure that would create a federal aviation police force to carry out these functions, thus compelling the House of Representatives to come up with an alternative to the Senate-passed bill. The Administration offered its owned legislative proposal, which was introduced by request in the House (H.R. 3858, 93rd Congress). The bill had much in common with the Senate-passed bill, but differed significantly with regard to law enforcement presence at airport screening checkpoints.

As congressional debate over aviation security and antipiracy measures dragged on, the looming threat of violent hijackings struck close to home. On February 22, 1974, Samuel Byck attempted to commandeer a Delta DC-9 aircraft at Baltimore-Washington International Airport (BWI), with the intent of crashing the airplane into the White House as a means to assassinate President Nixon. Just five days before, an Army private, who had washed out of Army flight school a year prior, had stolen a helicopter from nearby Fort Meade in Maryland and landed it on the White House lawn, perhaps giving Byck the idea of attacking the White House with an aircraft.[32] Fearing detection of a home-made suitcase bomb at the airport screening checkpoint, Byck shot and killed airport police officer George Neal Ramsburg and made his way on board the Delta jet. After the pilots told Byck that the aircraft could not move away from the gate because the wheels were still chocked, he shot them both, fatally wounding the copilot. After a standoff with police as the aircraft remained parked at the gate, Byck shot and killed himself. It was later noted that although "... Byck lacked the skill and self-control to reach his target, he had provided a chilling reminder of the potential of violence against civil aviation. Under a more relaxed security system, his suicidal rampage might have begun when the airliner was aloft."[33] The violent incident at BWI served as a poignant example of the violence in air piracy incidents for the ongoing debate in Congress over passenger screening. In a tape recording found after his death, Byck referred to his demonic plot as "Operation Pandora's Box," a fitting metaphor for the continuing challenge facing aviation security policymakers grappling with the challenges posed by violent aerial hijackings: "... once opened, this Pandora's box could never be completely sealed."[34]

Following the incident at BWI, the House went along with the tougher Senate bill, but dropped the language that called for a nationwide FAA airport security force.[35] The bill lingered for some time as Congress became embroiled in the Watergate hearings and the impeachment of President Nixon in the spring of 1974. A bill going along with the wishes of the Administration that airport and checkpoint law enforcement be left in the hands of state and local authorities emerged out of conference in July 1974 and was agreed to by both the House and the Senate. President Nixon signed the resulting Anti-hijacking Act of 1974 on August 5, 1974, just four days before he resigned from office. The Nixon Administration's stance on this matter shaped the U.S. aviation security system for years to come, creating a shared-responsibility model where the federal government's role was largely that of regulatory oversight. The operational security responsibilities were divided between airlines that provided screening functions and airports that provided law enforcement presence, typically through arrangements with state and local law enforcement authorities. This model of limited federal involvement would endure until 2001, when the 9/11 terrorist attacks prompted a rethinking of this approach. Yet, even to this day, despite the post-9/11 changes that have come about through federalization of security screening functions, law enforcement presence at airports and

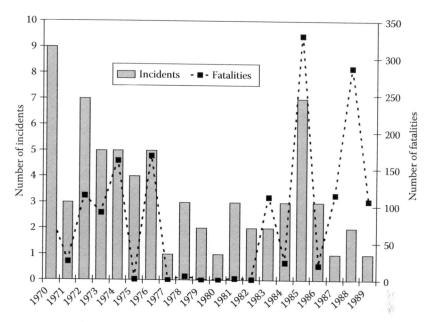

FIGURE 1.2 Worldwide aircraft bombing incidents and fatalities (1970–1989). (U.S. Department of Transportation, Bureau of Transportation Statistics.)

support at screening checkpoints still remain largely responsibilities of the individual airports and their respective state and local police agencies.

While the Act did not create a nationwide FAA airport armed security force as many in Congress at that time had wished, the law gave statutory authority to continue the course of action for aviation security that had been set forth by the Nixon Administration, which was widely supported by the Congress. Most significantly, it mandated in law the 100% physical screening of all passengers, providing statutory authority for the FAA's air carrier security requirements. As a deterrent against hijackings, the Act established that the death penalty could be applied in cases of air piracy incidents that resulted in a death.

By the late 1970s, it appeared that efforts to combat air piracy, primarily through metal detector and x-ray screening of passengers and carry-on luggage, were working quite effectively. Domestic hijackings had been significantly reduced, as had worldwide hijackings (see Figure 1.1). It also appeared that these security measures had been effective in preventing aircraft bombings worldwide by the late 1970s and early 1980s (Figure 1.2). However, events during the 1980s indicated that serious weaknesses in aviation security continued to exist, particularly in the international aviation arena on routes flown by U.S. flag air carriers.

THE LOOMING MENACE OF AIRCRAFT BOMBINGS

While domestic hijackings were troubling enough by themselves, the threat posed by potential bombings of aircraft was a particular concern because in-flight bombings had proven to be especially deadly. While the threat of aircraft bombings is most immediately associated with the decade of the 1980s, aircraft bombings have long been a threat to aviation security in the United States. However, aircraft bombings did not garner the attention of policymakers and federal officials charged with responsibilities for aviation security during the 1960s and 1970s to any degree remotely close to the attention that was given to aerial hijackings. Nevertheless, bombings were a continuing threat to commercial aviation long before the issue was brought to the forefront of U.S. policy debate by the December 21, 1988, bombing of Pan Am flight 103 over Lockerbie, Scotland.

Bombings of aircraft can be traced back to the early days of passenger airline service. The first aircraft bombing in the United States occurred in 1933, when a twin-propeller Boeing 247 passenger airliner operated by United Airlines exploded in flight and crashed near Chesterton, Indiana while en route from Cleveland to Chicago, killing all seven on board. While this is regarded as the first confirmed bombing of a commercial airline flight, no suspect was ever identified in the case. Isolated domestic aircraft bombing incidents continued throughout the pre-jet era. In 1955, a United Airlines DC-6, a four-engine piston propeller airplane, was destroyed by a dynamite bomb shortly after departing Denver, Colorado. John Gilbert Graham was convicted of the bombing and executed in 1957. His motive for the bombing was to kill his mother who was a passenger on the flight. She lost her life in the crash, along with 38 other passengers and 5 crewmembers. In a similar incident in 1949, a Canadian Pacific Airlines DC-3 had been destroyed by a bomb near Montreal, Canada, killing all 23 persons on board, including the intended target: the bomber's wife. Graham may have gotten his inspiration from this incident. Other bombing incidents involving targeted attacks and suicides ensued, exhibiting a possible pattern of contagion among aircraft bombing incidents, although certainly not to the degree evident among aircraft hijackings of the late 1960s and early 1970s.

Nonetheless, in the late 1950s and early 1960s, there was a series of suspected and confirmed aircraft bombing incidents with a similar motive: payouts from life insurance policies. In the first suspected, but unconfirmed, case involving the unsolved crash of National Airlines Flight 967 on November 16, 1959, it has been speculated, but never proven, that an ex-convict duped a friend from prison in a scheme to collect a life insurance payment. It is speculated that the suspect talked his friend into boarding a flight using a ticket purchased in the suspect's name and carrying a package containing a concealed explosive device. All 42 on board were killed when the aircraft crashed into the Gulf of Mexico en route from Tampa, Florida to New Orleans, Louisiana.

The first suspected suicide bombing of an aircraft in the United States occurred two months later when a passenger on board a National Airlines DC-6 en route from New York's Idlewild Field (now JFK International Airport) to Miami, Florida allegedly detonated a bomb he had carried on board. The airplane crashed near Wilmington, North Carolina killing all 34 persons on board. While the crash was determined to have been the result of a bomb, it was never confirmed whether the bomber was in fact a passenger on the flight.

Under similar circumstances, a Continental Airlines Boeing 707 was destroyed on May 22, 1962, over Missouri during a scheduled flight from Chicago O'Hare International Airport to what is now Kansas City Charles B. Wheeler Downtown Airport. All 45 on board were killed in the crash. Investigation revealed evidence of a bomb placed in the towel holder of an aft lavatory. Investigators also found evidence that passenger Thomas Doty—a married man with a young child, who was facing criminal prosecution for armed robbery—had purchased a large life insurance policy and dynamite shortly before the flight. This was the first documented bombing of a jet airliner in scheduled airline service.

On November 12, 1967, a bomb went off in the rear baggage compartment of an American Airlines Boeing 727, carrying 72 passengers and 6 crewmembers, while flying over Colorado en route from Chicago to San Diego. The airplane landed safely, and a man was later convicted of the bombing that targeted his wife, a passenger on the flight. A year later on November 19, 1968, another attempted bombing of a commercial jetliner took place in the skies over Colorado. A bomb exploded in an aft lavatory on board a Continental Airlines Boeing 707 as it was beginning its descent into Denver, but the airplane was able to land safely. The FBI arrested a passenger who had recently undergone brain surgery in connection with the incident. Senator Clifford Hansen of Wyoming was among the passengers on board. Fortunately, this was the last of these types of domestic aircraft bombing incidents.

Part of the success in reducing domestic bombings may be attributable to passenger screening measures implemented in the early 1970s. However, at that time, passenger baggage remained particularly vulnerable. In international aviation, bombing incidents continued with some regularity throughout the 1970s and 1980s (see Figure 1.2). Unlike the domestic bombings discussed above that were carried out by individuals with personal motives tied to insurance money, suicide, or revenge, bombings in the international aviation arena were often tied to terrorist groups seeking various political objectives. It is difficult to clearly identify any particular pattern among the international airline bombing incidents of the 1970s and 1980s as a whole. Bombing incidents involving U.S. and European flag carriers, however, were consistently linked to terrorist organizations in the Middle East. Many of these bombings were tied to hijacking events that later led to the destruction of the aircraft on the ground using explosives. These often did not result in fatalities. However, as these Middle Eastern terrorists were carrying out their campaign of aircraft hijackings in the late 1960s and early 1970s, they also targeted aircraft with in-flight bombs on several occasions beginning in 1970.

On February 21, 1970, a Swissair Convair 990 four-engine jet exploded after taking off from Zurich, Switzerland, on a scheduled flight to Tel Aviv, Israel, and crashed killing all 47 on board. The same day, an explosion rocked an Austrian Airlines Caravelle twin-engine jet departing Frankfurt, Germany, but the aircraft was able to return to the airport and landed safely. These two incidents, six months prior to the Dawson's Field hijackings were the beginning of a series of terrorist attacks against aviation carried out by the PFLP.

Bombings tied to anti-Israeli Arab terrorist movements continued throughout the early 1970s. On August 16, 1972, less than a month before the infamous massacre of Israeli athletes at the Munich Olympics by members of the Black September terrorist organization, two young British women were duped by three Arab men into carrying a bomb concealed in a phonograph aboard an El Al Boeing 707. The bomb exploded soon after the aircraft had taken off from Rome, Italy, but was able to return safely to the airport, perhaps because Israeli security reportedly had ensured that the phonograph containing the bomb was placed inside a blast-resistant cargo hold.[36]

In 1974, Middle Eastern terrorists brazenly targeted their campaign of bombings against a U.S. flag air carrier, likely in response to the United States' unwavering support for Israel. On September 8, 1974, TWA flight 841, a Boeing 707 en route from Tel Aviv, Israel to JFK International Airport in New York, blew up over the Ionian Sea, shortly after a scheduled stopover in Athens, Greece. The airplane had just departed on the second leg of its journey and its next scheduled stopover was to be Rome, Italy before continuing on to JFK. All 88 on board, including 79 passengers and 9 crewmembers were killed. The Arab National Youth Organization for the Liberation of Palestine quickly took responsibility for the bombing claiming that one of its members carried a bomb on board the airplane and set it off in flight.[37] At the time, it was the deadliest aircraft bombing and the most complex international accident investigation ever led by the National Transportation Safety Board (NTSB).

Despite initial skepticism over the claims that the airplane was brought down by a bomb, The NTSB issued a final report six months after the crash, concluding that the tragedy was likely caused by the detonation of a high-order explosive device placed in the aft cargo hold that damaged flight controls and rendered the aircraft uncontrollable. The NTSB issued four recommendations to the FAA for improving aviation security. These included: emphasizing coordination and support from the FAA to nations served by U.S. flag carriers on aviation security practices through an existing technical assistance program; establishing an overseas aviation security office at the FAA's international office in Brussels, Belgium; ensuring that air carrier security programs adequately addressed high-risk situations in international operations as well as in domestic operations; and, most notably, expediting the development and deployment of suitable explosives detection equipment to preclude the introduction of explosive devices on board aircraft.[38]

The FAA took some minimal action to address these recommendations, including disseminating audio/visual programs on explosives security to 53 countries serviced by U.S. flag air carriers, establishing a civil aviation security capability to oversee routes in Europe, Africa, and the Middle East and implementing air carrier security procedures for examining baggage, cargo, and mail placed on flights considered to be a high risk. With regard to deploying explosives detection equipment, in correspondence to the NTSB, the FAA acknowledged the need for such systems and indicated that "[a]ll techniques that have a possibility of being efficient in the detection of explosives are being pursued as fast as possible under current available resources."[39] The FAA indicated that it was pursuing research on explosive vapor detection, nuclear magnetic resonance, thermal neutron activation (TNA), and x-ray technologies. FAA's efforts in these areas, however, were limited, and little was done over the next 15 years to advance the capability to screen for explosives in baggage and cargo. The FAA's explosives research program was limited in its budget and resources and was not able to effectively develop field-deployable technologies that could effectively screen for explosives in operational settings.

Only by the late 1980s had x-ray equipment been deployed on a limited basis for the purpose of screening checked baggage and packages on high-risk international flights, but the ability of this technology to effectively identify improvised explosive devices (IEDs) was recognized as being limited. The longstanding failure to address this need left aircraft particularly vulnerable to the looming threat posed by explosive devices. While this threat failed to capture the interest of policy-makers in the 1970s to the extent that acts of air piracy did, by the end of the 1980s, the threat of aircraft bombings would, through tragedy, quickly become a key policy issue for the United States. However, by the late 1970s, fatal aircraft bombings appeared to have been almost completely eradicated as very few lost their lives through in-flight bombing incidents between 1977 and 1982 (see Figure 1.2). The relative calm in aviation terrorism, however, would be short lived as growing tensions in the Middle East in the early 1980s soon spurred more aerial violence.

THE 1980s: THE SHIFTING THREAT

Growing tensions in the Middle East in the early 1980s and the outbreak of war between Israel and Lebanon in 1982 intensified terrorist activity during the early and mid-1980s. In the spring of 1983, Shia militants bombed the U.S. Embassy in Beirut, Lebanon and, later that year, attacked a U.S. Marine Corps barrack in Beirut in two suicide truck bombing attacks. While terrorist acts against aviation did not show any particular increase in numbers during this time, events like the bombing of Gulf Air flight 771 on September 22, 1983, in the United Arab Emirates, and the 1985 hijacking of TWA flight 847 demonstrated the escalating violence and growing risks associated with international flight operations. Both of these incidents were directly tied to the situation in Lebanon and the growing power, influence, and ruthlessness of terrorist organizations in this region such as Hezbollah and the Abu Nidal Organization.

From a U.S. policy perspective, the most significant trend in the 1980s was the increased risk posed by aircraft bombings. While the number of worldwide airline bombing incidents in the decade of the 1980s, estimated as 24, was considerably less than the estimated 42 bombings that occurred in the 1970s, the bombing incidents of the 1980s were far deadlier. Specifically, it was estimated that the 42 bombings in the 1970s resulted in about 650 fatalities, whereas the 24 bombings in the 1980s resulted in approximately 1000 fatalities. This was largely attributable to more specific targeting of aircraft in flight, as opposed to aircraft on the ground, the targeting of larger aircraft including Boeing 747 jumbo jets, and more sophisticated bombing techniques and explosives that resulted in the complete in-flight destruction of several aircraft, killing all on board. The growing threat of aircraft bombings would drive U.S. aviation security policy during the late 1980s and throughout the 1990s, in the aftermath of the Pan Am flight 103 bombing on December 21, 1988. In testimony before a House subcommittee examining aviation security following the bombing of Pan Am flight 103, former FAA Director of Aviation Security, Mr. Billie Vincent stated that "[t]he nature of the threat to U.S. civil aviation changed from one of hijacking to a sophisticated sabotage threat in the early to mid-1980s .... In the same time period, the incidence of hijacking of the U.S. airlines dramatically decreased."[40] A synopsis of notable international aircraft bombing incidents and fatal aircraft bombings of U.S.-registered airliners during the 1980s is provided in Table 1.1.

The first significant aircraft bombing of the 1980s, and the most deadly aircraft bombing when it occurred, was the September 23, 1983, downing of Gulf Air flight 771. The flight had originated

TABLE 1.1
Notable Aircraft Bombings Since 1980

Date	Location (Route of Flight)	Aircraft Type (Airline Flight)	Details of Explosive Used	Event Description and Outcome
8/11/1982	Pacific Ocean, Near Hawaii (Narita, Japan to Honolulu, HI)	Boeing 747 (Pan Am flight 830)	Semtex IED placed under a cabin seat	Explosion in flight killed one and injured 15
9/23/1983	Near Jebel Ali, U.A.E., (Karachi, Pakistan to Abu Dhabi, U.A.E.)	Boeing 737 (Gulf Air flight 771)	Undetermined	Explosion in flight killed all 112 on board
1/18/1984	Karachi, Pakistan, (Karachi, Pakistan to Dhahran, Saudi Arabia)	Boeing 747 (Air France)	Believed to be about two-thirds to one pound of high explosive	Detonation during climb through 18,000 feet left a hole through the fuselage surrounding the aft cargo hold, no fatalities
6/23/1985	Atlantic Ocean Near Cork, Ireland (Montreal, Canada to London, Heathrow, UK)	Boeing 747 (Air India flight 182)	Undetermined	All 329 on board killed in the world's deadliest aircraft bombing
6/23/1985	Narita, Japan (Narita, Japan to Bangkok, Thailand)	Boeing 747 (Air India flight 301)	Approximately one pound of high explosive concealed in a radio	Denotation killed two baggage handlers and injured several others, 55 minutes to the destruction of Air India flight 182
4/2/1986	Over Argos, Greece (Rome, Italy to Athens, Greece)	Boeing 727 (TWA)	Semtex IED	Detonation in flight tore a hole in the fuselage and killed four passengers who were ejected during rapid cabin compression
5/3/1986	Colombo, Sri Lanka (Colombo, Sri Lanka to Male, Maldives)	Lockheed L-1011 (Air Lanka)	Several pounds of explosives	Detonation on the ground prior to a delayed departure killed 16 and injured more than 40
11/29/1987	Andaman Sea, (Abu Dhabi, U.A.E. to Bangkok, Thailand)	Boeing 707 (Korean Air flight 858)	PLXs concealed in a liquor bottle with C-4 charge, timer, and detonator concealed in a portable radio	Explosion over the Andaman Sea killed all 115 on board
12/21/1988	Lockerbie, Scotland, (London, Heathrow, UK to New York, NY–JFK)	Boeing 747 (Pan-Am flight 103)	Semtex IED concealed in a portable cassette player	Detonation in flight destroyed aircraft and killed all 259 on board and 11 persons on the ground
09/19/1989	Ténéré desert, Niger (N'Djamena, Chad to Paris-Charles de Gaulle Airport, France)	McDonnell-Douglas DC-10 (Union de Transportes Aériens–UTA flight 772)	Undetermined type placed in the forward cargo hold	An in-flight explosion caused the airplane to crash into the desert killing all 171 occupants
11/27/1989	Soacha (near Bogotá), Colombia (En route from Bogotá to Cali)	Boeing 727 (Avianca Airlines flight 203)	Explosive charge placed under a cabin seat	An in-flight explosion ignited fuel vapors in an empty fuel tank killing all 107 on board and three people on the ground

in Karachi, Pakistan. As the Boeing 737 was preparing to land at Abu Dhabi, United Arab Emirates, a bomb detonated in the baggage compartment. The plane crashed in the desert near Jebel Ali, United Arab Emirates, killing all 112 on board. It is suspected that the bomb was planted by terrorists belonging to the Abu Nidal Organization to punish the United Arab Emirates for failing to pay protection money to the group.[41] While the specific characteristics of the bomb were never determined, based on what is now known of the Abu Nidal Organization and its bombing tactics, the device likely consisted of Semtex high explosive attached to an improvised detonation device.

Four months later, a bomb exploded in one of the rear cargo holds of an Air France Boeing 747 as it departed Karachi, Pakistan for a flight to Paris, France with a stopover in Dhahran, Saudi Arabia. The explosion tore a large hole, two meters in diameter, in the fuselage, but the flight crew was able to quickly descend to 5000 feet to restore cabin pressure and returned safely to Karachi. The bomb was believed to have consisted of about two-thirds to one pound of high explosive. Fortunately, there were no fatalities among the 15 crewmembers and 246 passengers on board.

While the lives of those on board the Air France Boeing 747 were spared, the potential for mass casualties resulting from the bombing of a large jumbo jet were sadly realized a year and a half later. Air India flight 182, a Boeing 747 with a crew of 22 and 307 passengers on board, departed Montreal-Mirabel International Airport in Quebec, Canada on the evening of June 23, 1985 on its first leg of its scheduled journey to London Heathrow Airport in the United Kingdom and then on to New Delhi and Bombay, India. Seven hours into the flight, as the airplane cruised at 31,000 feet over the Atlantic Ocean southwest of Cork, Ireland, a bomb in the forward cargo hold exploded causing a rapid decompression and in-flight breakup. All 329 on board were killed in what remains the deadliest aircraft bombing incident in history.

Just one hour before the crash of Air India flight 182, half the world away, a bomb detonated in the cargo hold of another Air India Boeing 747 that was sitting on the tarmac in Narita, Japan. The explosion killed two baggage handlers who were loading the airplane for a scheduled flight to Bangkok, Thailand. Investigators linked the two events to a radical Sikh separatist terrorist organization that was believed to have been seeking revenge for the June 1984 attack on the Golden Temple Shrine in Amritsar by India's military forces to flush out Sikh militants. While the nature of the bomb that took down Air India flight 182 was never determined, the airplane at Narita was destroyed by approximately one pound of high explosive concealed in a portable radio. It is believed that a similar device took down Air India flight 182. The in-flight destruction of a Boeing 747 provided a grim reminder of the risk of mass casualties posed by IEDs concealed in passenger baggage or air cargo.

For U.S. policymakers, however, the threat of aircraft bombings largely remained an issue best dealt with through international efforts to punish the terrorists and take action against any nations that supported terrorist acts or sheltered terrorists from justice. In 1984, The Aircraft Sabotage Act of 1984 (see P.L. 98-473) was enacted to put in force elements of the multilateral Montreal Convention of 1971, making acts of sabotage against aircraft and aviation facilities punishable by the United States under an extraterritorial jurisdiction arrangement. The law gave the U.S. authority to prosecute certain aviation crimes, such as hijackings and aircraft bombings, including crimes committed in nonparticipating countries, when alleged perpetrators are found within the United States. The Act also increased the maximum sentence to 20 years and the maximum fine to $100,000 for hijacking, damaging, destroying, or disabling aircraft or navigational facilities, although certain incidents that resulted in loss of human life still carried with them the possibility of seeking the death penalty as provided for in the 1974 Anti-hijacking Act.

The legislation, while addressing gaps in U.S. ability to enforce international agreements pertaining to the prosecution of criminals and terrorists that commit acts against aviation, was limited in its practical application because countries like Libya and Algeria continued to provide safe haven to terrorists. The legislation did little to advance what was already achievable to pursue international terrorists under the existing international conventions, and without effective security measures in place at international stations of U.S. air carriers, terrorists operating in the Middle East were emboldened by the knowledge of the fact that they could carry out attacks against aviation largely beyond the reach of the U.S. legal system for all practical purposes. U.S. flag carriers operating in the Middle East were again seen as relatively soft targets for terrorist groups angry over U.S. presence in the region and rising animosities toward Israel. TWA, which operated routes throughout the Middle East and southern Mediterranean region was, again, particularly vulnerable.

The TWA Flight 847 Hijacking

On June 14, 1985, TWA flight 847, a Boeing 727 en route from Athens, Greece to Rome, Italy was hijacked as it cruised above the Mediterranean Sea. The hijackers, Lebanese terrorists calling themselves members of the Organization for the Oppressed of the Earth—widely regarded as a faction of Hezbollah—diverted the aircraft to Beirut, Lebanon. There, some hostages were exchanged for fuel, and the airplane was flown to Algiers, Algeria then back to Beirut after releasing additional hostages. The ordeal experienced by those passengers was reminiscent of the Dawson's Field hijackings that spurred radical changes in U.S. aviation security policy. But more significantly, the terrorists that hijacked TWA flight 847 demonstrated a new level of violence, torturing and publicly executing United States Navy Petty Officer Robert Dean Stethem, tossing his body to the tarmac from the airplane's exit door after shooting him in the head. Several passengers that the hijackers believed to be Jewish were handed over to members of Hezbollah before the airplane was ordered back to Algiers. The airplane returned to Beirut once more on June 16, and the following day, the hijackers abandoned the aircraft, transferring the remaining hostages to captivity with the Amal militia where they remained until June 30 when they were driven to Syria and released. The hijackers' demands focused on the release of several hundred Lebanese Shia Muslims held by Israel, and international condemnation of Israeli military action in Lebanon and U.S. military occupation and alleged actions in Lebanon, including the 1985 car bombing assassination attempt on Shia cleric Sayyed Mohammad Hussein Fadl-Allāh, which killed more than 60 people and injured about 200 and was linked to Central Intelligence Agency (CIA)-trained Lebanese mercenaries.[42]

While the TWA 847 hijackers fled and remained at large, one hijacker, Mohammed Ali Hamadei was picked up by West German officials in January 1987 as he tried to enter through Frankfurt airport using a fake passport and carrying liquid explosives. The fact that he was carrying liquid explosives was perhaps indicative of the shifting threat in the mid- to the late 1980s: a shift away from hijackings to in-flight bombings. In any event, the Reagan Administration had made international counter-terrorism a high priority for the Department of Justice and was initially highly confident that the West German government would extradite Hamadei to stand trial in the United States for the hijacking of TWA flight 847 and the murder of Robert Stethem, with the stipulation under a United States–German extradition treaty that he should not be subject to capital punishment if found guilty.

The hopes of extradition, however, were foiled when two German citizens were kidnapped in Beirut. The kidnappers demanded that the West German government should not extradite Hamadei to the United States, but instead release him in exchange for the two hostages. To the considerable chagrin of the Reagan administration and Justice Department lawyers who had built the case against Hamadei, the West German government subsequently refused to extradite Hamadei. Citing flexibility in its extradition treaty and the universal law principle, West Germany asserted that it had the authority to try Hamadei on hijacking and murder charges in Bonn, as provided for under the general terms of the Hague Convention and specific extradition arrangements between the United States and West Germany. For the German government, this was seen as a fortuitous flexibility in the law that allowed them to take a diplomatic course of action to protect the German hostages, who were eventually released, without fully giving into the kidnapper's demands. In 1989, Hamadei was convicted of the charges brought against him by the German government and sentenced to life in prison.[43]

While the U.S. government expressed satisfaction with the outcome of the Hamadei trial and sentencing in Germany, the case took an unexpected twist in 2005 when Hamadei was granted parole upon serving 19 years of his sentence, including time served prior to his conviction. Some have speculated that Hamadei's parole was bumped up and he was given safe passage to Lebanon as a gesture to gain the release of Susanne Osthoff, a German archeologist abducted in Iraq in late November 2005.[44] Despite repeated requests for extradition to the United States, upon release from prison in Germany, Hamadei was flown to Lebanon and remains a fugitive included among the FBI's list of most wanted terrorists.

ESCALATING VIOLENCE AND TERRORIST ANIMOSITY TOWARD THE UNITED STATES

Four months after the TWA 847 hijacking, on October 7, 1985, members of the Palestine Liberation Front (PLF) took over the cruise ship *Achille Lauro* as it sailed the Mediterranean en route from Alexandria, Egypt to Port Said, near the entrance to the Suez Canal. The terrorists ordered the ship to sail to Syria, and during the ordeal murdered a wheelchair-bound Jewish American, Leon Klinghoffer, execution style and threw his body overboard.

The following year, on September 5, 1986, four hijackers belonging to the Abu Nidal Organization stormed Pan Am flight 73, a Boeing 747, as passengers were boarding in Karachi, Pakistan. The flight crew escaped from the cockpit as hijackers took control of the cabin, prompting a standoff between the hijackers and Pakistani authorities. Frustrated that their demands that the flight crew return and fly them to Cyprus to obtain the release of Palestinian prisoners in that country were not met, the hijackers executed recently naturalized American citizen Rajesh Kumar. The leader of the hijackers, Zaid Safarini threatened to kill another passenger every 10 minutes until his demands were met. While he did not follow through with this threat, as night fell he ordered his fellow hijackers to open fire on the passengers and cabin crew who had been herded into the middle of the aircraft cabin, using automatic weapons and hand grenades. In the aftermath, 19 more people were killed, including one American, 50-year-old Surendra Patel, and seriously wounding several others. Contrary to widespread media claims that the passengers were killed as Pakistani forces stormed the airplane, the mass murder of these individuals was carried out without provocation, and Pakistani forces did not board the airplane until all those on board who were able to escape on their own accord had done so. The hijackers were arrested and sentenced to life in prison in Pakistan, but were later released. Safarini was captured by the FBI in Bangkok after being released from jail in Pakistan and was convicted and sentenced to life in prison in the United States.

It was later revealed that in addition to attaining the release of Palestinian prisoners held in Cyprus, the ultimate goal of the mission was to blow up the airplane over Israel, targeting some "sensitive strategic centre of the Zionist enemy and to blow it there with us inside [sic]." At their trial in Pakistan, the hijackers further proclaimed in a joint statement their "dream and desire to saturate the land of Palestine with our blood. That is why we planned to blow the plane over Palestine. No doubt, this time we failed but one day we will be successful."[45]

The execution-style murders of three Americans—Stethem, Klinghoffer, and Kumar—and the wanton rampage and mass murder of passengers on board the Pan Am aircraft exemplified a new level of animosity and violence toward U.S. citizens among Middle Eastern terrorists. This growing animosity toward Americans would later be instilled in others who would perpetrate the Pan Am flight 103 bombing in 1988 and the attack on the WTC in 1993, and in those who attacked America on September 11, 2001.

AERIAL SUICIDES AND AIRPLANES AS MISSILES

While the Pan Am flight 73 hijackers boasted of their unfulfilled dream to detonate the aircraft over an Israeli target in a suicide attack, the United States was soon confronted with incidents within its borders involving suicidal hijackers. The first of these cases occurred just over one year after the Pan Am flight 73 hijacking, on December 7, 1987. On that day, a Pacific Southwest Airlines (PSA) regional jet crashed near San Luis Obispo, California killing all 43 people on board.[46] Investigation revealed that a disgruntled former USAir employee, recently fired for alleged theft, used his employee identification badge, which had not been returned upon his termination, to bypass security armed with a handgun. During the flight, he shot his former supervisor who was a passenger on the airplane. He then forced his way into the cockpit where he shot the two pilots and then shot himself after putting the airplane into a crash dive.

In another incident on April 7, 1994, an off-duty Federal Express flight engineer attempted to hijack a FedEx DC-10 airplane and crash it into the company's Memphis, Tennessee headquarters. The mentally unstable hijacker boarded the airplane in Memphis under the guise of seeking free transportation (a practice known in the industry as deadheading) to San Jose, California. His only luggage was a guitar case that concealed hammers, mallets, a knife, and a spear gun. The flight crew fought back against the would-be hijacker, making a successful emergency landing in Memphis despite serious injuries to all three flight crewmembers.[47]

While these incidents did prompt some modifications to aviation security procedures, some of the preconditions that allowed these tragedies went unchecked. While efforts have been made to improve control of airport access credentials, those possessing them are still often allowed to bypass security screening, potentially allowing an employee to carry a firearm or weapon onto an aircraft as was the case in both of these incidents. In general, these incidents had no appreciable impact on aviation security policy or practice in the United States as policymakers remained primarily focused on the international terrorist threat to aviation during the decade of the 1980s.

U.S. Initiatives to Improve International Aviation Security

In an immediate response to the TWA 847 hijacking, Congress drafted legislation addressing international counterterrorism, or antiterrorism as it was referred to in the bill, and measures to improve foreign airport security. These measures were included as part of the larger International Security and Development Cooperation Act of 1985, a comprehensive foreign relations bill that had been introduced earlier that year. It was signed by President Reagan on August 8, 1985, and became Public Law 99-83. Title V of the Act, International Terrorism and Foreign Airport Security, addressed the specific measures designed to combat terrorism and terrorist acts carried out against aviation. The Act directed the Secretary of State to coordinate antiterrorism assistance to foreign countries and report annually to Congress on these initiatives. The Act also established a framework for imposing sanctions against those countries determined by the President to grant sanctuary or provide support to international terrorists, and specifically authorized trade sanctions against Libya. The Act also called for the establishment of an international antiterrorism committee and expressed the sense of Congress that international treaties should be negotiated to prevent and respond to global terrorist attacks and the use of terrorism should be condemned as an instrument for promoting political objectives. With regard to aviation security, the Act directed the FAA to assess the effectiveness of security at foreign airports, based on internationally established standards set by ICAO, particularly airports serviced by U.S. flag carriers and foreign carriers flying to and from the United States. The Act required the DOT to make publicly available lists of those airports found to have inadequate security and, in coordination with the Department of State, take action to suspend flight operations between the United States and any airports found to not provide adequate security. Any suspension of flight operations under the provisions of this Act could only be lifted if the FAA determined that adequate steps had been taken to correct security deficiencies and effective security could be maintained at the foreign airport. The Act also directed the Secretary of State to seek international agreements on effective measures to prevent aircraft hijackings and bombings and improve airport security.

Additionally, the Act directed the FAA to study options for an expanded air marshal program to deploy on international flights of U.S. air carriers. The Act provided the specific authority to FAA air transportation security officers to carry firearms on passenger airliners and make warrantless arrests to stop individuals from committing felony acts, including acts of air piracy or sabotage.

This authority led to the establishment of the air marshal program within the FAA, which was restricted, by statute, to covering international flight routes of U.S. flag carriers. Further, in response to the Air India bombing that occurred in the same month as the TWA 847 hijacking, the Act authorized appropriations for research and development of explosives detection technologies. While there was some recognition of the growing need for such technology, the limited public policy focus on research and development of explosives screening technology was arguably insufficient given the growing threat of aircraft bombings. More effective security measures were sorely needed at foreign air carrier stations to prevent aircraft bombings as well as aircraft hijackings.

THE ESCALATING THREAT OF AIRCRAFT BOMBINGS

The need for such action to improve security at foreign airports and along foreign routes serviced by U.S. flag carriers was again made all too clear the following year when a TWA Boeing 727 operating along the frequently targeted route between Rome, Italy and Athens, Greece experienced an in-flight bombing. The explosive device, consisting of about one pound of plastic explosive that had been placed under a seat cushion during a prior flight, possibly by a Lebanese woman with suspected ties to the Abu Nidal Organization and possible connections to PLO leader Yasser Arafat.[48] When the bomb exploded, it tore a gaping hole in the side of the jet, causing a rapid decompression of the cabin that ejected four American citizens from the aircraft, including a mother and her young infant, who fell to their deaths.

Two weeks later, on April 17, 1986, Israeli security officers conducting preflight interrogations of passengers boarding an El Al flight at London Heathrow Airport were able to foil another bombing attempt. After questioning and searching a pregnant woman of Irish nationality, the security officers discovered Semtex explosives and a timer in a bag given to the woman by her fiancé, Nezar Hindawi, a Jordanian national. While various theories have speculated that the Mossad, Israel's intelligence agency, may have had some foreknowledge of Hindawi's plot, the incident is frequently cited as an example of the potential effectiveness of extensive passenger profiling and interrogation in detecting potential security threats. Hindawi—who initially claimed that he was working for Syrian agents who had recruited him as a terrorist for the Palestinian movement, but at his trial suggested that he was really being set up by Israeli intelligence agents posing as Syrian operatives—was convicted by a British court for the attempted bombing and sentenced to 45 years in prison. In response to the incident, the United Kingdom ceased diplomatic relations with Syria.[49]

The growing risk of aircraft bombings was again put in the international spotlight on November 29, 1987, when a Korean Airlines Boeing 707, en route from Abu Dhabi, United Arab Emirates to Bangkok, Thailand blew up over the Andaman Sea killing all 115 on board. Two North Korean agents, a 70-year-old man and a 26-year-old woman, who had boarded the airplane at its origin in Baghdad, Iraq and got off in Abu Dhabi, were apprehended in Bahrain trying to travel on fake Japanese passports. While both agents swallowed cyanide capsules immediately upon being discovered, the woman survived. She admitted to planting an improvised explosive containing about three quarters of a pound of C-4 plastic explosive and about 25 fluid ounces of Picatinny Liquid Explosive (PLX) rigged to a time detonator housed in a portable radio.[50] In response, the United States condemned the bombing—carried out to discourage people from attending the 1988 Seoul Olympic Games—as a terrorist act and designated North Korea as a state sponsor of terrorism.

As evidenced by these and other aircraft bombing incidents and attempts in the mid-1980s, the risk posed by increasingly sophisticated terrorist bombs capable of downing large jets was a looming menace to aviation security, particularly to international flights. The potential for mass casualties stemming from these attacks posed a clear and present danger to aviation that far surpassed the risks associated with the wave of hijackings experienced in the 1960s and early 1970s. Yet, at this time, the U.S. aviation security system lacked the technology and resources to effectively detect improvised explosives, particularly explosive devices concealed in checked baggage placed in aircraft cargo holds, and consequently, passenger airliners remained highly vulnerable to this type of threat. Despite calls to develop and deploy systems for effectively detecting explosives in passenger baggage dating back to the TWA flight 841 investigation in 1974, options for screening baggage for explosives remained significantly limited and largely ineffective.

THE BOMBING OF PAN AM FLIGHT 103

On December 21, 1988, a bomb exploded on board Pan Am flight 103, a Boeing 747 en route from London to New York, killing all 244 passengers and 15 crewmembers on board and another 11 people in the town of Lockerbie, Scotland. Investigation revealed that the bomb consisted of a small quantity of Semtex plastic explosive that was placed with baggage in the forward cargo hold of the jumbo jet. The bomb is believed to have been hidden in a radio cassette player contained inside a suitcase that was transferred onto the airplane in Frankfurt, West Germany through the interline baggage transfer system. The bomb was likely detonated by a barometric trigger device as the airplane reached an altitude of 31,000 feet.

In the months prior to the Pan Am 103 bombing, intelligence information suggested that an attack against an aviation target operating in Europe was imminent. In late October 1988, West German authorities conducted raids against members of the Popular Front for the Liberation of Palestine-General Command (PFLP-GC) in Frankfurt and Neuss. Among items seized were radio cassette players that had been tampered with, including one that had been rigged as a bomb equipped with a barometric trigger. U.S. airlines operating at Frankfurt airport subsequently issued warnings about the device in a telex dated November 10, 1988. The telex provided specific detail about the construction of the device, noting that it would be very difficult to detect using x-ray screening. On November 18, 1998, the FAA followed with a similar bulletin to all U.S. international carriers warning about the device and the difficulty detecting such a device through x-ray screening.

In response to the radio cassette bomb threat, the FAA instructed the airlines to rigorously apply positive passenger bag match (PPBM) procedures that had been made mandatory on international flights as part of stepped up security measures implemented following the TWA 847 hijacking in 1985. The FAA was aware that Pan Am was frequently violating PPBM and screening requirements at major European hubs like London Heathrow and Frankfurt because of difficulties in reconciling interline transfers at these busy airports. Pan Am security officials indicated that they were under the impression that the airline had been granted a waiver allowing x-ray screening of interline baggage to be used in lieu of PPBM or physical searches. This would have been in line with accepted international standards that permitted either PPBM or x-ray screening of checked baggage. FAA inspections of Pan Am security at Frankfurt and Heathrow during 1988 did not note any specific violation of PPBM and baggage screening requirements, despite the knowledge that Pan Am was conducting x-ray screening in lieu of PPBM. This lack of any secondary means for preventing bombs not detected by x-ray screening was cited as a significant hole in security that the Pan Am 103 bombers were able to exploit. However, it should be duly noted that while PPBM may have thwarted the Pan Am 103 bombing, by itself it would be incapable of stopping a suicide bomber. Nonetheless, loopholes in the PPBM procedures at Frankfurt have been cited as a major security weakness that allowed the Pan Am 103 bombers to succeed in carrying out their mission of destruction.

Soon after the detection of radio cassette bomb devices by the West German authorities, the U.S. Embassy in Helsinki, Finland received an anonymous call on December 5, 1988 warning that a Pan Am aircraft departing Frankfurt for the United States would be bombed within the next two weeks. The male caller, characterized as having a Middle Eastern accent, identified two individuals tied to the Abu Nidal Organization who he said were responsible for constructing the bomb. The embassy notified the State Department in Washington and the Consulate Office in Frankfurt along with other agencies, including the FAA. The Consulate Office in Frankfurt subsequently notified Pan Am operations in Frankfurt, and the FAA issued a security bulletin regarding the threat to all U.S. carriers operating in Europe.

To borrow a quote by former CIA director George Tenet describing the time leading up to the September 11, 2001 attacks, in many respects the intelligence "system was blinking red"[51] at the time prior to the Pan Am 103 bombing as well. Yet little had been done to systematically address the continuing vulnerability to potential aircraft bombings. Prior to the Pan Am 103 bombing, Pan Am had responded to the threat information it had received by targeting Finnish passengers transiting through Frankfurt, because the Helsinki caller indicated that the bomb would be transported by a Finnish woman, the only detail that did not match the actual events that later transpired 16 days after the call. Pan Am, however, rejected the idea of augmenting x-ray screening of interline bags with PPBM or other security procedures in response to the threat largely because doing so, even on a limited or targeted basis, was considered too complicated given the increased passenger loads during the Christmas holiday season. When news of the Helsinki call reached the American Embassy in Moscow, embassy officials issued a travel warning to embassy employees and contractors, raising significant questions following the Pan Am 103 bombing as to why the public was not similarly made aware of the threat. Extensive investigation, however, failed to identify the caller or link the Helsinki call and the names provided by the caller to the Pan Am 103 bombing.

For investigators, prosecutors, and the victims' families, the years since the bombing have yielded a slow and painstaking process to determine the facts and circumstances of the tragedy and bring those responsible to justice. Initially, the CIA speculated on a variety of tips and claims of responsibility, but focused most heavily on the claim that the bombing was carried out by the Guardians of the Islamic Revolution, a faction of the Iranian military forces, as retaliation for the July 3, 1988, downing of Iran Air flight 655 over the Strait of Hormuz by the U.S. Navy AEGIS class cruiser *USS Vincennes*. As the investigation continued, the role of Libya and the Gaddafi regime slowly emerged. In 1990, Czechoslovakia President Vaclav Havel disclosed that the former Soviet block producer of the plastic explosive, Semtex, had supplied the Libyan government with about 1000 tons of the bomb-making material, the same material found in the West German raids and believed to have been used to take down Pan Am 103. In 1991, the United States and Britain issued formal criminal charges against two Libyan intelligence officers, Abdel Basset Al Megrahi and Al Amin Khalifah Fhimah. For several years, the Libyan government refused to turn these suspects over to authorities, despite U.N. Security Council resolutions condemning Libya's stance as well as imposing trade sanctions and U.S. restrictions on doing business with the country.

Ten years after the bombing, the effects of these actions pressed Libyan leader Muammar Gaddafi to distance himself from his past sponsorship of terrorism and negotiate arrangements for extraditing the two suspects to stand trial in The Hague, The Netherlands under Scottish law. In turn, U.N. trade sanctions against Libya were lifted. In 2001, Megrahi was found guilty and sentenced to life in prison, however Fhimah was acquitted. Megrahi has appealed his conviction to the Scottish Court of Criminal Appeal. Libya accepted responsibility for the actions of its officials, but did not outright admit to a role in the bombing. It did, however, provide compensation of about $8 million to the families of each of the victims of Pan Am 103. The United States has since removed Libya from its list of state sponsors of terrorism and has resumed diplomatic relations with the Gaddafi government. Despite the circumstantial evidence from the raids of Abu Nidal Organization sites in West Germany and known ties between Libyan leader Muammar Gaddafi and Abu Nidal, investigators have never established any concrete evidence linking any members of the Abu Nidal Organization to the Pan Am 103 bombing.

THE PRESIDENT'S COMMISSION ON AVIATION SECURITY AND TERRORISM

In August 1989, almost eight months after the Pan Am 103 bombing, President George H. W. Bush, bowing to pressure from Congress and concerned citizens, signed an executive order establishing the independent, bipartisan President's Commission on Aviation Security and Terrorism. The Commission was charged with the task of carrying out a comprehensive study and appraisal of aviation security practices and policy options and additional measures to prevent terrorist acts against aviation. The Commission was specifically instructed to place a particular emphasis on the Pan Am 103 bombing in reviewing and evaluating policy options for aviation security.[52] The Commission interviewed hundreds of aviation security experts and held five public hearings between November 1989 and April 2000.

The Commission concluded that "... the U.S. civil aviation system is seriously flawed and has failed to provide the proper level of protection for the traveling public. This system needs major reform."[53] The report criticized the FAA as being a reactive agency that had failed to anticipate and plan for future threats and had failed to adequately enforce security regulations and address air carrier security lapses, despite recognition of persistent unsafe security practices at Pan Am's international stations. The Commission concluded that the Pan Am flight 103 tragedy may have been prevented if stricter baggage reconciliation procedures and more extensive passenger screening and profiling techniques had been carried out. The Commission pointed to flaws in the FAA's apparent acceptance of Pan Am's procedures to use x-ray screening in lieu of interline PPBM reconciliation despite acknowledged weaknesses in the capability to detect well-concealed explosive devices through x-ray screening. Although the Commission did not specifically refer to this as a failure to adopt a multilay-ered approach to security, a key element of the post-9/11 U.S. strategy for aviation security, the sole reliance on x-ray screening at the Pan Am Frankfurt station in 1988 serves as a striking example of complete reliance on a single line of defense and the Pan Am 103 bombing as a case of a single point failure in a system that could have benefited from additional layers of security.

The Commission made numerous recommendations addressing international and domestic aviation security, handling of mail and cargo, FAA oversight of aviation security, research and devel-opment of aviation security technologies, coordination and sharing of intelligence and threat infor-mation, and measures to improve the treatment of families of the victims of terrorism. Major recommendations of the Commission included

- Pursuing a more vigorous counterterrorism policy, particularly with respect to nations sponsoring terrorists
- Creating a position of Assistant Secretary of Transportation for Security and Intelligence
- Elevating the FAA security office to a position where it would report directly to the FAA Administrator
- Establishing a system using federal security managers to oversee security operations at domestic airports
- Engaging the State Department in negotiations with foreign governments to ensure that U.S. air carriers operating overseas could fully comply with FAA passenger screening and other security requirements
- Having the FAA and the FBI cooperatively carry out security threat assessments at domes-tic airports
- Initiating research and development programs for technologies to detect small amounts of plastic explosives and improve the aviation security system's human and technical capabilities
- Developing consistent mechanisms for universally notifying the public regarding threats to civil aviation
- Establishing policies for special financial compensation for victims of terrorist acts
- Establishing policies and procedures for the State Department to respond to families of the victims of terrorism.

In general, the Commission's recommendations were quite comprehensive, addressing many facets of aviation security.

In specific, with regard to international security, the Commission urged the State Department to take on a more active role in negotiating aviation security measures in foreign airports and coordinat-ing international aviation security policies and positions. The Commission also recommended that the FAA take on an active role in providing technical assistance to improve security in foreign countries, particularly in high-threat regions, and urged the United States to press for tougher sanctions in response to terrorist acts against aviation, including attacks against airports and airline ticket offices. Domestically, the Commission recommended that all airport employees be required to pass criminal background checks as a condition of employment and urged the FAA to establish uniform mandatory reporting requirements and search procedures in response to bomb threats. The Commission also recommended additional training and standardized testing for ground security coordinators and standardized preflight security procedures. The Commission also recommended that, based on passenger risk assessments, domestic baggage associated with elevated risk passengers should be subject to security controls and PPBM procedures.

The Commission also addressed the threat of aircraft bombings posed by mail and cargo and made several recommendations to improve the security of cargo and mail carried on passenger aircraft. The Commission recommended that the U.S. Postal Service modify its regulations pertaining to mail security and screening to reduce the risk that a bomb placed inside mail could be loaded on an aircraft. The Commission also recommended that air carriers should be given the responsibility of screening cargo, instead of freight forwarders, and screening procedures should closely correspond to screening measures for checked baggage. The Commission also recommended that the FAA foster research and development of technologies to screen cargo for explosives and implement interim screening measures until such technology is able to be developed.

Looking specifically at the FAA, the Commission made several significant recommendations. The Commission noted that the FAA must develop stronger security measures for checked baggage, aircraft access controls, testing of security systems, the use of x-ray screening, and the prescreening of passengers. The Commission urged the FAA to take a leading role in researching human factors aspects of aviation security and take steps to improve the training of aviation security personnel. Within the FAA, the Commission recommended establishing an office of security that directly reported to the FAA Administrator. However, the Commission also recommended that a position of Assistant Secretary of Transportation for Aviation Security and Intelligence be established and given the authority and responsibility for developing an aviation transportation security policy and long-term strategy. The Commission also recommended that FAA security headquarters and field offices be fully and adequately staffed and that federal security managers in place at domestic airports and overseas locations "... should become the accountable entity for security."[54]

The Commission pressed for further research and development to enhance aviation security, particularly with regard to screening for explosives. Specifically, it recommended that the FAA gather the necessary expertise and resources to test effective explosives detection systems and establish an expert panel to oversee this initiative. It also recommended that the FAA undertake an intensive research and development program to study aircraft survivability to improve damage tolerance and determine the minimum amount of explosive material that could take down an airplane in order to set standards for detection technologies.

The Commission also directed several of its recommendations at improving intelligence gathering and dissemination related to security threats to aviation. The Commission recommended that the FAA and the FBI work cooperatively to assess vulnerabilities at U.S. airports. It also recommended moving the FAA's Intelligence Division to report directly to the proposed Assistant Secretary for Security and Intelligence position discussed above and establishing one or more CIA intelligence officers positions detailed to this office to coordinate national intelligence efforts with aviation security operations. Additional recommendations were designed to improve the coordination of threat notification and establish clear policies regarding processes and protocols for informing the traveling public regarding security threats to aviation. Several additional recommendations were made to improve the manner in which the government treats families of the victims of terrorist acts. The Commission also urged Congress to pass legislation that would require the FAA to carry out civil penalty proceedings whenever it is suspected that an air carrier's violation of FAA requirements may have contributed to a loss of life or serious injury.

The general theme of the Commission's report was that national will, and the resolve to take action to carry out that will, is the most critical element for defeating terrorism. The Commission emphasized that state sponsors of terrorism must be held accountable for their actions, and the United States must not allow terrorist attacks to influence or alter political or economic policies. The Commission recommended that steps should be taken to improve human intelligence-gathering on terrorist activity worldwide in collaboration with other nations. Also, the Commission emphasized that the U.S. government should develop a better understanding of how state-sponsored terrorism affects U.S. values and interests, and what measures are needed to effectively counter the terrorist threat, including working closely with other nations to isolate state sponsors of terrorism politically, economically, and militarily. The Commission expressed its view that the United States should be prepared to act—in possibly a preemptive manner as well as in a retaliatory manner—using either direct or covert means against state-sponsors of terrorism. Through these various recommendations, the President's Commission on Aviation Security and Terrorism established a framework for developing U.S. policy and strategy on aviation security and counterterrorism operations. After the release of the Commission's final report in August, 1989, Congress began drafting legislation to carry out many of the recommendations that had been made. These efforts resulted in the swift passage and enactment of the Aviation Security Improvement Act of 1990 (P.L. 101-604), which President George H. W. Bush signed into law on November 16, 1990.

The Aviation Security Improvements Act of 1990 (P.L. 101-604)

The Aviation Security Improvements Act of 1990 was sponsored by Representative James Oberstar, a member of the President's Commission on Aviation Security and Terrorism and a staunch advocate for aviation safety and security. Not surprisingly, the work of the Commission was clearly evident in the legislation, which was introduced less than two months after the Commission's report was released. The Act was the most significant piece of legislation on the subject of aviation security since the Anti-hijacking Act of 1974, and it addressed critical steps to enhance aviation security in recognition of the growing threats, particularly the threat of catastrophic aircraft bombings, like the Pan Am flight 103 bombing.

Congressional findings delineated in the Act noted that the current aviation security system was inadequate to address evolving terrorist threats and concluded that the United States should take immediate action to fully implement enhanced security measures targeting both U.S. and foreign air carriers. The Act created a special position of Director of Intelligence and Security within the DOT. This individual was given the responsibility for receiving, assessing, and distributing intelligence information; dealing with threats to transportation security; and developing policies, strategies, and plans for addressing transportation security threats. The Act also created a position of Assistant Administrator for Civil Aviation Security within the FAA. This individual was charged with the tasks of day-to-day management and operations related to civil aviation security. As specified in the Act, these functions were to be coordinated at the airport level by newly created federal security manager and foreign security liaison officer positions within the FAA. Specific measures to strengthen airport security called for in the Act included the strengthening of controls over checked baggage; strengthening of controls over individuals with access to aircraft; covert testing of security systems; measures to improve the reliability and performance of x-ray equipment; and measures to strengthen passenger prescreening.

As recommended by the Commission, the Act mandated preemployment background investigations for airport security personnel and air carrier personnel having unescorted access to aircraft, secured facilities, and restricted areas of airports. The Act also required the FAA to establish training standards for airport security personnel and to establish minimum staffing levels, language requirements, and education requirements for security-related positions, including ground security coordinators, supervisory security personnel, and airline pilots acting in the role of in-flight security coordinators.

The Act also directed the FAA in coordination with the FBI to conduct security threat assessments for the domestic air transportation system. In addition, it required the FAA to accelerate research on methods to deter terrorist attacks against civil aviation, with a special emphasis on protecting aircraft from the threat of explosives. The Act specifically tasked the FAA with identifying the types of explosives materials and the quantity of these materials that could cause catastrophic damage to commercial airliners. The FAA was to compare these findings with the detection capabilities that could reasonably be anticipated in the near future from emerging explosives detection technologies. The FAA was instructed to focus its efforts on identifying capabilities to screen items such as passengers, carry-on items, checked baggage, mail, and cargo to protect against such catastrophic explosives threats. The Act also directed the FAA to explore various methods to protect aircraft from the damage caused by on-board explosions. Additionally, the Act emphasized additional consideration of the role of human factors across all of these research initiatives.

A key provision of the Act required the FAA certification of any explosives detection equipment deployed to airports. The Act also created notification guidelines and proper channels for communicating aviation security threat information to the flying public. It also required the Administration to set criteria for international terrorism reporting, and required the CIA to designate one or more senior intelligence officers to liaison with the DOT, with the goal of creating better links between the intelligence community and those responsible for aviation security. The Act directed the FAA to conduct a study examining the feasibility of screening mail and cargo using the same procedures required for checked baggage and to assess explosive detection capabilities for screening mail and cargo. It also directed the Administration to seek bilateral agreements to achieve aviation security objectives worldwide, to vigorously pursue the improvements sought through the Foreign Airport Security Act including the foreign airport assessment program, and to work through the ICAO to improve aviation security internationally. The Act specifically directed the DOT to propose a comprehensive international aviation security program for training airport security personnel and to provide grants to certain nations for aviation security equipment. The Act also called for expanded use of canine teams for detecting explosives in the airport environment. Additionally, the Act addressed several recommendations of the Commission regarding government assistance to the families of victims of aviation disasters and acts of international terrorism.

THE 1990s: THE FAILURE TO IMAGINE AND ADEQUATELY PREPARE

Despite these various mandates to enhance aviation security both domestically and internationally, during the early 1990s, the FAA was stymied by inadequate funding and complex technical challenges that it was ill-equipped to handle, and it was distracted from its aviation security mission by an intense policy focus on failings related to its aviation safety oversight functions. Broadly speaking, government progress toward addressing the various aviation security initiatives sought also faced additional hurdles put in its path by complexities in the regulatory and international standards development processes. Some observers have been particularly critical of government efforts during the early to mid-1990s to address the recommendations of the President's Commission on Aviation Security and Terrorism and the mandates set forth in the Aviation Security Improvements Act of 1990. In the opinion of these critics "Congress and the President had duped the American public into believing they had buckled down and fixed a problem, when in fact the public was no more safe and secure than it had been the day Pan Am flight 103 exploded."[55] In hindsight, few can argue that the intentions of the President's Commission and the Aviation Security Improvements Act of 1990 were never fully and effectively carried out, setting up a variety of preconditions for the 9/11 terrorist attacks. In investigating the events leading up to the 9/11 tragedy, the 9/11 Commission focused intensely on these failures, latching onto an observation made by former Deputy Secretary of Defense Paul Wolfowitz who characterized the existing mind-set within the intelligence and aviation security community that dismissed the threat of suicide hijackers as a "failure of imagination."[56] The 9/11 Commission concluded that this failure of imagination was, in part, to blame for additional failures in policy, management, intelligence, counterterrorism, and aviation security capabilities that left the United States vulnerable to terrorist attacks against aviation.

Despite the policy interest in improving aviation security in the aftermath of the Pan Am flight 103 bombing, security issues were quickly overshadowed by airline safety issues. During the 1990s, the FAA came under intense scrutiny from both the media and the Congress over its role in managing and operating the air traffic control system in a safe and efficient manner and adequately regulating safety in the airline industry. First, there was the deadly runway collision on the night of February 1, 1991, at Los Angeles International Airport (LAX) that raised considerable concerns over the FAA's management and oversight of air traffic control operations. This was followed by a string of high profile airplane crashes in the mid-1990s that focused considerable attention on the FAA's role in regulating and overseeing the safety of the airline industry. The crash of a USAir aircraft departing New York's LaGuardia Airport (LGA) on March 22, 1992, was followed by two additional accidents involving USAir airplanes in 1994: The July 2, 1994, crash of a DC-9 that encountered wind shear during an aborted landing attempt at Charlotte International Airport (CLT), North Carolina, and the tragic in-flight loss of control of a USAir Boeing 737 airplane due to a rudder control malfunction while on approach to Pittsburgh International Airport (PIT) on September 8, 1994. These accidents focused considerable attention on the FAA's oversight of USAir in specific and the passenger airline industry in general. Also, on October 31, 1994, an American Eagle ATR commuter airplane, which was believed to have accumulated significant airframe ice and subsequently lost control, crashed over northern Indiana while in a holding pattern awaiting approach clearance to Chicago's O'Hare Airport (ORD). The crash, along with other incidents involving commuter flights, raised considerable questions about the safety of smaller aircraft and prompted calls in Congress for setting a single level of safety for all passenger flight operations: mainline carriers and commuter carriers alike. Then, in December 1995, the crash of an American Airlines Boeing 757 in the mountains of Colombia raised concerns over the safety and oversight of U.S. carrier international operations.

The scrutiny of FAA aviation safety oversight further intensified in 1996. On May 11, 1996, a DC-9, operated by the rapidly growing discount airline ValuJet, experienced an intense fire in one of its cargo compartments shortly after takeoff from Miami International Airport (MIA) and crashed in the Florida Everglades killing all on board. Congressional inquiry into the crash raised significant questions about the FAA's ability to regulate safety in an airline industry that was undergoing considerable change and faced with the FAA's conflicting mandates to regulate airline safety while also taking actions to facilitate the growth and expansion of the aviation industry. Amid all this concern over airline safety and the FAA's inadequacies in regulating, enforcing, and promoting commercial aviation safety, oversight of the FAA's aviation security responsibilities and its progress in carrying out the mandates of the Aviation Security Improvements Act of 1990 garnered relatively little attention. Faced with considerable concerns about aviation safety and the perception of a decreasing security threat to aviation, questions regarding what had been done to enhance aviation security had taken a backseat to debate over aviation safety policy.

As previously noted, terrorist incidents targeting U.S. carriers had declined considerably by the early 1990s. While there was a considerable uptick in worldwide airline hijackings in the early 1990s, this went largely unnoticed by policymakers in the United States. By 1992, the hijacking threat to U.S. airlines became virtually nonexistent. Following the Pan Am 103 bombing, U.S. aviation security policy and strategy was intensely focused on a single threat: the explosives threat. With regard to hijackings, for many policymakers, there appeared to be little reason to worry, and the data supported a view that the hijacking threat was a threat of the past. Throughout the decade of the 1990s, no U.S. air carrier airplanes operating either domestically or abroad were successfully hijacked. While none were bombed either, the bombing threat and its potential for mass casualties still loomed much more significantly in the minds of policymakers and senior aviation security strategists in Washington.

Since the early 1990s, the FAA had funded aviation security technology development, primarily aimed at projects for explosives detection systems. From 1991 to 1996, the FAA was spending about

$26 million annually, funding about 85 different projects for developing new explosives technology.[57] In 1993, the FAA published its first certification standard for explosives detection technologies specifying system performance criteria and human factors considerations for alerting operators regarding suspect items. However, deployment and operational use of explosive detection equipment remain quite limited throughout the early and mid-1990s. Effective aviation security technologies and procedural reforms to enhance detection of explosives carried in passenger bags were not adequately funded and largely remained a research and development effort that had limited impact on operational security practices throughout the early to mid-1990s.

Then, on the evening of July 17, 1996, an explosion on board TWA flight 800, a Paris-bound Boeing 747 departing JFK International Airport, lit up the sky over Long Island and raised immediate concerns that the threat of aircraft bombings had come to the U.S. homeland. Initial speculation that the in-flight explosion was the work of terrorists later proved false, but nonetheless, provided the necessary impetus to engage policymakers in renewed inquiries and debate over the progress made toward enhancing aviation security. Most significantly, President Bill Clinton asked Vice-President Al Gore to convene a special White House Commission to re-examine aviation security to address changing security threats. Immediately following the TWA 800 crash, President Clinton had asked the Commission to focus its attention on the issue of aviation security. However, as it became more apparent that the crash was an accident and not the result of a terrorist act, the Commission shifted its focus to also consider the FAA's regulatory oversight of air carrier safety and develop recommendations addressing aviation safety concerns.

THE GORE COMMISSION RECOMMENDATIONS REGARDING AVIATION SECURITY

On August 22, 1996, President Clinton signed executive order 13015 establishing the White House Commission on Aviation Safety and Security. Chaired by Vice-President Al Gore, the Commission became commonly known as the Gore Commission. President Clinton had instructed the Commission to develop and recommend a strategy for domestic and international aviation security and safety and gave the Commission six months to carry out this mission. The Gore Commission, in its final report to President Clinton issued in February 1997, concluded that the security threat against civil aviation was changing and increasing. It noted that the federal government must work cooperatively with private sector and local authorities to effectively carry out security responsibilities through partnerships to achieve desired goals and objectives.

The Gore Commission recommended improvements to security, not just to combat familiar threats such as explosives, but also to defend against emerging threats such as biological and chemical weapons and shoulder-fired missiles. The Gore Commission also asserted that "aviation security should be a system of systems, layered, integrated and working together to produce the highest possible levels of protection."[58] As discussed in extensive detail in later chapters of this book, the notion of a layered, integrated systems approach to aviation security has become a core principle for the present day aviation security strategy.

The Gore Commission's final report recognized the changing nature of the terrorist threat to aviation. Its first finding was that the emerging threat to aviation security was no longer just an overseas threat from foreign terrorists, citing the WTC bombing and the Oklahoma City bombing as examples of terrorism directed at targets within the United States. The second observation was that, in addition to well-established terrorists groups, terrorists were beginning to work alone or in "ad-hoc groups," and would likely resort to suicide attacks to carry out their missions, a chilling foreshadowing of the characteristics exhibited in the 9/11 attacks, four and a half years later. The report raised concern over the growing sophistication of the explosives threat to airliners, but also pointed to other emerging threats, such as biological and chemical agents, or the use of surface-to-air missiles to down an aircraft.

The Gore Commission issued a total of 31 specific recommendations to improve aviation security. Of these, 20 had been provided in an Interim Report issued on September 9, 1996, in hopes that they would prompt swift action from Congress and the FAA. An additional 11 were added with the release of the Gore Commission's final report on February 12, 1997. The final report concluded that improvements in aviation security had been stymied by a lack of government and industry cooperation and focus to resolve disputes over financing, effectiveness, technology, and potential impacts on operations and passengers. The Commission contended that enhanced security and efficient airline operations were both best achieved through cooperation among federal agencies, airlines, airports, airline employees, and law enforcement agencies. The Commission also considered the question of which federal agency was the most appropriate to have primary responsibility for aviation security. It concluded that the FAA was the appropriate agency to carry out that responsibility because of its extensive interactions and oversight of airlines and airports. However, the Commission noted that the FAA needed to significantly improve the manner in which it carried out its security mission and that the supporting roles of intelligence and law enforcement agencies in carrying out this mission must be more clearly defined and coordinated.

Foremost among its recommendations, the Gore Commission asserted that aviation security should be elevated in prominence to become a national security priority. The Commission also recommended substantial funding for capital improvements to aviation security. With regard to the looming threat of explosives, the Gore Commission called for expanded use of explosive detection system (EDS) technology and new policies and procedures for inspecting and screening U.S. mail carried on passenger aircraft. It also called for a comprehensive plan to address the potential threat of explosives placed in air cargo and recommended that the FAA work with industry to develop new initiatives in this area. The Commission recommended that the federal government purchase significant numbers of EDS equipment for screening checked baggage and upgraded x-ray systems for screening carry-on items and pursue the development of other innovative systems for explosives screening. The Commission recommended significantly expanding the use of explosives detection canine teams for airport security, noting that while bombs-sniffing dogs had been used in various settings, they had been only sparingly deployed for use in airports in the United States. The Commission also recommended implementation of full PPBM procedures for all domestic flights, as had been required for international flights, asserting that bag match was a critical component of a comprehensive, layered security program to protect against the explosives threat.

The Commission touted the potential benefits of automated passenger profiling systems for targeting high-risk passengers. The Commission noted that the FAA and Northwest Airlines were in the process of developing and testing an automated profiling system. It supported the continued development and implementation of that system, which came to be known as the CAPS system, for Computer-Assisted Passenger Screening, and later known as the Computer-Assisted Passenger Prescreening System or CAPPS. The Commission emphasized that profiling activity should not be based on race, religion, ethnicity, or other constitutionally suspect characteristics. Rather, it asserted that the profile should be based on measurable predictors of risk. While the purpose of the profile would be to select passengers for additional scrutiny, the Commission cautioned that searches based on the profiling system should be no more intrusive than those that could potentially be applied to all passengers. The Commission asserted that neither the airlines nor the federal government should maintain permanent records of those selected based on the profiling system and strict controls should be placed on access to the profiling system. The Commission, however, emphasized that these profiling systems should only remain in existence until EDSs could be reliably and fully deployed. In this regard, the Commission viewed these profiling techniques as being solely applicable to identifying explosives threats and did not fully consider their potential role in addressing the hijacking threat.

The Commission also emphasized that the FAA should work with industry to increase the professionalism of the aviation security work force, particularly screening personnel. The Commission specifically recommended that the FAA promulgate specific certification requirements for screening companies to improve the selection, training, and testing of airport security screeners. The Commission also recommended that the FAA aggressively pursue vigorous covert testing of security checkpoints to identify and correct weaknesses in screening techniques. As a result of this recommendation, the FAA significantly expanded its covert "red team" testing at airports. The Commission also emphasized that access to aircraft and secured areas of airports must be effectively controlled. It recommended that all airport and airline employees having unescorted access to secured areas of airports, as well as those performing screening duties and other security functions, should be subject to fingerprint-based criminal background checks.

The Gore Commission also commented on and made recommendations regarding some specific threats beyond the typical hijacking and explosives threats that had historically plagued commercial aviation. With regard to aviation-related information systems, it recommended strengthening security measures to protect aviation information networks and systems, such as electronic ticketing systems and air traffic control systems. The Commission also recommended the formation of an interagency task force to assess the potential threat of surface-to-air missiles to commercial aircraft. It also recommended that the U.S. Customs Service become more engaged in working with the FAA to jointly improve aviation security. As a result, the U.S. Customs Service deployed additional inspectors and investigators at major airports to assist with intelligence, criminal investigations, and counterterrorism efforts. The U.S. Customs Service also began to use more sophisticated technologies including large-scale x-ray scanners and radiation detectors, albeit on a relatively limited basis. The Commission also commented on information sharing, indicating that the FAA should pass on critical threat information received from intelligence sources to cleared airline and airport security officials so that they could take appropriate actions in response to this information. With regard to counterterrorism and intelligence, the Commission recommended significantly increasing the number of FBI agents assigned to counterterrorism investigations and providing antiterrorist assistance, including airport security training, to countries with airline service to and from the United States.

AVIATION SECURITY PROVISIONS IN THE FAA REAUTHORIZATION ACT OF 1996 (P.L. 104-264)

In parallel with the work of the Gore Commission, Congress used the ongoing FAA Reauthorization legislation being debated on Capitol Hill in 1996 as a vehicle to interject various provisions to enhance aviation security. Title III of the Act, added in response to the renewed emphasis on aviation security in the aftermath of the TWA flight 800 tragedy, addressed aviation security and included several mandates paralleling the recommendations of the Gore Commission. The intense focus on aviation safety and security following the ValuJet crash in the Everglades and the TWA flight 800 accident that year, prompted swift action on the bill that was signed into law by President Clinton on October 9, 1996.

Perhaps most notably, the Act mandated that the FAA certify security screening companies and improve the training and testing of aviation security screeners by developing uniform performance standards. The Act directed the FAA to carry out a study assessing whether certain aviation security responsibilities of air carriers, principally passenger screening, should be transferred to airports or to the federal government, and if so, how could this be best accomplished and funded. In response to this requirement, the FAA, in consultation with the airlines and airports and their respective advocacy groups failed to reach any consensus view and concluded that screening functions should be left in the hands of the airlines.

The Act also called for a study by the National Academy of Sciences examining weapons and explosives detection technologies and the potential use of hardened cargo containers to protect aircraft against the threat of in-flight explosions. The study group was instructed to provide formal recommendations regarding the most promising technologies for improving the efficiency and cost effectiveness of weapons and explosives screening. The Act also included a provision amending the Aviation Security Improvement Act of 1990, allowing the FAA to waive the requirement that airports only install FAA-certified explosives detection systems. This measure allowed for the interim deployment of noncertified explosives detection equipment until such systems could be certified and made commercially available, if it were determined that such equipment could significantly enhance aviation security. The Act also explicitly authorized the use of Airport Improvement Program (AIP) grants from the FAA and passenger facility charges (PFCs) collected by individual airports to be used for the design and improvement of airport facilities to enhance security and the purchase and the deployment of security equipment, including explosives detection systems.

The Act also expanded the scope of preemployment criminal history records check (CHRC) requirements to include aviation security screeners and supervisors and other individuals with aviation security-related responsibilities. The Act also directed the FAA, in coordination with the law enforcement and intelligence communities, to continue its development of computer-assisted passenger profiling programs. It also directed the FAA and the FBI to enter into formal agreements, establishing FBI aviation security liaisons for designated high-risk airports and conduct joint threat and vulnerability assessments at such airports at least every three years, or more frequently if deemed necessary. The Act also required airlines and airports to conduct their own vulnerability assessments on a periodic basis and directed the FAA to conduct audits of these assessments as well as unannounced inspections of airline and airport security systems to assess their vulnerabilities and effectiveness.

IMPACT OF THE GORE COMMISSION ON AVIATION SECURITY

In February 1998, one year after the release of the Gore Commission final report, the DOT released a status report outlining its progress in addressing the Commission's recommendations.[59] The report noted that President Clinton had publicly recognized aviation security as a national security priority and a major component of the U.S. strategy against terrorism. To directly address the role of aviation security in this national security strategy, the National Security Council had established a subgroup, headed by the DOT and consisting of all federal agencies with aviation security responsibilities, to specifically address the Gore Commission recommendations.

With regard to information sharing, the FAA establish channels for providing cleared airline and airport security personnel with access to classified information regarding threats to aviation security. The FBI significantly increased the number of agents assigned to counterterrorism operations. The FAA, in cooperation with the Department of State, began providing aviation security and anti-terrorism assistance to countries with airline service to the United States. The FAA also proposed, through ICAO, strengthened international aviation security standards.

In 1997, The Department of Defense (DOD) established an interagency task force to assess the surface-to-air missile threat to commercial aviation. Also, the DOT, in cooperation with the DOD, the Department of Energy, and other federal agencies, began to more closely assess the potential use of chemical, biological, and radiological weapons as terrorist threats to the aviation environment.

In 1998, the FAA began to phase in an industry-wide use of the CAPS system for behavioral profiling to identify high-risk passengers. This system was integrated with passenger bag match techniques to address the explosives threat on domestic as well as international flights. Additionally, the FAA began to deploy additional explosives detection systems and explosive trace detection devices to screen checked baggage on a limited basis. The combination of the CAPS system, passenger bag match techniques, and targeted electronic explosives detection screening was viewed as a layered, risk-based approach to addressing the threat of aircraft bombings.

LINGERING CONCERNS AND PERSISTING VULNERABILITIES

In the five years between the time the Gore Commission was established and the 9/11 attacks occurred, it is estimated that the United States spent about $500 million on aviation security technologies. This was a significant increase over the amounts spent on explosives detection technologies over the prior six years, equating to roughly a tripling of annual spending on aviation security equipment. Funding made available for aviation security technologies went primarily for deployment of EDS equipment for targeted screening of baggage and for research and development of technologies to improve checkpoint screening. Despite the emphasis on threats to airliners from bombs placed in checked baggage, the high cost and complexities of deploying EDS equipment left the U.S. aviation system significantly vulnerable to the explosives threat. As of September 11, 2001, the United States had installed only 177 EDS machines for screening checked baggage at various airports around the country and was screening less than 10% of checked baggage.[60]

Furthermore, little progress had been made on the Gore Commission recommendations for screening mail weighing more than one pound for explosives and other threat objects, citing concerns over impacts on the flow of mail service and the lack of statutory authority to scrutinize mail sealed against inspection. While the DOT had also established a baseline working group to address air cargo security, inspection methods for cargo were largely limited to documents checks to differentiate known from unknown shippers for the purpose of targeting inspections of cargo shipments originating from shippers that had not established a trusted relationship with air carriers, freight forwarders, or cargo consolidators.

Despite the considerable policy focus on aviation security in the late 1990s, the aviation system remained highly vulnerable to terrorist attacks. In 1999 and 2000, Congress began to scrutinize the FAA's progress in implementing the recommendations of the Gore Commission and the mandates to improve aviation security set forth in the FAA Reauthorization Act of 1996. What it found was troubling. The DOT Inspector General reported that, while the FAA was making some progress in deploying EDS equipment to airports, this equipment was significantly underutilized. At that time, each EDS machine was scanning about 250 bags per day, despite having the capability to screen that many bags in a two hour period. While the Inspector General found that the CAPS profiling system worked as intended, airline personnel did not always follow proper procedures to submit selectee baggage for EDS screening, and several airlines were using PPBM procedures in lieu of EDS screening, even though they had been instructed to submit all selectee bags for EDS screening at airports where explosives detection machines had been deployed. Of greater concern, covert testing revealed that airline personnel were often incapable of properly operating the EDS equipment and resolving threat alarms, and screeners often failed to detect threat items carried through checkpoints by covert testers. Also, the Inspector General found that, despite the improvements called for in the 1996 FAA Reauthorization Act, significant lapses in airport access controls continued to exist allowing covert testers to frequently penetrate into secured areas of airports or bypass screening checkpoints and board aircraft without being detected or challenged.[61]

Similarly, in testimony before the Senate Aviation Subcommittee in April 2000, General Accounting Office (GAO) Associate Director Gerald Dillingham reported that "... the chain of security protecting our aviation system has not one but several weak links."[62] Dillingham noted that, in 1987, screeners missed 20% of dangerous objects during covert FAA tests, while in 1978 screeners missed 13% of these items carried by covert testers. Although Dillingham did not publicly divulge covert testing results from more recent tests, he commented that screener detection was not improving, and, in some cases, was getting worse. Dillingham concluded that screener performance remained a serious concern. He attributed screener performance problems to rapid turnover and inattention to human factors considerations. Screener turnover averaged 226% annually at large airports, with some major U.S. airports experiencing turnover rates of over 300%. High turnover rates were attributed to low pay, minimal benefits, and the stress of the job. Screeners were typically making the same salaries as workers in fast food restaurants at large airports.

Dillingham commented that in other countries with highly effective screening practices, screeners were better qualified, received better pay and benefits, and screening responsibility was placed either with the airport or with the government and not with the air carriers. In 1996, Congress tasked the FAA with examining the feasibility of reassigning screening functions to either airports or the federal government. However, FAA consideration and evaluation of the issue through industry working groups and congressional hearings on this matter failed to reach a consensus regarding who should have responsibility for passenger and baggage screening. After considerable discussion, the status quo was maintained, and the job was left in the hands of the airlines, which farmed these security screening functions out to contract screening companies that were not yet under the direct regulatory oversight of the FAA.

THE AIRPORT SECURITY AND IMPROVEMENT ACT OF 2000 (P.L. 106-528)

In April 2000, Senator Kay Bailey Hutchison introduced the Airport Security and Improvement Act of 2000, a measure introduced largely in response to these troubling reports provided by the DOT Inspector General and the GAO and designed to improve and reemphasize security enhancements called for in the 1996 FAA Reauthorization Act. The Act was signed into law by President Clinton on November 22, 2000. The Act included a requirement that the FAA establish an industry-wide program for processing background checks required of airport and airline workers based on its ongoing pilot program. In response, the FAA in cooperation with the American Association of Airport Executives (AAAE) established the Transportation Security Clearinghouse (TSC), which serves to this day as the primary vehicle for processing aviation-related background checks and is credited with providing the capability to process the hundreds of thousands of background check renewals that were mandated following the 9/11 attacks. The Act also added several criminal offenses to the long list of the felony charges that would disqualify someone from being hired as an aviation screener or in other aviation-related positions requiring unescorted access to aircraft and secured areas of airports. The Act also provided specific guidelines for improving aviation security screener training, requiring a minimum of 40 hours of classroom instruction and 40 hours of on-the-job training, and successful completion of an approved on-the-job examination. Prompted by audits of airport security revealing significant lapses in secured-area access controls, the Act also mandated the FAA to set and impose sanctions for infractions of airport access control require-ments and directed the FAA to work with airport operators to identify and correct weaknesses in airport access control systems and procedures, correcting systemic problems no later than January 31, 2001. The Act also directed the FAA to correct any identified weaknesses in physical security measures at air traffic control facilities. The Act also sought to increase the screening of checked baggage using explosives detection equipment by adding a random process in addition to the CAPS selection process to select additional bags for screening at locations where deployed explosives detection equipment was underutilized.

HIJACKINGS AS A FORGOTTEN THREAT

In the absence of any successful domestic hijackings or any hijackings involving U.S. air carriers operating overseas during the 1990s, the air piracy threat continued to be viewed as a threat of the past. Progress on improvements to positive identification of passengers and intelligence information in the form of watch lists or no-fly lists was extremely limited. Critics noted that by 1998, Clinton Administration initiatives and mandates set forth and the FAA Reauthorization Act of 1996 were going nowhere, despite considerable rhetoric that the aviation security would be a top Administration priority during President Clinton's second term.[63] Critics have largely blamed inefficiencies at the FAA and lobbying efforts by the airline industry for stymieing efforts to enhance aviation security. In general, during the 1990s, the number of aviation security incidents impacting U.S. carriers dropped considerably compared to earlier decades. However, the aviation security threat never really went away. While global terrorists remained active and actively pursued aviation as a target, policy attention on terrorism had broadened in its perspective following the 1993 WTC Bombing and the 1995 Oklahoma City bombing. Aviation security was now competing for attention with growing policy concerns over the complexities of protecting citizens against terrorist attacks within the homeland. The WTC bombing in 1993, in particular, foreshadowed the growing threat of global terrorist activity within the United States. Ironically, the WTC bombing also foreshadowed the attacks against those buildings on September 11, 2001, using aircraft as weapons, a scenario that went tragically unimagined, leaving the aviation security system woefully unprepared for the events that unfolded that day.

REFERENCES

1. Martonosi, Susan Elizabeth. *An Operations Research Approach to Aviation Security*, Doctoral Dissertation, Massachusetts Institute of Technology, Sloan School of Management, September 2005.
2. Peter St. John. *Air Piracy, Airport Security, and International Terrorism.* New York: Quorum Books, 1991, p. 8.
3. Ibid.
4. Statement of Representative Ogden R. Reid, Before the Subcommittee on Transportation and Aeronautics, Committee on Interstate and Foreign Commerce, House of Representatives, Hearings on the Anti-Hijacking Act of 1973 (Part 1), Accompanying Skyjacking Fact Sheet, February 27, 1973.
5. Walter Cronkite. "The Skyjacking of 1970." *All Things Considered*, National Public Radio, September 9, 2003.
6. "1970: Hijacked Jets Destroyed by Guerrillas." *On This Day*, BBC News; Thomas J. Hamilton. "Last 6 Hostages Are Released; 19 Arabs Will Be Freed in Deal." *The New York Times*, September 30, 1970.
7. "Brinks Gives Bonus to Hijacking Hero." *The Hartford Courant*, September 18, 1970, p. 2.
8. Robert M. Smith. "President Asks Wider Use of Electronic Surveillance." *The New York Times*, September 12, 1970, p. 11.
9. "Nixon's Statement on Steps to Deal with Air Piracy." *The Washington Post, Times Herald*, September 12, 1970, p. A15.
10. "House Unit Tentatively Approves an Increase in Air-Passenger Taxes." *The Wall Street Journal*, September 23, 1970, p. 11.
11. Transportation Security Administration. *Our Mission: Law Enforcement*, U.S. Department of Homeland Security, Transportation Security Administration.
12. Paul Stephen Dempsey. "Aviation security: The role of law in the war against terrorism." *Columbia Journal of Transnational Law*, 41, 649–733, 2003.
13. Robert T. Holden. "The contagiousness of aircraft hijacking." *The American Journal of Sociology*, 91(4), 874–904, 1986. See also, Laura Dugan, Gary La Free, and Alex R. Piquero. "Testing a rational choice model of airline hijackings." In *Intelligence and Security Informatics, Lecture Notes in Computer Science*, P. Kantor, et al. (Eds). Vol. 3495. Heidelberg, Germany: Springer Berlin, 2005.
14. "Arizona Man Indicted in Hijacking of Plane." *The Washington Post*, June 9, 1970.
15. Federal Bureau of Investigation. *Famous Cases: Richard Floyd McCoy, Jr.—Aircraft Hijacking.* Available at: http://www.fbi.gov/libref/historic/famcases/mccoy/mccoy.htm
16. "The Real McCoy." *Time*, April 24, 1972.
17. "Accused Hijacker Held by FBI after Release by Cuban Government." *The Miami Herald*, June 15, 1975.
18. Jay Matthews. "Hijacker, Wanted in Murder, Enjoys Cuba Life." *The Washington Post*, January 7, 1975.
19. Gary Moore. "Hijacker Remains in Cuba: Michael Finney Talks of Exile." *The Miami Herald*, October 30, 1980, p. 1; R. Gregory Nokes. "Hijacker Detests Cuba." *The Washington Post*, April 26, 1977.
20. Robert F. Howe. "Years Later, Bank Killing Haunts Many; Manhunt Renewed in '72 Botched Holdup." *The Washington Post*, March 16, 1993, p. B3. See also, Ron Shaffer and Athelia Knight. "Tullers Chose to Risk Jail Rather Than Live in Cuba." *The Washington Post*, July 15, 1975.
21. Statement of G.M. Gross, Vice President, Southern Airways, Inc., before the Committee on Commerce, Subcommittee on Aviation, United States Senate, on the Administration's Emergency Anti-Hijacking Regulations, January 9, 1973.
22. Edmund Preston. *Troubled Passage: The Federal Aviation Administration during the Nixon-Ford Term, 1973–1977.* Washington, DC: U.S. Department of Transportation, Federal Aviation Administration, 1987, p. 42.
23. Ibid.
24. Ibid.
25. Ibid.
26. Ibid.
27. Statement of the Honorable John A. Volpe, Secretary, Department of Transportation, before the Committee on Commerce, United States Senate, on the Administration's Emergency Anti-Hijacking Regulations, January 9, 1973.

28. See The Anti-Hijacking Act of 1973 (S. 39, 93rd Congress).
29. Opening Statement by Senator Cannon, Committee on Commerce, Subcommittee on Aviation, United States Senate, on the Administration's Emergency Anti-Hijacking Regulations, January 9, 1973, p. 1.
30. Ibid., p. 2.
31. See note 27.
32. Richard L. Madden. "Soldier Lands a Stolen Copter on White House Lawn." *The New York Times*, February 18, 1974, p. 1.
33. Edmund Preston. *Troubled Passage*, see note 22, p. 53.
34. Ibid., p. 56.
35. Ibid.
36. "Women Duped into Taking Bomb to Their El Al Flight." *The New York Times*, August 18, 1972, p. 1; BBC News. "Aircraft Bomb 'Links' Explored." May 5, 2000.
37. "U.S.-bound Plane with 88 Crashes in Sea off Greece." *The New York Times*, September 9, 1974, p. 73.
38. National Transportation Safety Board. Aircraft Accident Report, Trans World Airlines, Inc., Boeing 707-331B, N8734, In the Ionian Sea, September 8, 1974. Report Number NTSB-AAR-75-7, Adopted March 26, 1975.
39. Federal Aviation Administration correspondence to the National Transportation Safety Board, Regarding Safety Recommendation A-75-4, April 16, 1975, National Transportation Safety Board Safety Recommendations Database.
40. U.S. House of Representatives, Committee on Government Operations, The Bombing of Pan Am Flight 103: A Critical Look at American Aviation Security, Hearings Before the Government Activities and Transportation Subcommittee of the Committee on Government Operations, House of Representatives, 101st Congress, September 25 and 26, 1989, Washington, DC: U.S. Government Printing Office, 1990.
41. "Abu Nidal behind Gulf Air Bombing in 1983: Report." *Agence France-Presse*, August 22, 2002.
42. William E. Smith. "Lebanon Blackmail in Beirut." *Time*, May 27, 1985.
43. David Kennedy. *The Extradition of Mohammed Hamadei*. Case Program, Kennedy School of Government, Project for the Study and Analysis of Terrorism, Harvard Law School, 1988.
44. "Germany Releases Hezbollah Hijacker Wanted by US." *Deutsche Welle*, December 12, 2005.
45. United States District Court for the District of Columbia. *United States v. Zaid Hassan Abd Latif Safarini*, Criminal Number 91-504 (EGS), Rule 11 Proffer of Facts.
46. National Transportation Safety Board. *Accident Brief, NTSB Identification DCA88MA008*.
47. David Hirschman. *Hijacked: The True Story of the Heroes of Flight 705*. New York: William Morrow & Co., 1997.
48. R. Jeffrey Smith. "New Devices May Foil Airline Security." *The Washington Post*, July 21, 1996, p. A1.
49. Jenny Booth. "El Al Bomber too Dangerous to Release, Court Rules." *Times Online*, UK, October 13, 2004.
50. Statement of Mr. Billie H. Vincent, Former Director of Civil Aviation Security, Federal Aviation Administration, Before the Government Activities and Transportation Subcommittee of the Committee on Government Operations, House of Representatives, Regarding the Bombing of Pan Am Flight 103: A Critical Look at American Aviation Security, September 25 and 26, 1989.
51. The 9/11 Report, p. 259.
52. The White House, "Commission on Aviation Security and Terrorism Formed—White House Statement (Transcript), August 4, 1989, U.S. Government Printing Office; George H.W. Bush, Executive Order 12686—Presidents Commission on Aviation Security and Terrorism, August 4, 1989.
53. Report of the President's Commission on Aviation Security and Terrorism, Washington DC, May 15, 1990, p. i.
54. Ibid., p. 122.
55. E. Marla Felcher. *U.S. Aviation Security Before and After the September 11 Terrorist Attacks*. A Report of the Century Foundation and Understanding Government. New York: The Century Foundation, 2004, pp. 31–32.
56. National Commission on Terrorist Attacks upon the United States. *The 9/11 Commission Report*, p. 336.
57. United States General Accounting Office. Aviation Security: Urgent Issues Need to Be Addressed. Statement of Keith O. Fultz, Assistant Comptroller General, Resources, Community, and Economic Development Division. Testimony before the Subcommittee on Aviation, Committee on Transportation and Infrastructure, House of Representatives, September 11, 1996.
58. White House Commission on Aviation Safety and Security. *Final Report to the President*. Office of the Vice President of the United States: Washington, DC, February 12, 1997.

59. U.S. Department of Transportation. White House Commission on Aviation Safety and Security, *The DOT Status Report*. February 1998.

60. Chris Yates, *Jane's Aviation Security—Standards and Technology*, 3rd Ed. Surrey, United Kingdom: Jane's Information Group, April 2002.

61. Statement of Alexis M. Stefani, Deputy Assistant Inspector General for Aviation, U.S. Department of Transportation, Aviation Security, Federal Aviation Administration, Testimony before the Subcommittee on Transportation and Related Agencies, Committee on Appropriations, U.S. House of Representatives, March 10, 1999.

62. Statement of Gerald L Dillingham, Associate Director, Transportation Issues, Resources, Community, and Economic Development Division, United States General Accounting Office. "Vulnerabilities Still Exist in the Aviation Security System." Testimony before the Subcommittee on Aviation, Committee on Commerce, Science, and Transportation, U.S. Senate, April 6, 2000.

63. Ibid.

2 The 9/11 Attacks and the Ensuing Policy Debate

The terrorist attacks of September 11, 2001, and the federal response to those attacks would come to shape aviation security policy and strategy in the United States. Following the attacks, the Bush Administration and Congress pondered and debated the best course of action for preventing future terrorist attacks against aviation and terrorist attacks using aircraft to target key facilities and infrastructure within the United States and made sweeping changes designed to strengthen aviation security and restore the confidence of the American people. Following the 9/11 attacks, the federal government made considerable changes to aviation security including the federalization of the screening workforce, 100% screening of checked baggage for explosives, significantly expanded lists of individuals to be denied aircraft boarding or subject to additional screening, deployment of large number of air marshals to protect flights, the creation of a program to arm airline pilots, and the hardening of cockpit doors, to name a few key initiatives. Despite the considerable cost and effort devoted to passenger airline security following the 9/11 attacks, some critics continue to raise concerns that significant weaknesses remain, and these weaknesses may be readily exploited by terrorist groups seeking to carry out aircraft hijackings and bombings.

Also, criticisms remain over policies and strategies that, in the opinion of some, have left considerable holes in other areas of the aviation security system. For example, concerns have been raised that airport workers, who are often allowed to bypass screening checkpoints, could slip a weapon or a bomb into the secured area of an airport. While the TSA is pursuing random screening of airport workers, airport access control policies and practices remain specific areas of concern for some. Also, some have argued that more need to be done to prevent terrorists from possibly placing a bomb inside of cargo placed on board passenger aircraft and to protect all-cargo aircraft from potential stowaway hijackers who could commandeer an aircraft to carry out a suicide attack. In response to these concerns, the TSA has imposed tighter regulations on the air cargo industry and some Members of Congress pushed for recently enacted legislation requiring the screening of all cargo placed on passenger aircraft by August 2010.

Policymakers have also raised considerable concerns that, faced with increased security measures at airports and on board aircraft, terrorists may carry out attacks against civilian passenger aircraft using shoulder-fired missiles and other standoff weapons capable of downing a large transport aircraft. In response to this threat, the State Department has engaged in an intensified effort to reduce worldwide stockpiles of these weapons, and a program was established within the Department of Homeland Security (DHS) to explore the use of military antimissile technology on civilian aircraft. Additionally, general aviation (GA) operations, which include all sorts of flying activity other than commercial passenger, cargo, and military operations, remain a concern for some, because these operations remain relatively open and easily accessible, thus posing unique security needs and requirements. While policy debates in the aftermath of the 9/11 attacks have focused most heavily on the security of passenger airline operations and threats originating from terrorists accessing the aviation system as commercial airline passengers, these various other threat scenarios have also been considered extensively in policy debate.

These threats and the existing vulnerabilities in the aviation system that they attempt to exploit have no simple solutions. Since 9/11, policymakers have been faced with difficult choices over implementing effective security measures while at the same time being mindful of potential impacts on the aviation industry, an industry that places a high value on the speed and efficiency of operations. This chapter will provide a general overview of the historical context, the policy debate, and course of action pursued by the United States in the aftermath of the 9/11 attacks.

In terms of the historical context of this policy debate, much of what is known about the terrorist attacks of September 11, 2001, and the events leading up to those attacks, was brought into the public light by the work of the 9/11 Commission. Therefore, the final report of the 9/11 Commission is generally regarded as the most significant authoritative source for information regarding the 9/11 attacks, the individuals and terrorist organizations responsible for carrying out those attacks. Therefore, the 9/11 Commission report[1] serves as a significant resource for the following discussion, augmented by other writings on the subject that are noted accordingly.

PRECURSORS TO 9/11

The precursors to the 9/11 terrorist attacks are rooted in the increasing animosities and threats of violence against the United States expressed by radical Islamic fundamentalists during the 1990s. These radical views reached the U.S. homeland in the early 1990s, brought here, in significant part, by Sheikh Omar Adbel Rahman, a Sunni Muslim cleric from Egypt referred to by many as the "Blind Sheikh." Despite having been implicated in the assassination of Egyptian President Anwar Sadat and expelled from his homeland, Rahman—the reputed leader of the radical Egyptian al-Gama'a al-Islamiyya or the Egyptian Islamic Group—was allowed to enter the United States on a tourist visa in 1990. Once here, he began preaching his radical views at mosques in and around New York City, advocating violence against Americans, particularly Jewish Americans. The Blind Sheikh and his followers began plotting terrorist attacks in and around New York City.

In September 1992, Ramzi Yousef, a Sunni Muslim extremist, entered the United States through JFK International Airport. Although his travel documents were considered suspect by immigration officials, he claimed political asylum. Yousef was granted temporary entry into the United States while awaiting a trial to determine the merits of this claim. Once in the United States, Yousef—who had recently attended a terrorist training camp in Afghanistan—associated himself with the Blind Sheikh and his followers. On February 26, 1993, Ramzi Yousef and coconspirators carried out the bombing of the World Trade Center (WTC) using an ammonium nitrate and fuel oil bomb that was packed into a rented truck which they parked in an underground garage under the north tower (Tower One). Yousef had originally plotted using chemical agents or radioactive material to maximize casualties and had envisioned that the bomb would topple both towers, killing perhaps 250,000 people.[2] Although the explosion was massive, the structure was able to withstand the force of the explosion. Six were killed and over 1000 were injured in the attack. While Yousef immediately fled the United States following the bombing, Rahman and his followers had ambitions of carrying out additional attacks.

Rahman and his followers conspired to carry out coordinated bombings of other prominent buildings and critical transportation infrastructure in the New York City metropolitan area. In addition to the WTC bombing, they plotted to attack the George Washington Bridge, the Holland and Lincoln Tunnels, the United Nations building, and Federal Plaza—the site of federal government offices in Manhattan—in a series of coordinated attacks.[3] These plots, however, were thwarted by a swift and effective investigation of the WTC bombing by the FBI that quickly led to the arrests of the Blind Sheikh and several of his followers. Despite this success, Yousef remained at large and would remain a considerable terrorist threat, turning his attention toward a plot targeting aviation.

BOJINKA PLOT

Following the WTC bombing, Yousef escaped to Pakistan, where he took part in the 1993 attempted assassination of Pakistani Prime Minister Benazir Bhutto, and then proceeded to Manila in the Philippines. While in the Philippines, Yousef and his uncle, Khalid Sheikh Mohammed, and other members of a terrorist cell in Manila concocted an elaborate, multipart campaign of terror they referred to as Operation Bojinka. The term Bojinka is believed to be a made-up word of unknown origin, perhaps inspired by the Serbo-Croatian word for a "boom" or an explosive sound. The first phase of the operation was a plot to assassinate Pope John Paul II during his planned visit to the Philippines for World Youth Day in January 1995. The assassination was to be followed immediately with a series of aircraft bombings targeting 12 U.S.-bound flights from Asia. Yousef and four other terrorists planned to board the first leg of these various flights and place bombs inside the life vests stored underneath their passenger seats. The terrorists would disembark at stopover points in Asia, leaving behind the explosive devices, linked to timed detonators, to blow up during the second leg of these flights while the airplanes were cruising at altitude over the Pacific Ocean.

To test this concept, on December 11, 1994, Yousef boarded Philippine Airlines flight 434, a Boeing 747, with scheduled service from Manila to Tokyo with a stopover in Cebu. On board, Yousef assembled an IED in one of the airplane's lavatories using liquid nitroglycerin concealed in a contact lens solution bottle, various other chemicals, a modified digital watch used as a timing/detonation trigger, and wires that had been concealed in his shoes. He then placed the device under his seat—a seat that would have been directly above the center wing tank on most Boeing 747s of similar age, but was located slightly forward of the tank on this particular airplane. Yousef disembarked in Cebu. As intended, the bomb exploded four hours later as the airplane cruised at 31,000 feet en route to Tokyo. The explosion killed the occupant of the seat, 24-year-old Japanese businessman Haruki Ikegami, and injured 10 others. Despite the damage to the airplane's flight controls, the airplane was able to make a successful emergency landing on Okinawa.

Based on the outcome, Yousef and others continued preparations for carrying out the first phase of the Bojinka plot, or the Manila air plot as it is referred to in the 9/11 Commission's final report, increasing the amount of explosives to increase the likelihood that the targeted aircraft would be destroyed. Had the plot been carried out successfully, the downing of 12 jumbo jets could have resulted in more than 3500 casualties. Following this, the terrorists contemplated a second phase of attacks against targets within the United States. Specifically, they planned to attack the CIA Headquarters in Langley, Virginia, either by loading a small GA airplane with explosives or by hijacking a large commercial airliner and flying the aircraft into the building. Also, in an early conceptualization of the September 11, 2001, attacks, the terrorists considered hijacking additional flights and targeting prominent buildings in the United States, such as the WTC, the Sears Tower in Chicago, the Transamerica Tower in San Francisco, the Pentagon, the United States Capitol, and the White House.

On January 6, 1995, just six days before the Pope's scheduled visit, the plot unraveled when the apartment that the terrorists were using to prepare their explosives caught fire. Extensive evidence, including bomb-making materials and instructions, along with Yousef's computer and floppy disks were found in the apartment. Investigators were able to crack encrypted files on the computer disks containing coded instructions and other details of the plot. Yousef immediately fled to Pakistan, followed soon after by Khalid Sheikh Mohammed. One month later, U.S. authorities caught up with Yousef in Pakistan after a friend whom he had previously tried to recruit for terrorist operations, Istaique Parker, provided information regarding Yousef's whereabouts in exchange for the $2 million reward that had been offered by the U.S. government. Yousef was returned to the United States where he was tried and convicted in New York for his role in the WTC bombing and the Bojinka plot. While Khalid Sheikh Mohammed remained at large, he was indicted in federal district court in Manhattan for his role in the Bojinka plot in January 1996. This resulted in him being placed on the FAA's "no-fly" list, an extremely small, select list containing the names of just 12 terrorist suspects prior to the 9/11 terrorist attacks, despite the fact that other government watch lists contained the names of thousands of known or suspected terrorists.[4]

RISING THREAT OF AL QAEDA

Meanwhile, on the other side of the globe in Sudan, Osama bin Laden, an Islamic militant from Saudi Arabia, was seeking to expand his emerging terrorist network and had set his sights on attacking the United States. Bin Laden had grand aspirations to unite and lead the various Islamic terrorist organizations. However, at this point, the U.S. intelligence community largely viewed bin Laden as a terrorist financier rather than a radical leader. Bin Laden came from a large and wealthy Saudi family, and his father was the owner of a large construction company in Saudi Arabia that was held in high regard by the Saudi royal family. However, after being ostracized by the Saudi government for his increasingly radical views and outspoken criticism, Osama bin Laden found refuge in Sudan, considered that at time to be a state sponsor of terrorism that had provided safe haven to terrorists and terrorists groups. While in Sudan, bin Laden, following in his father's footsteps, ran a legitimate construction business. However, he also worked relatively openly in establishing a terrorist financing network, training camps for Islamic terrorists, and a coordinating body for terrorist group alliances called the Islamic Army Shura.

To most observers in the United States, bin Laden was, at this point, largely an unknown figure among Arab terrorists. However, bin Laden's increasing affiliation with the Egyptian Islamic Jihad (EIJ) and its leader, Aymen al Zawahiri, contributed to his increasingly radical views against the United States. Although, it is generally believed that al Zawahiri, at that point in time, steered him away from strong rhetoric and direct threats against the United States out of fear that such talk might result in specific action by the United States or Israel to silence him.[5] While various sources have discussed possible connections between bin Laden and the WTC bombing, the planned attacks against New York City transportation arteries, and the Bojinka plot, the 9/11 Commission concluded that bin Laden's involvement in these operations was "at best cloudy."[6] What is apparent, however, is that during his time in Sudan, bin Laden concentrated his efforts on helping al Zawahiri and the EIJ. This made him an increasing concern for Egyptian intelligence and also for the Saudi government. The Egyptian government pressured the Saudis to revoke bin Laden's citizenship, which they did in March 1994.[7] By this time, bin Laden was becoming more and more of a perceived threat and his alliance with al Zawahiri and EIJ was becoming much more solidified. However, at the same time, the Sudanese government was coming under increasing international pressure to crack down on terrorists within its borders, particularly after the attempted assassination of Egyptian President Hosni Mubarak in 1995 by members of the Egyptian Islamic Group who were believed to have been provided with safe haven in Sudan and financial support from bin Laden. At the same time, economic woes brought bin Laden and his terrorist financing network close to ruin. Seeking ways to relieve international pressure that was causing a broader financial strain on the country of Sudan as a whole, Sudanese leaders began to negotiate options to expel bin Laden.

Facing possible financial ruin and increasing pressure from the Sudanese government, bin Laden uprooted and made his way back to Afghanistan in May 1996, a country he was intimately familiar with from his time spent there supporting the mujahedeen resistance against occupying Soviet military forces in the 1980s. When he returned in 1996, however, the country was divided. The fundamentalist Islamic Taliban ruled much of the country, but rival warlords controlled various regions. Although bin Laden did not initially receive a warm welcome from the Taliban—who continued to gain control of the country and implement a repressive regime based on fundamentalist Islamic teachings—he eventually won them over as he was able to run his terrorist recruitment, training, and operational planning openly and largely without interference from camps within Afghanistan.

On August 23, 1996, from a primitive cave in Tora Bora, Afghanistan, bin Laden issued a "fatwa" or edict, formally declaring war against the United States, citing the United States' continued support for Israel and its military presence in Saudi Arabia as specific offenses against the Muslim world that called for retaliatory action. It was from this very same stronghold along the Afghanistan–Pakistan border, eight years prior in September 1988, that bin Laden and his closest associates had coined the name al Qaeda ("the Base") for their newly formed group of global terrorists. Shortly after bin Laden issued his fatwa in 1996, Khalid Sheikh Mohammed came to him with a "portfolio of schemes" for attacking the United States, including the so-called planes operation, the unfulfilled second phase of the Bojinka plot involving suicide hijackings using commercial airplanes to hit strategic landmarks within the United States.[8] The two were prior acquaintances, although Khalid

Sheikh Mohammed, described as a corpulent, womanizing, world traveler, seemed to share little in common with the tall, lanky, and reclusive bin Laden, except, of course, for their strong animosity toward the United States and their mutual desire to wage war against America.[9]

By this time, the CIA had recognized the growing threat from bin Laden and al Qaeda. They had set up a listening post and intelligence analysis station at CIA Headquarters to monitor bin Laden, although initially their focus was on tracking terrorist financing. By the fall of 1997, CIA analysts had determined that bin Laden was much more than a terrorist financier and began identifying links between bin Laden and the Bojinka plot and other terrorist attacks, a strengthening al Qaeda military structure, various plans to attacks U.S. assets, and al Qaeda's specific interest in obtaining nuclear materials. They began to develop and plan an operation to capture bin Laden, but that plan was never approved or presented to the White House. As an alternative, the CIA began to pursue options to have the Saudi government pressure the Taliban to expel bin Laden from Afghanistan. Various efforts to capture or kill bin Laden were pursued only half-heartedly and none were successful in their objective. Even to this day, bin Laden has remained elusive and well protected from U.S. forces, despite extensive efforts to pursue him following the 9/11 attacks.

Unfettered by the possible repercussions of attacking U.S. interests, on August 7, 1998, al Qaeda operatives bombed the U.S. Embassies in Dar es Salaam, Tanzania and Nairobi, Kenya killing 257 people and injuring more than 5000.[10] On August 20, 1998, the United States retaliated with a series of cruise missile attacks against al Qaeda training camps near Khost, Afghanistan and a suspected chemical weapons facility in Khartoum, Sudan linked to bin Laden that was later determined to be a pharmaceuticals plant. Evidence that the facility was involved with chemical weapons production was based on limited CIA image intelligence and soil samples. It came under close scrutiny by the intelligence community because it was constructed by bin Laden's construction firm in Sudan, and it was operated by a close friend of bin Laden. Although it is known that bin Laden sought to acquire chemical weapons, as well as biological agents and nuclear weapons, during his time in Sudan, no one has been ever able to establish that the bombed facility was, in any way, connected to these efforts. In any case, the retaliatory actions carried out by the United States failed to stop or hinder bin Laden and al Qaeda to any significant degree.

The U.S. policy and strategy for dealing with the growing threat from al Qaeda was limited to these standoff attacks and continued contemplation of alternative ways to capture or possibly kill bin Laden. Bin Laden, on the other hand, apparently "wanted to lure the United States into Afghanistan, which was already being called the graveyard of empires,"[11] a reference to the Soviet Union's military failures in Afghanistan in the 1980s and the dissolution of the Soviet Union in 1991. The United States continued to explore various options for capturing or killing bin Laden, all to no avail, primarily due to a lack of agreement and conviction that such action needed to be taken as well as concern about potential diplomatic repercussions in the Muslim world among senior-level officials within the Clinton Administration. The intelligence community, nonetheless, remained convinced that al Qaeda was planning further attacks against U.S. interests, including some concern that the group may be planning for attacks within the U.S. homeland.

BUILDUP TO 9/11

As discussed in length in Chapter 1, Middle Eastern terrorists have had a specific fixation on attacking aviation targets overseas since the late 1960s, including both hijackings and bombings. However, insofar as the terrorist threat to aviation was concerned, throughout the 1990s, the FAA remained focused on the threat of aircraft bombings, with little apparent concern over the domestic hijacking threat. Evidence of the first phase of the Bojinka plot, presented at the trial of Ramsi Yousef, provided further support for this approach indicating a continuing terrorist threat of aircraft bombings. What the U.S. government knew or suspected about any al Qaeda plans to hijack aircraft prior to the attacks of September 11, 2001, however, remains a matter of considerable debate. While specific details of an al Qaeda plot to carry out suicide attacks were probably not known, government sources openly acknowledged the potential for such a scenario and federal intelligence and law enforcement agencies were aware of various indications of terrorist plans to carry out a major attack, perhaps within the United States.

On December 4, 1998, the CIA included in its Presidential Daily Brief intelligence analysis of information received from a friendly government, warning of a possible al Qaeda hijacking within the United States, carried out in coordination with the Islamic Group, as a means to barter for the release of the Blind Sheikh, Ramzi Yousef, and another coconspirator, all imprisoned in the United States.[12] The 9/11 Commission speculated whether this information, which remained classified until after the 9/11 hijackings, "might have brought more specific attention to the need for permanent changes in domestic airport and airline security procedures" if it were brought to the attention of key members of Congress.[13] Although it may have, it is important to note that this intelligence did not describe a suicide hijacking designed to use aircraft as weapons against key U.S. targets. Nonetheless, the threat may have prompted action to improve passenger and expand watch list screening for known or suspected terrorists and may have compelled FAA action to improve airline passenger screening practices and oversight. However, at the time, the Computer-Assisted Passenger Screening (CAPS) passenger prescreening process remained limited to selecting passengers for either bag matching procedures or EDS screening of checked baggage at airports where EDS equipment was available; the FAA's "no-fly" list contained a meager 12 names; FAA regulatory actions to improve the oversight of screening companies languished in the federal rulemaking process.

Following the bombing of the U.S. naval destroyer *USS Cole* in Aden, Yemen in October 2000, there was an incremental buzz of information flowing through the intelligence community regarding possible additional al Qaeda attacks, both overseas and possibly within the United States. By the late spring and early summer of 2001, the intelligence community was becoming increasingly concerned about imminent attacks, but had no specific details or actionable intelligence to pass along. On August 6, 2001, the CIA included in its daily brief to President Bush an attention-grabbing item with the headline "Bin Laden Determined to Strike in US." The brief, however, provided mostly historical information of bin Laden's desire to retaliate for the 1998 missile attacks, and his desire to strike within the United States as evidenced by the attempted millennium plot to bomb LAX. While the briefing did mention that there were some 70 ongoing FBI field investigations of suspected al Qaeda links within the United States, it provided no concrete information or actionable intelligence regarding the 9/11 plot or any other specific al Qaeda activity within the U.S. homeland.

Various unsubstantiated threats regarding targeting U.S. cities, and even the WTC, using aircraft as weapons had surfaced during the 1990s and in 2000 and 2001, but none appeared credible. Perhaps the clearest indication of the potential threat of suicide hijackings by Islamic terrorists linked to al Qaeda before 9/11 came from the December 24, 1994, hijacking of Air France flight 8969 in Algiers, Algeria by members of the Armed Islamic Group (Groupe Islamique Armé, or GIA). In the early 1990s, bin Laden had supported the GIA, providing them with weapons left over from the Afghan war that he smuggled through Sudan, seeking an all-out holy war to rid Algeria of non-Muslims. However, bin Laden reportedly withdrew his support because he felt that the massacres in Algeria would have a negative effect on his objectives of unifying Muslims jihadists under his umbrella organization.[14]

The hijacked Air France airplane, bound for Paris Orly airport, was diverted to Marseille, France after the flight crew was instructed to tell the hijackers that they did not have enough fuel to reach Paris. At Marseille, French commandos stormed the aircraft killing all four hijackers thus ending the ordeal. Investigation of the incident indicated that the hijackers most likely intended to crash the airplane into the Eiffel Tower or blow it up over Paris.[15] The plot was strikingly similar to the Abu Nidal Organization's hijacking of Pan Am flight 73 in Pakistan eight years prior, and occurred nine months after a mentally unstable FedEx flight engineer, flying as a passenger on a DC-10 cargo airplane, attempted to maim the flight crew, commandeer the airplane, and fly it into the company's Memphis, Tennessee headquarters. Perhaps because none of these attempted suicide hijackings succeeded in its objective, aviation security strategists and policymakers failed to take notice of the looming threat posed by suicidal hijackers.

Nonetheless, among government terrorism experts, the potential for a suicide aircraft hijacking was envisioned as one of many possible means for terrorists, and in particular al Qaeda, to attack within the United States. An unclassified government report issued in September 1999, two years prior to the 9/11 attacks, speculated on various forms of retaliation targeting the nation's capital that al Qaeda may have been contemplating to avenge the cruise missile attacks carried out by the United States in August 1998. The report, prepared by the Library of Congress' Federal Research Division, cautioned that "[s]uicide bomber(s) belonging to al Qaeda's Martyrdom Battalion could crash-land an aircraft packed with high explosives (C-4 and semtex) into the Pentagon, the headquarters of the CIA, or the White House," referencing Ramzi Yousef's plan to attack CIA headquarters in this manner and the established link between al Qaeda and Yousef in connection with a plot to assassinate President Clinton during his visit to the Philippines.[16] The reference to these connections between Yousef and al Qaeda and the contemplation of an al Qaeda-led suicide hijacking operation within the United States in this open source document indicate that government intelligence and counterterrorism agencies had most certainly contemplated such a scenario. Around the same time, in August 1999, however, the FAA's Civil Aviation Security intelligence office had assessed the threat of a suicide hijacking and concluded it to be an option of last resort for al Qaeda, because it would not offer the opportunity to achieve their presumed objective: to obtain the release of the Blind Sheikh and other key Islamic extremists in prison in the United States.[17] Also, according to Cathal Flynn, former Associate Administrator of Civil Aviation Security at the FAA, the capability of al Qaeda to pull off such an attack was not imagined. Mr Flynn concluded that "[t]here were disconnects. How would you coerce a pilot to fly into a building that's got people in it? . . . How would you do that? The notion of a full fledged al-Qaida member being a pilot . . . did not occur to me."[18] This failure to imagine a suicide hijacking led to inaction by the FAA: inaction that left the United States particularly vulnerable to such an attack.

In the fall of 1999, amid heightened concerns over possible terrorist targeting of U.S. aviation assets, the October 31, 1999, crash of EgyptAir flight 990 after departing JFK International Airport en route to Cairo, Egypt, raised immediate concerns over aviation security. The EgyptAir investigation focused on the apparent intentional actions of the relief first officer who was at the controls of the Boeing 767. However, failing to identify any link to terrorism, intelligence and counterterrorism efforts turned to addressing the numerous potential threats to the upcoming Year 2000 millennium celebrations.

In fact, al Qaeda had indeed been plotting a series of attacks against various worldwide targets to coincide with the Year 2000 millennium events, including an attack on an aviation target within the United States: the passenger terminal at LAX. Other planned attacks included the bombing of various tourist sites in Jordan, and the U.S. Navy destroyer *USS The Sullivans* while at anchor in Aden, Yemen. All of these plots failed. The LAX millennium bombing plot unraveled on December 14, 1999, when Ahmed Ressam, an al Qaeda operative, was arrested by U.S. Customs agents while attempting to enter the United States from Canada at the border checkpoint at Port Angeles, Washington after ferrying his car over from Victoria, British Columbia. Border agents, tipped off by Ressam's nervous behavior, searched his vehicle finding nitroglycerin and fuses hidden in his trunk. The case has been frequently cited as a prime example of how behavioral profiling techniques can serve as highly effective tools in the war against terrorism. The attack against the *USS The Sullivans* on January 3, 2000, failed when the attackers' small boat sank after being overloaded with explosives, and the plot to attack sites in Jordan was uncovered and broken up by Jordanian officials. The failures of the al Qaeda millennium plots left a false sense of security, leaving an impression that al Qaeda was not an organized, formidable threat and that counterterrorism efforts by the United States and others were highly effective against the threat posed. The fact that significant vulnerabilities in homeland security, and in aviation security in specific, continued to exist was not a priority concern among policymakers in Washington, DC. Meanwhile, al Qaeda operatives were planning a major attack against the United States by exploiting specific weaknesses in the aviation security system, weaknesses they apparently identified through systematic research, observation, and probing of that system.

PREATTACK PHASE: TERRORISTS IN OUR MIDST

By early 2000, the plan was already in motion. Al Qaeda had sent over two operatives, Nawaf al Hamzi and Khalid al Mihdhar, to California to learn English and to learn to fly. By May 2000, the two had largely given up on these objectives, but were quickly replaced by others more capable of meeting English language requirements and completing flight training. Specifically, in late May, al Qaeda has sent over three operatives from a terrorist cell in Hamburg, Germany—Mohammed Atta, Marwan al Shehhi, and Ziad Jarrah—for the purpose of obtaining flight training in the United States. They entered accelerated pilot training programs in Florida, and within six months the three had obtained commercial and instrument pilot ratings and exposure to jet aircraft operations through simulator training. While the terrorists advanced in their flight training within the United States, intelligence and counterterrorism efforts were diverted away from threats to the homeland when al Qaeda operatives bombed the U.S. naval destroyer, *USS Cole*, while at anchor in the port of Aden, Yemen on October 12, 2000. The attack on the *USS Cole*, while significantly bolstering al Qaeda support among radical Muslims, also served as the perfect diversion for the tightly held 9/11 plot.

While three al Qaeda operatives had successfully entered the United States and were well established in their flight training, a fourth member of the Hamburg cell selected to be a pilot, Ramzi Binalshibh, had failed to obtain a visa to enter the United States. However, a replacement was quickly found within the ranks of al Qaeda: a member who already had an FAA commercial pilot certificate, Hani Hanjour. Hanjour was sent to Arizona where he received some refresher training, followed by multiengine training and jet simulator instruction. The fact that all four of these al Qaeda operatives were able to receive the flight training needed to carry out their suicide missions at schools in the United States without raising any alarms has been cited by many as a particular failing of the aviation security and counterterrorism systems that existed prior to the 9/11 attacks.

Although none of these four 9/11 terrorists trained as pilots raised sufficient suspicion to prompt any of their flight school instructors to notify authorities, the actions of another al Qaeda operative, also sent to the United States for flight training, did. Zacharias Moussaoui, a French citizen of Moroccan descent, entered basic flight training in Oklahoma in February 2001 but abruptly stopped his training in May 2001. Even though he had logged only 50 hours of flight training in a small single-engine airplane and had not yet made a solo flight, he began making inquiries about obtaining training in Boeing 747 simulators, and subsequently enrolled in jet simulator training in Minnesota in August 2001. His instructor at the simulator training facility became suspicious and notified authorities, resulting in Moussaoui's arrest on immigration charges. While Moussaoui remained in jail, the FBI failed to establish a probable cause to search his notebook computer and other personal effects. When an FBI field agent and his supervisor in Minneapolis pressed the issue to get an emergency Federal Information Surveillance Act (FISA) warrant to search Moussaoui's computer and other personal effects, an FBI headquarter's agent handling the case claimed that the request was designed to get people "spun up." The Minneapolis supervisor retorted that that was exactly his intent to "... keep someone from taking a plane and crashing it into the World Trade Center."[19]

Despite this chilling premonition, the FBI failed to support this request thus eliminating a possible chance to unearth al Qaeda's 9/11 plot before it was carried out, despite having received information from French authorities linking Moussaoui to a Chechen rebel leader in late August. While the FBI did not pursue a FISA warrant against Moussaoui prior to the 9/11 attacks, they were apparently working on having him deported to France, where they believed French authorities had sufficient cause and authority to examine Moussaoui's computer. While the CIA also expressed an interest in the Moussoui case, briefing it to Director of Central Intelligence George Tenet on August 23, 2001, the CIA was apparently unable to identify Moussaoui as a terrorist or connect him with known al Qaeda operatives prior to the 9/11 attacks. Had the matter been pursued, as it was within two days after the 9/11 attacks, it would have been revealed that British intelligence had uncovered information that Moussaoui received training in an al Qaeda camp in Afghanistan. Armed with this information, the FBI may have been able to establish solid grounds for searching Moussaoui's belongings.

While the 9/11 Commission concluded that linking Moussaoui to the 9/11 hijackers would have been difficult to do within the span of one month, they noted that "publicity about his arrest and the possibility of a hijacking threat might have derailed the plot."[20] Also, had FAA intelligence officials been apprised of the Moussaoui case and heightened counterterrorism and intelligence concerns of a possible hijacking threat, this may have prompted specific action to step up aviation security operations. Instead, conducting business as usual at airport screening checkpoints, this last line of defense stood little chance of detecting or stopping the 9/11 attacks, where the hijackers armed themselves with nothing more than box cutters—deadly weapons in trained hands, but nonetheless items permitted to be carried on board passenger airliners. The 9/11 hijackers had apparently conducted surveillance flights within the United States, and they had encountered no problems carrying these utility knives through screening checkpoints.

9/11 ATTACKS

On Tuesday morning, September 11, 2001, four teams of al Qaeda trained hijackers, led by Mohammed Atta and the three fellow terrorists who had received flight training, took over four airliners during scheduled transcontinental flight from the East Coast to California: American Airlines flight 11, a Boeing 767 en route from Boston to Los Angeles; United flight 175, a Boeing 767, also en route from Boston to Los Angeles; American Airlines flight 77, a Boeing 757 en route from Dulles Airport in Virginia to Los Angeles; and United flight 93, a Boeing 757 en route from Newark, New Jersey to San Francisco.

After killing the flight crew of American Airlines flight 11, the hijackers crashed the airplane into the north tower of the WTC in New York City just before 8:47 a.m. About 15 minutes later, at roughly 9:03 a.m., the hijackers of United Airlines flight 175 crashed the airplane into the south tower of the WTC. Just before 9:38 a.m., the hijackers of American Airlines flight 77 crashed the third hijacked airliner into the Pentagon in Arlington, Virginia, impacting the building at a speed of about 530 miles per hour. At 8:42 a.m., just minutes before American Airlines flight 11 hit the WTC North Tower, United Airlines flight 93 took off from nearby Newark Airport, about 25 minutes behind schedule.

Unlike the other three aircraft that were attacked by a team of five hijackers, including one hijacker with pilot training on each flight, only four hijackers, including one hijacker trained as a pilot, were on board United Airline flight 93. Through numerous cell phone calls to friends and relatives, passengers on board the flight had learned the fate of the other aircraft and came to understand the hijacker's true intentions. As best as can be determined from available evidence, including information provided in the cell phone conversations and the words and sounds recorded on the cockpit voice recorder, a group of passengers fought back against the attackers, attempting to storm the cockpit and regain control of the aircraft from the hijackers. During the struggle, the hijackers attempted first to violently maneuver the airplane, apparently in an effort to throw the passengers off balance, and then put the airplane into a crash dive. The airplane crashed in a farm field near Shanksville, Pennsylvania, about 20 minutes flying time from its intended target: the United States Capitol, or perhaps alternatively, the White House, in Washington, DC.

By sunset on September 11, 2001, both WTC towers had collapsed and several other buildings in the WTC complex had suffered significant structural damage; the Pentagon had suffered significant damage to its west side, and almost 3000 victims had been killed in the attacks. Direct economic losses from the attack were enormous and the attacks had long-lasting impacts on the airline industry and the broader U.S. economy. It was the second known case of multiple, coordinated hijackings—the first being the Dawson's Field hijackings that had occurred 30 years prior. The U.S. government had not contemplated nor prepared for such a scenario, no less one involving suicide attacks using the hijacked aircraft as weapons against prominent buildings filled with people.

All evidence stemming from the 9/11 hijackings pointed directly to al Qaeda and bin Laden. However, bin Laden did not directly admit responsibility until October 2004 in a video aired by al Jazeera in which he indicated that he had personally directed the 9/11 hijackers. In that video, bin Laden noted that he was inspired by the destruction of towers in Lebanon during the 1982 war with Israel, a war that bin Laden viewed as being waged by the Israelis with the complicity of the U.S. government: "... it entered my mind that we should punish the oppressor in kind and that we should destroy towers in America in order that they taste some of what we tasted."[21]

TACTICAL RESPONSE ON SEPTEMBER 11, 2001

As it became apparent that multiple hijackings were in progress, the FAA coordinated with the North American Aerospace Defense (NORAD) to deploy military air defenses to intervene against the hijacked aircraft. At about 8:38 a.m., the FAA informed the NORAD Northeast Air Defense Sector (NEADS) in Rome, New York of the hijacking, and two Air National Guard F-15 fighter jets were scrambled from Otis Air Force Base (AFB) in Falmouth, Massachusetts. The F-15s were airborne by 8:53 a.m., nine minutes before the second airplane stuck the south tower, insufficient time to effectively acquire and engage the hijacked aircraft under the circumstances. The fighter jets briefly entered a holding pattern awaiting further instructions, and, by 9:25 a.m., they had established a combat air patrol (a CAP) over New York City.

NEADS received word of a second hijacked aircraft, United Airlines flight 175, from a call from the FAA's New York air traffic control center at approximately the same time that the airplane crashed into the WTC South Tower. Based on erroneous information that American Airlines flight 11 was still airborne and headed toward Washington, DC, NORAD subsequently ordered a pair of F-16 fighter jets from Langley AFB, in Hampton, Virginia, about 125 miles south-southeast of Washington, DC, to intercept the hijacked flight. The aircraft were initially sent toward Baltimore to attempt to intercept the aircraft. While NORAD remained unaware that United Airlines flight 77 had also been hijacked after departing Washington Dulles International Airport (IAD); controllers at Washington Reagan National Airport (DCA) informed the Secret Service of a suspicious inbound target and directed an unarmed National Guard C-130 cargo plane to intercept and track the target. Following the crash of American Airlines flight 77 into the Pentagon, the F-16s from Langley AFB set up a CAP over Washington, DC. NEADS was also informed of a Delta Airlines Boeing 767 that had departed Boston Logan airport and was suspected to have also been hijacked; however, it was never informed about United Airlines flight 93.

The same National Guard C-130 that had tracked American Airlines flight 77 as it flew into the Pentagon, continuing on its flight plan to Minnesota, was again the bearer of tragic news, being the first to report a sighting of smoke in the Pennsylvania countryside at the crash site of United Airlines flight 93. NORAD did not become aware of the fourth hijacked airplane, United Airlines flight 93, until it had already crashed. The 9/11 Commission concluded that NORAD remained unaware of the fourth hijacked aircraft, and the Langely F-16s—the only aircraft in a position to defend Washington, DC—lacked shoot-down authorization at that time. The 9/11 Commission, therefore, cast considerable doubt on NORAD's contention that military air defenses would have been able to effectively defend Washington, DC against the fourth hijacked aircraft had passengers on board not forced it down. The 9/11 Commission noted "that the nation owes a debt to the passengers of

United 93. Their actions saved the lives of countless others, and may have saved either the Capitol or the White House from destruction."[22] Additional fighter jets were subsequently launched with clear orders to fly "weapons free" and engage any perceived threat. The threat, however, had by then passed as all four hijacked aircraft had already crashed. The U.S. air defense system proved ineffective in responding to the attacks launched from within the nation's borders using airliners as missiles against strategic targets in major U.S. cities, a scenario that was never planned for or simulated in training exercises.

In addition to its *ad hoc* efforts to coordinate with NORAD, the FAA's most immediate tactical response to the terrorist hijackings of September 11, 2001, was to prevent further hijackings by first ordering ground stops and then by completely clearing the skies of aircraft. Shortly after United Airlines flight 175 hit the WTC South Tower, the FAA stopped all departures in the Northeast, and within minutes stopped all departures of flights into New York area airports or transiting New York area airspace. By 9:26 a.m., the FAA had issued a complete ground stop, banning the takeoff of all civilian aircraft in the United States. By 9:45 a.m., approximately one hour after the first aircraft had crashed into the north tower, the FAA ordered all aircraft to land at the nearest suitable airport as soon as practicable, effectively clearing the nation's skies of approximately 4,500 airborne flights being operated under instrument flight rules (IFR), and countless other small and mid-sized noncommercial aircraft operating under visual flight rules (VFR). By 12:15 p.m., the FAA reported that the airspace over the contiguous 48 states was virtually clear of all commercial and private aircraft.[23] Examining the tactical response to the 9/11 hijackings, the 9/11 Commission investigation concluded that "NORAD and the FAA were unprepared for the type of attacks launched against the United States ... [and] struggled, under difficult circumstances, to improvise a homeland defense against an unprecedented challenge they had never before encountered and had never trained to meet."[24]

Within two days, the FAA and the airlines began the process of reconstituting normal air traffic operations. While Transportation Secretary Norman Y. Mineta encouragingly stated that "[t]he reopening of our national airspace is good news for the travelers, for the airlines and for our economy,"[25] the impacts of the 9/11 attacks on the airline industry and the broader U.S. economy would be long lasting. Senior policymakers in the Bush Administration and in Congress immediately began to explore options for providing aid to the airline industry, restoring the confidence of the flying public, and developing effective aviation security policies, strategies, and measures to prevent future terrorist attacks against aviation or exploiting aviation to attack the U.S. homeland.

DOT RAPID RESPONSE TEAMS

On September 16, 2001, five days after the 9/11 terrorist attacks involving four hijacked airliners, then Secretary of Transportation Norman Y. Mineta announced the creation of two rapid response teams to assist DOT leadership in making informed decisions to improve aviation security, one focusing on airport security issues and the other on aircraft security with an emphasis on measures to protect the flight deck. Despite the name, the Rapid Response Teams were not made up of first responders, but rather, these teams were each comprised of a panel of senior leaders representing corporations and labor organizations in the airline and security protection industries. They were given the task of identifying the policy changes and strategic actions considered necessary to address the crisis in aviation security.

As directed by Secretary Mineta, these two rapid response teams reported their recommendations to the DOT on October 1, 2001, giving them roughly two weeks to deliver a plan of action that would shape aviation security policy and strategy for years to come. The Rapid Response Team on Airport Security issued a report containing five broad conclusions and 16 specific recommendations for strengthening airport security, and the Rapid Response Team on Aircraft Security issued a report containing six general conclusions and 17 specific recommendations for better protecting commercial aircraft against hostile threats.[26]

Conclusions and Recommendations of the Airport Security Rapid Response Team

The Airport Security Rapid Response Team concluded that a new federal law enforcement agency, housed within the DOT, should assume control of airport passenger screening and recommended the creation of such an agency. It also concluded that relevant law enforcement and intelligence information should be shared with those responsible for aviation security on a continual basis. The team recommended the integration of law enforcement and national security intelligence data with airline and airport systems, including passenger reservation systems, screening checks, employee background checks, employee and passenger identification systems, and airport access control protocols. The team recommended that all airlines and airports should designate a senior-level security officer with appropriate security clearance to receive and act on sensitive intelligence information. It also recommended that passenger prescreening performed using CAPPS be applied to all passengers. The team identified an urgent need to establish a nationwide program for voluntarily submitting information for vetting passengers who would be issued "smart" credentials, to expedite processing of the vast majority of travelers thus allowing aviation security resources to be focused most effectively—an idea that became known as the trusted traveler concept. This concept gave rise to the Registered Traveler (RT) program, which has not yet come close to attaining the objective of encompassing the vast majority of travelers as the Airport Security Rapid Response Team had envisioned.

The team also concluded that new technologies were needed to augment aviation security, and airport passenger screening and other security measures must be strengthened to ensure adequate protection. In specific, the team recommended new technologies for the positive identification of passengers, airport workers, and crews, and the detection of explosives. It emphasized that more effective passenger and baggage screening should be incorporated in airport security programs as soon as practicable. The team also recommended the creation of an aviation security technology consortium, including public and private sector participants, to identify, sponsor, and test new technologies. It also recommended that the DOD conduct an expedited review of classified technology programs with potential application to aviation security to identify and declassify, as appropriate, applications likely to be of value, so long as doing so would be consistent with national security objectives and requirements.

With regard to screening procedures, the team recommended that all persons, including airline employees and crews, and their carry-on items be screened at an approved screening checkpoint at all airport terminals with scheduled commercial air carrier service. It recommended the implementation of improved processes for checkpoint screening, limiting each passenger to one carry-on item, and allowing only ticketed airline passengers and authorized personnel to pass through airport screening checkpoints. The team recommended that LEOs or National Guard troops be posted at every screening checkpoint until the recommended new federal transportation security agency, what we now know as the TSA, became fully operational.

To improve access controls at airports, the team recommended that all commercial passenger airports revalidate identification and access control systems and associated identification cards that provide access to secured areas of airports. Additionally, the team called for a revalidation of airport worker background checks and CHRCs previously conducted on all persons granted access to secured areas of the airport. The team also recommended that key codes on all airport access doors be changed and all lock systems protecting secured areas of airports be rekeyed. It also urged an FAA review of all airport tenant exclusive-use and access control agreements to make necessary modifications with the objective of ensuring that a single entity is responsible for security in all areas of an airport.

In summary, the team focused its conclusions and recommendations on the creation of a new DOT aviation security agency; improved law enforcement and intelligence information sharing with aviation security officials, improved vetting of passengers, airport workers, and others accessing aircraft and secured areas of airports; identifying and deploying technologies to enhance passenger and baggage screening and airport security; making improvements to passenger and baggage screening procedures; and strengthening airport access control measures.

CONCLUSIONS AND RECOMMENDATIONS OF THE AIRCRAFT SECURITY RAPID RESPONSE TEAM

The Aircraft Security Rapid Response Team focused its efforts on identifying measures to improve in-flight security, with a particular emphasis on measures to prevent future aircraft hijackings. The team concluded that this could be accomplished through the installation of effective flight deck barriers and improved procedures for identifying airline personnel authorized to access the flight deck. The team specifically recommended that an appropriate barrier be approved within 30 days and its installation on all aircraft in the U.S. airline fleet be completed within 90 days, through urgent regulatory action providing the airlines with a simple, expedited method for approval and installation. The team also recommended that the industry identify and address the risks of rapid decompression and exit and rescue associated with these barrier devices and take steps to ensure adequate venting of a closed and locked flight deck door in the event of a rapid depressurization without allowing an intruder potential access to the flight deck via the venting feature. It urged that ongoing committee work to establish and harmonize cockpit door design standards be completed within 60 days. It recommended that future flight deck barrier design standards meet specific requirements for rapid decompression, flight crew rescue and exit, and protection from intrusion caused by blunt force, ballistics, fragmentation, or other explosive effects. The team recommended that the flight deck barrier design standard should be required for new aircraft types and as many elements of the new design as practical be retrofitted into the existing airline fleet.

With regard to flight deck access, the team recommended that airlines and pilots' unions develop procedures allowing gate and flight deck personnel to verify the credentials of noncompany pilots and flight engineers seeking to occupy the jumpseat in the cockpit, and that the FAA and the airline industry define requirements for a universal access identification system to validate, in real time, the identities of persons with legitimate access to aircraft and the flight deck. In addition to hardened flight deck barriers, the team recommended that industry evaluate the use of cameras and lighting outside the flight deck doors.

With regard to options for enhancing security within the airline cabin, the team enumerated several specific procedural actions for airlines and airline cabin crews to be immediately implemented to improve in-flight security, including

- Prohibiting passengers from loitering at the forward lavatory and galley areas
- Leaving curtains and dividers open between cabin sections to allow for unobstructed views
- Strictly enforcing seatbelt signs
- Reinforcing crew coordination to facilitate the reporting of suspicious activities to other crewmembers
- Suspending preflight beverage service to allow flight attendants to focus on passenger boarding
- Requiring the forward lavatory and the interphone to be operational before dispatching an aircraft for flight
- Positively identifying individuals seeking access to the flight deck, using peepholes, code words, or other similar methods
- Putting the jumpseat, in the cockpit, in the down position during flight if doing so inhibits access to the flight deck

The team also recommended that the FAA provide additional guidance on conducting cabin searches with the assumption that airlines would continue to conduct preflight cabin searches, and it urged these airlines to provide sufficient time and training for those personnel with cabin search responsibilities. The team emphasized that cabin search duties should not be assigned to flight or cabin crew. The team concurred with the recommendation of the Airport Security Rapid Response Team to develop a new federal security agency, and specifically recommended that this new agency be given the responsibility for conducting searches of aircraft cabins.

The team also concluded that all airline flight and cabin crews should be provided with effective training emphasizing defensive capabilities to address newly identified threats and that these changes to security training be incorporated into the annual curriculum for flight and cabin crew personnel. The team recommended that the airline industry, unions, and the FAA move swiftly to redesign security within 30 days, incorporate changes to the annual curriculum within 60 days, and provide security training to all crewmembers within six months thereafter. It also recommended that the FAA, in coordination with airlines and pilots, identify procedures to respond to attempted hijackings that could be incorporated into pilot training, such as including depressurization and rapid descent as defensive maneuvers to control a hijacker. The team also recommended that the airline industry work with the FAA to evaluate factors related to the use of nonlethal weapons and tactics for in-flight security and make recommendations for personal protection within six months. The team recommended the implementation of defensive capabilities, such as stun guns or tasers, in accordance with the recommendations of this evaluation, within one year after receiving the recommendations regarding how best to proceed. In the discussion of this recommendation, the following specific factors were presented:

- The appropriate type(s) of nonlethal defensive capabilities and the relative effectiveness of each
- Domestic and international rules and laws governing the use of nonlethal protective devices, and training and qualifying for all crewmembers in the use of such devices
- Weapons control (in a sealed/locked compartment on board the aircraft) and strict accountability procedures
- Standard operating procedures to maintain control of the situation after the device has been used
- Recurring maintenance and inspection of the devices
- Preventing passenger access to these devices

The Air Line Pilots Association (ALPA), as part of the team, in addition to these recommendations regarding nonlethal weapons, urged the FAA to formally present its reasons for or against arming pilots with lethal firearms.

The team also concluded that airlines should work in cooperation with the FAA to establish a system for disseminating government security advisories to crewmembers in a timely manner. It recommended that the airline industry develop feasible alternatives for emergency warnings within 30 days. The team also recommended the formation of a task force to identify methods for ensuring that the aircraft's transponder—a device that sends a unique aircraft identifying code to air traffic control radars—transmits continuously and cannot be shut off by terrorist hijackers, assuring a continuous transmission of a hijack signal, even if the fight deck-selected code or function is turned off. The 9/11 hijackers had disabled the airplanes' transponders, thus making the task of tracking the aircraft and coordinating air defenses more difficult.

In summary, the Aircraft Security Rapid Response Team placed a heavy emphasis on the use of flight deck barriers and procedural modifications to better restrict access to the cockpit. The team called for studies on the use of nonlethal weapons, on-board security cameras, uninterruptable transponders, and ALPA, in particular, sought official FAA guidance on the arming of airline pilots. Additionally, the team called for enhanced security training for flight crew and cabin crew and procedural changes to make it easier to detect and deter threatening behavior exhibited by passengers. The team supported the recommendation for a new federal aviation security agency, housed within the DOT, that it believed should assume responsibility for preflight security inspections of aircraft, as well as the screening functions recommended by the Airport Security Rapid Response Team.

The conclusions and recommendations of the two rapid response teams formed the foundation on which post-9/11 aviation security policy and strategy in the United States have been built. At the core of the rapid response team recommendations was the notion of creating an entirely new federal agency within the DOT that would be responsible for aviation security throughout the United States. This proposal paralleled ongoing congressional debate over options for strengthening aviation in the wake of the 9/11 attacks.

CONGRESSIONAL RESPONSE TO THE 9/11 ATTACKS

The most immediate question facing Congress following the 9/11 attacks was how to strengthen aviation security to prevent future suicide hijackings and restore public confidence in the security of the aviation system. A fundamental issue for policymakers was identifying and correcting the flaws in the aviation system that were exploited by the terrorists who carried out the 9/11 attacks. Although a complex set of preconditions contributed to the 9/11 attacks, Congress focused most heavily on the structure of divided responsibility for aviation security that existed under the system developed during the Nixon Administration, 30 years earlier. Under this system, prior to and on the day of the 9/11 attacks, airlines had the primary responsibility for screening airline passengers and their belongings for threat objects, while airports maintained responsibility for physical security of airport property and law enforcement support.

Under this scheme of airline responsibility for passenger screening, and because the commercial airport network is set up as a multipoint system where passengers can enter at any airport or airport terminal and can generally gain access to sterile areas beyond screening checkpoints at other airports and other airlines, there was no particular incentive for any one airline to invest more heavily in security screening than another. In essence, there was a diffusion of responsibility where airlines were not compelled to improve security. Some economists refer to this in game theory terms as a Nash equilibrium—so named for John Nash, the Nobel Prize-winning mathematician who demonstrated its generalized mathematical applicability—in which none of the airlines were compelled to adopt a strategy of investing in security because the potential payoff or benefit that could be realized by adopting such a strategy could be largely negated by the inaction of another airline to similarly invest in security. This phenomenon is often referred to as contagion by economists.

In such a situation, where operational and economic conditions breed inaction or failure to adopt an investment strategy among participating entities, some external force or externality must usually be introduced to spur investment or action to achieve a particular objective, such as strengthening aviation security. Externalities in the context of aviation security may include things such as public outcry for improved security or declines in passenger traffic because of broadly perceived inadequacies in aviation security and negative public reaction to significant security events; regulatory actions; or various forms of incentives for investing in security measures. Prior to the 9/11 attacks, the public generally gave little thought to airline security and the threat of terrorism, at least within the domestic U.S. market. In the international market, concerns still lingered regarding the threat of aircraft bombings, which was highlighted by the December 1988 bombing of Pan Am flight 103 and continued public concerns over aircraft bombings raised after the crash TWA flight 800 in July 1996 following an in-flight explosion later determined to have been the result of accidental causes. Hijackings, however, were largely regarded as a thing of the past, particularly among domestic flights in the United States. Thus, while there was some public pressure to enhance checked luggage screening for explosives, particularly along international routes, there was no particular public concern over the threat of hijackings of domestic flights or the adequacy of screening of passengers for threat objects.

With regard to regulatory actions to strengthen passenger screening and airline security, the FAA was moving slowly in this area, despite congressional mandates to establish and implement regulatory standards for screening companies. The FAA had only issued proposed rulemaking in the spring of 2001, five years after the statutory requirement for establishing such standards and oversight of aviation screening companies was set forth.[27] Therefore, prior to and on the day of the 9/11 attacks, the FAA had no regulatory framework in place for directly regulating, overseeing, or inspecting the operations of aviation screening companies that were under contract to the airlines to staff airport screening checkpoints with screening personnel. Although the FAA was slowly deploying EDSs for targeted and random screening of checked baggage on international flights, it had no specific programs in place to provide incentives to the airlines for otherwise improving existing aviation security screening measures. Thus, prior to the 9/11 attacks, there really were no particular external forces that would have compelled airlines in any way to improve the aviation security screening functions that they had responsibility for.

EXPANDING THE FEDERAL ROLE IN AVIATION SECURITY OPERATIONS

Following the 9/11 attacks, policymakers were faced with considerable pressure to consider the federalization of aviation security functions, particularly passenger screening functions. While an expanded federal role in aviation security had been considered previously, in the early 1970s and in the mid-1990s, operational responsibility for aviation security had been left in the hands of the airlines and the airports within the United States.

The Federal Aviation Authorization Act of 1996 (P.L. 104-264) had required the FAA to study and assess whether and, if so, how to transfer certain responsibilities, such as passenger screening, from air carriers to either airport operators or the federal government or to provide for a shared-responsibility model involving air carriers, airport operators, and the federal government. During the ensuing debate, proposals to either federalize security screening operations or make airport operators responsible for security screening were both evaluated but were ultimately dismissed for a variety of reasons.[28]

From the perspective of airport operators at the time, placing airports in charge of screening operations introduced logistic complexities and diffusion of responsibility among airports that they believed would erode security and increase the risk of terrorist infiltration of the aviation system. In 1996, Richard Marchi, Senior Vice President for technical and environmental affairs for the Airports Council International-North America (ACI-NA), speaking for his organization and the AAAE, the two primary trade organizations representing airports in the United States, summarized the airports' collective position on airport involvement in passenger screening at the time, stating that

> By interposing another controlling entity—an airport or federal employee—into the midst of the check-in process continuity is lost, and the suspect person and/or their baggage would have the opportunity to evade security measures such as a positive passenger/baggage match ... [Airline-managed screening] works because a single entity—in this case, the airline—is responsible for controlling all aspects of that passenger's screening process. If airport or federal government employees were to become responsible for effective screening of suspect passengers and/or baggage, they would multiply the number of points in the system where there must be a hand-off of responsibility and, in turn, multiply the number of opportunities for a miscue.[29]

Ultimately, the FAA elected to retain the system of airline-controlled screening operations while proposing increased federal involvement in research and acquisition of screening technologies such as EDSs and regulatory oversight of screening companies. Both the airlines and the airports supported this evolutionary approach that maintained the status quo with regard to airline responsibility for conducting screening operations while increasing federal involvement in the deployment of screening technologies and oversight of screening operations. However, to critics, maintaining the status quo was viewed as an indication that the FAA was simply too cozy with the aviation industry that it was charged with regulating.

In 1999, there were 66 private screening companies providing airport screening at the nation's commercial passenger airports.[30] Many of these contracts were on a month-to-month basis.

Furthermore, at some larger airports, multiple contracts were in place at a single airport, with multiple screening companies providing screening at security checkpoints in different parts of the passenger terminal. In 2000, the FAA reported that the average hourly wage for airport screeners was $5.75, and not all screeners received additional benefits. The FAA further noted that average annual turnover rates for screeners exceeded 100% in many locations. Also, at that time, there were no uniform standards for the selection, training, performance, and certification of private screening companies and their employees.[31] Such standardization had been recommended by the White House Commission on Aviation Safety and Security, and a requirement to certify screening companies and develop uniform performance standards was included in the Federal Aviation Authorization Act of 1996 (P.L. 104-848). However, the FAA was still working through the regulatory process to develop these standards when the 9/11 attacks occurred. Following the attacks, the policy debate largely characterized FAA efforts in this area as a failure, and policymakers immediately shifted their focus toward examining options for federalizing airline passenger screening operations.

Post-9/11 Debate over Federalizing Passenger Screening

Following the 9/11 attacks, those who advocated for federalizing aviation security functions, particularly passenger airline screening, predicated their position on two underlying arguments. First, they argued that the interconnected nature of the aviation system results in all airports and all system users benefiting from the security measures implemented at any particular airport. In the view of those advocating for a federalized screening force, this provided a compelling rationale for establishing a single entity responsible for security across the entire national aviation system. Second, in the aftermath of the 9/11 attacks, the potential positive benefits of effective aviation security for protecting the nation as a whole from future terrorist attacks became the focal issue for citizens, who collectively expressed a strong social demand for steps to be taken to improve aviation security. This provided an argument that aviation security could be viewed as a public good that all persons living in the United States could derive a benefit from, much like the security benefit derived from a strong national defense provided by the United States' armed forces.

Critics, however, voiced concerns that greatly expanding the federal role in aviation security could create a vast and ineffective bureaucracy that, in the end, would provide little or no improvement, but would cost significantly more.[32] While these concerns lingered in the minds of some, the post-9/11 debate centered on the need for strong and effective standards and practices for aviation security across the entire aviation system and the role of the federal government in either directly providing for that security or ensuring that it would meet or exceed a high standard for preventing, deterring, and detecting hijackings, bombings, and other potential threats to the aviation system.

It was argued that, without stringent regulatory requirements or other compelling external pressures, both airlines and airports would likely skimp on aviation security if given the responsibility to carry out operational security functions. For air carriers, this argument was based largely on the perceived inadequacies of airline-managed security screening before and at the time of the 9/11 attacks, and by examination of effective security practices in other countries around the world, almost all of which had put responsibility for aviation security either in the hands of the airport operators or the government, instead of the airlines.[33]

However, these arguments rested largely on a comparison of a proposed federalized system of aviation security to the way things were, rather than to the way aviation security could potentially be implemented in a more effective manner by airlines or airports under a more robust regulatory regime. These arguments did not fully explore the possibility that, with tighter regulatory control and oversight by the FAA, airline- or airport-managed aviation security screening functions could be effectively implemented. Problems with second party screening companies and their employment and management practices were a more central issue in the public policy debate and media coverage following the terrorist attacks of September 11, 2001, than the inadequacies of the FAA in establishing a more robust regulatory structure for aviation security and implementing better oversight and regulatory enforcement. The FAA had faced such criticisms with regard to safety following the crash of the ValuJet DC-9 in 1996. However, through various reforms to create a better regulatory and oversight system for aviation safety, the FAA has established a much more effective system of safety oversight that has resulted in a significant improvement in safety-related metrics over the past 15 years, despite some recent criticisms of that oversight system. We can, however, only speculate whether a similarly effective regime for regulating airline- or airport-operated security screening functions could have been equally effective as the system of federalized screening that was ultimately adopted in response to the 9/11 attacks. In any case, following the 9/11 attacks, airlines clearly viewed security operations as a significant liability, and they no longer wanted any specific responsibility for passenger screening functions.

With regard to airport operators taking over the aviation security screening function, some argued that airports, like airlines, would be likely to skimp on fully implementing effective security measures, largely because additional security measures at one airport would be seen as having limited benefit across the entire aviation system unless all airports adopted these measures uniformly. This viewpoint largely maintains that the airports, functioning largely in an autonomous fashion in setting up their aviation security screening programs, would all arrive at the lowest common denominator based on the supposition that the incremental costs of implementing additional security measures would be undermined by the fact that other airports had not taken similar steps. This view, however, ignores three important considerations. First, in the intense scrutiny of aviation security practices following the 9/11 attacks, airports would have been under considerable pressure from the public, the media, and policymakers to implement the best available practices and technologies for aviation security screening. Second, it fails to recognize the opportunity for the federal government to establish a robust and effective system-wide regulatory structure and regulatory oversight of airport-operated aviation security screening to ensure high levels of performance at all airports within the system, as has been done in several European countries.[34] Third, these arguments fail to fully consider that airports and airport authorities, unlike airlines, are typically run as not-for-profit, quasi-governmental entities without the competitive pressures faced by the airlines to keep operating costs to a minimum. Also, unlike the airlines, airports would likely have easier access to federal grants and bond revenue sources for raising the capital needed to improve security infrastructure and support airport-run security operations. Nonetheless, a conversion to airport-controlled security screening would likely have raised the hackles of the airlines, since they would have had to relinquish their control over these operations and would likely have faced increased costs passed on by airports in the form of PFCs, increased landing fees, or other facility charges to pay for additional airport-managed security measures.

Following the 9/11 attacks, the media focused intensely on airline passenger screening operations, exposing significant weaknesses in the hiring, retention, training, and performance of screeners working for third party security companies contracted by the airlines to operate airport screening checkpoints. Faced with the growing public concern over loss of public confidence in the airline-run passenger screening system, Congress moved swiftly to bring legislation to the floor that would require the federal government to takeover responsibility for the aviation security screening functions across the entire aviation system within the United States. Although policymakers and those in the airline industry largely agreed that the federal government should have responsibility for aviation screening, two issues remained. The issues were (1) what should the extent of the federal role in security screening operations be? and (2) which federal agency should have responsibility for screening functions?

In Congress, debate over the establishment of what would become the TSA focused heavily on the extent of federal involvement in screening operations and whether responsibility for aviation security should put in the hands of the DOT, which had more extensive knowledge of the aviation industry, or be placed with a law enforcement agency that may be more capable of integrating security with existing law enforcement functions. Whereas legislation considered in the House of Representatives, the Secure Transportation for America Act of 2001 (H.R. 3150, S. 1447 Engrossed

Amendment as Agreed to by the House, 107th Congress), proposed the creation of the TSA, to be housed within the DOT, it would have only required those supervising screening operations to be federal employees. In contrast, the Aviation Security Act (see S. 1447, 107th Congress), as passed by the Senate, sought to establish a federal screening workforce housed within the Department of Justice (DOJ). Provisions in the conference substitute that became the cornerstone of the Aviation and Transportation Security Act (ATSA; P.L. 107-71) created the TSA within the DOT and established the requirement for the TSA to assume existing screening contracts and convert to a security screening workforce composed entirely of federal workers, not just federal supervisors, within one year.

AVIATION AND TRANSPORTATION SECURITY ACT (ATSA, P.L. 107-71)

Following the 9/11 attacks, Congress moved swiftly to enact legislation to improve aviation security, and more broadly, security in all modes of transportation. As noted above, the focus of legislative debate centered on whether the security screening workforce at airports should be federalized. Although there was widespread agreement that the federal government should take on a more significant and direct role over security screening for passenger airline operations, there was considerable debate regarding whether the screeners themselves should be federal employees or whether they should be employed by contract firms under the direct control and supervision of federal security managers and coordinators. A related issue centered on what law enforcement powers would be given to any federal aviation security forces deployed to airports across the nation.

Just over two months after the 9/11 attacks, Congress passed the ATSA legislation that was signed into law by President Bush on November 19, 2001. Designed to correct weaknesses in aviation security exploited by the 9/11 hijackers as well as other potential vulnerabilities in transportation systems, ATSA established the TSA as a new organization within the DOT responsible for security matters across all modes of transportation. Highlights of ATSA included

- Establishing a federal security screener workforce under the TSA at airports
- Requiring explosive detection screening of all checked bags
- Deploying air marshals on all high-risk flights
- Hardening cockpit doors
- Requiring background checks for foreign flight students seeking advanced pilot training in large aircraft.

To pay, at least in part, for these new initiatives ATSA created two fee mechanisms to offset the costs of federal aviation security. The first of these, familiar to airline travelers, the passenger security fee was set at $2.50 per flight segment, with a cap of $5.00 per one-way trip. The second of these fee mechanisms, called the Aviation Security Infrastructure Fee (ASIF), is collected directly from the airlines. It is based on the inflation-adjusted amount airlines collectively paid for passenger screening in 2000, when they had responsibility for these functions. The TSA determines the proportional amount each airline is required to pay in ASIF fees based on its proportion of total passenger enplanements. The amounts collected from these two fee sources from 2002 to 2007 are shown in Figure 2.1. While collections in FY2007 totaled more than $2.5 billion from these two sources, these revenues cover less than 50% of the total amount spent by the TSA on aviation security and Federal Air Marshals. Various efforts by the Bush Administration and some in Congress to increase these fees have failed to garner widespread support in Congress. As a consequence, more than half of the total federal spending on aviation security each year is paid for out of the Treasury General Fund, which is supported by other revenue sources such as personal income taxes and corporate taxes. As previously mentioned, the notion that everyone in the United States has benefited in some way from strengthened aviation security, and it, therefore, provides a public benefit that should be funded, at least in part, by all, has been a central issue implicit in much of the post-9/11

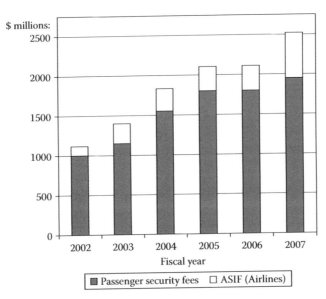

FIGURE 2.1   Revenues from passenger security fees and the ASIFs collected from airlines (FY2002–FY2007). (Data obtained from Transportation Security Administration, *TSA Historical Fee Collection Data*.)

public policy debate. However, the debate over an appropriate balance between the contributions from the General Fund and aviation-related security fee collections remains as a significant and complex issue. On the one hand, the amounts provided from the General Fund has come under scrutiny on account of increased deficit spending by the federal government. On the other hand, options to increase security fee revenues have met with resistance largely over concerns regarding the potential impact to the troubled airline industry, which has had to weather the post-9/11 downtown in passenger activity followed by rapidly escalating fuel prices. Many have argued that the airlines simply cannot afford increased security fees imposed on them directly or increases in security fees imposed on passengers that could make it more difficult for airlines to raise fares to cover fuel cost increases.

ATSA gave the newly created TSA broad authority to assess threats to security in all transportation modes, primarily focusing on aviation, and to implement appropriate security measures. In this regard, ATSA was seen as a comprehensive legislative vehicle for addressing transportation security with a specific emphasis on aviation security. ATSA established a Transportation Security Oversight Board, comprised of senior government officials responsible for transportation, law enforcement, national defense, and intelligence policy to oversee TSA's implementation of security regulations, review aviation security policies and plans, and facilitate the coordination and sharing of intelligence information with those responsible for aviation security. The Board was also charged with the task of exploring the technical feasibility of developing a common database of individuals who may pose a threat to transportation or national security.

In addition to establishing a federal screening workforce under the auspices of the TSA, ATSA required more stringent hiring qualifications and training requirements for aviation security screeners. While the Act made the screening workforce part of the federal government, it gave the TSA extensive flexibility in creating a personnel system and setting wage rates and benefits for screeners. While screeners were not given all of the benefits provided for other federal workers, the wages and benefits, including health and retirement benefits and paid leave, were a marked improvement over the low hourly wages that contract aviation security screeners were paid, often without additional benefits, under the airline passenger screening system in place prior to ATSA.

While ATSA federalized the screening workforce, it also included two provisions allowing airports to be staffed with private screeners. First, under a pilot program, five airports, one from each of the five designated airport risk categories (Category X, I, II, III, and IV), were selected to adopt a system using private screening companies closely supervised by the TSA. The pilot program was to run for a period of three years. Second, under an opt-out program, two years after the conversion to a federal screening workforce was completed, airport operators could, on an airport-by-airport basis, request conversion to TSA-approved private screening directly overseen by and under contract to the TSA. While all of the airports that participated in the pilot program elected to retain their private screeners, the option to privatize the screening workforce has not been popular with airports that were staffed with TSA screeners, and only a few smaller-sized airports have pursued this option.

Under both the private screening pilot program and the opt-out program, the pay and benefits provided to private screeners was required to be substantially the same as that provided to TSA screeners. Also, reflecting one of the recommendations of the Airport Security Rapid Response Team, ATSA gave the TSA the authority to establish a voluntary trusted traveler program to "expedite the security screening of passengers who participate in such programs, thereby allowing security screening personnel to focus on those passengers who should be subject to more extensive screening."[35]

With respect to the screening of checked baggage, ATSA established an ambitious deadline, requiring that all checked baggage be screened using EDSs or other acceptable electronic screening methods by December 31, 2002, roughly 13 months after enactment. The deadline was eventually extended by the Homeland Security Act of 2002 (P.L. 107-296) for an additional year when it became apparent that the TSA would be unable to acquire and deploy enough EDS systems to meet this deadline.

ATSA's related provisions regarding air cargo screening and security have been the subject of considerable concern and debate over the interpretation of the legislative language. With respect to commercial airline operations, ATSA directed the TSA to assume responsibility for the screening of cargo and mail, along with passenger baggage. It stated that the screening of such items shall be carried out by TSA federal screeners, but it granted a specific exception to cargo items screened under known shipper programs. These known shipper programs—established in the late 1990s based on recommendations of an industry working group convened by the FAA to examine options for improving air cargo security—relied on databases maintained by airlines and freight forwarders listing established shipping customers whose supply chain security practices had been determined to meet acceptable criteria. In interpreting this aspect of the legislation, the TSA established procedures in which only cargo received from known shippers could be placed on passenger aircraft. This practice was frequently decried by critics who regarded the lack of routine physical screening of cargo placed on passenger aircraft as a gaping hole in passenger airline security. Under this interpretation, responsibility for securing and inspecting cargo shipments placed on passenger airliners was left in the hands of the airlines and freight forwarding companies, and cargo shipped on passenger aircraft was largely exempted from routine physical inspection. Security for all-cargo operations was also left largely in the hands of the airlines and freight forwarding companies. ATSA, however, called for the implementation of a system to screen, inspect, or otherwise ensure the security of shipments transported in all-cargo as soon as practicable. Citing the impracticality of screening all mail placed on passenger aircraft, the TSA kept in place the FAA's post-9/11 prohibition on carrying U.S. mail items weighing more than one pound on passenger airplanes as an operational means to provide for the screening of mail required under ATSA.

The Federal Air Marshal Service (FAMS) was greatly expanded under ATSA and organizationally placed in the new TSA. The TSA was given broad powers to deploy appropriately trained and equipped federal air marshals on all scheduled passenger flights. Under the requirements of ATSA, FAMS must be deployed on every "high-risk" flight, which may include nonstop, long-distance flights, such as those targeted on September 11, 2001, even if the flight is fully booked. Specific determination of which flights are regarded as high risk was left up to the TSA Administrator. FAMS coverage of airline flights, as well as the specific number of FAMS and details of their operations, is a closely guarded secret. What is known is that there are thousands of air marshals who work in teams to cover both domestic and international flights. This is in stark contrast to the 33 air marshals who were employed by the FAA on September 11, 2001.[36] However, in terms of the size of this force relative to the number of daily passenger airline flights, FAMS coverage today is probably less than what it was in the early 1970s when the air marshals served as a single line of defense against hijackers. It should be recognized, though, that today, FAMS are one element of a multilayered strategy that includes passenger name checks against lists of known and suspected terrorists, physical screening of all passengers and baggage, hardened cockpit doors, and so on.

While ATSA established the TSA and gave it full responsibility for assuming the operational functions to carry out passenger screening and deploy federal air marshals, most other commercial aviation security responsibilities remained in the hands of the airlines and airport operators. ATSA created the positions of federal security managers within the TSA, now known as federal security directors or FSDs, assigned to commercial passenger airports to coordinate day-to-day security functions between the TSA, the airports, and the airlines. ATSA called for various actions to improve access controls to secured areas of airports, and it directed the airlines to implement expanded flight and cabin crew security training. ATSA also required airlines to enhance their flight crew and cabin crew security training. Although the Act did not outright authorize the controversial proposal to arm airline pilots to protect aircraft against attempted hijackings, it did order a DOJ study on the potential application of less-than-lethal weapons, like tasers, for in-flight security. Pending the results of this study, ATSA authorized the arming of flight crews with less-than-lethal weapons. The Act left the more controversial proposal for arming of pilots with lethal firearms up to the decision of the TSA and the individual airlines, allowing pilots to be armed only if the TSA approved and administered the training, and only if the air carrier employing the pilot agreed. However, at the time, the Bush Administration did not support the concept, and airlines largely opposed it out of concerns over liability.

HOMELAND SECURITY ACT OF 2002 (P.L. 107-296)

While the Bush Administration remained skeptical of the proposal to arm pilots, many in Congress backed the concept, spurred, in part, by widely held perceptions that missteps in standing up the TSA and implementing the requirements of ATSA had left commercial airliners still considerably vulnerable to another terrorist attack. Amid continuing debate in Congress over the implementation of ATSA and consideration of additional options to strengthen aviation security, there was broad bipartisan support of a measure to allow trained pilots to carry firearms to defend the flight deck against potential hijackers. Initially, a provision to set up a two-year test program that would limit participation to 2% of eligible airline pilots was proposed. However, this measure was later amended to allow all passenger airline pilots to participate in a permanent program to train and arm pilots. This provision was ultimately incorporated into the Homeland Security Act of 2002 (P.L. 107-296) in provisions referred to as the Arming Pilots Against Terrorism Act. This Act established the Federal Flight Deck Officer (FFDO) program for training, deputizing, and arming passenger airline pilots. The Act also redefined the requirements for airline crew security training based on complaints that the programs developed by the airlines to meet the training requirements mandated by ATSA were minimal and did not provide adequate information or development of security-related skills that would help thwart a real-world hijacking attempt.

The Homeland Security Act of 2002 (P.L. 107-296) is, however, more widely recognized for mandating the largest reorganization of government agencies and functions since World War II by creating the DHS. Under ATSA (P.L. 107-71), the TSA had been placed in the DOT, although there was considerable debate over whether it should be more appropriately aligned with law enforcement functions, such as under the auspices of the DOJ, where it would be more closely tied to the investigative, law enforcement, domestic intelligence, and infrastructure protection and domestic preparedness functions of the FBI. The fact of the matter was that, across the entire federal government, law enforcement functions and other functions related to homeland security were broadly divided across the various cabinet-level departments. The U.S. Customs Service, which had a significant role in international aviation operations and air and marine interdiction along the U.S. borders, was housed in the Department of the Treasury. However, Immigration and Naturalization Services, which often had a closely coordinated role in vetting international airline passengers, fell under the DOJ. Like the TSA, the U.S. Coast Guard, which often took on a role similar to the U.S. Customs Service air and marine interdiction operations, was housed in the DOT. Other functions related to homeland security were similarly spread across the federal government in arrangements that often had more historical and political meaning than functional significance.

The question of where to best house the newly created TSA was a matter of considerable debate during the development of legislation to create the DHS. While the Bush Administration sought to bring the TSA into the proposed DHS, alternative legislative proposals had a more narrow view of the role of DHS, limiting its role to border security, emergency preparedness, and response functions, leaving the TSA within the DOT.[37] The arguments for keeping the TSA within the DOT were largely predicated on the belief that this would allow for better integration with the DOT's aviation policy office and the FAA, which had primary responsibility for the regulation of airlines and airports. Critics of this view, however, argued that, in the post-9/11 context, more stringent steps were needed to effectively implement aviation security, and more closely aligning aviation security functions with law enforcement and border protection functions would enhance these efforts. This view ultimately won out.

However, another issue emerged: whether to keep the TSA intact as a distinct entity or merge some or all of its functions with other components of the newly created DHS. At the time, considerable concerns had been raised over whether the structure and management of the newly created TSA was capable of executing the tasks mandated under ATSA. Several policymakers therefore contemplated whether it would be better to start anew and viewed the creation of the DHS as a possible opportunity to assimilate the TSA functions into another more capable entity. Apparently, much of this was spurred by widespread disagreements that quickly emerged between the man chosen to head the TSA, former Secret Service Director John Magaw, and both senior White House officials and key Members of Congress over how the TSA should be run. There was considerable concern expressed by Secretary Mineta and several Members of Congress that Magaw's law enforcement style approach to aviation security was alienating the airlines and their customers, the flying public whose confidence the DOT and the airlines were trying desperately to restore.[38] Magaw saw things differently and believed that the tactics used by his former agency, the Secret Service, to protect the President and the White House could be adopted to protect passengers and airliners from future terrorist attacks, and he viewed the mandates contained in ATSA as clear indications that Congress intended for this kind of approach.

In Congress, however, there was growing concern that moving the TSA into the proposed DHS and potentially integrating it into a law enforcement agency, like the Customs Service for example, could compound the perceived problems encountered during the TSA's first year under Magaw's leadership. As the situation played out, Magaw was asked to resign immediately following the July 4, 2002 shooting at LAX by a lone gunman, the first incident of aviation terrorism occurring within the United States following the 9/11 attacks, which drew criticism and debate over the TSA's ability and responsibility to protect airports and respond to such attacks. Magaw was replaced by former Coast Guard Commandant Admiral James Loy, who remained at the helm of the TSA through the completion of its task of hiring and training the new federal screening workforce nationwide, an effort that was in high gear by the summer of 2002, as well as the deployment of explosives detection equipment for screening 100% of checked baggage at all airports nationwide.

Congress was put somewhat more at ease by Loy's style and approach and agreed to adopt the Administration proposal to place the TSA within the DHS. However, the Homeland Security Act provided specific protections to keep the TSA intact for at least two years, rather than dismantle it and start a new, a move that could have potentially integrated the TSA with another component of the DHS that may not have been as sensitive to the concerns of the airports and the airlines, nor particularly familiar with the operational constraints and considerations of the commercial airline environment. By November 2002, the fledgling TSA had grown in size to almost 60,000 employees, including about 53,000 federal screeners deployed at airports nationwide, thus meeting the statutory mandate in ATSA to stand up the federal screening workforce within one year. The large workforce of frontline screening personnel made TSA the largest entity within the DHS. While the TSA met the one-year deadline for deploying the federal screener workforce nationwide, the Homeland Security Act gave the TSA a one-year extension on the deadline to screen all checked baggage using explosives detection equipment, recognizing that there simply was not enough time to produce and deploy enough systems to meet the original December 31, 2002 deadline.

By December 31, 2003, the TSA had for the most part, met the deadline for EDS screening at all but a few large airports. At a few large airports, the TSA continued to rely on alternative methods, like hand searches and passenger bag matching procedures, but by the late spring of 2004, almost all checked bags were routinely passing through EDS machines. However, to meet this statutory requirement, bulky EDS machines were haphazardly placed wherever space could be found in airports, often in the middle of passenger terminals. The result was far from optimal and the placement of EDS equipment was inefficient and often unsightly. The long-term solution was to integrate the EDS machines with airport baggage handling conveyer systems, particularly at larger airports in an approach known as in-line EDS. However, Congress received testimony that the price tag for competing in-line EDS solutions at all airports across the United States would be in the range of $3 billion to $5 billion.[39] Airports began raising concerns that spending for modifications to accommodate EDS equipment as well as other security projects would take priority over, and take money away from, needed capacity expansion projects. Therefore, coming up with a mechanism for funding these efforts became a priority for Congress.

VISION 100: THE CENTURY OF AVIATION REAUTHORIZATION ACT (P.L. 108-176)

The solution that Congress came up with for funding in-line EDS projects at airports was the Aviation Security Capital Fund (ASCF). This fund was created under a provision in the 2003 FAA Reauthorization Act, called Vision 100—the Century of Aviation Reauthorization Act of 2003 (P.L. 108-176), a title recognizing the 100th anniversary of powered flight and the Wright brothers first flight at Kitty Hawk, North Carolina on December 17, 1903. The Act authorized up to $500 million per year through FY2007 to be appropriated to this fund and required that the first $250 million in aviation security fee collections, established under ATSA, be deposited in this fund each year through FY2007. Authorization for the fund was later extended through 2028 by the Implementing Recommendations of the 9/11 Commission Act of 2007 (P.L. 110-53). Vision 100 gave the TSA the authority to issue grants to airports for projects to integrate baggage EDSs with baggage conveyer systems; reconfigure terminal baggage areas as needed to install EDSs; deploy EDSs behind the ticket counter, in baggage sorting areas, or in line with baggage handling systems; and for other aviation security-related capital improvement projects. Vision 100 set the federal share of costs for such projects at 90% for large and medium hub airports, and at 95% for all other airports, and set guidelines for the allocation of ASCF monies for these projects. However, in contrast to authorization language in Vision 100, appropriations language from FY2005 to FY2007 limited the federal share of these project costs to 75% for medium and large hub airports and 90% for other airports.

Establishing the ASCF as a funding stream for airport security-related projects, Vision 100 repealed the existing authority to use AIP grants or PFCs collected by airports to fund airport security projects. There had been growing concerns that security spending would take AIP grant money away from needed projects to expand airport capacity and address airline delays and congestion. The ASCF was seen as a separate, dedicated stream of funding for airport security enhancements, particularly modifications to baggage handling systems to accommodate and streamline checked baggage screening systems and operations. However, recognizing that the ASCF could not provide for sufficient funding in the near term to fund all airport projects to accommodate and integrate the EDS equipment, Vision 100 formally endorsed the use of letters of intent (LOIs), which are essentially promises to reimburse airports in part for costs incurred for in-line EDS construction projects according to a prioritization lists as future year funding becomes available. The LOIs were viewed as a means to encourage near-term airport investment in in-line EDS integration with reimbursement from the TSA to follow.

Another growing concern within Congress was the size of the TSA workforce. Faced with intense pressure to meet the deadline to stand up the federal screening workforce and considerable uncertainty about increased staffing needs, particularly for baggage screening operations, and screener schedules, the TSA over-hired. Also, because the TSA's staffing allocations across airports had not been optimized, some airports were significantly overstaffed while others, particularly large airports in major metropolitan areas, had staffing shortages that contributed to long delays at security checkpoints during peak travel periods. Congress pressed the TSA to develop a more optimal staffing allocation among the airports and placed a cap of 45,000 on the total number of full-time-equivalent (FTE) screener positions. The cap actually became a sore point between congressional authorizing committees and appropriators. In the view of the authorizing committees, the cap was seen as an artificial constraint that limited the TSA's ability to determine appropriate staffing levels. Appropriators, however, viewed the cap as a necessary measure for maintaining an efficient workforce and concentrating on improved procedures and technologies that would further improve upon the efficiency of screening operations. Although Vision 100 included a provision lifting the cap, it was soon put back in place in subsequent appropriations legislation.

Vision 100 authorized flight crewmembers of all-cargo airlines to voluntarily participate in the FFDO program implemented to train and deputize armed pilots to guard aircraft cockpits against hostile attacks. The FFDO program was initially limited to pilots working for passenger airlines, but cargo pilots had pointed out that large cargo airplanes could be an attractive target for suicide hijackers and that security for all-cargo aircraft was not as elaborate as the security in place for passenger airliners. Vision 100 also expanded the FFDO program to include other flight crewmembers, such as flight engineers, in addition to pilots. In addition, Vision 100 expanded the security training of airline flight and cabin crewmembers by including a TSA-administered advanced self-defense training program that flight and cabin crew could voluntarily attend. Under these provisions, the airlines remained responsible for providing mandatory basic security training, while the TSA was required to develop and provide a voluntary advanced self-defense training course for airline crewmembers.

Amid growing concerns over the privacy implications of various homeland security initiatives to detect known and suspected terrorists, and particular concerns over the use of airline passenger data, Vision 100 required the Government Accountability Office (GAO) to review the proposed Computer-Assisted Passenger Prescreening System II (CAPPS II) passenger prescreening system and prevented the TSA from fully implementing this program until the TSA certified that a variety of issues pertaining to civil liberties, privacy, data protection, system security, system performance, and system oversight had been adequately addressed. The TSA has since scrapped the CAPPS II program and is developing an alterative prescreening system called Secure Flight. However, through various other acts of legislation, these same requirements, as well as additional requirements restricting the use of commercial data collected on individuals, such as databases used by the consumer credit industry, have been placed on whatever passenger prescreening system the TSA ultimately deploys.

Vision 100 also modified the background check requirements for foreign pilots seeking flight training in the United States. The Act transferred the duties of conducting these background checks from the DOJ to the TSA. The provisions require flight schools or instructors to provide notification and identification information for individuals seeking training in smaller aircraft, weighing less than 12,500 pounds, and require background checks be completed before training can be initiated in larger aircraft. The legislation also authorized fee collections to offset the costs of conducting these background checks. It also established a specific redress process for pilots, mechanics, or other licensed aviation professionals whose certification is denied, suspended, or revoked on the grounds that they pose a risk to aviation security. It also required the implementation of security programs for air charter operations involving aircraft weighing more than 12,500 pounds and the promulgation of regulations to ensure the security of foreign and domestic aircraft repair stations. Further, the Act required the TSA, in coordination with the FAA, to complete a security review and audit of foreign repair stations that work on air carrier aircraft and aircraft components. It also required the FAA to provide a justification to Congress for establishing an Air Defense Identification Zone (ADIZ) around a city where pilots are required to use special communications and operating procedures to enable air traffic controllers to identify potential security threats. While the congressional authorizing committees were more sympathetic to the concerns of GA pilots and implemented this measure in response to these concerns, appropriations legislation had taken action to place additional flight restrictions over Disney theme parks and over venues for major sports events, drawing the ire of GA groups who noted that these specific measures provided no real security but created considerable hassles for pilots.

By the end of 2003, an extensive statutory framework had been established through ATSA, the Homeland Security Act of 2002, and Vision 100. While the TSA had made considerable strides to address the statutory mandates of these laws, efforts were heavily focused on passenger and baggage screening. Concerns remained over other aspects of aviation security, including airport access controls, air cargo security, and the security of GA operations. Even with regard to screening operations, which were a major focus of the TSA in the two years following the 9/11 attacks, considerable concerns remained over the challenges in screening passengers and carry-on items for explosives and the need to better optimize explosives screening operations for checked baggage. Moreover, the United States had not yet devised a comprehensive strategy for addressing these numerous challenges. These continuing challenges and the need for a central strategy for addressing them represent a major focus of the bipartisan 9/11 Commission's findings and recommendations regarding aviation security, which are discussed in Chapter 3.

REFERENCES

1. National Commission on Terrorist Attacks upon the United States, *The 9/11 Commission Report*, July 22, 2004, U.S. Government Printing Office.
2. Lawrence Wright. *The Looming Tower: Al-Qaeda and the Road to 9/11*. Alfred A. Knopf: New York, 2006.
3. Ibid.
4. National Commission on Terrorist Attacks upon the United States, *The 9/11 Commission Report*.
5. Lawrence Wright. *The Looming Tower*.
6. See note 4, p. 60.
7. See note 5.
8. Ibid., p. 236.
9. Ibid.
10. "U.S. Embassy Bombings." United States Department of State.
11. See note 5, p. 272.
12. See note 4.
13. Ibid., p. 344.
14. See note 5.
15. See note 4.
16. Rex A. Hudson, *The Sociology and Psychology of Terrorism: Who Becomes a Terrorist and Why?* Federal Research Division, Library of Congress, September 1999.
17. See note 4.
18. The Associated Press. "Panel: FAA Downplayed Suicide Scenario." *The New York Times*, January 28, 2004.

19. See note 4, p. 275.
20. See note 4, p. 276.
21. Osama bin Laden video tape, al Jazeera, October 29, 2004, as translated and transcribed in Lawrence Wright, *The Looming Tower*, p. 151.
22. See note 4, p. 45.
23. Federal Aviation Administration. *September 11, 2001—The FAA Responds.*
24. See note 4, p. 45.
25. U.S. Department of Transportation. Statement of U.S. Secretary of Transportation Norman Y. Mineta, September 13, 2001.
26. U.S. Department of Transportation. *Meeting the Airport Security Challenge: Report of the Secretary's Rapid Response Team on Airport Security,* October 1, 2001; U.S. Department of Transportation. *Meeting The Aircraft Security Challenge: Report of the Secretary's Rapid Response Team on Aircraft Security,* October 1, 2001.
27. Department of Transportation, Federal Aviation Administration, "Certification of Screening Companies (Proposed Rule)," *Federal Register,* 65(3), January 5, 2000, pp. 560–611.
28. U.S. Department of Transportation, Federal Aviation Administration, *Study and Report to Congress on Civil Aviation Security.*
29. As quoted in U.S. Department of Transportation, Federal Aviation Administration, *Study and Report to Congress on Civil Aviation Security.*
30. Federal Aviation Administration, Office of Aviation Policy and Plans, Operations Regulatory Analysis Branch (APO-310), *Draft Regulatory Evaluation, Initial Regulatory Flexibility Determination, Trade Impact Assessment, and Unfunded Mandates Determination—Notice of Proposed Rulemaking, Certification of Screening Companies,* FAA Docket FAA-1999-6673, April 1999.
31. Ibid.
32. Robert S. Kirk. *Selected Aviation Security Legislation in the Aftermath of the September 11 Attack,* CRS Report for Congress RL31150. Washington, DC: Congressional Research Service. Updated December 14, 2001.
33. U.S. General Accounting Office. *Aviation Security: Terrorist Acts Illustrate Severe Weaknesses in Aviation Security,* Statement of Gerald L. Dillingham, Director, Physical Infrastructure Issues, Before the Subcommittees on Transportation, Senate and House Committees on Appropriations, September 20, 2001, GAO-01-1166T.
34. Ibid.
35. P.L. 107-71, Sec. 109.
36. See note 4.
37. Robert S. Kirk. *Department of Homeland Security: Should the Transportation Security Administration Be Included?* Congressional Research Service, The Library of Congress, Washington, DC, Updated July 24, 2002, Order Code RS21244.
38. Greg Schneider and Sara Kehaulani Goo. "Twin Missions Overwhelmed TSA," *The Washington Post,* September 2, 2002, p. A1.
39. See U.S. Government Accountability Office. Statement of Cathleen A. Berrick, Director, Homeland Security and Justice. *Aviation Security: Better Planning Needed to Optimize Deployment of Checked Baggage Screening Systems.* Testimony Before the Subcommittee on Economic Security, Infrastructure Protection, and Cyber security, Committee on Homeland Security, House of Representatives, July 13, 2005, GAO-05-896T.

3 Policy Refinement in Response to the Evolving Terrorist Threat

In the spring and early summer of 2004, nearly three years after the 9/11 attacks, many policymakers seemed to be growing increasingly frustrated with what they perceived as the slow pace at which aviation security improvements mandated in legislation were being implemented. There was also growing concern among some lawmakers that the TSA lacked a clear direction and strategy for fulfilling its duties to identify and implement transportation security needs. Various threats, incidents, and gaffes related to screening operations concerned some that significant vulnerabilities may still exist in the aviation security system, which was proving costly to operate. Policymakers in Washington wanted to see demonstrable improvements from the TSA. They also eagerly awaited the release of the 9/11 Commission's findings and its recommendations for improving aviation security with the hopes of turning these recommendations into actionable items that could be drafted into legislation for Congress to consider.

THE 9/11 COMMISSION AND ITS IMPACT ON AVIATION SECURITY POLICY

Congress had established the independent 9/11 Commission and charged it with the tasks of examining the facts and circumstances of the 9/11 attacks and making recommendations to strengthen aviation security and counterterrorism efforts to prevent future terrorist attacks. In November 2002, shortly after passing the Homeland Security Act of 2002 (P.L. 107-296), Congress included language in the FY2003 Intelligence Authorization Act (P.L. 107-306) that established the National Commission on Terrorists Attacks Upon the United States (commonly known as the 9/11 Commission). The bipartisan 9/11 Commission, led by former New Jersey Governor Tom Kean and former Indiana Congressman Lee Hamilton, was charged with the responsibilities of examining and reporting on the facts and causes of the September 11, 2001, terrorist attacks and presenting its findings, conclusions, and recommendations for corrective measures to prevent future acts of terrorism to the President and the Congress.

The 9/11 Commission concluded its investigation and released its final report on July 22, 2004.[1] Its final report was widely disseminated and was generally held in high regard by the public and Members of Congress. While some have questioned whether the 9/11 Commission fully and diligently carried out the objectives of its charter, the most widely held criticisms have centered on whether the 9/11 Commission was given sufficient time to conduct an in-depth investigation and fully consider the findings and recommendations offered by its staff, and whether the Commission was unencumbered by political pressures.[2] Despite some criticism, the work of the 9/11 Commission has served a significant role as a basis or justification for subsequent aviation policy decisions. Although the formal 9/11 Commission completed its work upon release of its final report in July 2004, some members of the Commission and Commission staff established the 9/11 Public Discourse Project, a privately funded initiative to continue the work of the Commission, largely by focusing on public education and dissemination of key elements of the Commission's investigation. The 9/11

Public Discourse Project provided an unofficial forum for the 9/11 Commission members to voice their observations and views on homeland security matters, including the federal response to the Commission's recommendations. This project concluded in December 2005, although some members of the Commission have remained active in advocating for reforms to further enhance homeland security and intelligence functions.

Upon release of the 9/11 Commission's final report in July 2004, Congress took an immediate interest in examining the report, holding hearings regarding the Commission's findings, and crafting actionable recommendations made by the Commission into legislative proposals. While Congress had already addressed aviation security issues, mostly through The Aviation and Transportation Security Act (ATSA; P.L. 107-71) and Vision 100 (The Century of Aviation Reauthorization Act; P.L. 108-176), the recommendations of the 9/11 Commission provided additional options for Congress to consider for enhancing aviation security. Crafting these recommendations into law became a top priority immediately following the release of the Commission's final report. Again, when Democrats took over majority control of Congress at the beginning of 2007, they made revisiting the 9/11 Commission report and implementing 9/11 Commission recommendations that had not yet been fully carried out a top priority. Thus, in terms of recent U.S. policy regarding aviation security and counterterrorism, the work of the 9/11 Commission has played a pivotal role.

AVIATION SECURITY-RELATED RECOMMENDATIONS OF THE 9/11 COMMISSION

The 9/11 Commission delineated its recommendations regarding aviation security in a section of its final report titled "A Layered Security System." As suggested by this title, the 9/11 Commission concluded that the TSA should implement a multilayered security system that takes into consideration the full array of possible terrorist tactics. The 9/11 Commission noted that these various layers of security must each be effective in their own right and must be coordinated with other layers in a manner that creates redundancies to catch possible lapses in any one layer. This conclusion closely parallels aviation security mandates under ATSA and the TSA's concept of "concentric rings of security" and its layered approach to aviation security, which are discussed in detail in Chapters 4 and 5 of this book.[3]

The 9/11 Commission made recommendations in six areas pertaining to aviation security: (1) enhancing passenger prescreening; (2) improving measures to detect explosives on passengers; (3) addressing human factors issues at screening checkpoints; (4) expediting deployment of in-line baggage screening systems; (5) intensifying efforts to identify, track, and screen potentially dangerous cargo; and (6) deploying hardened cargo containers on passenger aircraft to protect against explosives threats from cargo and checked baggage. In addition to these six aviation-specific recommendations, the 9/11 Commission also issued an overarching recommendation for transportation security policy to set priorities based on risk and implement the most practical and cost-effective deterrents, assigning appropriate roles and missions to federal, state, and local authorities, as well as to private stakeholders. In addition, the 9/11 Commission concluded that "[m]ajor vulnerabilities still exist in cargo and GA security. These, together with inadequate screening and access controls, continue to present aviation security challenges."[4] While the Commission identified potential threats posed by inadequate access controls to secured areas of airports and GA operations, it did not issue any specific recommendations pertaining to these risks. Also, while the 9/11 Commission acknowledged concerns raised by previous and current administrations over possible shoulder-fired missiles attacks against commercial airliners, it did not make any specific recommendations regarding this threat. In the following discussion, the six aviation-specific recommendations of the 9/11 Commission are discussed in depth.

ENHANCING PASSENGER PRESCREENING

On September 11, 2001, passenger prescreening consisted of three measures: the CAPPS; answers to two security-related questions asked by airline ticketing and gate agents (namely, "Have your bags been under your control since you packed them?" and "Has anyone unknown to you asked you to carry any items aboard this flight?"), and the presentation of photo identification to airline personnel. More than half of the 9/11 hijackers were identified as "selectees" based on CAPPS criteria. However, there was little consequence to their selection because, at the time, prescreening was used solely as a tool to screen for individuals that might try to bomb a passenger jet using methods similar to those employed in the bombing of Pan Am flight 103 by conducting PPBM or explosives detection screening of checked baggage for elevated risk travelers. The procedures were not set up to defend against either a suicide bombing or a suicide hijacking. While the CAPPS system is still in use, its purpose has since been expanded to screen for these threats as well by triggering secondary screening of passengers and carry-on items. CAPPS is maintained directly by the airlines as part of their security programs and uses computer algorithms to identify "selectees" based on matching passengers' behaviors tied to their ticket purchase and passenger name record (e.g., paying by cash, paying with someone else's credit card who is not traveling with the individual or has a different last name, and/or buying a one-way ticket) to hijacker and bomber profiles.

The 9/11 Commission recommended that improved passenger prescreening capabilities should not be delayed while the argument about a successor to CAPPS continues. The 9/11 Commission further recommended that the prescreening system should utilize the larger set of watch lists maintained by the federal government. Developing a government-run system to vet passengers against terrorist watch lists has been a long-delayed and controversial endeavor that remains uncompleted more than four years after this recommendation was issued by the 9/11 Commission. Under current implementation plans, the TSA began rolling out domestic passenger prescreening against a consolidated terrorist watch list in FY2009, and it will eventually integrate this with prescreening of passengers on international flights, a function currently performed by the Bureau of Customs and Border Protection (CBP).

IMPROVING MEASURES TO DETECT EXPLOSIVES ON PASSENGERS

Heightened concerns over the potential use of IEDs to destroy passenger airliners were brought to public attention soon after the 9/11 attacks, by the December 2001 attempted shoe bombing incident aboard an American Airlines flight from Paris to Miami. Concerns over IEDs were again raised by the media in October 2003 when a college student, Nathaniel Heatwole, sneaked banned items and materials resembling plastic explosives aboard passenger jets. While neither of these high-profile incidents was cited in the 9/11 Commission report, the 9/11 Commission acknowledged persisting weaknesses in the ability to detect explosives on passengers by formally recommending that the TSA and Congress give priority to improving detection of explosives on passengers. The 9/11 Commission further recommended that, as a start, all individuals selected for secondary screening undergo explosives screening.

The need to address these recommendations was punctuated by terrorist attacks that occurred one month after the release of the 9/11 Commission's final report, just as Congress was convening hearings to assess the policy implications of the 9/11 Commission's recommendations. On August 24, 2004, two Russian passenger jets were destroyed by IEDs believed to have been carried aboard by two female suicide bombers with ties to Chechen rebel forces. As the U.S. Congress convened hearings to consider the findings and recommendations of the 9/11 Commission, these bombings brought the threat posed by IEDs in the airline cabin, and the vulnerabilities of the current passenger screening system in the United States to such attacks, to center stage during the ensuing policy debate over options for addressing the 9/11 Commission's recommendations through legislative action. On the following day, the House Subcommittee on Aviation convened one of many congressional hearings on the findings and recommendations of the 9/11 Commission, this one looking specifically at the recommendations to improve aviation security. At that hearing, John Lehman, a member of the 9/11 Commission, testified to the "… very real threat of a suicide bomber now that the whole protocol of dealing with hijackings makes the concept of gaining control of an airplane far more difficult. The likelihood of a suicide bombing is commensurately higher."[5] The TSA concurred that that threat of explosives carried by passengers demanded immediate attention to improve the capability to detect explosives at passenger checkpoints.

However, at the time, checkpoint screening technologies and procedures had changed little since the early 1970s and provided quite limited capabilities to detect explosives carried on passengers. While carry-on items, and now shoes as well, are being x-rayed as a matter of routine and could be subjected to secondary chemical trace detection screening methods, passengers are typically only screened using metal detectors that are incapable of sensing the presence of explosives and other nonmetallic threat items. In response to the 9/11 Commission recommendations and the growing threat of aircraft bombings, the TSA expedited the development and testing of technologies to address the specific vulnerability of the screening system to the threat of IEDs carried through passenger checkpoints, although significant questions remain regarding the TSA's deployment strategy for these technologies. Initially, the TSA quickly commenced operational tests of walk-through explosives trace detection (ETD) portal systems that offer the capability to detect bomb-making chemicals on individuals using chemical trace detection methods. These systems have been operationally tested in various transportation settings including airport passenger screening checkpoints, but have suffered from reliability issues that have raised questions about their wide-scale deployment. Other possible methods for detecting explosives on passengers involve the use of whole body imaging (WBI) systems using either low-dose x-ray backscatter or other techniques, such as millimeter wave imaging technologies. WBI technology, however, has been slow in gaining acceptance and is considered somewhat more controversial because these technologies are capable of rendering a nude or seminude image of the scanned individual, which is regarded by some as being overly intrusive. To address these concerns, the TSA has worked with systems developers to incorporate modesty or privacy filters that degrade the images generated by these systems to protect individual identities and prevent imaging of private areas in a manner that attempts to strike a balance between effective screening and respect for individual privacy. The TSA has also established policies and procedures for remote viewing and analysis of screened images and immediate deletion of images to ease fears over individual privacy. Alternatives to using these technologies include the use of bomb-sniffing dogs and pat-down searches of individuals, both of which are also viewed objectionably by some.

Of these various alternatives, the TSA appears to be moving forward with a strategy of deploying WBI systems at large airports. In field tests of these systems, the TSA has offered them as an alternative means for conducting secondary screening, allowing passengers to choose WBI screening instead of a physical pat-down search. In the interim, until a suitable technology is identified and deployed system-wide to screen passengers for explosives threats, pat-down searches of elevated risk passengers continue to be the primary method for explosives screening at passenger checkpoints.

ADDRESSING HUMAN FACTOR CONSIDERATIONS AT SCREENING CHECKPOINTS

The 9/11 Commission also recommended that the TSA conduct a human factors' study to understand problems in screener performance and set attainable objectives for improving performance at screening checkpoints. Screener performance deficiencies have been highlighted by various audits and investigations that have revealed poor screener performance among both federal and contract screeners during covert testing at screening checkpoints.[6] The TSA has launched several initiatives to address these concerns. For example, the TSA has greatly expanded the use of threat image projection (TIP), a system that tests screener on-the-job performance by projecting images of threat objects on x-ray monitors. Using data from TIP, researchers can assess certain human performance needs in aviation security. The TSA has also been examining ways to improve recurrent training for screeners. Key human factors issues that pose significant challenges to optimizing the performance and efficiency of passenger and baggage screening include screener selection and training, fitness for duty factors such as fatigue and alertness, and human interaction with screening technologies. In addition to these factors, workplace ergonomics and occupational safety have become significant issues, particularly among baggage screeners, because of high rates of on-the-job injuries that have led to high costs for workers compensation and lost work that impacts screener staffing and training, particularly at larger airports.

EXPEDITING DEPLOYMENT OF IN-LINE BAGGAGE SCREENING SYSTEMS

The 9/11 Commission recommended that the TSA expedite the installation of in-line baggage screening systems. Since the total cost of integrating and optimizing EDS equipment deployment at all passenger airports is estimated to exceed $4 billion, it is anticipated that it could be more than 15 years to complete the integration of baggage screening systems nationwide given the historic funding levels of $250 million annually provided since the Aviation Security Capital Fund (ASCF) was created for this purpose in 2003. To address the funding challenges of improving airport infrastructure to accommodate EDS equipment, letters of intent (LOIs) issued to airports by the TSA were established as a vehicle to leverage limited federal funding by stretching obligations over several years. LOIs were initially authorized in appropriations legislation as a means for TSA to convey to airports its intent to obligate future funds for the purpose of EDS integration. In addition to streamlining the baggage screening process, making it more efficient and capable of meeting the increased demand for air travel anticipated in the future, it is hoped that the completion of in-line EDS integration will reduce staffing needs for baggage screeners and mitigate on-the-job injuries associated with repeatedly lifting and moving heavy baggage.

The 9/11 Commission also recommended that "[b]ecause the aviation industry will derive substantial benefits from [in-line EDS] deployment, it should pay a fair share of the costs."[7] However, defining that fair share has been a significant point of contention. Airlines already indirectly pay the federal share of EDS integration, because the first $250 million annually must come directly from aviation security fees paid by the airlines and their passengers. Airports also pay a portion of the costs. Under the scheme adopted by Vision 100, large- and medium-sized airports contribute 10% of the cost while small airports contribute 5%. However, the TSA has sought to instead set this airport share at 25% for large- and medium-sized airports and at 10% for small airports, an approach that airports oppose, arguing that the federal government should fully cover the cost of the federally imposed mandate for explosives screening of checked baggage. In FY2006 and FY2007, these higher percentages for airport contributions were set in appropriations language, as sought by the administration in FY2006 and for large- and medium-sized airports in FY2007. In FY2008, appropriations language was silent on the matter, leaving the airport share of costs at the lower level set by Vision 100. The 9/11 Commission did not specifically say what they would consider to be a more equitable contribution from industry. However, the recommendation implies that members of the Commission believed that industry had not been paying its fair share of the costs for in-line EDS. It can, however, be argued that the funding mechanisms put in place do require the industry to pay a considerable amount of the cost. It can also be argued that, given other economic pressures, such as rising fuel costs, the airline industry, in particular, is not well positioned to take on additional security-related costs. The economic pressures on the airline industry may also make it increasingly difficult for airports to raise capital to provide additional funding for these security-related projects.

INTENSIFYING EFFORTS TO IDENTIFY, SCREEN, AND TRACK CARGO

The 9/11 Commission recommended that the TSA intensify its efforts to identify suspicious cargo and appropriately screen and track potentially dangerous cargo in aviation as well as in maritime operations. Stemming from recommendations of the Aviation Security Advisory Committee (ASAC), a standing committee of aviation stakeholders representing labor and industry, the TSA unveiled a strategic plan for cargo security in November 2003. That plan consists a multilayered risk-based approach with four key strategic objectives: (1) enhancing shipper and supply chain security; (2) identifying elevated risk cargo through prescreening techniques; (3) identifying technologies for performing targeted air cargo inspections; and (4) securing all-cargo aircraft through appropriate facility security measures.[8] Goals of the plan include prescreening air cargo shipments in order to determine their level of relative risk; working with industry and federal partners to ensure that 100% of items considered to pose an elevated risk are inspected; developing and ensuring that new information and technology solutions are deployed; and implementing operational and regulatory programs that support enhanced security measures. The 9/11 Commission recommendations seem to imply that it concurs with TSA's overall approach as outlined in this strategic plan but feels that progress toward achieving these objectives must be accelerated, and perhaps, augmented.

Debate in Congress over air cargo security has focused on the level of physical screening or inspection of cargo needed to adequately mitigate the risks posed by cargo placed on passenger aircraft. This debate culminated in the passage of legislation in 2007, as part of the Implementing Recommendations of the 9/11 Commission Act of 2007 (P.L. 110-53), that requires the physical screening or inspection of all cargo placed on passenger aircraft by August 2010, with an interim requirement that 50% of all such cargo be physically screened or inspected by January 2009. The technologies and procedures to meet this mandate are currently a matter of considerable debate and concern among affected entities in the air cargo industry. In coordination with efforts underway to address these screening requirements, the TSA and the air cargo industry are implementing technologies and procedures to improve the tracking of air cargo and prevent tampering along the supply chain, particularly after cargo items have been inspected and cleared for placement on aircraft.

Deploying Hardened Cargo Containers

In addition to these various steps designed to improve cargo security, the 9/11 Commission specifically recommended the deployment of at least one hardened cargo container on every passenger aircraft that also hauls cargo to carry suspicious cargo. This concept had been previously considered by the FAA and the National Research Council (NRC) of the National Academies. While containers able to withstand blasts from bombs of the size that took down Pan Am flight 103 have been available for some time, the cost and weight of these units have been deterrents to implementing them in airline operations. Moreover, using just one hardened cargo container per passenger aircraft still leaves the system open to potential vulnerabilities. From a policy standpoint, it remains unclear what criteria would be used to permit shipment of elevated risk cargo in hardened cargo containers instead of simply preventing those items from being shipped on passenger aircraft altogether.

Risk-Based Prioritization as the Basis for Transportation Security Policy

In addition to the aviation-specific recommendations discussed above, the 9/11 Commission also issued an overarching recommendation to establish risk-based priorities for protecting all transportation assets. Based on this assessment of risks, the 9/11 Commission recommended that the TSA select the most practical and cost-effective approaches for implementing defenses of transportation assets and develop a plan, budget, and funding to implement this effort. The plan, according to the 9/11 Commission, should assign roles and missions to federal, state, and local authorities, as well as to private stakeholders.

While the risk-based approach to aviation security is nothing new, in the post-9/11 context, it came to be viewed as the principal policy tool for effectively allocating limited resources. What was lacking at the time the 9/11 Commission made this recommendation, however, was a unified strategic plan for aviation security. To a large extent, ATSA, and subsequent legislation amending ATSA, set the strategy for aviation security following the terrorist attacks of September 11, 2001. The TSA's initial focus was on meeting the mandates of ATSA, particularly deploying air marshals and federal screeners. Once the TSA had stood up its operational components, met key legislative mandates, and had achieved some level of normal operations, it was able to devote additional time and resources to developing a comprehensive strategy for aviation security, which is considered in detail in Chapter 4.

While this strategy has now been set forth, it is most appropriately viewed as an evolving strategy, requiring continual attention to adapt to shifting adversary threats and tactics as well as any advances in security technologies and capabilities, and any changes to U.S. policy regarding homeland and aviation security.

The 9/11 Commission findings and the subsequent aviation security strategy developed by the TSA and the DHS duly note that, while aviation security relies extensively on cooperation and the integration of shared responsibilities, challenges persist in defining roles and allocating resources for state and local participation and industry involvement. At airports, the local role is defined in the airport security program, which includes access control measures, badge and identification systems, and physical security plans. These security programs are tailored for each airport location. Physical security of the airport site is ultimately the responsibility of airport operators, whereas the TSA maintains the overall role of aviation security oversight and regulatory enforcement as well as direct responsibility for passenger and baggage screening. The role of local governments, and in some cases state authorities, in aviation security involves both law enforcement support for airport site security and law enforcement presence at screening checkpoints, provided through arrangements with the airport as laid out in each airport's TSA-approved security plan. Passenger air carriers must also participate in security through procedures and training for ground operations and in-flight security, carrying out security inspections of aircraft, securing aircraft, and so on. In air cargo and GA, security measures rely heavily on the direct participation of aircraft owners and operators, while the federal role is one of oversight and enforcement of aviation security requirements.

While implementing aviation security already involves federal, state, local, and industry participation, what the 9/11 Commission observed was a clear need for a unified strategy for assigning roles and missions to each stakeholder based on careful consideration of costs and logistics, and adopting a systems approach to define how each element contributes to the overall security strategy. In light of these 9/11 Commission recommendations, attention has been devoted to improving the strategic planning, resource allocation, and integration of federal, state, local, and private sector resources for aviation security. Continuing efforts in these areas may be needed as the national strategy for aviation security continues to evolve.

NATIONAL INTELLIGENCE REFORM AND TERRORISM PREVENTION ACT OF 2004 (P.L. 108-458)

The National Intelligence Reform and Terrorism Prevention Act (IRTPA) of 2004 (P.L. 108-458) addressed through legislation a large number of the recommendations made by the 9/11 Commission, as well as additional provisions to strengthen homeland security. The Act, which was signed into law on December 17, 2004, contains numerous provisions related to aviation security, many directly addressing the concerns and recommendations of the 9/11 Commission discussed above.

The IRTPA of 2004 required the DHS to develop, prepare, implement, and update as needed a National Strategy for Transportation Security as well as modal-specific security plans, including a plan for aviation security. It required the modal security plan for aviation to include a threat matrix outlining each threat to the U.S. civil aviation system and the corresponding layers of security in place to address these threats. It also required the development of a plan for mitigating impacts and reconstituting the aviation system in the event of a terrorist attack.

As previously noted, the threat of explosives carried through passenger screening checkpoints was a particular concern of the 9/11 Commission and a focus of congressional interest, intensified by the bombings of two Russian airliners in August 2004, shortly after the release of the 9/11 Commission report. In response to these concerns, the IRTPA of 2004 directed the TSA to give a high priority to developing, testing, improving, and deploying airport checkpoint screening technologies to detect nonmetallic, chemical, biological, and radiological weapons, and explosives on passenger and carry-on items. It also required the DHS to create a formal strategic plan for the deployment and use of explosive detection equipment at airport screening checkpoints. The Act required the TSA to initiate a pilot program to test advanced airport checkpoint screening systems. The Act also required the TSA to prohibit airline passengers from carrying butane lighters and any other objects considered by the TSA to be inappropriate carry-on items. This was the first time a specific prohibited item had been named in statute, and it reflected a particular concern in Congress over speculation that Richard Reid may have been successful in detonating his shoe bomb had he had a lighter instead of just matches. Two years later, Congress, though an appropriations provision, gave the TSA the authority to lift the ban on butane lighters, which it subsequently did based on its assessment that other actions taken had sufficiently reduced the risk posed by butane lighters.

The IRTPA of 2004 also required the TSA to conduct a human factors' study to better understand problems with screener performance and take such action as may be necessary to improve the job performance of airport screening personnel. It also required the TSA to develop and report to Congress on standards for determining appropriate screener staffing levels at airports that provide necessary levels of security and keep passenger wait times to a minimum. The Act also called for a study to assess the feasibility of integrating operations of the screening workforce and other aviation security-related functions, to coordinate these activities and increase their efficiency and effectiveness.

With regard to baggage screening, the Act authorized the TSA to take necessary action to expedite the installation and use of in-line baggage screening equipment at airports. It also required the TSA to establish a schedule to expedite this activity and study cost-sharing options among federal, state, and local governments, and the private sector for integrating in-line baggage screening systems. The Act increased the authorization for the ASCF by authorizing up to $400 million per year through FY2007, in addition to the initial $250 million deposited from aviation security fee collections as established by Vision 100. It also authorized the expenditure of $100 million for research and development of improved EDSs and directed the TSA to develop a plan and guidelines for implementing these next generation systems.

In recognition of the 9/11 Commission recommendation to move forward with a federally operated system to check passenger names against terrorist watch lists, the IRTPA of 2004 required the TSA to begin testing of an advanced passenger prescreening system by January 1, 2005. Although the Act did not provide a deadline for the completion of testing this prescreening system, it requires the TSA to begin to assume the role of passenger prescreening and checking passenger names against terrorist watch lists no later than 180 days after such testing is completed. The Act also required the TSA to establish redress and remedy procedures for passengers who are delayed or denied boarding because of being falsely identified or targeted by the system, and required the TSA to ensure that the number of such false positives is minimized. The Act also required the TSA to establish an oversight board and implement other safeguards to ensure the security and integrity of the system and to address and resolve privacy concerns. The Act also required that the DHS prescreening of international flights to or from the United States be conducted prior to departure rather than after the aircraft is already airborne and en route to the United States. It further required that individuals seeking FAA certificates, such as pilot and aircraft mechanic ratings, as well as individuals seeking to obtain unescorted access to airport secure areas and air operations areas be screened against the consolidated and integrated terrorist watch list. The Act also required the TSA to establish a process allowing air charter and leasing companies to voluntarily submit information regarding prospective customers seeking to use aircraft weighing more than 12,500 pounds for prescreening.

With respect to furthering the use of biometric technologies for aviation security applications, the Act required the TSA to issue guidance for the use of biometrics in airport access control systems. It also required the TSA to establish a biometric credential and authentication procedures for identifying LEOs authorized to carry firearms on board passenger aircraft. The Act authorizes $20 million, in addition to any other authorized amounts, for research and development of biometric technologies for aviation security. Further, it required the FAA to begin issuing tamper-resistant pilot licenses with a photograph of the bearer. The license is to be capable of accommodating a digital photograph, a biometric, or any other unique identifier considered necessary for identification purposes. The Act also authorized $1 million to establish a center of excellence in biometric technologies.

The IRTPA of 2004 required the Federal Air Marshal Service (FAMS) to continue operational initiatives to protect the anonymity of Federal air marshals. The Act also provided for the training of LEOs who are authorized to carry firearms on passenger aircraft on in-flight counterterrorism and weapons handling procedures and in the identification of fraudulent identification documents such as passports and visas. The Act also encourages the President to pursue international agreements to enable the maximum deployment of FAMS on international flights, and authorizes the DHS to provide air marshal training to foreign law enforcement personnel. In addition, it directed the TSA to study the application of readily available wireless communication technologies to enable cabin crewmembers to discreetly notify the pilot in the case of a security breach or safety issue occurring in the cabin.

The IRTPA of 2004 also contained several provisions for mitigating the threat from shoulder-fired missiles to commercial aviation, a continuing concern that was not specifically addressed in any of the 9/11 Commission recommendations. Specifically, the Act directed the President to urgently pursue international treaties to limit the availability, transfer, and proliferation of Man-portable Air Defense Systems (MANPADSs), such as shoulder-fired missiles, worldwide. The Act also directed the President to continue to pursue international arrangements for the destruction of excess, obsolete, and illicit MANPADS stockpiles worldwide. It also required the DHS to assess the vulnerability of aircraft to MANPADS attacks and to develop plans for securing airports and aircraft from this threat. The Act also required the FAA to establish a process for expedited certification of missile defense systems for commercial aircraft.

With regard to air cargo security, the IRTPA of 2004 authorized $200 million each year through FY2007 for improved air cargo and airport security related to the transportation of cargo on both passenger aircraft and all-cargo aircraft, and $100 million per year through FY2007 for the research, development, and deployment of technologies to better identify, track, and screen air cargo. The Act established a grant program to encourage the development of advanced air cargo security technology. It also required the TSA to issue a final rule on its proposed regulations to strengthen the security of air cargo operations for both passenger and all-cargo aircraft. It required the DHS, in coordination with the DOD and the FAA, to report on the threats posed by international cargo shipments bound for the United States and provide an analysis of the potential for establishing secure facilities along established international aviation routes for the purposes of diverting and securing aircraft believed to pose a security threat. It also mandated a pilot program to evaluate the use of blast-resistant cargo containers and authorized $2 million for this purpose. In addition to these air cargo security provisions in the IRTPA of 2004, the Department of Homeland Security Appropriations Act for FY2005 (P.L 108-334, Sec. 513) directed the DHS to research, develop, and procure certified systems to inspect and screen air cargo on passenger aircraft at the earliest date possible and amend security directives and procedures to, at a minimum, triple the percentage of cargo placed on passenger aircraft that is physically inspected. Subsequent appropriations acts have included language seeking further investment in technologies to increase the percentage of air cargo placed on passenger aircraft that is subject to physical screening.

TSA REGULATIONS TO STRENGTHEN AIR CARGO
AND THE PUSH FOR 100% CARGO SCREENING

Congress had continued to push the TSA to move forward with its strategy for securing both air cargo placed on passenger aircraft and operations involving all-cargo aircraft, as required under ATSA. Many critics of the TSA's approach, however, had voiced concerns that existing air cargo security regimens largely amounted to a framework for the air cargo industry to police itself using the known shipper framework, with little oversight from the TSA. Legislation passed by the Senate in the 108th

Congress (see the Air Cargo Security Act, S. 165 [108th Congress]) had sought to create a consolidated known shipper database (KSD), require the vetting of air cargo workers, and strengthen physical security measures and security training for air cargo operations. The Senate had originally included the provisions of this legislation in the IRTPA of 2004. However, while the bill was being debated, the TSA introduced proposed rulemaking in the fall of 2004 that proposed to accomplish these same objectives.[9] Therefore, Congress settled on language setting a deadline for TSA to finalize and implement these rules for the air cargo industry. Despite the requirement, the TSA missed the deadline by over a year, and even then, had to grant specific extensions and waivers to the industry to meet background check and training requirements for air cargo handlers and agents of freight forwarding companies. Nonetheless, the objectives originally sought to strengthen air cargo security outlined in the original Senate bills are now largely being achieved though implementation of the TSA's air cargo security regulations.[10]

While these air cargo regulations were largely viewed as the framework for industry to carry out its security responsibilities as envisioned under the TSA's risk-based air cargo strategy, critics continued to voice concern that the risk-based model left a large percentage of air cargo carried on passenger aircraft unchecked for explosives threats. A particularly outspoken critic of the TSA's approach to air cargo security was Representative Ed Markey of Massachusetts, who pushed for legislation to require 100% screening of all air cargo placed on passenger aircraft. While Representative Markey's legislative proposals for air cargo screening had gained considerable bipartisan support in the House, they were adamantly opposed by the air cargo industry and the TSA, which warned that imposing a requirement to physically screen or inspect all air cargo placed on passenger aircraft would require screening technologies with capabilities that did not yet exist, in order to meet this requirement without significantly impacting delivery schedules and logistics and without imposing a significant cost and operational burden on the air cargo industry. While these concerns prevented the legislation proposed by Representative Markey from moving forward in the 108th and 109th Congresses (2003–2006), the concerns he raised were shared to some degree by appropriators who included language in appropriations measures calling for tripling the amount of air cargo screened in FY2004, and thereafter, incrementally improving the technology and capability to screen more and more cargo placed on passenger airplanes. Congressional appropriators also secured funding for additional TSA air cargo regulatory compliance inspectors and the research and development of explosives screening technologies tailored to the need of air cargo operations and shipments. In Congress, air cargo has remained a particularly salient issue in discussions and debate over aviation security.

LINGERING CONGRESSIONAL POLICY CONCERNS

Democrats in Congress, as well as some Republican members of Congress, had continued to voice concerns over the Bush Administration's efforts on homeland security, including the TSA's progress on implementing the legislative mandates set forth to strengthen aviation security. Identified gaps in aviation security noted by Democratic Members of the House Committee on Homeland Security included perceived lapses in screening capabilities and performance that allowed dangerous items to continue to pass through checkpoints and aboard passenger airliners; the lack of routine screening for cargo placed on passenger airplanes, the lack of routine screening or physical inspection of airport workers having access to restricted and secured areas of airports and to aircraft, and the lack of effective measures to protect aircraft against an attack using a shoulder-fired missile.[11] In response to these perceived gaps, Democrats in Congress set forth a strategy for homeland security that included, among other things, establishing a unified terrorist watch list, setting priorities based on threats and vulnerabilities, keeping track of foreign nationals that enter and exit the United States, and providing for comprehensive aviation security including a screening process for cargo placed on passenger airplanes, improved airport perimeter security, and the deployment of missile protection systems for passenger aircraft as soon as technically feasible.[12]

In many regards, the objectives set forth were generally in line with Bush Administration policies and goals for aviation security, but there were some important differences. While both sides generally agreed that priorities should be based on threats and vulnerabilities, a fundamental tenet of the risk-based approach to aviation security views on the allocation of resources and the need for certain measures to reduce vulnerabilities often differed widely. Regarding both the need for countermissile technologies and the need to enhance cargo screening, Democrats in Congress and the Bush Administration held considerably different views, although both sides acknowledged that vulnerabilities continued to exist in these aspects of commercial aviation operations. Whereas positions expressed by Democratic party policies and writings have characterized countermissile systems as a much needed defense for protecting passenger airliners, the Bush Administration has favored near-term efforts to reduce existing stockpiles of these weapons worldwide, but nonetheless, agreed to pursue a multiyear research, development, test, and evaluation (RDT&E) program to examine the feasibility of adapting military countermissile technologies for use on civilian aircraft. Now that this program has concluded, how to proceed and whether passenger airliners should be equipped with these systems, which are costly to acquire and maintain, remain a rather controversial policy issue. While this issue remains unresolved, the debate over approaches to screening cargo has resulted in legislative action mandating the screening of all cargo placed on passenger aircraft, rather than the risk-based approach of selective screening advocated by the Bush Administration and the TSA. By August 2010, all cargo placed on passenger screening must undergo some form of physical screening or inspection, although the procedures through which this will be accomplished and the impacts it will have on air cargo operations and logistics remain as issues of particular concern among entities in the air cargo industry.

Another key difference of opinion between Democrats in Congress and the Bush Administration centered on their positions regarding whether TSA screeners and other security personnel, now collectively known as Transportation Security Officers (TSOs), should be given the right to collective bargaining. Under ATSA, the TSA Administrator was given broad authority to set up a personnel management system for screeners separate from the personnel management system for other TSA employees, whose personnel system was modeled after the FAA personnel management system: a system that grants considerable power to labor organizations to negotiate salaries and other benefits. Since the creation of the TSA, the Bush Administration has maintained that granting collective bargaining rights to screeners would be detrimental to homeland security because it would likely lead to long-running and costly contract negotiations, and possible impasses between the TSA and labor officials, that would detract from the organization's mission. The continued strife between the FAA and air traffic controllers over labor contracts has served as a case-in-point, in the Bush Administration's view, that collective bargaining would be a considerable hindrance to creating an effective screening workforce.

During the 108th and 109th Congresses (2003–2006), the Republican majority not only supported this view, but had unsuccessfully sought legislative options to restructure the TSA and provide incentives for airports to adopt the model of TSA-managed contract screening operations, using private screeners, as provided for under the opt-out provision of ATSA. In particular, legislation considered by the House Committee on Homeland Security in 2006 sought to create a separate Airport Screening Organization within the TSA to carry out the operational functions of passenger and baggage screening. By separating out TSA's regulatory oversight function of aviation security from screening operations and promoting the use of private screening partners, the bill was crafted to address, in part, a concern expressed by some over the TSA's dual role as both the policymaker and regulator of aviation security and the provider of airport security screening.[13] The bill also sought to create various performance goals for private screening operations as well as incentives for private screening entities that meet or exceed performance expectations. Additionally, to provide airports with an incentive to request private screeners, the measure (H.R. 4439, 109th Congress) sought to authorize grants to airports to cover aviation security costs of up to 90% of the annual cost savings realized by converting to private screeners, subject to the availability of appropriations, as an incentive to pursue private screening alternatives that would result in cost savings to the federal government. However, when Democrats gained majority party status in both the House and the Senate in 2007, the attention shifted toward options for providing additional incentives to, in their opinion, improve job satisfaction within the existing structure of the TSA screener workforce. Toward this objective, they immediately sought to modify ATSA to bring TSA screeners under the personnel management system covering other TSA employees, and in so doing, extend collective bargaining rights to the screener/TSO workforce.

As previously noted, another long-standing difference in policy views has centered on the approach to securing cargo placed on passenger airliners. In 2003, the TSA established a strategic plan for air cargo security predicated on continued use of known shipper programs coupled with tightened physical security around air cargo operations areas and the air cargo supply chain, and additional risk-based tools for selecting high-risk shipments either for further screening and inspection for preventing certain shipments from being placed on passenger aircraft. To implement these initiatives, in 2006 the TSA established new regulations for the air cargo industry to create an industry-wide database of known shippers, required background checks for air cargo workers and certain employees of freight forwarding companies that arrange for the shipment of items on passenger aircraft, and increased physical security measures and security training for air cargo operations.[14] The TSA's slow progress in finalizing these regulations and stepping up its enforcement efforts with respect to air cargo became a continuing source of frustration for both Republicans and Democrats in Congress, who used appropriations legislation as a vehicle to require increased screening of cargo placed on passenger aircraft and to expand the workforce of TSA regulatory compliance inspectors assigned to air cargo operations. Through appropriations legislation, Congress also pressed for additional research and testing of explosives screening technologies for screening cargo placed on passenger aircraft. In response, the TSA had increased the amount of air cargo that was physically screened, and was at work trying to conceptualize and develop a risk-based tool to conduct targeted screening of such cargo. Some in Congress, however, continued to view the lack of mandatory physical screening of air cargo placed on passenger airliners as a significant vulnerability and pushed for legislation to mandate 100% physical screening of air cargo placed on passenger aircraft.

This issue, along with additional proposals to address uncompleted recommendations of the 9/11 Commission and strengthen other aspects of aviation and homeland security was touted as a top priority when the 110th Congress convened in January 2007. Legislation moved swiftly through the House and Senate, but stalled out when the White House Office of Management and Budget (OMB) issued strongly worded statements of administration policy on both bills, indicating that if a bill presented to the President included provisions allowing TSA screeners to unionize and requiring the screening of all air cargo placed on passenger aircraft, the President's senior advisors would recommend that he veto the bill. Congress heeded this warning by stripping out the provisions that would have granted TSA screeners collective bargaining rights and reworded provisions regarding screening requirements for air cargo, providing additional flexibility that appears to allow shippers to perform the screening functions using TSA-approved methods of screening and inspection. Satisfied with these concessions and compromises, the Implementing Recommendations of the 9/11 Commission Act of 2007 moved through the bicameral conference to resolve differences between the House and Senate versions of the bill in the early summer of 2007, and President Bush signed the measure into law (P.L. 110-53) on August 3, 2007.

IMPLEMENTING RECOMMENDATIONS OF THE 9/11
COMMISSION ACT OF 2007 (P.L. 110-53)

The Act requires that by August 2010, three years from enactment, the TSA must screen 100% of all cargo placed on passenger aircraft, with an interim requirement that 50% of such cargo must be screened by January 2009. The legislation specifies that the screening must involve some sort of physical examination or nonintrusive observation methods, such as the use of x-ray, EDS and/or ETD technology, or the use of explosives-sniffing canine teams or physical searches combined with manifest verification. The legislation allows for the implementation of a TSA program to certify shipping methods used by shippers to meet these requirements, thus providing the option of approved screening and inspection programs carried out by shippers, rather than TSA screening of all pieces of cargo placed on passenger aircraft. While this would eliminate the need for expanding the TSA workforce to handle cargo screening, it may place a considerable burden on the air cargo industry that may significantly impact cost and schedules. Implementation of this requirement remains a central issue in ongoing aviation security policy debate.

Addressing the 9/11 Commission recommendation for expediting in-line EDS integration, the Act reauthorized the ASCF through FY2028, and further authorizes additional discretionary funds of up to $450 million annually from FY2008 through FY2011 for in-line EDS integration projects. The Act also addressed the 9/11 Commission recommendation for improving the detection of explosives and passenger screening checkpoints by establishing an Airport Checkpoint Screening Fund, providing $250 million security fee collections for use in conducting research and development and procuring and deploying technologies for detecting explosives at screening checkpoints. However, this fund, unlike the ASCF, was only authorized for one year in FY2008. The TSA has generally not favored the use of these types of dedicated funding mechanisms because they can impose considerable constraints on budget planning and execution. In FY2009, the funding of checkpoint technology and support reverted back to the discretionary funding mechanisms favored by the TSA. The Act also required the TSA to submit the strategic plan for deployment of checkpoint explosives detection technologies, originally required by the IRTPA of 2004 (P.L. 108-458), to Congress within 30 days, and required the TSA to begin implementing the plan by August 2008.

The Act also addressed the 9/11 Commission recommendations for enhancing passenger prescreening by requiring a plan for the TSA to assume responsibility for checking airline passenger names against the consolidated terrorist watch list maintained by the federal government, providing a timeline for testing the system to accomplish this function, explaining how prescreening of domestic and international flights will be integrated, and describing how the system will comply with privacy rights pertaining to information collected by the federal government on individuals. The legislation calls on the GAO to independently review the process though which passengers wrongly placed on the no-fly and terrorist watch lists can appeal and seek remedy, how the TSA will protect private passenger information, progress toward integrating domestic and international passenger prescreening functions, and an assessment of when the domestic passenger prescreening system will realistically be completed. The Act also requires the DHS to establish an Office of Appeals and Redress to provide passengers wrongly identified as a threat with a timely and fair process to correct erroneous information and maintain records to authenticate the identity of the individual and mitigate future delays or travel disruptions that result from being falsely identified as a threat.

As highlighted by this most recent major piece of legislation addressing aviation security, the issues of passenger prescreening, cargo screening and security, the detection of explosives at passenger checkpoints, and the completion of in-line EDS integration efforts stand out as the most prominent policy issues regarding aviation security. Along with these issues, policymakers remain keenly interested in efforts to improve airport access controls and perimeter security, as well as ways to protect commercial passenger aircraft from the threat posed by shoulder-fired missiles and other standoff weapons, and options for strengthening the security of GA operations, particularly operations involving large aircraft and GA aircraft flying into the United States from foreign countries. It is expected that these will remain central policy issues for aviation security and specific topics for congressional oversight in the years to come. Evidence of a continuing terrorist threat to the aviation system within the United States, and to U.S. airlines operating in foreign countries suggests that a continually evolving national strategy and robust national aviation security policies are needed to address the shifting terrorist threat, reduce existing vulnerabilities in the aviation system, and prepare to respond swiftly and effectively to mitigate the consequences of a possible attack and reconstitute the operations of the aviation system.

CONTINUING TERRORIST THREAT

As discussed above, aviation security has been a significant policy issue for the U.S. federal government in the seven years since the 9/11 attacks. Since the 9/11 attacks, the United States and its allies in the war against terrorism have faced a continuing threat from al Qaeda as well as other global and domestic terror threats. A detailed timeline of significant terrorist attacks, including major terrorist acts against aviation, along with significant aviation security legislation and regulatory action is presented in Figure 3.1. While various threats exist, al Qaeda remains the most significant threat to aviation security globally. Within the U.S. homeland, there has been growing concern over home-grown terrorists, particularly among those who might share ideological objectives with al Qaeda and others who espouse radical Islamic views and animosities toward the U.S. government and its policies. In addition to these threats from Sunni Muslim radicals supporting al Qaeda, there is also concern that growing tensions between Israel and Lebanon may heighten the risk of terrorist attacks from the Lebanese Shia Muslim group Hezbollah, which has been historically associated with numerous terrorist attacks against aviation targets.

The United States is faced with a broad range of continuing threats to aviation. While the greatest threat is perceived to be from potential bombings of aircraft, suicide hijackings and attacks using aircraft as weapons against ground targets remain a risk not only for commercial passenger and all-cargo airlines, but for GA operators as well. Both airports and aircraft may be targeted by chemical

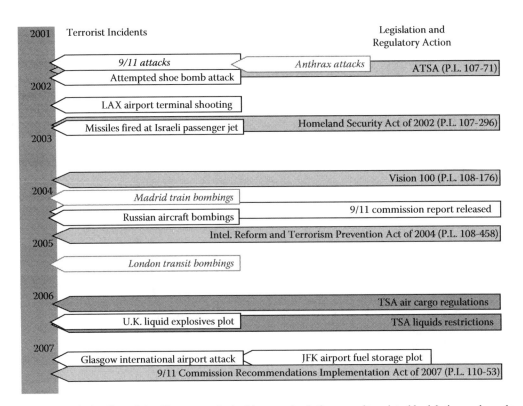

FIGURE 3.1   A timeline of significant terrorist incidents and aviation security-related legislation and regulatory action since the September 11, 2001 attacks.

or biological weapons attacks, and unsecured areas of airport terminals are particularly vulnerable to these types of threats as well as to shootings and bombings using conventional munitions and explosives. Additionally, faced with enhanced security measures surrounding passenger airline operations, terrorists may resort to the use of shoulder-fired missiles or other standoff weapons to target passenger aircraft. Present-day aviation policy and security must fully consider this broad array of potential terrorist attack scenarios to assess the overall risk picture and determine the most appropriate course of action. The continued campaign of terror since the 9/11 attacks suggests that al Qaeda and others have a continued interest in attacking aviation and transportation targets throughout the world using a broad range of terrorist weapons and tactics. The following discussion provides a brief synopsis of key terrorist attacks since 9/11 that illustrate the range of potential threats to aviation. Many of these key events have been directly linked to al Qaeda. However, some, such as the anthrax mail attacks of September and October 2001, in particular, are not believed to be linked to al Qaeda, but nonetheless highlight the continuing threats and potential vulnerabilities in homeland and aviation security.

Post-9/11 Anthrax Attacks

On the heels of the 9/11 attacks, the U.S. Congress, along with various media outlets were targeted by anthrax attacks using the U.S. mail system. In August 2008, a civilian scientist at the U.S. Army Research Institute of Infectious Diseases (USAMRIID), Fort Detrick, Maryland, who was under investigation by the FBI for possible involvement in the anthrax attacks committed suicide. While the FBI contends that this individual, Bruce Ivins, acted alone in carrying out the anthrax attacks largely based on a considerable amount of circumstantial evidence,[15] the case remains both intriguing and controversial. The first mailings of five anthrax-laced letters were postmarked September 18, 2001, one week after the 9/11 attacks. Two more anthrax-laced letters were mailed in early October 2001. The attacks killed five out of the more than 20 confirmed victims of the attacks. While these attacks have not been linked to al Qaeda, their timing immediately after the 9/11 attacks suggests that whomever was responsible wished to further exploit the acute public concern over terrorism immediately following the 9/11 attacks, either to continue the campaign of terror begun on 9/11 or to highlight the vulnerabilities of the United States to biological attacks of this kind. While most experts believe that the attacks have no apparent connection to al Qaeda and the 9/11 attacks, the anthrax attacks most certainly had the effect of broadening policymakers views regarding the potential threats that the United States and its allies may face in the war against terrorism, and brought the risk of chemical and biological attacks to the forefront of the debate, along with efforts to strengthen security in the air transportation system. Recognizing the air transportation system's unique vulnerabilities to chemical and biological attacks has been part of the policy discussion on aviation security ever since. However, considerable vulnerabilities to chemical and biological attacks remain in the air transportation system.

Attempted Shoe Bombing of American Airlines Flight 63

While al Qaeda did not appear to play any role in the anthrax attacks of 2001, three months later it became clear that al Qaeda sought to continue its campaign of terror against the United States, again by targeting the air transportation system. On December 22, 2001, Richard Colvin Reid, a 28-year-old British national, boarded American Airlines flight 63, a Boeing 767 with scheduled service from Charles de Gaulle Airport in Paris, France to Miami, Florida. As the airplane cruised above the Atlantic Ocean en route to Miami, Reid lit a match in an attempt to ignite a fuse attached to an explosive device hidden in his shoes.[16] A flight attendant, Hermis Moutardier, alerted by passengers who had smelled smoke, observed Reid's actions. Thinking that he was trying to light a cigarette, she informed him that smoking was not permitted on the aircraft. A few minutes later, she again observed Reid acting suspiciously and asked him what he was doing. He grabbed her, at which point she observed a lit match and a shoe with a fuse attached in his hands. He began to fight with her, and she yelled for help. A second flight attendant, Christina Jones, came to her aid, trying to subdue Reid who continued to resist. Observing the altercation, some passengers assisted the two flight attendants, eventually subduing and restraining Reid, who was then sedated by a medical doctor who was a passenger on the flight. The flight diverted to Boston Logan Airport in Massachusetts, where Reid was placed under arrest.

The FBI determined that both of Reid's shoes contained a mixture of pentaerythritol tetranitrate (PETN) high explosive compound, one of the ingredients in Semtex, and triacetone triperoxide (TATP), a high explosive that has been linked to other terrorist bombings. While some have noted that the peroxide-based TATP has become popular among terrorists because it cannot be detected by explosives detection equipment designed to look only for nitrate-based explosives, this clearly was not the reason Reid and his accomplices selected it, since his shoes also contained PETN, a nitrate-based high explosive. Rather, the TATP in Reid's shoe was intended as a primary explosive or trigger for the shoe bomb devices because of its propensity to detonate when ignited. The FBI determined that the explosives in Reid's shoes were present in sufficient quantities to easily destroy the aircraft if ignited in the pressurized aircraft cabin. Reid, who was linked to al Qaeda—reportedly having trained alongside Ahmed Ressam, the would-be LAX millennium plot bomber, in 1998, and issued his assignment to bomb American Airlines flight 63 by Khalid Sheikh Mohammed—was tried and convicted in federal court in Boston for the attempted aircraft bombing and was sentenced to life in prison. It was later determined that a second bomber, 22-year-old British national Said Badat, was to carry out an identical shoe bombing attack against another U.S.-bound airliner.[17]

Soon after, *Wall Street Journal* reporter Daniel Pearl traveled to Pakistan with the objective of investigating and reporting on Richard Reid's ties to al Qaeda, but he was captured, tortured, and executed by terrorists. At a March 10, 2007, military tribunal at the U.S. Naval Base, Guantanamo Bay, Cuba, Khalid Sheikh Mohammed—who was captured in 2003 and held as an enemy combatant—provided a written statement claiming that he had personally decapitated Pearl.[18]

AL QAEDA'S POST-9/11 AMBITIONS

At that tribunal, Khalid Sheikh Mohammed also admitted to serving in various senior leadership positions in al Qaeda, serving as a member of the al Qaeda Council and as the director for al Sahab (the Clouds), an al Qaeda media outlet that fed al Qaeda-sponsored information and propaganda to the Al Jazeera Arab-language media network. His testimony provides a glimpse into al Qaeda's extensive set of plans for attacking the United States and Israel following the 9/11 attacks, including numerous operations targeting aviation.

Khalid Sheikh Mohammed stated that he personally directed and planned the 9/11 attacks and the "shoe bomb operation to down two American airplanes."[19] He admitted responsibility for the November 2002 attempted downing of an Israeli charter jet using two shoulder-fired missiles, both of which missed their intended target. He also indicated that he had personally orchestrated a plot involving a second wave of suicide attacks using aircraft to target the Library Tower (the U.S. Bank Tower) in Los Angeles, the Sears Tower in Chicago, the "Plaza Bank, Washington State [sic]" (a possible reference to a skyscraper in Seattle), and the Empire State Building in New York City.[20] He also claimed to be planning a similar attack against the Israeli city of Elat, using aircraft leaving from Saudi Arabia. Other plots against aviation targets described in his statement included the planned destruction of an El-Al aircraft in Bangkok, Thailand, and an attack against London Heathrow Airport.

Hitting aviation targets was just part of the continued campaign of terror that Khalid Sheikh Mohammed and other al Qaeda terrorists had allegedly been contemplating following the 9/11 attacks, including numerous planned attacks in the U.S. homeland. Khalid Sheikh Mohammed indicated that, under his direction, the group also plotted to assassinate former U.S. Presidents, bomb suspension bridges in the New York City area, destroy the New York Stock Exchange and other financial targets, destroy the Sears Tower in Chicago using fuel trucks, and had also conducted surveillance to assess the feasibility of attacking nuclear power plants in the United States. He indicated that he was also responsible for various al Qaeda plans to attack significant targets throughout the world including: U.S. Naval vessels and merchant ships in the Strait of Hormuz, the Strait of Gibraltar, and the Port of Singapore; the Panama Canal; significant targets in the United Kingdom including the Houses of Parliament (Big Ben); the United States and Israeli embassies in India, Asia, and Australia; and targets within Israel.

While Khalid Sheikh Mohammed's testimony provides an eye-opening glimpse into the breadth of the sinister plotting against aviation and other targets being contemplated by al Qaeda, it is difficult to say how advanced the planning for these attacks was or whether these admissions largely reflect the boasting of an individual seeking to establish the importance of his role in the al Qaeda organization. In any case, U.S. military action in Afghanistan immediately following the 9/11 attacks was likely effective in disrupting the core command and control functions of al Qaeda, at least temporarily, thus preventing any ongoing planning and preparation for further planned attacks against the U.S. homeland. One thing that appears certain from publicly available sources is that the airline shoe bombing plot in December 2001 was part of a second wave of attacks against U.S. aviation targets that was orchestrated by al Qaeda's central command. The fact that al Qaeda again chose to attack aviation targets immediately following the 9/11 attacks—when there was an acute focus on strengthening aviation security both within the United States and in Europe, where the aircraft were targeted—suggests a continued fixation on carrying out terrorist attacks against aviation. This long-standing fixation on attacking aviation was further demonstrated by the attempted shoot down of an Israeli charter jet in Mombasa, Kenya the following year, in November 2002, and in the number of planned or conceptualized attacks, gleaned from the claims of Khalid Sheikh Mohammed, specifically targeting aircraft and airports.

It is interesting to note that while Khalid Sheikh Mohammed claims to have hatched the 9/11 plot, the concept of attacking prominent landmarks and buildings with aircraft may have been on al Qaeda's plan books for some time before he pitched the idea to Osama bin Laden. For example, an Egyptian radical named Mohammed Ibrahim Makkawi, a former colonel in the Egyptian special forces, reportedly warned an Egyptian lawmaker of a plot to crash an airliner into the Egyptian parliament building right before he left Cairo in 1987 to join forces with Dr. Ayman al Zawahiri in Afghanistan. At the time al Zawahiri was the leader of the Egyptian Islamic Jihad, an extremist group in Egypt that sought to overthrow the Egyptian government. He was banished from Egypt in 1985 after the Egyptian government failed to link him to the assassination of President Anwar Sadat. Al Zawahiri is generally regarded as being the ideological leader of al Qaeda, and second in command behind bin Laden. Mohammed Ibrahim Makkawi is thought to have assumed the *nom de guerre* Saif al Adl (Sword of Justice), and is considered to be a senior military commander and weapons and tactics expert in the al Qaeda organization. He was indicted for his role in the 1998 U.S. Embassy bombings and is on the FBI's list of most wanted terrorists. His early warnings of an attack against the Egyptian Parliament using a commercial airliner provide evidence of a long-standing desire among Islamic radicals tied to al Qaeda to not only attack aviation targets, but also to use aircraft as weapons against strategic ground targets.

While al Qaeda clearly had ambitions to carry out additional terrorist attacks against the United States, including specific plans to attack aviation targets after the 9/11 attacks, the U.S. homeland has been spared from additional terrorist attacks against aviation attributed to al Qaeda. The only attack within the U.S. homeland involving aviation, in the seven years since the 9/11 attacks, formally classified as a terrorist attack, was the July 4, 2002, shooting attack at LAX. In that incident, a lone gunman, Hesham Mohamed Hadayet, opened fire at the El Al ticket counter using a .45-caliber handgun killing two and wounding four others before being shot and killed by an El Al security guard. While Hadayet was never linked to any terrorist group, the incident was regarded as a terrorist act because he was motivated, in part, by anti-Israeli views and opposition to U.S. Middle

Eastern policies. While this remains an isolated incident, shootings as well as bombings in the unsecured areas of airports remain as specific concerns because these areas of airports may be regarded as soft targets compared to aircraft and secured areas that are more tightly guarded by stringent screening procedures and access control measures.

This incident highlighted the persisting vulnerability of unsecured areas of airports, including curbside drop-off and pickup locations and ticketing counters to shootings, bombings, and other possible terrorist attacks, including attacks using chemical weapons or biological agents. Following the LAX shootings, many were reminded of the terrorist attacks at Rome, Italy and Vienna, Austria airports in December 1985. On December 27, 1985, terrorists opened fire on passengers using assault rifles and threw hand grenades into the crowds around the El Al and TWA ticket counters in coordinated attacks at these two airports. In Rome, four terrorists killed 16 people and injured about one hundred others before police returned fire killing three of the perpetrators and wounding and capturing the fourth. In Vienna, three assailants opened fire killing two and injuring many others. They escaped by car, with police in pursuit. The police caught up with the three, killing one and capturing the other two. The men were believed to have been a part of the Abu Nidal Organization. The incidents were the deadliest attacks targeting an airport, although numerous other shootings and bombings of airports, as well as airline ticket offices, are included among official databases of worldwide terrorist incidents.[21]

While airports, and aviation targets in general, have often been attacked in historic terrorist incidents, since the 9/11 attacks, further attacks or even unveiled plots and attempted attacks against aviation targets within the United States have been relatively limited in number. While much of the policy discussion regarding aviation security in the United States since the 9/11 attacks has focused on perceived weaknesses in aviation security policies, strategies, and measures, little acknowledgment has been given to the fact that the U.S. aviation system has remained a highly secure mode of transportation.

The success in preventing additional terrorist attacks since 2001 has been the topic of considerable debate and speculation. Have the military actions of the United States in Afghanistan and Iraq had an impact on disrupting the al Qaeda command structure and diverting their efforts to supporting insurgents in Iraq and Afghanistan? Have U.S. foreign policies been effective in isolating and neutering state sponsors of terrorism? Have the United States' controversial domestic intelligence efforts had an impact on disrupting terrorist activity within the homeland? Have efforts to better track terrorist travel had an impact on preventing terrorists from entering the United States? Have law enforcement and counterterrorism efforts been effective in detecting terrorist activity and preventing terrorist acts from being carried out? Have the extensive resources and investments to improve aviation security made the aviation system in the United States highly resilient to the full spectrum of terrorist plots and tactics? Or have we simply been lucky?

While the prevention of terrorism appears to be the result of more than just luck, it is impossible to pinpoint what the impact of these specific policies and initiatives, either individually or in combination, have been. What most experts do agree on, however, is that for this success to continue, aviation security policies, strategies, and approaches must continually evolve and adapt to new terrorist threats and tactics, because most experts also agree that the U.S. aviation system and U.S. air carrier aircraft operating abroad remain high-profile targets in the eyes of terrorist groups.

EVOLVING TERROR THREAT

This long-standing terrorist fixation on aviation appears to pose a continuing threat despite the considerable policy and strategy focus on enhancing aviation security, both within the United States and among our allies in the war against terrorism, in the years since the 9/11 attacks. This continued threat was clearly demonstrated in August 2006 when a plot to attack U.S.-bound airliners from the United Kingdom using improvised liquid explosive devices was detected and disrupted by British authorities.

The UK Airplanes Bombing Plot

On August 10, 2006, a plot to bomb seven U.S.-bound passenger airliners from the United Kingdom using improvised liquid explosive devices was uncovered and broken up by British authorities. Operating from a flat in east London, a group of eight terrorists planned to disguise peroxide-based liquid explosives in plastic soft drink bottles to smuggle them on board the aircraft. They intended to extract the soft drink and inject the liquid explosive into the bottles using syringes, sealing the needle holes so that the bottle tops would remain unopened. The terrorists planned to inject a mixture of hydrogen peroxide and other organic compounds, combined with Tang, providing a sugar content to produce a hotter and more powerful explosion. Each of the terrorists intended to carry two of these bottles, one to serve as a backup in case security screeners confiscated one of the bottles. The men planned to detonate the liquid explosive using a hexamethylene triperoxide diamine (HMTD) detonator rigged to some sort of electric spark trigger from an electronic device, such as a disposable camera flash bulb, while the airliners were cruising at altitude above the Atlantic Ocean.[22] Scientists at the Sandia National Laboratory, working in cooperation with the DHS, conducted testing of the liquid explosive and detonation methods the terrorists planned to use and found the improvised explosive to be extremely powerful.[23]

The plot bore many striking similarities to the Bojinka plot and the attempted shoe bombing by Richard Reid, but provided insight into new terrorist tactics designed to elude tightened security measures at screening checkpoints. The fact that the plotters intended to use hydrogen peroxide-based explosives and detonators appears to reflect a deliberate attempt to elude possible chemical trace detection methods in use at the time, which were designed to search exclusively for nitrate-based explosives. Also, the plot, like the London transit bombings, pointed to a continued threat from so-called homegrown Islamic radicals, living in major western cities and countries.

A total of seven flights bound for the United States and Canada were targeted by the plot. The plot, by design, targeted flights that would all be airborne and over the Atlantic Ocean at the same time, in a coordinated fashion, offering little chance to prevent any of the bombings once the targeted flights had departed. Shortly before their arrest, several of the suspects made martyrdom videos describing their motivations for the attack as revenge against the United States, and British and Jewish accomplices, for actions in Iraq, Afghanistan, and Palestine.[24] The making of the videos, which was observed by British intelligence agents, who had placed listening devices inside the flat being used as the group's operational headquarters, tipped British authorities off to the fact that the plot was entering an advanced stage of planning and the attacks could be imminent. British authorities subsequently moved in and apprehended the members of the group, thus averting what could have been the most significant terrorist attack since 9/11.

Following the plot, the TSA took immediate action to ban liquids carried through airport screening checkpoints and deployed Federal Air Marshals on board of all U.S.-bound flights from Heathrow for a period after the attacks, out of fear that there may have been additional terrorists who had not been apprehended that could follow through with the execution of the plot. While the plot was broken up by effective British intelligence work before it could be executed, the incident stands out as a stark reminder of the capabilities, resourcefulness, and reach of U.S. adversaries in the ongoing war with global terrorists. The plot also stands out as a clear indicator that terrorist groups continue to have a keen interest in attacking commercial passenger aviation targets, contrary to some speculation that terrorists would shift their focus to attacks against softer targets as was the case with the March 11, 2004, Madrid passenger rail bombings and the July 7, 2005, London transit bombings.

Terrorists in the United Kingdom again demonstrated a continued fixation on attacking aviation targets in the June 30, 2007, bombing attack of the passenger airline terminal at Glasgow International Airport in Glasgow, Scotland. In that attack, terrorists rammed a sport utility vehicle (SUV) loaded with propane canisters through the main airport terminal entrance in an attempted suicide bombing. While one of the assailants died from burns sustained in the attack no one else was killed, although about five people in the airport terminal were injured in the attack. British authorities connected the attack at Glasgow International Airport to IEDs found in vehicles parked in central London two days prior, indicating that the attack was likely part of a larger plot to carry out coordinated attacks against prominent sites in the United Kingdom.[25] While plots of this sophistication have not been detected within the U.S. homeland, various incidents and investigations have pointed to a growing threat from homegrown terrorists operating within the United States as well.

HOMEGROWN TERRORIST THREATS IN THE UNITED STATES

In June 2007, a group of aspiring terrorists in New York were arrested after their group was infiltrated by an undercover LEO following leads provided by an informant about the group's aspirations. The men were allegedly conspiring to blow up a fuel farm and pipeline that supplied jet fuel to the John F. Kennedy International Airport (JFK) and other New York area airports. The alleged ringleader of the group had previously worked at JFK. While the group had conducted extensive surveillance and planning, they had not acquired explosives, and many experts have brought into question the seriousness of the threat posed by this group as well as the likelihood that the type of attack they were planning would have had any degree of success in destroying jet fuel storage and distribution systems for the New York area airports.

As exemplified by this plot, the continuing terrorist threats to civil aviation are complicated by an apparent rise in domestic sympathizers with terrorist movements like al Qaeda. While such domestic terrorist plots that have been detected to date have often failed to establish solid links between these homegrown groups and al Qaeda, the growth of a domestic insurgency is both alarming and indicative of a shifting global trend toward a more decentralized terror network, where the historic core of al Qaeda and its radical Islamic teachings serving more as an inspiration, providing general guiding principles and broad objectives for loosely knit terrorist cells and like-minded individuals and groups, rather than a center for planning and execution of terrorist attacks.

At the same time, recent national intelligence estimates warn that the core al Qaeda organization is again strengthening its capability to pre-9/11 levels, and it desires to carry out attacks within the United States as well as in Europe.[26] Central elements of al Qaeda have apparently found safe haven in the tribal areas of Pakistan, along the Afghan border, where they have been able to strengthen their core command and control functions. Additionally, U.S. intelligence sources consider Hezbollah in Lebanon a growing threat that may be contemplating carrying out attacks against U.S. interests overseas, or even an attack within the United States. Intelligence analysts surmise that attacks within the United States would most likely target locations of political or economic importance, or critical infrastructure with the objectives of "producing mass casualties, visually dramatic destruction, significant economic aftershocks, and/or fear among the US population."[27] Since both al Qaeda and factions of Hezbollah have targeted aviation in the past, and since aviation targets offer the potential to achieve all of these terrorist objectives, the air transportation system should be regarded as a prime target for these terrorist organizations.

While numerous steps have been taken since the 9/11 attacks to strengthen aviation security both within the United States and internationally, the terrorist threat remains high. While various reports of terrorists casing U.S. domestic flights have surfaced since the 9/11 attacks, the August 2006 interdiction of the terrorist cell near London Heathrow airport that was plotting to bomb U.S.-bound flights with improvised liquid explosive devices has provided clear and compelling evidence of the continuing terrorist threat to civil aviation. In addition to plotting domestic attacks, such as the foiled plot to attack fuel farms at JFK airport, domestic sympathizers and affiliates of al Qaeda may aid foreign terrorists in gaining access into the United States and may provide them with resources to carry out attacks within the United States.

An analysis by the New York City Police Department (NYPD) concluded that the terrorist threat in the post-9/11 climate comes predominantly from radicalized homegrown terrorists and terrorist groups.[28] The analysis notes that worldwide terrorist plots carried out since the 9/11 attacks have been conceptualized, planned, and carried out by "unremarkable" individuals who have attacked within their country of residence using al Qaeda and radical Islamic ideologies as their inspiration and motivational framework. The pressures for radicalization appear to be more pronounced in foreign countries, particularly countries in Europe, where second and third generation Muslims have often failed to assimilate into the culture and society of their country of residence and have become disenfranchised. In contrast, within the United States, immigrant populations have typically had an easier time assimilating into mainstream culture, thus reducing, to some degree, these incubators for radicalization. The analysis, however, concludes that radicalization pressures are also present to a certain degree within the United States, and extremist views and social networking capabilities with like-minded individuals through the Internet may facilitate the radicalization process throughout the world, including within the United States. The NYPD report concludes that "[t]he internet is now a tactical resource for obtaining instructions on constructing weapons, gathering information on potential targets, and providing spiritual justification for an attack."[29]

Besides fact gathering and social networking with like-minded individuals on the Internet, the radicalization process may be facilitated by various informal venues for camaraderie and socialization that the NYPD study refers to as "radicalization incubators." These sites where like-minded individuals often congregate may include cafes, cab driver hangouts, flophouses, prisons, student associations, hookah (water pipe) bars, and book shops. Initially, during an exploratory self-identification phase, otherwise "unremarkable" individuals leading ordinary lives may begin to explore radical Islamic views through use of the Internet and by seeking out the camaraderie of others at these various venues. This exploration is often triggered by a variety of catalytic events—such as the loss of a job or a perceived lack of opportunity for upward mobility; alienation and isolation; experiencing real or perceived racism; political unrest or hostile actions against Muslim populations; or personal losses such as the death of a close family member or friend—although experience indicates that this is not always the case.

As individuals become more radical in their views and beliefs, they may enter an indoctrination phase of radicalization in which beliefs are intensified and solidified, culminating with firm belief in the ideological conclusion that militant jihad is necessary to support and further the cause. The solidification of this view may then be followed by a process referred to as "jihadization" in which a group of like-minded indoctrinated individuals accept their duty to carry out jihad, and as a group begin the process of operational planning to participate in jihad or carry out a terrorist attack, including possible suicide missions. The NYPD report notes that, while the self-identification and indoctrination phases of radicalization are relatively slow and can evolve over a period of two to three years, the jihadization process can occur in a relatively short time span of only a few months, or in some cases, in a matter of weeks. Particularly in the case of suicide missions, or martyrdom operations as they are viewed and referred to by these terrorist groups, group leadership will often seek to execute these plans quickly after they are divulged to the participants to avoid possible attrition from those who have second thoughts about the prospect of dying for their cause. This provides a compelling explanation for why British authorities moved so swiftly to apprehend those involved in the liquid explosives plot in 2006, recognizing that the recording of martyrdom videos suggested that the plot was very close to being carried out.

Since the 9/11 attacks, counterterrorism operations have identified numerous terrorist groups and individuals with links to al Qaeda operating within the United States. Examples include the so-called Lackawanna Six terrorist cell, based near Buffalo, New York, whose members were found guilty of providing terrorist support to al Qaeda; a Detroit-based sleeper cell that may have be planning to carry out an attack against Disneyland in Anaheim, California; and a group of radical Islamists living in New Jersey who were planning to attack the Fort Dix military installation using automatic weapons, as well as the previously discussed group that was plotting the attacks of the fuel storage and distribution facilities at JFK airport. As previously noted, linking these groups to al Qaeda or a common terrorist movement has proven difficult for prosecutors. Nonetheless, these cases serve to illustrate the potential threat of attacks that may be launched from within the United States. This evidence of a continued interest among terrorists to conduct operations within the United States and to specifically target aviation assets provides evidence that, while the United States has not experienced a major terrorist attack within the U.S. homeland in the seven years since 2001, those responsible for aviation security must be constantly vigilant. Moreover, the U.S. aviation security policies and strategies should seek the most effective and efficient means possible to detect, deter, prevent, and respond to the evolving terrorist threat and possible future attacks targeting the aviation system.

AN ASYMMETRIC THREAT INTENT ON DIMINISHING OUR RESOLVE

In addition to becoming an increasingly homegrown threat, terrorism, whether it be spawned by global movements like al Qaeda or carried out by homegrown groups espousing radical ideologies, has been described as posing an asymmetric threat. The term asymmetric threat generally refers to various potential attacks that can be made by an adversary whose funding, manpower, and resources is vastly smaller than the entity it seeks to attack or wage war against.

Faced with such an asymmetric threat, security strategies and approaches must become arguably more complex to address the increasingly uncertain nature of the threat. The various security measures put in place to protect and defend against terrorist threats must be both comprehensive to protect against the full range of potential threats and also effective against these various threats. While aviation security has always had to deal with the uncertain nature of threats posed by terrorists seeking to carry out bombings and hijackings, the tactics and objectives of the 9/11 attacks, the shoe bombing plot, and the liquid explosives plot indicate that present-day terrorist adversaries desire to execute well-thought-out plans and methods for defeating elaborate security measures and sophisticated threat detection technologies. While asymmetric threats posed by terrorists pose a continuing risk to aviation security, the notion of asymmetric threats is nothing new. Military history is rife with examples of asymmetric warfare, including the tactics of the Continental Army during the Revolutionary War and those of the Viet Cong during the Vietnam conflict.[30] What these experiences suggest is that, while asymmetric warfare in various forms has been around for a long time, these tactics have proven to be highly effective in eroding the morale and weakening the resolve of forces with superior technologies, training, and capabilities compared to their adversaries.

Perhaps the clearest example of the use of terrorism as an asymmetric tactic was the widespread use of bombings, including some bombings of civilian targets, by the Provisional Irish Republican Army (IRA), in addition to sniper attacks and other guerilla tactics carried out by the IRA against British forces. Beginning in the mid-1970s, the Provisional IRA adopted a strategy known as the "Long War," designed to include an enduring campaign of attacks carried out by numerous small, self-sufficient terrorist cells that could not be easily identified, infiltrated, or stopped by British forces. Despite periodic truces and cease fires, the IRA's "Long War" spanned more than 20 years, until the Belfast Agreement or Good Friday Agreement of 1998 brought about constitutional change and power sharing in Northern Ireland.

In his 2006 State of the Union Address, President Bush described the ongoing conflict with Islamic extremists as "a long war against a determined enemy."[31] While the term "long war" has often been used in describing military conflicts and its use by the Bush Administration appears to have no specific connection to the Provisional IRA's adoption of the term in the 1970s,[32] from the standpoint of terrorist tactics, the parallels between strategies and methods employed by the Provisional IRA and those adopted by al Qaeda, particularly in terms of the use of small, stealthy cells to carry out attacks, are striking and capture the essence of the asymmetric threat posed by these groups. The groups also appear to share a common strategy in the sense that their tactics are largely designed to primarily have a psychological and social impact, rather than a significant military impact. Again, the objective of asymmetric terrorist tactics appears to be largely one of weakening the resolve of the superior power. However, in the case of al Qaeda, and like-minded Islamic radicals, the ultimate objective of their campaign of terror is less clear, but appears to be tied to loosely defined goals of lessening or eliminating western and U.S. influences in the Islamic world, and the elimination of Israel.

Whereas the Provisional IRA targeted aviation only on a limited basis, aviation has long been a primary target of Middle Eastern and radical Islamic terrorist groups, including al Qaeda. Attacks against aviation targets arguably offer a considerable degree of psychological and social impact, the type of impact and attention sought by terrorist organizations. Intense media interest in aviation disasters offers terrorists a global audience for voicing their message and seeking support for their cause. The 9/11 attacks and the various al Qaeda plots and attacks since, including several plots and attempted attacks against aviation targets, reflect the asymmetric nature of the terrorist threat to aviation and the terrorist's continued interest in attacking aviation targets.

Arguably, the notion of a "long war" or a protracted campaign of terror provides a strategic advantage to terrorist adversaries in the sense that they can wear down the resolve of security forces by behaving unpredictably and at irregular intervals over long periods of time, breeding complacency during periods of calm intermingled with potentially demoralizing defeats if security measures are breached allowing attacks to be successfully carried out. For this reason, many policymakers argue that terrorism cannot be defeated by security measures alone, regardless of how effective those security measures may be. These policymakers argue that security must be complemented by sanctions against those states that harbor or otherwise provide aid to terrorist groups, and/or military action to eliminate terrorist threats and disrupt or disable the command and control structure of terrorist organizations. The use of military force to combat al Qaeda and the Taliban regime in Afghanistan immediately following the 9/11 attacks exemplifies the overwhelming view among federal policymakers in the Bush Administration and in Congress that military action was a necessary part of the global war against terrorism, along with enhanced security measures and expanded counterterrorism efforts. Thus, aviation security is but one small part of the overall U.S. strategy to combat global terrorism, and spending on aviation security is relatively small compared to national defense and counterterrorism efforts tied to the global war on terrorism. Nonetheless, spending on aviation security since the 9/11 attacks has been considerable, and future directions for enhancing and optimizing approaches to security seek even larger investments over the next 15 years to further strengthen aviation security against terrorist threats.

COST OF PROTECTING AVIATION

While terrorists groups appear to have a specific interest in continuing to target the aviation system, defending and protecting this system and its assets against asymmetric threats is complex and resource intensive because terrorist adversaries behave in ways that can be difficult to predict and difficult to detect. Terrorists apparently achieve and maintain these stealthy, unpredictable characteristics by operating in small, close-knit cells or groups, and by observing defensive postures of security systems through probing and other observational techniques and adapting their strategies accordingly, all characteristics of an asymmetric threat. In terms of aviation security, what this means is that security systems need to be robust against a wide array of threats and be capable of quickly adapting to new potential threats based on intelligence information. Robust security systems, however, tend to be extremely costly and can be resource and labor intensive because policymakers and strategists typically seek to make these systems highly capable of defending against the entire gamut of potential threats.

Additionally, the widely held view that security can largely be achieved through a variety of technology solutions can have the effect of perpetuating a cycle of costly research, development, testing, acquisition, and deployment of the latest security technologies. A careful evaluation of the threats and existing vulnerabilities of the aviation system to these threats can help direct technology investment using a risk-based framework. The risk-based framework will be discussed in greater detail later in this book, but generally involves a deliberative examination and prioritization of threats and available vulnerability reduction measures based on the likelihood and severity of possible attack scenarios. While risk-based analyses can help to define aviation security technology investment strategies, the breadth of potential threats and the difficulty in detecting and defending against various types of threats, like the threat of explosives in particular, point to a conclusion that effective, robust security is often unavoidably costly and resource intensive.

The extensive spending by the United States on aviation security since the 9/11 attacks, nonetheless, raises considerable policy questions over how future funds and resources should be best allocated in a risk-based fashion, as well as what revenue sources should be used to pay the cost of effectively securing the air transportation system in a manner that demonstrates fiscal responsibility and accountability to taxpayers and users of the aviation system. To address these policy questions, it is useful to examine more closely the costs incurred by the United States to protect its aviation system.

The extensive measures to protect aviation following the 9/11 attacks have been extremely costly. TSA spending on aviation security between FY2002 and FY2008 totaled nearly $40 billion dollars, more than $6 billion annually. Additionally, airports, airlines, air cargo companies, and other elements of the aviation industry have collectively spent billions of dollars to improve physical security and surveillance capabilities, administer security training to employees, and comply with new federally mandated security regulations.

Prior to the 9/11 attacks, aviation security was primarily funded by the airlines. It is estimated that the airlines were spending about $450 million annually for passenger screening contracts.[33] In addition, the FAA received appropriations totaling about $180 million annually in FY2000 and FY2001. The majority of this funding was going toward the research, acquisition, development, and deployment of EDSs, primarily for targeted use on international routes and, on a limited basis, for screening the baggage of domestic passengers selected by passenger prescreening procedures under the CAPPS. These funds also went to fund the FAA's aviation security intelligence and oversight functions, and the FAA's air marshals program, which had just 33 marshals operating solely on international flights. Estimated expenditures by the FAA and the airlines for passenger and baggage screening and related security activities, such as law enforcement support and security checkpoints, from 1996 to 2001 are summarized in Figure 3.2. These amounts are estimated based on FAA

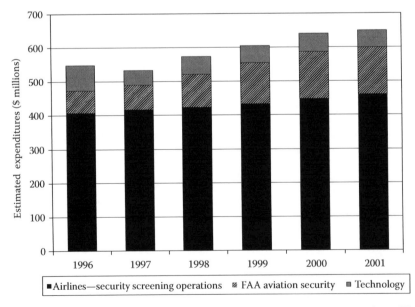

FIGURE 3.2 Estimated pre-9/11 expenditures for aviation security screening operations, FAA aviation security activities, and related federal research, development, and procurement of screening technologies (1996–2001).

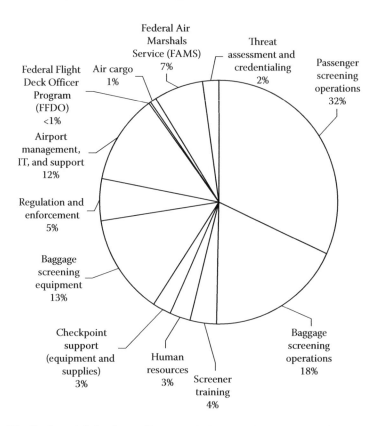

FIGURE 3.3 Distribution of federal spending on aviation security-related activities based on FY2003–FY2008 appropriations amounts.

appropriations and analysis by the U.S. GAO* of air carrier costs for passenger and property screening in 2000.[34] Following the 9/11 terrorist attacks, ATSA mandated that these functions be transitioned to the newly created TSA.

Annual spending on aviation security following the 9/11 attacks increased more than 10-fold compared to estimated spending on aviation security in FY2000 and FY2001. Much of this spending has been driven by the mandates of ATSA, particularly the mandates requiring federalization of passenger and baggage screening operations, and the mandate that 100% of all checked baggage be subject to electronic screening or acceptable alternative screening methods. Not surprisingly, passenger and baggage screening operations make up 50% of the total appropriations to the TSA for aviation security (Figure 3.3). Figure 3.3 displays the breakout of aviation security spending over the years from FY2003 to FY2008 and provides some interesting insights into aviation security policy and its budgetary implications. More detailed appropriations amounts for all TSA budget activities in FY2007 and FY2008 are provided in Table 3.1.

It is not particularly surprising that direct costs for passenger and baggage screening operations comprise 50% of the TSA total budget given that these functions are extremely labor intensive and these budget activities primarily represent the salaries and benefits paid to the TSA screener/TSO workforce that includes almost 45,000 full-time equivalent (FTE) positions. A sizable portion of the additional TSA aviation security budget is spent in support of these day-to-day screening

---

* The U.S. government agency known as the GAO changed its name from the General Accounting Office to the Government Accountability Office in 2004. The first time Government Accountability Office appears (for a cited report from 2004 or later) it should be spelled out. (Everyone in public policy just knows the organization as the GAO).

TABLE 3.1
**Appropriations for TSA Aviation Security-Related Budget Activities
(FY2007–FY2008)**

Budget Activity	FY2007	FY2008
	\$ Millions	
Aviation security		
Screening partnership program (private screening contracts)	149	143
Passenger and baggage screeners salaries and benefits	2470	2636
Screener training and equipment	244	224
Human resource services	207	182
Checkpoint support (equipment and supplies)	173	250
Explosives detection equipment purchase and installation	279	294
Screening technology maintenance	222	264
Operations integration	23	25
Regulation and enforcement	218	256
Airport management, IT, and support	666	652
FFDOs program and crew training	25	25
Air cargo security	55	73
Airport perimeter security	0	4
ASCF	250	250
FAMS	714	770
Transportation Threat Assessment and Credentialing (TTAC)		
Secure flight	15	50
Crew vetting	15	15
RT program (fees)	3	4
Transportation security support functions		
Intelligence	21	21
HQ administration	294	293
Information technology	210	209
Totals	6253	6640

operations. Baggage screening equipment accounts for about 13% of the TSA's total budget. This budget activity includes the purchase and installation of expensive explosives detection machines, primarily full-sized EDS machines that range in price from $900,000 to $1.3 million a piece. Redesigning airport baggage handling systems to accommodate these EDS machines and integrate them in line with baggage conveyors has also been a costly endeavor, and this 13% slice of the TSA aviation security budget also includes funds placed into the special ASCF established specifically to provide federal funds and federal reimbursements to airports for construction projects to accommodate and optimize the installation of EDS equipment. This does not, however, reflect the full cost of these activities between FY2003 and FY2008 because airports are expected to pay a share of the cost, and also because many airports are still awaiting reimbursement for the anticipated federal share of projects initiated during this time frame, that are expected to be covered by future year funding of either the ASCF or, possibly, additional appropriations amounts to cover costs related to in-line EDS integration and optimization.

In addition to the costs of baggage screening equipment, another 3% of the TSA budget has gone toward the cost of passenger checkpoint equipment and supplies. This cost is largely driven by screening equipment needs, such as magnetometers and x-ray machines, but also reflects costs for various consumable supplies, such as disposal inspection gloves worn by TSOs, as well as certain durable items, such as plastic bins for placing coats, shoes, and laptop computers in to move through the x-ray machines. In the coming years, this aspect of the TSA budget may experience a push for specific increases as the TSA seeks to attain improved capabilities for detecting explosives on passengers and to better streamline and modernize passenger screening checkpoints. In addition to these costs, the cost of training screeners accounts for about 4%, and human resources functions tied to the screening workforce account for another 3% of the TSA budget for aviation security. All totaled, functions directly tied to passenger and baggage screening account for nearly 75% of the TSA's aviation security spending.

Another 12% of TSA aviation security spending has gone toward airport management, information technology systems installation and upkeep at airports, and other airport support functions. These budget activities also support the TSA's screening functions, but more broadly encompass the TSA's coordination and oversight of airport-wide security. The TSA itself, however, is not responsible for airport perimeter security, surveillance, and access controls, as these are primarily the responsibilities of each individual airport and airport operator. Airports' spending on these functions has increased significantly since the 9/11 attacks, but because this spending is not tied to federal appropriations for TSA budget activities or funded out of federal accounts, it is not reflected in Figure 3.3 or Table 3.1. The federal government has, however, reimbursed some airports for their law enforcement presence and support at screening checkpoints, and these reimbursement agreements are reflected as a relatively small part of the TSA's regulation and enforcement functions. These arrangements have been made in lieu of creating a large law enforcement force within the TSA to deploy to airports, and law enforcement at airports remains primarily a local or state agency responsibility. The TSA, however, has overall regulatory responsibility of the security aspects of all airports, airlines, and other elements of the aviation industry, and these regulatory functions account for the majority of spending on regulation and enforcement activities that account for roughly 5% of the TSA budget. This funding primarily pays for the salaries and benefits of the TSA's workforce of regulatory inspectors. Regulation of the air cargo industry, however, has been treated separately, and these air cargo regulatory activities as well as spending on various pilot programs for screening cargo placed on passenger aircraft accounts for another 1% of TSA spending. While the new mandate to screen all cargo placed on passenger aircraft by January 2010 will likely increase spending on air cargo regulatory activity to some degree, under current plans, the actual screening functions are to be conducted by shippers and cargo freight forwarding companies, and therefore, air cargo security functions will largely be paid for and carried out by industry partners and not the TSA. Therefore, the impact on the overall TSA budget for these activities is likely to be relatively limited and air cargo security is likely to remain a considerably small component of the overall TSA budget.

As the above discussion has suggested, while the TSA's regulatory and oversight functions are a limited part of the overall TSA budget, aspects of aviation security that the TSA has operational responsibility for, such as passenger and baggage screening, impose much more significant costs on the federal budget. In addition to its screening functions, the TSA also has operational responsibility for the FAMS that has accounted for about 7% of the overall TSA budget over the years from 2003 to 2008. However, it should be noted that for some portion of this time frame, the FAMS was taken out of the TSA and placed inside the CBP. For the purposes of this budget analysis, appropriations for FAMS were included as part of the total federal funding for aviation security-related budget activities.

Following the 9/11 attacks, the FAMS expanded dramatically from a small group of 33 marshals to a forces of thousands. Funding for the air marshals service has accounted for about 7% of federal aviation security funding. In contrast to the relatively costly measures of passenger and baggage screening and FAMS, the related initiative of training and deputizing airline pilots to carry firearms to defend cockpits against possible hijacking attempts under the Federal Flight Deck Officer (FFDO) program and training flight attendants in self-defense carries a comparatively small price tag of about $25 million annually, much less than 1% of the overall TSA budget. While the FFDO program remains controversial, as some still continue to question the safety and security aspects of arming pilots, it stands out as a particularly cost-effective layer of security, primarily because it utilizes pilots who are already salaried by the airlines, thus requiring only limited federal investment in training and issuing firearms to pilots who voluntarily participate in the program.

In addition to these various aviation security budget activities, various threat assessment and credentialing functions are conducted by the TSA to strengthen aviation security. These include work on the long-delayed and controversial Secure Flight program to replace passenger no-fly and secondary screening selection (selectee) lists, as well as programs to vet foreign students who apply for flight training in the United States and foreign and domestic airline crews and pilots. These functions account for roughly 2% of TSA spending. In addition to this, the TSA is involved in coordinating the background checks required of all airport and airline employees and air cargo workers with unescorted access to secured areas of airports and aircraft. However, this program is funded entirely through fees paid by the workers or their prospective employers and imposes no additional cost to the federal government.

The fees paid by airports and airlines is but a small part of the overall spending by the aviation industry and related entities for establishing aviation security programs and complying with federal regulations pertaining to aviation security. Every airline, airport, and air cargo freight forwarder, along with several other aviation entities, such as companies that charter business jets, are required to set up and implement TSA-approved security programs. Each of these programs is tailored to the particular airport, airline, or operator, and therefore, the costs of establishing and implementing these programs vary widely, although each must adhere to a certain set of TSA-established standards. These security programs will be examined in more depth in chapters covering airport security, in-flight security, and air cargo, as well as to some degree with regard to those GA operators, such as companies that charter business jets, that are subject to federally mandated aviation security regulations. The total cost of these various programs, however, is difficult to gauge but has certainly totaled billions of dollars in the years since the 9/11 attacks.

One particular concern over all this aviation security spending that has taken place since the 9/11 attacks is how it is all being coordinated and prioritized in a cohesive fashion to ensure that the money is well spent. The next chapter examines in depth the U.S. strategy for aviation security that has slowly emerged following the 9/11 attacks and was first put into a comprehensive framework in 2006 and 2007. This strategy and the underlying policy continue to evolve and are likely to play an important role in determining future directions for investment intended to further strengthen aviation security.

REFERENCES

1. National Commission on Terrorist Attacks upon the United States. *The 9/11 Commission Report*, New York: W.W. Norton & Co., 2004.
2. For example of a work criticizing alleged political influencing and manipulation of the work of the 9/11 Commission see Philip Shenon, *The Commission: The Uncensored History of the 9/11 Investigation*, New York: Twelve, Hachette Book Group USA, 2008.
3. Transportation Security Administration. *Budget Estimates: Fiscal Year 2004*, March 2003.
4. National Commission on Terrorist Attacks upon the United States. *The 9/11 Commission Report*, p. 391.
5. Transcript of Hearing Before the Subcommittee on Aviation, Committee on Transportation and Infrastructure, House of Representatives, 108th Congress, *9/11 Commission Report: Review of Aviation Security Recommendations*, August 25, 2004, p. 26.
6. See, for example, Statement of Clark Kent Ervin, Inspector General, U.S. Department of Homeland Security, before the Committee on Transportation and Infrastructure, Subcommittee on Aviation, U.S. House of Representatives, April 22, 2004.
7. See note 4, p. 393.
8. Transportation Security Administration. *Air Cargo Strategic Plan*, November 2003.
9. Department of Homeland Security, Transportation Security Administration. Air Cargo Security Requirements; Proposed Rule, *Federal Register, 69*(217), November 10, 2004, pp. 65258–65291.

10. Department of Homeland Security, Transportation Security Administration. Air Cargo Security Requirements, Final Rule, *Federal Register, 71*(102), May 26, 2006, pp. 30477–30517.
11. Democratic Members of the House Select Committee on Homeland Security, Jim Turner, Ranking Member. *America at Risk: The State of Homeland Security, Initial Findings.* Washington, DC, January 2004.
12. *Democratic Strategy on Homeland Security, Making America Safer: Closing the Security Gap.*
13. See, for example, Robert W. Poole, Jr. *Airport Security: Time for a New Model.* Policy Study 340, Los Angeles, CA: Reason Public Policy Institute, January 2006.
14. See note 10.
15. Lara Jakes Jordan and Matt Apuzzo. "US: Ivins Solely Responsible for Anthrax Attacks." *The Associated Press*, August 6, 2008.
16. United States District Court, District of Massachusetts. United States of America v. Richard Colvin Reid, a/k/a Abdul-Raheem, a/k/a Abdul Rareem, Abu Ibrahim.
17. Michael Jacobson. "They Trained. They Plotted. Then They Bailed." *The Washington Post*, March 23, 2008, p. B3.
18. United States Department of Defense. *Verbatim Transcript of Combatant Status Review Tribunal Hearing for ISN 10024* (Unclassified), March 10, 2007.
19. Ibid., p. 18.
20. Ibid.
21. For a comprehensive database of terrorism incidents see National Consortium for the Study of Terrorism and Responses to Terrorism (START), *Global Terrorism Database*, available at http://www.start.umd. edu/data/gtd/.
22. Peter Wright, Congressional Quarterly, "Chilling Details Emerge from Trans-Atlantic Terror Plot Hearing," Reprinted in Transportation Security Administration *News & Happenings*, Updated April 8, 2008.
23. "Plot Would Have Killed Thousands." *ABC News*, August 6, 2007.
24. "'Bombers' made martyr videos." *The Sun (UK)*, April 4, 2008.
25. "Terror Plot: Glasgow and London Attacks Were Carried Out by Same Men." *The Daily Mail*, July 3, 2007.
26. National Intelligence Council. *National Intelligence Estimate: The Terrorist Threat to the US Homeland*, July 2007.
27. Ibid.
28. Mitchell D.Silber and Arvin Bhatt. *Radicalization in the West: The Homegrown Threat.* Police Department, City of New York, 2007.
29. Ibid.
30. Michael Rubin. "Asymmetrical Threat Concept and Its Reflection on International Security," *Presentation to the Strategic Research and Study Center (SAREM) Under the Turkish General Staff, Istanbul, Turkey*, May 31, 2007.
31. President George W. Bush, *State of the Union Address by the President*, United States Capitol, Washington, DC, January 31, 2006.
32. See Bradley Graham and Josh White, "Abizaid Credited with Popularizing the Term 'Long War'." *The Washington Post*, February 3, 2006, p. A8, for background on the use of the term "Long War" in reference to the war on terrorism.
33. See U.S. Government Accountability Office, *Aviation Fees: Review of Air Carriers' Year 2000 Passenger and Property Screening Costs*, April 2005, GAO-05-558.
34. Ibid.

4 The U.S. Strategy for Combatting Terror Threats to the Aviation Domain

The U.S. strategy for aviation security that has emerged as part of the global war on terrorism is predicated on two principal goals: (1) deterring or mitigating security risks and (2) minimizing disruption to the flow of passengers and goods that travel by air. The strategy employs a risk-based and multidimensional, multilayered approach to securing aviation assets from attack and exploitation by terrorists and criminal elements. While the strategy is evolutionary in its thinking, building upon preexisting approaches to aviation security, it seeks to provide a unified framework for implementing aviation security policies that largely did not exist prior to the September 11, 2001, terrorist attacks.

In the years leading up to the terrorist attacks of September 11, 2001, the United States lacked a comprehensive national policy and strategy for aviation security. The approach to aviation security was largely shaped by past events—such as the bombing of Pan Am flight 103 in December 1988 and aviation security policy debate in the aftermath of the TWA 800 accident—rather than a comprehensive evaluation of the full range of security risks. The 9/11 Commission concluded that the terrorist attacks of September 11, 2001, revealed failures of imagination, policy, capabilities, and management by both the FAA and the U.S. intelligence community.

Following the September 11, 2001, attacks, U.S. aviation security policy and strategy was closely linked to the mandates of ATSA (P.L. 107-71), which emphasized sweeping changes to the security of passenger airline operations. While the importance of strategic planning was recognized, it was not a priority. The 9/11 Commission Report[1] concluded that the TSA had failed to develop an integrated strategy for the transportation sector and mode-specific plans, prompting Congress to mandate the development of these strategies and plans in the IRTPA of 2004 (P.L. 108-458). While the TSA has developed these strategies and plans, the documents have been considered security sensitive limiting public discourse on the DHS strategy for aviation security. However, in June 2006, President Bush directed the DHS to establish and implement a national strategy for aviation security and an accompanying set of supporting plans.

Under the framework for national aviation security policy established by the President, the DHS has developed a publicly available national strategy for aviation security that addresses threats to aviation using a risk-based methodology to complement the overarching National Infrastructure Protection Plan (NIPP) and seeks to deter and prevent terrorist attacks against aviation, mitigate damage and expedite recovery, and minimize the impact of a future terrorist attack to the aviation system. The strategy seeks to achieve these objectives by engaging domestic and international partners and carrying out specific actions set forth in a series of supporting plans for operational security, surveillance and intelligence, threat response, system recovery, and coordination.

Questions, however, remain regarding whether these plans are comprehensive, adaptable, sustainable, and adequately coordinated with budgetary decisions and resource allocation. Specific issues include the validity of the strategy's underlying risk assumptions, the capability of security technologies and programs to meet future needs and system demands, whether the strategy is sufficiently forward-looking and not reactive in its approach, the extent to which the strategy provides a comprehensive framework for a robust aviation security system, and the degree to which strategic objectives and approaches align with budget priorities and resource availability.

PRE-9/11 APPROACHES TO AVIATION SECURITY

Before the terrorist attacks of September 11, 2001, the U.S. approach to aviation security had largely been shaped by past events such as the bombing of Pan Am flight 103 in December 1988 and the aviation security policy discussions in the aftermath of the TWA flight 800 accident. During the 1990s and up until the 9/11 attacks, the U.S. approach to aviation security was undergoing a reactive shift in strategy, placing an emphasis on addressing the threat of aircraft bombings aboard commercial airliners, albeit with limited resources and a much slower time frame compared to actions taken following the terrorist attacks of September 11, 2001. Based on past incidents and events and intelligence analysis of the terrorist threat to aviation, the hijacking threat was not seen as significant and took a backseat to efforts addressing the threat of aircraft bombings.

In April 2001, the FAA issued a strategic plan for civil aviation security titled "A Commitment to Security." The vision was for the FAA and the U.S. aviation security system to be "[r]ecognized as the world leader in civil aviation security—identifying and countering aviation-related threats to U.S. citizens worldwide."[2] The strategic goal stated in the plan was to ensure that "[n]o successful attacks against U.S. civil aviation" occur.[3] In comparison to the breadth and depth of the post-9/11 focus on aviation security, the desired key results stated in this document in retrospect seem quite modest and this goal tragically unattained. The pre-9/11 strategic plan sought to improve on checked baggage and checkpoint screening performance and utilize a combination of EDS screening and PPBM techniques to vet 100% of checked baggage. In addition to improving technical capabilities to detect explosives in checked baggage, strategies identified by the FAA included

- Establishing security screening operations and training standards which, at that time, did not exist
- Ensuring that federal air marshals were available to protect selected high-risk flight, although their number had dwindled to 33 at the time of the 9/11 hijackings[4]
- Ensuring that certified explosives canine teams were available at major U.S. airports
- Establishing preparedness and crisis management to respond to incidents that may occur

The FAA Civil Aviation Security Strategic Plan also sought to improve air cargo security, primarily to reduce the transport of dangerous goods, a response to concerns raised by the May 11, 1996, crash of ValuJet flight 592 in the Florida Everglades caused by improperly transported oxygen generators that ignited an intense cargo fire. The strategic plan sought to achieve this objective largely through industry training and education and targeted inspections of dangerous goods transportation areas. Despite the emphasis on preventing aircraft bombs carried in passenger luggage, the potential threat of a bomb placed in air cargo was not mentioned in the strategic plan. Also, while the strategic plan addressed internal FAA security, the emphasis of this strategic element was on handling and protection of sensitive information and maintaining up-to-date background checks and clearances for employees in security-sensitive positions. While the strategic plan did identify the completion of facility security assessments and the protection of information systems among key results sought, it did not convey any insight regarding the potential threats and vulnerabilities of air traffic facilities to physical attack or FAA information systems to physical or cyber attack.

The FAA's pre-9/11 strategic plan also identified several key results regarding external relationships including improved communications with Congress, the aviation industry, foreign governments, the OMB, and the Department of Transportation, Office of Inspector General (DOT OIG). The strategic plan, however did not specifically address relationships with federal law enforcement agencies and the intelligence community, factors that became a central focus of post-9/11 homeland security policy debate. The strategic plan also did not address relationships and coordination with the military for incident response, a major deficiency in the FAA's response to the hijackings on September 11, 2001, and an area of considerable focus during post-9/11 strategic planning.

While the FAA strategic plan for aviation security failed to adequately consider all security risks, the 9/11 Commission concluded that the terrorist attacks of September 11, 2001, revealed failures in imagination, policy, capabilities, and management both on the part of the FAA and the U.S. intelligence community. Although the brunt of the criticism levied by the 9/11 Commission was directed at the U.S. intelligence community, it faulted the FAA for focusing too heavily on the threat of bombings and for not involving the FAA's Civil Aviation Security intelligence functions in the FAA's policy-making process. The 9/11 Commission pointed out that the suicide hijacking threat was imaginable, and it was in fact imagined by FAA Civil Aviation Security intelligence analysts in 1999 but largely dismissed as being unlikely.[5] The 9/11 Commission faulted Congress as well for becoming entrenched in debate over airline passenger service issues while failing to focus attention and resources on the terrorist threat to the aviation system. The FAA Civil Aviation Security Strategic Plan released in April 2001 serves as evidence that the FAA did not create a comprehensive strategy for protecting the aviation domain from the full spectrum of terrorist threats and did not effectively prioritize and allocate resources to reduce the vulnerability of the aviation system to possible terrorist attacks.

POST-9/11 ACTIONS ADDRESSING AVIATION SECURITY POLICY AND STRATEGY

Immediately following the terrorist attacks of September 11, 2001, aviation security policy and strategy debate was closely linked to the legislative process leading to the swift passage of the ATSA (P.L. 107-71). With regard to strategy and policy, ATSA gave the newly created position of Undersecretary of Transportation for Security (now known as the TSA Administrator or more formally as the Assistant Secretary of Homeland Security, TSA) specific authority and responsibility for assessing threats to transportation and developing policies, strategies, and plans for dealing with these threats to transportation security.[6] However, the primary emphasis of ATSA was on the security of passenger airline operations, and the immediate focus of the newly created TSA was to meet congressionally established requirements and deadlines for deploying air marshals, federalizing airport security screeners, and implementing 100% EDS screening of checked baggage. While the importance of establishing a comprehensive policy and strategy for aviation security was recognized by many policymakers, a strategic plan for protecting the aviation domain was slow to take shape.

In 2002, as these mandates for enhancing passenger airline security set forth in ATSA were being carried out and while Congress debated legislation to create the DHS, the Bush Administration began examining U.S. policies for protecting the homeland against future terrorist attacks in a broader context, considering other infrastructure and assets beyond the aviation domain that may be at risk. In July 2002, President Bush issued the National Strategy for Homeland Security and in February 2003, the President issued the National Strategy for the Physical Protection of Critical Infrastructures and Key Assets. However, neither of these strategies offered specific details on aviation security strategy nor did they specify how aviation security plans and programs fit into these broader strategies for protecting the homeland and its critical infrastructure and key resources (CI/KR) from terrorist attacks.

On July 22, 2004, the 9/11 Commission released its final report, concluding that the TSA had failed to develop an integrated strategy for the transportation sector and mode-specific plans to carry out this strategy. The 9/11 Commission recommended that the U.S. strategy for transportation security should be predicated on a risk-based prioritization for allocating limited resources to protect transportation infrastructure in a cost-effective manner, assigning roles and responsibilities for federal, state, regional, and local authorities, as well as private stakeholders.[7] Following the release of the 9/11 Commission's final report, Congress made addressing the recommendations of the report a key legislative priority, reflecting many of the Commission's recommendations in the IRTPA of 2004

(P.L. 108-458). The Act specifically required the DHS to develop, prepare, implement, and keep up-to-date a comprehensive national strategy for transportation security and mode-specific security plans. Reflecting 9/11 Commission recommendation language, the Act required the strategy to assign risk-based priorities and realistic deadlines for implementing practical and cost-effective defenses against security threats, setting forth agreed-upon roles and missions for federal, state, regional, and local authorities and mechanisms for private sector cooperation and participation.

Under the requirements established in the Act, the National Strategy for Transportation Security was to be accompanied by mode-specific security plans, including an aviation mode-specific plan. The modal security plan for aviation was required to include a threat matrix outlining each threat to the U.S. civil aviation system and the corresponding layers of security in place to address these threats. The plan was also required to include details for mitigation and reconstitution of the aviation system in the event of a terrorist attack. As required by law, updates to the strategy and the mode-specific plans must be transmitted to Congress every two years. These strategy documents have been designated as security-sensitive information as provided for in the Act. Consequently, they have had limited distribution beyond the DHS and the homeland security committees in Congress and limited public discourse on the DHS approach to developing a national strategy for aviation and transportation security.

However, in June 2006, President Bush issued policy guidance directing the DHS to establish and implement a national strategy for aviation security and a series of supporting plans for implementing this strategy.[8] Unlike prior strategies and plans that were either too broad in scope or limited in distribution, the policy, strategy and supporting plans developed under this Presidential directive have been made available to the public, thus offering unique insight into the strategic direction and approach to aviation security being pursued by U.S government. These documents are also much more comprehensive in their consideration of security in the aviation domain compared to prior strategy documents and therefore provide a more thorough picture of U.S. policy and strategy for mitigating threats involving aviation.

THE NATIONAL AVIATION SECURITY POLICY

The National Aviation Security Policy represents the overarching aviation-specific components of The National Strategy for Homeland Security. That strategy call for the DHS to serve as the focal entity for managing and coordinating border and transportation security initiatives "... to prevent the entry of terrorists and the instruments of terror, while facilitating the legal flow of people, goods, and services on which our economy depends."[9] The policy, however, addresses a broader spectrum of threats to the air domain that include not only specific threats to the homeland, but also threats to national security interests both within the United States and abroad. Therefore, in addition to the overall responsibility for homeland security and aviation security for which the DHS and the TSA are directly responsible, the National Aviation Security Policy also involves matters concerning the DOD, the Department of State, the DOJ, and a variety of other federal, state, and local agencies and private entities, and relies on close coordination with and continued cooperation from other nations.

On June 20, 2006, President Bush issued Homeland Security Presidential Directive 16 [HSPD-16/National Security Presidential Directive 47 (NSPD-47)] establishing new U.S. policy, guidelines, and implementation of actions to address threats to the air domain. The document broadly defines the air domain as the global airspace and all aircraft operating within that airspace including both manned and unmanned vehicles, as well as all people and goods being transported by such aircraft, and all supporting aviation infrastructure. The policy objectives set forth in HSPD-16 endeavor to prevent terrorist acts and other hostile actions either directed at or exploiting elements of the aviation domain while also minimizing the impact on air commerce and fostering the economic growth and stability of the aviation industry. The statement of policy notes that

> [t]he United States must continue to use the full range of its assets and capabilities to prevent the Air Domain from being used by terrorists, criminals, and other hostile states to commit acts of terrorism

and other unlawful or hostile acts against the United States, its people, property, territory, and allies and friends, all while minimizing the impact on the Aviation Transportation System and continuing to facilitate the free flow and growth of trade and commerce in the Air Domain. These efforts are critical to the global stability and economic growth and are vital to the interests of the United States.[10]

The stated policy specifies that the United States, in cooperation with international partners, will take all necessary and appropriate actions, consistent with applicable laws, statutes, and international agreements, to enhance the security and protect the United States and U.S. interests in the air domain. The implementation of this policy is to be consistent with a risk-based prioritization of aviation security strategies and tactics. Activities to support this policy objective specifically cited in this directive include

- Protecting critical transportation networks and infrastructure from terrorist attacks and other hostile, criminal, and unlawful acts and reducing the vulnerability of the air domain to these types of possible attacks or exploitation
- Improving situational awareness of security issues affecting the air domain and facilitating and enhancing information sharing to improve detection of threats and appropriate responsive actions
- Ensuring seamless, coordinated efforts relating to aviation security among federal, state, tribal, and local agencies and authorities
- Enhancing the resilience of the air transportation system to a terrorist attack, including the capability to rapidly recover from such an attack and minimize impacts on economic, transportation, social, and governmental systems
- Countering the proliferation of standoff weapons, such as shoulder-fired missiles, that pose significant risks to both civilian and military users of the air domain by terrorists, criminals, and other hostile groups and individuals
- Enhancing international relationships and promoting the integration of other nations and private sector partners in an improved global aviation security framework

Implementation of this policy is to be coordinated through the President's Homeland Security Council (HSC) Border and Transportation Security Policy Coordination Committee (BTS PCC). The policy established a requirement for the Secretary of Homeland Security to develop an overarching national strategy for aviation security and supporting plans to carry out this strategy.

HSPD-16 directed the DHS to implement this policy through the creation of an overall national strategy for aviation security. The directive explicitly called for the development of a national strategy for aviation security that is adaptive to changing threat levels and types of threats, and it is rooted in a risk-based, multidisciplinary, and global approach to aviation security. The directive required that the national strategy, along with its supporting plans, include, at a minimum, risk-based approaches to address the following threats:

- Attacks using aircraft against ground-based targets, including possible attacks using aircraft to deliver or transport chemical, biological, radiological, nuclear, or explosive (CBRNE) weapons
- Attacks using standoff weapons, such as shoulder-fired missiles or other MANPADS
- Attacks using on-board explosive devices and other conventional and nonconventional weapons to directly target aircraft
- Hijackings and air piracy
- Physical or cyber attacks on aviation critical infrastructure and facilities, such as air traffic control facilities and networks and navigation systems

The policy gives the Secretary of Homeland Security the leadership responsibility for developing the national strategy for aviation security and coordinating federal agency activities for protecting the aviation domain. The directive also identifies several specific action items to be addressed in supporting mode-specific plans to implement the national strategy for aviation security. The required plans include

- The Aviation Transportation System Security Plan
- The Aviation Operational Threat Response Plan
- The Aviation Transportation System Recovery Plan
- The Air Domain Surveillance and Intelligence Integration Plan
- The International Aviation Threat Reduction Plan
- The Domestic Outreach Plan
- The International Outreach Plan

The National Strategy for Aviation Security, along with several of these supporting plans was publicly released on March 26, 2007. The International Aviation Threat Reduction Plan and the Aviation Transportation System Recovery Plan were not released at that time, but may be released to the public in the future.

SECURITY THREATS TO AVIATION

The National Strategy for Aviation Security identifies three origins or sources of threats to the air domain: terrorist groups, hostile-nation states, and criminals. The strategy document points out that while physical attacks from terrorist groups pose the most prominent threat, terrorists may also use criminal tactics to move operatives, weapons, explosives, or possibly weapons of mass destruction (WMDs) through the aviation system. The strategy notes that "[s]uch threats are particularly worrisome in areas of the world where governments are weak or provide safe haven to terrorists."[11] Further, hostile-nation states may directly sponsor international terrorism directed against aviation by providing funding, training, weapons, explosives, supplies, and other material support to carry out attacks against the air domain. Also, the presence of criminal elements with extensive knowledge of the aviation sector, both within the United States and in foreign countries, poses a persistent threat to aviation and could provide potentially violent domestic groups or international terrorists with specific capabilities to exploit weaknesses in aviation security. Therefore, these three threat origins or sources cannot be viewed as being mutually exclusive, as they may combine in various forms to carry out attacks either directly against aviation assets or by exploiting elements of the air domain to prepare for or carry out attacks against the homeland or U.S. interests abroad.

The strategy document defines three primary categories of threats against the aviation domain based on the target of the threat. These consist of threats involving aircraft; threats to aviation infrastructure; and threats involving hostile exploitation of air cargo. A variety of tactics may be used to attack these targets including hijackings, bombings, shootings, and criminal tactics such as smuggling of persons and weapons. A synopsis of the relationships between threat origins or sources, aviation targets, and tactics for attacking these aviation targets is presented in Figure 4.1.

AIRCRAFT-RELATED THREATS

Aircraft threats may be directed at aircraft or may involve the use of aircraft to attack other targets, as was the case in the terrorist attacks of September 11, 2001. The strategy document notes that large passenger aircraft have historically been at the greatest risk from terrorist attacks, including both hijackings and bombings, because terrorists have perceived that attacks against such aircraft have significant potential to cause catastrophic damage and mass casualties and disrupt the aviation system. The document, however, notes that terrorists may also seek to attack all-cargo aircraft, especially large all-cargo aircraft that are considered attractive as weapons to attack ground-based

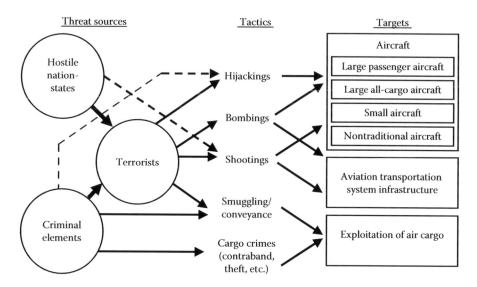

FIGURE 4.1   Aviation security threat sources, tactics, and targets.

targets in 9/11-style attacks. All-cargo aircraft, and the air cargo system in general, may also be attractive to terrorists or criminals as a means of conveyance for weapons, explosives, or other supplies. The strategy considers large transport aircraft, both passenger airliners and to a lesser extent all-cargo aircraft, to be at risk from possible attacks using shoulder-fired guided missiles or other standoff weapons.

The strategy also indicates that small aircraft face both the threat of direct attack as well as the threat that they may be used as weapons to attack ground targets. While the strategy notes that small aircraft appear to be relatively unattractive targets for attacks by themselves because they carry few passengers, it cautions that terrorists may use a wide variety of small aircraft, such as business jets and helicopters, to destroy ground targets, especially critical assets and infrastructure. The most formidable threat comes from the potential use of small aircraft to either transport or deliver a WMD payload. The strategy also notes that small aircraft are also used by transnational criminal elements to carry out illegal activities, such as drug and weapons smuggling, and pose a considerable challenge for border protection.

Finally, the strategy recognizes that nontraditional aircraft, such as unmanned aircraft, ultralights, and aerial-application aircraft (i.e., crop dusters), may be used as either weapons or means of conveyance for WMDs. The strategy states that terrorists may employ such aircraft for missions that are limited in range, require limited accuracy, and have a specific and small target. For example, crop dusting aircraft have been regarded as a potential threat for dispersing a chemical or biological agent. The strategy notes that such tactics deserve very close monitoring.

THREATS TO AVIATION INFRASTRUCTURE

The strategy maintains that reported threats to aviation infrastructure, including airports and air navigation facilities are relatively few. The strategy notes that air navigation facilities, in particular, have a low public profile and are resilient to attack due to a robust multilayered design that can be quickly reconstituted, thus limiting psychological and economic impacts stemming from an attack. The strategy, however, notes that there is a wide variety of potential threats to aviation infrastructure. The strategy notes in particular the potential threat to concentrations of individuals at major airport passenger terminals. Terrorists may attack passenger terminal buildings with explosives, as was attempted at Glasgow International Airport, Scotland in June 2007 and in several other histori-cal incidents.[12]

The strategy concludes that attacks against other facets of aviation infrastructure, such as GA airports and air cargo handling areas, are less likely to materialize, largely because attacks against these facilities would generally not offer the opportunity to target large number of people and would therefore have a more limited psychological impact. The strategy, however, was released a few months before U.S. law enforcement authorities arrested members of a suspected home-grown terrorist cell who were plotting to bomb jet fuel storage tanks at New York's JFK and the network of jet fuel distribution pipelines in the New York City area. While the actual vulnerability of this infrastructure to such an attack remains debatable, the plot highlighted the possibility that aviation jet fuel storage facilities and distribution systems at major U.S. airports may be at risk. While the sophistication of this particular plot has been questioned,[13] in general, the potential threat to fuel farms and pipelines and other critical aviation infrastructure—where an attack could have a dramatic effect capturing considerable public attention and potentially disrupting the avia-tion system on a large scale—may deserve further attention from policymakers and aviation secu-rity strategists.

THREATS INVOLVING EXPLOITATION OF AIR CARGO

The strategy recognizes that the large scale, diversity, and complexity of the air cargo industry make it potentially vulnerable to exploitation by terrorists. The strategy, however, concludes that post-9/11 actions to enhance air cargo security have been effective in reducing the threat of stowaways aboard air freighters that could carry out a 9/11-style suicide hijacking and the threat of explosives. Nonetheless, the strategy recognizes that the enhanced regulatory framework for air cargo security[14] is not immune to exploitation, and the air cargo system, in general, has been exploited for years by criminal elements. In addition to possible threats to all-cargo aircraft noted above, the threat of ter-rorist infiltration of air cargo handling operations and facilities remains a threat that could lead to exploitation of the air cargo system as a means of conveyance for terrorist operatives, and conven-tional weapons, WMDs, explosives, weapon components, and other terrorist items. While not dis-cussed specifically by the strategy, it should be noted that all sorts of criminal activities, possibly including cargo-related crimes in the aviation domain, could provide revenue sources to support terrorist organizations, particularly in regions where government oversight and security measures are weak.

THE RISK-BASED FRAMEWORK

The U.S. National Strategy for Aviation Security is predicated on a risk-based, multidisciplinary, and global approach to ensure that resources allocated at the federal, state, and local levels and by private sector aviation interests provide the greatest potential to detect, deter, and prevent attacks against aviation and mitigate the consequences if an attack does occur. This risk-based approach or methodology is described in detail in the NIPP and the NIPP Transportation Sector Specific Plan (TSSP), which were made available to the public in May 2007.[15] The NIPP is designed to be a com-prehensive, integrated plan for protecting critical infrastructure and was required under Homeland Security Presidential Directive Number 7 (HSPD-7) as a mechanism for establishing uniform poli-cies, approaches, guidelines, and methodologies for infrastructure protection and risk management activities across various sectors of homeland security including the transportation sector and avia-tion, which falls under the responsibility of the TSA. In general, the NIPP serves to define a com-mon framework for identifying critical assets, conducting risk assessments, and developing and implementing a risk reduction and mitigation initiatives based on the results of these assessments. The TSSP applies this risk-based framework across the entire transportation sector, including the aviation domain.

The system-based risk management framework outlined in the TSSP describes risk as a function of threat, vulnerability, and potential consequences and analyzes security risk by taking into account all three of these factors. Specific methods for assessing risk will be considered in more detail in Chapter 5. The TSSP highlights the interdependencies of the transportation system, and the aviation sector as an element of this broader multimodal transportation network in examining the vulnerabilities to attack as well as the planning, coordination, and collaboration of resources for protecting against attacks and responding to attacks if they occur. The plan also highlights various dependencies of the transportation sector on other critical infrastructure sectors, most notably the energy sector. The plan also recognizes that the criticality of the transportation sector is due, in part, to the fact that so many other sectors of the economy are dependent on it for the movement of goods and people. The TSSP consequently emphasizes the identification and mitigation of strategic risks, defined as those risks that can cause disruption among multiple groups of stakeholders and can have far-reaching, long-term effects on the economy, the environment, and public confidence. Examples of strategic risks to transportation include disruption of a major node in the transportation network, use of the transportation network to deliver a WMD, or release of a biological agent at a major passenger facility. From these examples, it is relatively clear that certain elements of the aviation domain, particularly those facilities that handle large number of passengers and large volumes of high-value cargo, have significant strategic security risks associated with them. Also, with regard to maintaining public confidence, continued confidence in the security of the passenger airline industry as a strategic risk element has been a major focus of post-9/11 aviation security policy.

The transportation sector approach to risk management adheres to an underlying vision for risk-based decision making that seeks to establish a balance between security and freedom. The approach involves a systematic process for protecting CI/KR that involves

- Identifying CI/KR and associated risks
- Analyzing and prioritizing plans of action based on analysis and assessment of risk
- Implementing protective programs
- Measuring the effectiveness of actions taken
- Continually improving plans and initiatives to enhance protection of CI/KR based on the analysis of measured effectiveness

Across the transportation sector, and with regard to applying the system-based risk management framework to aviation, the approach is intended to manage threats, vulnerabilities, and consequences across both the physical and the cyber (i.e., information technology space) domains. The approach is intended to address both system-level risks that affect the interconnections and interdependencies of elements that comprise the entire aviation system, as well as asset-specific risks that focus more specifically on risks associated with specific facilities and resources. The goals outlined in the TSSP include

- Preventing and deterring terrorist acts against transportation systems
- Enhancing the resilience (i.e., the ability to absorb damage without catastrophic failure) of the U.S. transportation system
- Improving the cost-effective use of resources allocated to transportation security

The risk-based methodology seeks to achieve these three overarching goals by prioritizing resources based on risk. This approach is designed to include inputs from global, state and local, and private sector entities in developing programs for CI/KR protection and for coordinating and prioritizing research and technology development using risk-based priorities and methods.

The TSSP calls for setting evolving strategic risk objectives (SROs) that address the overarching goal of "... continuously improving the risk posture of the national transportation system ...."[16]

The process of setting these SROs relies on inputs from the intelligence community, expert judgment, and futures analysis related to the impact or consequences of various threat scenarios on human health and safety, the economy, and the ability to carry out critical missions such as delivering public services, as well as the potential effects on public confidence. The DHS defines the materiality of a potential risk as a function of threat likelihood and the relative size of potential impact taking into consideration these various factors (Figure 4.2). Strategic risks are those risks considered to meet some criterion level based on the combination of event likelihood and consequence or extent of potential impact. While strategic risks represent those threats with greatest materiality (i.e., high-likelihood, high-impact events), the DHS notes that threats having high likelihood but lower relative consequence and threats having a high potential consequence but a low likelihood still represent significant areas of consideration for homeland security policy and strategy development. Ultimately, determination of materiality is recognized as a qualitative or subjective process, and the TSSP indicates that techniques to assess threats in this manner will draw upon a wide array of technical and policy experts from government, industry, and academia using focus groups, interviews, and analytic sessions.

After identifying system risk objectives, the risk-based methodology includes a multistep system-based risk management process to identify available action-oriented countermeasures. These options can then be prioritized, and based on this prioritization, security programs can be developed and implemented. Progress can be measured using a variety of core metrics including tallies of assets and asset risk ratings, and the percentage of assets reduced from high risk. Also, assessment of the alignment of sector and mode-specific security needs and research and development plans can help to determine the extent to which these efforts are addressing existing and emerging risk-based needs and requirements.

A wide variety of risk-based transportation sector security assessment tools have been developed to assist security strategists and planners. These consist of self-assessment tools and government site evaluations, reviews, and analytic tools examining either risk as a whole or specific risk elements and subcomponents. Some specific tools being implemented to assess risk in the aviation domain include government-facilitated site visits and comprehensive reviews, web-based Vulnerability Identification Self Assessment Tool (VISAT) modules for airports, and the FAA's Information

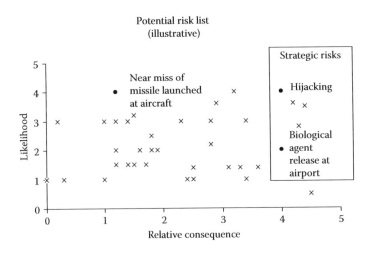

FIGURE 4.2 An illustration of materiality mapping of potential threats highlighting examples of aviation-specific threats. (Data obtained from Department of Homeland Security, *Transportation Systems: Critical Infrastructure and Key Resources Sector-Specific Plan as Input to the National Infrastructure Protection Plan*, May 2007, p. 48.)

Systems Security Program (ISSP) for air traffic control systems and related functions. Communication and dissemination of this information to sector stakeholders is seen as a critical component of the risk-based strategy.

STRATEGIC OBJECTIVES

Relying on the risk-based framework, the National Strategy for Aviation Security identifies five strategic objectives to guide aviation security activities. These include

- Deterring and preventing terrorist attacks and criminal or hostile acts in the air domain
- Protecting the homeland and U.S. interests in the air domain
- Mitigating damage and expediting recovery if an attack against aviation occurs
- Minimizing the impact of an attack on the aviation system and the broader U.S. economy
- Actively engaging domestic and international partners

According to the strategy for aviation security, terrorist attacks will be deterred and prevented by maximizing shared awareness of domestic and international airspace, aviation infrastructure, and individuals having access to the aviation system. This shared information will be used to detect adversaries seeking to attack aviation, denying them safe havens where they can operate unobstructed, denying them freedom of movement, preventing them from entering the United States, and identifying, disrupting, and dismantling their capabilities to attack aviation targets. It is believed that terrorists and criminals will continue to target the air domain as a means of attacking the United States and U.S. assets. An attack may cause casualties and damage to specific nodes of critical infrastructure within the aviation system, but could also have broad-reaching impacts on the economy, and perhaps the ability to deploy military forces. Therefore, the strategy seeks to establish a system of protection that considers not only individual elements of the aviation system, but also their connections and interdependencies.

While the principal goals of the strategy are to deter and prevent attacks, the strategy also seeks to prepare for and have in place contingencies for mitigating damage and expediting recovery. In the event of an attack, it seeks to minimize impacts, possibly by isolating portions of the aviation transportation system, to ensure public safety while maintaining continuity of air commerce and minimizing any ripple effects that could impact other transportation modes or other sectors of the economy. For example, the ability to expeditiously detect and identify possible WMD agents, react swiftly without endangering first responders, treat those that may be injured, contain and minimize damage, rapidly reconstitute operations, and mitigate long-term consequences through effective decontamination measures are viewed as critical steps that must be carried out effectively to minimize the impacts of a possible attack.

The strategy also identifies a need for diverse and flexible response options, for example, allowing for the selective restriction or suspension of air traffic on local or regional levels as necessary, and providing decision makers with tools and resources to effectively close and reconstitute the aviation system and take other appropriate steps to prevent further attack. In general, the strategy seeks an overall approach to implementing security measures whose normal operations will minimize impacts on the flow of goods and people through the air transportation system while at the same time providing a high level of protection tailored to the unique needs of the aviation sector. The current strategy indicates that it will rely on the use of new and emerging technologies, such as biometric solutions for access controls, and will also increasingly rely on partnerships between government and the private sector to collaborate and coordinate on the planning and implementation of security measures and incident response. The strategy also seeks to foster cooperative partnerships and alliances with other nations and private entities abroad to improve global aviation security by strengthening international efforts.

STRATEGIC ACTIONS

The strategy notes that specific actions to protect aviation assets are necessary because the air domain is uniquely susceptible to exploitation and disruption. This vulnerability is primarily a consequence of the air domain's global span, the volume of air traffic handled, and the fast pace of aviation operations. According to the strategy, terrorists have a continued desire and have the capability to exploit vulnerabilities and adapt to changes in aviation security to carry out attacks either within the United States or against U.S. interests throughout the world. The strategy concludes that "security of the Air Domain can be accomplished only by employing all instruments of national power in a fully coordinated manner in concert with other nation states."[17] The strategy defines five broad strategic actions:

- Maximizing domain awareness
- Deploying layered security
- Promoting a safe, efficient, and secure aviation transportation system
- Enhancing international cooperation
- Assuring continuity of the aviation transportation system

In the following discussion, each of these broad strategic actions will be explained and briefly discussed.

MAXIMIZING DOMAIN AWARENESS

Initiatives to maximize domain awareness center on improving abilities to collect, analyze, integrate, and disseminate information from intelligence, law enforcement, and surveillance data, as well as open source data from industry, the public sector, and international partners. Also, developing a more complete shared situational awareness of the air domain hinges on expanding ongoing efforts to make available operations information such as data on aeronautical and navigational systems and flight operations in addition to intelligence, surveillance, and reconnaissance of these various operations. Ongoing initiatives to improve domain awareness include improvements to flight surveillance and the monitoring of integrated information regarding a flight, such as aircraft type, crew and passenger information, air marshals and armed pilots and any domestic and foreign law enforcement that may be on board, and also possible remote monitoring of data from on-board sensors. Also, with regard to supply chain security, the DHS plans to create more robust information collection and dissemination regarding persons and cargo through regulatory actions and private industry initiatives. Further, the DHS hopes to improve supply chain awareness worldwide through cooperative efforts with international partners.

The strategy indicates that the U.S. government is committed to continually improving sensor technologies, analytical capabilities, human intelligence (HUMINT) collection, and the integration of various information processing tools for monitoring security in the air domain. The strategy endeavors to improve processes for disseminating information to public and private partners to improve overall security situation awareness. With the cooperation of international partners, a key strategy objective seeks to monitor aircraft, air cargo, and persons of interest from the point of origin, during a flight, and at the point of entry into the United States to ensure security and, if needed, interdict or divert aircraft.

DEPLOYING LAYERED SECURITY

Layered security has been a linchpin of the U.S. approach to aviation security, and the strategy identifies the layered approach to aviation security as a critical enabler for deterring and preventing terrorist attacks and reducing the vulnerability to other potential threats to the air domain. The TSA has described the layers of aviation security as concentric circles protecting the core elements of the air domain, whether aircraft or CI/KR.

As shown in Figure 4.3, multiple layers of protection exist to protect passenger airliners from hijackings and bombings, including: passenger prescreening and airline employee vetting; airport surveillance and law enforcement; physical screening for threat objects on passengers, carry-on and checked baggage; and various on-board measures such as air marshals, armed pilots, and hardened cockpit doors. These layers, according to the strategy, can operate in combination to serve as a force multiplier that can deter potential attacks. Similarly, multifaceted layered approaches are being implemented to protect the aviation domain from other threats, such as threats posed by air cargo operations, and threats from shoulder-fired missiles and other standoff weapons.

The strategy calls for several actions to continually build upon the existing layered framework for aviation security. These actions include aligning aviation security programs and initiatives to create a more comprehensive and cohesive system based on scalable, layered security measures with enhanced capabilities to identify, intercept, and defeat threats to the aviation system either in the air or on the ground. The strategy calls for action to expand partnerships with public- and private sector entities to train and equip security forces to provide physical security for key assets and critical aviation infrastructure on the ground. In collaboration with state and local governments, the strategy seeks to prioritize critical facilities, infrastructure, and venues based on risk. The strategy also seeks to sponsor further development of emerging capabilities for detecting WMDs, as well as capabilities for reducing aircraft vulnerability to attack and increasing the survivability of aircraft that may come under attack. The strategy calls for enhancing procedures for identifying or targeting designated flights of interest and coordinating procedures for monitoring such flights and initiating any necessary operational response. The strategy also seeks to enhance and expand capabilities to assess risks posed by individuals with access to the air domain, such as airport workers, air cargo

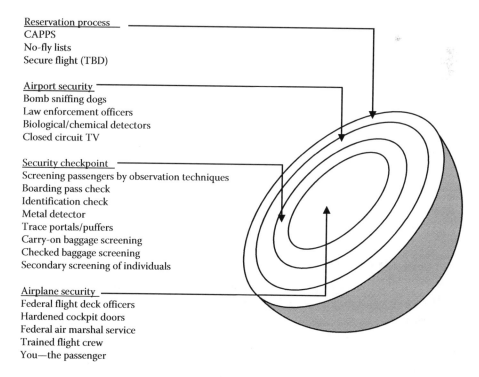

FIGURE 4.3 The layered approach to passenger airline screening. (Data obtained from Transportation Security Administration.)

workers, and airline crewmembers. Additionally, applying risk-based methods, the strategy seeks to develop effective techniques for detecting and preventing possible attacks against aircraft using standoff weapons, such as shoulder-fired missiles.

Promoting a Safe, Efficient, and Secure Aviation System

The strategy seeks to promote an aviation security system that protects the U.S. homeland and interests in the air domain while, at the same time, is efficient and minimizes impacts on the aviation transportation system and the broader U.S. economy. The strategy seeks to accomplish several actions to promote a safe, efficient, and secure aviation transportation system. The strategy calls for the U.S. government to assume the function of checking passenger names against terrorist watch list information prior to departure, a function that has been carried out domestically by the airlines using government-supplied no-fly and selectee lists. The utility of checking passenger manifests of flights that overfly, but do not land in, the United States against terrorist watch lists will also be assessed and implemented if deemed necessary. The strategy also seeks the furtherance of air cargo security measures for all-cargo carriers, passenger airlines, and freight forwarders (i.e., indirect air carriers) for both domestic and international routes. The strategy also calls for action to improve airspace security and security measures pertaining to air traffic management. Further improvements in aviation and aviation supply chain security will be examined using a risk management strategy and various outcome-based standards, incentives, and market mechanisms may be contemplated to encourage private sector self-assessments and initiatives to improve supply chain security practices. The strategy also calls for action to strengthen the detection of individuals with malicious intent who may try to obtain clearance or credentials granting access to secured or restricted areas of the aviation transportation system.

Fostering International Cooperation

The strategy recognizes that improved cooperation with international partners will be a critical enabler for achieving strategic objectives to deter and prevent attacks in the air domain. It concludes that new initiatives are needed to ensure that all nations fulfill agreements to prevent and respond to terrorist or criminal actions. Specific actions to promote international cooperation include initiatives to improve sharing of information regarding aircraft registry and owner information and more transparency of the air cargo supply chain. The strategy also calls for enhancing mechanisms for responding to threats to the air domain that may span international boundaries and jurisdictions including implementation of anti air piracy conventions and other international aviation security arrangements. The strategy seeks to promote adoption of international standards and best security practices among international partners through international organizations, such as the ICAO and global industry participation. The strategy calls for the United States to continue its efforts to provide aviation and airport security assistance, training, and consultation to international partners to enhance aviation security capabilities worldwide.

Assuring Continuity of Operations

The strategy notes that actions to assure the continuity of operations address strategic objectives of mitigating the consequences of an attack and expediting the recovery of the aviation transportation system. Assuring continuity of operations relies on effective development and dissemination of, training on, and coordination of contingency plans for response, recovery, and reconstitution. Specific actions called for include the development of response and recovery protocols for aviation consistent with the Federal Emergency Management Agency's (FEMA's) National Incident Management System (NIMS). These efforts will also be aligned with the National Preparedness Goal (NPG) to establish readiness priorities, targets, and metrics. The strategy calls for action to enhance emergency preparedness, including prestaging of resources, coordinating and planning exercises for first responders, and planning to reconstitute the aviation system following an attack or other significant incident.

The strategy also calls for developing effective means for mitigating the operational and economic consequences of an attack, including plans for suspending or restricting flight operations in segments of the national airspace system (NAS), and developing near-term as well as long-term recovery strategies for implementation following an attack. Working with public, private sector, and international partners, participating federal agencies will seek to identify and address any gaps in recovery capabilities in an effort to reduce direct and indirect costs stemming from a terrorist attack against aviation. By coordinating contingency and continuity plans, the strategy endeavors to reduce or prevent any prolonged and systemic disruption to the aviation system following a possible attack or other security-related incident.

STRATEGIC ROLES AND RESPONSIBILITIES

The complexity and scope of the global aviation transportation system requires cooperation among federal, state, and local government entities, international agreements and cooperation, and the participation of various industry and other private sector stakeholders to prevent, respond to, and recover from possible attacks involving aviation assets. The leading and supporting roles and responsibilities of these various entities are guided by existing laws and regulations, specific authorities to act, desired outcomes or objectives, and the availability of assets and capabilities to address aviation security needs and requirements.

At the highest levels of federal government (i.e., among cabinet-level leadership), the Secretary of Homeland Security has responsibility for coordinating national aviation security programs. In general, responsibilities of the DHS include risk analysis and reviews of aviation security programs; coordination of aviation security law enforcement operations; border protection including monitoring of cross-border aviation operations and inspections and controls at all ports of entry including airports; coordinating efforts to assess and prioritize security measures for CI/KR; developing security technologies to protect against threats such as explosives, carry-on weapons, and shoulder-fired missiles; coordination of aviation security measures and incident response; and information sharing to support and improve the global aviation security network.

Within the DHS, the TSA has the statutory responsibility for security across all modes of transportation, including aviation where it has extensive operational responsibility for passenger airline security screening activities as well as strategic planning and regulatory responsibilities for all other aspects of security. The TSA collaborates with DOT entities, and in particular the FAA, on transportation and aviation infrastructure protection and security issues. The TSA administers a variety of programs to support aviation security including: the National Explosives Detection Canine Team Program that trains and deploys canine teams for explosives detection in aviation and other transportation modes; the FFDO program that trains and deputizes armed pilots to defend commercial airliner flight decks from hostile actions; checkpoint and baggage screening carried out by TSA-employed TSOs; the use of aviation security inspectors to ensure regulatory compliance among aviation operators and related industries; the FAMS and the explosives operations division to respond to potential explosives threats. Additionally, the TSA maintains an intelligence function to coordinate and provide notice regarding threats to transportation, vetting passengers and aircrews, foreign students seeking flight training in the United States, airport workers, and other populations that may pose a threat to aviation or transportation security. During a national emergency, the TSA has the responsibility of coordinating transportation security-related responsibilities and activities of other departments and agencies in all modes, including aviation.

The TSA's Office of Intelligence (OI) plays a central role in the transportation threat assessment process. It is the only federal entity focused solely on transportation and aviation security threat assessment. As such, it has developed a wide range of threat assessment products, based on analysis of intelligence information provided by the National Counterterrorism Center (NCTC) and other components of the intelligence community. These include a transportation intelligence gazette; comprehensive transportation-related threat assessments; annual modal threat assessments for all transportation modes including aviation; special threat assessments for specific events; weekly intelligence reports; suspicious incident reports; intelligence notes on transportation-related terrorist trends, incidents, and tactics; and transportation situational awareness notes on notable transportation-related terrorist information.

While the TSA has broad authority and responsibility for both domestic and international aviation and transportation, CBP has the specific primary mission of preventing terrorists and terrorist weapons from entering the United States. CBP also provides radar tracking and monitoring to support the FAA and the DOD in protecting airspace around Washington, DC and throughout the continental United States. The United States Coast Guard (USCG) conducts aviation operations for law enforcement and national security, including the specific mission of providing aerial patrols and aircraft interdiction in the National Capital Region around Washington, DC. The DOD is, however, ultimately responsible for deterring, defending against, and if necessary, defeating aviation threats within the United States and to U.S. interests globally. To meet this mission, the DOD operates as part of the NORAD Command to monitor, deter, and detect potentially hostile actions. The DOD also maintains a capability to respond to aerial threats by keeping a significant number of fighter aircraft on alert, carrying out airborne fighter patrols over the homeland, and deploying ground-based missile defense systems around Washington, DC and other areas as warranted.

Whereas the DOD has responsibility for airborne threats, potential criminal and terror threats to aviation by individuals or groups of individuals is primarily the responsibility of the law enforcement arm of the DOJ, the FBI. The FBI's Civil Aviation Security Program (CASP) and counterterrorism units have been involved extensively in efforts to uncover and prevent terrorist operations to attack or exploit civil aviation in the United States. The FBI has deployed over 500 airport liaison agents (ALAs) to about 450 airports with commercial passenger service to respond to aviation-related incidents and threats and participate in vulnerability assessments and planning at the airport level of analysis.

There are a myriad of other agencies and organizations that play important roles in operational aviation security. The intelligence community, coordinated through the Office of the Director of National Intelligence (ODNI), plays an important role in assimilating and assessing intelligence—including signal intelligence (SIGINT), imagery intelligence (IMINT), and human intelligence (HUMINT) collection and analysis—regarding threats to aviation security. Additionally, other DHS components, including the FEMA, the Domestic Nuclear Detection Office (DNDO), and the Office of Infrastructure Protection (OIP) have various responsibilities related to infrastructure protection and critical incident response in the aviation domain. Also, the Department of Energy provides scientific and technical expertise regarding nuclear weapons, radiation detection capabilities at airports to detect possible nuclear weapons or radiological materials, and coordinating response to any radiological contamination resulting from a possible nuclear or radiological attack.

The DHS Science and Technology (S&T) Directorate maintains research and development programs to enhance aviation security, especially to address explosives threats and threats to aircraft from shoulder-fired missiles. Also, the multiagency Joint Planning and Development Office (JPDO) has responsibility for designing and overseeing the implementation of the future air transportation system, including its security components. In addition to these efforts, the Department of State has overall responsibility for outreach and coordination with foreign governments to enhance cooperation in improving aviation security. Ongoing State Department efforts include initiatives to improve data sharing for advance passenger prescreening, and programs to reduce stockpiles of standoff weapons, including shoulder-fired missiles, which pose a threat to civil aircraft. Also, the Department of Commerce and the DOT play a role in international trade negotiations and by developing U.S.

policy and regulation regarding international flight operations, aviation trade, and negotiating related security issues.

In addition to the federal role, a variety of industry advisory groups have been established to provide insight and recommendations for guiding transportation security policy and practice. Most notably, the ASAC exists to support the TSA by providing advice and developing recommendations for improving aviation security methods, equipment, and procedures. The ASAC has been in existence since before September 11, 2001, and advised the FAA on aviation security matters, and has continued in this role, now supporting the TSA in its role as the lead federal agency for aviation security issues. Also, the NRC and the Transportation Research Board (TRB), components of the National Academies, provide venues for information sharing and analysis of transportation security policies and practices among researchers, practitioners, and other subject matter experts. Additionally, airports, airlines, and other aviation industry stakeholders as well as state and local security and law enforcement entities play an important role in shaping and carrying out the national aviation security policy and strategy, largely by working in cooperation and coordination with the TSA to design and execute aviation mode-specific security plans and fulfilling various aviation security roles and responsibilities.

AVIATION MODE-SPECIFIC PLANS

The DHS had developed a suite of aviation mode-specific plans that serve as a general framework for implementing the National Strategy for Aviation Security under normal operating conditions, during the transgression of a terrorist attack involving the aviation domain, and during recovery and reconstitution of aviation system functions and services following a potential attack (Figure 4.4).[18] Specifically, the Aviation Transportation System Security Plan most directly addresses the day-to-day security measures and programs to reduce the vulnerability of the air transportation system to terrorist actions or other criminal acts. This plan is augmented by the Air Domain Surveillance and Intelligence Integration Plan that coordinates intelligence gathering, analysis, and dissemination within the air domain. In addition, the International Aviation Threat Reduction Plan and the International Outreach Plan provide a framework for working with other nations to improve the global aviation security network with an emphasis on outreach to promote the implementation of effective security practices worldwide.

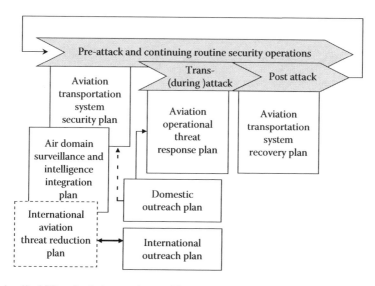

FIGURE 4.4   Applicability of aviation mode-specific supporting plans and their interrelationships.

Upon recognition that a terrorist or criminal attack targeting or using aviation assets is transgressing (i.e., entering a trans-attack period), the Aviation Operational Threat Response Plan would be activated. This plan considers specific actions and concepts of operations for mitigating the consequences of a broad array of attack scenarios. This plan is augmented by the Domestic Outreach Plan that considers the involvement and coordination of state, local, and tribal government resources and private sector entities in responding to such an event, focusing most specifically on strategies for incident communications as well as the dissemination of threat information during routine operations. An Aviation Transportation System Recovery Plan is also being developed by the DHS to facilitate rapid recovery following a possible terrorist attack or similar disruption to the air transportation system. The goal of the recovery plan is to mitigate the operational and economic impacts of such events on the aviation system.

AVIATION TRANSPORTATION SYSTEM SECURITY PLAN

The DHS notes that the Aviation Transportation System Security Plan builds upon the existing system of interdependent, interlocking layers of security. These interdependent layers involve numerous federal roles, including identifying threats and threat countermeasures; identifying and mitigating vulnerabilities and risks to the air domain; establishing and enforcing regulations, policies, and procedures for aviation operators and related industries; and applying security measures for passenger airline operations. Airlines and other aircraft operators, airports, the shipping industry, law enforcement agencies, and others all play important roles in this multilayered system.

The plan emphasizes the need for the aviation security system to be both scalable and flexible, providing capability to address a broad array of current and future threats, including attacks using aircraft as weapons against ground-based targets; the use of aircraft to transport or deliver CBRNE agents; attacks against aircraft using standoff weapons such as shoulder-fired missiles; aircraft bombings; hijackings; and physical attacks and cyber attacks against aviation infrastructure such as airports and air traffic control facilities. The plan categorizes vulnerabilities to such threats in three broad categories: passenger, employee, and crew security assurance; threat object detection and interdiction; and infrastructure protection.

The plan relies upon a risk-based, layered approach to prevent the air domain from being attacked or from being exploited to commit attacks against U.S. infrastructure and assets. The plan seeks to develop enhancements to the existing security system that will better facilitate secure and efficient travel and commerce, both nationally and internationally. These objectives are intended to support the five broad strategic actions outlined in the National Strategy for Aviation Security.

Guiding Principles

The plan is predicated on a variety of guiding principles. First, it is acknowledged that effective aviation security involves a multilayered system, with each layer effectively reducing the likelihood or probability of a successful attack. While any one of the layers could potentially be compromised, together they combine to reduce overall risk and enhance security. Under the plan, the DHS intends to address, enhance and further strengthen all major layers and systems critical for reducing security risks to aviation. At each level or layer in the overall system, the objective is to maintain a degree of randomness or unpredictability in order to prevent discovery of security measures and techniques and to provide an alternative means of disrupting terrorist plots and criminal acts. The plan recognizes that aviation security is vital to the national interests of the United States. It also recognizes that the aviation security system must be continuously assessed and modified to address changes in the "highly dynamic and adaptive terrorist threat."[19] The goal, however, is to be proactive rather than reactive emphasizing the importance placed on accurately predicting how terrorist strategies and tactics may evolve over time and adapting security approaches to address emerging threats. While the Aviation Transportation System Security Plan is focused on reducing the vulnerabilities to attacks against the air domain, the plan asserts that recommendations and plan components must take into consideration all three risk elements (i.e., threat, vulnerability, and consequence). The plan also asserts that scalable, flexible security measures will help build the resiliency of the air domain. The plan seeks continued cooperation among various federal agencies, state and local authorities, and with foreign partners to further enhance the strength of aviation security measures pursued.

Goals and Requirements

The plan categorizes aviation system vulnerabilities in three broad categories: passenger, employee, and crew security assurance; threat object detection and interdiction; and infrastructure protection. The plan identifies numerous goals to build upon existing aviation security infrastructure and operations in these three key areas.

Passenger, Employee, and Crew Security Assurance

The plan calls for adequate and effective methods for identifying and appropriately vetting all individuals accessing the aviation transportation system, including airline passengers, airline and airport employees, and aircraft crewmembers. While the plan notes that broad challenges exist, particularly with regard to assuring the security of those individuals having on-the-job access to aircraft and airport air operations areas, it sets forth several specific objectives and planned actions for enhancing current measures to vet individuals accessing the air transportation system.

The plan specifically addresses the goal of implementing predeparture vetting of international passengers and crews against no-fly and selectee lists, a mandate set forth in the IRTPA of 2004 (P.L. 108-458) which was fully implemented in the summer of 2007. The plan also set a target of implementing Secure Flight—the long-delayed system for the TSA to assume the role of screening passenger names against consolidated terrorist watch lists from the airlines—by December 31, 2008. The plan also called for the consolidation of all DHS redress programs by the end of FY2007, a task that has now been accomplished. The plan calls for the enhanced use of biometrics for employee and airport vendor identification to improve airport physical security programs. The plan also calls for the TSA to assume responsibility for verification of passenger identification when passengers present themselves at airport checkpoints, a function previously carried out largely by airport contractors, and to implement behavioral observation techniques both at and beyond the security checkpoint, an objective that may require considerable personnel resources to fully implement.

In coordination with these DHS initiatives, the DOJ will work to consolidate watch list data and watch list vetting processes and work to ensure that the Terrorist Screening Database (TSDB) is thorough, accurate, and continuously up-to-date. Additionally, the Department of State will work with foreign nations to negotiate agreements regarding access to passenger data for U.S.-bound flights prior to aircraft departure. On this issue, successful negotiations with the European Union (EU) led to formation of a formal agreement between the United States and the EU in 2007 allowing for the sharing of passenger name record (PNR) data for flights from EU countries to the United States in a manner that meets the operational and technical requirements set forth by DHS to appropriately vet passengers on such flights against the consolidated TSDB prior to departure.

Threat Object Detection and Interdiction

The detection of threat objects carried by passengers has been a central focus of U.S. policy and strategy for aviation security following the 9/11 terrorist attacks. Key statutory changes included the federalization of the passenger and baggage screening workforce and a mandate for 100% EDS screening of all checked baggage. More recently, a requirement for implementing physical screening of all cargo placed on passenger aircraft by August 2010 was included as part of the Implementing Recommendations of the 9/11 Commission Act of 2007 (P.L. 110-53). In addition to these statutory obligations, the plan identifies several objectives for enhancing threat object screening at passenger checkpoints, for checked baggage, for air cargo, and on board aircraft, as well as generally applicable initiatives to improve threat detection capabilities across the entire air domain. Specific actions called for in the plan are listed below:

1. Passenger checkpoints
   • Improving checkpoint and baggage screening technologies to detect a broader array of CBRNE threats as well as exploring on-board aircraft detection, identification, containment, and mitigation technologies
   • Exploring the use of future modular, interchangeable checkpoint detection units that can be quickly reconfigured to adapt to changes in the threat picture while minimizing the space requirements or "footprint" of passenger checkpoints and designing for easy maintainability
   • Deploying in-line EDS for screening carry-on items
2. Checked baggage
   • Working to harmonize checked baggage screening processes and standards with Canada and, more broadly, seeking to harmonize passenger and baggage screening technologies and protocols internationally
3. Air cargo
   • Strengthening the vetting process for shippers and other elements of the air cargo supply chain and enhancing physical security of the cargo supply chain by improving indirect air carrier (i.e., freight forwarder) security programs and working thorough international supply chain security initiatives covered under the Customs-Trade Partnership Against Terrorism (C-TPAT)
   • Using risk-based prescreening measures to identify elevated risk international cargo shipments and utilizing technology, canine teams, and inspections procedures to carry out 100% inspection of targeted air cargo
   • Expanding the use of the Automated Commercial Environment Advanced Trade Data Initiative to vet international air cargo shipments and supply chain information
   • Exploring possible recommendations for statutory, regulatory, organizational, or policy changes to increase the advanced notice period for electronic cargo manifest data for inbound air freight shipments to the United States
4. In flight
   • Conducting further research on terrorism tactics, such as the use of small explosive charges, to breach secured areas of an aircraft, such as the flight deck
5. Broadly applicable elements of the plan
   • Developing and implementing strategies to prevent CBRNE attacks against airports and critical air traffic control facilities and coordinating the development of CBRNE detection capabilities for the air domain
   • Establishing national explosives detection canine team standards and expanding the use of canine teams for explosives detection throughout the air transportation system
   • Developing a risk assessment methodology for chemical and biological threats and issuing guidance to aviation facilities and stakeholders for mitigating chemical and biological threats in the air domain
   • Developing an evaluation system for assessing layered approaches to threat detection and interdiction

Aviation Infrastructure Protection

In addition to enhancements to current practices for vetting individuals accessing the air transportation system, and improvements to detecting and preventing the introduction or use of threat objects in the air domain, the Aviation Transportation System Security Plan seeks to strengthen protections of air transportation system infrastructure such as airports and air traffic control facilities. While post-9/11 aviation security legislation and policy has emphasized measures to protect against threats to commercial airliners, the threat to aviation infrastructure, including airports and CI/KR necessary for maintaining a safe, secure, and efficient air transportation system, has also been recognized.

The plan seeks to protect aviation infrastructure from a wide array of attacks, and other disruptions, including cyber attacks or sabotage to remotely located navigation and communications facilities through multilayered, cooperative approaches to security. The threat posed by shoulder-fired missiles and other standoff weapons is identified as a particular concern, and various initiatives to mitigate this threat are included in the consideration of protecting aviation infrastructure and system operational elements.

The plan calls for a variety of specific actions, including improving the vetting of persons boarding U.S.-bound flights; examining options to enhance airspace security and establish security programs for GA aircraft; pursuing options to counter the smuggling of and terrorist attacks using shoulder-fired missiles and other standoff weapons; continuing efforts to assess vulnerabilities to standoff weapons attacks at U.S. airports and expanding the program to assess these vulnerabilities at foreign airports; continuing the ongoing exploration of various technologies to counter the threat posed by shoulder-fired missiles; developing criteria for designating or targeting high-risk flight or "flights of interest"; and increasing the ability to detect and monitor aircraft, including GA aircraft, entering U.S. territorial airspace. The plan also calls for cooperative research and development of technologies to address cyber attacks, radio-frequency jamming, electromagnetic pulse attacks and other related threats to aviation information technology, communications, and navigation systems.

As a participant in implementing the National Strategy for Aviation Security, the FAA has committed to enhancing security measures to protect critical air traffic control and navigation infrastructure from both physical attacks and possible cyber attacks. The FAA is also working with the DHS, particularly CBP and the TSA, to strengthen vetting procedures and monitoring of inbound international flights, including GA flights. Further, the FAA is engaged in efforts to enhance its capability to rapidly reconfigure airspace based on changing security requirements. The FAA indicates that it will support DHS aviation security and DOD defense operations through restructuring airspace, diverting aircraft, imposing ground delays and stops, and implementing other air traffic management and airspace security strategies to fit operational needs. The FAA will also seek to improve the existing notification system, the Notices to Airman or NOTAM system, to provide greater capability to support the need to quickly disseminate aviation security-related information to aircraft and airport operators and other stakeholders who may require such information.

The FAA also seeks to improve its systems and processes for tracking and monitoring actions and sanctions for security-related airspace violations to better ensure consistency and the appropriate use of punitive measures to deter future airspace violations. The FAA will also continue to explore options for enabling access to certain flight restricted areas, such as the airspace around Washington, DC, for properly vetted aircraft and flight crews. Additionally, the FAA will continue to examine strategies for further improving the use of flight data and aircraft operator information to enhance situational awareness of air traffic for security purposes. To aid in positive identification and monitoring of aircraft operations, the plan calls for statutory or regulatory action to reinforce aircraft operator's use of aircraft call signs or registration numbers including provisions for enforcement action in cases of noncompliance. Also, the FAA, in coordination with the JPDO and other partners in the initiative to modernize air traffic control technologies and procedures, will seek to identify and leverage communications, navigation, and surveillance (CNS) technologies and infrastructure to strengthen aviation and airspace security.

In addition to these initiatives, the plan calls upon the DOD to maintain its state of alert to protect aviation assets. Also, the plan will rely on continuing efforts initiated by the State Department to strengthen controls over standoff weapons that pose a threat to civil aircraft, especially shoulder-fired missiles. Additionally, the plan calls on the intelligence and law enforcement communities to coordinate efforts for establishing intelligence indicators and warning criteria for standoff weapons attacks and the sharing of threat information, thus enabling effective responses to threats. The plan also seeks to foster continuing interagency cooperation and assistance from private sector partners in developing aviation security components of the Next Generation Air Transportation System (NGATS or NextGen).

The plan concludes that, in addition to a need for continued coordination, cooperation, and information-sharing among federal, state, local, and private entities involved in operating and securing the air transportation system, "... funding and resources must be allocated to maintain and enhance current security measures, and resources must be available to research and employ new measures as appropriate."[20]

THE AIR DOMAIN SURVEILLANCE AND INTELLIGENCE INTEGRATION PLAN

In addition to the Aviation Transportation System Security Plan that outlines the core strategic actions and day-to-day aviation security functions to implement the aviation security strategy, the Air Domain Surveillance and Intelligence Integration Plan outlines the strategic actions pertaining to the collection, analysis, and dissemination of intelligence to establish persistent situational knowledge and awareness of air domain security-related threats, vulnerabilities, and capabilities. The plan calls for close coordination and integration of aviation security-related intelligence, information, and surveillance data to facilitate shared situational awareness of air domain security among federal, state, and local agencies and foreign governments.

The plan seeks to improve and develop new capabilities to allow for persistent, effective monitoring of all aircraft, cargo, people, and infrastructure of interest when needed, in a manner that is consistent with the protection of civil liberties and privacy rights. The aim is to collect, analyze, and disseminate information regarding terrorist-related threats, tactics, and potential targets to a wide range of policymakers and operational decision makers through various integrated domain awareness and information sharing solutions. This is anticipated to be achieved through the development of a shared U.S. government air domain awareness capability that can be tailored to user requirements and is compatible with approaches being developed for other domains.

Guiding Principles

The guiding principles of the Air Domain Surveillance and Intelligence Integration Plan include the detection and prevention of threats at early stages of development; a unified, coordinated effort among federal, state, local and private entities, and international partners; the ability to provide accurate, real-time information sharing and integration capabilities with adequate safeguards to protect individual privacy and proprietary information; and enhancement of the safe and efficient flow of commerce in the air domain through active, responsible use of information sharing capabilities.

Considerations and Assumptions

The plan recognizes that threats are continually evolving and thus require constant monitoring and adaptation of collection and analysis methods and timely dissemination of up-to-date intelligence information. The plan also recognizes that information sharing initiatives must comply with laws, directives, and other plans and policies as well as international obligations and agreements, particularly those regarding the rights and freedoms of individuals. As needed, laws and policies may need to be assessed to determine if they present any specific obstacles to achieving desired plan objectives. The plan also seeks to develop solutions that are compatible with overall future visions and plans for modernizing the NAS under the NGATS. Also, the plan seeks to harmonize efforts for surveillance and intelligence information sharing in the air domain with ongoing and planned initiatives for other transportation modes to achieve an overall goal of an integrated domain awareness architecture.

The plan acknowledges that threats may emerge with little or no warning and may involve singular or multiple attacks that could be geographically dispersed. Also, threat actors may exhibit complaint behavior—going along with rules, procedures, and norms and, in general, blending in with others—prior to an attack, thus adding to the unpredictability and difficulty in identifying threats. The plan assumes that the various federal, state, local, and international participants in aviation security will act collaboratively and cooperatively to improve information sharing and pooling or resources. The plan also assumes that systems will evolve to reflect changes in technology and policy as well as changes in the threat environment.

Achieving Air Domain Awareness

The overarching objective of the plan is to achieve the capability to provide those having operational aviation security responsibilities with a comprehensive, robust, shared awareness and understanding of activity, threats, and significant security-related events taking place in the air domain. Achieving this capability hinges on extensive collaboration and cooperation among federal, state, and local entities as well as private sector stakeholders and international partners. The plan considers the following components to be essential elements for realizing this objective:

- Air domain intelligence and information
- Air domain surveillance
- Integration and analysis of intelligence and surveillance data
- Sharing of air domain awareness

Air Domain Intelligence and Information

Air domain intelligence and information consists of data gathered regarding aircraft, cargo, people, and infrastructure in the air domain in concert with intelligence information, including information gathered from SIGINT and HUMINT, and other information regarding current and emerging threats. Specific actions sought to enhance the security picture in the air domain include improving the collection and dissemination of data on passengers, crews, aircraft, air cargo, and aircraft ownership; refining intelligence collection and analysis requirements and methods in the air domain through periodic reviews; aligning regulatory and information technology requirements of passenger prescreening systems—including the Advance Passenger Information System (APIS) and Secure Flight—for vetting passengers and crews; utilizing biometric identification technologies to assist in positively identifying airline and airport employees; expanding the use of prescreening system to vet flight manifests of aircraft that overfly, but do not land in, the United States; and partnering with other cooperative nations to identify and monitor transnational aviation threats.

Air Domain Surveillance

With regard to surveillance within the air domain, the plan seeks to integrate and facilitate the sharing of air surveillance data. The plan seeks to identify, develop, and deploy new detection and surveillance technologies to address current and future threats, including threats from cruise missiles, low-altitude low-observable aircraft, including both manned and unmanned aircraft, as well as standoff weapons such as shoulder-fired missiles. The plan seeks to refine efforts and capabilities to detect, monitor, track, and identify all aircraft operating within U.S. airspace in a manner that enhances security as well as safety. The plan calls for the FAA and the DHS to review air surveillance capabilities, any existing limitations in these capabilities, and identify critical surveillance coverage areas. The plan also seeks to ensure that surveillance capabilities provide adequate coverage of aircraft ground movement on airport surfaces, including the monitoring of potential standoff weapon launch sites around airports. The plan considers options for improving surveillance capabilities to include not only ground-based radar systems, but a variety of sensor capabilities including ground-based, elevated, and airborne radar and electro-optical and infrared (EO/IR) systems. The plan also seeks improvements in portable WMD and standoff weapons detection capabilities, which may include radiation detection capabilities as well as a broad array of radar, electronic, and optical sensing and imaging platforms. The plan seeks to integrate these various capabilities across all of North America under the Security and Prosperity Partnership for North America.

To support the development of technologies and processes to achieve these strategic objectives, an air surveillance implementation and integration plan is sought. The plan is expected to provide details regarding the maintenance and enhancement of existing surveillance capabilities; options for improving low-altitude surveillance in areas of national interest; interagency responsibilities for monitoring, tracking, and identifying both cooperative and noncooperative aircraft; solutions for addressing any identified gaps in surveillance coverage; initiatives for developing next generation surveillance capabilities; options for transitioning to future surveillance technologies; and standards, technical requirements, and resources for integrating and disseminating air surveillance data and coordinating this data with multimodal geospatial surveillance and intelligence data.

Integration and Analysis of Intelligence and Surveillance Data

By integrating intelligence information with air domain surveillance data, the plan hopes to achieve an improved awareness of the air domain thereby providing policymakers and operational leadership with the capability to make better informed decisions regarding the allocation of resources and specific measures to protect the aviation domain from perceived threats. The plan calls for intergovernmental coordination to support the sharing of intelligence information and other data related to aviation security. To achieve this integration, the plan seeks to network existing surveillance systems to achieve shared situational awareness capabilities. The plan also recognizes that existing regulatory barriers to information sharing and systems interoperability also need to be addressed to optimize integration and fusion of intelligence and surveillance data. In addition to addressing possible regulatory barriers, the plan seeks to clarify legal authorities, policies, and interagency agreements to allow for the processing, fusion, and sharing of intelligence, law enforcement, and commercial aviation security data. The plan also seeks to establish a common information technology architecture for processing and integrating intelligence and surveillance data in a manner compatible with similar initiatives, such as the Defense Department's Global Information Grid network and information management architecture. As part of this objective, the plan envisions an automated system for data integration of flight information and tracking and databases from aviation, law enforcement, and intelligence sources. The plan also calls for a review of how to best align intelligence resources and capabilities with aviation security operations centers. The plan also seeks advancements in the automation of processes and tools to facilitate collaborative analysis and fusion of flight operational data to better detect anomalies and aid human analysis efforts. Similarly, the plan seeks capabilities for aiding in the detection of anomalies that may be indicators of a potential threat among data pertaining to aircraft, cargo, and people in the air transportation system. Also, the plan seeks specific capabilities to correlate and merge sensor data to identify potential threats and generate automated alerts.

Sharing of Air Domain Awareness

These integration initiatives are intended to facilitate the development of a comprehensive awareness of air domain operations and potential security threats related to those operations. Sharing of this awareness, however, is also dependent on the development of a secure, accessible, common architecture for data networking and information sharing. The plan seeks to establish an information sharing framework that provides authorized users with access to net-centric or network-enabled, secure information in real-time or near-real-time. To achieve this objective, the plan calls for the development of a data sharing architecture with standards for web-based information storage and access, interoperable communications standards, information assurance capabilities across all access and classification levels among the various authorized participating entities, and interoperable system capabilities that allows for the transfer of data between sensors, platforms, and personnel. It is envisioned that achieving this network-centric shared information awareness capability will allow for effective exploitation of intelligence and surveillance information to defend the air domain against attack and provide the capability to expose and defeat any identified weaknesses or vulnerabilities among terrorist groups or other adversaries.

In summary, the Air Domain Surveillance and Integration Plan provides guidance for maximizing the awareness and understanding of the air domain and actual or potential security threats to the air domain. The plan seeks to achieve this objective by enhancing both intelligence and surveillance capabilities, as well as the tools and techniques for integrating and fusing this information and disseminating it to policymakers and aviation security operational leadership to allow for better preparedness and response to security threats.

THE INTERNATIONAL OUTREACH AND INTERNATIONAL AVIATION THREAT REDUCTION PLANS

The International Outreach Plan has been developed in recognition of the global nature of international aviation, and recognition that weaknesses in aviation security in other countries could jeopardize U.S. interests and national security both beyond the borders of the United States as well as within the homeland. In recognition of this, the International Outreach Plan emphasizes the key role of the State Department to use its diplomatic resources and influence to promote and improve cooperation with foreign countries, international and regional organizations, and international private sector entities engaged in aviation operations to enhance global aviation security. The key underpinnings of the plan include a consistent, coordinated U.S. policy regarding aviation security activities and enhanced outreach to foreign governments and entities for improving global aviation security practices.

To foster improved international relations addressing aviation security issues, the plan calls for establishing unified, consistent U.S. foreign policy positions emphasizing aviation security as a key priority for international policy and promoting initiatives for bilateral and multilateral discussions and agreements to advance aviation security. The plan seeks to promote international best practices in aviation security on a global scale, and it encourages the use of U.S. diplomatic missions abroad to build support for U.S. aviation security initiatives and establish partnerships with foreign governments and international stakeholders. The plan seeks to establish mechanisms for coordinating technical assistance, training, and resources to promote effective aviation security in developing nations and critical regions. The plan also seeks to establish effective mechanisms for information sharing among cooperating nations to facilitate the detection of threats and appropriate operational and law enforcement responses to these threats.

These actions are intended to align international efforts with objectives and actions specified in the International Aviation Threat Reduction Plan, a plan that has not been made publicly available. The International Outreach Plan is also designed to coordinate with the elements of the Domestic Outreach Plan to establish protocols for communicating and coordinating resources with foreign partners to respond to threats or security-related events that may occur in the air domain. While the International Outreach Plan emphasizes operational aviation security, surveillance, and intelligence integration and sharing, the Domestic Outreach Plan, discussed later focuses primarily on incident communications strategy and critical incident management, and therefore it is more closely aligned with the objectives and actions set forth in the Aviation Operational Threat Response Plan.

THE AVIATION OPERATIONAL THREAT RESPONSE PLAN

The Aviation Operational Threat Response Plan provides the overarching guidance for directing immediate actions in response to the full range of potential terrorist threats to components of the aviation system. Elements of the plan would be put into action upon receipt of actionable intelligence, surveillance, or other information indicating that a security-related incident is transpiring or an imminent threat exists. The plan does not address the steady-state or day-to-day operational aspects of aviation security that are covered primarily in the Aviation Transportation System Security Plan. Examples of events that could trigger implementation of the Aviation Operation Threat Response Plan include transpiring attacks to use aircraft as weapons against ground targets, attacks using standoff weapons such as shoulder-fired missiles, and attacks against aviation infrastructure such as airports and air traffic control facilities, including the potential use of WMDs at these sites. The plan covers strategic objectives and actions to immediately counter and react to transpiring threats against aviation, but does not consider system recovery that is covered by the Aviation Transportation System Recovery Plan.

The purpose of the plan is to coordinate response to threats in the air domain and augments the general framework of the National Response Plan (NRP), which is now known as the National Response Framework (NRF). The NRP or NRF establishes a broad-based all-hazards approach for critical incident management that establishes the structure for interagency coordination and integration with state, local, and tribal governments and the private sector in responding to large-scale domestic incidents. The framework sets incident management priorities such as saving lives and protecting property, mitigating damage, and ensuring continued homeland security, emphasizing local response by first responders. The framework outlines the federal role in large-scale events that can exceed local or state response capabilities and provides a general coordination structure for multiagency coordination and integration of response.[21] The Aviation Operational Threat Response Plan, along with the associated Domestic Outreach Plan, provides specific objectives and actions for implementing this response framework to large-scale threats and other events in the air domain.

Specifically, the plan orchestrates the coordinated effort of various entities that play a role in protecting aviation infrastructure and assets, and people in the aviation system. These may include military and homeland security airborne interception and interdiction of threat or suspect aircraft; surface-to-air weapons systems operations for ground-based defense of critical sites; on-board law enforcement response on flights; aviation law enforcement and counterterrorism response at airports and other ground-based sites; and responsive security measures pertaining to airspace and air traffic management, such as security-related ground holds and diversions.

Guiding Principles

The plan is predicated on the assumption that any airborne threat within U.S. airspace or approaching U.S. borders is a potential threat to national security which the U.S. government must be prepared to meet using an appropriate, coordinated response. The plan maintains that coordination and responsive action should be swiftly initiated upon receipt of sufficient intelligence or other information indicating that a threat is transpiring. Frontline operators and entities that encounter threats should take appropriate actions within their capacity and authority to eliminate or mitigate the identified threat, including the use of deadly force if appropriate. The plan also directs those entities encountering threats to notify, consult with, and coordinate continued or follow-up response with other agencies and entities if the threat continues or for postresponse recovery actions if the threat is neutralized. In responding to threats, the plan places priority on the preservation of life and minimizing related risks to the public; preventing and defeating transpiring attacks; minimizing impacts on the air transportation system; apprehending perpetrators of threats and attacks against aviation; and gathering threat-related intelligence and evidence to aid in the prosecution of attackers and to aid in improving aviation security measures to prevent future threats and attacks.

Considerations and Assumptions

The operational threat response plan envisions that information sharing among various agencies and entities will be maximized to take full awareness of shared situational awareness and facilitate the coordination of actions. The plan recognizes the strategic importance of international trade and commerce. Like the Air Domain Surveillance and Intelligence Integration Plan, the Aviation Operational Threat Response Plan recognizes that threats and attacks may occur with little or no warning or indicators of an impending threat or attack. The plan assumes that private industry stakeholders and other nations will support and cooperate in carrying out appropriate threat response actions outlined in the plan to the extent that they are capable.

Concept of Operations

The operational threat response plan is intended to utilize the capabilities and resources of the existing integrated national command centers of the various participating agencies and entities and interoperable communications tools to facilitate effective information exchange. A lead agency would be designated based on the nature of the threat and the specific response. DHS agencies, including the TSA, are expected to be prepared to take on either a leading or supporting role. It is likely that the TSA would assume a primary role in coordinating domestic threats to the air domain, although this may not necessarily be the case in all circumstances. CBP may also take on a leading role in response to certain airborne threats, particularly those involving inbound international flights. Also, the USCG has been given responsibility for airborne interdiction in the National Capital Region around Washington, DC, and therefore may play a significant role in the response to airborne threats in that area of operations, while the Secret Service may play a leading role in response to possible airborne threats involving movements of the President or other special events of national security interest. Upon determination that a threat to aviation infrastructure or other elements of the aviation domain involves nuclear or radiological materials, the DNDO may take on a more central role in coordinating an operational response.

The lead agency would be responsible for coordinating the full range of aviation security activities in response to a threat or attack in a manner that would ensure unity of effort among the various entities, and in a manner that will allow for the orderly transition of leadership to other agencies, such as FEMA and the FBI, for follow-on activities such as recovery, mitigation, and postevent investigation. The lead agency would be responsible for tactical planning and mission execution as the threat response is carried out, and coordination across the various agencies and entities involved in the response. The lead agency would also be expected to maintain close coordination with intelligence sources for the development and dissemination of evolving threat assessments, and involve the Department of State to assess the role of foreign affairs in the threat response. The lead agency would also be responsible for public affairs activities, except in cases where consideration of foreign affairs issues would make it more appropriate for the Department of State to take on the primary role in coordinating public affairs regarding the event and the response.

The various federal agencies serving in a supporting role during an operational threat response would provide expertise to aid in crisis management and coordination activities orchestrated by the lead agency. Supporting agencies would be responsible for keeping the lead agency apprised of their support and response capabilities and lend support for intelligence gathering, investigation, mitigation, and recovery activities as part of the coordinated response. Supporting agencies would be expected to coordinate with the lead agency on all public affairs matters, an issue of particular concern in recognition of past missteps by DHS agencies in handling public affairs during the operational response to significant events.[22]

Various agency protocols have been established or are being developed for coordinating operational response under this plan. These protocols include details of how agency contact information would be continually updated and shared by integrated command centers; processes for information flow and senior-level decision making by government officials; guidelines for coordinating activities and conferences; considerations for maintaining continuity of operations; a matrix of agency participation and roles; and guidance on coordination with the aviation industry. It is anticipated that various aviation threat scenarios will be incorporated into future DHS national threat exercises. Under this plan, the DHS, in coordination with other federal departments and agencies, is expected to develop methods for observing and evaluating vulnerabilities and consequences, agency capabilities, airspace control measures, and communications and coordination effectiveness. The plan notes that operational threat response is not simply a "last line of defense," but can serve to enhance the deterrent effects of the overall aviation security strategy, and significantly mitigate the potential consequences of terrorist actions that threaten the air domain.

The Domestic Outreach Plan

The Domestic Outreach Plan augments the Aviation Operational Threat Response Plan by outlining a framework for incident communications in the aviation domain, focusing most specifically on incidents that are more specific and limited in scope for which major elements of the NRP/NRF, such as the external affairs annex, are not activated. The plan is designed to fulfill the role of opening communications channels with aviation stakeholders and the public in the event of a threat or attack against the air transportation system. It builds upon lessons learned regarding communications and coordination from efforts carried out under HSPD-5, *The Management of Domestic Incidents*, HSPD-7, *Critical Infrastructure Identification, Prioritization, and Protection*, and HSPD-8, *National Preparedness*, tailoring the elements of these directives to the aviation community.

The strategic objectives include facilitating stakeholder engagement in strategic planning and operational response, and implementing a communications strategy to be activated in the event of a threat or attack to the aviation system that is capable of providing rapid transmission of information to state, local, and tribal governments, and private sector entities. Stakeholder engagement is centered around the use of two coordinating bodies as called for in HSPD-7: the Aviation Government Coordinating Council (AGCC) and the Aviation Sector Coordinating Council (ASCC). Whereas the AGCC, under the guidance of the TSA, would conduct outreach and coordinate stakeholder involvement in implementing the plan among federal and state officials, the ASCC, a self-organized body of owners and operators in the aviation industry, is expected to develop and coordinate a private sector plan and strategy for responding to aviation threats and coordinating threat response with private entities in other critical infrastructure sectors. Under the plan, both the AGCC and the ASCC are expected to work cooperatively to educate and inform stakeholders regarding all aspects of the National Strategy for Aviation Security and the various supporting plans, although the emphasis appears to be on operational threat response. Various messages and materials to support stakeholder education and engagement are anticipated under this initiative, some which may also be used for public education and media relations.

The plan also calls for the development of communications strategies to respond to threats, attacks, and other critical incidents in the aviation sector. The communications strategy seeks to provide and receive accurate, timely information to and from aviation industry stakeholders and maintain active participation in the coordinated response among the various entities that play a critical role in operating the air transportation system. Communications channels and key federal entities engaged in this initiative include the DHS Office of Public Affairs and Office of Legislative and Intergovernmental Affairs, as well as the DHS Office of State and Local Government Coordination and the DHS Private Sector Office. These offices are expected to provide coordination and support to DHS operational agencies including: the TSA—which will be primarily responsible for intelligence dissemination, policy, operational decision making and coordination with industry partners during critical incidents as well as during day-to-day aviation security operations—as well as CBP, the USCG, and Immigration and Customs Enforcement (ICE), which are anticipated to support these efforts. The FAA will play a key role in the federal government response to prevent, respond to, and recover from attacks against the aviation domain in its role in oversight and operation of the NAS. This will involve close coordination and collaboration both with DHS as well as with local, state, and private sector entities. Other federal agencies involved in law enforcement and counterterrorism (e.g., FBI, DOJ), intelligence gathering and dissemination (e.g., CIA), and economic regulation (e.g., Department of Commerce, DOT) also play important roles in coordinating with the private sector and are represented on the AGCC. The AGCC, in coordination with private sector entities working on the ASCC, is the primary vehicle for establishing and maintaining the policies and plans for effective information dissemination to state, local, and private entities regarding air transportation security and the coordination of communications and critical incident response.

The final component of the overall aviation mode-specific supporting plans is the Aviation Transportation System Recovery Plan. This plan would be put into action following an attack to reconstitute the air transportation system and minimize the impacts of an attack on air transportation and the broader economy. While the details of this plan have not yet been made available to the public, a DHS synopsis indicates that the plan incorporates recommended measures to mitigate the operational and economic effects of an attack in the air domain. Reflecting on the impacts of the 9/11 attacks, it is likely that a considerable focus of such a plan would be placed on restoring confidence among airline passengers that adequate measures can be quickly and effectively implemented following an attack to prevent future attacks against aviation. The plan may also consider various operational measures available to quickly, safely, and effectively reconstitute routine operations of the NAS so as to minimize the impact on air commerce.

ISSUES FOR CONSIDERATION

While the national policy and strategy for aviation security and the supporting mode-specific plans provide an important framework for structuring aviation security measures in the United States, these documents themselves should be viewed with a critical eye to identify potential shortcomings in underlying assumptions and approaches. Potential weaknesses in the U.S. policy and strategy for aviation security fall into five broad issue areas:

- The validity of underlying risk assumptions made in developing the aviation security policy, national strategy, and mode-specific plans.
- The adequacy of considerations regarding the sustainability of the aviation security system and its various components.
- Whether the policy and strategy are forward-looking (i.e., proactive), or rather, do they perpetuate a reactive approach to security planning in the aviation domain.
- The extent to which the policy and strategy provide a comprehensive framework for developing and maintaining a robust aviation security system.
- The extent to which objectives and approaches outlined in the national strategy align with budgetary processes and resource availability to ensure that strategic objectives can be adequately met.

These issues are discussed in further depth below.

THE VALIDITY OF UNDERLYING RISK ASSUMPTIONS

Determining the validity of the various risk models and assumptions that have been used to set aviation security policy and strategy is a difficult task. These risk determinations have largely arisen from restricted access intelligence information and other limited distribution sources, thus constraining the ability to engage in open public discourse on the validity of their underlying evidence and assumptions. Nonetheless, some critics have argued that these risk assumptions and resulting policy and strategic decisions may be based on inaccurate and incomplete analysis. For example, some have noted that federal intelligence and security agencies are "inexperienced with and uninterested in statistics."[23] This has led some to argue that the use of statistical techniques to study terrorism data is sorely needed, although it has been questioned whether the federal government has necessary capability and expertise to assess the reliability of available data, and use reliable methods to perform statistical analyses.[24] Instead, some have argued that "security agencies seem to advance policies without any empirical basis," relying instead on anecdotal evidence, political pressures, or "gut feelings."[25] Such a basis for setting policy and establishing strategies for homeland security and aviation security can result in inappropriate estimates of risk—overstating the risk of certain scenarios while underestimating the risk of others. While it appears that efforts are being made to better document global terrorism incidents and perform statistical analyses to identify risk trends, more comprehensive efforts to look specifically at security risk across the aviation domain still appear to be needed to provide better guidance for developing and refining aviation security policies and strategies.

Consideration of System Sustainability

One seemingly unavoidable reality for aviation security strategists is the continued growth in demand for air travel and air commerce. The FAA estimates that the number of airline passengers will increase at an annual rate of about 3.4% domestically and about 4.7% for international flights over the next 12 years.[26] This anticipated growth could strain passenger and baggage screening operations in the future if it is not adequately planned for. Similarly, growth in air cargo volume is expected to increase at an average annual rate of 3.5% domestically and by 6.7% on international routes through 2020. Strategies and initiatives to enhance the security of air cargo operations and screen air cargo shipments must, therefore, also consider these growth projections in carrying out policies, strategies, and plans for enhancing air cargo security. Air traffic is also expected to increase about 3.8% with a growth of about 3.7% in GA operations expected. Airspace security strategies and approaches may need to consider this growth in flight operations in devising effective security programs and procedures for protecting airspace over areas considered critical for national security.

It remains unclear, however, whether this anticipated growth in aviation operations is being adequately planned for in the context of national strategies and mode-specific plans for aviation security. The strategies indicate that they will evolve with shifting threat and vulnerability characteristics on the basis of ongoing risk assessments. However, the degree to which the changing nature, size, and scope of aviation and air travel is being considered in these risk assessments remains a significant issue for policymakers and aviation security strategists.

With regard to the sustainability of aviation security technologies, specific strategies for maintaining deployed technologies and phasing-in next generation screening technologies have not yet been clearly defined. While plans for enhancing aviation security under the comprehensive NGATS initiative envision extensive improvements to aviation security by 2025, the roadmap to achieving these capabilities has not yet been fully defined. According to the future concept of operations for aviation and airport security, significant security transformations will include

- Integrated dynamic risk management solutions
- Biometric technologies for airport access controls
- Smaller footprint, multithreat detection capabilities for screening passengers and baggage
- Network-enabled environmental sensors to detect and warn of CBRNE threats at airports
- Rapidly deployable, reconfigurable screening systems to meet temporary and intermittent screening requirements
- On-board aircraft safety modifications and ground-based systems and procedures to protect flights from shoulder-fired missiles
- Network-centric information sharing capabilities for data mining and decision support to aid security operations personnel and security analysts
- Capabilities to allow for CBRNE screening of all air cargo items not packed in secured areas or securely conveyed to aircraft[27]

While all of these objectives are reflected to some degree in the National Strategy for Aviation Security and the supporting plans. Congress may have a particular interest in how the strategic plan aligns with NGATS aviation security initiatives and the vision for aviation and airport security over the next 18–20 years.

A Proactive or a Reactive Approach?

Some experts have expressed concern that the DHS may be relying too heavily on "gut feelings" and anecdotal evidence in pursuing certain courses of action reflected in aviation policies, strategies, and plans. Similarly, some have questioned whether the DHS and the TSA approach to aviation security has taken on too much of a reactive stance, failing to strategically plan resource allocation based on robust and thoughtful risk analysis, instead allowing high-profile events and media reaction to potentially influence decision making.

For example, using the TSA's response to the foiled liquid explosives plot in August 2006 by restricting carry-on liquids, some critics have argued that the Administration is allowing single events and the media and public attention they generate to shape policy decisions.[28] The TSA has defended its actions in response to the liquid explosives threat, making available to the public documentation and demonstrations of the formidable threat posed by improvised liquid explosive devices. However, liquid explosives have long been known by security experts to pose a formidable threat to aircraft, yet U.S. aviation policy and strategy before this plot was uncovered had not included any specific near-term measures to screen passengers for liquid explosives.

Critics argue that reacting to single events is nearsighted and goes against the very purpose of developing strategies and plans in the first place, which is to be proactive in assessing threats and directing resources to mitigate associated vulnerabilities. On the contrary, if these strategies and underlying plans are to be adaptive, they should be able to shift rapidly in response to changing threat characteristics and changing threat levels. Reviewing the TSA response to the liquid explosives plot may provide more specific insights into whether this response was a reasonable adaptive approach to mitigate unforeseen risks or a case of taking immediate, and arguably questionable, actions in an effort to restore and maintain public confidence in aviation security. If it is determined that the TSA's actions in response to the liquid explosives plot represented a well–thought-out example of an evolving strategy that can respond quickly and effectively to emerging threats, then perhaps additional questions need to be asked regarding why the emerging threat of liquid explosives was not foreseen prior to widespread public disclosure of information regarding the failed liquid explosives plot in the United Kingdom. A more detailed examination of the deliberations and decision making regarding liquid explosives, both before and after receiving knowledge of the foiled plot can perhaps provide unique insights and "lessons learned" to aid security analysts and senior policymakers in developing strategic and tactical decision-making tools to improve upon the U.S. response to future emerging threat situations.

Critics argue that the government must replace its practices of responding to single threats with more systematic approaches for improving homeland security. A lingering concern is that if aviation security policies and practices, and more broadly homeland security policies and practices, remain too reactionary, terrorists may be able to exploit this approach. Terrorist may be able to trigger reactionary responses by providing misinformation about intended targets or attack methods. This may lead to haphazard allocation or reallocation of resources that could be wasteful and inefficient and could even result in resources being redirected in a manner that could make the system more vulnerable to attack. In other words, terrorists may be able to more easily exploit a reactionary approach to aviation security by using diversionary tactics that may increase vulnerabilities in other areas or aspects of the air domain.

Consideration of Whether the Strategy Is Comprehensive and Robust

In 2004, the GAO issued recommendations regarding the desired characteristics of national strategies to combat terrorism.[29] The desired elements of such strategies identified by the GAO included

- A purpose, scope, and methodology
- A definition of the problem and an assessment of the associated risk

- An identification of the goals and supporting or subordinate objectives and activities to meet these goals, and performance measure to evaluate progress toward achieving these goals
- An identification of resources, costs, and a risk management analysis to determine where resources and investments should be targeted
- A clear definition of organizational roles, responsibilities, and coordination
- A discussion of how a particular strategy relates to other strategies and how plans, activities, and objectives will be integrated to meet the stated goals of the various related strategies

While the GAO used these criteria to evaluate various national security, homeland security, counterterrorism, and infrastructure protection strategies that had been developed prior to 2004, the National Strategy for Aviation Security had not been developed at that time and has not subsequently been evaluated against these desired elements. At first glance, the aviation security strategy appears to contain or address many of these desirable characteristics. Where the strategy and supporting plans may be lacking, however, is in

- Fully defining the methodology for evaluating risk and carrying out the strategy
- Fully documenting associated cost estimates and resource requirements
- Providing sufficient detail regarding roles, responsibility, and coordination, particularly among nonfederal entities that are expected to participate in execution of the various mode-specific plans
- Clearly indicating how the various components fit into the hierarchy of national security, homeland security, and counterterrorism strategies and plans and how the elements of these various plans may be integrated both within and beyond the aviation domain

Additionally, one of the key required features of the National Strategy for Aviation Security is that it must be adaptive. Consequently, the national strategy and its supporting plans and documents are likely to evolve over time to address changes in threats, intelligence, terrorist tactics and capabilities, as well as new security technologies and capabilities. It is also likely that the strategy and its supporting plans will sometimes need to change quickly in the face of imminent threats.

ALIGNMENT OF STRATEGIC OBJECTIVES WITH BUDGETARY PLANNING AND RESOURCE ALLOCATION PROCESSES

As a final consideration, within the federal government, there is a particular interest in assessing how the national strategy and supporting plans align with budgetary decisions and resource availability, particularly in the context of the annual budget and appropriations process. This could be a key consideration as elements of the current strategy call for some considerable expansion of the TSA's roles and responsibilities. For example, DHS objectives for the TSA to assume passenger identification functions and carry out behavioral observation both at and beyond airport screening checkpoints is likely to be human resource intensive and therefore may need further scrutiny in the context of budget and resource prioritization. Also, technology advancements for checkpoint, baggage, and cargo screening are also being sought by both Congress and the Administration. Additionally, new and proposed statutory requirements may also expand the functions of the TSA and other federal agencies. For example, provisions in the Implementing the 9/11 Commission Recommendations Act of 2007 (P.L. 110-53) require the swift phase in of air cargo inspections to achieve 100% inspections of all cargo carried on passenger air carrier aircraft within three years. This mandate is likely to have significant cost and resource implications not only for the federal government, but also for the airline and air cargo industries. Aligning this initiative with ongoing strategic plans for risk-based profiling and targeting of cargo shipments and investment in cargo screening technologies is likely to be a topic of considerable interest in the context of the federal budget process over the next several years. As new threats emerge and the U.S. aviation security strategy evolves, policymakers and aviation security strategists will likely face continuing challenges to ensure that adequate funds are available to support new aviation security needs and requirements and adequate resources are available to carry out new roles and responsibilities assigned to the various entities involved in implementing the National Strategy for Aviation Security.

REFERENCES

1. National Commission on Terrorist Attacks upon the United States, *The 9/11 Commission Report* (Authorized Edition), New York: W.W. Norton & Company.
2. Federal Aviation Administration, *A Commitment to Security, Civil Aviation Strategic Plan 2001–2004*, April 2001, p. 3.
3. Ibid., p. 11.
4. See note 1, p. 85.
5. Ibid., p. 345.
6. See Title 49 U.S. Code, § 114.
7. See note 1, p. 391.
8. President George W. Bush, *National Security Presidential Directive/NSPD-47, Homeland Security Presidential Directive/HSPD-16, Subject: Aviation Security Policy*, Washington, DC: The White House, June 20, 2006.
9. White House Office of Homeland Security, *National Strategy for Homeland Security*, July 2002, p. 22.
10. See note 8, p. 3.
11. U.S. Department of Homeland Security, *The National Strategy for Aviation Security*, March 26, 2007, p. 9.
12. See Ariel Merari, "Attacks on Civil Aviation: Trends and Lessons," in Paul Wilkinson and Brian M. Jenkins (Eds.), *Aviation Terrorism and Security*, Portland, OR: Frank Cass, 1999, for an overview of historical incidents.
13. See especially, Bruce Schneier, "Portrait of the Modern Terrorist as an Idiot," *Wired*, June 14, 2007.
14. See 71 *Federal Register*, 30510 et seq., May 26, 2006.
15. Department of Homeland Security, *Transportation Systems: Critical Infrastructure and Key Resources Sector-Specific Plan as Input to the National Infrastructure Protection Plan*, May 2007, Arlington, VA.
16. Ibid., p. 45.
17. *National Strategy for Aviation Security*, p. 16.
18. The text of the supporting plans, along with the *National Strategy for Aviation Security*, can be viewed or downloaded at (http://www.dhs.gov/xprevprot/laws/gc_1173113497603.shtm).
19. *Aviation Transportation System Security Plan*, p. 4.
20. Ibid., p. 15.
21. U.S. Department of Homeland Security, Press Office, *Fact Sheet: National Response Plan (NRP)*, January 6, 2005.
22. See, for example, Spencer S. Hsu, "Fake FEMA Briefing Costs Official New Assignment," *Washington Post*, October 30, 2007, p. A3.
23. Zack Phillips, "A Feel for Numbers," *Government Executive*, October 1, 2007, p. 52.
24. Ibid., p. 54.
25. Ibid., p. 54.
26. Federal Aviation Administration, Aviation Policy and Plans, *FAA Aerospace Forecasts, Fiscal Years 2007–2020*.
27. Joint Planning and Development Office, *Security Annex, Concept of Operations for the Next Generation Air Transportation System* (Version 2.0), June 13, 2007.
28. Zack Phillips, "One Hit Wonders," *Government Executive*, October 30, 2006.
29. U.S. Government Accountability Office, *Combating Terrorism: Evaluation of Selected Characteristics in National Strategies Related to Terrorism*, Statement of Randall A. Yim, Director, Homeland Security and Justice Issues before the Subcommittee on National Security, Emerging Threats, and International Relations, Committee on Government Reform, U.S. House of Representatives, February 3, 2004, GAO-04-408T.

5 Evaluating and Managing Security Risks

As discussed in the previous chapter, the U.S. strategy for aviation security is built upon a general risk management framework and applies a multilayered approach to mitigating security risks. This framework recognizes that terrorist threats and other threats to aviation security cannot be completely eliminated. However, through effective management and allocation of security resources and available technologies, these risks can be managed and the threat sufficiently mitigated to what most would regard as acceptable levels. Of course, what constitutes an acceptable level of risk has been a matter of considerable policy debate. However, most concede that, given limited resources, policy decisions based on perceived risk are necessary, not only within the context of aviation security by itself but also in the broader context of homeland and national security. That is, at the broadest level of policy decision-making, trade-offs between aviation security and other homeland security priorities—such as port security, border security, critical infrastructure protection, and detection and prevention of CBRNE attacks against major population centers and other critical targets—must be evaluated. While the focus of this book is the evaluation and mitigation of security risks in the aviation domain, the risk evaluation and mitigation concepts discussed here may be applicable to risk evaluation processes carried out in the broader context of homeland security policy.

RISK ASSESSMENT METHODS

Security risk is generally regarded as a function of the nature of the threat, the vulnerabilities to attack inherent in a given system, and the consequences associated with a particular attack scenario. In general terms, one can represent this as

$$\text{Risk} = f(\text{Threat, Vulnerability, Consequence}).$$

That is, risk is some function, f, of the three risk parameters: threat, vulnerability, and consequence.

The threat to a given system as well as the vulnerability of that system can both be defined in terms of their probability or likelihood of occurrence. Consequence, however, is a variable that is more appropriately defined operationally in terms of potential impact or severity. In a risk framework, this is often accomplished by developing a scale of consequence severity. Alternatively, in developing a cost-benefit analysis for assessing the economic implications of a policy option, consequence can be framed in terms of monetary impact. In either case, whether consequence is operationally defined in terms of a rating of severity of consequence or a monetary amount associated with the projected cost of an event or scenario, the risk equation is often described in terms of the multiplicity of the three risk factors. This can be expressed as

$$\text{Risk} = \text{Threat} \times \text{Vulnerability} \times \text{Consequence}.$$

In assessing risk, subject matter experts may utilize a rating scale or evaluation system in which threat, vulnerability, and consequence are defined by ordinal or interval-scale descriptors of these three elements that comprise security risk. An ordinal scale would be one in which the values simply represent a rank ordering of the descriptors on the given scale of either likelihood or severity of consequence. In an interval scale, it would be assumed that the steps in between values adhere to some constant scale factor. For example, if a likelihood rating of four represented a judgment that an event was considered twice as likely as an event given a rating of two, and an event rated a two was considered twice as likely as an event rated a one, then the rating scale would be an interval scale. In practice, these types of rating scales are really ordinal in nature since risk judgments are largely subjective and therefore do not represent consistent differences between rankings. However, they are typically treated as interval scales to mathematically evaluate risk scores. Using such a rating method, a risk matrix can be developed. Typically, risk matrices for aviation and industrial safety applications only consider two variables: (1) the vulnerability of the system to certain failures and (2) the severity of the consequences associated with such a failure.[1] This approach can be extended to the aviation security domain, or, more broadly, to the homeland security domain, by also including a consideration of the fundamental element of security risk: the threat. The result is a three-dimensional risk matrix such as the one shown in Figure 5.1. In this risk matrix, categories and descriptors from a typical risk matrix used in the aviation safety domain have been adopted for analysis of aviation security risk. System vulnerability is evaluated by placing the known or per-ceived probability of a security breach or system failure into one of six categories, from extremely unlikely (i.e., "highly improbable") to very likely (i.e., "frequent"). The categorical descriptors include (1) highly improbable, (2) improbable, (3) remote, (4) occasional, (5) probable, and (6) fre-quent. These same descriptors can also be used to categorize the perceived security threat. In the risk matrix shown, the consequence of a perceived threat exploiting a vulnerability can be rated in terms of one of four descriptors ranging from negligible to catastrophic. The specific consequence descriptors, in order of severity, are (1) negligible, (2) marginal, (3) critical, and (4) catastrophic. These scales illustrate the process, although, in practice, scales with fewer or larger numbers of categories and different descriptors may be developed to suit the particular needs and preferences for conducting a specific risk assessment.

Each cell of the risk matrix represents some combination of threat rating, vulnerability rating, and severity of consequence rating. In some cases, it may be desirable to compute a single risk score that is either the product of these three factors or the product of each factor multiplied by some factor weight. For example, in making a comparative analysis of risk among various threat scenar-ios, if the vulnerability was regarded as being twice as important in the analysis compared to the threat and the severity of consequence, then the vulnerability score would be multiplied by two, the weighting factor, before being multiplied by the threat and severity scores. If such an analysis is

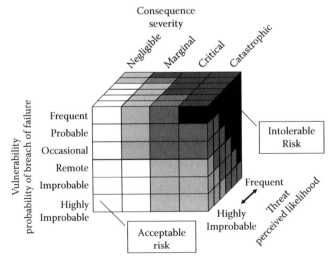

FIGURE 5.1 A three-way risk matrix indicating rating-scale descriptors of threat, vulnerability, and consequence.

performed to derive an overall risk score, then an underlying implicit assumption is being made that the ratings for each of the risk parameters are represented by an interval scale, and therefore differences between rating scores are measured on a ratio scale with an absolute zero value, so that differences between numerical scores have some comparative significance.

In performing a security risk assessment, a wide variety of scenarios could be evaluated by subject matter experts along these dimensions of threat, vulnerability, and consequence. Each scenario could be rated and placed into one of the (Threat × Vulnerability × Consequence) cells in the risk matrix. Scenarios based on threats and vulnerabilities that are highly improbable, improbable, or remote and have negligible or marginal consequences are likely to be regarded as acceptable risks. On the other hand, cases where experts perceive a high probability that terrorists would attempt to carry out a particular threat scenario, the probability of a breach or failure of available security measures to prevent such an attack is high, and the severity of the outcome or consequence is considered critical or catastrophic are likely to be viewed as having an intolerable or unacceptable risk. When intolerable risks are identified, from a public policy standpoint, there is typically widespread agreement that additional risk mitigation is necessary to safeguard the flying public and the aviation system. In the context of aviation security policy and strategy discussed in the previous chapter, these types of risks, which are likely and have a high severity of consequence associated with them, are viewed as strategic risks. In between acceptable risks and intolerable, unacceptable, or strategic risks, however, is the proverbial "gray area," where risk is not at fully acceptable levels but it is not completely intolerable, either. Typically, in such cases, further action to reduce risk as much as possible to fully acceptable levels would be prescribed. However, high costs and limited resources available to devote to such risk mitigation efforts in the face of competing homeland security needs make for difficult policy decisions. In such policy debates, risk evaluation methods can serve to provide a basis for resource allocation by prioritizing risk mitigation alternatives not only within aviation security but also in the broader context of homeland security.

Much of the current aviation security policy debate has been the product of differing views regarding the extent to which further mitigation and risk reduction is needed in those gray areas where there are considerable differences of opinion regarding the degree and nature of security risk. Specific areas where risk assessment and related policy have been particularly contentious include passenger prescreening, air cargo security, protecting passenger airliners from the threat of shoulder-fired missiles and other standoff weapons, as well as security risks associated with GA operations. Each of these issues is discussed in later chapters devoted specifically to these particular topics. The risk model is equally applicable for evaluating the costs and benefits of various mitigation options for airport security, passenger and baggage screening, and in-flight security, which are also considered in depth in the context of the risk analysis framework in separate chapters of this book.

USING THE RISK-BASED FRAMEWORK TO DETERMINE A RISK VALUATION AND ASSESS COSTS AND BENEFITS

The general risk matrix framework—using rating scales of threat, vulnerability, and consequence—may be particularly beneficial as a tool for airport managers, airline security coordinators, federal security officials, and other operational managers to provide a general assessment of security risk and rank order–specific threat scenarios and vulnerabilities for the purposes of prioritizing resource allocations. However, to directly compare the cost of security measures to the expected benefits to be derived from specific security enhancements—an important consideration in policy debate—it is necessary to use probability estimates to describe the threat posed by a particular attack scenario, as well as the vulnerability to such a scenario, and quantify the severity of the consequences in economic terms. So far, the risk elements of threat and vulnerability have been discussed in terms of using descriptive ratings or scores to quantify the elements of risk in relative terms. An alternative means of computing risk would be to represent threat and vulnerability in terms of their probability or likelihood of occurrence. Severity of consequence, measured in terms of direct and indirect monetary costs associated with an expected outcome of such a terrorist attack scenario being successfully carried out, can be incorporated into the equation to yield a cost-based risk evaluation.

In other words, instead of using a five- or seven-point scale or some other rating scheme to quantify the level of threat and perceived vulnerability as discussed earlier, these parameters could be couched in terms of probability values ranging between zero and one, or 0% to 100%. For example, a terrorism expert might conjecture that the probability or likelihood of a terrorist plot to attack an airport within the United States using conventional explosives over the next 10 years might be 25%. This can be represented as

$$P_T = 0.25,$$

where P_T is the probability value assigned to a given threat, T, which, in this case, is the threat of an airport bombing.

As previously discussed, however, risk is not determined solely by the probability of an attack, but it is also dependent on the vulnerability to such a threat. Continuing with the example above, an aviation security expert might surmise that, despite stepped-up law enforcement presence and surveillance at airports and placement of physical barriers to prevent attacks using explosives-laden vehicles, a moderate vulnerability nonetheless exists because airport terminal drop-off points and check-in and ticketing areas are open public spaces. She may consequently assign the vulnerability to such an attack among U.S. airports at 50%, meaning that any conceivable terrorist bombing of the airport would have a 50% chance of causing notable structural damage or loss of life. This can be expressed in terms of probability as

$$P_V = 0.50,$$

where P_V is the probability that a specific vulnerability, V, can be exploited by a terrorist attack or other security breach.

In statistical terms, vulnerability expressed in terms of a probability value, P_V, is actually the conditional probability of a successful attack given that a particular threat scenario has been attempted. In this example, the joint or combined probability that an attack using a particular threat scenario, an airport bombing, is attempted and is successful is the product of the two individual probabilities.

So, $P_{T \text{ and } V} = P_T \times P_V$, and therefore

$$P_{T \text{ and } V} = 0.25 \times 0.50 = 0.125 \text{ or } 12.5\%,$$

where $P_{T \text{ and } V}$ is the probability of being attacked (the threat) *and* the attack being carried out successfully (the vulnerability). This represents the likelihood of a successful attack being carried out compared to the event space of all possible outcomes including no attack, an unsuccessful attack, and a successful attack, with the probability of a successful attack being computed to be 12.5%.

As stated previously, the vulnerability expressed as a probability value, P_V, is the conditional probability of a successful attack *given* that a particular threat scenario has been attempted. This can be expressed by the following relationship:

$$P_{V|T} = P_{T \text{ and } V}/P_T = (P_T \times P_V)/P_T,$$
$$P_{V|T} = (0.25 \times 0.50)/0.25,$$
$$P_{V|T} = 0.50,$$

where $P_{V|T}$, read as the probability of vulnerability V being successfully exploited *given* that threat scenario T has been attempted, is the conditional probability of a successful attack given a threat attempt.[2] Assuming that the threat, T, and the vulnerability, V, are independent of each other—a reasonable assumption in most cases—the conditional probability $P_{V|T}$ will always be equal to the probability of V alone, P_V, as shown by this calculation.

The risk posed by such an event is a function of both the likelihood or probability of a specific attack scenario, the threat, and the degree of vulnerability measured in terms of the likelihood that an attack could successfully exploit known security weaknesses. In the simplest terms, this can be represented by the joint probability of the aviation system, or in this case an airport, being vulnerable (the vulnerability) and the system or an airport being attacked (the threat). This joint or combined probability, calculated above, is simply the product of these two factors. In other words, whereas the value representing the threat component is the likelihood of an attack, whether successful or not, the product of this threat value times the vulnerability value yields the overall probability or likelihood of a successful terrorist attack.

The result of the combined probability of being attacked and the degree of vulnerability, expressed as the conditional probability of a successful attack, can then be multiplied by the consequence, expressed in monetary terms, to derive a risk valuation. For this example, a monetary valuation of risk can be calculated by expressing the severity of consequence in terms of its financial impact. This financial impact valuation of severity of consequence would typically reflect both direct losses, including any expected loss of life expressed in monetary terms and direct costs resulting from the physical destruction of property as a result of an attack, as well as indirect financial impacts on the aviation industry and the broader economy. For the purposes of continuing the example of the airport bombing threat described above, assume that economists predict the financial impact resulting from a terrorist bombing of an airport to consist of $250 million in direct costs and $750 million in indirect economic damage to the airline and tourism industries as well as financial impacts to the local economy in the city of occurrence. Thus, the total severity of consequence in terms of financial impact would be $1 billion. According to the risk model, the monetary risk, R, tied to an explosives attack at an airport can be computed using the following equation:

$$R = P_T \times P_V \times S_C,$$

$$R = 0.25 \times 0.5 \times \$1,000,000,000,$$

$$R = \$125,000,000$$

where S_C is the severity of a particular consequence, C, expressed in monetary terms.

The computed risk value, R, may be referred to as either the unmitigated risk or the residual risk that remains after currently implemented security measures, such as stepped-up law enforcement presence at airports and installed physical barriers, have been taken into account.

So, in this illustrative analysis, the unmitigated or residual risk of an airport bombing is calculated to be $125 million dollars.

To continue this illustration, let us imagine that a policymaker has learned about initiatives to use large-scale x-ray scanning systems specifically designed for scanning trucks as a means for screening for explosives, WMDs, and contraband at border checkpoints. He argues that these systems should also be put in place at the busiest 20 airports in the United States to screen large trucks approaching the airport terminals. This raises a fundamental policy question: Would it be beneficial to do so? Whether something is beneficial or not can be a value-laden judgment. However, the question can be examined more objectively in the risk-based cost-benefit framework by examining how much of the residual or remaining risk of an airport bombing would be reduced or mitigated by implementing this proposal.

Continuing this example, imagine that a team of homeland security analysts are asked to determine the projected monetary risk reduction that can be achieved by implementing this proposal. The team's research indicates that the primary benefit would be a reduction in the direct costs of an attack, based on their conclusion that most large truck bombs would be effectively stopped and detected at a proposed x-ray screening checkpoint. Instead of an estimated $250 million in direct costs before implementation, the analysts believe that the direct costs of an attack would drop to $100 million, based on the premise that if the truck scanners were put in place, the threat would most likely involve smaller vehicles that would cause less damage. Also, the indirect costs, which are primarily derived from a collective psychological response to an event, would also drop because the event would likely be less severe in nature and would not deter air travel to the same extent. The analysts may conclude that the indirect costs would drop from $750 million to $400 million. Thus, the severity of consequence tied to the proposed action would total $500 million ($100 million in direct costs and $400 million in indirect costs), which is $500 million less than, or half of, the estimated $1 billion severity of consequence based on the hypothetical analysis of current security measures.

In addition to reducing the severity of consequence, the vulnerability itself would also decrease as a result of the proposed action. In this example, the analysts may determine that the vulnerability may diminish from a 50% chance that an explosives attack at an airport would be successful to a 30% chance. In other words, P_V would drop from 0.50 to 0.30. Finally, the probability of an attack, the threat component, may also change based on terrorists' perceptions of how effective this approach would be at thwarting an attempted airport bombing. In this example, the analysts may assume that the initiative will be perceived as being a moderately effective measure, and it would reduce the threat of an airport bombing over the next 10 years from 25% to 20%. In other words, P_T would be reduced from 0.25 to 0.20. This reflects the deterrent effects of the proposed action. The analysts are now able to compute a new projected risk valuation based on implementing the hypothetical proposed action to deploy x-ray truck scanners at major airports. This can be expressed in the following equation, where the subscript A is used to indicate that this is the risk valuation being computed for a given alternative or action:

$$R_A = P_{T(A)} \times P_{V(A)} \times S_{C(A)},$$

$$R_A = 0.20 \times 0.30 \times \$500,000,000,$$

$$R_A = \$30,000,000.$$

So, in this example, the analysts would estimate the residual risk after deployment of the truck x-ray scanners to be $30 million. The risk reduction, or benefit, B, associated with implementing this proposal would simply be the difference between the estimated residual risk or unmitigated risk before implementation of the proposed action (i.e., the deployment of truck x-ray scanners) and the estimated residual risk after implementation. That is,

$$B_A = R \times R_A,$$

$$B_A = \$125,000,000 - \$30,000,000,$$

$$B_A = \$95,000,000,$$

where B_A is the benefit tied to alternative or action A, which in this example is the proposed deployment of truck x-ray scanners.

In this example, the total benefit associated with the proposal would be $95 million over the 10 year time span used as the basis for the calculation. Thus, if the costs of implementing the proposal, amortized over 10 years, are less than $95 million, the proposal would be regarded as being cost beneficial. However, if the 10-year costs exceed $95 million, the proposal may be regarded as exceeding the risk reduction benefit that it would yield. Given that 20 airports were slated to get the systems under the proposal, the per airport cost for system acquisition, operation, and maintenance over the 10-year time span should not exceed $4.75 million, an average (mean) cost of $475,000 per airport per year, if the proposal is to be considered cost beneficial. This type of analysis for computing risk using a probability-based cost valuation is mathematically no different than the risk matrix model and computation of risk scores described previously. However, it offers the advantage of establishing a monetary valuation for risk. In this regard, risk can be evaluated not only on a comparative basis but also in monetary terms that can be compared and contrasted with funding for security mitigation measures in a cost-benefit framework. Risk-based cost-benefit analysis is an important tool for assessing aviation security policy and strategy alternatives.

It should be noted, however, that often—including in the many policy and strategy debates cited in this book—risk valuation is not fully assessed or calculated in this fashion. The primary reason for this is that considerable uncertainty exists and there could be widespread policy disagreement regarding the extent of the threat and the degree of vulnerability. Therefore, the potential monetary costs representing the severity of an expected outcome are sometimes the only parameter formally estimated in examining the costs and benefits of a given security strategy. The discussion of threat and vulnerability is frequently couched mostly in descriptive terms. Nonetheless, the risk-based framework, both for the purpose of general strategic risk assessment and also for assessing the costs and benefits of various policy options or approaches, has important conceptual underpinnings for understanding risk in the context of aviation security and, more broadly, homeland security. Presently, the TSA, the DHS, and others are working to develop more sophisticated analytical models for better understanding the dynamics of threats, vulnerabilities, and program costs within the context of the risk-based analytical framework.

APPROACHES FOR DEVELOPING COMPLEX MODELS OF RISK IN THE AVIATION SECURITY DOMAIN

While the example provided above considered risk only in terms of the basic elements of probability theory to illustrate the application of the basic risk model framework, more complex models of risk can be developed to examine threats and vulnerabilities and to address resource allocation among existing and proposed approaches to aviation security. The TSA, in cooperation with the Boeing Corporation, has undertaken a research initiative aimed at developing more complex risk models under a program it calls the Risk Management Assessment Tool (RMAT). The system relies on Monte Carlo simulation methods to estimate risk probabilities.[3] The Monte Carlo method derives its name from the world-renowned gambling casinos located in the city of Monte Carlo, Monaco. Like repetitive rolls of the dice at Monte Carlo's gambling tables, the Monte Carlo method uses repeated probabilistic or stochastic simulations of events and possible outcomes. In the case of the TSA's RMAT, the primary purpose is to assess the vulnerability of the aviation security system to a wide array of threat scenarios, so the focus is primarily looking at security vulnerabilities in the aviation domain. The RMAT is being developed under the auspices of the United States Commercial Aviation Partnership (USCAP), a government–industry partnership applying operations research solutions to aviation security challenges.

The RMAT is part of a larger set of risk-based systems engineering and econometric modeling tools that have been used to provide "what if" analyses to support aviation security policy decision-making.[4] Over the past several years, these modeling tools have been used to evaluate the impact of public fear on passenger demand for air travel, the impact of security fees on passenger demand, security screener staffing requirements and impacts of staffing levels on passenger checkpoint throughput, and the operational and economic impacts of expanding airport worker credentialing and screening requirements and implementing enhanced security measures for air cargo operations. The developers of these tools assert that the application of operations research techniques and econometric models to aviation security policy analysis under this program has helped policymakers make better informed decisions resulting in effective use of limited resources to improve security while identifying multi-billion-dollar savings compared to less efficient alternatives. Nonetheless, it is important to note that policy decisions are made based on a broad array of considerations, including political and economic considerations that do not always favor an optimal solution based on models such as these that attempt to define operational parameters and determine probable outcomes using objective, empirical methods of analysis.

Another theoretical framework that can be used to more specifically model and evaluate threats, but may also provide insights regarding vulnerabilities, is game theory. Game theory applies mathematical models to understanding strategic decisions in response to opponents' or competitors' decisions and actions. Game theory studies optimal decision behavior in an interactive system. In the context of aviation security, and more generally homeland security, game theory appears to be most applicable to understanding how terrorist tactics may evolve in response to U.S. homeland security and aviation security strategies. For example, it is intuitive that if sufficient security measures to protect commercial airliners from passenger hijackings were implemented, terrorists would seek alternative methods of attack or might seek out alternative targets to attack. However, what specific shifts in terrorist strategy would occur would largely depend on the terrorists' assessment of vulnerabilities to various attack scenarios across the aviation system, which can be represented mathematically in probabilistic or stochastic terms. Various game models of homeland security terrorist threats and security risks have been developed. For example, researchers at Stanford University have constructed game models based on the perception of terrorist knowledge and perceptions and likely responses of the U.S. government and societal responses.[5] Also, the DHS has conducted various simulations of hypothetical terrorist attack scenarios. For example, the TOPOFF 2 project examined the response and impact of a combined radiological "dirty bomb" attack in Seattle and the release of a biological agent at ORD.[6] Examining possible terrorist tactics within the framework of game theory can help security strategists better understand potential terrorist threats and threat dynamics in response to an evolving system for aviation and homeland security.

A combination of approaches such as Monte Carlo techniques and game theory can be utilized to determine values for quantifying the probability of a given threat scenario as well as the vulnerabilities to such scenarios. In addition to these methods, complex risk models can be constructed to examine and compare the relative risk of various threat scenarios both within aviation as well as in comparison to security risks associated with other transportation systems and other critical infrastructures and assets.

The difficulty in this process, however, is estimating the parameters of the equation. Operationally defining the threat element is particularly problematic and particularly contentious. The nature and extent of a particular threat may be difficult to establish and even more difficult to quantify in probabilistic terms. Vulnerabilities may often be underestimated, either because the extent of the vulnerability inherent in a system is not fully understood or because inherent vulnerabilities could be downplayed for political reasons to avoid criticism and challenges over the presence of unmitigated vulnerabilities and the policy implications associated with acknowledging such unmitigated vulnerabilities. On the other hand, vulnerabilities may, in some cases, be exaggerated in order to justify or gain support for implementing a particular security measure or course of action. While the risk-based cost-benefit approach provides a useful framework for analyzing policy decisions, it is nonetheless susceptible to limitations in estimating cost and benefit parameters or outright gaming of the process to achieve a result consistent with a particular policy viewpoint or position on a particular course of action. Policy analysts sometimes refer to this as the "garbage in, garbage out" phenomenon, because providing unreliable or slanted parameter estimates into the risk-based cost-benefit framework will yield unreliable, biased results that could lead to poor policy decisions and the pursuit of an inappropriate course of action.

These concerns aside, risk estimates can be made for specific attack scenarios using the risk equation, or, by summing or averaging the risk estimates for all possible risk scenarios considered, one can derive an overall risk estimate for the entire system. For example, risk estimates can be derived for the potential of a shoulder-fired missile attack against a civilian airliner in the United States. This risk estimate, along with risk estimates for hijackings, bombings, and other scenarios with various outcomes and consequences, could be used to derive an overall risk picture or risk estimate for the civil aviation domain. Despite the difficulty associated with quantifying the risk posed by specific attack scenarios, these activities play an important role in developing aviation security policy and strategic approaches.

Defining the threat element of the equation is largely a matter that falls in the realm of the intelligence community. Understanding vulnerability and adapting security systems to minimize vulnerabilities, on the other hand, are largely the responsibility of those charged with the task of overseeing and implementing aviation security functions. Without specific intelligence information, however, an accurate picture of the threat variable is difficult to establish, and consequently a comprehensive risk picture for determining policies and strategies for deploying aviation security resources cannot be fully developed. Nonetheless, from an operational standpoint, the threat element is often put aside, and the focus of operational security reviews is typically on conducting vulnerability assessments. For example, the TSA has conducted vulnerability assessments to examine the vulnerability of large airports in the United States and some major overseas airports to shoulder-fired missile attacks targeting airliners. Also, the TSA has created vulnerability self-assessment tools for operators of GA airports to assess site security. Absent a formal consideration of threat, risk is generally regarded as the combination of vulnerability and consequence. In examining a GA airport, for example, the security risk of an airport that handles large business jets that is in close proximity to a major urban center is intuitively greater than the risk associated with a small, short grass strip airport in a rural part of the country. Specific vulnerabilities and consequences associated with particular facilities or aviation infrastructures can be identified through formal vulnerability assessment tools and processes.

While vulnerability assessments are important activities at the operational level, some consideration of the nature and extent of the perceived threats to aviation security operations is needed to evaluate and set policies regarding aviation security, determine how resources and funds will be apportioned to aviation security among the various homeland security needs, and identify how these resources and assets can be applied within the context of aviation security to address specific vulnerabilities that could be exploited under various perceived threat scenarios. However, because the nature of the threat is often ambiguous, considerable debate and disagreement among policymakers with regard to aviation security resource allocation have resulted. For example, various policymakers have called for additional steps to be taken: to protect airliners from shoulder-fired missile attacks, to mitigate the risks associated with explosives introduced in air cargo placed on passenger airplanes, and to reduce the risk of attacks against critical infrastructures and population centers carried out using GA aircraft. These specific issues and the policy debate surrounding them will be examined in detail in designated chapters of this book focusing specifically on these ongoing aviation security challenges.

MITIGATING AVIATION SECURITY RISK

So far, methods to measure and assess aviation security risk have been discussed at length. Based on assessments of risk, using the risk evaluation tools and cost-based risk valuation methods described above, policymaker and security strategists can evaluate risk across a wide variety of threat scenarios and allocate resources to mitigate risk in a manner commensurate with the degree of assessed risk. Approaches to deterring and preventing attacks and mitigating the consequences of a potential attack have involved multiple layers or facets of protection to reduce the chances of a successful attack based on the predicate that systems having built-in redundancies or multiple layers of protection tend to be more resilient to failures, human errors, or deliberate attacks.

In addition to incorporating multiple layers of protection, distributed networks or decentralized systems also tend to be highly resilient to failures among elements or nodes of the system, because the entire system is not wholly dependent on the functioning of each of its elements. To some degree, modern complex technological systems have some degree of independence as well as a certain limited amount of interdependence. In general, such systems have been extremely vulnerable to attacks, but the impact of an attack on the entire system is typically limited.[7]

Many aspects of modern, large-scale systems, including many components of the aviation transportation system, exhibit these decentralized but interdependent characteristics. Therefore, the air transportation system and its component systems, like other complex distributed systems, are relatively tolerant or resilient to externalities, such as accidents, errors, and malicious attacks, that can disrupt these systems but are nonetheless vulnerable to the consequences of these events. For example, well-coordinated cyberattacks and cyberterrorism threats may be capable of crippling the Internet computing capabilities of a specific corporation or government agency. If large enough, such an attack could have ripple effects that could slow performance for other Internet users, but it would be highly unlikely that an attack could be of such a scale to cause major disruption to the entire Internet, which is highly distributed and, for the most part, highly decentralized. So too is the case with aviation. Consider, for example, a catastrophic accident that shuts down a major U.S. airport for a length of time over the course of a day. Air traffic to and from that airport would, of course, be disrupted until the airport reopened and traffic flows and flight operations could be reconstituted. Traffic to other airports may also be disrupted to some degree, particularly if the closed airport is the principal hub for a major airline. In such a case, the inability to position aircraft to meet later flight schedules may have a cascading effect, resulting in delays and cancellations at other airports. However, the U.S. aviation system is sufficiently large and highly distributed. Therefore, such an event, while catastrophic to those whose lives are directly impacted, would typically have a rather limited impact on the aviation system as a whole, at least from a systems perspective. Typically, the aviation system has been capable of quickly reconstituting operations following such catastrophes. Notwithstanding the complete air traffic system shutdown following the 9/11 terrorist attacks, past experience suggests that even after relatively significant catastrophes, the aviation system as a whole can be reconstituted in a matter of hours at most, and flight operations at directly impacted airports and facilities can typically be reconstituted in a few days, time. The distributed and redundant, multilayered nature of the aviation system and safety and security features built into that system make it relatively tolerant or resilient to disruption. In addition to the distributed nature of the aviation system, its multilayered approach to safety and security not only makes it more resilient to attack but also makes it less likely that an attack could be successfully carried out. The multilayered strategy involves a deliberate strategic approach to engineering complex systems to make them less prone to failures and attacks that exploit inherent weaknesses or gaps that cannot easily be eliminated in a cost-effective manner.

THE MULTILAYERED APPROACH TO AVIATION SECURITY

In James Reason's discourse on risk management, Reason notes that all complex systems are prone to certain weaknesses and gaps in defensive layers that are designed for safety or security.[8] While Reason focuses most of his discussion on safety risk posed by gaps or vulnerabilities in complex systems, his model for risk reduction is equally relevant in discussing complex security systems such as aviation security. In his view of complex systems, Reason compares the various weaknesses and gaps in complex systems to the holes in a stack of sliced Swiss cheese. In this metaphor, each slice of cheese can be considered a layer of protection designed into a system, and the holes in the cheese represent gaps or weaknesses in these layers.

Complex systems are typically designed to have multiple or redundant layers, so that a failure or breach of one layer, because of its inherent weaknesses or gaps, does not result in a catastrophic failure to the entire system. Systems engineers sometimes talk of failures at one level or layer that are catastrophic to the system as single point failures, and it is always a design objective to either eliminate or mitigate the consequences of such single point failures on the system. This is often accomplished by multiple or redundant layers of defense or protection that serve to nullify or lessen the severity of a failure at another layer in the system. Strictly from the standpoint of probability or likelihood, then, the fewer layers that are built into a system, the greater the chance that a failure or breach of a single layer will be catastrophic to the system. Thinking back to the Swiss cheese metaphor for a second, imagine stacking various numbers of slices together. If one were to stack just two slices together, chances are probably pretty high that one or two of the holes in each of the slices might overlap so that there is a contiguous hole through the stack. But, if someone were to stack 10 slices of cheese together, then the probability that there would be a contiguous hole through the entire stack of slices is likely to be quite low. Thus, the more slices that are placed on top of each other, the less likely it would be that the holes in slices would all line up so that something, an ant for example, could find its way through the entire stack. Similarly, in a security system, the more layers of protection that exist, the less chance that the entire system would be compromised by an attack. Thus, failures by one layer of the system to thwart an attack that slips through a hole in that particular layer would likely be trapped or captured by some other layer of security built into the system, provided that sufficient effective layers of security exist.

Reason fashioned his Swiss cheese model largely as an explanation for accidents in complex systems, and Reason refers to the potential paths through his layers of metaphorical Swiss cheese as accident trajectories. Similarly, experts in the aviation security domain speak of threat trajectories when discussing terrorist tactics or methods of operation that have been attempted or may be used by terrorists or criminal elements actively seeking to commit intentional acts to attack or exploit aviation assets or disrupt air commerce. While Reason focused primarily on system vulnerabilities that could lead to accidental system failures, the underlying causes he identifies that give rise to system vulnerabilities, or what he calls *active failures* and *latent conditions*, have important implications for security as well.

In Reason's model, active failures are the more immediate lapses or failures of a system that can have near-term adverse effects. Active failures can be the result of either accidental causes, such as human errors, or intentional violations. Examples in the aviation security realm might include the accidental disruption of power at a screening checkpoint metal detector that goes unnoticed, or the intentional propping of an access door leading to secured area, an intentional violation of security rules to facilitate access for a parcel delivery. Intentional violations may also be the result of criminal or terrorist acts. That intentionally propped door might not have been the result of someone trying to facilitate access for a benign purpose, but might have been left in that state to allow criminals' access to commit theft. Similarly, an airport worker permitted to bypass checkpoint screening procedures might illegally carry a weapon into a secured area of an airport. That worker may do so because he or she may feel threatened by a coworker, or may do so to pass the weapon on to a terrorist intending to carry out an attack against an aircraft. Thus, various threats to aviation security may exploit the same vulnerabilities in the system. These threats can thus be described as sharing a common threat vector, although the motives behind these specific threats may be quite different. The motive behind the exploitation of a given security vulnerability thus plays into both the nature of the threat and the consequences of the event in defining the overall risk picture of a given scenario.

In Reason's model, these active failures predominantly occur at what he calls the "sharp end" of the system, in other words by front line personnel like security checkpoint screeners or airport ramp workers. Reason's model includes another class of vulnerabilities, which he refers to as latent conditions. Reason asserts that these latent conditions are the product of strategic and top-level policies and decisions made by governments, regulators, systems designers, and managers who set local policies and practices. These latent conditions often do not manifest themselves unless combined with more immediate factors and circumstances such as active failures by front-end operators. In the case of security threats, latent conditions that become known to attackers can be exploited to defeat a security system. In the case of aviation security, take for example the "common strategy" used across the airline industry for responding to hijackings prior to and on September 11, 2001. That strategy, predicated on past history of hijackings that largely ended peaceably through negotiation, was to acquiesce to hijacker demands while airborne in an effort to reach a peaceable negotiated resolution to the hijacking situation on the ground. The 9/11 hijackers were able to exploit this latent condition, presumably knowing that they would meet minimal resistance from the flight and cabin crew when they carried out their hijackings. Similarly, a policy of allowing short-bladed knives, like box cutters, through airport screening checkpoints and on aircraft allowed the 9/11 hijackers to either carry or have passed to them weapons to carry out their attacks on the flight crews of the commandeered aircraft. Latent conditions identified as being factors in the 9/11 terrorist attacks include

- Lack of an extensive list or database of terrorist names for vetting airline passengers
- Limited use of behavior-based passenger prescreening only to positive bag match procedures (i.e., assuring that the elevated risk passenger boarded the aircraft prior to placing his/her baggage on board) and not requiring that targeted passengers undergo additional or secondary screening at passenger checkpoints
- Lack of direct regulatory oversight of aviation screening companies
- High turnover and limited training of aviation security screeners
- Permitted items' list that included dual use items, such as box cutters, which could easily be used as lethal weapons
- A very limited number of air marshals or sky marshals (reported as being fewer than 40 at the time of the 9/11 attacks) and limited deployment of those marshals on flights
- The common strategy training and procedures used by flight and cabin crews for handling hijacking situations that emphasized passive nonresistance
- Inadequate procedures and training for interagency coordination of response and airspace control between the FAA and the military

In the previous chapter, the various elements of aviation security to protect from threats to commercial passenger aircraft were described in terms of the TSA's onion metaphor, with each successive layer of the onion representing a protection, whether passenger prescreening, physical screening measures, or in-flight protections. These elements can similarly be viewed in terms of Reason's Swiss cheese metaphor as shown in Figure 5.2. In this metaphor, each layer has inherent weaknesses or holes that could potentially be exploited by attackers. For example, passenger prescreening suffers from the fact that passenger name lists may be incomplete and may not include all terrorists or terrorist aliases. It may also suffer from an inability to accurately identify fraudulent or stolen identities in all cases, thereby potentially allowing a terrorist operative to elude this element of security. Also, physical screening may have holes or weaknesses stemming from technology limitations that

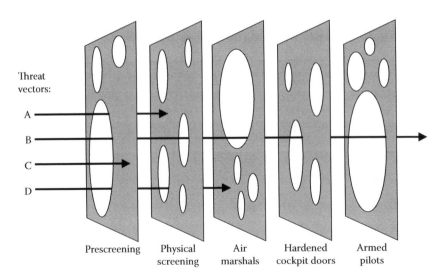

FIGURE 5.2 The Reason "Swiss cheese" model as a metaphor for the multilayered approach to passenger airline security.

do not allow for accurate screening of all threat types—such as nonmetallic weapons and certain types of explosives, including liquid explosives—carried by persons passing through screening checkpoints or in carry-on items. In-flight measures also have limitations that can be viewed as holes in these layers of defense. For example, air marshals cannot cover every flight leaving many flights without this layer of on-board protection. Also, while hardened cockpit doors are a deterrent, they are not impenetrable. In addition, the surrounding bulkhead is not reinforced, and on some aircraft, there are other means to access the cockpit. Like air marshals, armed pilots cannot be placed on all flights, leaving additional holes that could potentially be exploited. Based on these considerations, it is apparent that many holes exist, despite numerous initiatives to enhance these various security layers. But, what are the chances that all of these vulnerabilities could be successfully exploited in an attempted attack? To answer this question, basic probability theory can again be used to quantify the joint or combined probability of an outcome in which all of these layers are defeated in a single attack, assuming that the probabilities that the various layers of defenses could individually fail can be reasonably estimated. To illustrate, the following hypothetical values will be used to assess vulnerability of passenger airliners to a hijacking:

- The probability that prescreening against terrorist watch lists and for behavioral indicators of terrorist activity failing to detect an attacker is 50% (prescreening failure).
- The probability of an attacker getting needed weapons or explosives to carry out the hijacking plot past airport screening is 20%, and the probability that he could have a cohort airport or airline employee circumvent screening and pass these threat items to him undetected beyond the checkpoint is 30% (weapons and explosives).
- The chance of an air marshal team being on a targeted flight is 25% and the probability that that air marshal team could successfully stop an attack is 95% (air marshal failure).
- The probability that a hardened cockpit door fails to sufficiently delay an attack to prevent a successful hijacking is 20% (cockpit door failure).
- The probability of an armed pilot being on board the targeted fight is 10% while the probability that he or she could successfully stop an attack if on board is 90% (armed pilot failure).

Based on these estimates, the overall probability, P, or likelihood of a successful breach of all layers can be found by the following equation:

$$P = p(\text{prescreening failure}) \times p(\text{weapons and explosives}) \times p(\text{air marshal failure})$$
$$\times p(\text{cockpit door failure}) \times p(\text{armed pilot failure}),$$

$$P = (0.50) \times (0.20 + 0.30) \times (1 - (0.25 \times 0.95)) \times (0.20) \times (1 - (0.10 \times 0.90)),$$

$$P = 0.025$$

or roughly a 2.5% chance that an attempted attack would successfully breach all of these layers of protection.

This computed probability of breaching all the layers can be regarded as the overall system vulnerability to a passenger hijacking and could be used as the vulnerability value in assessing risk using the risk equation discussed earlier. Note that, based on the descriptions above, the overall probability of a breach of any given layer may be either additive or the product of the various factors considered for that particular security layer, depending on how the factors were framed or discussed. For example, regarding a checkpoint breach, a threat item could get beyond the checkpoint either because there was a failure to detect the object during screening *or* because screening was circumvented by a cohort such as an airport or airline employee. In this "either, or" case, the probabilities are additive. In the case of the air marshal protection and also in the case of armed pilots, the overall probability of these particular layers successfully thwarting an attack is dependent on the air marshal team or armed pilot being on board the aircraft *and* the air marshal team or armed pilot successfully defending the aircraft against an attack. In such a case, the two independent factors (being on board *and* successfully defending against an attack) comprise an overall joint probability that the given layer of protection will effectively thwart a terrorist attack on board and is found be calculating the product, or multiplying, the two probability values associated with these two factors. Because the overall equation seeks to calculate the probability that these various layers are successfully breached in an attack instead of the probability of successfully defending against an attack, in cases where the calculated probability of a successful defense is given, this value is subtracted from one (1) to determine the estimated probability that the given layer—either the air marshal protection or the use of armed pilots, for example—would be defeated. This calculation assumes that all of the layers and security measures are independent of each other, which turns out to be a reasonable assumption for consideration of most layered security applications including the security measures in place for protecting passenger airliners.

What is particularly notable about this illustration is that while the probability of breaching any single layer is seemingly quite high, the probability of successfully defeating all five layers is relatively low. In fact, so long as additional layers have some capability to prevent an attack and so long as they are not completely redundant or duplicative of other layers, then the more layers of security added will continue to increase the chances of a successfully stopping an attack and the odds of a successful attack will continue to decrease. The problem, of course, is that each layer of security adds incremental operational cost but has a diminishing marginal or incremental return on investment in terms of the additional threat reduction it will provide. Also, each incremental layer of security potentially imposes additional delays and hassles on air travelers and other users of the system. Therefore, a key policy objective is determining what combination of security layers or measures offers the most cost-effective and least disruptive approach to providing effective security to prevent terrorist attacks or other exploitations of aviation security systems by terrorists or criminals.

EVALUATING THE EFFECTIVENESS OF MITIGATION MEASURES AND SECURITY SYSTEMS

Using the tools described above to assess risk policymakers can make better informed decisions regarding the allocation of resources to mitigate risk to acceptable levels. However, understanding the elements of risk alone does not provide an adequate picture of whether and specifically how these risks can be dealt with. Upon examining aviation security risk using techniques such as those described above, questions remain regarding whether effective technologies and operational procedures are available to mitigate the identified risks based on policy and strategic priorities. Questions may also arise regarding whether available options are cost effective, and what combinations of available options would provide an optimal solution for mitigating identified security risks in the most effective and efficient manner, taking into consideration factors such as

- The effectiveness of available security measures in deterring terrorists and preventing attacks against aviation assets
- The availability of technologies and security measures to address policy objectives and strategic priorities
- Any inefficiencies in the flow of passengers and goods through the air transportation system resulting from implementation of specific security measures
- The cost of implementing security measures under consideration
- The potential benefit that can be obtained from an available option or alternative course of action

Assessments of the costs and benefits tied to specific security measures have previously been discussed in the context of the risk management framework. In the following discussion, methods for evaluating the effectiveness of security measures and their impact on aviation system efficiency will be considered. Systems engineering and operations research provides an array of tools and methods for addressing system performance and efficiency. The following discussion provides a broad overview of selected approaches for examining the performance of aviation security systems in terms of their effectiveness and efficiency, explaining how examining risk mitigation strategies from a systems perspective can benefit from careful engineering and economic analysis. The discussion focuses on a limited number of specific models and tools that are particularly well suited for explaining and examining strategies, technologies, and operational procedures for implementing an effective aviation security system. One particularly useful approach to examining and understanding the performance of aviation security from a systems perspective is signal detection theory (SDT), which is particularly useful for describing the ability of aviation security measures to detect threats in the context of an imperfect, uncertain environment where threats are often difficult to distinguish from nonthreats. Besides the ability to detect threats, aviation security systems are also evaluated on their efficiency because minimizing the impact of these security measures on the flow of goods and people through the air transportation system is often regarded as a competing objective with implementing effective security. Therefore, tools and approaches for evaluating the impact of security measures on aviation system efficiency will also be briefly considered.

APPLYING SDT TO EVALUATING THE PERFORMANCE OF AVIATION SECURITY SYSTEMS

In evaluating the performance of technological systems, the theory of signal detection is a particularly useful tool. SDT provides a specific analytic framework for evaluating situations in which a decision must be made between two alternatives in the face of uncertainty. Aviation security is well suited for signal detection analysis because it involves numerous decision points or nodes where a choice between two alternatives must be made in an uncertain environment. In signal detection parlance, the item to be detected is the "signal," and uncertainty regarding the presence of a signal arises because of "noise." This "noise" is not necessarily acoustic noise, although SDT is often applied to experiments involving human ability to detect sounds in a noisy environment. Rather the "noise" refers to both items in the environment, referred to as external noise, that might resemble the signal of interest as well as imprecision in the equipment or techniques being used or limitations in human performance that can be regarded as internal noise.

SDT concepts that will be introduced here are broadly applicable to various scenarios in security and law enforcement as well as more specifically in the assessment of aviation security practices. A listing of signal detection terms presented in a matrix of possible system states and decision outcomes in presented in Table 5.1. These concepts and terms will be more fully discussed below, but

TABLE 5.1

System States and Terminology Used in the Application of SDT to Aviation and Homeland Security Applications

System Response/Diagnosis	Reality/Actual State of World	
	Threat	Nonthreat
Signal "Threat"	Hit True positive Correct detection	False alarm False positive Type I error
Signal "Not a Threat"	Miss False negative Type II error	Correct rejection True negative

in general SDT applies when there are two possible states and two possible decision outcomes, producing a two-by-two matrix of possible system state-decision response combinations.

Security and law enforcement personnel evoke signal detection concepts frequently in carrying out their jobs without even realizing it, particularly in reference to using criminal and terrorist databases and threat detection technologies. Law enforcement personnel, for example, often speak of getting a "hit" when running a name through a criminal database, although in the field, LEOs and security screeners rarely differentiate a true "hit" from a "false positive." In the context of such databases, false positives, which occur when individuals are misidentified by a targeting system, have become a major concern for policymakers as well as privacy rights advocates because high levels of these false positives can snarl a system and may also cause undue hassle for individuals erroneously fingered by these systems.

Both "hits" and "false positives," which are sometimes also called "false alarms," are central elements of the SDT framework. Essentially, SDT is a mathematical model for examining a system's capability to accurately detect something. In the case of criminal or terrorist databases, the database systems are designed to detect criminals or terrorists. SDT is a means for evaluating how well those databases do their job of detecting these elements. In the context of security systems, and aviation security in particular, SDT's applicability is far reaching. Besides couching criminal and terrorist databases in a SDT framework, SDT can be used to analyze baggage screening systems, checkpoint screener human performance, automated airport perimeter monitoring systems, canine explosives detection teams, passenger prescreening systems and protocols, passenger behavioral observation methods, and so on. Further, application of SDT is scalable, so researchers can examine the detection performance of an entire system or the performance of individual components of that system within the SDT framework. For example, passenger screening checkpoints consist of various technologies including magnetometers, passenger bag x-ray machines, explosives detection portals, ETD machines, and other new technologies to detect weapons and explosives that are being developed and field tested. SDT can be used to describe the performance of the entire passenger checkpoint or any of these individual components. Most typically, however, systems engineers will apply SDT at the component level of analysis. At this level of analysis, parameters can be more tightly controlled under test conditions to determine and compare the performance of a given piece of equipment, either to other competing or alternate systems or to established benchmarks.

In the signal detection framework, systems or components are analyzed at the level of a binary decision—a choice between two alternatives. Aviation security systems are readily adaptable to such an analysis because they typically involve decisions of this kind. Any person purchasing an airline ticket either poses a potential threat or does not. Any bag passed through an x-ray scanner or an automated explosives detection machine contains either an explosive device or a threat object or it does not. Any notable, suspicious action taken by a passenger and observed by an air marshal either constitutes a valid threat to the flight or it does not. Each of these examples has two possible states, either there is a threat or there is not, and the security task involves a binary, or two-choice, decision—deciding whether a threat exists or not.

In classic SDT discussions, researchers speak of detecting signals among a cacophony of background noise. For example, an early application of SDT was the evaluation of naval sonar operators' ability to detect enemy ships on a sonar screen amid varying degrees of background noise or clutter on the sonar display. In applying signal detection to security applications, valid threats to security, such as the enemy ships on the sonar screens, are regarded as the signals that are to be detected, and everything else is considered noise. For example, in the case of checked baggage screening, explosives materials or explosives devices are the signals that are to be detected, and everything else—clothing, toiletries, food items, gifts, and other items placed in checked luggage—is considered noise. In this context, an EDS must thus make a binary choice—deciding whether a piece of baggage contains explosives materials or does not in the context of picking out a threat among distractors or noise that can potentially confuse the system.

To illustrate the application of signal detection concepts to aviation security, consider the task of detecting a firearm in carry-on baggage. At present, this task is performed by human screeners who interpret x-ray images of these carry-on items. The signal to be detected is the firearm as well other prohibited items. The uncertainty in performing this task is introduced by a variety of external and internal noise sources. In terms of the x-ray equipment, external noise largely comes from the clutter of the display from the variety of personal effects that people carry on airplanes. Electronic devices and nonthreat metallic objects can make the image particularly cluttered or noisy. Noise internal to the x-ray equipment used includes limitations in the ability to effectively penetrate certain materials and the limited capability to resolve or distinguish between subtle differences in the density of various materials. For the human screener, external noise would include distractions in the environment created by passengers, fellow screeners, acoustical noise and other distractions at the checkpoint, external pressure to keep wait times to a minimum, and so on. For the human screener, internal noise in the decision process could be caused by fatigue, emotional state, limitations of visual acuity, and so on.

Each component of the larger aviation security system makes thousands or tens of thousands of decisions of this kind every day. Given that there are two possible states of reality—the object in question is a threat or it is not—and a decision must be made whether a threat exists or not, then there are four possible outcomes or system states for any decision (see Table 5.1). If there really is a threat, and the system indicates a threat, then the system is said to have made a "hit," which is sometimes also referred to as a "true positive" or a "correct detection." If there is no threat and the system does not indicate a threat, then the system is said to have made a "correct rejection" or indicated a "true negative." In either case, the system made a correct diagnosis. Given that threats are rare events, the "true negative" case is the most common outcome. In fact, "true negatives" are typically so routine that they are rarely given very much thought at all. For checkpoint screeners working the x-ray scanner for carry-on items, clearing a bag diagnosed to not be a threat becomes the normal flow of operations. On the other hand, "hits" are big deals; they are rare but significant events. For example, detecting a weapon or banned item at a checkpoint requires intervention and possible law enforcement action. Similarly, getting a valid hit on the "no-fly" list when someone checks in for a flight is a relatively rare occurrence, but something that warrants immediate action to insure that the individual is denied boarding and proper law enforcement authorities are notified to intervene.

DETECTION CRITERIA AND SYSTEM ERRORS

System errors are a matter of particular interest in describing and analyzing aviation security systems. The consequences of not detecting an explosive device packed in a suitcase, an example of a "miss" or a "false negative," could be catastrophic. On the other hand, having too many "false alarms" or "false positives," where the system indicates a threat when no actual threat exists, could snarl and backlog the system and could create considerable nuisances and hassles for both screeners and system operators, as well as for passengers and other users of the aviation system. False positives are sometimes referred to as Type I errors, while false negatives are sometimes referred to as Type II errors. This designation stems from the application of inferential statistical nomenclature. Specifically, diagnoses made by a system, such as an EDS can be viewed as testing one of two hypotheses: A null hypothesis (denoted H_0) against an alternative hypothesis (denoted H_1). In the case of security systems, the statistical null hypothesis is that no threat is present, whereas the alternative or test hypothesis is that a threat is present. Type I errors occur when the null hypothesis, H_0, is falsely rejected. In the case of security systems, this occurs when the system signals a threat, but no threat is actually present. On the other hand, Type II errors occur when the null hypothesis, H_0, is not rejected, but is, in fact, false. In security systems, this occurs when the system fails to signal a valid threat.

While both types of errors have their inherent drawbacks, from an operational standpoint there is a tradeoff between these two kinds of errors. If the system has a very low threshold for signaling a threat, referred to in signal detection parlance as a "liberal" criterion, then the system will be capable of detecting most threats, but it will also generate more "false positives." If the criterion is set too liberally, the number of false positives may become an intolerable nuisance to both system operators, such as security screeners, and users of the system, primarily airline passengers. Everyone that has gone through a metal detector at an airport security checkpoint is probably familiar with this, at least on a conceptual level. If the criteria used by the metal detector are set too low, or too liberally, then it can be set off by belt buckles, coins, and other small metallic objects that are not threats. If, on the contrary, the system is more permissive in letting items by, that is, more "conservative" in its decision criteria for signaling that something is a threat, then such a system will generate fewer false positives but also fewer hits or correct detections. In other words, the system will have more misses or failures to detect a valid threat.

In an aviation security system, the potential consequences of a failure to detect a valid threat could be catastrophic, and therefore, setting the system to be too conservative in its decision criterion is not likely to be acceptable. For any given system, then, there are two ways to mitigate the possibility of failing to detect a valid threat—either by (1) setting a more liberal decision criterion for signaling a threat or by (2) building in additional layers of security so that other systems can serve to catch any threats that a given system might miss. Both of these techniques are used in aviation security systems to varying degrees. In the case of security checkpoints, secondary screening using hand-wand metal detectors and pat-down searches are applied on certain passengers as a redundant layer of security. In practice, these secondary screening methods are also used to resolve alarms during primary screening to differentiate a valid hit from a false positive. However, in this context, the reference is more specifically made to redundant secondary screening carried out based on either random or targeted selection of passengers to provide a second layer of screening to lower the probability that threat objects missed during primary screening will make it beyond screening checkpoints. Also, the criterion used on metal detector machines may be shifted to a more liberal decision criterion to change the security posture in light of intelligence information indicating an elevated threat level. These are examples of the two ways for mitigating potential failures to detect valid threats for existing, already deployed systems. There is a third way to reduce the potential for such errors and that is to deploy improved systems that have a greater capability to detect a threat.

SYSTEM SENSITIVITY

This capability of a given system to detect a threat is referred to in signal detection terminology as a system's sensitivity. Sensitivity is a measure of a system's performance, and SDT provides a specific means for mathematically determining the sensitivity of a given system. Conceptually, the sensitivity metric is arrived at first by plotting the number of "hits" on the y-axis against the number of "false positives" or "false alarms" on the x-axis thus generating a plot of hits as a function of false positives or false alarms. Recall that if the criterion of a given system for indicating that a threat exists is shifted, to be either more liberal or more conservative, then the number of hits and false positives will be altered. If the criterion becomes more conservative, then the system will generate fewer false positives, but it will also get fewer hits. Conversely, if the criterion becomes more liberal, then the system will generate more hits and more false positives as well. In between, the system will strike more of an even balance between the number of hits and the number of false positives it signals. By shifting the systems decision criteria, one could obtain multiple data points—pairs of hits and false alarms generated by the system—at different decision criteria levels. These data points could be plotted on the graph of hits as a function of false positives, generating a curve referred to as a Receiver Operating Characteristic (ROC) function (Figure 5.3).

An alternative way of generating such a curve without altering the decision criterion is to have the system or a human operator provide an indication of the degree of confidence in making the decision to indicate either a threat or a nonthreat. A similar technique is to have the system or

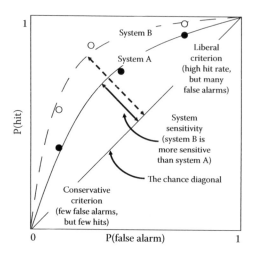

FIGURE 5.3 The ROC curve showing the concepts of system criterion and the comparison of system sensitivity among two alternative aviation security systems.

the system operator, such as a security screener, use a rating scale to indicate the perceived likelihood that a threat is believed to be present. For engineered systems, the method of shifting the system criterion can be more easily employed in tightly controlled laboratory settings to determine system sensitivity. For example, consider an ETD system that is designed to identify the presence of explosives based on chemical analysis of samples obtained by swabbing objects such as carry-on baggage. In the laboratory, a researcher could systematically shift the criterion, measured in parts per million (ppm) of an element found in high explosives, and test the system using a variety of samples including both high explosives (valid threats or signals), and other materials (nonthreats or noise). Based on this testing, an ROC curve could be generated. In comparing two competing systems, ROC curves could be generated for both systems under the same controlled experimental conditions.

For human operators, such as checkpoint screeners, however, rating systems are often a preferred means for generating ROC curves.[9] Consider a human performance evaluation testing the sensitivity of screeners viewing x-ray images of scanned carry-on items. Because it is difficult to manipulate or control a human operator's criterion used in making judgments, a researcher might instead ask the screeners participating in such an evaluation to rate their confidence or indicate the likelihood that sample bags contain threat items using a rating scale, say a one-to-five scale where one indicates only "slightly confident" or "highly unlikely" and five indicates "highly confident" or "highly probable." The proportion of hits and false alarms that were assigned each confidence rating can then comprise five separate data points, and a curve can be fitted through these five points.

Once the ROC curve is plotted, the sensitivity of the system can be assessed. Visually, system sensitivity is the difference between the ROC curve and what is referred to as the chance diagonal. The so-called chance diagonal is the line through the points where the proportion of hits and false alarms are equal, which would be the expected outcome if the system had no diagnostic capability whatsoever and was just guessing whether items were threats or nonthreats. Sensitivity, then, is essentially a measure of how much better the system does compared to just chance alone or simply making a random guess as to whether a threat exists or not. Mathematically, there are two common ways to compute sensitivity. The first, referred to as the d-prime or d' measure of sensitivity assumes that the underlying distributions of "signal" and "noise" follow a normal bell-shaped curve. When such an assumption can be made, the value d' measures the distance between the two distributions. In the case of security applications, it measures the average or mean difference between threats and nonthreats using some particular assessment measure or technique for quantifying the degree of threat, such as the amount of an element or compound found in explosives materials detected in a sample (Figure 5.4). Note that the value of d' is independent of the criterion selected for signaling that something is a threat or is not a threat, as the criterion for such a decision can be set anywhere within the range of possible threat scores or values depending on system capabilities and system objectives regarding the tradeoffs and costs associated with misses and false alarms. Values for d' can be computed using available computer statistics programs or look-up tables published in various texts,[10] and are equal to the difference between standardized values of hits and false alarms. Values of d' range from 0 to around 5–5.5, although in practice, most systems or measures considered in the aviation security context for which d' scores could be determined or estimated would likely have d' values that fall in the range between 0.50 and about 3.0.

While normal, or bell-shaped curve, distributions are convenient for describing the conceptual approach to SDT, they cannot be readily employed in all applications where SDT can be used to describe or evaluate aviation security measures and approaches. In many cases, the underlying distribution among nonthreats and threats is unknown or would likely violate assumptions of normality. That is, the distribution of values would not conform to a typical bell-shaped curve. In these cases, alternative systems can be compared by determining and comparing the area above the chance diagonal formed by connecting the available data points for a given system along with the (0,0) and (1,1) points. In some cases, however, only a signal data point of hits and false alarms generated by a given security system may be available. In these instances, an alternative metric for computing sensitivity called A-prime (A'), can be calculated using the following equation:

$$A' = 1 - \frac{1}{4}\left(p(\text{False positive})/p(\text{Hit}) + p(\text{Miss})/p(\text{Correct rejection})\right).$$

As seen from the equation, A' has an upper limit or maximum value of 1. Also, somewhat less obviously, A' has a lower limit of 0.5, which falls along the chance diagonal shown on the plot of the ROC curves in Figure 5.3. So, any detection system where a hit rate and a false alarm rate can be determined can be described by an A' sensitivity value ranging between 0.5, a value no better than simply guessing, and 1.0, a score only attainable if the system had 100% hits or correct detections of target items

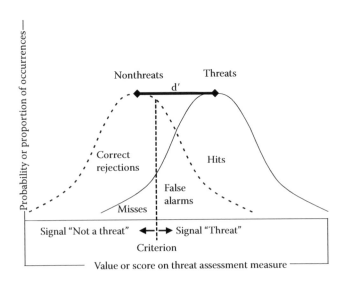

FIGURE 5.4 The hypothetical normal distribution of security threats compared to nonthreats along some quantifiable threat assessment metric, showing the relationship of a system's decision criterion to possible decision outcomes (hits, misses, correct rejections, and false alarms) and sensitivity as a measure of the system's ability to distinguish threats from nonthreats.

and no false alarms. In practice, perfect systems and perfect operating conditions rarely exist. While actual data on the sensitivity, hit rates, and false alarm rates for aviation security system are not publicly disclosed, depending on the application, A' values are likely to range between 0.70–0.95.

Intuitively, sensitivity values for automated screening systems are likely to be higher than sensitivity values for human-in-the-loop systems such as x-ray screening of carry-on bags, although this may not necessarily be the case in all circumstances. Certain other aviation security functions performed by human operators and observers, such as behavioral observation techniques to spot suspicious behavior, may be difficult to accurately gauge the sensitivity of, even in controlled simulations or studies, and are virtually impossible to quantify in real world settings. While it may not be possible to actually determine sensitivity values for security measures such as these, thinking about these approaches conceptually in terms of the signal detection framework may nonetheless be beneficial for framing policy debate over the tradeoffs between correct identifications and false alarms. For certain aviation security systems, particularly screening technologies, whether they are fully automated or require human-in-the-loop decision-making, SDT provides an essential tool for evaluating and comparing system performance.

For example, assume that a certain model of explosives detection equipment is found to signal a false alarm or false positive 20% of the time. The same machine is found to accurately detect sample explosives threats 95% of the time. Based on this, the probability of a correct rejection is one minus the probability of a false positive, which in this example is 80%, and the probability of a miss is one minus the probability of a hit, which is 5%. Thus, the value of A' in this example can be calculated as follows[11]:

$$A' = 1 - \frac{1}{4}\left(\frac{0.20}{0.95} + \frac{0.50}{0.80}\right),$$
$$A' = 0.932.$$

The value of A' by itself does not have a lot of meaning; however, it is extremely useful as a single metric for making comparisons among competing systems. Say, for example, another EDS is marketed boasting a "98% accuracy" in detecting explosives threats, meaning that it has a hit rate of 0.98. Compared to the 95% hit rate of the system considered previously, this seems like a considerable improvement. However, what this comparison has failed to include is a consideration of the false alarm rates between the systems. What if the false alarm rate for this system is 30%? If so, then the system sensitivity, measured by A', would be

$$A' = 1 - \frac{1}{4}\left(\frac{0.30}{0.99} + \frac{0.01}{0.70}\right),$$
$$A' = 0.921.$$

So, despite the improved accuracy or ability to detect valid explosives threats, this system is not more sensitive than the first because of its higher false alarm rate. From a policy standpoint, however, tradeoffs between hit rates and false alarm rates must be weighed, and in such evaluations, the concern over false alarms is often tied not so much to their overall number, frequency, or probability of occurrence. Rather, it is often more closely tied to their impact on air transportation system efficiency. In the following discussion, the impact of security measures in general along with impacts related to system-generated false alarms will be considered in the context of available measures for quantifying their impact on system efficiency.

ASSESSING THE IMPACT OF SECURITY MEASURES ON AIR TRANSPORTATION SYSTEM EFFICIENCY

Although the current discussion is primarily focused on measuring the performance of security systems in terms of the risk reduction or risk mitigation, it is widely recognized that many security measures have a broad spectrum of impacts, mostly on air transportation system efficiency, but also potentially on the convenience and privacy of passengers and shippers who rely on the air transportation system for travel and commerce. In the context of aviation security in the current post-9/11 climate, considerable attention has been given to the potential impact of additional security measures on the flow of goods and people throughout the air transportation system. A wide variety of operations research tools exist for examining the impact of aviation security measures on air transportation system efficiency.

The aviation security strategy seeks primarily to maximize effectiveness in terms of reducing risk to the air transportation system and second to optimize efficiency of the system. A variety of efficiency metrics exist including passenger wait times at checkpoints and baggage throughput through explosives detection screening processes. Staffing efficiency, typically measured in terms of required man-hours, is also a key metric as personnel compensation and benefits are a primary contributor to operating costs in aviation security systems that tend to be very labor intensive. So, if a new technology or screening technique provides equivalent levels of performance or effectiveness compared to current approaches but can improve efficiency and reduce workforce demand, such a system may provide a benefit that outweighs its additional cost. For example, more costly EDSs that have higher throughput rates may be cost advantageous because at these higher throughput levels, fewer machines may have to be purchased to meet the same level of demand for baggage screening. Similarly, improved system reliability can reduce maintenance down-time of individual systems, thereby reducing the number of backup systems that must be purchased and made available to continually meet baggage screening demand and 100% baggage screening requirements established by law. Finally, tieing this back to the earlier discussion on performance, improved system sensitivity can lead to fewer false alarms at an equivalent level of security with no reduction in hit rate or the ability to detect true positive threat items. Reduced false alarms may, in turn, allow for improved system throughput because fewer alarms would need to be resolved. Fewer false alarms could also allow for possible reductions in manpower requirements, because resolving alarms tends to involve human intervention and can often be labor intensive. This may also be true in the case of terrorism watch lists as additional, more robust details are provided on individuals within PNRs, allowing the vetting process to better distinguish between actual persons of interest that would generate hits and individuals with identical names or similar personal details that may generate false alarms. Reducing false alarms in the passenger prescreening process, where passengers are checked against terrorist watch lists, can reduce workforce requirements in terms of law enforcement response to investigate signaled threats as well as the processing to provide redress and remedy to adjudicate individuals falsely identified by such records check processes. Passenger prescreening will be considered in greater depth in the next chapter on exploiting intelligence and counterintelligence information, and passenger and baggage screening techniques and technologies will be examined in further detail in Chapter 7.

In other applications of the risk-based framework to aviation security measures, the impacts on air transportation system efficiency are highly complex and not easily defined, but are nonetheless important considerations. For example, in terms of reducing aircraft vulnerability to shoulder-fired missile attacks, the option of equipping commercial aircraft with electronic countermeasures based on military technology is under consideration. However, the operations and sustainment costs and logistics associated with deploying these systems in the context of commercial airline operations remain central issues for determining whether this approach can be cost effective. Similarly, the impact of airspace restrictions for GA aircraft on air traffic control procedures and functions is an important consideration in assessing the impact of these actions on flight operations and air traffic control efficiency, but it is extremely difficult to quantify and measure. Also, with regard to air cargo security, questions remain regarding how and where to apply screening and physical security measures along the supply chain in a manner that will minimize impacts to the flow of goods being transported by air while at the same time providing effective security to prevent the introduction of explosives or incendiary devices on to aircraft and prevent terrorist and criminal exploitation of the air cargo system. Each of these various topics will be discussed in detail in the context of the risk management framework in later chapters.

MITIGATING THE CONSEQUENCES OF AN ATTACK

Besides reducing or mitigating the degree of aviation security risk, largely by reducing vulnerability to an attack, policymakers and aviation security strategists are also examining ways to mitigate the consequences of a possible attack in order to minimize its potential impact and quickly reconstitute the aviation transportation system and its operating capabilities should an attack occur. Resilience is a multidimensional construct for assessing the ability of organizations and communities to mitigate hazards and contain the impacts of catastrophic events, such as disasters or terrorist attacks, that may occur in order to reconstitute activities, minimize disruption, and take actions to mitigate the impacts of possible future attacks or other catastrophic events. This has been described among disaster preparedness experts in terms of four factors, referred to as the R4 framework of resilience.[12] These factors include

- Robustness—the ability of the system to withstand attacks or other catastrophic forces without significant degradation or loss of performance
- Redundancy—the extent to which alternative systems or system components can substitute for affected facilities and infrastructure following an attack or other catastrophic event
- Resourcefulness—the ability to assess and prioritize needs and available solutions and mobilize required resources including monetary resources, equipment, facilities, information, technology, and personnel
- Rapidity—the capability to quickly restore system functions and minimize losses and service disruptions

These elements can be examined across four domains of analysis: (1) the technical domain, which refers primarily to the actual workings of the system; (2) the organizational domain, which refers to the entities and institutions that manage the system, such as airlines, airports, the FAA, and the TSA; (3) the social domain, which refers to impacted individuals, such as air travelers and airport workers, local communities, and geographic regions and their specific vulnerabilities; and (4) the economic domain, which can examine economic impacts at various levels of analysis from impacts on local communities to broader impacts on global markets. Collectively, these four domains of analysis, technical, organizational, social, and economic are referred to by the acronym TOSE.

Various measures of TOSE disruption can be used to evaluate or predict resilience. These measures can be plotted as a function of time in a time-series analysis, which can provide an assessment of how some variable changes over time. In this manner, variables of interest can be examined preevent and postevent using either actual data if an event occurs or forecast data based on simulations and other estimates to examine how particular scenarios may impact the aviation system or system components, organizational entities involved in air transportation, as well as indicators of social and economic impact. For example, using a scenario of an attack on a major air traffic control facility, researchers could examine technical impacts in terms of disruption to the ability to handle air traffic. In this example, organizational impacts may be examined in terms of impacts on FAA air traffic controller staffing and the FAA's ability to shift operations to alternative facilities. Broader social impacts could be examined in terms of how the resulting service disruption may effect people's use of air transportation, and finally, economic impacts could be examined in terms of direct costs associated with the attacks as well as any indirect costs tied to disruptions in air traffic operations. A general framework for examining aviation system resilience in the context of the 4R-TOSE framework is provided in Table 5.2.

For quantifiable measures, say for example passenger boardings or enplanements as they are referred to in the airline industry, resilience can be measured by examining the change in values of

TABLE 5.2

Examples of Elements in the R4-TOSE Framework for Conceptualizing and Evaluating Resilience of the Air Transportation System to a Terrorist Attack or other Catastrophic Event

R4 Component	Technical (T)	Organizational (O)	Social (S)	Economic (E)
Robustness	System performance	Staff performance	Impact of event on behavior of affected individuals and communities	Response of economic markets
Redundancy	Availability and use of alternative systems	Staffing flexibility and available staffing alternatives	Alternative transportation resources and options available to a community	Other components of the broader economy that can mitigate sector-specific or mode-specific impacts
Resourcefulness	System diagnostics, failure protection, and error tolerance capabilities	Management decision-making and its impacts on system performance	Ability of communities to adapt to alternative transportation arrangements and procedural changes	Market-based or regulatory protections to mitigate impacts on economic markets
Rapidity	Time course of reconstituting system operations	Time course of shifting organizational resources to adapt and respond to an event	Time course of changes in social/ behavioral indicators (e.g., passenger boardings)	Time course of change in economic indicators

this variable over time. Researchers refer to the initial immediate drop off in such a value immediately after a catastrophic event followed by a gradual recovery to preevent levels as the "resilience triangle."[13] This time course specifying the rapidity or pace of recovery to baseline levels that existed prior to the event provides a key indicator of resilience. Note, however, that while the air transportation system may be highly resilient to attack and able to reconstitute operations to preevent levels rather quickly, lasting psychological impacts may result in the time course of social and economic recovery to proceed at a much slower pace.

ADAPTIVE SYSTEMS APPROACHES TO AVIATION SECURITY

As alluded to in the earlier discussion on risk-based cost valuation, the risk picture is constantly shifting as perceived threats evolve and new threats are identified. The risk picture can also change as a function of new technologies and new approaches to address existing vulnerabilities and mitigate the consequences of potential terrorist attacks. As these measures are implemented, they not only alter the vulnerability of the aviation system to certain types of attacks, but may also alter the threat based on terrorists' perceptions of how effective these measures may be. For example, certain changes in security measures or security posture may cause terrorists to seek out softer targets, either within the aviation domain or perhaps in other transportation modes or other critical infrastructure sectors. Understanding and modeling these shifting risk dynamics using simulation and modeling tools is a critical function for making effective recommendations regarding aviation security policy and strategy in the broad context of homeland security and national defense.

An overarching strategic goal is to build an effective security network consisting of robust, resilient, and adaptable security systems that have a high degree of diagnostic capability and are cost effective. In this chapter, a variety of risk-based tools and practices have been considered for assessing how candidate systems and systems-of-systems that comprise the aviation security network will effectively function both by themselves and in coordination with other elements of aviation security. These tools include

- General risk models and risk-based evaluation tools for examining threats, vulnerabilities, and consequences
- Risk-based cost valuation tools for assessing the cost effectiveness of various security technologies and approaches using the risk framework
- Probabilistic models and simulations using techniques such as Monte Carlo methods and game theoretic approaches to assess complex risk dynamics
- Assessing how and to what degree multilayered approaches effectively reduce security vulnerability using probability-based models
- Applying the SDT framework to assess the nature of system errors, and system sensitivity and operational performance
- Using various metrics and operations research approaches to assessing aviation security system efficiency
- Relying on available models and techniques for conceptualizing and evaluating system resilience to assess the capability of the aviation domain and the aviation security network to rapidly reconstitute its systems and organizations and minimize the impact of an attack on society and the economy

By continuously applying these various tools and analytic approaches to study the evolving aviation security risk picture and available technologies and resources to protect against and mitigate calculated risks, aviation security strategists and policymakers can implement adaptive, multilayered, risk-based approaches to aviation security. In the upcoming chapters, these methods, models, and metaphors will be used to examine specific aviation security challenges in the age of global terrorism. These challenges include

- Exploiting intelligence information to effectively direct security resources and using available intelligence and counterterrorism data to adequately vet airline passengers and individuals with access to the air transportation system in a manner that does not unduly intrude upon the privacy and civil liberties of individuals
- Effectively utilizing the suite of available technologies and procedures for screening passengers and carry-on possessions and developing effective risk-based investment strategies for the research and development of future checkpoint screening technologies to protect against a broad array of existing and emerging threats
- Continually fostering improvements in the efficiency and effectiveness of passenger baggage screening technologies and procedures to detect explosives, incendiary devices, and other evolving threats
- Supporting and enhancing available in-flight security measures such as the FAMS, armed pilots, cabin crew training, hardened cockpit doors, and flight monitoring and surveillance technologies
- Developing effective risk-based airport security programs, utilizing advanced security technologies and procedures to implement effective physical security measures, surveillance, and robust access control systems to protect aircraft and sensitive areas of the airport and critical components of the aviation system
- Implementing effective strategies to minimize the terrorist threat posed by shoulder-fired missiles and other standoff weapons to civil aviation

- Developing and implementing robust risk-based strategies for securing the air cargo supply chain in a manner that balances security requirements with the efficient and expedient flow of goods through the air cargo system
- Applying effective and cost-efficient risk-based approaches to securing the broad array of GA operations in a manner that does not unduly impede or restrict access to airports and airspace or cause undue economic burdens to specific segments of the GA industry

It is important to bear in mind that all of these challenges remain ongoing, unresolved issues as evidenced by the continuing policy debates on these specific topics. They are difficult challenges that are critical to address in developing timely and effective policies and strategies for combatting the persistent and emerging threats to aviation we face in the age of global terrorism.

REFERENCES

1. See, for example, U.S. Department of Transportation, Federal Aviation Administration, *Introduction to Safety Management Systems (SMS) for Airport Operators*, Advisory Circular No. AC 150/5200-37, Washington, DC: February 28, 2007.
2. For a more complete discussion of probability theory consult a probability and statistics text such as Hays, William L., *Statistics*, Fourth Edition, Fort Worth, TX: Holt, Rinehart and Winston, Inc., 1988.
3. Dizzard, Wilson P. III, "TSA Rolls Dice on Risk Model," *Government Computer News*, June 4, 2007, p. 1.
4. Peterson, Robert M., Raymond H. Bittel, Christopher A. Forgie, William H. Lee, and John J. Nestor, "Using USCAP's Analytical Models, the Transportation Security Administration Balances the Impacts of Aviation Security Policies on Passengers and Airlines," *Interfaces, 37*(1), pp. 52–67, 2007.
5. Elisabeth Paté-Cornell, *On Signals, Response, and Risk Mitigation: A Probabilistic Approach to the Detection and Analysis of Precursors*. In James R. Phimister, Vicki M. Bier, and Howerd C. Kunreuther (Eds), *Accident Precursor Analysis and Management: Reducing Technological Risk Through Diligence*, Washington, DC: The National Academy of Engineering of the National Academies, The National Academies Press, 2004.
6. Ibid.
7. Albert, Réka, Hawoong Jeong, and Albert-László Barabási, "Error and Attack Tolerance of Complex Networks," *Nature, 406*, 378–382, July 27, 2000.
8. James T. Reason, *Managing the Risk of Organizational Accidents,* Burlington, VT: Ashgate, 1997.
9. Swets, John A., "Measuring the Accuracy of Diagnostic Systems," *Science, 240*, 1285–1293, June 3, 1988.
10. See, for example, Green, David. M. and J. A. Swets, *Signal Detection Theory and Psychophysics*, Los Altos, CA: Peninsula Press, 1988 (first published in 1966 by John Wiley & Sons, Inc., New York).
11. See, for example, Wickens, Christopher D., *Engineering Psychology and Human Performance*, Second Edition, New York: Harper Collins, 1992.
12. Tierney, Kathleen and Michel Bruneau, "Conceptualizing and Measuring Resilience," *TR News*, Number 250, May–June 2007, Washington DC: Transportation Research Board of the National Academies, pp. 14–17.
13. Ibid.

6 Exploiting Intelligence and Counterterrorism Information

The use or exploitation of intelligence information in the context of aviation security has two principal objectives. The first is to inform security personnel and others with a need to know regarding credible threat intelligence. This information can allow security managers to adapt security postures and implement procedures to respond to specific threats and alert frontline security personnel to the potential that certain types of threats or attacks may be imminent. The second use of intelligence and counterterrorism information in the context of aviation security is to assess the risk of individuals being granted access to the air transportation system, whether they be pilots, air traffic controllers, mechanics, airport workers, airline employees, or airline passengers. Vetting the identities of such individuals against available information on known and suspected terrorists, and in some cases against criminal records, provides an essential first layer of defense for identifying those individuals who should not be granted access to aircraft or other components of the air transportation system. It also may serve as a means for identifying those individuals who present an unknown or elevated security risk and therefore should receive additional scrutiny, either through more detailed investigation or through more thorough physical screening procedures before being granted access to portions of the air transportation system.

This chapter examines how intelligence and counterterrorism information gathered from a broad array of intelligence, law enforcement, and homeland security sources can be analyzed, synthesized, integrated, and disseminated to improve aviation security with a particular emphasis on the tracking of terrorist travel and the use of government terrorist watch lists to prescreen airline passengers and others accessing aircraft and secured areas of the air transportation system. While this chapter briefly discusses the intelligence process, it is primarily concerned with conveying a general understanding of how fused, or synthesized, intelligence information is disseminated and how this information may be best exploited to improve aviation security.

AN OVERVIEW OF INTELLIGENCE GATHERING AND ANALYSIS

Figure 6.1 provides an overview of how intelligence information is collected, analyzed, disseminated, and exploited in the context of aviation security. The intelligence community deals with a broad array of information regarding potential terrorist threats in various forms that can typically be categorized into one of three primary source categories: signal intelligence (SIGINT), imagery intelligence (IMINT), and human intelligence (HUMINT). Other forms of intelligence information may be categorized as measurement and signature intelligence (MASINT) or open source intelligence (OSINT). While OSINT plays an important role in the context of counterterrorism and homeland security intelligence, MASINT plays a more limited role in information gathering regarding terrorist operatives and nonstate groups. Collectively, these various delineations of intelligence based upon its source characteristics define the various intelligence gathering disciplines.

In the context of counterterrorism intelligence gathering, SIGINT refers primarily to the interception of communications signals such as telephone conversations, e-mails, text messages, and so

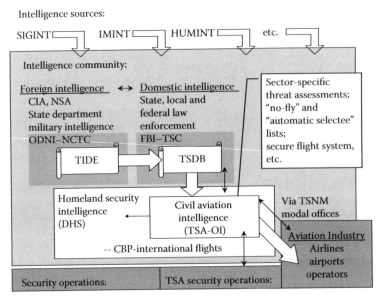

FIGURE 6.1 An overview of intelligence information gathering, the intelligence community, and their relationship to aviation security operations. SIGINT, signal intelligence; IMGINT, imagery intelligence; HUMINT, human intelligence; ODNI, Office of the Director of National Intelligence; NCTC, National Counterterrorism Center; FBI, Federal Bureau of Investigation; TSC, Terrorist Screening Center; TIDE, Terrorist Identities Datamart Environment; TSDB, Terrorist Screening Database; TSA-OI, TSA Office of Intelligence; TSNM, Transportation Sector Network Management; CBP, Customs and Border Protection.

forth, transmitted over communications channels, including telecommunications networks. Since this intelligence gathering primarily deals with communications, it may sometimes be referred to as COMINT for communications intelligence, a subset of the broader SIGINT category that also includes various forms of electronic intelligence (ELINT). In addition to SIGINT, the intelligence community gathers IMGINT from various aerial platforms, including manned and unmanned reconnaissance aircraft, and satellites. In reference to intelligence collected on terrorist groups, IMGINT may consist of aerial or satellite tracking of activity at suspected terrorist training sites or operations bases in places like Afghanistan.

Although IMGINT, and more especially SIGINT, can provide valuable information regarding terrorist operatives, their movements, and possible terrorist plots, most intelligence experts believe that a richer source of information can be gained through interpersonal interaction or HUMINT gathering. HUMINT can be gathered from various sources, such as foreign government and business contacts, using a variety of techniques. Although, in the context of dealing with nonstate groups such as terrorist organizations, meaningful HUMINT may only be achievable by using clandestine means to infiltrate these groups. Clandestine HUMINT may be able to provide information about group membership, group structure, group leadership, and group plans and aspirations to carry out acts of terrorism, including possible plots to carry out attacks against aviation targets.

In addition to clandestine intelligence operations, the intelligence discipline of collecting and analyzing OSINT has a specific importance in the context of counterterrorism intelligence, particularly in the current age of ubiquitous Internet communications. It is known that terrorist groups have used the Internet extensively to disseminate propaganda, recruit new members, exchange information regarding ideologies, conduct fundraising, and to make threats and issue warnings.[1] Such information may provide important clues regarding ongoing plots or terrorist attacks in the planning stages.

Additionally, terrorist groups may use online chat rooms or other social networking resources to discuss ideologies with potential recruits, concoct and coordinate terrorist plots, and exchange information on how to plan and carry out attacks. The Internet likely functions as a key training resource for terrorist groups who may be able to gain information online about bomb making, information on chemical and biological weapons (e.g., how to make deadly ricin toxin extract from castor beans that could be released on board an aircraft), or how to launch a shoulder-fired missile. Therefore, besides providing OSINT, the Internet may provide important SIGINT traces that can potentially be followed to try to identify terrorist networks. For example, by looking at Internet traffic to sites that provide specific information on constructing IEDs or carrying out attacks using deadly chemical or biological agents, as well as chat room and social networking exchanges about such topics, intelligence analysts may be able to trace terrorist networks and identify suspect individuals. However, because computer savvy terrorists may be able to effectively cloak their locations and identities while using the Internet, sophisticated electronic tracing and forensic techniques may be needed to uncover the identities and location of suspected terrorists who communicate and disseminate information over the World Wide Web.

Once intelligence information in its various forms is gathered, it is integrated and analyzed by the intelligence community. At the federal level, intelligence obtained from foreign sources, pertaining to foreign nations and overseas groups has historically fallen primarily under the purview of the CIA as well as the Department of State's Bureau of Intelligence and Research (INR). Other key intelligence agencies involved in the collection and analysis of foreign intelligence include the National Security Agency (NSA), and other military intelligence components of the DOD. Domestic intelligence and counterterrorism related to threats and terrorist organizations that operate solely within the United States, on the other hand, fall under the jurisdiction of various law enforcement agencies and are coordinated at the federal level by the FBI. Since the 9/11 attacks, however, there has been a specific policy emphasis on facilitating greater interaction and coordination among the intelligence community and law enforcement leading to the creation of the NCTC within the ODNI. The NCTC is now the central federal entity responsible for coordinating national and international counterterrorism intelligence.

INTELLIGENCE REFORMS IN RESPONSE TO THE GLOBAL TERROR THREAT

The global war on terrorism and the multinational reach of global terror networks like al Qaeda have raised unique policy questions regarding the distinction between international and domestic intelligence. In response, statutory and administrative changes have been made to adapt and modify the legal and administrative distinctions and barriers that have historically existed between the international intelligence community and domestic intelligence and counterterrorism functions carried out by federal, state, and local law enforcement. Reshaping the federal intelligence community and federal counterterrorism law enforcement functions was a central focus of recommendations made by the 9/11 Commission and a central policy issue behind the passage of the IRTPA of 2004 (P.L. 108-458). As the federal government has endeavored to move forward in implementing these changes, improving information sharing and coordination among the various federal, state, and local entities involved in intelligence and counterterrorism functions remains a central policy issue for addressing the global terror threat.

Establishing a clear bridge between intelligence functions and aviation security operations, the 9/11 Commission concluded that disrupting terrorist travel was as powerful a weapon as targeting their financing.[2] The 9/11 Commission, however, concluded that, prior to the 9/11 attacks, the intelligence community did not view the use of terrorist watch lists as an integral part of intelligence work.[3] To prevent future terrorist attacks, the 9/11 Commission recommended that the United States significantly expand its intelligence work related to terrorist travel and integrate this work with threat countermeasures, such as aviation security initiatives, to prevent future attacks.

In close parallel with the recommendations for reforming the intelligence community made by the 9/11 Commission, President Bush had issued Homeland Security Presidential Directive 6 (HSPD-6) in September 2003. The directive established the multiagency Terrorist Threat Integration

Center (TTIC) to consolidate terrorist screening functions that were previously performed across various agencies. In 2004, the TTIC was renamed the NCTC under reforms included in the IRTPA of 2004 (P.L. 108-458), and it was placed under the direct control of the newly created ODNI.

Under the Act, the ODNI was established to oversee and coordinate the activities of the entire U.S. intelligence community, encompassing both foreign and domestic intelligence. As defined in the Act, it oversees and coordinates the work of: the CIA; the NSA; the Defense Intelligence Agency (DIA); the National Geospatial-Intelligence Agency (GIA); the National Reconnaissance Office (NRO); other DOD offices that specialize in national intelligence through reconnaissance programs; the intelligence components of the Army, Navy, Air Force, and Marine Corps, the FBI, the Department of Energy, and the Coast Guard; the INR at the Department of State; the Office of Intelligence and Analysis (OI&A) at the Department of the Treasury; and the DHS OI&A, which coordinates homeland security entities concerned with the analysis of foreign intelligence information.

As a key component of the ODNI, the NCTC is charged with maintaining the Terrorist Identities Datamart Environment (TIDE), a single repository for all international terrorist-related data maintained by the U.S. government, replacing the TIPOFF database previously maintained by the State Department. Under the provisions of the IRTPA, the primary functions of the NCTC consist of

- Analyzing and integrating all U.S. intelligence pertaining to terrorism, except that relating to purely domestic terrorist groups
- Strategic planning for counterterrorism activities across agencies
- Assigning roles and responsibilities among federal agencies for counterterrorism activities
- Providing access to intelligence information and intelligence-related support to agencies conducting assigned counterterrorism missions
- Serving as the shared central knowledge bank regarding known and suspected terrorists and terrorist organizations and their goals, strategies, capabilities, and social networks

The TIDE provides a centralized repository of intelligence information for carrying out these various elements of its mission to coordinate counterterrorism intelligence.

HSPD-6 also created the Terrorist Screening Center (TSC), a component of the FBI, charged with maintaining the consolidated terrorist watch list, known as the TSDB. The NCTC shares international terrorist data stored in TIDE with the TSC, which are culled and included in the TSDB as deemed appropriate. In addition to maintaining the TSDB, the TSC is also responsible for disseminating information about known and suspected terrorists to federal agencies and state and local law enforcement as appropriate, handling and coordinating suspected encounters with known and suspected terrorists and their supporters who are reported by various homeland security and law enforcement agencies, and for providing around-the-clock support for homeland security and law enforcement agencies accessing TSDB records. In the aviation mode, the TSC supports the terrorist screening activities of the TSA and CBP, as well as the Department of State's Bureau of Consular Affairs, which provides visa issuances to foreign air travelers.

At the state and local law enforcement levels, state-run information and intelligence fusion centers perform the role of collecting, analyzing, synthesizing, and, as appropriate, disseminating information gathered regarding possible terrorist operatives and their activities in various jurisdictions. Fusion centers have been established in all 50 states and the District of Columbia, as well as in several U.S. territories, following the 9/11 attacks in response to state-led initiatives to improve intelligence information sharing paralleling federal initiatives to improve coordination among intelligence agencies, federal law enforcement agencies, and DHS components.

Information from these state-run fusion centers is shared with federal agencies, which is coordinated at the federal level by the FBI. Suspected terrorists or other individuals believed to pose a threat to homeland security operating within the United States that may come to the attention of law enforcement agencies, and these state-run fusion centers that are brought to the attention of the FBI may be nominated for inclusion in the consolidated TSDB. In addition, federal law enforcement, homeland security, and intelligence agencies may nominate individuals who come to their attention for inclusion in the TSDB. The TSDB consolidates domestic and international terrorist records into a single database that is accessible to federal agencies, state and local law enforcement, and certain foreign governments that have entered into terrorism information-sharing agreements with the United States.[4]

As of September 2008, the TSDB contained data on about 400,000 individuals, of which about 3% referenced U.S. persons (citizens and legal permanent residents).[5] Due to aliases and name variants, however, the TSDB includes over one million records on these individuals.[6] The TSA is one of many users of the TSDB records, which are used to generate the "no-fly" list of individuals who are to be denied aircraft boarding, and the "automatic selectee" list of individuals who are required to undergo additional security screening prior to boarding a commercial passenger aircraft. While the TSA has historically disseminated these lists to the airlines to check PNRs against these lists, the TSA is moving forward with implementing a system called Secure Flight, which will require airlines to submit PNR data to the TSA so that airline traveler data may be compared against terrorist watch list data in checks run by the federal government. Passenger prescreening based on terrorist watch list information and the Secure Flight implementation is discussed in further detail later in this chapter.

TSA'S ROLE IN TRANSPORTATION SECURITY INTELLIGENCE

The TSA's role in transportation security intelligence is, however, much broader than just comparing passenger data to names contained in terrorist watch lists. Although the TSA is not a primary intelligence gathering or analysis agency, through its OI (TSA-OI), it works closely with the intelligence community to further analyze and disseminate, as appropriate, intelligence information related to threats and vulnerabilities to aviation and other transportation modes. ATSA (P.L. 107-71) specifically mandated that the TSA receive, assess, and distribute transportation security-related intelligence information, and assess threats to transportation systems. The Act established the TSA as the primary liaison between intelligence and law enforcement communities with respect to coordinating federal, state, and local response to threats against transportation systems, including threats to aviation security. To execute these functions the TSA established the TSA-OI.

The TSA-OI's objectives are to provide intelligence support to aviation security operations and other field level components of the TSA so that appropriate actions can be taken to protect the transportation sector from credible threats. In the aviation mode, actionable intelligence—meaning analyzed intelligence information indicating a credible threat for which specific actions can be taken to defend against—may be disseminated to FSDs overseeing airport security, and security officials for airports and airlines. This information may also be packaged and disseminated to provide information to frontline security personnel, such as federal air marshals, TSA screeners, armed pilots participating in the FFDO program, and security personnel employed by airports, airlines, and other aviation operators as deemed appropriate.

In addition to the primary role of the TSA-OI in analyzing and disseminating intelligence information relevant to aviation security, CBP maintains a vital role in assessing potential threats posed by passengers on international flights with a specific focus on its primary mission objective: to prevent terrorists and terrorist weapons from entering the United States. Across the various DHS components, including the TSA and CBP, the dissemination and exploitation of intelligence information gathered from various sources is coordinated through the DHS OI&A.

While other DHS agencies play an important role in assessing intelligence information about terrorist threats, the TSA-OI is the primary DHS entity focused on intelligence directly related to transportation security. As such, it coordinates closely with components of the intelligence community; other DHS entities; other federal agencies, including the DOT and the FAA; state and local law enforcement; airport operators; the airlines; and various other transportation industry partners. Functionally, the TSA-OI is divided into two distinct components: the Intelligence Watch and Outreach (IW&O) Division and the Transportation Intelligence Analysis (TIA) Division (formerly known as the Current Intelligence and Assessments Division or CI&A).

The IW&O Division performs continuous (24/7) monitoring of transportation security intelligence to support security operations, such as passenger screening and FAMS operations, and to provide crisis management and critical incident response assistance as needed. To accomplish these objectives, the TSA has deployed full-time liaison officers at various intelligence community and law enforcement centers including the DHS OI and Analysis, the NCTC, the CBP's National Targeting Center (NTC), the NSA, the Drug Enforcement Agency's El Paso Intelligence Center (EPIC) Air Watch, and the TSC.[7] The TSA intelligence officers detailed to these centers apply their expertise regarding the transportation sector to analyze and assess the stream of intelligence information to identify credible threats to transportation, including potential terrorist threats to aviation.

The IW&O Division also plays an important role at the TSA's Transportation Security Operations Center (TSOC), which monitors security situations across the entire transportation network on a continuous (24/7) basis. In addition to providing intelligence support to unfolding incidents, the IW&O presence at the TSOC disseminates warnings and notifications of credible and imminent threats to the transportation sector through appropriate channels to other components of the TSA and to federal, state and local law enforcement, and aviation industry entities.

While the IW&O Division deals with the continual flow of intelligence data and provides short-term intelligence support for unfolding situations, the TSA-OI's TIA Division provides long-term strategic planning based on intelligence assessments and disseminates a wide variety of intelligence products for transportation sector security personnel. These products include the Transportation Intelligence Gazette (TIG); the Weekly Field Intelligence Summary (WFIS); Suspicious Incident Reports (SIRs); specialized analytic assessments on terrorist groups, weapons, tactics, and trends; modal threat assessments; and other special reports and intelligence products to support the TSA and the intelligence and law enforcement communities.[8]

Within the TSA, the TIA Division provides intelligence support to the TSA's Transportation Sector Network Management (TSNM) modal offices, which serve as the primary liaisons to private industry components, such as airports, airlines, and other aircraft operators. The CI&A Division also supports TSA security operations, which oversee passenger and baggage screening operations and other operational aspects of airport and air cargo security, and the FAMS. The unit also conducts vulnerability assessments of the transportation sector, including the so-called red team testing of passenger and baggage screening, airport access controls, and other aviation security measures.

While the primary function of the TSA-OI is to analyze and disseminate intelligence information to support aviation security functions, various intelligence gathering efforts in the aviation environment can help in tracking the movements of suspected terrorists and analyzing patterns of security breaches and other anomalies that could indicate specific threats or vulnerabilities. For this reason, there has been a particular policy interest in exploiting information available in the aviation environment to track terrorist travel. There has also been a specific interest in synthesizing and exploiting data from diverse security, law enforcement, and intelligence sources working in the aviation domain to construct and analyze a robust stream of security sensor and intelligence data that may be utilized to identify specific patterns indicative of possible threats and vulnerabilities that may be otherwise overlooked.

TRACKING TERRORIST TRAVEL IN THE AVIATION MODE

Almost two million passengers travel on domestic and international flights during the course of a typical day. Detecting and tracking terrorist travel amid this high volume of air passenger traffic has become an issue of considerable interest since the 9/11 attacks, alongside other high-priority objectives, such as tracking international terrorist financing and monitoring the communications of suspected terrorist operatives. In addition to controversial electronic surveillance initiatives by intelligence agencies, intelligence analysis of airline passenger travel patterns could reveal connections among known and suspected terrorists and others who may otherwise remain unknown to the intelligence and law enforcement communities. However, the use of passenger lists, travel itineraries, and other information contained in PNRs, created by the airlines whenever flight reservations are made, for such purposes is also considered highly controversial. Privacy advocates have consistently cautioned policymakers and the public over the potential dangers of government-led data mining of travel records for such purposes, fearing that government-maintained databases and data mining techniques present a potential infringement upon privacy rights, that travel records and the analysis of such records could be used for purposes other than counterterrorism, that data security breaches could potentially compromise private information contained in these records, and that innocent individuals could potentially be falsely targeted by systems designed to identify suspicious patterns in airline passenger records.

In addition to the TSA, CBP and ICE play a central role in vetting and tracking about 250,000 international passengers who arrive on international flights every day. Passenger prescreening systems, such as the CBP's APIS and its Automated Targeting System (ATS), as well as the much discussed TSA's Secure Flight system, which are all described in further detail below, could be utilized to detect and search for possible trends in terrorist travel. Individual travel patterns available through records maintained by these systems could be further analyzed to possibly establish links among terrorist operatives and potentially uncover terrorist networks and cells.

For example, close examination of travel itineraries could reveal patterns among individuals with suspected ties to terrorism. While not enough intelligence or counterterrorism data may exist to establishing reasonable cause for preventing these individuals from boarding passenger airplanes, they could be required to undergo more thorough secondary screening at airport checkpoints. The travel records of such individuals could be compared to other suspected terrorists, as well as other travelers to attempt to identify possible interpersonal connections between suspected terrorists and between suspected terrorists and other individuals who may not be known to the law enforcement and intelligence communities as being possible threats.

Upon analyzing personal travel data, patterns may emerge. For example, a suspected member of a terrorist cell in New York may travel to Seattle via Chicago. The same day, a suspected member of a terrorist cell in Los Angeles may travel to Indianapolis via Chicago. They may meet and exchange information during their stopovers in Chicago. Amidst the myriad of data collected on passengers flying on any given day, it would be almost impossible to make any connection between these two individuals. If however, the same two individuals have common travel connections months later, a pattern may emerge. Say, for example, the same suspected New York terrorist cell member travels to Tampa via Atlanta two months later, and the suspected Los Angeles terrorist cell member has a return trip from Atlanta to Los Angeles on the same day, having flown to Atlanta two days prior. These two instances of these individuals crossing paths at different airports on different days may provide an indication that the two suspects are linked. Travel records provided for passenger prescreening would indicate that these two suspected terrorists had overlapping travel plans on two separate occasions. This intelligence may allow analysts to infer a possible link between these two individuals, particularly if other intelligence collected on these individuals would support such a conclusion. Additional intelligence information could be added to these bits of information to increase the understanding of the terrorist network and demonstrate how these two hypothetical terrorist cells, one in New York and one in Los Angeles, may be collaborating.

While terrorist watch lists and other intelligence data may be utilized in combination with airline passenger data and PNR records to track the movements of suspected terrorist operatives through the air transportation system, the potential that passenger prescreening system could be applied for such purposes has raised considerable concerns among privacy advocates. A number of legal questions remain regarding the use of such travel data to detect suspicious patterns without specific legal grounds for monitoring or surveillance of records detailing the movement of individuals, particularly when those individuals are U.S. citizens or permanent residents. Although the mining of travel records provides a potentially promising yet controversial opportunity for intelligence and counterterrorism agencies, from the standpoint of aviation security, the use of watch lists has instead focused primarily on how such systems can be implemented to prevent individuals posing a clear security risk to air transportation from boarding aircraft or being granted access to secured areas of airports, and from being granted access into the United States aboard inbound international flights.

AIRLINE PASSENGER PRESCREENING AND TERRORIST WATCH LISTS

Watch lists have also been used as a means to focus limited aviation security resources by targeting additional screening measures on those individuals who have been identified through prescreening as posing an elevated risk to aviation security. This is accomplished through the use of an "automatic selectee" list containing the names of those individuals who are required to undergo secondary screening.

The use of the "automatic selectee" list has been viewed as one of several tools allowing the TSA to focus the additional security resources needed to conduct more detailed secondary screening on those passengers believed to pose a greater security risk. To meet these objectives, the DHS has developed various systems to check the names and identifying information of passengers, airline crews, airport workers, and others seeking access to areas of the air transportation system against the TSDB, the federal government's consolidated repository of records on known and suspected terrorists worldwide. The following discussion examines the U.S. policies and strategies for implementing terrorist watch list prescreening of airline passengers in depth. An examination of the use of terrorist watch list screening, along with the use of criminal history background checks, to screen airport workers and airline crews is provided in Chapter 9 in the context of commercial airport access control systems and perimeter security.

One specific means for exploiting intelligence information to improve aviation security, and a central focus of policy debate regarding the use of intelligence in the context of aviation security, is the utilization of terrorist watch lists to prescreen passengers to assess whether those seeking transportation on commercial passenger aircraft may pose a threat or represent an elevated risk to aviation security because of their known or suspected involvement with or ties to terrorist groups. Considerable controversy continues to surround U.S. policies regarding air passenger prescreening and terrorist watch list checks and the implementation of those policies. These controversies have centered on concern over privacy, data security, the potential misuses of traveler personal information, and the potential impacts of false positive matches on passengers who are wrongly delayed or denied boarding or subjected to additional screening because of misidentifications.

Efforts to expand and improve passenger prescreening since the 9/11 attacks have been significantly impacted by continuing concerns over the adequacy of measures to protect flyers' personal information and not infringe upon their civil rights. Critics of passenger prescreening approaches have argued that the TSA's ever-expanding vision for prescreening was to include data mining of commercial and government databases to look for indicators that someone may pose a threat, and searches of notoriously inaccurate criminal databases. These concerns were spurred by vague statements issued by the TSA as to how it might authenticate passenger identity and check for possible links to terrorism along with media reports linking passenger prescreening to controversial proposals, such as the DOD's Total Information Awareness (TIA) program to detect terrorists by mining personal data. This controversy ultimately led the TSA to scrap its originally proposed enhanced passenger prescreening system, CAPPS II, in August 2004, and pursue enhanced prescreening capabilities under a new system called Secure Flight.

While Secure Flight has been touted to be a significantly scaled down approach to prescreening compared to the CAPPS II development, concerns over data security and redress procedures for passengers falsely identified by the system have also delayed its development and deployment. Through appropriations legislation enacted over the past several years, Congress has prohibited the TSA from fully deploying the Secure Flight program until these ongoing concerns were adequately addressed. The legislation also prohibited the TSA from using commercial data, such as credit records or credit scores, or the transfer of passenger data to a nonfederal entity. While commercial databases have the potential to provide a rich set of personal information to help authenticate the identity of passengers and minimize the number of false alarms or individuals erroneously targeted by the system, concerns have been raised about the TSA's past handling of passenger data in a manner that was not fully explained to the public. These concerns lead to specific restrictions on the transfer of personal data between the government and private entities other than the initial exchange of selected information from PNRs obtained from the airlines.

Privacy advocates have also raised considerable concerns over the ATS, a data mining program for assessing the risk of all international travelers, as well as freight carried on international flights. Public disclosure regarding the scope of this program and associated data collection and data retention policies, in November 2006, renewed debate over whether certain passenger information collection and analysis practices unduly infringe upon privacy rights, or whether they are necessary actions to assess terrorism risks to aviation.

While recognizing these concerns over flyer's privacy rights, expansion of the federal government's efforts and role in effectively utilizing terrorist watch lists and passenger prescreening tools to strengthen aviation security has been widely supported by policymakers and aviation security experts in response to the 9/11 terrorist attacks. The 9/11 Commission recommended that air passengers be more comprehensively screened against available U.S. government terrorist watch lists, and that U.S. border security systems be expanded and integrated with other homeland security systems to expand the network of screening points to include the nation's transportation systems, including the air transportation system, and access to critical infrastructure facilities.[9] While interest in passenger prescreening and the use of terrorist watch lists has been a central focus of post-9/11 U.S. aviation security policy, various passenger prescreening initiatives had been put in place prior to the 9/11 attacks as tools to detect possible aircraft bombings.

PRE-9/11 PASSENGER PRESCREENING INITIATIVES

Limited capabilities to prescreen airline passengers existed prior to the 9/11 attacks. These capabilities consisted of a government generated "no-fly" list and the Computer-Assisted Passenger Screening (CAPS) system which applied various rule-based algorithms to ticket purchasing characteristics to assess passenger risk. While these two prescreening tools were available prior to the 9/11 attacks, they were quite limited in their scope and capability. For example, on September 11, 2001, the "no-fly" list contained only 12 names, even though other government terrorist watch lists contained tens of thousands of names.[10] Since then, considerable resources have been devoted to expanding and improving upon systems and protocols for screening passengers against terrorist watch lists.

COMPUTER-ASSISTED PASSENGER PRESCREENING SYSTEM

The use of terrorist watch lists for prescreening airline passengers was extremely limited prior to the 9/11 attacks, in part because of concerns raised by the intelligence and law enforcement communities over disseminating this data to the airlines. As a result, the FAA had instead focused on developing a risk-based assessment tool to prescreen passengers based on airline ticket purchasing and flight reservation information. In the mid-1990s, the CAPS system evolved out of recommendations stemming from reviews of aviation security following the bombing of Pan Am flight 103 in December 1988 and the explosion of TWA flight 800 in July 1996. Prior to the 9/11 attacks, the primary intent of the system was to assess passenger risk and implement PPBM or explosives detection screening of baggage checked by those passengers designated by the CAPS system as posing an elevated risk.

The 1996 FAA Act (P.L. 104-264) authorized the development of the CAPS system as a means to profile passengers using tools developed cooperatively by the FAA and the airlines, with the assistance of the intelligence and law enforcement communities. In parallel with the legislative debate over the 1996 FAA Reauthorization Act, the FAA and airline partners had already initiated the development of the CAPS system, and the FAA's interest in pursuing an automated passenger profiling system for commercial aviation was reflected in the recommendations of the Gore Commission on aviation safety and security.[11] The FAA and Northwest Airlines developed and conducted initial tests of the CAPS system in 1996 and 1997. Field testing continued through 1998, and in 1999, the FAA required all major U.S. air carriers to implement CAPS on their computerized reservation systems.

The operational concept behind CAPS centers on the identification and selection of high-risk airline passengers based on certain characteristics identifiable through analysis of data elements contained in PNR records. The CAPS systems examine specific elements of these PNR records for indicators of possible security risk, such as booking a one-way ticket, paying with cash, or paying with a credit card issued to someone not traveling on the itinerary. Addressing broad civil rights concerns regarding prescreening and profiling practices in security applications, the DOJ's Civil Rights and Criminal Divisions, along with the FBI, thoroughly reviewed the CAPS system during its initial testing in 1998. These assessments found that the risk assessment criteria used in CAPS were not based on characteristics related to race, ethnicity, gender, or religion.[12] Instead, CAPS looks exclusively at ticket purchasing patterns and other unique markers in the PNR, although continued concern has been voiced by some that the use of certain PNR data elements, such as special meal requests, may target specific ethnicities. While some CAPS risk criteria have been speculated on and discussed in open media sources, the specific PNR data elements searched by CAPS and the decision criteria used to determine risk have not been made public.

After its initial launch, the CAPS system was renamed CAPPS, presumably to make it clear that the system played no direct part in physically screening passengers, carry-on items, or checked baggage. Rather, the system's purpose at the time was to perform a risk-based prescreening of passengers to apply PPBM and explosives detection screening of checked baggage in a targeted manner. Since the 9/11 attacks, the emphasis and purpose of the system has shifted to prescreening passengers prior to arriving at a screening checkpoint to determine which passengers and passenger baggage should undergo more detailed screening and inspection. The CAPPS system is largely invisible to the public, and was virtually unheard of before the 9/11 attacks. Since the 9/11 attacks, however, much broader public awareness of CAPPS and its risk criteria (such as purchasing a one-way ticket) for selecting passengers for additional screening has resulted from media coverage of passenger prescreening and related controversies. Nonetheless, the TSA has elected to maintain CAPPS as a component of air passenger prescreening and an element of its multilayered strategy for airline security. The federal government, however, does not collect, analyze, or maintain records of passenger travel using CAPPS, as the system resides exclusively on the various airline-maintained reservations systems, such as Sabre and Amadeus.[13]

While nine of the nineteen 9/11 hijackers were selected by CAPPS for additional baggage screening, it is notable that, on September 11, 2001, CAPPS was not used to select passengers or their carry-on items for additional screening or inspection at passenger checkpoints.[14] This is a direct reflection of pre-9/11 policy decisions emphasizing the threat of aircraft bombings and failing to recognize the potential threat of aircraft hijackings. Since the 9/11 attacks, however, the role of CAPPS has been expanded to include identification of high-risk passengers for additional checkpoint screening as well, recognizing the continued threat of aircraft hijackings.

Some statisticians have also suggested that, in addition to simply prescreening individual passengers, an entire flight could be prescreened using similar criteria. For example, if the number of passengers who purchased one-way tickets on a given flight is much higher than the norm or if an unusually large number of passengers paid cash, then this may be regarded as a flight with elevated risk based on these and other criteria.[15] Policies could be established in terms of how to respond to such estimations of heightened risk on a flight-by-flight basis, such as assigning air marshal teams to flights based on risk scores for individual flights using such criteria in combination with other factors such as the size of aircraft, or risk factors associated with the origin, destination, or route of flight.

"No-Fly" and "Automatic Selectee" Lists

Although the TSA has elected to continue using CAPPS as an element of passenger prescreening, many aviation security experts believe that CAPPS by itself is quite limited as a risk assessment tool because of the limited information that can be gleaned solely from selected PNR data, and because of open source discussions of the decision criteria used by the system that arguably compromise its effectiveness. Security experts have therefore recommended utilizing available government databases and information on individuals with suspected ties to terrorism to the maximum extent possible during the passenger prescreening process.

Since its creation following the 9/11 attacks, the TSA has provided airlines with the "no-fly" and "automatic selectee" lists for use in identifying passengers who are to be denied boarding or who require additional scrutiny prior to boarding. While the FAA also maintained and utilized a "no-fly" list prior to the 9/11 attacks, since those attacks, the utilization of terrorist watch lists has grown exponentially in size and in importance within the scope of aviation security policy.

The "no-fly" watch list is a list of persons considered to pose direct threats to U.S. civil aviation. Aircraft bombings in the late 1980s, including most prominently the 1988 bombing of Pan Am flight 103, prompted the U.S. government to develop this list in 1990. It was initially administered jointly by the FBI and the FAA, but the FAA assumed sole responsibility for maintaining and disseminating the list to airlines in November 2001, soon after the 9/11 attacks. At that time, the FAA also instituted the "automatic selectee" list. As the names of these lists imply, travelers found to be on the "no-fly" list are to be denied boarding and referred to law enforcement, while those on the "automatic selectee" list, like those passengers identified as posing an elevated risk based upon the CAPPS assessment, are automatically selected for secondary security screening before being cleared to board.

Under ATSA (P.L. 107-71), the newly created TSA assumed administrative responsibility for both the "no-fly" and "automatic selectee" lists. As the FAA did before TSA, the TSA has continued to distribute these lists to U.S. air carriers. In turn, the airlines have been required, as part of their TSA-approved security programs, to compare PNR data against these lists at the time of ticketing and check-in to assess and indicate to security screeners or airline personnel whether a traveler should be subjected to additional screening or denied aircraft boarding. In general, these lists are downloaded on a routine basis into a handful of computer reservations systems that are used by most U.S. air carriers. However, a few smaller carriers have continued to rely on printouts of the lists to manually compare passenger data against these watch lists.

Within the TSA, the TSA-OI is responsible for resolving potential matches to the "no-fly" list when brought to its attention by an airline, a responding law enforcement entity, or an operational field component of the TSA. In the case of individuals on the "automatic selectee" list, no further action is typically taken if the secondary screening process does not indicate anything suspicious. However, flights with "automatic selectees" on board may be monitored at the TSOC and any air marshals or armed pilots on board may be made aware that these individuals are on board the flight as a preemptive measure.

According to the FBI, the "no-fly" and "automatic selectee" lists were consolidated into the TSDB sometime in the latter half of FY2004.[16] While these two lists have expanded considerably since the days immediately following the 9/11 attacks, they still represent a relatively small subset of the entire TSDB. Since not all known and suspected terrorists are considered threats to civil aviation, there are a number of ongoing policy issues to be considered in determining what records contained in the TSDB should be included in the "no-fly" and "automatic selectee" lists and establishing criteria for deciding which list to place an individual on. Moreover the TSC may, in some cases, be reluctant to release the full list of known and suspected terrorists to the airlines because of data security concerns.

In the fall of 2008, the TSA reported that the "no-fly" and "automatic selectee" lists together contained less than 16,000 names.[17] It indicated that fewer than 2500 of these names comprised the "no-fly" list, and less than 10% of these names referred to individuals who reside in the United States.

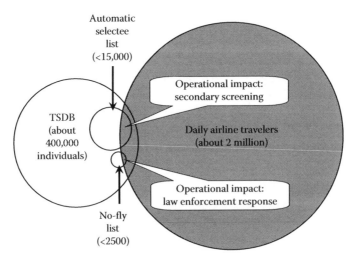

FIGURE 6.2   A comparison of the TSDB and the operational impact of the "automatic selectee" and "no-fly" lists to the number of daily airline travelers. *Note*: The areas of the representative circles are not to scale.

According to the TSA, the larger TSDB from which these lists have been created contains about 400,000 names, as previously noted. So, while almost two million people fly on commercial airliners domestically or on international flights to and from the United States on a daily basis (about 700 million annually), only a very small percentage of these travelers are likely to be selected for additional screening because they are on the "automatic selectee" list, and even fewer would be denied boarding because their name is on the "no-fly" list (Figure 6.2).

As shown in Figure 6.2, only those whose names are contained on these lists and who fly on a given day would have an additional operational impact on aviation security resources, requiring either secondary screening of those individuals identified as being on the "automatic selectee" list or a law enforcement response to assess the threat posed by individuals whose names match a "no-fly" list record. Since only a small percentage of individuals on these lists reside in the United States, most of those selected for additional screening or denied boarding are likely to be the result of a false positive match. However, the TSA's efforts to reduce the size of these lists and the requirements for providing additional personal information, including full name and date of birth, as part of the Secure Flight system initiatives, discussed in further detail below, are generally regarded as positive steps toward minimizing the number of false positives generated by the passenger prescreening process.

The TSA has provided the aforementioned statistics on the "no-fly" and "automatic selectee" lists and the TSDB to counter claims made by the American Civil Liberties Union (ACLU) that the number of names on these lists and in these databases has now exceeded one million. The TSA has noted that the ACLU likely did not distinguish between database records, where there can be multiples for each name listed in the TSDB, and likely failed to account for a name-by-name scrub of the TSDB that took place in the fall of 2007.

Policy disagreements between the DHS and privacy advocates and civil libertarian groups, such as the ACLU, regarding the use of terrorist watch lists and airline passenger prescreening systems have been a central focus of ongoing controversies. With respect to the "no-fly" and "automatic selectee" lists, these advocacy groups have expressed particular concern over false positives generated by these lists that can potentially cause aggravation and disrupt the travel of law abiding individuals with no ties to terrorism. As more and more individuals began to complain about instances of being wrongly delayed or denied aircraft boarding because of these passenger prescreening procedures, particularly in the 2003–2004 time period, the "no-fly" and "automatic selectee" lists became the subject of increased media scrutiny. In some cases, misidentifications included members of Congress, such as Senator Edward Kennedy and Representatives John Lewis and Don Young, and other prominent individuals, and even a four-year-old boy.[18] In other cases, misidentifications on international flights have led to costly diversions in which air carrier flights were prohibited from entering U.S. airspace or prevented from continuing to their destinations. In the midst of these controversies that accompanied the expansion of the TSA "no-fly" and "automatic selectee" lists, the 9/11 Commission recommended that the use of these terrorist watch lists for airline passenger prescreening be improved without delay.

To improve aviation security, the 9/11 Commission more broadly recommended that the Congress and TSA give priority to screening passengers for explosives.[19] At a minimum, the 9/11 Commission recommended that all passengers referred for secondary screening be thoroughly checked for explosives. Arguably, the considerable resources needed to implement such an approach would necessitate a robust prescreening process for carefully selecting only those passengers believed to pose the greatest risk to aviation security for secondary screening, while minimizing false positives. To improve air passenger prescreening, the 9/11 Commission formally recommended that

- The "no-fly" and "automatic selectee" watch lists be improved without delay
- The actual watch list prescreening process be transferred from U.S. air carriers to the TSA
- Air passengers be screened against the larger set of U.S. government watch lists (principally the TSDB)
- Air carriers be required to supply the needed information to test and implement government-operated passenger prescreening using terrorist watch lists

THE CAPPS II DEVELOPMENT EFFORT

When the 9/11 Commission report was released in July 2004, the TSA had already been working for almost two years on a new passenger prescreening system called the CAPPS II. This system was intended to replace the airline-operated systems for checking passenger names against the government-issued "no-fly" watch list and the "automatic selectee" watch list. In addition, some proposals for CAPPS II implementation also included sophisticated data mining approaches that would query both government-maintained and commercial databases to authenticate the identity of passengers and assess their security risk. As such, the CAPPS II concept included watch list checks as well as risk-based assessments of passengers, potentially using extensive amounts of available data on prospective air travelers that went far beyond the information available solely from PNR records and the limited risk-based profiling techniques available under existing CAPPS prescreening methods.

The CAPPS II concept was therefore especially controversial. Critics argued that the TSA's ever-expanding vision for prescreening constituted an unprecedented government-sponsored invasion of privacy. This and other controversies ultimately led TSA to scrap CAPPS II in August 2004, soon after the release of the 9/11 Commission final report, and pursue enhanced prescreening capabilities under a new system called Secure Flight. Prompted in part by the 9/11 Commission's recommendations, the TSA unveiled plans to discontinue the development of CAPPS II in favor of a new system dubbed Secure Flight.[20] In parallel with this move, Congress included several provisions related to air passenger prescreening in the IRTPA of 2004 (P.L. 108-458), requiring

- The TSA to assume the airline passenger prescreening function from U.S. air carriers, after it establishes an advanced passenger prescreening system for domestic flights that utilizes the watch lists integrated and consolidated in the TSDB
- The DHS to prescreen passengers on international flights against the TSDB prior to departure

- The TSA and the DHS to establish appeals procedures by which persons who are identified as security threats based on records in the TSDB may appeal such determinations and have such records, if warranted, modified to alleviate such occurrences in the future

At least with respect to the mandate for government-run prescreening of domestic airline passengers against the TSDB, the Secure Flight system under development was viewed as the tool for meeting this requirement. For international flights, however, CBP was already at work adopting its APIS system for predeparture passenger record checks, as described in further detail later in this chapter. While CBP currently prescreens international flights through the APIS system, the TSA plans to eventually incorporate international passenger prescreening under the Secure Flight system as well.

SECURE FLIGHT SYSTEM DEVELOPMENT

While the TSA touted Secure Flight as a significantly scaled down approach to passenger prescreening compared to CAPPS II, focused solely on watch list checks of airline passenger data and streamlined identity authentication, the program has also been beset with problems and has been repeatedly delayed. In March 2005, the U.S. Government Accountability Office (GAO) reported that, while the TSA had begun developing and internally testing Secure Flight, it had not fully determined "data needs and system functions," despite ambitious timelines for program implementation.[21] Consequently, the GAO report cast doubt over whether TSA would meet its original initial operational deployment date for Secure Flight of August 2005. The TSA, in fact, did not meet that deadline, and in February 2006 the TSA announced that it was restructuring or "rebaselining" the Secure Flight program.

The Secure Flight program had become bogged down in many of the privacy and data protection controversies and administrative challenges that had plagued its predecessor, CAPPS II. In July 2005, the GAO reported that the TSA had not fully disclosed its use of passenger data during its initial testing of Secure Flight.[22] The GAO's critiques of the Secure Flight implementation have been of particular interest because Congress, through various appropriations acts, has prohibited the DHS from spending any appropriated funds on the operational deployment of Secure Flight, or any successor system used to prescreen aviation passengers, until the GAO reports that certain conditions have been met pertaining to data protection, privacy assurances, and the establishment of an appeals process for passengers. However, the GAO has not been the only government watchdog agency finding fault with the Secure Flight development. In August 2005, the DOJ Office of Inspector General reported numerous problems in coordinating the development of the Secure Flight program with the TSC.[23] Also, in September 2005, the identity authentication element of the Secure Flight program, under which the TSA planned to compare PNR data (for domestic flights) with commercially available data to verify passenger identities, was dropped apparently over privacy concerns. Congress later included language in subsequent appropriations acts barring the use of any commercial data in the Secure Flight system and restricted the TSA from disseminating any data contained in the Secure Flight system to any commercial entities. Adding further controversy and criticism to the TSA's management of the Secure Flight development, the DHS's Privacy Office issued a report in December 2006, finding that the TSA had not accurately described its use of personal data under the Secure Flight program in public notifications required under the Privacy Act.

Two and a half years after the TSA announced that it would "rebaseline" the Secure Flight development efforts, after having worked through a number of issues and controversies, the TSA published the much awaited final rule detailing the planned operational implementation of Secure Flight on October 28, 2008.[24] Under this final rule, the TSA is now moving forward with the operational implementation of Secure Flight to compare passenger data provided by the airlines against the TSDB. Operational implementation, however, is proceeding in small steps with no specifically defined timetable for milestones and could be a rather lengthy process. In the end state, Secure Flight implementation is eventually expected to replace the process of providing the "automatic selectee" and "no-fly" lists to the airlines for prescreening passengers.

The Secure Flight program will apply to passenger airlines offering scheduled passenger service and public charter flights that operate to and from about 450 commercial passenger airports throughout the United States. These airlines will be required to submit passenger data to the TSA beginning 72 hours prior to the flight and, thereafter, continue to provide passenger data as soon as it becomes available. The airlines must also submit this required information for any nonemployee seeking access to the sterile area beyond the security screening checkpoint, such as an individual assisting a special needs traveler or escorting an unaccompanied minor to or from an aircraft.

Operating under Secure Flight, the airlines will be required to collect from all passengers and individuals seeking access to the airport sterile area their full name, date of birth, and gender. The airline must also request from travelers any known traveler or passenger redress number provided by the TSA and, if these numbers are provided by the passengers, then the airline must transmit them to the TSA. The TSA Secure Flight final rule explains that this known traveler number would be a unique number assigned to a traveler for whom the federal government has already conducted a threat assessment and was found to not pose a security threat. Since the TSA eliminated the requirement for security threat assessments for passengers participating in the voluntary RT program effective July 30, 2008, it does not appear that the known traveler number field will be propagated with RT number data at this point. It is not believed that RT participation will, at present, have any impact on the name-based threat assessment process to be conducted under the Secure Flight program. The airline must also transmit passport numbers, itinerary information, record locator data, and various other reference numbers if these data are available. For a complete list of Secure Flight Passenger Data (SFPD) (Table 6.1).

Once received, the TSA will use an automated process to compare this passenger data against the consolidated TSDB. A schematic diagram outlining the Secure Flight passenger prescreening process is presented in Figure 6.3. The TSA does not maintain its own watch list. Rather, the TSA is a customer of the TSC, and in consultation with the TSC compiles the "no-fly" and "automatic selectee" lists from the consolidated TSDB. Under the Secure Flight system, the TSA will similarly continue to rely on the TSDB to determine whether to deny a passenger boarding or subject the passenger and his or her property to additional physical screening.

When the Secure Flight process returns an indication of an exact or reasonably similar match, a TSA intelligence analyst will review additional available information in an effort to reduce the number of false positive matches. If the TSA determines that a probable match exists, it will forward these results along with the passenger information to the TSC to provide confirmation of the match. According to the procedures set forth in the Secure Flight final rule, if the TSA or the TSC cannot make a definitive determination based on the data the airline customer provided at the time of his or her ticket purchase or flight reservation, notification would be sent to the airline to require the passenger to present a verifying identity document (VID)— such as an unexpired driver's license or a passport—when checking in at the airport. If the TSA determines that the passenger data provided is a match to the Secure Flight selectee list, it will inform the airline. The airline, in turn, will be required to identify the passenger and his or her baggage for enhanced screening. This is typically carried out by making a notation on the individual's boarding pass to indicate to security screeners that the individual is to undergo secondary screening procedures. The TSA may also inform an airline that a passenger is to be placed in "inhibited status," meaning that he or she cannot be issued a boarding pass and cannot enter the sterile area of an airport. This is equivalent to the current procedures for handling matches to the "no-fly" list, and such events would typically trigger a law enforcement and/or security response to question the individual further and assess the validity of the watch list match.

TABLE 6.1

A Comparison of Available PNR Data Elements Transmitted to DHS for the APIS and Secure Flight Passenger Prescreening Systems

PNR Data Elements	APIS (International Flights)	Secure Flight
Full name	X	X
Date of birth	X	X
Gender	X	X
Redress number		If available
Known traveler number		Future option
Passport number	X	If available
Passport country of issuance	X	If available
Passport expiration	X	If available
PNR record locator	X	
Origin—airport code	X	X
Airport of first arrival (international passengers)	X	X
Final foreign airport (international passengers)	X	
Airline carrier code	X	X
Flight number	X	X
Date of aircraft departure	X	X
Time of aircraft departure	X	X
Date of aircraft arrival	X	X
Time of aircraft arrival	X	X
Citizenship	X	
Country of residence	X	
Status on board flight	X	
Travel document type	X	
Alien registration number	X	
Address while in United States (inbound foreign international passengers only)	X	
Reservation control number		X
Record sequence number		X
Record type		X
Passenger update indicator		X
Traveler reference number		X

Source: Department of Homeland Security, Transportation Security Administration, "Secure Flight Program; Final Rule," *Federal Register, 72*, pp. 64018–64066, October 28, 2008.

Note: Other PNR data fields not transmitted to DHS include available frequent flyer and benefit information (i.e., free tickets, upgrades, etc.); all available payment/bill information; date of reservation/issue of ticket; baggage information; seat information; additional travel status and relevant travel history; ticketing information, including ticket number, one-way tickets and Automated Fare Quote (ATFQ) fields; airline code share information; all historical changes to the PNR; and so on.

OPERATIONAL IMPLEMENTATION OF SECURE FLIGHT TERRORIST WATCH LIST CHECKS

The TSA plans to implement Secure Flight in two distinct phases. The first phase will encompass only domestic flights, while the second phase will include international departures and arrivals as well as commercial international flights overflying any of the 48 contiguous states. The TSA indicated that it would conduct initial operational field testing in early 2009 to thoroughly test the reliability of data transmission connections for receiving passenger data from the airlines and sending screening results back to the airlines, and to assess the performance of the watch list screening

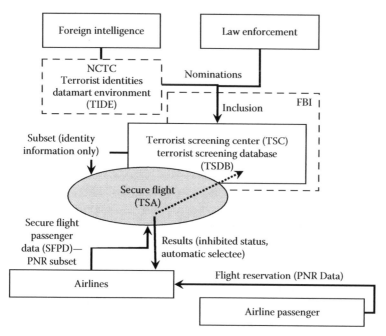

FIGURE 6.3   A schematic of the Secure Flight passenger prescreening system for checking passenger data against terrorist watch list data derived from the TSDB.

process under operational conditions. The TSA has not provided specific information regarding how long operational testing will take or when Secure Flight will become fully operational. However, the TSA noted that the phase in is likely to occur at a different pace for different airline operators.

During the time that an airline is participating in operational testing of Secure Flight, it will be required to continue the process of checking passengers against the "no-fly" and "automatic selectee" lists provided by TSA. As a result, the TSA will continue to produce these lists for distribution to the airlines until all airlines have completed operational testing of the domestic portion of Secure Flight and the TSA assumes full responsibility for comparing passenger data against the terrorist watch list.

For international flights, CBP will continue to check passenger names against terrorist watch lists under the APIS predeparture protocols described below until Secure Flight is fully implemented for international flights. The airlines will, however, transmit data for both domestic and international flights using a single transmission DHS portal, even though the two systems have slightly different data requirements and different timetables for the delivery of data. A comparison of the required data elements of PNRs for Secure Flight and APIS is provided in Table 6.1.

Overflights represent a new category of covered operations that will require transmission of passenger data for screening against the terrorist watch list and will encompass operators who may not operate flights to and from the United States. Overflights refer to flights that transit through the airspace above a geographic area but do not originate or land at an airport in that area. As noted previously, Secure Flight requirements will only be applied to those overflights transiting through airspace over the contiguous 48 states, and will not include aircraft overflying Alaska or Hawaii. According to the final rule, the phase in incorporating overflights into the Secure Flight system will coincide with the phase in of international flights. However, a specific time frame for this implementation has not been provided.

PRESCREENING OF INTERNATIONAL PASSENGERS

Under the current plan for Secure Flight, once fully implemented, it will be utilized for prescreening passengers traveling on both domestic and international flights. However, until that occurs, passengers on international flights will continue to be prescreened against U.S. government terrorist watch list information through CBP's APIS. APIS is a component of the CBP's Interagency Border Inspection System (IBIS), a comprehensive system for border inspections and records.

The collection of data on international flights is subject not only to U.S. law, but also to the laws of countries of flight origin, and various international treaties and agreements. Negotiations with foreign countries and multinational groups can, and have, proved to be challenging, as various different nations and cultures have differing views and expectations regarding the use of personal information for security purposes. After extensive negotiations with the EU, the United States entered into a multilateral agreement under which the CBP is being provided with specific PNR data elements, a subset of all available PNR data, for travelers on international flights from EU countries. On July 26, 2007, the EU and the United States reached a permanent agreement, under which selected PNR data may be collected and stored by CBP for up to seven years in an active file and eight years thereafter in a dormant file.[25] Since flights from EU countries make up a significant portion of international air travel to the United States, this agreement has been viewed as an important achievement for strengthening aviation security on international routes, and it has established a framework for continued international cooperation in the use of terrorist watch list data in the context of aviation security.

The APIS system requires U.S. flag and foreign airlines to transmit selected passenger and crewmember data for international flights in an electronic format to the CBP Data Center. The required data includes both personal identity information and other travel information contained in the PNR collected during each traveler's ticket purchase or reservation. The PNR data elements required to be submitted to the CBP Data Center include a person's full name, date of birth, gender, country of residence, and country of citizenship. Additional travel data elements, including items such as carrier code, airport of first arrival, status on board (e.g., checked-in, boarded), data and time of arrival, and foreign airport code, are also required to be submitted. For a complete listing of PNR data elements required by APIS, and by the TSA's Secure Flight system, see Table 6.1. Using the APIS system, CBP cross references this passenger data against law enforcement, customs, and immigration databases, as well as terrorist watch list records derived from the TSDB.

Prior to the 9/11 attacks, APIS data had been collected voluntarily from the airlines in an effort to streamline and expedite the clearance process for passengers upon arrival in the United States. However, following the 9/11 attacks, the collection and transmission of international passenger data was mandated by ATSA (P.L. 107-71) for commercial passenger flights arriving in the United States, and by the Enhanced Border Security and Visa Reform Act of 2002 (EBSVERA; P.L. 107-173) for both international arrivals and departures.

Since February 2008, all air carriers flying on international routes to and from the United States, including U.S. flag and foreign air carriers, have been required to provide CBP with the required APIS data prior to departure for both inbound and outbound international flights.[26] Air carriers may provide this information either in batch form, no later than 30 minutes prior to securing the aircraft doors for departure, or as each passenger checks in for the flight, up until the time the aircraft doors are secured. Air carriers are encouraged to begin transmitting available APIS data 72 hours prior to a flight.

RISK-BASED TARGETING OF INTERNATIONAL AIR TRAVELERS AND SHIPMENTS

While the risk-based targeting of passengers under the existing CAPPS system is only resident on the reservation systems of U.S. flag air carriers, CBP has established its own risk-based assessment tools for prescreening all international passengers as well as cargo and other goods shipped into the United States aboard passenger and all-cargo aircraft, as well as by other means of conveyance.

Given the sheer volume of people and goods seeking entry into the United States every day at airports and other points of entry, it has been considered impractical to physically inspect all persons and goods entering the United States. Therefore, in the mid-1990s, the U.S. Customs Service (now CBP) developed a decision support tool known as the ATS to assist border inspections, with an emphasis on interdicting illegal drugs and other contraband. Prior to the 9/11 attacks, the scope of the ATS was limited to the cargo industry, targeting shipment methods that had been linked to drug and contraband smuggling. After the 9/11 attacks, however, CBP shifted the focus of the ATS program to targeting known and suspected terrorists and terrorist activities and broadened the scope of the program to include terrorism risk assessments of both passengers and cargo shipments.

In the context of aviation security, CBP's NTC uses ATS to analyze trade data and air cargo shipments, as well as airline crew and passenger data to focus its inspection resources on those individuals and goods considered to pose the highest risk. The NTC was established on October 21, 2001, with the primary mission of providing continuous (24/7) tactical targeting and analytical support for CBP's frontline counterterrorism efforts. Its primary tool for applying intelligence information to the border inspections functions is the ATS. At the NTC, bits of intelligence information, referred to as "lookouts," are continually analyzed to provide tactical targeting of border inspection activities.

Within the aviation mode, the NTC relies on the ATS to prescreen inbound and outbound air cargo shipments, and inbound and outbound passengers on international flights. In some instances, ATS targeting assessments and underlying intelligence information may be shared with foreign customs authorities who have entered into data sharing agreements with the United States to aid in the worldwide tracking and targeted inspections of elevated security risk passengers and goods.

With regard to cargo shipments, the ATS system assigns risk scores to using a weighted scoring method that considers data patterns and trends.[27] Shipments scoring above a defined threshold risk score may be selected for further inspection at airports or other ports of entry. The specific rules and criteria are constantly evaluated and adjusted based on intelligence information. However, these details are not made available to the public for security reasons.

For applying risk-based targeting to international airline passengers, CBP requires air carriers and vessel operators to transmit PNR data to the NTC, in addition to the APIS data requirements discussed above. Through ATS-Passenger, the air passenger module or component of the ATS system, the NTC analyzes PNR data by comparing it to a number of law enforcement, customs, and immigration systems and databases. ATS-Passenger, however, does not assign a score to determine an individual's risk as the ATS system does for cargo shipments. Rather, it compares PNR data for all travelers against available law enforcement, homeland security, and intelligence and counterterrorism systems and databases to identify probable watch list matches as well as suspected patterns of suspicious activity. The DHS claims that these efforts have had a measurable success, resulting in the identification of known and suspected terrorists and criminals, as well as travelers attempting to enter the country using fraudulent documents or stolen passports, all of whom may have otherwise gone undetected.

IMMIGRATION CONTROLS AT INTERNATIONAL AIRPORTS OF ENTRY

In addition to the use of APIS and ATS, immigration control systems play an important role in screening individuals seeking entry into the country, including many travelers from Europe, Asia, Africa, the Middle East, and elsewhere who arrive in the United States on commercial airliners. For prospective international travelers, the visa issuance process, operated by the Department of State's Bureau of Consular Affairs, provides an initial prescreening opportunity of those individuals seeking entry to the United States, thus allowing for checks of their personal information against the TSDB and other available terrorist watch lists and lookouts. Such checks may prevent those posing a threat that are known to the U.S. intelligence community from purchasing an airline ticket on a flight to the United States, at least using their own identity or a known alias.

To facilitate travel and tourism, however, a small number of countries, including several European countries along with Australia, New Zealand, Japan, Brunei, the Republic of Korea, and Singapore, have entered into agreements with the United States under the Visa Waiver Program (VWP). Additionally, citizens from Mexico, Canada, and Bermuda, as well as citizens from the Bahamas entering through preclearance facilities at the airports in Nassau and Freeport, do not require visas to enter the United States. Also, citizens of the Federated States of Micronesia, the Marshall Islands, and Palau, in the South Pacific, may enter the United States bearing only a valid passport.

To enhance homeland security and expedite the entry processing of foreign nationals, the DHS has developed the US-VISIT (United States Visitor and Immigrant Status Indicator Technology) program. US-VISIT is a primarily intended as a biometric identity verification program that relies on digital fingerprint records of foreign nationals entering the United States. The system relies on a number of databases, maintained primarily by CBP, to identify potential terrorist threats posed by those seeking entry into the United States. These databases include the Arrival and Departure Information System (ADIS), the passenger processing component of the Treasury Enforcement Communications System (TECS), and the Automated Biometric Information System (IDENT).

ADIS is the central database for storing personal information, biometrics, and entry/exit data on non-U.S. citizens.[28] The biographic data contained in ADIS is derived from passenger manifests and PNR data submitted by the airlines through APIS. TECS is a comprehensive, multipurpose law enforcement data repository. The passenger processing component of TECS that feeds data to the US-VISIT program includes IBIS, which supports name-based lookouts derived from the INTERPOL crime database and the FBI's National Crime Information Center (NCIC) database, as well as CBP's APIS. Finally, the IDENT system is a repository for digital photograph and fingerprint records and biographical information on immigration law violators and non-U.S. citizens with serious criminal records. While there appears to be some considerable overlap between the US-VISIT process and the APIS process, the US-VISIT system provides additional redundancy as well as some new capability for potentially detecting and preventing individuals who pose a national security risk from entering the United States through various ports of entry, including international airports.

Presently, while US-VISIT plays an important role at international points of entry at airports, its significance with regard to aviation security appears somewhat more limited because it is not used to screen passengers prior to boarding an international flight. However, future expansion of the program anticipated to include the use of the system for confirming a foreign visitor's exit from the United States. Exit tracking may be of particular benefit to aviation security by alerting security officials regarding individuals who have overstayed their visa, made unusual changes to their itinerary, or present other unique factors that may be indicative of possible elevated security risk. The extent to which exit tracking of foreign visitors will assess such factors under US-VISIT, however, has not been defined.

As previously noted, all international travelers, including travelers on outbound flights, are now vetted using the APIS program as mandated by EBSVERA (P.L. 107-173). However, while the APIS screening of outbound flights compares PNR data to watch list records, it does not appear to look for other possible risk factors related to the travel status of the individual. While it is unclear whether US-VISIT or some other system may look at travel status and other factors in assessing passenger risk prior to aircraft boarding, such an approach may be capable of further enhancing aviation security.

Moreover, to prescreen noncitizens visiting the United States temporarily under the VWP, DHS has recently issued an interim final rule for the Electronic System for Travel Authorization (ESTA) that will allow the department to prescreen travelers from VWP countries against consular records and terrorist watch lists. A provision in the Implementing Recommendations of the 9/11 Commission Act of 2007 (P.L. 110-53) mandated the creation of ESTA as a tool for enhancing the security of the VWP. The system is intended to address the inherent risks associated with allowing visa waiver eligible passengers to travel to the United States before making any initial determination of eligibility to enter the country, as is typically done when foreign citizens apply for a visa.

Under ESTA, which became fully operational in January 2009, individuals traveling under the VWP are required to complete an electronic version of the CBP I-94W nonimmigrant visitor form prior to travel.[29] Historically, this form was typically filled out on board the aircraft while en route to a U.S. destination and presented to CBP upon arrival at the airport of entry. Under ESTA, VWP-eligible individuals seeking to travel to the United States, must submit this information using the Internet prior to purchasing a ticket, or a perspective traveler may apply through an airline or travel agency at the time of making an airline reservation.

The ESTA system compares the information provided by prospective travelers against the TSDB and law enforcement databases, using the TECS system, and against an INTERPOL database of lost and stolen passports and travel documents to make a determination regarding travel eligibility before the passenger boards a U.S.-bound flight. Travel eligibility determinations are typically provided by ESTA almost instantaneously in response to an application and are valid for multiple entries for up to two years or until the traveler's passport expires, but can be revoked at any time. The ESTA determination, however, is just a travel eligibility determination, and it does not guarantee admissibility into the United States upon arrival. If an applicant is found to be ineligible to travel to the United States by an ESTA determination, they may apply to a U.S. Department of State Consular Affairs office to obtain a visa and remedy any misidentification that may have caused them to be found ineligible. By statute, however, ESTA determinations are not subject to judicial review by the courts.

For the purposes of aviation security, the ESTA process appears to complement the functions of APIS. As such, it may provide an additional layer of security to catch inconsistencies that may indicate an elevated risk that might otherwise go undetected. Thus, while ESTA's primary purpose is to strengthen customs and immigration control at international airports and other ports of entry, it appears to have an ancillary benefit of prescreening certain prospective airline travelers even before their records would be subjected to an APIS predeparture inquiry. In this role, ESTA appears to provide a redundant layer of security in the passenger prescreening process that may prevent individuals who pose a risk to aviation security from even seeking to purchase an airline ticket for a flight to the United States. ESTA may also provide an additional targeting capability by providing advance indications regarding ticket purchases by individuals whose travel documents or personally identifying information may suggest an elevated risk that may warrant additional scrutiny by aviation security officials, although there is no indication at this time that ESTA has been linked to airline passenger prescreening and risk assessment processes.

PRESCREENING OF AVIATION WORKERS AND GENERAL AVIATION PASSENGERS

While much of the focus on DHS prescreening initiatives to date has centered on airline flights, including both international and domestic flights, other policy initiatives have focused on expanding the use of terrorist database checks and prescreening to other facets of aviation. The IRTPA of 2004 (P.L. 108-458) specifically required preemployment terrorist watch list screening for pilots, mechanics, and other requiring FAA certification, and of airport workers requiring unescorted access to secured areas of commercial passenger airports. In response to this mandate, the use of the terrorist watch list checks to screen airport and air cargo workers has already been incorporated into the background check procedures for these individuals, which are described more fully in Chapter 9 on airport access controls, and in Chapter 11 on air cargo security.

In addition to these applications, there has been additional interest in expanding passenger prescreening and watch list check procedures to other operations, such as charter flight operations, aircraft rentals, and flights of large corporate and fractionally-owned general aviation (GA) aircraft. P.L. 108-458 also contains provisions requiring the DHS to set up a program allowing aircraft charter and rental companies to submit the names of prospective customers seeking to charter or rent aircraft weighing more than 12,500 pounds to the TSA for vetting against the consolidated terrorist watch list on a voluntary basis. Additionally, under a TSA proposal for enhancing the security of large GA aircraft operations, passengers on all aircraft weighing more than 12,500 pounds—which includes most business jets and larger jet aircraft—would be required to be vetted through the consolidated terrorist watch list using a prescreening system like Secure Flight.[30] In considering such proposals, the feasibility and implementation costs are likely to be weighed against the potential security threat posed by general aviation. Such proposals may also be examined with respect to whether using prescreening for GA and charter flights may provide adequate security in lieu of screening passengers for such flights, since physical screening of passengers and baggage is an option that many familiar with GA operations consider to be impractical and, in many cases, unnecessary.

POLICY ISSUES RELATED TO PASSENGER PRESCREENING AND TERRORIST WATCH LIST CHECKS

While the various systems discussed above—which are specifically designed to exploit intelligence information to prescreen airline passengers and others seeking access to the air transportation system against government records of known and suspected terrorists, criminals, and others posing a threat to national security—appear to provide great promise and opportunity for enhancing aviation security, there are a number of policy issues related to the implementation of these systems and the government-maintained databases that underlie the prescreening process. These issues include

- The accuracy and reliability of the underlying intelligence databases and watch lists, most notably TIDE and the TSDB, that form the bridge between the intelligence community and passenger prescreening applications
- The operational impacts of both false positive matches and potential failures to detect terrorist operatives or other individuals posing a potential threat to aviation security prior to aircraft boarding
- The timeliness and effectiveness of redress and remedy procedures to mitigate the impacts of false positive matches on misidentified airline passengers

ACCURACY AND RELIABILITY OF UNDERLYING TERRORIST DATABASES

The overall effectiveness of passenger prescreening against terrorist watch lists is ultimately dependent on the accuracy and reliability of the underlying watch lists and intelligence information. The accuracy and reliability of this data is a reflection of the extent to which the intelligence community is capable of providing comprehensive information regarding all individuals worldwide known to pose a threat to aviation and national security, while providing sufficiently accurate details to minimize misidentifications and false positive matches during the passenger prescreening process. Since the TIDE database, which is maintained by NCTC, is the principal source of lookout records on international terrorists included in the TSDB, a key issue related to the success of passenger prescreening measures is whether the intelligence community is appropriately sharing terrorist information with the NCTC, and whether this information is being adequately analyzed and integrated into TIDE. Another issue is whether the TSC is receiving comprehensive and timely updates to TIDE, reflecting the most current and reliable intelligence information for inclusion in the TSDB. Addressing database accuracy remains an ongoing concern directly involving both the TSC and the NCTC.

In essence, at each of these layers in the terrorist information collection, integration, and dissemination process, adequate quality assurance (QA) mechanisms are needed to continually assure the integrity and accuracy of available intelligence information. The TSA and its Secure Flight system, as well as the CBP and APIS and other DHS users and watch list systems, can, in large part, be viewed as end users or access portals to these consolidated terrorist databases. While the TSA, CBP, and other DHS entities will need to provide their own QA to ensure that they accurately process and compare PNR data to these terrorist watch lists, QA of the TSDB will largely be the responsibility of the TSC and will require close continued cooperation between the TSC and the various DHS components it supports, including the TSA.

FALSE POSITIVE MATCHES AND POTENTIAL FAILURES TO DETECT TERRORIST THREATS

The accuracy and reliability of underlying intelligence information and terrorist databases constructed from that information has a direct bearing on the overall reliability and error rate of passenger prescreening systems. Recall from the discussion in the previous chapter that with any detection or screening system, such as Secure Flight or APIS, there are essentially two classes of errors that can be made. The first type of error, termed a Type I error or a false positive, occurs when a system erroneously signals a match. In the case of Secure Flight, such an error would occur when someone with no affiliation to terrorists is flagged by the system and either subjected to additional screening measures or denied aircraft boarding. In other words, a Type I error would occur anytime someone is misidentified by the system when the individual, in fact, poses no threat to aviation security. The second type of error, termed a Type II error or a false negative, occurs when the system fails to detect or identify that which the system has been designed to look for. In the case of passenger prescreening systems, such an error would occur if a known or suspected terrorist or someone posing a threat to aviation was not identified by the system and boarded a flight without additional scrutiny.

Broadly speaking, a Type II error could be the result of either a gap in intelligence information, or a specific problem with the prescreening system or process itself. So, a Type II error may occur because the intelligence community had no specific knowledge about the threat posed by a specific individual; knew of the threat, but failed to include the individual in the terrorist database; or the prescreening system itself may have failed because of a data coding error, such as a badly misspelled name that failed to generate a watch list match to the PNR data provided by the individual. Another potential cause of a Type II error might be a failure of the system to detect fraudulent personal information presented by an individual posing a threat to aviation. For example, if a terrorist were to use a stolen identity to travel on board a passenger aircraft, the failure to authenticate the individual's identity and identify him as a potential threat can also be regarded as a Type II error. Since the intelligence gathering, terrorist watch list, and passenger prescreening functions in combination represent a broad-based system of systems, identifying the root cause of possible Type II errors for this overarching system would require detailed analysis of the potential failure modes for each of the component elements and processes of this broader system.

While Type II errors and their possible root causes are of considerable concern to intelligence experts and aviation security officials, many policymakers have focused more intently on the concerns raised over Type I errors and their potential impacts on the traveling public. During the development of CAPPS II, the TSA had issued an estimate that the total number of passengers flagged by the system would be reduced from a rate of about 15% under existing CAPPS protocols and use of the "no-fly" and "automatic selectee" lists to a rate of about 5%.[31] Since the large majority of passengers flagged by the system are not linked to terrorist organizations, Type I errors would be expected to decrease by a proportional amount—about a 10% reduction, based on the estimates provided. Additional reductions in Type I errors may be realized as continued improvements are made to intelligence data in the consolidated watch list and if identity authentication protocols are implemented into Secure Flight to better differentiate passengers who may have the same name or similar biographical information to an individual on the watch list. Improvements in detecting terrorists and reducing the likelihood of a Type II error, on the other hand, could be realized as improvements are made to the quality of intelligence data in the consolidated watch list.

However, it is important to note that with imperfect intelligence data and limited capabilities to authenticate individual identities, there will always be a tradeoff between committing Type I and Type II errors. Recognizing this tradeoff has been a crucial consideration in designing and assessing the system architecture for Secure Flight and other passenger prescreening applications. There are two key factors of the system's design and implementation that influence this tradeoff between Type I and Type II errors.

The first factor is the sensitivity of the system. In the case of Secure Flight, system sensitivity is largely determined by the accuracy and completeness of intelligence information contained in the consolidated terrorist watch list. System sensitivity is also dependent on the robustness and completeness of data in that watch list and in the PNR data that allows the system to differentiate the identities of individuals on the watch list from others who may have identical or similar names or common biographical information.

The second, somewhat more subtle, factor that affects the propensity for Type I and Type II errors is the criteria used by the system for making a decision to indicate a match between a passenger's data and a watch list entry. In the Secure Flight system, decision criteria are imposed at multiple levels. At the first level, there are criteria imposed for including an individual on the underlying consolidated terrorist watch list that the system will rely on, the TSDB. Since the TSDB is consolidated and used for multiple intelligence and homeland security functions, the criteria for including someone on such a list might be quite broad. However, adopting relatively broad criteria could result in large number of people being included. This may negatively affect aviation security operations in that the misidentification and additional scrutiny of individuals who are not likely to pose a threat to the aviation system could tax limited airport security screening resources. That is, unacceptably high number of Type I errors or false positives may occur if the criteria for signaling a match and denying passenger boarding or requiring secondary screening are set too low. On the other hand, adopting overly stringent criteria for prescreening passengers may lead to a Type II error or *false negative* in which a terrorist infiltrates the aviation system undetected.

In developing Secure Flight, a key question policy issue has centered on how much personal information is needed to set criteria for the system in order to provide reasonable assurances that Type II errors are minimized without creating unacceptable levels of Type I errors or unnecessarily infringing upon the privacy of airline passengers. The policy decision in response to this question is largely reflected in the PNR data fields required from the airlines for Secure Flight and APIS, which have been made as a result of extensive deliberations and debate involving the U.S. Congress, various DHS components, the intelligence community, the Department of State, the EU, and other foreign nations.

From the standpoint of adopting and implementing aviation security policy, the system's sensitivity or robustness and the criteria implemented for selecting individuals for additional screening or denying boarding can be framed in terms of the costs and benefits associated with both Type I and Type II errors. In the case of passenger prescreening systems, regardless of the criteria used or the robustness of the system, Type I errors are likely to be much more common than Type II errors, simply because only a very small percentage of air travelers are likely to be known or suspected terrorists. While more than 600 million passenger board commercial airliners each year, the consolidated watch list has been reported to contain about 400,000 individual identities, most referring to individuals who live and operate outside the United States, and as previously noted, the number of unique individuals on the "automatic selectee" and "no-fly" lists totals less than 16,000, most of whom reside overseas. Therefore, particularly with regard to implementing Secure Flight for domestic aviation, Type I errors will be far more likely than Type II errors by several orders or magnitude.

While Type II error may be highly uncommon, the potential costs associated with just one Type II error may far outweigh the potential costs of more frequent Type I errors, although this is difficult to quantify. While the costs of Type I errors—comprised chiefly of the impact of inconveniencing misidentified passengers, the cost of additional security measures to screen or interrogate misidentified passengers, and costs associated with rectifying grievances filed by misidentified passengers—should be relatively easy to gauge, the potential costs of Type II errors are extremely difficult to quantify. This is because the costs of a Type II error—allowing a terrorist board a passenger flight undetected—is highly dependent on the performance of other layers in the aviation security system.

To elaborate, there would only be a clear cost associated with committing a Type II error during the prescreening process if additional failures occurred in the multilayered aviation security system. If there is relatively high confidence that the screening process is capable of detecting and preventing the carriage of threat items that could be used to carry out a hijacking or bombing, and in-flight security measures—such as air marshals, hardened cockpit doors, and armed pilots—are believed to be effective, then the potential cost of failing to detect a terrorist in the prescreening process may be offset by these additional layers of security. However, if these additional security measures were unable to thwart a terrorist plot and another major catastrophe—like the 9/11 hijackings or the bombing of Pan Am flight 103—were to occur, this chain of failures in security, including the failure to detect the terrorists during prescreening, could result in multibillion dollar direct costs and lasting economic impacts to the aviation industry.

Potential vulnerabilities in additional security layers, such as passenger screening or in-flight security measures, are likely to heighten concern over the likelihood of potentially disastrous consequences resulting from a Type II error during the prescreening process. While the 9/11 Commission gave no specific justification for its recommendation to expedite the deployment of the follow-on system for CAPPS, heightened concerns over a failure of the entire aviation system, particularly with respect to detecting explosives, is a possible motivation for issuing this recommendation.

Ultimately, a key consideration for policymakers in the administration and in Congress has centered on whether the costs of Type I errors—resulting in occasional misidentifications and additional scrutiny of some passengers—are outweighed by the benefits of reducing the probability of a Type II error—allowing a terrorist to board a passenger aircraft undetected. As one expert surmised, in the current context of heightened aviation security in the aftermath of September 11, 2001, "... [T]he growth in danger from Type II errors necessitates altering our tolerance for Type I errors. More fundamentally, our goal should be to minimize both sorts of errors."[32] Designing Secure Flight to maximize the detection of terrorists trying to board a passenger flight, while minimizing misidentifications of passengers who pose no threat to aviation, is an obvious goal. However, it is important to point out that tradeoffs must be made in setting criteria for the system that will maximize the likelihood of detecting terrorists while keeping misidentifications and their impact on security resources and airline passengers within acceptable levels.

PASSENGER REDRESS PROCEDURES

Type I errors, or false positives, are largely recognized by policymakers and system designers as unavoidable and undesirable tradeoffs that go hand-in-hand with efforts to improve aviation security through the use of passenger prescreening and the use of terrorist watch lists. Recognizing this tradeoff, considerable policy attention has been given to available options for minimizing the number of false positives by improving system sensitivity and minimizing the impacts of false positives on those passengers who are delayed or denied aircraft boarding or subjected to additional security screening as a consequence of the passenger prescreening process. These policy concerns have led to extensive efforts to create a timely and effective process for addressing passenger complaints and providing remedies to those passengers erroneously targeted by the passenger prescreening process.

Passengers who believe that they have been wrongly delayed, denied boarding, or subject to additional screening as a result of the "no-fly" or "automatic selectee" lists, the Secure Flight system, APIS, or any other DHS prescreening system and the processes that they apply to screening passenger data against terrorist watch list information and other government databases may seek redress from the DHS. Provisions in the Implementing Recommendations of the 9/11 Commission Act of 2007 (P.L. 110-53) required the DHS to establish a single Office of Appeals and Redress to establish a timely and fair process for individuals who believe they have been delayed or prohibited from boarding a commercial aircraft because they were wrongly identified as a threat. The provisions further established a requirement to maintain records of those passengers and individuals who have been misidentified and have corrected erroneous information.

To handle and resolve the complaints of passengers and meet these statutory requirements, the DHS Office of Appeals and Redress established the DHS Traveler Redress Inquiry Program

(DHS TRIP) as a mechanism for addressing watch list misidentification issues and other situations where passengers feel that they have been unfairly or incorrectly delayed or denied aircraft boarding or identified for additional security screening at airport screening checkpoints, ports of entry, or border checkpoints, or when seeking to access other modes of transportation. The DHS TRIP program allows passengers seeking redress, or their lawyers or other representatives, to file complaints, either by using an Internet online system or by completing and mailing a complaint form. After completing the online questionnaire or mailing the complaint form, the DHS will request supporting information within 30 days. Filers are given a control number that allows them to track the status of their inquiry using the Internet. The DHS will make a final determination and respond to the filer.

If the DHS investigation in response to a complaint finds that the traveler has been delayed due to a misidentification, the response will describe the steps taken to resolve this issue. Often, the traveler may be required to retain a copy of the DHS response letter and present it during the check-in process when traveling on airline flights. Under the Secure Flight system, passengers who have gone through the redress process may be issued unique redress numbers that they would provide to the airline at the time of flight reservation, ticket purchase, or check-in to assist in identity validation and confirmation of the remedy action taken as a result of the redress process. The PNR data submitted to the Secure Flight system include a data field for this redress number, which the airlines must forward to the TSA if it is provided by the traveler.

The DHS cautions, however, that the steps taken in accordance with the DHS TRIP process may not resolve all future travel-related concerns. For example, the traveler may be selected for additional screening based on a variety of factors or at random. Presently, individuals may be singled out for secondary screening for a variety of reasons, including use of the "automatic selectee" list as well as by CAPPS or by random processes (Figure 6.4). The TSA argues that these multiple decision criteria for secondary screening, including some amount of random selection, make it more difficult for terrorists groups to probe airport security measures to figure out which cell members are not on the "automatic selectee" list. However, the use of CAPPS and random processes may lead some

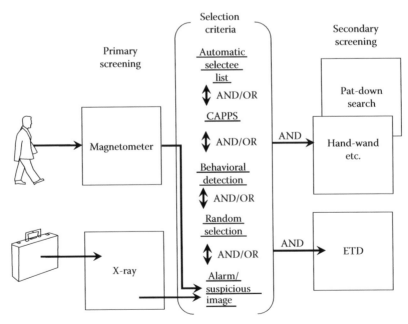

FIGURE 6.4 The various selection criteria utilized for selecting passengers and their carry-on items for secondary screening.

passengers to mistakenly believe that they have been wrongly placed on the "automatic selectee" list. In any event, the DHS TRIP provides a process to seek remedy, although it may be more limited in its capacity to assist passengers singled out for reasons other than being misidentified as matching a terrorist watch list record. Under DHS TRIP, if a passenger disagrees with the resolution decision made by the DHS, he or she may take further steps to appeal the decision.

FUTURE DIRECTIONS FOR EXPLOITING INTELLIGENCE INFORMATION TO STRENGTHEN AVIATION SECURITY

While passenger prescreening and the use of terrorist watch lists has been at the forefront of U.S. aviation security policy and strategy following the 9/11 attacks, advances in data mining and data fusion technologies and capabilities may steer future policy and operational decisions toward the development of more advanced capabilities for analyzing and exploiting a broader array of intelligence and security data. In response to the global war on terrorism along with technology advances in the ability to collect, store, and analyze all sorts of security and intelligence data, there has been an increasing need to sift through and analyze vast amounts of such data in efficient and effective ways. In response to this need, intelligence and security systems solutions have been focusing on data mining capabilities to parse through data and identify otherwise hidden anomalies and trends, as well as unique data fusion capabilities to synthesize security and intelligence data into meaningful units of analysis that can be assessed in decision-making processes to evaluate security risk and apply appropriate security responses to individuals or events determined to pose an elevated security risk. Such capabilities can aid in identifying new and emerging threats and quickly adapting aviation security measures to respond to these threats.

USING INTELLIGENCE INFORMATION TO IDENTIFY TERRORIST NETWORKS

Advances in data storage and data analysis capabilities coupled with advanced computer-based techniques for culling through vast databases make possible the identification of anomalies and trends in travel and financial data that can point to criminal or terrorist activity. The use of computer data mining capabilities coupled with the use of sophisticated social network analysis and the application of network theory can allow intelligence analysts to identify connections that can potentially link individuals involved in terrorism or other criminal activity that may be trying to hide their affiliation or relationship with other persons of interest.

For example, following the 9/11 terrorist attacks, researchers have used social network analysis to identify the specific relationships between the hijackers and the manner through which they communicated and plotted the attacks.[33] Social network analysis examines group structures by defining relationships or ties between various individuals, who are referred to as nodes. The closeness among individuals, as well as the role of the individual within a group, can be revealed by determining how many intermediary nodes or steps lie along known communication links, establishing what is commonly referred to as the degrees of separation between individuals.

Starting with information on two of the 9/11 hijackers, Nawaf al Hazmi and Khalid al Midhar, links between all 19 of the 9/11 hijackers were established based on information made public after the attacks. These two particular hijackers are of specific interest in examining the 9/11 hijackings and how the use of social network theory and analysis may have been capable of unveiling the plot before it was carried out because both al Hazmi and al Midhar had come to the attention of the CIA at least one and one-half years prior to the attacks because of their ties to Walid bin Attash (a.k.a. Khallad), the suspected mastermind of the October 2000 USS Cole attack in Aden, Yemen. Attash was already under surveillance by intelligence operatives well before this attack, and he, along with these two hijackers, were observed together by intelligence sources at a suspected meeting of al Qaeda operatives in Kuala Lumpur, Malaysia in January 2000.[34]

Network analysis, performed after the 9/11 attacks, revealed that all 19 of the 9/11 hijackers as well as convicted terrorist Zacarias Moussaoui were within two steps or two degrees of freedom from these two individuals. In other words, any one of them communicated to another through, at most, just one intermediary, and many were in some form of direct communication with each other. Further analysis of the specific links between the hijackers and their associates gave some indication that Mohamed Atta had a leadership role in the network. Following the attacks, additional information on Atta led to the conclusion that he was, in fact, the overall leader of the group.

Doing this type of analysis in a post hoc, or after the fact, manner is much more tractable because the facts and circumstances of a terrorist attack will undoubtedly uncloak many of the previously unidentified connections between terrorist operatives. In terms of using intelligence data to unveil terrorist networks before terrorist groups attack, the task is far more daunting. This is because each and every person is connected to tens of thousands of people by two steps or degrees of separation. Social networks grow exponentially as they move away from the original focus, and so individuals can be linked to hundreds of thousands of people by only three degrees of separation. This means that two criminal or terrorist operatives masking their relationship to each other could blend into a sample of hundreds of thousands of people simply by using two intermediaries to relay all of their communications and financing through. Studies have shown that, at least among Internet savvy users of online social networking and instant messaging systems, there are only about six or seven degrees of separation between all system users.[35] Therefore, without any *a priori* knowledge of existing ties between individuals, intelligence analysts would need to cull through vast amounts of data to identify trends that may establish such a link.

Nevertheless, improving technologies to cull and analyze vast amounts of intelligence and security sensor data provide new opportunities to identify and thwart terrorists in their tracks and respond to new and emerging threats. Some researchers, however, have suggested that new approaches to data fusion and data logic may be needed to best exploit this vast array of information, including the considerable amount of security information available through airport security monitors and sensors and other surveillance and intelligence gathering capabilities present in the aviation domain.

DATA FUSION IN THE AVIATION ENVIRONMENT

In the context of the global war on terrorism, considerable public policy attention has been given to improving capabilities to synthesize surveillance and intelligence data in a process called data fusion. Data fusion refers to the combining or integration of data from multiple sources, including screening technologies and sensors, to derive a more complete analysis of a potential threat. Information fusion, however, occurs at a higher level of data aggregation and analysis. It involves the synthesis of intelligence gathering from a broad array of information sources including state, local, and federal law enforcement and counterterrorism units, the intelligence community, and homeland security components including CBP and ICE Officers, FAMS, and TSA TSOs, including those specifically training as Behavioral Detection Officers (BDOs).

With regard to conducting surveillance of potential threats and collecting intelligence information on the movements of known and suspected terrorists, the airport environment may play an important role. This is because major airports are considered potential terrorist targets and are also a nexus for travel, particularly international travel. Therefore, surveillance activities at airports, combined with watch list checks of travelers and workers, may provide important inputs into the data stream of intelligence information gathering. Also, because of the specific interest in detecting and preventing terrorists from entering into the United States, CBP and ICE operations at international airports, along with State Department checks of foreign citizens requesting entry into the United States, are major components of both collecting and using intelligence information to detect and track terrorist travel and travel activity of other individuals of interest. Since most international travel from Europe, Asia, Africa, and the Middle East relies on commercial passenger airlines, the tracking of international airline passengers is a vital component of intelligence and homeland security efforts to track international terrorist travel and prevent known or suspected terrorists from entering into the United States.

In addition to the tracking of travelers, integration and fusion of data from the myriad of cameras, sensors, access control systems and other surveillance technologies in the airport environment may provide valuable information regarding potential threats as well as latent vulnerabilities that may otherwise go undetected. Therefore, the fusion or synthesis of intelligence information from these various aviation-related sources, as well as information about suspected terrorist operatives from other diverse sources, is a key function of intelligence and counterterrorism activities in the age of global terrorism. Airport surveillance activities carried out by airport security, state and local law enforcement presence at airports, and by federal agencies including the TSA, ICE, and CBP, may provide important intelligence data for monitoring and tracking terrorists, criminals, and others who may seek to attack or exploit the air transportation system.

As airports incorporate new screening and surveillance technologies, there will likely be a growing need and a growing desire to integrate data from these various sources in order to provide a more complete security picture and create opportunities to identify potential threats that may otherwise go unnoticed. Similarly, as new techniques for behavioral observation and encoding intelligence information emerge, new needs and opportunities for information fusion are anticipated to better collect and analyze information provided from a wide range of law enforcement, intelligence, and security sources potentially allowing for a more complete picture of threats and vulnerabilities. Therefore, homeland security experts, including those inside the DHS and the TSA, have identified a growing need for both data and information fusion to meet future aviation security challenges.

In 2007, the TSA sponsored a study by the NRC of the National Academies to examine the needs and opportunities for using data fusion techniques to improve airport and aviation security. While the focus of the study was on data fusion in the airport security environment, the observations and findings of the study appear to have broader applicability to a wide array of homeland security data and counterterrorism intelligence information fusion. To carry out this study, the NRC formed the Committee on Assessment of Security Technologies for Transportation, which examined the issue and made several recommendations to the TSA.[36] As a result of the study, the Committee recommended the TSA accomplish the following:

- Perform a formal analysis to select a data fusion approach to address the goals of increasing threat detection rates, increasing system throughput, and/or reducing false alarm rates
- Establish a set of system-level fusion requirements for checked baggage screening, security checkpoint, and airport access control systems, complete a systems engineering analysis incorporating data fusion into these components of airport security, test and validate these data-fused systems against projected threats, building in assumptions regarding future system configurations and unique facility characteristics, and update system requirements and capabilities to reflect any future advances in technology and data fusion capabilities
- Establish partnerships or contracts with leading integrators and manufacturers to develop strategies and standards for integrating airport security components, checkpoint screening technologies, checked baggage screening systems, and airport access control systems and procedures
- Develop formal mechanisms or processes for entering and coding human observational data with security system data
- Implement selected data fusion systems through a series of phased-in deployments using an operational testbed and/or selected test airports, relying on these initial trials to enhance data fusion systems rolled out on a larger scale in later implementations[37]

DATA LOGIC AND CURRENT DATA FUSION PRACTICES

In making these recommendations, the Committee drew a distinction between decision data fusion and parametric data fusion. In decision data fusion, binary decisions of security system components may be aggregated together using AND logic, meaning that multiple system components must signal a threat in order for the entire system to signal a threat. Alternatively, signals from various system components may be considered separately using OR logic, meaning that if any one component or another signals a threat, then the entire system would code the event as a threat. In complex security systems, decision data fusion networks might have various combinations of AND and OR logic.

A common example of data fusion in the aviation security environment is the checkpoint screening process with secondary screening (see Figure 6.4). This screening process typically involves an AND logic structure in which an alarm during initial screening is resolved or verified through secondary screening, and the system will only indicate that a validated threat exists if both the primary screening process and the secondary screening process signal that a threat is present. Certain individuals are automatically selected for secondary screening based on name-based or behavior-based risk assessments, but the system is largely designed to indicate a validated threat only if these indicators are confirmed by a threat detection during secondary screening. Such a system is designed to reduce the false alarm rate. However, in this example, as in many cases using AND logic, this reduction in false alarm rate can come at the expense of an increase in missed detections. This is particularly true if the primary screening techniques or initial security components for assessing risk are less sensitive than secondary systems, which is often the case.

Alternatively, an OR logic structure can be implemented in certain cases. For example, one component of security screening for cargo to be conveyed on passenger aircraft is the KSD. If a cargo item is found to have come from someone other than a known shipper that has been vetted through TSA-established protocols, then it cannot be placed on passenger aircraft. Documents inspection is another component or layer of the cargo security system, and items may be prevented from being placed on a passenger aircraft if a spot inspection of the cargo manifest reveals inconsistencies or errors, even if the goods came from known shipper. In such an instance, the security system relies on OR logic because either the KSD or the documents inspection process can signal an alert that would prevent the item from being placed on a passenger aircraft.

The OR logic has the advantage of reducing missed detections because all components of the system look at and make a binary decision regarding whether a threat is present or not. While OR logic may increase the number of false positives in many cases, this is highly dependent on the sensitivity and criteria of the individual system components involved in threat assessments. Nonetheless, the more tests used to assess whether a threat is present increases the likelihood that one of these tests may yield a false positive. In addition to potentially increasing false positives, the main disadvantage of using OR logic is that it will typically increase system resource requirements and decrease throughput rates, because it is designed to have multiple components of the security system look at everything, or at least look at a sizable portion of all individuals or items passing through security based on random or targeted selection processes. The NRC Committee found that most currently deployed TSA security systems rely on decision data fusion networks using either AND logic or OR logic or some combination of these logic structures.

PARAMETRIC DATA FUSION NETWORKS

Since AND logic decision data fusion networks may suffer from increased missed detections, and OR logic decision data networks can be resource intensive and time consuming, the Committee recommended that the TSA should instead look more toward designing parametric data fusion networks to incorporate into various security systems of the future. In a typical parametric data fusion network, system components do not simply register binary (threat or no threat) decisions, but provide likelihood estimates that an individual or item is a threat. These likelihood estimates, pooled from various security system components or sensors, can be combined to create some mathematical risk score (presumably using parametric equations to combine the various likelihood estimates).

For example, one might examine how the use of current behavioral indicators programmed into the CAPPS process might be combined with risk scoring of observations made by BDOs evaluating an individual as they proceed through a checkpoint. The CAPPS system could code the risk posed by an individual, based on ticket purchasing methods and other indicators contained in their PNR, on a scale indicating threat likelihood. Similarly, BDOs could use various scoring methods to rate or code threat probability based on observable behavioral markers displayed at the checkpoint. Using parametric data fusion, the CAPPS risk score could be combined with the BDO threat likelihood estimate to establish a combined risk score for an individual. This aggregated risk score could be used as the basis for additional screening or further observation to establish the intent of the individual.

While the NRC Committee noted that parametric data fusion can often offer advantages for increasing threat detections and reducing false alarms compared to decision data networks, this may not always be the case. The Committee therefore recommended that the TSA conduct formal analyses to select a most suitable sensor data or intelligence information fusion approach for each given application, considering the impacts of available data and information fusion options on detection rates, false alarm rates, system resource requirements, and system throughput.

ONGOING INITIATIVES FOR IMPROVING DATA FUSION PRACTICES

In future aviation security systems it is likely that we will see various combinations of decision data and parametric data fusion, using more complex network structures to more thoroughly evaluate threats. It is also likely that these fusion networks will be designed to look at threats not only at the level of the individual or the single item level of analysis, but also at more aggregated levels of analysis. In other words, threat assessments may be made on various scales building from the individual level of analysis, looking at very specific elements, such as individual passengers or cargo shipments, to highly aggregated security threat assessments of the entire aviation system on a national or global scale.

Several ongoing research projects provide opportunities for integrating these various data fusion techniques to optimize the performance of future aviation security systems. Projects include command, control, communications, computation, and intelligence (C4I) testbeds for networking airport security sensors; the design of fusion systems for on-airport vehicle tracking, combining elements such as global positioning system (GPS) tracking and surface surveillance radar; integrated motion-detection and camera sensor platforms for monitoring air cargo operations areas; integrated tracking systems for smart container and baggage using radio-frequency identification (RFID) tracking and GPS vehicle tracking; screening checkpoint command and control including airport-wide RFID tracking of carry-on items carried by selectees considered to pose an elevated security risk; and airport access control systems using biometric identifiers and access control tracking using legacy access control systems such as magnetic card swipe and numeric key code locks.

The NRC Committee cited additional opportunities for data fusion in aviation security systems including passenger prescreening; baggage tracking and baggage screening; identification of explosives and hazardous materials; RFID tracking of baggage and cargo; integrated checkpoint screening; classification of threat objects enabling dynamic threat assessment and alerting capabilities; visualization methods to understand patterns in fused data to enable enhanced situational awareness and assessment; and integrated access control systems using biometrics.

These various initiatives and opportunities center on data fusion at relatively low levels of analysis, for example, at a single screening checkpoint. Further fusion and integration of security system data at more aggregate levels of synthesis may also provide options for analyzing security status at higher levels of analysis, for example, providing a total picture of security status at a large airport, or airspace security situational awareness at a regional level, like the National Capital Region around Washington, DC, or across the entire U.S. airspace system, which can be monitored at locations like the TSA's TSOC.

So far, this discussion has focused on alternative approaches that appear most readily applicable to sensor data fusion. Sensor data fusion refers to the aggregation of data collected from various sensor technologies such as imaging systems for detecting explosives in baggage and cargo, biometrics and access control systems for tracking the authentication and movement of individuals in the aviation system, identity systems for authenticating and vetting individuals seeking access to areas of the aviation system, and monitoring sensors for detecting motion and tracking goods, vehicles, aircraft, and individuals as they move through the transportation system. There are also considerable amounts of intelligence and counterterrorism data collected from various law enforcement and intelligence sources, mostly related to the security risk of individuals and organizations, which may also benefit from the various alternative approaches to data fusion and synthesis discussed above. By incorporating various data and information fusion strategies and approaches to the process of analyzing both security sensor data and intelligence data, aviation security operations may be able to benefit from a clearer picture and a better understanding of the security risk posed by individuals and items present in the aviation security system. In the future, policymakers and aviation security strategists are likely to consider various approaches to data and information fusion and analysis strategies to best exploit intelligence information to strengthen aviation security. While terrorist watch lists are likely to remain an integral part of the U.S. strategy for aviation security, future policy directions are likely to seek broader solutions to more fully exploit security and intelligence data to guide tactical and strategic decisions for adapting aviation security resources and techniques to respond to shifting terrorist threats.

REFERENCES

1. See, for example, Gabriel Weimann. "www.terror.net, How Modern Terrorism Uses the Internet." Washington, DC: United States Institute of Peace. Special Report 116, March 2004.
2. National Commission on Terrorist Attacks upon the United States, *The 9/11 Commission Report: Final Report of the National Commission on Terrorist Attacks upon the United States*, Washington, 2004.
3. National Commission on Terrorist Attacks upon the United States, "Three 9/11 Hijackers: Identification, Watchlisting, and Tracking," Staff Statement No. 2, Washington, 2004.
4. Statement of Donna A. Bucella Director, Terrorist Screening Center, before the Senate Committee on Homeland Security and Governmental Affairs, Hearing on Passport Vulnerabilities, Washington, June 29, 2005.
5. Written Statement of Rick Kopel, Principal Deputy Director, Terrorist Screening Center, Before the House Committee on Homeland Security, Subcommittee on Transportation Security and Infrastructure Protection, September 9, 2008.
6. Ibid.
7. Transportation Security Administration. Testimony by William Gaches, Assistant Administrator for Intelligence, Before the U.S. House of Representatives, Subcommittee on Intelligence, Information Sharing, and Terrorism Risk Assessment, June 14, 2006.
8. Ibid.
9. National Commission on Terrorist Attacks upon the United States, *The 9/11 Commission Report*.
10. Ibid.
11. See *White House Commission on Aviation Safety and Security: Final Report to President Clinton*, February 12, 1997.
12. Anthony Fainberg. "Aviation Security in the United States: Current and Future Trends." *Transportation Law Journal*, 25, Spring 1998.
13. Ibid.
14. See note 9.
15. David L. Banks. "Statistics for Homeland Defense." *Chance, 15*(1), 8–10, 2002.
16. U.S. Department of Justice, Federal Bureau of Investigation, Criminal Justice Information Services (CJIS) Division, "Terrorist Screening Center Consolidates Data for Law Enforcement Needs," *The CJIS LINK*, 7(4), 1–2, October 2004.
17. Transportation Security Administration. *Myth Buster: TSA's Watch List is More Than One Million People Strong.*
18. Sara Kehaulani Goo. "Committee Chairman Runs Into Watch-List Problem: Name Similarity Led to Questioning at Anchorage and Seattle Airports, Alaska Congressman Says," *Washington Post*, September 30, 2004, p. A17; and "Hundreds Report Watch-List Trials: Some Ended Hassles at Airports by Making Slight Change to Name," *Washington Post*, August 21, 2004, p. A08; "4-Year-Old Boy on Government 'No Fly' List," *The New York Times*, January 5, 2006.

19. See note 9.
20. U.S. Department of Homeland Security, Transportation Security Administration, *TSA to Test New Passenger Pre-Screening System*, Washington, August 26, 2004.
21. U.S. Government Accountability Office, *Aviation Security: Secure Flight Development and Testing Under Way, but Risks Should Be Managed as System is Further Developed*, GAO-05-356, March 28, 2005, p. 17.
22. U.S. Government Accountability Office, *Aviation Security: Transportation Security Administration Did Not Fully Disclose Uses of Personal Information during Secure Flight Program Testing in Initial Privacy Notices, but Has Recently Taken Steps to More Fully Inform the Public*, GAO-05-864R, July 22, 2005.
23. U.S. Department of Justice, Office of the Inspector General, *Review of the Terrorist Screening Center's Efforts to Support the Secure Flight Program*, Audit Report 05-34, August 2005, p. 41.
24. Department of Homeland Security, Transportation Security Administration, "Secure Flight Program; Final Rule," *Federal Register, 72*, pp. 64018–64066, October 28, 2008.
25. U.S. Department of Homeland Security, *Statement By Homeland Security Secretary Michael Chertoff On A New Agreement With The European Union for Passenger Name Record Data Sharing*, July 26, 2007.
26. Department of Homeland Security, Bureau of Customs and Border Protection. "Advance Electronic Transmission of Passenger and Crew Member Manifests for Commercial Aircraft and Vessels, Final Rule," 72 *Federal Register, 72*, pp. 48320–48353, August 23, 2007.
27. U.S. Department of Homeland Security, *Privacy Impact Assessment for the Automated Targeting System*, August 3, 2007, p. 7.
28. U.S. Department of Homeland Security, *Privacy Impact Assessment for the Arrival Departure Information System (ADIS)*, August 1, 2007, p. 2.
29. Department of Homeland Security, "Changes to the Visa Waiver Program to Implement the Electronic System for Travel Authorization (ESTA) Program," *Federal Register, 73*(11), pp. 32440–32453, June 9, 2008.
30. See Department of Homeland Security, Transportation Security Administration. "Large Aircraft Security Program, Other Aircraft Operator Security Program, and Airport Operator Security Program; Proposed Rule." *Federal Register, 73*(211), pp. 64790–64855, October 30, 2008.
31. Sara Kehaulani Goo. "U.S. to Push Airlines for Passenger Records," *The Washington Post*, January 12, 2004, p. A1.
32. Testimony of Paul Rosenzweig, Senior Legal Research Fellow, Center for Legal and Judicial Studies, The Heritage Foundation Before the U.S. House of Representatives, Committee on Transportation and Infrastructure, Subcommittee on Aviation Regarding the Transportation Security Administration's Computer-Assisted Passenger Prescreening System (CAPPS II). March 17, 2004.
33. Patrick Radden Keefe. "Can Network Theory Thwart Terrorists?" *The New York Times Magazine*, March 12, 2006. Also see, Valdis Krebs, *Connecting the Dots—Tracking Two Identified Terrorists*, available at orgnet.com.
34. Wright, Lawrence. *The Looming Tower: Al-Qaeda and the Road to 9/11*. New York: Alfred A. Knopf, 2006.
35. Jure Leskovec and Eric Horvitz. "Planetary-Scale Views on an Instant Messaging Network." Microsoft Research, Redmond, Washington. Microsoft Research Technical Report MSR-TR-2006-186.
36. National Research Council, Committee on Assessment of Security Technologies for Transportation. *Fusion of Security System Data to Improve Airport Security*. Washington, DC: The National Academies Press, 2007.
37. Ibid.

7 Passenger and Baggage Screening

The passenger and baggage screening functions of the TSA account for about two-thirds of all federal spending on aviation security. At present, about three-quarters of this amount goes toward the salaries, benefits, and training of screening personnel, while the remaining one-quarter is devoted to the acquisition, installation, and upkeep of screening equipment. New initiatives to expand the role of TSA personnel beyond traditional physical screening of passengers and their belongings, as well as initiatives to improve screening efficiency and effectiveness through the deployment of new technologies, will likely require considerable investment and resources. However, policymakers and aviation security planners are still working on a comprehensive plan for evolving airline passenger and baggage screening functions to incorporate new technologies, capabilities, and procedures to more effectively and efficiently detect explosives, weapons, and other threat objects as well as individuals who may pose a threat to aviation security.

Over the next several years, the TSA will likely face continuing challenges to address projected growth in passenger airline travel while maintaining and improving upon the efficiency and effectiveness of passenger and baggage screening operations. Addressing these challenges raises a number of significant policy issues related to allocating resources and funding passenger and baggage screening initiatives, adequately addressing human performance issues in the design of future passenger and baggage screening systems, and developing effective strategies for deploying next generation screening technologies.

POLICY CONSIDERATIONS FOR AVIATION SECURITY SCREENING

The TSA faces a number of ongoing challenges to maintain and improve upon the effectiveness and efficiency of passenger and baggage screening functions. These challenges include

- Addressing projected airline passenger traffic growth and its anticipated impacts on screening operations
- Optimizing screening efficiency and throughput and minimizing passenger wait times.
- Identifying and addressing potential airport space constraints for screening checkpoints and checkpoint equipment
- Improving the capability to detect explosives at passenger checkpoints as recommended by the 9/11 Commission and called for in legislation
- Integrating in-line EDSs to optimize baggage throughput and reduce workplace injuries
- Developing strategic plans for addressing identified technology and human factors needs related to passenger and baggage screening
- Defining funding requirements to implement these strategic plans

Key policy considerations regarding the strategies and approaches for addressing these ongoing challenges are discussed below.

AIRLINE PASSENGER TRAFFIC GROWTH

Currently, across the United States and its territories, passenger screening is conducted at about 450 airports. In total, there are more than 750 screening checkpoints and slightly more than 2000 screening lanes at these airports.[1] The FAA projects that domestic passenger traffic will increase at an average annual rate of about 2.8% and international passenger traffic will increase at a rate of approximately 5% per year through 2020.[2] Based on these projections, passenger volume at screening checkpoints is expected to increase by more than 25% over the next eight years, although an economic slowdown could moderate the pace of this growth to some degree. In 2006, the TSA reported that it had screened over 700 million passengers and other individuals accessing the secured areas of airports in the United States. If airline passenger traffic grows as predicted, then the TSA will likely be screening over one billion people annually by 2019, or perhaps sooner if initiatives to conduct random and targeted screening of airport employees, currently being conducted under pilot programs at selected airports, are expanded across the entire aviation system. Significant resources will likely be needed to address future screening needs to accommodate this growth without causing an operational impact on screening efficiency and effectiveness.

SCREENING EFFICIENCY AND PASSENGER WAIT TIMES

With respect to screening efficiency, the TSA has set an objective of keeping average passenger wait times to 10 minutes or less ever since its inception in 2002. While the average wait times aggregated across the entire aviation system have generally met this objective, wait times at larger airports, particularly at the 50 busiest airports, often exceed 10 minutes.[3] Passengers frequently experience long waits in screening checkpoint queues, particularly during peak periods at the nation's busiest airports.

At many larger airports, space constraints and other design considerations have limited the TSA's ability to add additional screening lanes and reconfigure checkpoints to better optimize the flow of passengers. This has resulted in lengthy wait times during peak periods, sometimes exceeding 40 minutes, at many of the nation's largest airports. Wait times are not just a problem at large airports as smaller regional airports may also face challenges with large seasonal fluctuations in passenger volume coupled with screening lane and workforce limitations that limit the ability to respond to spikes in passenger traffic. Therefore, in addition to accommodating projected future growth in passenger volumes, the TSA faces ongoing challenges at various airports to improve upon the overall efficiency of passenger screening operations and meet stated wait time objectives without sacrificing performance.

SPACE CONSTRAINTS AT AIRPORTS

Space constraints at airport terminals are likely to become an increasing concern for the TSA as it seeks to increase the number of screening lanes to meet anticipated growth in the volume of airline passengers. These constraints are also likely to become an increasingly important issue as the TSA moves forward with initiatives to reconfigure checkpoints over the next several years to accommodate new screening technologies. The TSA is also seeking to expand the footprint of the screening checkpoint queue and screening lanes to provide a more relaxed atmosphere for travelers and to provide BDOs with additional space to mingle and interact with passengers in an effort to improve the detection of suspicious behavior and possible hostile intent. These factors may combine to result in a considerably larger footprint for screening checkpoints compared to current configurations, particularly at older airports constructed when passenger volume was considerably less and the footprint of screening checkpoints was quite small.

Optimizing the layout of screening checkpoints at these airports may require a considerable investment in redesigning and expanding airport facilities to accommodate proposed future changes to screening checkpoints. Particular challenges may be encountered at smaller regional airports that have limited capability to expand, as well as at large airports with older terminals that were not initially designed with these new security challenges in mind.

IMPROVING EXPLOSIVES DETECTION AT PASSENGER CHECKPOINTS

The 9/11 Commission recommended that the TSA give priority attention to implementing technology and procedures for screening passengers for explosives. Provisions to improve checkpoint technologies to detect explosives were included in the IRTPA of 2004 (P.L. 108-458). In response, the TSA initially pilot tested walk-through trace detection portals, known as explosives trace portals (ETPs), and implemented procedures for conducting pat-down searches of passengers for explosives. Full deployment of the walk-through trace detection portals, or puffer machines, for use in secondary screening of selected passengers had been part of the TSA's strategy for screening passengers for explosives. However, this initiative was put on hold due to maintenance issues with deployed systems. The TSA has since been working to identify strategies and technologies that more completely address the explosives threat posed by passengers and carry-on items.

Provisions in the Implementing Recommendations of the 9/11 Commission Act of 2007 (P.L. 110-53) required the TSA to finalize within 30 days the strategic plan for checkpoint explosives detection required by the IRTPA of 2004, and to fully implement the plan within one year of enactment. The Act also contains provisions eliminating the cap previously imposed by legislation on the system-wide number of TSA screeners and requiring specialized training for screeners on security skills, such as behavioral observation and analysis, explosives detection, and document examination. The Act directed the TSA to hire sufficient personnel to ensure adequate aviation security and reduce average security-related delays to less than 10 minutes. The Act also created a separate "Checkpoint Security Screening Fund," specifying that $250 million in security fees collected during FY2008 be deposited into this fund to be used for research, development, deployment, and installation of equipment to improve the detection of explosives at passenger checkpoints. The Act also directed the TSA to carry out a pilot study to examine technologies to improve the security at access control doors and exit lanes for secured areas of airports.

In addition to keeping up with increased volumes of people passing through airport screening checkpoints and improving upon screening efficiency, the TSA continues to face considerable challenges in addressing 9/11 Commission's recommendations and subsequent legislative mandates to improve the detection of explosives on passengers and in carry-on items. There are lingering concerns that, without a significant investment to improve the detection of concealed explosives and nonmetallic weapons at passenger checkpoints, considerable vulnerabilities will persist. The TSA is pursuing a wide variety of technologies to address the challenge of detecting explosives at passenger screening checkpoints. These technologies include walk-through ETD portals, WBI systems, bottle liquid scanners, cast and prosthesis scanners, shoe scanners, advanced technology (AT) x-ray systems, and EDSs tailored for carry-on screening applications. These various technologies will complement, and in some cases may replace, existing checkpoint tools such as magnetometers, hand wands, and ETD equipment.

Under the TSA's current budget plans, in the near term, deployment of this technology will be concentrated at the nation's largest airports and will often be limited to use on those passengers selected for secondary screening or to resolve alarms set off during primary screening. Full-scale deployment of technologies to screen all passengers and carry-on items for explosives and other concealed threats will involve a considerably larger investment over the long term. While these various technologies have reached a level of maturity where they can be operationally deployed, achieving an end state in which all passengers are screened unobtrusively to detect a broad range of threat objects raises a number of policy issues related to the privacy of passengers as well as the long-term investment strategy for implementing future checkpoint concepts.

IN-LINE EDS INTEGRATION

In addition to the challenges that the TSA faces to improve on the efficiency and effectiveness of passenger and carry-on screening, considerable challenges remain regarding checked baggage screening operations. First, airports and the TSA have been engaged in ongoing efforts to integrate EDS equipment with baggage conveyor systems to optimize in-line screening solutions. However, at current funding levels, the GAO has estimated that these ongoing efforts will not be completed system-wide until 2024 if future funding remains consistent with historic funding levels for these activities.[4] In recognition of this continuing funding need, the Implementing Recommendations of the 9/11 Commission Act (P.L. 110-53), includes a long-term, 20-year reauthorization of funding for in-line baggage system installation and integration, extending authority for the ASCF and other funding mechanisms for in-line EDS integration through 2028. The Act also directed the TSA to take further steps to prioritize airport EDS integration projects.

Also, the TSA is currently facing mounting sustainment and repair costs for the large number of EDS systems that were deployed in 2002 and 2003 to meet the December 31, 2003, deadline for screening 100% of checked baggage using explosives detection equipment. The TSA is also beginning to deploy next generation EDS equipment that yield fewer false positives and have significantly improved throughput capabilities. Full deployment of these systems, along with in-line EDS integration, will likely result in a significant improvement to baggage screening efficiency. However, considerable investment over the next several years will likely be needed if policymakers want to accelerate ongoing efforts for deploying more efficient baggage screening equipment and integrating this equipment with airport baggage handling systems.

STRATEGIC PLANNING FOR ADDRESSING TECHNOLOGY AND HUMAN FACTORS NEEDS

The challenges to improving screening capabilities are reflected in the 9/11 Commission's recommendations to improve the detection of explosives on passengers, address human factors considerations related to screener performance, and expedite the installation of in-line baggage screening equipment.[5] Four years after these recommendations were issued, the GAO reported that only limited progress had been made in fielding explosives detection technologies at passenger checkpoints, and the TSA did not have a strategic plan for the acquisition and deployment of screening technologies.[6] Moreover, covert testing at passenger checkpoints continues to provide evidence that, despite the considerable federal spending on airline passenger screening since the 9/11 terrorist attacks, the system remains vulnerable, particularly to the threat posed by adversaries attempting to sneak IEDs, or the components to assemble such devices, through security checkpoints and on board passenger airliners. These vulnerabilities reflect the lack of adequate technologies deployed at checkpoints capable of detecting explosives materials, as well as limitations in screener performance that is influenced by a variety of human performance factors.

PROJECTED COSTS AND FUNDING ISSUES

Deploying new checkpoint technologies will likely cost more than $500,000 per screening lane, based on average unit costs for candidate technologies. This cost only considers the direct costs for screening lane technology acquisition and installation and does not include additional costs associated with expanding or reconfiguring airport terminals to accommodate new checkpoint designs. Given that there are more than 2000 screening lanes in operation throughout the United States, the total cost to upgrade screening checkpoints is likely to exceed one billion dollars in equipment costs alone. Additionally, the cost to operate and maintain this screening equipment is likely to be in the tens of thousands of dollars each year per checkpoint. Based on these rough estimates, it appears that current funding levels of about $250 million per year for checkpoint technology equipment and maintenance will not support a full-scale, near-term deployment of emerging passenger checkpoint technologies. Policymakers may consider various funding options to expand or accelerate the deployment of these checkpoint technologies. If these options are not pursued, it will likely take several years to fully deploy these new technologies and reconfigure passenger screening checkpoints at the nation's passenger airports.

At present, the TSA has adopted a strategy of focusing its efforts to deploy new checkpoint screening technologies on larger airports. However, since the aviation screening system in the United States operates using a single gateway concept, meaning that passengers are only screened once at their originating airport, focusing investments solely on larger airports could result in persisting vulnerabilities at smaller regional airports. These vulnerabilities may further persist without a strategy and commitment to future funding for system-wide deployment of AT systems for detecting explosives and nonmetallic threat items at checkpoints.

The TSA also faces unique funding challenges related to checked baggage screening. EDSs are the backbone of the TSA's baggage screening function at larger airports, but these machines are extremely costly to purchase, install, and maintain. The wave of EDS machines deployed in the 2002 and 2003 time frame to meet the mandate of 100% screening of checked baggage have been in service for more than five years now, requiring additional maintenance and service-life extension costs. Additionally, the TSA is refining its strategy for investment in newer EDS equipment to replace these older, slower systems. Newer systems can increase baggage throughput by up to 300%.[7] However, these systems are costly. Standard EDS machines cost between $900,000 and $1,300,000 each.

In addition to the cost of acquiring and maintaining EDS machines, redesigning airport baggage handling systems to integrate EDS in line with baggage conveyors is extremely costly. The GAO estimates that making the needed changes to integrate EDS equipment at all airports in the United States where EDS equipment is deployed will not be completed until 2024 if future funding remains consistent with historic funding levels for these activities.[8] While Congress took the unusual step of including a 20-year reauthorization of funding for in-line EDS integration through 2028 and directed the TSA to take further steps to prioritize airport EDS integration projects as part of the Implementing Recommendations of the 9/11 Commission Act of 2007 (P.L. 110-53), without additional funding the task of optimizing baggage screening throughout the aviation system in the United States will not be completed for many years. In 2009, additional funding for passenger and baggage screening was provided in the American Recovery and Reinvestment Act of 2009 (P.L. 111-16). The bill specified an additional $1 billion for aviation security screening, of which the TSA has designated $700 million for optimizing baggage screening and the other $300 million for acquiring checkpoint explosives screening technologies.

CHECKPOINT SCREENING HUMAN PERFORMANCE

The aviation security system is a human system that relies extensively on human perception, performance, decision making, and judgment. This is particularly true with regard to checkpoint screening functions that rely extensively on human operators and screeners to detect and resolve potential threat items. An underlying challenge related to proposed checkpoint expansion and enhancements is addressing ongoing human performance concerns to improve upon the detection of dangerous items at checkpoints and incorporate human factors considerations in the design and operator training for next generation checkpoint technologies and procedures.

Screener performance continues to be a concern as covert testing results have repeatedly demonstrated existing weaknesses in screening procedures and capabilities that could potentially be exploited to attack the aviation system. These weaknesses may reflect a combination of policies, procedures, technology capabilities, and screener human performance, although screener human performance has been emphasized as a particular concern that can be affected by various factors. A wide range of human factors considerations pertaining to screening procedures, training, fatigue and alertness, human perception and detection capabilities, and judgment and decision making can have a significant effect on the overall effectiveness of passenger checkpoint screening as well as baggage screening operations.

Passenger checkpoint screening at the nation's airports is carried out by about 30,000 screeners who make up about 60–65% of the total TSA screener workforce. The screening workforce has long been regarded as a highly fallible and vulnerable element of the aviation screening system. This should not be construed as a reflection on the dedication and commitment of individual screeners to performing this critical job function. Rather it reflects a combination of the complex challenges faced by screeners, limitations in human perception and performance, resourceful adversaries who may employ artful concealment methods, and competing job pressures to accurately detect threat objects while maintaining an efficient flow of passengers through security checkpoints. Adversaries seeking to carry out hijackings or bombings by carrying explosive devices, bomb-making components, or handheld weapons through screening checkpoints may attempt to exploit various limitations on human perception and performance that may compromise security. A variety of factors may contribute to these human performance limitations, including inadequate training, lack of motivation and job satisfaction, fatigue, and workplace conditions, as well as general human perception and performance limitations.

POTENTIAL IMPACTS OF RESPECTING PRIVACY ON SCREENING PERFORMANCE

Balancing individuals' rights and expectations of privacy with screening effectiveness is a particular human performance challenge. Criminals and terrorists have been known to conceal items in private areas of the body, especially in the small of the back above the buttocks and high on the thigh. Screeners need to carefully inspect these areas during pat downs to adequately check for dangerous items. Also, women's underwire bras can set off magnetometers, and bras have been used to conceal dangerous items. One of the most intrusive and most controversial aspects of secondary screening is the use of pat-down inspections to check selected passengers or to resolve magnetometer alarms. Specific complaints over pat-down techniques have centered on allegations of inappropriate touching and unprofessional or rude conduct by screeners. More general complaints have focused on privacy concerns and perceptions that the pat-down procedures were intrusive and humiliating.[9]

A Department of Homeland Security, Office of Inspector General (DHS OIG) investigation and audit of pat-down screening procedures found that the TSA adequately advised passengers of their rights under the pat-down procedures and appropriately accommodated those rights.[10] The DHS OIG also found that TSA screeners were adequately trained in pat-down inspection procedures and, based on TSA records, additional screening procedures were performed on proportionate numbers of male and female passengers. Finally, the DHS OIG found that the TSA had implemented procedures to investigate and resolve passenger complaints regarding the screening process. Specifically, the TSA maintains a screening Performance Management Information System (PMIS) where recorded complaints are logged. Operations research analysis teams and FSDs review complaints logged in the database to track trends and identify areas of concern and take appropriate actions, including possible disciplinary actions, to resolve specific issues. Complaints involving allegations of discrimination based on color, race, gender, religion, or national or ethnic origin are forwarded to the TSA's Office of Civil Rights for further investigation. Despite considerable concern raised by some regarding inappropriate use of or behavior during pat-down screening procedures, the DHS OIG found no systematic problems with the technique.

Nonetheless, privacy groups, such as the ACLU, continue to express concern over potential intrusion on individual rights and alleged cases of sexual harassment and abuse of passengers, particularly female passengers, by TSA screeners.[11] These concerns, however, raise a significant challenge for the TSA: to maintain high levels of security, which necessitate resolving all alarms and screening in detail those passengers ascertained to pose an elevated security risk, while maintaining the privacy rights and dignity of passengers identified for these secondary screening measures.

The principal option under consideration for addressing these concerns is the use of WBI technologies, discussed below. While these technologies offer a potential alternative to pat-down screening techniques, they too, raise privacy concerns because the images generated by these systems can reveal private areas, physical characteristics that individuals may wish to keep private, as well as prosthetics and other assistive medical devices.

In the sometimes chaotic and fast-paced environment of the passenger checkpoint, pat-down searches may be rushed and certain areas may be overlooked. The difficulty in detecting threat items on passengers is compounded by the requirements to respect the privacy of individuals as well as social and cultural norms and individual differences regarding interpersonal contact and expectations of privacy and modesty. Some have also noted cultural sensitivities toward handicaps and disabilities and point out that screeners are sometimes hesitant to perform intrusive searches, particularly on individuals wearing various prosthetics.[12] Terrorists and criminals can and have exploited these aspects of individual privacy by concealing prohibited items in body cavities and near private areas of their bodies, and could also exploit a screener's reluctance to perform thorough searches of prosthetic devices. Covert testers also use these methods to conceal simulated threat items in an effort to test screeners' abilities to detect items under real-world conditions and identify vulnerabilities in checkpoint screening that can potentially be reduced through procedural modifications and/or changes to screener training. These covert tests have revealed weaknesses in screener performance to detect weapons, simulated explosives, and components of explosive devices.

COVERT TESTING

Much of the concern over the performance of airport screening operations has arisen from information that has been made public regarding the results of covert testing operations. Covert testing using rudimentary mock bombs and guns started soon after screening checkpoints were first established in the early 1970s. Following the bombing of Pan Am flight 103 in December 1988, the FAA began more sophisticated "red team" tests to identify weaknesses in screening performance and other aspects of aviation security. The term "red team" harkens back to the Cold War era military exercises where red teams—so designated in reference to the Soviet Union's red flag and the association of red with communist groups—adopted strategies and tactics of an enemy force in simulations and war games.

The use of aviation security red team testing was suspended for a period of time following the 9/11 attacks, largely over concerns that red team practices could potentially put testers in danger or cause significant panic among passengers because of the acute focus on aviation security and the lingering public fear following the attacks. In 2003, the TSA's Office of Internal Affairs and Program Review (OIAPR) resumed covert testing of passenger screening checkpoints, checked baggage screening operations, and airport access control measures. This function now falls under the responsibility of the TSA's Office of Investigations (TSA-OI). In addition to nationwide covert testing conducted by the TSA-OI, FSDs at each airport also perform local covert testing. The local testing was initially called the Screener Training Exercises and Assessments (STEA), but is now known as the Aviation Screening Assessment Program (ASAP). The testing program has been revamped to better reflect the types of threat objects that may be used by terrorists based on the latest intelligence and threat information.

The TSA conducts more than 2500 covert tests of passenger screening checkpoints annually in an effort to continually identify vulnerabilities and take corrective action to improve checkpoint screening.[13] While specific test results are considered security-sensitive information, various media leaks of test results suggest that failure rates are often quite high, particularly with respect to screeners missing simulated IEDs and explosive components. In 2004, it was reported that TSA covert testing failure rates were comparable to those observed in 1987, when screeners failed to detect about 20% of concealed items during on-the-job performance testing.[14] However, the TSA has noted that the testing methods used prior to the 9/11 attacks were in no way comparable to newer methods. More concerning results have since been reported regarding tests conducted in 2006. In those tests, TSA screeners reportedly missed fake bombs 75% of the time at LAX, and 60% of the time at ORD.[15]

The TSA contends that while, on the surface, the results appear discouraging, they reflect the challenge of highly sophisticated concealment methods being used by testers to uncover specific system vulnerabilities so that corrective action can be taken. According to the TSA "... as security officers adapt and begin to consistently discover covert testing methods, testers start all over again, creating more difficult and harder-to-detect tests. This years' long game of cat and mouse more closely simulates real terrorist probing and operations and keeps officers alert and informed of the latest techniques and improvements."[16] The TSA points out that this type of testing is fundamentally different from the static, unchanging performance evaluations that were employed prior to the 9/11 attacks. Since the present day test protocols are constantly changing, the TSA has primarily used them to provide a snapshot of specific vulnerabilities in the system. It has not systematically assessed whether screener performance is improving or getting worse over time, although it asserts that improvements have been made. The covert testing methods are primarily used as a tool for assessing and identifying areas where performance improvements are needed and are potentially achievable through additional training, operational emphasis, or procedural redesign.

Concern over advance warning of covert tests and screener performance evaluations has been a long-standing issue. While media reports have suggested that some recent TSA covert tests were leaked to screeners, the TSA maintains that its procedures are designed to minimize the likelihood that screeners will be tipped off regarding a covert test operation while providing appropriate notification to TSA airport level management and local law enforcement to ensure that the tests are conducted safely. Nonetheless, cases of screeners being tipped off regarding covert testing have been documented. For example, in 2004, the DHS OIG found that screeners at the Jackson-Evers International Airport in Mississippi had been given information regarding upcoming covert tests, including details about the gender and race of the testers, the type of test items being used, and the location of test items on the tester and in carry-on and checked baggage.[17] Also, it was revealed that in April 2006, TSA headquarters staff used an internal electronic communications system to provide field level personnel with heads up information regarding possible covert testing operations, providing details regarding testing methods.[18] The TSA responded that it was investigating the allegations, but preliminary findings indicated that the internal communication regarding the testing was considered suspicious by a headquarter's official who decided to forward it to FSDs at airports across the country, but the email was recalled 13 minutes after it was sent. Based on these findings, the TSA concluded that the dissemination of information regarding the upcoming covert test did not appear to be a deliberate attempt to tip off screeners or screening supervisors. TSA Administrator Kip Hawley testified that there was nothing to indicate that anyone within the TSA attempted to tip off airport security screeners regarding covert testing in this incident.[19] Congress has considered legislation (see H.R. 5909, 110th Congress; H.R. 2200, 111th Congress) that would specifically prohibit advance notice of covert testing to security screeners.

In addition to concerns over possible advance warning of covert tests, concerns have also been raised that the TSA does not have adequate processes in place to systematically document causes of covert testing failures and carry out appropriate remedial action. A GAO audit of TSA's covert testing programs, including covert testing of passenger screening, baggage screening, and airport access control systems, found that the TSA-OI has failed to systematically record, document, and inform management of causes for test failures as would be expected if federal government standards for internal control were fully implemented.[20] The GAO further noted that the TSA lacked a systematic process to ensure that recommendations by TSA-OI are fully considered, and management decisions for adopting or rejecting these recommendations are appropriately documented. While the TSA-OI made numerous recommendations to the TSA's Office of Security Operations during the period reviewed (March 2003–June 2007), the GAO found that often, in more than 40% (18 out of 43) of cases, TSA management either took no action or it was unclear how the action taken addressed the recommendation. The lack of a formal process made it difficult to assess how the recommendations related to covert testing results, and in turn, how actions taken remedied problems identified by the TSA-OI. The GAO concluded that without such a process, the TSA's ability to strengthen aviation security based on the findings and recommendations of covert testers is limited. It recommended that the TSA establish a system for documenting the results and recommendations stemming from covert testing and formally track actions taken in response to these recommendations.

In addition to the internal covert testing and screener performance evaluations performed by the TSA, both the DHS OIG and the GAO independently conduct periodic audits and inspections of TSA screening functions that often include covert testing methods. While many of the details of these audits are considered security sensitive, the results of these tests have provided Congress and observers with important insights regarding the persisting vulnerabilities at airport passenger screening checkpoints.

Most notably, in a series of covert tests conducted in 2007, GAO investigators demonstrated that, even when proper procedures were followed, checkpoint screening often failed to detect concealed explosives and components that could be used to construct an explosive device potentially capable of downing an airliner.[21] For these tests, the investigators constructed two improvised devices: An IED, consisting of a liquid explosive that would be triggered by a low-yield detonator (i.e., a blasting cap); and an improvised incendiary device (IID), constructed from commonly available products including a liquid component. The investigators obtained the materials to construct these devices at local stores and over the Internet, spending less than $150. The investigators then employed various methods to conceal these items on their persons and in carry-on baggage, demonstrating that it is possible to pass either a constructed device or the components to build an IED or an IID through airport screening checkpoints without detection.

The GAO noted that the specific security weaknesses exploited in these covert tests, which were not divulged for security reasons, were identified by reviewing publicly available information, including information often shared through the Internet and readily available to terrorist groups. By exploiting these weaknesses, the investigators were able to pass these components, including banned liquid items, through various security checkpoints. While the investigators were subjected to secondary screening for unrelated reasons in some instances, pat-down searches and other secondary screening methods failed to detect the improvised explosives or prohibited items. In other instances, screeners challenged the covert testers for failing to fully comply with various procedures, including procedures regarding permissible quantities and packaging of liquids. However, in all cases, screeners failed to detect or prohibit the carriage of IED and IID components, including liquid components. The GAO concluded that its "tests clearly demonstrate that a terrorist group, using publicly available information and few resources, could cause severe damage to an airplane and threaten the safety of passengers by bringing prohibited IED and IID components through security checkpoints."[22] In reviewing these results, the TSA has acknowledged checkpoint vulnerabilities related to human performance, screening procedures, and checkpoint technologies. The GAO asserted that improvements in these areas may further reduce the risks to commercial aviation posed by IEDs and IIDs.

While the GAO's specific recommendations focusing on ways to improve screener detection of threat objects made to the TSA were not publicly divulged, the GAO also urged the TSA to take the following broad actions to enhance checkpoint screening operations:

- Establish dedicated airport screening lanes to handle those passengers posing an elevated risk and for those passengers with special needs
- Introduce more aggressive, visible, and unpredictable checkpoint procedures, such as random pat-down and hand-wand screening
- Continue to develop new technology at checkpoints to better detect concealed items

These recommendations for action reflect a continuing concern that, despite considerable investment in checkpoint screening technologies and personnel since the terrorist attacks of September 11,

2001, significant vulnerabilities persist in checkpoint screening operations. In testimony before the House Committee on Homeland Security on November 14, 2007, former DHS Inspector General Clark Kent Ervin stated that "the sad fact is that for all the dollars and attention that has been focused on screener performance since 9/11, study after study … shows that it is just as easy today to sneak these deadly weapons past screeners [as] it was on 9/11."[23] While Ervin's conclusions have been somewhat controversial and widely disputed by the DHS and the TSA, his general recommendations parallel various initiatives put forward by the Congress and the Administration to improve screener performance. Specifically, Ervin recommended extensive training and frequent retraining of screeners under simulated real-world conditions; remedial action for screeners and supervisors who fail performance tests and termination of those employees who habitually perform on a subpar level; and system-wide deployment of next generation screening technologies, such as WBI and advanced x-ray systems. These recommendations reflect specific needs for improvements in human factors and training for screening personnel as well as investment in screening technologies. The TSA is actively pursuing an approach to address checkpoint screening technology and human factors through its recently launched checkpoint evolution initiative.

THREAT IMAGE PROJECTION

In addition to covert testing, which tests screener performance in detecting concealed threat items under operational conditions, the performance of screeners that inspect x-ray images of carry-on items is routinely monitored and evaluated using a technology called TIP. This technology provides the capability to overlay virtual, computer-generated, threat objects over x-ray images of passenger's screened property during normal screening operations or to present virtual images of baggage containing concealed threat items. TIP was first fielded by the FAA in 1999. Following the terrorist attacks of September 11, 2001, TIP was discontinued as an operational performance tool over concerns that screener responses to TIP images would increase delays amidst the heightened focus on aviation security threats. However, viewing the technique as a valuable operational testing and performance tool, the TSA reintroduced TIP in late 2003 using a greatly expanded database of threat images said to be more representative of weapons and concealment tactics that may be used by terrorists.

In comparison to the FAA TIP system prior to the 9/11 attacks which had about 200 images in its database, the TIP system in use by the TSA today has over 2000 images,[24] with new images constantly being added based on identified threats and concealment methods identified through intelligence and field operations. Fielded x-ray equipment in use at screening checkpoints is TIP-ready. That is, these machines are designed to store and display TIP database images, and are therefore referred to as TIP-Ready x-ray or TRX equipment. These systems are networked and linked into TSA laboratories that create and distribute new TIP imagery periodically based on intelligence regarding new threat items and concealment methods.

On TRX equipment, images of weapons and explosives are projected on the x-ray images of actual bags being screened. This is carried out for several purposes. First, by providing periodic threat images to the screeners, the system promotes alertness and acts as a mitigation for boredom and complacency, two factors that can have a significant negative impact on human performance. Second, the ability to collect data regarding screening performance and screener sensitivity in real-world settings serves as an invaluable tool for human factors researchers studying screener performance. For example, these researchers can look at performance as a function of time of day and time on shift, to best optimize the scheduling of shifts and breaks for screeners. Researchers can also use the TIP data to identify particular threat items or methods of concealment that are often missed, and in response can tailor recurrent screener training and requalification to emphasize and correct specific weaknesses, either on a system-wide, an airport-by-airport, or even on an individual screener level. Third, TIP provides a quantifiable means to evaluate the performance of screeners at individual, work group, airport, or system-wide levels of analysis. As such, it can be used to track progress over time and can be used to document deficient levels of individual performance that establish grounds for dismissal. TIP has been one of the most significant technology changes to carry-on screening since x-ray screening techniques were first implemented in the early 1970s, and it directly addresses human performance aspects of checkpoint screening functions.

However, TIP is limited in its scope and provides data on only one aspect of screening operations. For example, TIP does not provide data on whether proper procedures were carried out once a threat object was suspected and flagged by the x-ray screener, whether ETD systems were properly used to conduct secondary evaluations of suspected explosives, and so on. Also, TIP does not provide any data on the screening of passengers themselves or their checked baggage; it only provides data on the screening of carry-on baggage. Nonetheless, TIP is widely regarded as an important screener evaluation tool, and it will likely remain an integral part of AT x-ray equipment deployment in the future.

X-RAY IMAGERY AND CARRY-ON BAGGAGE SCREENING PERFORMANCE

Current generation x-ray systems provide significantly higher resolution than systems that were deployed at airports in the 1990s and prior. However, these systems only provide a single view angle, typically an overhead view, of screened items. Nonetheless, in addition to increased image resolution, image coloration and other image enhancement features allow screeners to more easily differentiate organic and metallic materials and provide the capability to use color contrast to better differentiate certain elements of the x-ray image. For example, the coloration allows organic materials to stand out from inorganic materials making it easier to detect dense organic matter that may be indicative of an IED, and provides differential coloration of metals to allow for easier detection of metallic weapons. Newer x-ray systems allow for a wide array of image enhancement functions to highlight or turn off and declutter certain features in a process known as image "stripping."

However, some research has shown that individual image enhancements do not necessarily improve IED detection compared to viewing of the original x-ray image, suggesting that the greatest advantage derived from current single-view x-ray systems may be their improved image resolution.[25] Nonetheless, viewing multiple image enhancements in combination—such as stripping out organic items or metallic items, or displaying a negative image—can potentially help resolve image ambiguities and possibly improve detection. While currently deployed x-ray systems have these capabilities, time pressures at busy screening checkpoints may often preclude detailed examination using various combinations of these image enhancement capabilities.

Object orientation in the x-ray view is often a key determinant to whether a threat object will be recognized or detected. Prohibited items, such as guns and knives, presented at odd viewing angles can often be missed, even by highly trained screeners. At present, the main tool to address detection performance of objects presented at difficult-to-recognize view angles is through the use of computer-based training using TIP imagery of threat items presented at various view angles. Since threat object recognition and detection is a skill that is likely to continually improve with experience and exposure to both TIP imagery and artfully concealed real-world threat items, retention of high-performing experienced x-ray screeners is likely to remain a key component of maintaining high levels of screening performance.

Research has also shown that preemployment screening to assess aptitude for interpreting x-ray images, recognizing objects and detecting prohibited items can substantially increase x-ray screening performance.[26] Thus, with regard to establishing and maintaining effective x-ray image screening performance, it appears that a specific emphasis should be placed on screener selection and training, as well as initiatives to retain high-performing x-ray image screening personnel. Besides improvements in screener selection and training in methods of performing pat-down searches and interpreting x-ray images, addressing additional human factors issues related to the screener work setting—including fatigue, motivational factors, and environmental considerations, such as lighting, noise, and operations tempo—may also yield improvements in the ability to detect threat items and individuals with hostile intent.

With regard to advancements in screening technology, next generation AT x-ray systems are capable of providing multiple image views, usually two views that provide both an overhead view and a profile view of the x-rayed item. Some of these systems also incorporate computer image interpretation algorithms that automatically search for, and either highlight or alert the operator to suspected threat items such as explosives and weapons. These features, however, can often be viewed negatively by operators and can slow the screening process if they generate high numbers of false alarms. The specific performance characteristics of AT x-ray systems being acquired and deployed by the TSA, including information about their false alarm rates, is not publicly available, but remain important considerations in the selection of systems and system features for operational deployment.

PASSENGER CHECKPOINT EFFICIENCY

While the ability to detect threats is the primary metric for evaluating passenger checkpoint system performance, maintaining checkpoint efficiency has also been given a high priority. However, the well-documented phenomenon of speed-accuracy tradeoffs in human performance highlight the fact that increasing system throughput can lead to missed threats and a deterioration of system effectiveness. Therefore, policymakers and aviation security strategists have sought a balance that will allow passengers to typically experience reasonable times standing in queue to pass through airport security while maintaining high levels of threat detection. While research and engineering has focused on optimizing screening lane efficiency and effectiveness, long-standing wait time objectives have been set by policy, largely based on what is regarded as reasonable to expect by the traveling public.

PASSENGER WAIT TIMES

It has been the DOT's and the TSA's long-standing goal that passengers should not wait, on average, more than 10 minutes to pass through an airport security checkpoint. This can be traced back to the objectives laid out for checkpoint efficiency by Transportation Secretary Norman Mineta in 2002 as responsibility for checkpoint screening functions was being turned over to the TSA.[27]

The challenge in determining the number of checkpoints that will meet these specified wait time criteria largely derives from the variability and fluctuation in daily and hourly passenger volumes. Typically, a representative busy hour is picked to model the passenger demand for screening. The TSA has identified a variety of methods for selecting the busy or peak hour to be used in modeling passenger screening demand. Data can be derived from either annual enplanement forecasts or from airline flight schedules, with adjustments made for the percentage or amount of passengers who are transferring from other flights and do not impose demand on the screening checkpoints.

The number of checkpoints required can then be estimated based on the modeled passenger demand for checkpoint screening for a representative busy hour divided by the hourly throughput achievable from a single checkpoint. For example, if the model predicted 3000 passengers per hour, and the achievable throughput per screening lane was 300 passengers per hour (five passengers per minute), then 10 screening lanes would provide an optimal number with no excessive queuing. However, this may result in excessive capacity during nonpeak periods.

Space requirements for queuing passengers awaiting to pass through screening checkpoints, known as queue length requirements, can be assessed by determining passenger average arrival rates over the selected busy hour, multiplied by the average or expected wait time, divided by the number of checkpoint lanes to process these passengers. For example, if it were expected that 3000 passengers would arrive during the hour, the arrival rate would be 50 passengers per minutes. If the target wait time was 10 minutes, the total queue size would be 500 passengers, and in a 10 screening lane configuration, that would translate to 50 passengers in queue per lane. According to design guidelines issued by the TSA, space allocation for queues should provide somewhere between 7 and

15 square feet per person,[28] resulting in a total square footage allocation for queuing passengers of between 3500 and 7500 square feet in this example.

In this manner, the TSA can determine the optimum number of screening lanes and gauge the space allocation requirements for queuing passengers to meet peak passenger demand loads. However, space constraints at airports may prevent achieving these objectives, at least without overcrowding passengers in queue, which can heighten aggravation and tension making it more difficult to spot suspicious individuals. Crowding may also heighten security risks because these overcrowded queues could become prime targets for a shooting or bombing attack. In various locations, unique airport factors may have a notable impact on the optimum number of screening lanes as well as the configuration of those lanes. More significantly, airport space limitations and other factors limiting available resources to set up and staff screening lanes may result in less than optimal numbers of screening lanes.

Wait time objectives are a key consideration in determining the number of screening lanes and screeners needed across the nation's airports. The screening lane requirements, in turn, drive space requirements at airports for housing security checkpoints and terminal layouts to accommodate passenger screening operations. The TSA models its staffing allocation and screening lane requirements using a model that attempts to screen 85% of passengers within the 10 minute target time frame based on passenger volumes projected for each airport's peak travel month.[29] The TSA notes that on only about 7% of days out of the year will passenger volumes exceed these levels, resulting in expected wait times of more than 10 minutes. Predictably, many of these days occur during peak travel periods during the Thanksgiving and Christmas holiday times.

While this model, which forms the basis of the TSA's staffing allocation, is designed to minimize the number of passengers experiencing waits of more than 10 minutes, in practice many more passengers experience waits of longer than 10 minutes. At the busiest airports, designated as security category X and category I airports, average wait times have consistently exceeded the 10 minute goal (Figure 7.1). Since these larger airports account for more than three-quarters of passenger boardings, a good portion of airline travelers routinely experience wait times in excess of the 10 minute goal. While the average wait times at these large airports are a few minutes greater than the 10 minute target, lengthy wait times, sometimes exceeding 40 minutes, are not uncommon during peak travel periods at major airports. However, consistent peak period waits of

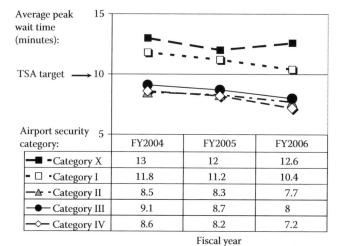

Airport security category:	FY2004	FY2005	FY2006
■ Category X	13	12	12.6
□ Category I	11.8	11.2	10.4
△ Category II	8.5	8.3	7.7
● Category III	9.1	8.7	8
◇ Category IV	8.6	8.2	7.2

Fiscal year

FIGURE 7.1 Average peak passenger wait times at screening checkpoints. (Data obtained from U.S. Government Accountability Office. *Aviation Security: TSA's Staffing Allocation Model Is Useful for Allocating Staff among Airports, but Its Assumptions Should Be Systematically Reassessed.* February 2007, GAO-07-299.)

more than 40 minutes are often grounds for further examination from a TSA optimization team to identify staffing, screening lane, or other resource issues that may be contributing to these long waits.[30] The GAO has recommended that the TSA establish a mechanism for periodically assessing the assumptions of its screener staffing allocation models as it continues to refine and optimize screener staffing and screening lane requirements to maintain and improve the efficiency and throughput of passenger screening lanes.[31]

POTENTIAL SECURITY RISKS OF CHECKPOINT INEFFICIENCIES

Despite various efforts to improve checkpoint efficiency and reduce passenger wait times, checkpoint lines remain vulnerable terrorist targets for bombings, shootings, or the potential release of chemical or biological agents because they often consist of large congregations of individuals in the "nonsterile" portion of the airport terminal, prior to screening for possible threat items. Inefficiencies at screening checkpoints that result in long screening queues and congestion in airport terminals introduce unique vulnerabilities that may be mitigated through various efforts to increase checkpoint efficiency, but may also be mitigated by specific design considerations to minimize congestion and isolate long screening queues from open, accessible areas of the airport terminal. Toward this objective, airport and security checkpoint queue design might consider options for better restricting access to security screening lines and better controlling access to the areas in and around checkpoints to address these vulnerabilities. Additional streamlining of passenger screening checkpoints may further reduce these vulnerabilities. In addition to streamlining checkpoint procedures, the TSA is examining ways to integrate next generation screening technologies as part of its new "checkpoint evolution" initiative.

QUEUING PRACTICES AND PROCEDURES

For some time, responsibility for passenger screening checkpoint queues has been a contentious issue. Previously, the TSA had taken a much more limited role in controlling and monitoring the lines that formed in front of security checkpoints. Airports had the primary responsibility for controlling access to these lines, and on an airport-by-airport basis, procedures varied for queuing, including whether to set up dedicated lines for elite travelers (e.g., first and business class travelers), and for airline crews. Access controls for security screening queues were primarily a function carried out by airport contract employees serving as document checkers. More recently, the TSA has been hiring and deploying TSOs to serve as document checkers, eliminating the need for airport document checkers to control access to screening lines. The TSA has adopted the title of TSOs for the TSA screener workforce to better reflect the more diversified job functions and roles of these employees, including document checking, behavioral observation, and bomb appraisal functions. In addition, the continued expansion of the RT program, which potentially offers the opportunity for streamlined checkpoint processing for passengers who voluntarily submit background information for vetting by the TSA, is also changing the manner in which screening lines operate.

At many airports, queues to enter screening checkpoints have been designed to provide "elite" flyer lanes that the airlines make available to first class, and sometimes to business class, travelers as well as to their best customers who have reached certain status levels in airline frequent flyer programs.[32] The airlines maintain that they have the right to offer elite passengers curbside-to-curbside perks, including dedicated queues to enter checkpoint screening lanes. However, some people have complained that security screening is paid for equally by everyone through equivalent passenger security fees and Treasury general fund contributions, and therefore, all passengers should receive equal treatment. However, the TSA contends that separating seasoned passengers familiar with screening procedures from others benefits everyone through better efficiency and resource allocation at the screening checkpoints.[33] More recently, the TSA has moved forward with a system of lane self-selection or tailored screening lanes, allowing expert travelers to select expedited lanes, while families traveling with small children and individuals needing additional assistance are funneled through screening lanes better equipped to handle these traveler's special needs. Also, the RT program offers participants dedicated checkpoint lanes for expedited processing, or the opportunity to move to the front of normal checkpoint screening lines, depending on the airport. Whether these concepts will replace or complement "elite" flyer lanes remain an issue for the TSA, airlines, and airports as they seek to determine the best model to accommodate travelers and expedite the screening process. The tailored screening lane initiative and the RT program are described in further detail below.

THE TAILORED SELF-SELECT SCREENING LANE INITIATIVE

In an effort to explore ways to make checkpoint screening queuing processes more efficient and expedient for passengers, the TSA field tested an initiative for passengers to self-select among one of three designated screening lanes based on their knowledge and experience with TSA screening procedures and the number of carry-on items in their possession. In field tests of this concept at the Salt Lake City, Utah, Airport and Denver International Airport, the TSA adopted a skiing analogy, setting up a "Black Diamond" fast lane for expert travelers who are completely familiar with screening procedures and are traveling with a single carry-on bag. A "Blue Square" lane has been designated for frequent flyers somewhat familiar with TSA procedures, or more experienced flyers who have multiple carry-on items. Finally, a "Green Circle" lane has been established for families with small children, parents carrying infants and toddlers in strollers, and others needing special assistance, as well as those unfamiliar with checkpoint security procedures who require additional guidance. For some travelers, lane selection is constrained. For example, those carrying multiple bags are not allowed to choose a Black Diamond lane, and those traveling with small children or strollers are routed to the Green Circle lane. However, other travelers are free to self-select their lane. For this reason, choosing a Black Diamond lane might not always be the fastest route if it is often chosen, particularly if it is chosen by individuals who really do not have a full understanding of the security screening procedures and restrictions. This could lead to frustration and aggravation among delayed passengers expecting a streamlined process by choosing the expert lane. While this is a difficult issue to address, passenger checkpoint experiences among all travelers, including expert travelers, may be improved through passenger education.

The TSA has noted that in the pilot program, passengers choosing the Black Diamond lanes experienced significantly reduced wait times. Smoother operations in other lanes were also observed. For example, the TSA attributes a reduction in the confiscation of prohibited items to families feeling less rushed and having more time to prepare for the screening process. The TSA contends that "[s]ecurity is best served by a calm screening environment . . ."[34] and has indicated that it is seeking to expand this initiative to additional airports that will be selected based on airport and airline support, and consideration of checkpoint configuration and passenger characteristics.[35] By the end of FY2008, the TSA expanded the use of these self-select lanes to 32 airports and has now expanded family lanes to all commercial passenger airports. According to TSA observations, since implementing the program, expert lanes have seen an average 21% increase in throughput (with some as high as 40%), while alarm rates for lanes designated for families and those needing extra assistance have been reduced by an average of 11%.[36]

THE RT PROGRAM

In addition to the tailored self-select screening lanes, the TSA considers the RT program as another potential means to streamline checkpoint processing of participating passengers who pose a known low risk, allowing the TSA to better concentrate its resources on screening passengers of unknown or elevated risk. The RT concept was recommended by airlines and airports soon after the 9/11 attacks as a means to vet and clear trustworthy travelers and allow security screening efforts to concentrate on those passenger of unknown risk, or particularly, passengers posing an elevated risk. It was initially believed that such a system could encompass most of the flying public, allowing security screening efforts to be highly focused on those travelers who were not part of the program. Within weeks after the 9/11 attacks, the DOT's Airport Security Rapid Response Team included among its recommendations the urgent need to establish a nationwide program for voluntarily submitting information for vetting passengers who would be issued "smart" credentials to expedite processing of the vast majority of travelers, thus allowing aviation security resources to be focused more effectively, an idea that became known as the "trusted traveler" concept. The recommendation was reflected in statutory language included in ATSA (P.L. 107-71) and gave the TSA the authority to pursue a voluntary system for passenger vetting and identity authentication using biometrics.

So far, the RT program has been quite limited in its scope, available primarily to frequent travelers at a small number of airports under a pilot program. As of December 2007, the TSA estimated that only about 64,000 individuals were participating in the RT pilot program, a very small fraction of the tens of millions of annual airline travelers. The TSA, however, began expanding the RT program in the summer of 2008 beyond the original 19 airports that participated in the pilot program. RT is now available to any airport that requests it.

The RT program was originally implemented under a public–private partnership model, in which volunteer passengers, who submit background information for vetting along with biometric data, are issued biometric identity cards issued by private service providers once cleared through the background check process, which is coordinated by the TSA. The TSA has since dropped the background check process and now describes the RT program as strictly a private sector enterprise.[37] Under the program, the RT vendors are responsible for card issuance and identity verification of program participants as they enter screening checkpoints; however, security screening remains the responsibility of the TSA. In some airports, RT participants are simply given preemptive queuing into screening lanes used by all other passengers.

From its experience during pilot testing, the TSA determined that the security threat assessment conducted on RT applicants is largely redundant with terrorist watch list checks conducted on all passengers each time they fly, and found that other elements of the background check performed "are not core elements in determining threats."[38] Therefore, under the fully deployed RT program, the TSA decided to eliminate the additional elements of the background check process and do away with the $28 fee it passed on to RT applicants to offset related costs.[39] While the RT program is now available to all airports, its future now seems somewhat more uncertain as the benefits to both the TSA and program participants based on experience during pilot testing appear to be much more limited than originally anticipated.

Moreover, just as the TSA announced nationwide availability of the RT program in the summer of 2008, it took action to temporarily suspend Verified Identity Pass, Inc., which serves as a vendor for the RT program under the brand name Clear®, from processing new applications after a laptop computer containing unencrypted applicant personal data from about 33,000 RT applicants was reported missing from San Francisco International Airport (SFO). This potential data breach prompted the TSA to suspend further enrollment in the Clear Identity Pass RT program while it conducted audits of Verified Identity Pass, Inc., data security procedures. The suspension was quickly lifted after the laptop was recovered and the company put in place procedures to encrypt all enrollee personal data.[40] This incident and the potential threat of data breaches, however, raise considerable questions about the protection of private information under such programs during a time when there is considerable anxiety over identity theft. Security breaches such as this may cause potential applicants to reconsider whether the potential benefits of moving more quickly through security lines with fewer hassles are worth the risk of potential identity theft. Data security, therefore, appears to be another key issue for the future direction of the RT program.

Questions also remain regarding how hassle-free RT security lines are and how much time RT participants really save at security checkpoints. According to the TSA, it is up to individual airports to determine if they wish to participate in this program. As TSA moves forward with RT, the airline industry, which once backed this program as a means to reduce hassles for frequent flyers, now characterizes the manner in which it is being implemented as having limited and questionable benefit.

At some airports, like Orlando International Airport (MCO), RT program participants have been used to test out emerging technologies, such as shoe scanners, allowing them to reduce or eliminate some of the hassles associated with passenger screening. The concept has been to provide RT participants with some form of expedited screening experience as an incentive for participation. However, the TSA has largely concluded that these preliminary technologies tested under the RT program were not reliable enough to offer such anticipated benefits.[41]

The use of the program as a testbed for streamlined screening technologies and procedures has thus only provided limited benefits and reductions in travel hassles to participants. Nonetheless, some RT vendors have been pushing forward with the concept of promoting the RT program as an opportunity to stimulate the development of advanced screening technologies, particularly technologies that can improve checkpoint efficiency. For example, Verified Identity Pass, Inc., has offered technology developers a $500,000 prize for the development of technologies that can further streamline checkpoint processes, focusing on the scanning of shoes, laptops, and outer garments.[42] The company indicates that it would pursue partnerships with the winning developer to obtain TSA certification of promising new technologies and would ultimately seek to purchase systems for screening RT participants.

While the potential benefits of the RT program have not yet been fully realized, Congress has directed the TSA to establish an international RT program that incorporates biometrics and e-passport technologies to be used in conjunction with US-VISIT and the VWP. Under the existing RT program, some international carriers have been participating for outbound flights originating from JFK and Newark Liberty airports. The future of both domestic and international RT implementation remains an issue of particular interest with regard to how this program may be able to someday work in coordination with other screening initiatives to streamline the process for certain passengers, thereby facilitating a risk-based allocation of screening resources to focus on those passengers who present an unknown or elevated risk.

OPTIONS FOR FURTHER STREAMLINING PASSENGER CHECKPOINT PROCEDURES

Additional efficiencies may be gained in passenger checkpoint screening if some current requirements could be met using more expedient alternatives. Two procedural requirements in particular are believed to be major factors in decreasing passenger throughput and increasing the so-called hassle factor: The requirements to remove shoes for x-ray screening and the requirement to remove laptops and other large portable electronics, such as portable DVD players, from carry-on baggage so that they can be screened separately. Eliminating these requirements, or taking steps to streamline these aspects of the screening experience, is therefore seen as having a potentially significant impact on improving checkpoint efficiency.

Shoe scanners that may eliminate the need to remove shoes for scanning were initially tested on participants in the RT pilot program in 2007. However, the model manufactured by GE tested under the RT program was found to not meet TSA's detection criteria and further testing of the systems was suspended.[43] However, in August 2008, the TSA initiated field testing of a different model shoe scanner, the L3 PassPort, at LAX. The shoe scanner systems currently under evaluation use ETD methods and puffs air over the shoes to collect samples for analysis.[44] The systems are designed to detect traces of nitrate-based and peroxide-based explosives, but they do not generate an image of the shoe or screen for metals.[45] During field testing, the TSA will still require passengers to remove their shoes after being scanned by the machines to make sure the technology does not miss any explosives threats.[46] However, pending the outcome of these trials, shoe scanners may eventually be deployed to airports nationwide potentially allowing most passengers to keep their shoes on during the entire screening process.

The TSA has also approved certain laptop carrying cases that are specifically designed to allow laptop computers to remain in the bag as they pass through the x-ray scanner. The TSA requires that the bag designs provide an unobstructed x-ray image of the laptop computer by itself.[47] This is accomplished through the use of a pull out or flip out laptop sleeve or compartment that allows the laptop to be scanned by itself, away from the other compartments and contents of the carry-on bag. Passengers are instructed to place only the laptop in this sleeve to avoid the laptop image from being obscured by power cords, peripheral devices, or other items stowed in the carry-on bag. Since use of the TSA-approved laptop cases is voluntary and requires an investment by travelers, it may be some time before this has any meaningful impact on improving checkpoint efficiency. For business travelers, however, the reduced hassle of not having to remove then repack laptop computers may be seen as a considerable incentive by itself to purchase one of these cases, even if it does not guarantee shorter wait times at screening checkpoints.

CHECKPOINT PROCEDURES FOR LIQUIDS

In addition to checkpoint delays caused by laptop and shoe screening requirements, TSA limitations on liquids carried through security checkpoints, implemented in 2006, has resulted in considerable confusion, delays, and hassles for airline passengers.

Immediately following the detection of the terrorist plot targeting airliners bound for the United States and Canada from London's Heathrow Airport in August 2006, the TSA responded by banning the carriage of all liquids and gels by passengers through airport screening checkpoints. The total ban on liquids and gels remained in effect for several weeks. During this period, limited exceptions were made for breast milk for babies, liquid medicines, and other liquids regarded as being medically necessary. Beverage purchased beyond the screening checkpoint were not included in the ban, largely because the threat of passing bomb-making materials to an airline passenger using liquids purchased from vendors in the secured areas of airport terminals was considered minimal. Also, other security measures, such as background checks for airport workers, were viewed as limiting the possibility that terrorists might exploit beverage distribution to airport vendors as a means to get liquid explosives beyond airport security checkpoints.

In September 2006, the TSA relaxed the passenger liquid ban to some degree, establishing specific quantity limits and special procedures for carrying liquids through screening checkpoints. The TSA refers to these procedures as the "3-1-1 for carry-ons" concept, with the objective of providing a simple-to-remember memory aid for travelers. Under 3-1-1, travelers are allowed to carry through the checkpoint liquids in bottles with a liquid volume of *three* ounces or less, are limited by how many of these bottles will comfortably fit within a *one* quart clear plastic bag, with a limit of *one* such bag per traveler. The TSA has made extensive efforts to educate and inform the public regarding these procedures, and has been exploring the use of tailored screening lanes to separate passengers who might be unfamiliar with these procedures from seasoned air travelers seeking an expedited process to get through airport screening.

By November 2006, the EU, along with Canada and other countries in Europe, Asia, and the South Pacific, adopted the 3-1-1 protocols in an effort to harmonize international aviation security procedures with TSA procedures. The TSA believes that roughly half of the world's aviation travelers must adhere to these procedures for carrying liquids through security screening checkpoints.

The 3-1-1 procedures were designed to allow the carry-on of liquid toiletry items in specified quantities for passengers traveling on short trips and not checking baggage and for making reasonable accommodations to allow for accessible liquid medicines and toiletry items on longer flights. However, placing liquids in checked baggage is still preferred. In addition to these allowable liquids, passengers are allowed to bring on board liquid medicines, as well as baby formula and food, breast milk, and juices to provide for a traveling infant. These items are allowed in reasonable quantities exceeding the three-ounce limit imposed on other liquids and are not required to be placed in the quart-sized bag.

The TSA has responded to public criticism over the liquids ban and subsequent 3-1-1 procedures by pointing out the significance of the liquids explosives threat. However, an aspect of the liquids ban that has raised considerable criticism of the TSA is that the threat posed by liquid explosives was widely understood prior to the U.K. liquids bombing plot. Liquid explosives had been used in the downing of Korean Airlines flight 858 in November 1987, and Ramsi Yousef used an improvised liquid explosive device to bomb Philippine Airlines flight 434 in December 1994, smuggling the chemicals on board in a contact lens solution bottle. He and his coconspirators planned to use similar liquid explosive devices, assembled in aircraft lavatories, to destroy as many as twelve U.S.-bound aircraft from Asia as part of the so-called Bojinka plot concocted by Yousef and his uncle, Khaled Sheikh Mohammed. Authorities believe that the U.K. liquids explosives plotters similarly sought to assemble liquid explosive devices in aircraft lavatories. Despite the previous attacks involving liquid explosives, it was only after this plot was uncovered by British authorities that the TSA felt compelled to take action and impose significant constraints on the carriage of liquids through screening checkpoints and on board aircraft.

While it appeared unlikely that security procedures for carrying liquids on board aircraft would be significantly modified or relaxed until new technologies capable of reliably detecting liquid explosives could be developed, tested, and fully deployed at airports, the TSA announced that it would begin phasing out restrictions on liquids in carry-on by the fall of 2009.[48] TSA Administrator Kip Hawley has indicated that, by the end of 2010, passengers should be able to again carry liquids through screening checkpoints, but would be required to place bottles and other liquid containers through x-ray machines separately.

PASSENGER EDUCATION AND INFORMATIONAL MATERIALS

Public education and easily accessible, easy-to-understand information regarding security proce-dures and requirements may play an important role in improving checkpoint efficiency. The TSA has launched several initiatives to inform the public regarding specific checkpoint requirements, procedures, and limitations. The efforts to inform passengers regarding the 3-1-1 policy on liq-uids serves as a prime example of how the TSA has made considerable efforts to provide the traveling public with adequate information regarding screening and security procedures to make passengers experiences as efficient and hassle-free as possible, given current policies, strategies, and approaches to screening. However, many security procedures remain confusing, in part, because they have changed in response to changing threat assessments, or have been applied inconsistently in the past.

Public education is likely to increase in importance as the TSA rolls out various new checkpoint screening technologies over the next several years. While some of these technologies have been field tested on a limited basis at various airports across the country, ongoing initiatives to deploy these systems nationwide represent the most significant change to the passenger checkpoint experi-ence since mandatory use of magnetometers and x-ray screening of carry-on items was imple-mented 35 years ago.

THE EVOLUTION OF CHECKPOINT DESIGN

To address the challenges of improving screening performance, enhancing the capability to detect explosives, and increasing checkpoint efficiency and throughput, the TSA is testing new checkpoint concepts that integrate emerging screening technologies and address various operational and human factors needs. In March 2008, the TSA launched an initiative called *Checkpoint Evolution* encom-passing a variety of planned improvements to airport screening checkpoints. TSA Administrator Kip Hawley noted that "[t]his is the first significant change to the checkpoint since the 1970s," a reference to the fact that the layout of airport screening checkpoints in the United States has remained relatively unchanged since they were first put in place in the early 1970s.

A Checkpoint Evolution Team at the TSA has developed a prototype concept for the checkpoint of the future that was showcased on the TSA website. The prototype future checkpoint concept entered operational testing and evaluation at BWI Airport, in Terminal B, which services Southwest Airlines, in April 2008. This prototype includes multiview AT x-ray equipment, millimeter wave WBI portals used for continuous random screening, and liquid bottle scanners.[49] However, the investment strategy and deployment schedule for deploying various future checkpoint concepts currently under evaluation remains unclear.

In addition to potentially improving the efficiency and effectiveness of the screening process, proposed changes to the screening checkpoint may help reduce congestion at "soft target" locations such as airport lobbies. Various design elements of the proposed future checkpoint provide potential mitigation of the threat of explosives carried through the security checkpoint and possibly for the threat of shootings or bombings in and near the checkpoint queue. By designing more streamlined queuing processes, and queuing areas that are better separated from the public spaces of the airport terminal, the TSA hopes to achieve enhanced capabilities for surveillance and behavioral detection of potential threats of this kind.

The TSA is also seeking to implement methods to make the screening checkpoint a calmer environment in hopes that this will allow screeners and BDOs to more easily spot suspicious behaviors. TSA Administrator Kip Hawley noted that "[c]alm allows things to stand out more. It creates a better environment to observe hostile intent."[50] According to the TSA, a calmer checkpoint environment can also help to ease perceived time pressures and other distractions that may hinder screener performance.

Elements of the future screening checkpoint queuing area design include mood lighting, soothing music, improved signage to direct and instruct passengers, and museum-style storyboards that convey personal stories of various TSA screeners (Figure 7.2). In the prototype, panels and informational

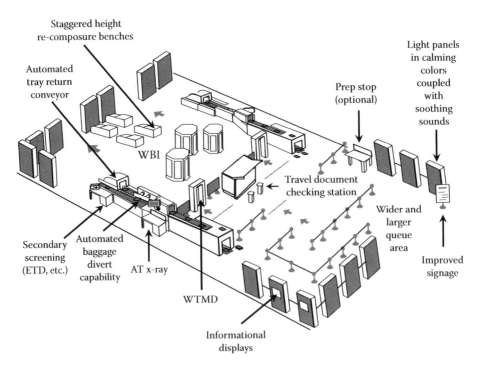

FIGURE 7.2 The prototype design of the checkpoint evolution concept. Key to abbreviations: ETD, Explosives Trace Detection; WBI, Whole Body Imaging; WTMD, Walk-Through Metal Detector; AT x-ray, Advanced Technology x-ray.

boards also function as barriers to better separate the checkpoint queue from the rest of the passenger terminal. The queuing area also includes a "prep stop," providing passengers with a location to discard or recycle any trash or prohibited items and to organize and bag other items prior to screening. Travel document checking stations, staffed by TSA document checkers, will be positioned at the transition between the queue and the screening lanes.

In the screening lanes, various technologies and procedures to streamline the screening process are included in the future checkpoint concept. For processing carry-on bags, the prototype system integrates an automatic conveyor and bin return system. The proposed automated conveyor system will have the capability to separate alarm items (i.e., suspicious items that require additional scrutiny) from cleared carry-on items. Cleared items will proceed down the conveyor to a collection area where passengers can gather their possessions. One highlighted feature of the prototype system is the use of sensitive cameras in the collection area to identify and alert passengers when items, including items as small as coins, are left behind in the conveyor bins. Once the bins are emptied, the system would automatically return them via a reverse-direction conveyor belt to the beginning of the conveyor for reuse, thus eliminating the labor-intensive function of moving and stacking bins currently performed by TSOs. On the back end of the future checkpoint configuration, the TSA plans to install "recomposure benches," to allow passenger to reassemble their items that may have been removed or opened during the screening inspection process, and an "end zone" where travelers can regroup with their families or others traveling with them before proceeding to their boarding gate.

Two significant challenges to implementing the proposed checkpoint evolution concept are the acquisition and sustainment costs and airport space requirements. Future funding to carry these checkpoint evolution concepts beyond initial field testing is yet to be determined. These checkpoint evolution concepts are being field tested in conjunction with other initiatives to deploy next generation checkpoint screening technologies aimed at addressing lingering concerns over the limited ability to detect explosives on passengers and in carry-on items. The TSA's investment strategy for these next generation checkpoint technologies is an area of considerable policy interest.

NEXT GENERATION CHECKPOINT TECHNOLOGIES

Since the early 1970s, passenger screening checkpoints have relied almost exclusively on the use of magnetometers, or walk-through metal detectors (WTMDs), as the sole means for primary screening for weapons and other prohibited or dangerous items being carried by passengers. These machines induce pulsed magnetic fields and sense any interruption or disturbance in those fields, usually caused by the presence of metallic objects, as individuals pass through these detectors.[51] These devices, however, are not capable of detecting explosives or nonmetallic threat items. Also, checkpoint screening of carry-on items for explosives, weapons, and other threats is carried out using x-ray systems that are limited in their ability to assist human operators detect objects or make determinations regarding potential threats based on the x-ray image.

In its final report, the 9/11 Commission recommended that "[t]he TSA and the Congress must give priority attention to improving the ability of screening checkpoints to detect explosives on passengers."[52] Congress responded by including language in the IRTPA (P.L. 108-458), directing the DHS to "... give a high priority to developing, testing, improving, and deploying, at airport screening checkpoints, equipment that detects nonmetallic, chemical, biological, and radiological weapons, and explosives, in all forms, on individuals and in their personal property."[53] The legislation also directed the TSA to develop a strategic plan for deployment of explosives detection equipment at airport checkpoints, including technologies such as walk-through explosives detection portals, document scanners, shoe scanners, and x-ray backscatter devices. These various technologies are discussed in further detail below.

The Implementing Recommendations of the 9/11 Commission Act of 2007 (P.L. 110-53) reiterated the requirement for developing this strategic plan, and also established a Checkpoint Screening

Security Fund, requiring that $250 million collected from passenger and airline security fees be deposited in this fund in FY2008. Funding for Checkpoint Support, which encompasses checkpoint technology acquisition has been maintained at the $250 million level for FY2009 (see P.L. 110-329).

One potential concern over the TSA's deployment strategy for these enhanced technology systems is that large Category X and Category I airports are slated to be the first to get these new technologies. The strategy reflects a view that focusing efforts on the largest airports will encompass the greatest number of passengers and the highest-risk flights. The aviation screening system in the United States, however, operates using a single gateway concept, meaning that passengers are typically only screened once at their originating airport. Terrorists may exploit knowledge that smaller airports may not have the same level of advanced checkpoint technologies as larger airports to try to minimize detection. Such concerns may prompt additional policy debate over whether focusing on the largest airports first is the best strategy, or if targeted or accelerated deployment of these technologies to include small- and mid-sized airports could provide an alternative strategy for minimizing such a threat.

Over the past few years, the TSA has been field testing a wide variety of checkpoint technologies aimed at improving the screening of passengers and carry-on items, particularly to address the need for improving the detection of explosives at passenger checkpoints. A summary of some of the key emerging checkpoint technologies that are now reaching technical maturity for field testing and deployment in airport settings is provided in Table 7.1. These technical approaches include

TABLE 7.1
Emerging Checkpoint Technologies

Emerging Technology	Description	Estimated Per Unit Acquisition Cost
AT x-ray	X-ray systems with advanced visual detection capabilities including multiview imaging and automated explosives detection algorithms	$199,845
WBIs	Imaging systems using x-ray backscatter or millimeter wave imaging technologies to inspect for concealed weapons and explosives under passenger clothing. These units can be used in place of metal detection wands and physical pat-down inspections	$256,872
BLSs	A new handheld detection capability to discriminate explosives or flammable liquids from common benign liquids carried by passengers or in carry-on items	$42,419
Cast and prosthesis imagers	Specially designed low-dose x-ray backscatter devices to screen casts and prosthetic limbs for possible concealed weapons and certain explosives	$56,567
Shoe scanner systems	Devices to scan shoes for explosives using nuclear quadrupole resonance imaging techniques. Field tested under the RT program but found to not yet meet minimum detection standards	Not specified
ETD portals	Walk-through portals using ETD methods to inspect passenger for trace indicators of explosives	$211,924
Automated carry-on bag EDS	Automated detection capability for inspecting bags for explosives and weapons using CT-based solutions. Seen as a possible means for either complementing or replacing current manual x-ray image analysis processes	$506,778

Source: Compiled from Transportation Security Administration, *Congressional Justifications—Aviation Security*, FY2008 and FY2009.

explosives chemical trace detection methods; WBI systems; AT x-ray capabilities; and other methods, such as computed tomography (CT)-based EDSs and the use of magnetic resonance imaging (MRI) technologies for detecting explosives and other threat objects in carry-on items.

ETD TECHNOLOGIES

Several technologies that use various ETD methods are available for screening passengers and carry-on items for explosives. Available ETD technologies that may be considered for checkpoint use include ETD machines tailored for checkpoint screening lane use to screen carry-on items; handheld bottled liquids scanners that use ETD screening methods; and walk-through ETD portals for screening individuals.

ETD Machines

ETD machines have been a fixture at aviation screening checkpoints and for checked baggage screening at smaller regional airports since the TSA assumed responsibility for passenger screening. These systems are capable of detecting minute quantities of elements found in explosive compounds using a variety of techniques—including mass spectrometry, gas chromatography, chemical luminescence, and ion mobility spectrometry—to measure the chemical properties of vapor or particulate matter sampled from passengers, carry-on items, checked baggage, or cargo. It is generally believed that ETD systems will continue to play a central role in the screening of carry-on items to detect traces of explosives for items belonging to individuals singled out for secondary screening, or items flagged for additional screening based on the analysis of the TSA screener viewing the x-ray image of the item during the primary screening process.

Bottle and Liquid Explosives Scanners

Following the August 2006 U.K. aircraft liquid bombing plot, the TSA has been keenly interested in identifying an effective technology for detecting explosives in liquids and flammable liquids without requiring direct contact with a sample. Observers have noted that it would have been extremely difficult to detect liquid explosives, like those the terrorists had planned to use, employing checkpoint screening technologies and techniques in place at that time.[54] Since then, the TSA has been working with a number of vendors of bottled liquid scanner (BLS) technology to identify candidate systems for field testing.

So far, two handheld units, the Fido PaxPoint developed by ICx Technologies and the SABRE 4000 developed by Smiths Detection have been acquired by the TSA for field testing. The SABRE 4000 relies on ion mobility spectrometry, a common trace detection method proven effective in detecting minute quantities of explosives and chemical weapons. The Fido PaxPoint uses a different trace detection technology that relies on amplifying fluorescent polymers, a technique that utilizes a film lining that reacts when exposed to minute quantities of explosives. The sensitivity of these devices is considered to be sufficient enough to detect explosive traces and vapors through bottles and other sealed containers, including peroxide-based explosives as well as nitrate-based explosives. These units cost roughly $43,000 each. Under the TSA's proposal for FY2009, it intends to deploy a cumulative total of 250 of these units, which will enable them to be available at roughly two-thirds of all screening lanes at Category X and Category I airports. This, however, is considerably scaled back from earlier estimates that the TSA would acquire a cumulative total of 800 of these units by the end of FY2008.[55] Both devices have been deployed in field tests at several large airports.

While these devices also have the capability of detecting chemical warfare agents, it appears that the TSA is primarily interested in the explosives detection capabilities of these devices and has not formally addressed the potential threat of chemical attacks in airline passenger cabins, although chemicals like Sarin and VX nerve agent have been used in nonaviation terrorist attacks in the past.

The TSA has also considered various other technologies capable of detecting liquid explosives through a sealed container that use x-ray quadrupole resonance imaging, acoustic/ultrasound, Raman spectroscopy, and electromagnetic resonance techniques. Researchers are also working on laser irradiation techniques for detecting peroxide-based explosives.[56] These various techniques, however, can encounter difficulty in accurately identifying explosives through opaque containers and tend to yield relatively high numbers of false positives making them impractical for deployment at airport screening checkpoints given the current state of technology maturity of these systems.[57]

Walk-Through ETD Portals

In 2004, the TSA initiated pilot testing of walk-through ETD portals. When passengers pass through these semienclosed portals, puffs of air are blown at them to provide airborne samples of elements on their person. The samples are automatically collected and analyzed by the unit to detect the presence of explosives using ETD techniques. The system relies on an ion mobility spectrometry process that provides versatile detection of both positive and negative ions using a proprietary ion "trap."[58] The system is capable of detecting a broad spectrum of explosives in a matter of a few seconds. Citing reliability problems, the TSA has suspended further deployment of these systems, and was reportedly reassessing how to proceed.[59] The TSA has not sought to acquire additional trace portal systems, focusing instead on testing and deployment of WBI technologies, which are discussed in further detail below.

WBI TECHNOLOGIES

As part of the TSA's overall approach to improving the detection of explosives and nonmetallic weapons at passenger checkpoints, it is currently exploring the use of WBI technologies for detecting concealed items carried by passengers. WBI solutions offer an integrated approach to passenger screening insofar as these technologies can reveal concealed items carried by a person, including traditional metallic weapons, nonmetallic weapons, and explosive devices. These systems, however, cannot provide an indication of whether a concealed item is made of explosives material. Nonetheless, detection of a concealed item can alert screeners to conduct more thorough screening to determine the specific characteristics of the item through methods such as ETD or walk-through explosives detection portals.

The TSA is continuing to study specifically how WBI technologies could be integrated with other technologies in future checkpoint screening solutions. The Transportation Security Laboratory (TSL), a component of the DHS S&T Directorate, has been mulling a concept it refers to as the "tunnel of truth." This future checkpoint concept, which would submit passengers to a battery of screening techniques while being transported on a moving walkway, incorporates WBI technologies along with trace detection portal technologies.[60]

Because of the ability to detect a broad array of concealed items, many view WBI systems as a candidate technology for primary screening as part of a system such as the future "tunnel of truth concept," although in current field testing, the TSA is providing this technology solely as an option for passengers selected for secondary screening as an alternative to a pat-down search and as a procedure applied to individuals randomly selected for secondary screening.

Since WBI technologies are regarded by some as highly invasive, critics of these systems have argued that they should only be used in limited circumstances. For example, the ACLU has urged Congress to ban the use of WBI technologies as a method for primary screening. The ACLU maintains that "[p]assengers expect privacy underneath their clothing and should not be required to display highly personal details of their bodies."[61] The ACLU has also raised concerns that, if used as a primary screening method, WBI technologies would, in their opinion, cause unnecessary delays by increasing the number of questionable items detected on persons passing through the checkpoint that would need to be resolved through additional screening techniques such as explosives detection portals and conventional metal detectors. The ACLU maintains that these technologies require "a tremendous invasion of privacy with little speed or efficiency gains."[62]

It should be noted, however, that while these technologies may be considered by some as being more invasive, they offer a potential capability for detecting nonmetallic threat items, particularly explosives, that does not currently exist with magnetometer screening. In this regard, WBI systems directly address 9/11 Commission recommendations and congressional mandates to develop and deploy capabilities to detect nonmetallic threat items at airport screening checkpoints. It is therefore, arguably inappropriate to directly compare these WBI systems to current screening checkpoint technologies that do not have the capability to address these mandates.

The TSA is currently field testing two candidate WBI technologies for use in detecting explosives and nonmetallic weapons carried by passengers at airport screening checkpoints. The first of these technologies is known as x-ray backscatter technology and involves images generated by detecting radiation reflected off objects irradiated with x-rays. The second technology, millimeter wave imaging technology generates images by examining reflections of extremely high-frequency electromagnetic waves. Both technologies have the capability of penetrating objects that can normally conceal objects in a visual scene, including clothing, baggage, and even steel containers and automobiles. Broadly speaking, both of these technologies offer the potential for unobtrusive monitoring and scanning capabilities for security applications, including possible covert scanning applications in the aviation security context and perhaps in other homeland security applications. In addition to potential use at airport screening checkpoints, both x-ray backscatter and millimeter wave technologies are also being considered for screening air cargo, carry-on items, checked baggage, and also for screening vehicles parked near airport terminals and vehicles entering access-controlled areas. While there is a broad array of potential security applications for these technologies, this discussion focuses on the use of these technologies for screening passengers at airport screening checkpoints. Some concerns over this specific application of these technologies include protection of personal privacy, ability to detect items hidden in private and concealed areas on an individual, and possible health concerns regarding exposure to radiation emitted during the screening process.

X-Ray Backscatter Imaging Systems

Unlike traditional x-ray machines that measure the x-ray absorption pattern of different materials, x-ray backscatter technology works by emitting an x-ray beam and measures the scatter or reflections of the beam. The key difference is that organic materials do not absorb much of the x-ray, allowing the beam to mostly pass through. This characteristic makes traditional x-rays, which measure absorption characteristics, a poor choice for differentiating organic material. X-ray backscatter systems, on the other hand, do a much better job of differentiating organic materials, because different chemical elements in the materials deflect these beams quite differently. This makes backscatter a well-suited technology for detecting organic explosives in either solid or liquid form as well as drugs. The ability to provide high-quality imaging of organic matter, however, raises privacy concerns because x-ray backscatter technology can accurately image body parts normally concealed under clothing. This has raised considerable concerns among privacy advocates, as noted above, and it has resulted in the TSA requiring that specific privacy filters and special operating procedures be put in place to maintain the privacy of individuals being imaged by these systems. The use of x-ray backscatter devices may also generate some concern over public health and safety because these devices emit ionizing radiation, albeit in very small doses. It is estimated that each scan exposes an individual to 10 microRems of radiation, which is about 1% of the radiation exposure experienced every day. The system in use in pilot testing by the TSA meets American National Standards Institute (ANSI) requirements and is regarded as safe for all passengers, including small children and pregnant women.[63] The x-ray backscatter technology also provides an alternative to traditional x-ray machines for screening carry-on items, and systems are available that use backscatter technology for inspecting carry-on items. However, the TSA's present initiatives to acquire and deploy AT x-ray systems for carry-on screening do not include x-ray backscatter solutions, relying instead on high-resolution x-ray systems capable of providing multiple image views.

Millimeter Wave Imaging Systems

Millimeter wave screening technologies refer to an array of screening devices capable of creating high-detail images of items otherwise visually concealed. These devices emit electromagnetic waves in the 30–300 gigaHertz frequency range, that are capable of penetrating a variety of items that cannot be seen through, including clothing, vehicles, and shipping containers. For this reason, millimeter wave technologies potentially have a broad array of security applications, including the screening of individuals, vehicles, shipping containers, baggage, or other items presented at screening checkpoints. The screening devices capture the reflections of these waves as they bounce off visually concealed items. Depending on the composition of the material, some of the energy will be reflected and some will be absorbed. While metals and the human body tend to be highly reflective and will appear light or white in the generated image, materials such as plastics, ceramics, and organic materials, including organic explosives, will be partially reflective and seen as partially transparent in the image generated using this technology.[64] The resolution of current millimeter wave imaging systems allows for a relatively high-detail image to be generated. However, like x-ray backscatter screening of individuals, images must be generated from multiple view angles because millimeter waves are largely reflected by the human body and do not penetrate through the body to see items concealed on the other side. Also, like x-ray backscatter technology, millimeter wave imaging systems can detect concealed items, but cannot analyze the composition of those items. Therefore additional screening techniques would be needed to determine whether a detected item contained explosive material. According to the vendor, the millimeter wave screening technology currently being evaluated by the TSA can scan individuals in about two seconds.[65]

Since the millimeter wave signals emitted by these devices are nonionizing and are emitted at very low power levels, health and safety concerns have not been a significant issue related with this technology. While some still question the potential health effects of exposure to electromagnetic energy, the TSA points out that the millimeter wave imaging systems currently being field tested emit 10,000 times less energy than a typical cell phone transmission.[66] For TSA screeners, occupational exposure is regulated by Occupational Safety and Health Administration (OSHA) regulations and standards, and exposure to the traveling public would be expected to be much lower than these levels in most cases.[67]

AT X-Ray Equipment

The TSA has been using the term AT x-ray to refer to a wide range of possible next generation x-ray screening systems to be deployed for screening carry-on items at passenger checkpoints. The TSA has been field testing three different systems that provide a variety of enhanced features including improved image resolution, multiple views, and automatic explosives detection capabilities. The TSA has requested funding through FY2009 to deploy more than 900 of these systems, primarily at Category X and Category I airports. The TSA anticipates that it will have deployed enough of these units to provide coverage of 60% of lanes at these larger airports by the end of FY2009. The systems cost, on average, about $200,000 each.

Other Candidate Technologies and Applications for Aviation Security Screening

Various other technologies have been suggested as options for screening carry-on items. For example, some vendors have developed small-footprint CT-based scanners tailored for passenger checkpoint use that have throughput rates on the order of 400 bags per hour and include automated explosives and weapons image detection algorithms. CT-based systems are also capable of generating 3-D or multiangle images of scanned items for image analysis by screeners. While these systems offer some unique advantages over AT x-ray by incorporating automated EDS detection algorithms, and allowing for the viewing of 3-D images or viewing the item from virtually any perspective, they are considerably more expensive than available AT x-ray systems. A key policy issue is whether the potential enhancements these technologies offer compared to AT x-ray provide benefits that justify the cost difference. This may be a difficult question to answer depending on testing methods and assumptions. Findings may indicate that CT-based systems for passenger checkpoint screening may provide unique benefits in some instances, but at present, the TSA appears to favor the use of AT x-ray technologies to replace current generation x-ray systems in most, if not all, instances.

Also, the DHS S&T Directorate has been working with Los Alamos National Laboratories to develop and test ultralow field MRI scanning capabilities to screen for threat items. Researchers have developed a prototype system that may eventually be integrated into checkpoint screening systems to establish a reliable liquid explosives detection capability. The system, called SENSIT (for "sense it"), is being specifically designed to identify and differentiate fluids by including a database of MRI signatures for both threat and nonthreat liquid items. Possible advantages of using ultralow field MRI technology are that it is considered noninvasive, it is widely regarded as being safe for human exposure, and it can potentially be integrated with the existing airport screening checkpoint architecture.[68]

Millimeter wave technology, discussed above in reference to WBI systems, also has the potential of being adapted for use in screening carry-on items, although it is not clear that it would provide any advantages over AT x-ray systems. Millimeter wave systems, however, have another potential application in covert, passive scanning of objects. For example, patrol vehicles could potentially use millimeter wave scanning systems to inspect vehicles standing at passenger pick-up and drop-off points for suspect items, such as possible explosive devices. In the terminal, such technology also has potential application for the remote inspection of unattended or otherwise suspect items from a distance using, for example, robotic sensor platforms. However, such potential applications of this technology pose considerable policy and legal questions regarding individual privacy rights and reasonable cause for search. At present, therefore, the application of this technology in the aviation security domain appears to be limited to consensual searches of passengers conducted at screening checkpoints.

SCREENING AIRPORT WORKERS

While the major emphasis of these emerging checkpoint technology initiatives is to improve threat object detection capabilities and the efficiency of the screening process for airline passengers, concerns have been raised that airport workers who access sterile and secure areas are often exempted from screening procedures as a matter of routine. Pilot tests of programs for screening workers on either a mandatory or on a random basis has raised questions over how such requirements may impact equipment and staffing needs if implemented on a nationwide basis. The screening of airport workers remains a significant issue in policy debate over approaches to airport security screening measures.

The lack of mandatory screening for airport workers has been an issue of debate for some time. At most airports, identification checks, along with random or targeted screening, are used in lieu of 100% physical screening for airport workers. It has been estimated that nationwide about 600,000 such workers access secured areas of airports each day. Some policymakers have expressed particular concern over these practices, noting that this lack of checkpoint screening of airport workers creates vulnerabilities in which workers, or individuals with counterfeit or stolen worker identification, could pass threat objects into secured airport areas or travel on aircraft without being subjected to security screening. Acknowledging these concerns, the TSA and airport operators, however, have voiced concerns that full checkpoint screening of airport workers would be very time consuming and would significantly impact limited security screening resources and the TSA's ability to process airline passengers through screening checkpoints.[69]

While procedures vary from airport to airport, prior to 2007, only MIA had implemented a system requiring 100% physical screening of all airport workers accessing secured areas. However, a security incident in the spring of 2007 brought the issue to national attention. On May 5, 2007, the TSA was alerted to possible weapons on board a Delta Airlines flight from Orlando, Florida to San Juan, Puerto Rico after Orlando police received a tip through their anonymous crime hotline.[70] The TSA ordered that the flight be reverse-screened upon arrival in San Juan.[71] All passengers, carry-on items, and checked baggage were screened again as the passengers disembarked in San Juan. The search unveiled 14 guns—13 semiautomatic handguns and a .22 caliber rifle—and eight pounds of marijuana in a carry-on bag toted by a Comair employee traveling on the flight.[72] He and others accomplices, also employees of Comair in Orlando, were able to smuggle these items on board the airplane because their access credentials allowed them to bypass passenger screening checkpoints. The incident highlighted the long-debated insider threat posed by airline employees who are not routinely screened before accessing sterile and secure areas of airports.

Following the incident, the TSA ramped up employee screening and security measures.[73] However, neither the TSA nor Congress has required airports to implement 100% screening of all airport employees. As noted above, only MIA had a program in place prior to this incident to screen 100% of airport employees accessing secured areas. Following the incident, MCO implemented a similar program. However, at other airports, screening is conducted only on certain airport workers or, more typically, is carried out on a random basis if at all.

The TSA has been pilot testing various techniques for random and targeted screening of airport workers accessing secured areas of airports under its Aviation Direct Access Screening Program (ADASP). The ADASP was initiated in July 2006, and according to the TSA, the program places an emphasis on unpredictable, random screening of airport employees, items carried by them, and vehicles passing through airport access points. The ACI-NA asserts that the random, unpredictable nature of worker screening under the ADASP will make it difficult for terrorists to ascertain and exploit operational patterns.[74] Moreover, the TSA emphasizes that its personnel can be "surged" on very little notice to step up airport worker screening in response to threat intelligence or other indicators of heightened risk.[75] Therefore, both the TSA and the industry support the risk-based, random screening concept being developed under the ADASP as opposed to a more costly and resource intensive effort to conduct 100% screening of airport employees, similar to what was implemented in Miami and Orlando.

As noted above, both MIA and MCO have implemented full screening programs for airport workers, requiring all those accessing sterile and secured areas to undergo physical inspection. Additionally, a pilot program at Boston Logan International Airport (BOS) requires 100% physical screening of airport workers and vehicles accessing the airfield. While 43 TSA screeners were added to staff five airfield checkpoints at BOS, an airport official speculated that a full-time requirement to screen all airport workers at airport perimeter checkpoints and at designated terminal checkpoints prior to accessing sterile area may require as many as 1300 additional TSA screeners at BOS alone.[76] However, it is important to point out that, unlike the statutory requirement for TSA screening of passengers, no such requirement exists for airport worker screening, so this function could be conducted by private screening vendors. In any case, system-wide implementation of 100% airport worker physical screening may require tens of thousands of new screener personnel, whether they be TSA screeners or private screeners.

The TSA maintains that through a layered security approach, relying on extensive background checks, access controls, surveillance, and law enforcement presence at airports, adequate security can be maintained without implementing 100% screening of all airport workers. The TSA believes that stepped up random screening of workers can provide an additional layer of security to augment these other long-standing layers of airport security.

In addition to random selection techniques, additional steps are under consideration, including the use of behavioral profiling techniques for targeting physical inspections of airport workers.[77] For example, at several Florida airports and in San Juan, Puerto Rico, the TSA has augmented the

ADASP program with Saturation Security Teams (SSTs) that rove through sterile and secure areas of airports using behavioral observation techniques to evaluate and select airport workers for on-the-spot random inspections.

The TSA has also been mulling the idea of creating a voluntary program, allowing certain "certified employees" who undergo more extensive background checks to be exempt from routine, but not random, inspections. Some familiar with airport operations have also pointed out that certain categories of workers—such as maintenance workers who must routinely pass into and out of sterile and secured areas—often carrying tools, knives, and other items that could be used as deadly weapons. Repeatedly screening such individuals throughout the day may be labor intensive and arguably ineffective against preventing certain kinds of weapons from being carried into sterile and secured areas. Additional background checks and vetting of these workers may provide an option for exempting them from routine screening every time they access sterile and secured areas of airports.

SCREENING AND VETTING OF AIRLINE CREWS

While the TSA has been testing various procedures for screening airport employees, it has also moved forward to develop a system for validating the identity of airline crews as a means for sterile area access in lieu of physical screening at security checkpoints. The 9/11 Act (P.L. 110-53) required the TSA to assess the feasibility of creating a credentialing and identity verification system to allow airline flight crews access to the sterile areas of airports, and if feasible, initiate implementation of such a system. Since the 9/11 attacks, flight and cabin crews have been required to undergo physical screening at airport checkpoints, largely over concerns that terrorists or criminals could gain access to secured areas of airports or to air carrier aircraft by impersonating airline crewmembers, particularly pilots. Pilots and flights attendants and organizations representing these groups have complained that while they were required to pass through screening checkpoints whenever accessing sterile areas of airports, other airport and airline workers have been allowed to bypass screening, despite the fact that pilots and flight attendants were required to pass the same background checks as airline workers.[78] Nonetheless, the TSA had expressed specific concerns about the level of access pilots, as well as flight attendants, have to aircraft and cockpits, fearing that an imposter dressed as an airline crewmember could gain access allowing them to sabotage or hijack an aircraft if such an individual was allowed to bypass screening checkpoints.

Similar concerns were also raised about allowing crewmembers from other airlines from riding on the cockpit jumpseat. Prior to the 9/11 attacks, it had been a long-standing industry practice to allow flight crew personnel from other airlines to ride in the cockpit as a means of transportation to position pilots, and sometimes flight attendants, for their flight assignments. Most major airlines had reciprocal agreements with the other airlines to allow for this. However, after the 9/11 attacks, this practice was terminated because there was no industry-wide system to authenticate the credentials of flight crews from other airlines. Airline crews were, therefore, often required to fly standby on a space-available basis to commute to and from their flight assignments.

As a result of an industry need to provide jumpseat access privileges on other airlines in order to maintain efficient crew positioning, an industry-wide database, called the Cockpit Access Security System (CASS), was developed. It was field tested beginning in 2003 and received TSA approval for full operational deployment in September 2005. This database is maintained by ARINC, Inc. using human resources data provided by the individual airlines. The system provides gate agents identity verification of flight crewmembers by transmitting an up-to-date photograph and background information to compare with employee credentials using a secure Internet-based interface.

For flight crew sterile access area pilot testing, the TSA has leveraged the investment in the development of CASS to develop a system called crewPASS. The system relies on secure Internet access to the CASS database via TSA checkpoint computer terminals positioned at exit lanes to validate the identity of airline flight crewmembers. The testing is being conducted at BWI, PIT, and

Columbia (S.C.) Metropolitan Airport. It is currently limited in participation to uniformed flight crewmembers. Further evaluation of the program, including whether to extend participation to cabin crewmembers, will be made based on the results of this testing. The TSA is continuing to study ways to further enhance airline crew identity validation, and it is assessing how this program may be able to enhance security by reducing the number of individuals requiring physical screening, allowing screeners and BDOs to better focus their efforts on detecting suspicious items and suspicious behaviors.[79] Nonetheless, flight crewmembers participating in crewPASS will still be subject to random screening and behavioral observation.

Additionally, in September 2008, the TSA launched a separate test of a biometrics-based access control system for flight crews.[80] The system, known as SecureScreen, is being tested on about 200 Southwest Airlines pilots based at BWI airport. The pilots participating in the testing are being issued biometric identity cards that store fingerprint data, a digital photograph, and personally identifiable security information. Card readers have been installed at TSA security checkpoints at BWI to verify pilot identities, allowing pilots to bypass routine security screening. However, pilots participating in the test may still be subject to random or targeted screening as a secondary layer of security.

CHECKED BAGGAGE SCREENING

In addition to the challenges associated with screening passengers, airport workers, and airline crews, the TSA continues to face considerable challenges in its efforts to optimize checked baggage screening operations and perform costly maintenance and upkeep on this equipment. While airports are, for the most part, meeting mandated requirements to inspect checked bags with explosive detection equipment 100% of the time, airports are continuing to struggle with the daunting task of integrating these systems into baggage handling and sorting facilities. To address these needs, Congress established (in Vision 100, P.L. 108-176) an ASCF with a mandatory funding level of $250 million annually and a total authorized funding level of $500 million per year through FY2007. These funds are provided directly to airports in the form of grants to carry out capital improvement projects to integrate and optimize EDS equipment installations. This funding is separate from the purchase and maintenance of the EDS and ETD equipment, which is a TSA responsibility funded through annual discretionary appropriations.

In general, EDS equipment serves as the primary means for explosives screening of checked baggage at large airports, while ETD systems are used to perform secondary inspections when the EDS alarms of a potential explosives threat. At small-sized airports where the installation of larger-sized and more costly EDS is not considered necessary, ETD systems are used for primary explosives screening of all checked baggage. In total, the TSA has deployed over 2000 EDS machines, and almost 6000 ETD machines to about 450 commercial passenger airports throughout the United States and its territories.

According to the TSA, over 530 million pieces of checked luggage were screened using EDS equipment in 2006. Over 85 million pieces were opened for inspection, corresponding to an alarm rate of roughly 16%. Since there have been no publicly reported incidents of actual bombs placed in checked baggage, this roughly corresponds to the system-wide false alarm rate for primary checked baggage screening techniques using EDS.

A concern raised by some experts regarding the implementation of explosives detection screening of all checked baggage is the relatively high false alarm rate of current EDS equipment and the potential impact that this may have on baggage throughput. TSA procedures call for additional screening of all bags that generate EDS alarms using techniques such as hand searches, canine inspections, or inspections using trace element detection equipment. A more detailed examination of the CT images captured by the EDS system has not been approved by the TSA as an acceptable means of resolving EDS alarms. Consequently, the TSA relies heavily on the use of ETD systems and hand searches, both time-consuming and labor-intensive processes, to resolve EDS alarms.

Relatively high false alarm rate for EDS screening poses continuing challenges for the TSA to resolve alarms in an effective and expedient manner and, to some extent, impacts the number of EDS and ETD machines needed to maintain operational efficiency.

In addition to creating the ASCF, Congress also gave the TSA the authority to issue LOIs to airports, committing future funding toward in-line EDS integration projects. Despite these measures, efforts to integrate EDS systems at all airports have been progressing slowly, prompting the 9/11 Commission to recommend that the TSA expedite installation of these in-line baggage screening systems. Provisions to expedite and increase funding for in-line baggage screening were included in the IRTPA (P.L. 108-458). Meeting funding needs for airport security projects and setting priorities amid budgetary constraints remain ongoing challenges for Congress. In particular, the House Appropriations Committee noted that, as of the spring of 2008, only slightly more than half of the largest airports in the United States (45 out of 82 Category X and Category I airports) have optimized the installation and integration of their checked baggage EDSs. Of these, only 18 have optimized baggage screening configurations at all of their terminals, while the remaining 27 have only optimized these systems at some of their terminals. The other 37 large airports have suboptimal baggage screening solutions, with equipment that is not integrated with baggage conveyors. Some of these airports continue to house bulky EDS machines in lobbies and ticket counter areas, creating potential security and traffic flow issues. Provisions in the Implementing Recommendations of the 9/11 Commission Act (P.L. 110-53) extended the mandatory funding of the ASCF through 2028, and authorized an increased discretionary funding level of $450 million in FY2008 through FY2011 for in-line baggage screening. The measure also requires the TSA to prioritize airport in-line EDS projects based on risks and other considerations.

PROPOSED STRATEGY FOR BAGGAGE SCREENING OPTIMIZATION

In 2006, the TSA called on the ASAC, a standing committee of aviation industry advisors to the TSA, to form a working group to study the technology and fiscal challenges associated with baggage screening. In response, the industry partners represented on the ASAC convened a Baggage Screening Investment Study (BSIS) working group to identify and review funding and financial options.

The BSIS is a key input to the TSA's investment strategy for its Electronic Baggage Screening Program (EBSP).[81] The BSIS concluded that the total cost to implement this strategy, beginning in FY2006 and completing the optimized nationwide baggage screening initiative by FY2025 would be $23.3 billion, or roughly $1.22 billion annually. Of the total estimated program cost, the TSA expects that $19.7 billion (roughly 85%) would be paid by the federal government, while the remaining $3.6 billion (about 15%) would be paid for by airports and tenant airlines.

The BSIS working group failed to reach a consensus regarding cost sharing for continually meeting the 100% checked baggage screening mandate of ATSA, a reflection of the fact that airlines and airports generally maintain that the federal government should be solely responsible for all funding needs to meet this mandate. However, the group proposed a variety of funding mechanisms to help accelerate the acquisition, deployment, and optimization of baggage screening solutions. One option proposed by the group called for establishing a $3 billion voluntary tax credit bond (TCB) program allowing airports or airlines to fund infrastructure improvements to accommodate optimized EDS baggage systems. TCBs are bonds on which the federal government pays "interest" in the form of credits against federal income tax liability.[82] The Congressional Budget Office (CBO) notes that while TCBs result in higher costs to the federal government in cases where they are proposed as an alternative to traditional appropriations, these bonds may offer savings to the federal government compared to certain tax-exempt bonds if the TCBs are structured to meet conditions explained in the CBO study.[83] Tax-exempt bonds are popular vehicles for airports to raise capital for infrastructure improvement projects.

The working group estimated that the effective share of facility modification costs paid for by the airports and airlines would be about 25% under its TCB proposal. It also recommended the continuation of federal appropriations of at least $435 million annually for EDS purchase and installation.

The working group recommended that these funds include money for facility modification grants for those airports and airlines that do not participate in the voluntary TCB program. It proposed that appropriators combine EDS purchase and installation funds as a single line item to provide the TSA with increased flexibility to fund installation projects. It also recommended increased flexibility in airport PFCs to include the use of PFCs for the modification and construction of baggage handling systems and related infrastructure to accommodate EDS screening systems, and the use of PFCs to repay debts incurred under the proposed TCB program.

These proposals, however, mostly appear to require specific congressional action to raise security fees and/or increase PFC flexibility. The airlines, however, have opposed security fee increases and Congress has not moved forward with legislation to authorize additional security fees. The airlines have also resisted efforts to increase PFC flexibility, although their opposition appears to be more specifically tied to concerns over proposals to use PFC money to fund airport access projects, such as public transportation to and from airports, which could shift funds away from airport infrastructure spending that supports air carrier operations.[84] Finally, the concept of establishing a voluntary TCB mechanism has not been taken up in legislation. Currently, discretionary appropriations for EDS/ETD purchase and installation and the use of the ASCF to provide grants to airports to accommodate in-line EDS solutions serve as the funding mechanisms to support baggage screening optimization initiatives. This approach, however, has been criticized by some airports that have been frustrated over the slow pace of funding for in-line EDS integration projects and the uncertainty over federal reimbursements to those airports that have funded these types of projects up front using their own money in anticipation of eventually receiving reimbursement for the majority of the costs from the federal government.

OPTIONS FOR REDUCING BAGGAGE

It is estimated that the TSA currently screens more than one billion checked bags on an annual basis. As passenger volume is expected to increase at an average annual rate of about 3% per year,[85] the volume of baggage subject to screening is anticipated to increase at a similar rate. Similar increases in the number of carry-on items that must undergo screening are also anticipated. If passenger behavior regarding baggage remains unchanged, these increases will likely necessitate additional investment in screening equipment and increased physical space needs at airports to accommodate additional EDS and ETD machines for checked baggage screening and expand the number of passenger screening lanes.

One possible alternative approach to address concerns over the projected growth in baggage required to be screened is to somehow modify passenger behavior with regard to baggage amounts, such as by placing specific limits on the number of carry-on or checked baggage. At least in terms of carry-on baggage this idea is not new. Immediately following the 9/11 attacks, the DOT Rapid Response Team on Airport Security recommended that carry-on luggage should be limited to one carry-on bag and one personal item such as a purse or briefcase.[86] While this recommendation roughly parallels current airlines rules, these rules are not strictly enforced.

However, tighter restrictions on carry-ons, particularly the ban on carrying liquid items on aircraft imposed in August 2006, initially had the effect of increasing the volume of checked baggage. Some airlines claimed that they were experiencing an increase of as much as 25% in checked baggage soon after the liquids ban was put into effect, resulting in considerably increased labor costs to the airlines for baggage handling.[87] As restrictions on carrying liquids were eased and the TSA implemented its 3-1-1 policy, however, this spike in the volume of checked baggage eased to some degree.

Recently, some airlines have begun assessing fees for checked baggage, largely as a means to offset rising fuel costs. From a screening perspective, this would be expected to have an opposite effect than the liquids ban by creating a monetary incentive for passengers to carry-on items rather than check baggage. Airlines have long charged fees for oversized baggage or baggage exceeding a certain weight, typically over 50 pounds on domestic flights, with some airlines providing higher free weight allowances on international flights and for first class and business class travelers and frequent flyers. However, since the economic deregulation of the airline industry in 1978, baggage allowances and fee setting practices have largely been left up to the individual airlines. At present, several airlines are charging fees for additional checked baggage but allow one free checked bag, while others are charging fees for all checked bags. These baggage fees, as well as possible baggage limits, may play a significant role in resource demand and resource allocation for passenger and baggage screening. Checked baggage fees could result in increased volumes of carry-on luggage as passengers seek to avoid these fees, which in turn could result in increased workload at passenger checkpoints and a corresponding reduction in workload for checked baggage screening operations. While the fees could reduce overall baggage screening workload to some degree by prompting some passengers to pack lighter, the effect would largely be consumer driven based on pricing rather than the result of any specific policy or strategy to curtail growth in passenger and baggage screening workload.

The fees, however, may make the option proposed by some of preshipping or separately shipping baggage, sometimes using cargo aircraft, a potentially more attractive option for some airline passengers. While the concept has yet to attract any major market appeal, two companies have established services where passengers can check in their bags at off-site locations or can participate in door-to-door pickup and delivery service from home, office, or destination hotels.[88] The TSA verifies the security processes of these companies to ensure adequate controls and safeguards for keeping baggage secure in much the same way that it reviews the procedures of freight forwarding companies in the air cargo industry to ensure adequate supply chain security measures are in place and are followed. As more and more airlines begin charging fees for baggage service, paying additional shipping charges for origin to destination preshipping of checked baggage items may become an option that will appeal to a wider number of travelers.

Reportedly, both the TSA and airport managers liked the concept because it can reduce peak demand and time pressure for baggage screening and it can potentially reduce congestion in airport terminals if passengers do not need to check baggage upon arrival, and with a preprinted boarding pass can proceed directly to the screening checkpoint.[89] However, like the airlines checked baggage pricing strategies, the impacts of this program on checked baggage screening are being driven completely by market forces rather than any specific policy or agenda for streamlining aviation security operations. Policymakers may consider how these options may be more formally integrated into initiatives to improve passenger and baggage screening processes, perhaps through formal public awareness and education regarding these options or through specific incentives to passengers for opting to use such services or to companies that provide these services.

FIREARMS IN CHECKED BAGGAGE

While the greatest risk associated with checked baggage is from explosives, regulations allowing the transport of secured and unloaded firearms in checked baggage introduce a potential vulnerability. Firearms carried in checked baggage present unique security concerns because they offer a mechanism for getting weapons beyond security checkpoints that could potentially be exploited by terrorists or criminals seeking to use firearms to carry out an aircraft hijacking or some other attack within the sterile or secured areas of an airport. Firearms and ammunition are permitted to be carried in checked baggage, so long as the firearm is shipped unloaded and weapons and ammunition are carried in a secured hard-sided case. Passengers checking firearms must properly declare these weapons to the airline when they check-in and check their baggage. While the weapons are secured, there remains some concern that these allowances and procedures could be exploited to slip a weapon into the secured area of an airport with the assistance of a baggage handler or other airport worker. There is also some concern over the possible theft of these weapons while they are in transit.

At present, the TSA has no formal mechanism or process for tracking checked firearms and ensuring their security, leaving this primarily up to the airlines. The TSA also does not have a formal process for investigating or tracking cases of lost or stolen firearms from checked baggage, leaving this largely in the hands of local law enforcement. However, such incidents are often not reported by the owner or traveler until arrival at the destination when the firearm is reported missing, raising jurisdictional issues regarding at what point in transit the firearm was lost or stolen. Policymakers and aviation security strategists may explore options for strengthening the positive control and tracking of checked firearms while in transit, including the possible application of tracking and security technologies to prevent possible loss or theft of firearms in the sterile and secured areas of the air transportation system.

SCREENER WORKFORCE ISSUES

As passenger demand increases at existing airports, and as new airports begin to add passenger service, there will be an increasing need to hire additional screeners to maintain or improve upon current levels of screening efficiency and performance. Retaining high-performing screeners will also likely be a high priority for maintaining and improving upon the efficiency and effectiveness of screening operations. New technologies and streamlined screening procedures using these future checkpoint and baggage screening technologies may offset future screener workforce needs to some degree, particularly with respect to baggage screening operations. However, the extent to which improvements in passenger screening technologies and procedures will reduce staffing needs in the coming years is difficult to assess until new technologies further mature and until operational tests and models of operational use provide a clearer indication of anticipated improvements to checkpoint and baggage screening efficiency and effectiveness.

While various emerging screening technologies have the potential to streamline screening operations and reduce the demand for screeners, recent initiatives by the TSA have sought to broaden and diversify the role of its frontline workforce beyond traditional screening functions. As previously noted, the TSA now refers to its frontline workforce at airports as TSOs to reflect the more diversified roles and job functions performed by these personnel. These additional duties, in combination with expansion to meet expanding passenger demand, have led to a sizable increase in the TSA workforce over the past few years. By the end of FY2009, the TSA estimates that it will have 49,697 FTE positions for TSOs, about an 8% increase over the 45,897 FTE positions it counted at the end of FY2007.[90] The expansion of the TSO workforce and the broadening role of this workforce are likely to be issues of increasing interest for policymakers and aviation security strategists in the coming years.

BROADENING ROLES FOR TSOs

In addition to traditional passenger and baggage screening operations, officers are now serving as travel document checkers (TDCs), BDOs, and bomb appraisal officers (BAOs), and are performing additional duties including random and targeted screening of airport employees.

BDOs have recently become an integral component of the TSO workforce. These officers receive specific behavioral observation training under the TSA's Screening Passengers by Observation Techniques (SPOT) program. SPOT utilizes nonintrusive behavior observation and analysis techniques to identify passengers who may pose a security threat, which is sometimes referred to as a form of behavioral profiling. The SPOT program evolved from early initiatives to implement behavioral observation techniques developed by the Massachusetts State Police for use at BOS, called the Behavior Assessment Screening System (or BASS). The TSA has trained and deployed more than 650 BDOs, who are deployed at about 40 major airports throughout the United States.

While various techniques and tools are available for trained behavior detection officers, these officers typically have limited interaction with passengers. Mostly through observation, rather than direct interaction, these officers attempt to detect various physical and physiological indicators that people sometimes exhibit as a manifestation of their fear of being discovered. Decisions must be made based on limited observational data looking for behavioral indicators that can often be mis-interpreted. Some individuals may exhibit suspicious behavior based on fears of flying or fears of crowds, while terrorists and criminals may specifically train and practice techniques to conceal any behavioral markers of their intent. Thus, the potential for both missed indicators of potential threats as well as false positives is significant while using these types of techniques. Also, BDOs work under the pressure of knowing that they can potentially run afoul of safeguards to protect against profiling on the basis of ethnicity, race, religion, or other characteristics that may be challenged on constitutional grounds of equal treatment and violation of civil rights statutes.[91] Systematic patterns of singling out individuals of Middle-Eastern appearance based on observed behaviors, for example, may result in challenges to behavioral observation practices if it can be demonstrated that BDOs have a tendency to more closely observe individuals fitting a certain pro-file based on their appearance, including their ethnicity or particular clothing that may indicate an ethnic or religious affiliation. The ACLU, for example, has raised concerns that the techniques include many highly subjective elements that could result in behavioral profiling being applied in a discriminatory manner.[92] The TSA maintains that the BDOs are trained to focus on objective behavioral indicators and not subjective judgments. They receive four days of classroom instruc-tion followed by 24 hours of on-the-job training at airports before being qualified as a BDO.[93]

Despite the inherent limitations faced by BDOs, TDCs, and other screening officers resulting from their limited interaction with passengers and the difficulty distinguishing potential hostile intent from other behavioral manifestations of stress or fear, these individuals have been credited with several positive detections of dangerous criminals and other suspicious individuals. For exam-ple, in March 2008, a TDC at Minneapolis-St. Paul International Airport was credited with aiding police in apprehending a murder suspect after suspecting that the California driver's license the individual presented as identification was a forgery.[94] Also, on April 1, 2008, BDOs working at MCO identified and tracked a passenger acting suspiciously. After the passenger checked his bag-gage, they quickly inspected it and summoned a BAO who assessed that the individual had what appeared to be bomb-making materials in his baggage. The suspicious passenger was placed under arrest and a bomb squad was called in.[95] These real-world examples of how the use of TSOs with specific training as BDOs and BAOs can successfully contribute to detecting and responding to suspected threats has added credibility to these programs, which are now established components of the TSA's airport security workforce.

SCREENER RETENTION

When the TSA was first established and charged with the task of federalizing airport screeners across the United States, ATSA gave the TSA Administrator broad authority to establish standards for the hiring and retention of security screening personnel. Improving screener retention was viewed as a key objective for the TSA as it stood up the federalized screening workforce in 2002. Reducing screener turnover, which has significant implications for screener training, training costs, and on-the-job performance still remains an issue of considerable interest.

Screener turnover rates have long been regarded as an impediment to effective aviation security. As screeners gain more and more on-the-job experience and additional training, they tend to become increasingly more proficient in detecting threats and more efficient at conducting screening operations. High attrition rates can, therefore, lead to poorer system performance and decreased efficiency. Additionally, attrition can results in considerably increased costs to continually recruit, hire, and train new screeners. The TSA estimates that the costs incurred to assess, hire, and train one screener totals about $10,000. With a screening force of more than 45,000, a change of 1% in the annual attrition rate can result in an increased cost or a savings of about $4.5 million per year in training costs alone.

There are two components to the overall screener attrition numbers: Voluntary attrition, which reflects a variety of personal and professional reasons for leaving, and involuntary attrition, which reflects the TSA action to downsize its workforce in certain locations or to dismiss certain TSOs who cannot perform their duties effectively or are otherwise are determined to be unsuited for employment in a security-related position.

While involuntary attrition can often be reduced through more effective staffing allocation models and improved applicant selection processes, employee screening techniques, and hiring practices, voluntary attrition problems on an organizational level can often be remedied by addressing work-related factors that may be attributing to attrition. These factors may include a lack of opportunity or the perceived lack of opportunity for career advancement, inflexible or irregular work schedules, or real or perceived inequities in pay and benefits compared to the broader labor market. Immediately following the 9/11 attacks, the low pay and lack of benefits for private screeners were regarded as a major factor influencing high turnover rates and much of the debate over federalizing the screening workforce centered on the concept of providing the screening workforce with better compensation to reduce attrition and, in turn, improve the effectiveness of the screening performance across the aviation system.

Voluntary attrition among TSA screeners has been significantly lower than screener attrition prior to the 9/11 attacks which, in many cases, exceeded an annual rate of 100%. Overall voluntary screener attrition has been reduced to below 20% annually, and the retention rate is even better for full-time screening staff. For full-time TSOs, the voluntary attrition rate has dropped to below 12%.[96] Attrition rates for part-time TSOs, which make up about one-quarter of the total TSO workforce, is notably higher. Having a relatively high percentage of part-time workers, however, can help the TSA better match its staffing levels to airline flight schedules that have peak activity levels in the morning and in the late afternoon and early evening. An alternative to part-time work is split-shift full-time work. While split shifts are used to some extent, these arrangements tend to be a less appealing alternative to workers, particularly at larger airports in major metropolitan areas where commuting times to the airport are usually much greater. The TSA notes that, through FY2007, the average (mean) length of time that full-time and part-time TSOs had been with the TSA was 3.5 years, and 44% had been with the TSA for five years or more. However, average (mean) time with the TSA among just part-time TSOs was only 1.3 years, and only 6.2% of part-time TSOs had been with the TSA for more than five years, reflecting the considerably higher attrition rates for part-time TSOs.[97] Reducing attrition rates among experienced, high-performing screening and security personnel remains an ongoing challenge for the TSA.

SCREENER HIRING STANDARDS

In addition to federalizing the screening workforce in an effort to improve screener pay and benefits, legislation set specific screener hiring standards, largely as an effort to improve screener performance and reduce rates of involuntary attrition. Specifically, provisions in ATSA require screeners to have either a high school diploma, a general equivalency diploma (GED), or a combination of education and work experience providing the prerequisite skills and knowledge to perform screening functions. The TSA accepts one year of experience as a security guard, an aviation screener, or an x-ray technician in lieu of a high school diploma or GED. ATSA also requires screeners to be proficient in English. In addition to these requirements, the TSA requires screeners to have good vision correctable to within acceptable limits, no color blindness, good hearing, blood pressure within acceptable limits, the ability to repeatedly lift and carry items weighing up to 70 pounds, and the mental ability to interpret x-ray images. These requirements conform to ATSA guidance that the TSA establish qualification standards for screening personnel. Screeners also cannot have a criminal history that includes convictions within the past 10 years of any disqualifying felony offenses. Under ATSA, federal screener positions were initially limited to only U.S. citizens; however, language in the Homeland Security Act of 2002 (P.L. 107-296) expanded the eligibility to include noncitizen U.S. nationals, which primarily encompasses individuals from American Samoa.

TSA STAFFING NEEDS

ATSA set no specific limits and established no particular guidelines with respect to the staffing of airport screening checkpoints, requiring only that the TSA deploy sufficient numbers of federal screeners to conduct screening of all passengers and property at commercial passenger airports. By November 2002, when aviation security screening had been fully turned over to the federal government, TSA had hired enough screeners to fill about 54,600 FTE positions. In 2003, the TSA subsequently developed a staffing allocation model, which relies on computer modeling and simulation methods, for systematically determining screener staffing needs at all commercial passenger airports. However, from FY2003 to FY2007, the TSA was constrained by a congressionally imposed cap, limiting the system-wide number of FTE screeners to 45,000. This cap was lifted in FY2008.

Since FY2008 when the screener cap was lifted, TSA screener staffing levels have risen slightly above the 45,000 FTE level. However, this increase largely reflects the creation of new positions for BDOs, BAOs, TDCs, and additional screeners needed for airport worker screening initiatives. Through adjustments to its screener staffing models, the TSA has been able to fund over 1000 additional FTEs to function as travel documents checkers. Additionally, over 650 BDOs have been deployed, mostly at the largest airports, and BAOs have been deployed at over 100 airports.

In 2007, the TSA adjusted its screener staffing allocation model to reduce the number of screeners per screening lane at large airports from 5.5 to 4.25. It also reduced staffing requirements for baggage screeners from three screeners per EDS machine to two, reflecting the considerably improved throughput of newer EDS equipment that is now being deployed. The TSA also made improvements to the model to account for paid time off, time spent in training, and time spent performing ancillary nonscreening job duties. While the new model reduces the number of screeners performing checkpoint and baggage screening duties, it adds to its tally screening personnel assigned to screen airport workers, as well as BDOs and BAOs. To reflect this broader scope of duties performed by TSA line personnel, they are now referred to officially as TSOs.

In addition to the growth in passenger air travel, TSOs are taking on additional duties and specialized job functions. The TSA has been taking over travel document inspection functions and has been deploying BDOs and BAOs. In addition to these new specialties, wide-scale deployment of WBI technologies is likely to increase the need for screeners specially trained for reviewing the images generated by these devices. However, used solely as secondary screening tools, these technologies will replace the need for pat-down inspections in many cases. Therefore, the overall impact of deploying these technologies on TSA staffing requirements is not a straightforward assessment. However, if it is the ultimate intent to screen all persons passing through checkpoints for explosives and nonmetallic weapons through the use of WBI or other technologies, then the impact on staffing would likely be quite substantial.

The GAO found that while most Category X and Category I airports were staffed at or near levels determined by the staffing allocation model, among smaller airports there was a much greater variance between staffing needs determined by the model and actual staffing levels. Thirty eight percent of Category III and IV airports were staffed below 90% of their allocation, while 23% of these airports were overstaffed by 10% or more.[98] Improving and optimizing screener staffing allocation among commercial passenger airports remains a significant challenge that has a direct bearing on the effectiveness and efficiency of screening operations. Current trends suggest that, over the near term, passenger activity may become more concentrated at larger airports potentially placing a greater strain on screening operations at those airports that are already experiencing average wait times in excess of the 10-minute target. Further adjustments to screener staffing allocations may be needed to address these anticipated airline industry trends. The TSA may need to look more closely at its strategies for recruiting and retaining high-performing screeners in major metropolitan areas where these larger airports are located, a task that has proved to be a challenge in the past but may be improved upon through various career advancement initiatives that have been put in place.

SALARIES, BENEFITS, AND CAREER ADVANCEMENT INITIATIVES

The TSA has adopted a new career progression program, potentially providing a clearer path to job growth for those hired as TSOs. The model consists of a five step progression through various merit-based promotion opportunities. The TSA maintains that the majority of attrition occurs at the lower pay grades due to a perceived lack of career advancement opportunities. The TSA hopes that by more clearly defining the career progression and offering a broader range of opportunities for career advancement, it can improve the retention of experienced, trained, high-performing TSOs.

TSO pay is considerably higher than most security guard positions, which are typically paid at an hourly wage rate and usually with fewer benefits. In addition to their salaries, TSOs receive most federal employment benefits including health benefits and participation in the federal employee retirement system. In 2007, the TSA extended full-time health benefits to part-time screeners, a move that could help improve recruitment and retention of hard-to-fill part-time positions, particularly at large airports. While it is difficult to make direct comparisons, it is estimated that the salaries and benefits of TSA screeners, in constant dollars, is about three times that of private screeners who were employed by contract screening companies prior to the 9/11 attacks.

The TSO workforce is compensated using a performance-based pay system. The TSA has also used performance bonuses as a retention tool for screeners who demonstrate high levels of on-the-job performance. In 2006, the TSA launched the Performance and Accountability Standards System (PASS) to evaluate screener personnel and serve as the basis for performance-based pay. The system, however, has been criticized for being based on testing that does not adequately reflect actual job duties. In 2008, the TSA announced changes to the PASS system to address some of these criticisms. The changes include an elimination of a test on standard operating procedures, modifications to the TIP-based image testing to more closely correspond to screener training, and the use of a numeric score rather than the use of five broad subjective performance categories.[99] Critics remain concerned that screeners still have no avenue to appeal a negative evaluation outside the TSA, and they argue that the system is prone to favoritism because supervisors can assign additional duties to their favorite employees, which can boost their performance ratings considerably.

Labor groups maintain that extending collective bargaining rights to TSA screeners would address many of these lingering concerns. However, under an agency order issued by the TSA in January 2002, screeners may not form collective bargaining units.[100] Options to extend collective bargaining rights to screeners have been controversial. For example, provisions in both the House-passed and Senate-passed versions of the Implementing the 9/11 Commission Recommendations Act of 2007 (H.R. 1, 110th Congress) included language that would have eliminated the separate personnel management system for TSA screeners, thereby having the effect of extending collective bargaining rights available to other TSA employees to TSA screening personnel. The language, which was the subject of a veto-threat, however, was dropped from the final bill, which became P.L. 110-53.

REDUCING WORKPLACE INJURIES

Workplace injuries and disability claims have posed a challenge for the TSA. Particularly among baggage screeners, lifting and repetitive motion injuries have been common causes of work-related disabilities. Besides the direct cost of worker compensation for on-the-job injuries, the temporary or permanent loss of trained screeners to injuries can have an operational impact on staffing. The TSA must plan for projected injury rates in order to assure adequate staffing of baggage screening operations as well as passenger screening checkpoints. Based on 2006 claims, the TSA identified 58 large airports that accounted for 80% of all worker compensation claims. The TSA focused its mitigation efforts on these larger airports, where the workload and pace of operations, as well as specifically identified work hazards, contributed to workplace injuries. The TSA has substantially reduced the number of workers' compensation claims compared to FY2004 levels, when over 15,000 claims were filed.

To reduce workplace injuries, the TSA implemented safe-lifting classes, safety training programs, preshift stretching programs, spot checks to reinforce best practices, safety posters, safety newsletters, and recognition programs to encourage and reward safe practices at airports. The TSA's Office of Occupational Safety, Health, and Environment has implemented an agency-wide QA process to monitor and track worker compensation claims.[101] Also in January 2006, the TSA made nurse case management of work-related injuries available at all commercial airports. Since implementing the program, the average work days lost due to injury has dropped 55%, from about 45 days prior to 20.5 days after nurse care management implementation.[102]

Long-term initiatives to further reduce workplace injuries may involve the further deployment of in-line baggage systems to further reduce lifting requirements as well as the use of assistive devices to reduce lifting requirements. For example, a variety of mechanical arms, and even powerful vacuum systems for baggage handling, are available and can be used to significantly reduce the weight of baggage and other items that TSA screeners must lift to perform their job functions. Requirements for screening of air cargo placed on passenger aircraft may intensify interest in these types of assistive technologies.

WHISTLEBLOWER PROTECTIONS

Whistleblower protections have long been regarded by many as an important tool in the aviation industry for encouraging and supporting employees who report conditions affecting the safety or security of operations by extending certain protections against disciplinary actions and possible retaliation by employers and coworkers. However, TSA screeners and other TSOs are not explicitly granted the same whistleblower protections as other federal employees, raising concerns among some that those with specific knowledge of situations or practices that compromise security of the air transport system may be reluctant to divulge that information for fear of reprisal or disciplinary action.

Under the terms of a 2002 agreement between the TSA and the U.S. Office of Special Counsel, TSOs can use the same channels other federal employees use to disclose information regarding violations of law, violations of rule or regulation, gross mismanagement, gross waste, fraud, and abuse, and situations that create a substantial and specific danger to public health and safety. The Office of Special Counsel reviews whistleblower disclosures of this sort and makes nonbinding recommendations to the TSA.

Under a 2008 memorandum of agreement with the Merit System Protection Board (MSPB), TSOs can now appeal Office of Special Counsel decisions to the MSPB, a component of the federal government that adjudicates appeals of various agency actions taken against federal employees. However, labor leaders representing government employees have complained that this does not extend full whistleblower protections to TSOs, because they have no further avenue to appeal negative decisions issued by the MSPB or resulting actions imposed by the TSA against TSOs in federal court.[103] They have also raised concerns that the arrangement entered into by the TSA is voluntary and not set in statute and that the MSPB's role has been negotiated with the TSA, limiting MSPB control over the process. Broader whistleblower protection bills introduced in the 110th Congress (H.R. 985 and S. 274) sought to extend statutory whistleblower protections to TSOs. Whistleblower protections, along with collective bargaining rights, remain as specific policy issues of interest for federal policymakers. These various screening workforce issues, along with emerging checkpoint technology deployment, checkpoint reconfiguration, and checked baggage screening optimization, remain as key aviation security policy issues that will likely figure prominently in strategic planning and oversight of TSA programs over the next several years.

REFERENCES

1. United States Government Accountability Office. *Aviation Security: TSA's Staffing Allocation Model Is Useful for Allocating Staff among Airports, but Its Assumptions Should Be Systematically Reassessed*, February 2007, GAO-07-299.
2. Federal Aviation Administration, *FAA Aerospace Forecast: Fiscal Years 2008–2025.*
3. United States Government Accountability Office, *Aviation Security: TSA's Staffing Allocation Model*, GAO-07-299.
4. U.S. Government Accountability Office. *TSA Has Strengthened Efforts to Plan for the Optimal Deployment of Checked Baggage Screening Systems but Funding Uncertainties Remain*, Statement of Cathleen A. Berrick, Director, Homeland Security and Justice Issues, Before the Subcommittee on Aviation, Committee on Transportation and Infrastructure, House of Representatives, June 29, 2006, GAO-06-875T.
5. National Commission on Terrorist Attacks Upon the United States. *The 9/11 Commission Report*, Washington, DC, July, 2004.
6. U.S. Government Accountability Office, *Transportation Security Administration Has Strengthened Planning to Guide Investments in Key Aviation and Surface Transportation Security Programs, but More Work Remains*, Statement of Cathleen A. Berrick, Director, Homeland Security and Justice Issues, Before the Committee on Commerce, Science, and Transportation, U.S. Senate, May 13, 2008, GAO-08-487T.
7. Department of Homeland Security, Transportation Security Administration, *Fiscal Year 2009 Congressional Justification: Aviation Security.*
8. U.S. Government Accountability Office, *TSA Has Strengthened Efforts to Plan for the Optimal Deployment of Checked Baggage Screening Systems but Funding Uncertainties Remain*, GAO-06-875T.
9. Department of Homeland Security, Office of Inspector General, *Review and Audit of the Transportation Security Administration's Use of Pat-Downs in Screening Procedures (REDACTED)*, November 2005, OIG-06-10.
10. Ibid.
11. American Civil Liberties Union, *TSA Pat-Down Search Abuse*, New York, December 21, 2004.
12. Jeanne Meserve and Mike M. Ahlers, "TSA Tester Slips Mock Bomb Past Airport Security," *Cable News Network (CNN)*, January 28, 2008.
13. Transportation Security Administration, *Fiscal Year 2009 Congressional Justification, Transportation Security Support.*
14. Sara Kehaulani Goo, "Airport Screeners Do Poorly, Panel Told," *The Washington Post*, April 23, 2004, p. A8.
15. See note 12.
16. Transportation Security Administration, *Covert Testing: Why Is Covert Testing Important?*
17. Department of Homeland Security, Office of Inspector General, *Letter Report: TSA's Management of Aviation Security Activities at the Jackson-Evers International Airport*, August 2007, OIG-07-73.
18. Honorable Bennie G. Thompson, Chairman, Homeland Security Committee, U.S. House of Representatives, "Cover Blown: Did TSA Tip Off Airport Screeners about Covert Testing," Statement Released November 14, 2007.
19. "TSA: Airport Screeners Weren't Tipped Off," *Air Safety Week*, November 19, 2007.
20. United States Government Accountability Office, *Transportation Security: TSA Has Developed a Risk-Based Covert Testing Program, but Could Better Mitigate Aviation Security Vulnerabilities Identified Through Covert Tests*, August 2008, GAO-08-958.
21. United States Government Accountability Office, Statement of Gregory D. Kutz, Managing Director, Forensic Audits and Special Investigations, and John W. Cooney, Assistant Director, Forensic Audits and Special Investigations, *Aviation Security: Vulnerabilities Exposed through Covert Testing of TSA's Passenger Screening Process*, Testimony Before the Committee on Oversight and Government Reform, House of Representatives, November 15, 2007.
22. Ibid., p. 10.
23. Statement of Clark Kent Ervin before the Committee on Homeland Security, House of Representatives, *Cover Blown: Did TSA Tip Off Airport Screeners about Covert Testing?* November 14, 2007.
24. Transportation Security Administration, *Aviation Security System of Systems: THEN and NOW.*
25. Adrian Schwaninger, "X-ray Imagery: Enhancing the Value of the Pixels," *Aviation Security International*, October 2005, pp. 16–21.
26. Ibid.
27. Remarks of Norman Y. Mineta, Secretary of Transportation, Travel and Tourism Industry Unity Dinner, Washington, DC, March 6, 2002.

28. Transportation Security Administration, *Recommended Security Guidelines for Airport Planning, Design and Construction*, Revised June 15, 2006.
29. See note 1.
30. Ibid.
31. Ibid.
32. Sara Kehaulani Goo, "First Class Fast Lane," *The Washington Post*, August 2, 2005, p. D01.
33. Ibid.
34. Transportation Security Administration, *TSA Announces Expansion of "Diamond" Self-Select Lanes*, Press Release, March 5, 2008.
35. Ibid.
36. Transportation Security Administration, *Black Diamond Self Select Lanes, Helping Passengers Move at Their Own Pace*.
37. Transportation Security Administration, "Registered Traveler Interoperability Pilot Program," *Federal Register, 73*(147), pp. 44275–44278, July 30, 2008.
38. Transportation Security Administration, "TSA Lifts Cap and Eliminates Fee on Registered Traveler," Press Release, July 24, 2008.
39. See note 37.
40. Transportation Security Administration, "Update on Verified Identity Pass, Inc. Clear®'s Registered Traveler Enrollment," Press Release, August 11, 2008.
41. Ibid.
42. "Clear Offers 500 K Prize for New Checkpoint Technology," *Aviation Week's Airports*, 26(1), pp. 1–2, January 8, 2008.
43. Transportation Security Administration, "Status Update on Testing of General Electric Kiosk for Registered Traveler," *TSA News & Happenings*, October 9, 2007.
44. Benet Wilson, "TSA Tests L3 Shoe Scanners at LAX Airport Checkpoints," *Aviation Daily*, August 7, 2008.
45. Steve Surjapurta, "May We Leave Our Shoes On at Airport Security?" *Tripso Travel News*, August 1, 2008.
46. Art Marroquin, "Airport Security to Test Shoe Scans," *LA Daily News* (Los Angeles, CA), August 2, 2008.
47. Transportation Security Administration, "New Security Simplifying Laptop Bag Procedures," *TSA News & Happenings*, July 29, 2008.
48. Thomas Frank, "TSA likely to ease restrictions on liquids in 2009," *USA Today*, October 28, 2008.
49. Transportation Security Administration, "Checkpoint Changes to Improve Security and Calm Process," *TSA News & Happenings*, April 28, 2008.
50. Thomas Frank, "TSA Tries Soothing Screening Process," *USA Today*, March 30, 2008.
51. Tim L. Hudson and Matthew J. Frankel, "Staying Ahead of the Game: The Future is Now for Advanced Passenger Screening," *Airport Magazine*, April/May 2007, pp. 46–50.
52. National Commission on Terrorist Attacks Upon the United States, *The 9/11 Commission Report* (Authorized Edition), New York, NY: WW. Norton & Company. p. 393.
53. P.L. 108-458, Sec. 4013; 49 U.S.C. §44925.
54. Norman Shanks and Steve Wolff, "The Liquid Bomb Threat," *Air Safety Week*, August 21, 2006, p. 1.
55. "TSA Adds More Bottle-Screening Devices at Airport Checkpoints, *Aviation Daily*, November 16, 2007.
56. "New Analytical Tool Developed for Liquid Explosives Detection," *Science Daily*, October 13, 2006.
57. Kevin Bullis, "A Better Liquid-Explosives Detector," *MIT Technology Review*, December 1, 2006.
58. General Electric, "The United States Transportation Security Administration (TSA) has Installed the GE EntryScan3 Walk-through Explosives Detector to Screen Passengers at Boston Logan Airport's Terminal a Security Checkpoint," September 9, 2006.
59. Eric Lipton, "Screening Tools Slow to Arrive in U.S. Airports," *The New York Times*, September 3, 2006.
60. "TSA Tunnel of Truth May Come Your Way," *Airport Magazine*, August/September 2008, p. 66.
61. Statement of Timothy D. Sparapani, ACLU Legislative Counsel, Before the Senate Committee on Commerce, Science, and Technology, Regarding the U.S. Transportation Security Administration's Physical Screening of Airline Passengers and Related Cargo Screening, April 4, 2006.
62. Ibid.
63. American Science and Engineering (AS&E), Inc., *TSA Z Backscatter Pilot*. Billerica, MA: AS&E.
64. D.M. Sheen, D. L. McMakin, H. D. Collins, T. E. Hall, and R. H. Severtsen, *Concealed Explosive Detection on Personnel Using a Wideband Holographic Millimeter-Wave Imaging System*. Proceedings of SPIE—Volume 2755 Signal Processing, Sensor Fusion, and Target Recognition V, Ivan Kadar and Vibeke Libby (Eds), pp. 503–513, June 1996.
65. L3 Communications, *Active Millimeter Wave Screening*, L3 Communications, Security and Detection Systems, Woburn, MA.

66. Transportation Security Administration, *Millimeter Wave.*
67. See, especially, 29 CFR §1910.97—Nonionizing radiation.
68. "Detecting Liquid Explosives," *Air Safety Week*, November 19, 2007.
69. "Technical Corrections Bill Passes out of Subcommittee," *Aviation Daily*, Vol. 352, No. 35, p. 3, May 19, 2003.
70. Armen Keteyian, Pia Malbran, and Phil Hirschkorn, "14 Guns And 8 Bags Of Pot On A Plane, Lax Security For Airport Workers Leads To Arms And Drug Smuggling," *CBS News*, March 8, 2007.
71. Testimony of Kip Hawley, Assistant Secretary, Department of Homeland Security, Transportation Security Administration, Before the United States House of Representatives, Committee on Homeland Security, Subcommittee on Transportation Security and Infrastructure Protection, April 19, 2007.
72. See note 70.
73. See note 71.
74. Testimony of Greg Principato, President, Airports Council International—North America, Hearing on Aviation Security: The Necessary Improvements to Secure America's Airports, Before the Subcommittee on Transportation Security and Infrastructure Protection, Committee on Homeland Security, House of Representatives, April 19, 2007.
75. See note 71.
76. "New Screening Program Begins Test At Logan," *The Boston Globe*, May 7, 2008.
77. Ibid.
78. Transportation Security Administration's Screening of Airline Pilots: Sound Security Practice or Waste of Scarce Resources, Hearing Before the Subcommittee on Economic Security, Infrastructure Protection, and Cybersecurity of the Committee on Homeland Security, House of Representatives, One Hundred Ninth Congress, First Session, May 13, 2005. Serial No. 109-13, U. S. Government Printing Office, Washington, DC, 2005.
79. Transportation Security Administration, "TSA Announces Launch of Expedited Screening for Flight Deck Crew Members," Press Release, July 17, 2008.
80. Kathleen Hickey, "TSA Tests Biometrics for Pilots," *Government Computer News*, September 18, 2008.
81. Transportation Security Administration, *Synopsis: Baggage Screening Investment Study*, September 2006.
82. Congressional Budget Office, *Tax-Credit Bonds and the Federal Cost of Financing Public Expenditures*, July 2004.
83. Ibid.
84. CRS Report RL33891, *Airport Improvement Program: Issues for Congress* by Robert S. Kirk.
85. Federal Aviation Administration, *FAA Aerospace Forecast, Fiscal Years 2008–2025.* Washington, DC: Federal Aviation Administration, Aviation Policy and Plans.
86. U.S. Department of Transportation, *Meeting the Airport Security Challenge: Report of the Secretary's Rapid Response Team on Airport Security*, October 1, 2001.
87. Marilyn Adams, "Fliers Board Faster As Fewer Carry On Bags," *USA Today*, August 29, 2008.
88. Robert Poole, "Bag Check Options," *Airport Policy and Security Newsletter* (Issue 33), Los Angeles, CA: The Reason Foundation, March 2008.
89. Ibid.
90. Transportation Security Administration, *FY2009 Congressional Justification, Aviation Security.*
91. See, especially, 42 U.S.C. Chapter 21.
92. Eric Lipton, "Faces, Too, Are Searched at U.S. Airports," *The New York Times*, August 17, 2006.
93. Transportation Security Administration, "BDOs SPOT More than Just Opportunities at TSA," *TSA News & Happenings*, May 8, 2007.
94. Transportation Security Administration, "TSO Honored by Police, Helped Apprehend Murder Suspect," *TSA News & Happenings*, April 17, 2008.
95. Bianca Prieto, "How TSA Captured Bomb Suspect at OIA," *The Orlando Sentinel*, April 4, 2008.
96. Transportation Security Administration, *The Facts on TSO Attrition Rates*, July 22, 2008.
97. Ibid.
98. See note 1.
99. Brittany R. Ballenstedt, "TSA Makes More Modifications to Screener Pay System," *Government Executive*, March 27, 2008.
100. Transportation Security Administration, "TSA's Loy Determines Collective Bargaining Conflicts with National Security Needs," Press Release, January 9, 2003.
101. Transportation Security Administration, *Quarterly Scorecard a Key to Injury Reduction.*
102. Ibid.
103. Alyssa Rosenberg, "TSA Extends Whistleblower Protections," *Government Executive*, February 27, 2008.

8 Airline In-Flight Security Measures

The layered approach to aviation security that begins from the point of sale of an airline ticket extends beyond the passenger and baggage screening systems and includes several in-flight measures on board commercial passenger aircraft. Some of these measures, such as the specially trained FAMS and cockpit security barriers have been significantly improved in response to the terrorist attacks of September 11, 2001. Other measures, such as the FFDO program, enhanced security training for flight and cabin crews, and the deployment of hardened cargo containers are new initiatives introduced since 9/11. Future measures to further improve aircraft survivability and provide hardened locations to contain explosives discovered in flight, and even systems to remotely guide a hijacked aircraft to a safe landing are some of the possible options for further enhancing in-flight airline security that are being considered by systems engineers, regulators, and policymakers. The evolving terror threat to aviation security is also focusing attention on ways to prevent or mitigate possible nonconventional attacks against aircraft in flight, including the dispersal of chemical or biological agents in the aircraft cabin.

This chapter discusses the various in-flight security measures that have been put in place or are under consideration to reduce the vulnerability of various threats, including hijackings, attempted bombings using devices located in the airline cabin, unruly passengers, and attacks using nonconventional weapons such as chemical and biological agents. Immediately following the 9/11 attacks, several recommendations for strengthening in-flight security were proposed and many were swiftly pursued. As discussed in Chapter 2, immediately following the 9/11 attacks, the DOT assembled rapid response teams of senior aviation industry leadership to make recommendations for airport and aircraft security.

The specific conclusions and recommendations of the Rapid Response Team on Aircraft Security focused on the following elements:

- Hardening of cockpit doors
- Monitoring and surveillance of the aircraft cabin
- Deploying federal air marshals
- Arming airline flight crewmembers on a voluntary basis
- Training airline crews to handle in-flight security situations
- Addressing the coordination of armed law enforcement personnel
- Credentialing and identity verification procedures for individuals authorized to carry firearms on board commercial passenger aircraft and/or access the flight deck[1]

These recommendations largely reflect the major ongoing policy and strategic issues for the in-flight components of aviation security and have been addressed, to some extent, through aviation security legislation enacted since the 9/11 attacks. Most notably, this legislation and corresponding regulatory changes have led to the hardening of cockpit doors, stricter security procedures for cockpit access, the deployment of thousands of federal air marshals, federal training for volunteer airline pilots to carry firearms to defend the cockpit from possible attacks, and security and self-defense training for airline cockpit and cabin crews. Despite these steps, a variety of issues remain regarding the U.S. policy and strategy for the in-flight component of airline security. These include the consideration of various security technologies, ranging from in-flight video monitoring of the airliner cabin to autonomous flight control systems that can be engaged in response to a hijacking attempt to safely land an aircraft without human intervention, potentially eliminating the threat of an aircraft being used to attack a ground target. Policy considerations also include issues regarding identity validation and coordination among law enforcement personnel that are authorized to fly while armed; the proposed use of secondary flight deck barriers to protect the cockpit during times when cockpit doors are opened in flight; the possible use of special bomb-containment areas on board in the event that a suspected explosive device is found in flight; and approaches for preventing and responding to possible security threats involving in-flight dispersal of a chemical or biological agent.

HARDENED COCKPIT DOORS

Provisions in ATSA (P.L. 107-71) prohibit access to the flight deck of passenger aircraft except by authorized persons. ATSA also required that flight deck doors and locks be strengthened and that these doors remain locked while the aircraft is in flight, except when necessary to permit access and egress by authorized persons. The FAA required interim modifications to flight deck doors and provided temporary regulatory relief from certain airworthiness standards to quickly improve the intrusion resistance of the flight deck. These short-term measures principally consisted of door modifications for stronger internal locking devices that can only be unlocked from inside the flight deck and reinforced bars to hinder any attempted forced entry into the cockpit.

On January 15, 2002, the FAA published a final rule establishing new standards for the design of flight deck doors and access doors for crew rest areas to protect airline flight crew areas and flight decks from intrusion and penetration by small arms fire or fragmentation devices, such as grenades.[2] The FAA reported that full deployment of hardened cockpit doors meeting these specifications on about 10,000 U.S. passenger airliners and foreign aircraft flying to and from the United States has been completed and, in all but a few special instances, the doors were in place by the April 9, 2003, deadline set in the regulations.

While the regulations called for a considerable strengthening of the doors, doorframes, and locking mechanisms, there was no requirement to further strengthen other components of the bulkheads that separate cockpits from the passenger cabin. Some have, therefore, expressed concern that cockpits may still be vulnerable to attack from grenades, fragmentation devices, or improvised explosives detonated in the forward cabin or forward lavatory. While options for further hardening cockpit bulkheads may be considered for future aircraft design, the heavy weight of these dividers may limit their acceptance by airlines. There has been little consideration of the option of retrofitting airliner cockpit bulkheads to further strengthen them. In general, the sense is that the threat to the cockpit from explosives or fragmentation devices is best mitigated through effective screening of passengers and carry-on items for explosives, noting that these devices pose a threat to the integrity of the entire aircraft fuselage as well as to the cockpit bulkhead.

Following the FAA's promulgation of its final regulations for improving flight deck door intrusion and penetration resistance, a significant concern raised by air carriers was the cost of fitting the passenger air carrier fleet with hardened cockpit doors meeting the regulatory requirements. Although FAA's original estimate placed the cost of installing the doors at about $13,000 per aircraft, the airlines reported that retrofit door installations typically had cost between $30,000 and $50,000 per aircraft depending on the size and composition of their fleet.[3] Congress initially appropriated $100 million dollars to the FAA to be disbursed to air carriers as reimbursement for cockpit door installations in FY2003 Appropriations (see P.L. 108-7) and subsequently made available an additional $100 million for this purpose in the FY2003 Emergency Wartime Supplemental Appropriations Act (P.L. 108-11) as part of the larger package to compensate airlines for security-related costs.

In response to air cargo industry objections to requiring that all-cargo jets also be equipped with hardened cockpit doors, language in the Consolidated Appropriations Resolution for FY2003 (P.L. 108-7) limited FY2003 funds for hardening cockpit doors to passenger aircraft only. While the FAA's implementation plan originally called for hardening cockpit doors on all-cargo aircraft equipped with cockpit doors as well, the FAA has since rescinded this proposed requirement for all-cargo aircraft and limited the requirement to passenger aircraft with 20 or more seats. Hardened cockpit doors, therefore, are still not a requirement for all-cargo jets, although all-cargo operators must demonstrate that they have other security measures in place to ensure that unauthorized individuals are not allowed access to aircraft.

SECONDARY FLIGHT DECK BARRIERS

While the initiative to strengthen cockpit doors has long been completed, concerns have been raised about potential security vulnerabilities that arise when the cockpit door is opened, even for brief periods, for pilots to take lavatory breaks, change out crews on long flights, receive meal and beverage service from flight attendants, or on rare occasions, to deal with in-flight mechanical problems. Various airlines and airline crews have devised procedures for blocking aisles with food or beverage carts to impede access to the flight deck when the flight deck door is opened. However, many have argued for a more permanent solution. Some have pointed out that El Al airlines has equipped aircraft with a double-door system, in which a second door can be closed and locked blocking access to the forward lavatory area during times when the primary cockpit door must be opened. In the United States, advocates for additional barriers, however, have sought a less expensive solution using gates that would not completely close off the forward lavatory and aisle areas, but would provide a considerable impediment to anyone attempting to pass over these barriers and attempt to access the cockpit. In the summer of 2007, the ALPA published a position paper urging the U.S. and Canadian governments to require secondary flight deck barriers on all air carrier aircraft by 2010.[4] In that document, ALPA called for a standard that the secondary barrier should be capable of delaying anyone trying to attack the cockpit by at least five seconds. While the TSA has agreed that the barrier designs appear to offer increased security at a relatively low cost, it recommended against mandating their use citing concerns over the frail economic conditions of the airlines that would be asked to bear the cost of deploying these barriers.[5]

On October 22, 2007, Representative Steve Israel introduced legislation (H.R. 3925, 110th Congress) that would require the FAA to issue an order requiring airlines to install secondary barriers, and require that these barriers remain locked whenever the cockpit door is opened. The legislation also contains language aimed at all-cargo aircraft and small commuter aircraft that are not equipped with hardened cockpit doors, requiring such barriers on these aircraft as well, but leaving it to the pilot's discretion as to when the flight deck barrier would be locked. Similarly, in 2004, Representative Israel had introduced legislation (H.R. 4801, 108th Congress) requiring the installation and use of secondary cockpit doors on air carrier aircraft whenever the cockpit door is open.

The proposed legislation has won the praise of ALPA which remains focused on seeing that secondary barriers are installed on both passenger and all-cargo aircraft.[6] However, while United Airlines took the initiative to begin equipping some of its fleet with secondary flight deck barriers beginning in the fall of 2004,[7] other airlines have not followed suit. The barriers installed on United Airlines aircraft cost around $25,000 each and consist of multiple metal cables stretched between two metal rods that can be locked in place as needed. These devices range in height from about five to six feet high. While they could be scaled by a would-be attacker in some cases or the cables could potentially be cut, they appear to offer a degree of deterrence along the lines of the proposed ALPA standard of delaying an attacker trying to gain access to the cockpit by five seconds or more. Other vendors have indicated that they could produce secondary barriers that would cost less than $10,000 installed.[8] However, since no specific performance standard or design criteria for secondary barriers yet exists, it is difficult to say exactly what it would cost to equip airliners with TSA and FAA-certified devices in large quantities. Based on this range of costs, equipping the U.S. air carrier fleet might run between $100 and $250 million all totaled, assuming about 10,000 passenger and all-cargo aircraft in service for U.S. commercial air carrier and regional operators and foreign carriers flying to the United States that may be affected by the requirement. This cost remains a primary concern in the debate over whether secondary flight deck barriers should be required.

FLIGHT DECK ACCESS PROCEDURES

In addition to hardened cockpit doors and, in some cases, secondary barriers, effective protection of the cockpit is also highly dependent on effective procedures for preventing unauthorized access to the flight deck, particularly while in flight. In addition to requiring hardened cockpit doors, ATSA requires these doors to remain locked at all times during the flight, except when necessary to allow authorized personnel to enter and exit. Meeting this mandate required refinement of procedures for opening and securing doors and for establishing effective communication between flight crews and cabin crews.

More significantly, the mandate required the development of a system to assess and validate the identity of individuals seeking authorized access to the flight deck. Individual airlines were able to rely on their internal access credential systems for flight crews, maintenance workers, and other employees to validate those employees with authorized access to the cockpit. In general, the required flight crew, other pilots, flight attendants, mechanics, and airline management personnel may access the cockpit with the permission of the airplane's captain. Airline check pilots or check airmen performing periodic in-flight evaluations of flight crewmembers are granted full access to the cockpit and this access is not at the discretion of the captain. Additionally, FAA inspectors performing formal inspections of cockpit operations must be granted access to the cockpit, and TSA inspectors must also be granted access to the cockpit if conducting specific cockpit security inspections. Other federal officials, such as certain FAA employees, NTSB investigators, TSA officials, Secret Service agents, and in certain circumstances, other homeland security and LEOs may also be granted access to the cockpit, but typically at the discretion of the pilot in command. Federal officials with authorized access to the cockpit are issued special credentials that must be validated by the boarding agent when seeking permission to occupy the cockpit jumpseat, and these officials must comply with TSA-approved airline protocols and procedures for requesting and obtaining cockpit access. These various procedures to validate the identity and cockpit access authorization of airline employees and federal officials were strengthened following the 9/11 attacks to minimize the risk that terrorists could exploit such access to compromise the layers of in-flight and cockpit security measures that have been put in place since.

However, a long-standing industry practice prior to the 9/11 attacks had been to allow flight crews of other airlines to ride inside the cockpit on the jumpseat as a means to position crews for their flight assignments at various airports across the air carriers network. One significant barrier to continuing this practice following the 9/11 attacks and the subsequent mandate in ATSA for validation of those seeking authorized access to the cockpit was the lack of an industry-wide database for crewmember identification.

To address this need, the airline industry and engineering solutions vendor ARINC, Inc. developed a secure Internet-based system, called the CASS, which allows airline gate attendants to quickly determine whether employees of participating airlines are authorized to access an aircraft's cockpit to ride on the cockpit jumpseat. Airlines first sought to create the system in the summer of 2003 and worked with the TSA and the FAA to launch a pilot test of the concept, which was initiated in 2004. After extensive development and testing of the system, the TSA granted final approval for the CASS system in September 2005 and the system was fully implemented in February 2006.[9] The system serves as an Internet-based interface, accessible from gate agent computer terminals, which integrates information from participating airlines' human resources databases to provide employee information and photographs of airline crew for validation against airline-issued identification provided by the crewmember seeking authorized cockpit access. Over 60 U.S. airlines, including all major passenger carriers, are using the CASS system to allow for reciprocal access to aircraft jump-seats to facilitate flight crew positioning.[10] At present the system is limited to flight crews, but may eventually be expanded to include cabin crew personnel and possibly other airline personnel.

VIDEO SURVEILLANCE OF THE AIRLINER CABIN AND IMPROVED CABIN–COCKPIT COMMUNICATIONS

Hardened flight deck doors and the restricted access to the cockpit under current security regulations and procedures have the potential negative consequence of making communication and coordination between flight crews in the cockpit and cabin crews on board an airliner more challenging, particularly during security situations or in-flight emergencies. ATSA permits the FAA to develop and implement the use of video monitors or other devices to alert pilots to cabin activity. It also directs the FAA to revise procedures used by cabin crew to notify the flight deck of security breaches and other emergencies using switches or other devices or methods. Additionally, the Homeland Security Act of 2002 (P.L. 107-296) requires air carriers to provide flight attendants with methods for discreet, hands-free, wireless communications with the pilots. The FAA, in coordination with the TSA, continues to examine feasible technologies and operational procedures for monitoring and communications between the cockpit and cabin.

While video is a viable option for improving cockpit security awareness, the use of video monitoring on board aircraft is not required. However, passenger aircraft with hardened cockpit doors must have some means for viewing the area outside the cockpit door, and flight crews must visually verify that any person requesting access to the flight deck is not under duress using an approved viewing device. Also, airlines must provide an FAA-approved means for the cabin crew to notify the flight crew of suspicious activity or security breaches in the cabin.

On August 15, 2007, the FAA issued a final rule requiring flight deck door monitoring and crew discreet alerting systems.[11] The rule sets a performance standard giving airlines the option to choose a variety of methods and technologies to meet these requirements. In terms of monitoring the area outside the flight deck, the rule allows for the use of video monitoring devices, optical peepholes or viewports, or other types of viewing devices. With regard to discreet communications, the FAA's position is that the intercom/interphone systems installed on most airliners can provide for discreet communications, despite concerns raised by some that it may be difficult to use the interphone discreetly, the system could be easily compromised, and it could be difficult for cabin crewmembers to reach an interphone in certain circumstances. Critics of the FAA decision, such as the Professional Flight Attendants Association and the Association of Professional Flight Attendants, had hoped instead for a requirement to provide cabin crewmembers with wireless communication devices. The FAA, however, cautioned that such devices could be taken away by an attacker and then could possibly be used to gain unauthorized access to the flight deck. The FAA further cautioned that the loss or theft of one of these devices could compromise an airline's entire in-flight security system. The FAA did not, however, rule out the possibility of approving a wireless system to meet the requirements for discreet communication between cabin crewmembers and the flight deck.

UNINTERRUPTABLE AIRCRAFT TRANSPONDERS

Language in ATSA also authorizes the FAA administrator to develop and implement methods to ensure the continuing operation of aircraft transponders in the event of an emergency. Aircraft are equipped with radio transmitters called transponders that respond to air traffic control radar interrogation signals by sending back a discrete aircraft code and other information, such as aircraft call sign and altitude. Modern airliners have transponders installed that automatically transmit information about the call sign and aircraft type to air traffic control facilities. Aircraft transponders also have the capability for pilots to input unique codes for in-flight emergencies and for hijackings to alert air traffic controllers of certain in-flight situations. In the case of hijackings, transponders offer pilots a potential means of alerting air traffic controllers regarding the hijacking in a discreet manner under situations where pilots may be unable to otherwise alert anyone on the ground that a hijacking is in progress. Most importantly, transponders serve as the principal means for providing a signal allowing air traffic controllers and airspace security monitors to track the position and movement of an aircraft in flight, including suspected and confirmed hijacked aircraft.

In the case of the 9/11 hijackings, the terrorists disabled the transponders of the hijacked airplanes to make it more difficult to track these aircraft. While the transponders were turned off, the hijacked aircraft were not completely invisible to air traffic controllers, because their radar displays still include primary surveillance radar (PSR) returns acquired when rotating radar antennas on the ground receive reflections off of the body of the aircraft. These primary radar returns, however, provide no information about the type of aircraft, its call sign, or its altitude. On a cluttered radar display, with many other aircraft, it may be difficult for controllers to continually track an aircraft with an inoperative or intentionally disabled transponder.

While the provision in ATSA authorizes the FAA to take appropriate action to ensure that aircraft transponders that report aircraft position and altitude information cannot be turned off in flight during an emergency, such as a hijacking, this objective is difficult to achieve in practice because doing so may significantly limit a flight crew's ability to diagnose and correct transponder problems during normal flight operations. For safety reasons, access to power circuitry for electric-powered avionics and equipment is a standard design feature of modern aircraft. Even circuits for required safety equipment, such as cockpit voice and data recorders, can be accessed from the flight deck and can, therefore, be interrupted or disabled by someone with ill intent. For example, in the December 19, 1997, crash of a SilkAir Boeing 737 in Indonesia, the NTSB uncovered evidence suggesting that the cockpit voice and flight data recorders were intentionally switched off, possibly by the airplane captain, perhaps to cover up the intentional downing of the airliner in a suspected suicide.[12]

Pilots often need legitimate access to transponder devices to reset power and system modes when they malfunction and fail to continuously provide aircraft position information in response to air traffic control radar interrogations. For this reason, pilots often need to have access to the full functionality of transponder units, including the capability to shut these units off as needed. While engineers could design transponders to become uninterruptable in certain emergency states, doing so may require some input from the pilot to indicate that an emergency state exists, particularly in the case of a hijacking, which cannot be detected automatically by the aircraft's systems. Even if transponders were designed to include such an uninterruptable mode, because they require continuous electric power, a hijacker with knowledge of the system may still be able to cutoff power to the unit and render it useless. Even if the transponder had some sort of backup power source, such as a stand-alone integrated battery, this too could potentially be defeated by a knowledgeable hijacker with adequate time available by accessing and disabling the unit itself. Placing the unit in a location that is difficult to access in flight could minimize these potential risks. However, the FAA has not yet certified or required design modifications to transponder systems to improve their security.

FUTURE SYSTEMS FOR AIRCRAFT SURVEILLANCE

The FAA is currently working on an integrated navigation and surveillance system called Automated Dependent Surveillance-Broadcast (ADS-B), which is expected to replace radar surveillance and the use of transponders as the primary means for aircraft surveillance in the next 10–15 years. Work on ADS-B complicates the issue of uninterruptable transponders because once ADS-B is fully deployed, transponders may become largely obsolete. However, ADS-B introduces its own unique policy and technology issues regarding airspace security surveillance.

The proposed transition away from radar-based air traffic surveillance raises considerable policy questions regarding the future capability to monitor air traffic for security purposes. This is because, unlike radar that provides a means to monitor all aircraft using primary radar returns (i.e., passive radar reflections off of the airframe), the ADS-B system fully relies on aircraft transmissions to monitor air traffic. If an aircraft is noncompliant (i.e., if ADS-B equipment is intentionally disabled), it would be invisible to those monitoring ADS-B-transmitted positions and tracks, such as air traffic controllers and airspace security monitors. Similarly, aircraft that suffer a loss of power or some other system failure affecting the ADS-B device would be invisible to ADS-B ground monitoring stations and other aircraft monitoring ADS-B signals. Without a radar system to back up ADS-B surveillance, there would be no identifiable means to passively monitor the position and track of these aircraft.

No specific decisions have been made regarding the continued operation of radar sites after the proposed switch over to ADS-B surveillance. Some have speculated that, while the FAA would likely retain some radar sites as a backup means of surveillance, particularly in the busy airspace around major airports, FAA-maintained long-range radars in remote areas, including areas that provide border surveillance capabilities, may be decommissioned. Thus, DHS agencies and/or the NORAD Command might need to assume responsibility for maintaining these radar sites, and/or invest in initiatives for enhancing or expanding their own surveillance capabilities to monitor flight activity along the border and within U.S. airspace to detect and track noncompliant or suspicious aircraft. With regard to surveillance of flights along the U.S. borders, if sufficient capabilities to conduct passive surveillance of air traffic, using radar or other technologies, are put in place, then ADS-B might actually facilitate the detection of suspicious flight activity by allowing easier identification of noncompliant aircraft detected by other means of surveillance that are not transmitting their position and identification through ADS-B.

THE FEDERAL AIR MARSHAL SERVICE

The FAMS has its roots in the Sky Marshal Program of the late 1960s and early 1970s. However, at the time of the 9/11 attacks, the FAA's air marshals totaled only 33 in number and their mission was limited to covering certain high-risk international flights.[13]

Following the 9/11 attacks, the FAMS was greatly expanded under ATSA and organizationally placed within the newly created TSA. Within one year after the 9/11 attacks, the FAMS grew from the small cadre of 33 air marshals to a force of thousands, although a specific headcount remains classified. The TSA was given broad authority to deploy appropriately trained and equipped federal air marshals on any scheduled passenger flight. Marshals must be deployed on every "high-risk" flight, which may include nonstop, long-distance flights, such as those targeted on September 11, 2001, even if the flight is fully booked. Under provisions in ATSA, airlines are required to provide seating for on-duty air marshals at no cost to the U.S. government or to the marshal. Additionally, airlines must provide transportation on a space available basis to off-duty air marshals traveling to an airport nearest the marshal's home upon the completion of his or her security duties at no cost to the marshal or to the U.S. government.

Air marshals receive law enforcement availability pay (LEAP) equal to 25% of their base pay as entitled to under ATSA in addition to their base salary and locality pay, and in return are expected to work, on average, 50-hour workweeks. Federal air marshals, like most other federal LEOs, face mandatory retirement at age 57, and may retire upon completion of 20 years of service.[14] Consequently, DHS policy specifies that individuals over the age of 37 cannot be hired as federal air marshals, unless they have previously served in a qualifying federal law enforcement position.

Post-9/11 Air Marshal Hiring and Training

In the first year after the 9/11 attacks, as the FAMS grew rapidly, the adequacy of FAMS training and preparedness was brought into question. In order to quickly expand the air marshal program after September 11, 2001, the FAA and, subsequently, the TSA abbreviated the training for air marshal recruits, reducing the initial training course from a 14 week course to a five week course for candidates without law enforcement experience and a one week course for those with law enforcement experience. Reportedly, about 1400 of the initial cadre of post-9/11 air marshal recruits came from other federal law enforcement positions, raising some concerns that the more lucrative pay being offered by the TSA was causing a drain on other federal law enforcement agencies that suddenly faced staffing shortages at a time when they were being called upon to step up policing efforts to combat potential terrorist threats on the ground.[15]

Immediately following the 9/11 attacks and the call to greatly expand the air marshal program, the FAA reported receiving more than 50,000 applications for the FAMS program from citizens eager to join in the efforts to prevent future terrorist attacks. Air marshal applicants hired under this abbreviated and accelerated training program were later required to complete an additional four week advanced training program that included emergency evacuation and flight simulator training. Additionally, the advanced marksmanship requirement was dropped, but air marshal candidates were still required to pass the pistol range test at the highest level required for any federal law enforcement agency. The initial wave of new air marshal hires were provisionally hired with expedited secret clearances until full investigations for their required top secret clearances could be conducted. While a backlog of security investigations delayed issuance of top secret clearances for many air marshals, as of November 2003, the GAO reported that only about 3% of all air marshals were still awaiting their top secret clearances.[16] By July 2002, the Administration's deadline for fully deploying federal air marshals, thousands of air marshals had been trained and deployed. Information on the exact number of federal air marshals is classified, as is specific information on air marshal training programs and operational aspects of FAMS.

FAMS applicants must meet strict hiring standards, with all but 6% of those hired having attended some college, and 78% holding either a bachelors degree or an advanced degree. New hires into FAMS are now largely limited to filling vacant positions as the result of retirements or attrition. These new hires go through extensive training including basic law enforcement training conducted at facilities in Artesia, New Mexico, and specialized training provided at the Artesia site and at facilities near Atlantic City, New Jersey. In addition to classroom training in law enforcement and TSA regulations and procedures, air marshals receive specialized training in basic marksmanship, reactive firearms techniques, and advanced firearms handling scenarios in aircraft cabin mockups. The full training program costs more than $40,000 per recruit.[17] While new hires receive intensive training to become air marshals, there has been considerable speculation and controversy over whether FAMS recruitment and hiring has kept pace with attrition rates or whether the numbers of FAMS has been dwindling over the last few years.

CONTROVERSIES REGARDING AIR MARSHAL FORCE SIZE AND FLIGHT COVERAGE

In the first few years following the 9/11 attacks, the attrition rate among air marshals was relatively high, at about 10%. More recently, the TSA has indicated that attrition rates since the air marshal program was expanded following the 9/11 attacks have settled down to about 6.5% annually, a rate comparable to other federal law enforcement agencies. Based on these statistics, it might be surmised that either those air marshals hired on during the initial wave of hiring who realized that the air marshal program was not for them have left the FAMS to find other work and have been replaced by individuals more satisfied with the job and the organization or the TSA has corrected some of the problems leading to higher attrition rates in the early days of the expanded air marshal program. However, media reports criticizing the FAMS program have painted a very different picture, suggesting that large numbers of air marshals have left the program since 2002, not all of which have been replaced, leaving the organization with a limited ability to provide adequate coverage of airline flights. Despite a sizable budget for FAMS, air marshal coverage of airline flights and the effectiveness of the program remain controversial issues that are difficult to address because of limited public information available regarding the program.

While the official number of air marshals is regarded as security-sensitive information, a report in the Christian Science Monitor in December 2005 stated that "[a]fter peaking at 4,800 in 2002, sources say, the force shrank dramatically, due to attrition and compounding health problems from excessive flying," and placed the total number of air marshals at about 3000, but noted that only about two-thirds of these actually operate on the front lines covering airline flights on a routine basis.[18] However, with this and many other media accounts of the FAMS, the TSA, and the DHS have discounted these numbers and accompanying claims of an overworked, understaffed force as being inaccurate, noting that media sources, often disgruntled frontline air marshals, do not have the full picture and access to system-wide staffing numbers and scheduling information. In 2004, the TSA had acknowledged that it had fewer air marshals on the payroll than previously, but argued that improved efficiencies in scheduling enabled FAMS to cover more daily flights, noting that more than 5% of commercial airline flights were dispatched with FAMS aboard.[19]

However, in an April 2008 Cable News Network (CNN) investigative report, it was reported that FAMS fly on less than 1% of daily commercial airline flights in the United States.[20] The report quoted sources that had estimated FAMS staffing levels at some major field offices, such as Dallas, Texas, Seattle, Washington, and Las Vegas, Nevada, have decreased by more than 40% compared to their peak levels reached in the 2003 time frame. The TSA disputed these claims and stated that attrition rates have been holding steady at about 6.5% annually in recent years. It did not provide a statement of the percentage of flights that have FAMS on board, but retorted that the FAMS cover, not hundreds, but thousands of daily flights. The article pointed out, however, that the TSA may be considering a flight to be covered if it has either FAMS on board, or an armed pilot, or another armed LEO; so this does not provide an accurate picture of FAMS deployment by itself.

The TSA acknowledges that it is not capable of covering a large percentage of flights given the budgetary limitations on FAMS, despite comparatively large appropriations amounts, which comprised about 11% of annual federal spending on aviation security in FY2008 and FY2009. Consequently, from a strategic perspective, FAMS is used in a risk-based manner, deploying on flights based on specific threat intelligence and on threat and vulnerability assessments to determine which flights have the highest risk. ATSA left it up to the TSA to determine which flights are considered high risk. However, the statutes require FAMS to be deployed on all high-risk flights, raising questions about what specific criteria are used by the TSA to determine whether a flight is high risk.

Since flight risk is constantly changing, the number and characteristics of high-risks flights are also likely to change over time in response to changes in threats and vulnerabilities. While the greatest threat would still appear to be to large, wide-body aircraft, such as those used in the 9/11 terrorist attacks, and international flights originating outside the United States, like the flights targeting in the attempted shoe bombing in December 2001 and the liquid explosives plot uncovered in August 2006, specific threats may change from day-to-day based on specific intelligence information.

In terms of the vulnerability component of risk, other efforts to strengthen aviation security, including hardened cockpit doors and the deployment of armed pilots have arguably reduced the risk posed to domestic flights, but to what degree is hard to gauge. As was the case in the 1970s when airline security screening resulted in the obsolescence of the sky marshals of that era, it can be argued that the present day FAMS do not serve as critical of a role as they did immediately following the 9/11 attacks, before hardened cockpit doors could be fully deployed and before the creation of the program to arm volunteer airline pilots. However, in the current context, policymakers are not asking for the FAMS to be scaled back, and the FAMS annual budget has been growing at a steady pace from 2002 to 2009. Based on this, the apparent disconnect between the level of budgetary resources being provided to FAMS and the allegations of minimal FAMS coverage of airline flights remains a particularly controversial issue.

While little is known about actual FAMS scheduling and coverage of flights, by intention so as to not provide this critical information to those seeking to carry out hostile actions against aircraft, it is known that the FAMS budget has been growing at a rate largely in line with annual unavoidable cost adjustments, such as inflationary costs and salary increases, suggesting that the number of employees in FAMS is likely holding steady. The CNN report, however, stated that air marshals whom the investigative reporters spoke with question where the money is really going based on their observations of dwindling numbers in their ranks and their perception of limited coverage of airline flights.[21]

In FY2008, FAMS received an appropriation of $770 million, for salaries, training, equipment, and travel expenses for frontline air marshals and whatever administrative support is required to maintain the operation of the FAMS organization, and in FY2009 the total appropriation for FAMS increased to $819 million. How this translates to total numbers of air marshals and flight coverage remains largely unknown and highly controversial because it is cloaked in secrecy for security reasons. Lingering policy questions remain regarding what the appropriate level of coverage should be and how this compares to actual FAMS deployment levels and flight coverage.

It was reported in 2004 that the average total salary, compensation, annual recurrent training, overhead expenses for a deployed air marshal was about $170,000.[22] Applying estimated annual salary adjustments and comparing the resulting per air marshal cost estimate to the total FAMS appropriations can provide an estimate of the FAMS force size. However, what remains unknown is how many of these air marshals are flying the line on a routine basis. For those who are on active flight status, FAMS fly, on average, 181 days out of the year (roughly 15 days per month) and spend about 900 hours per year in flight, according to the TSA. These statistics roughly match the duty schedules of line pilots flying for major airlines in the United States. On a typical duty day, an air marshal will spend about five hours in flight.

When not flying, air marshals participate in recurrent training and periodic firearms requalification. Recently, FAMS have also been deployed on multimodal Visual Intermodal Prevention and Response (VIPR) teams. These VIPR teams are deployed on a periodic basis to protect passenger rail, mass transit systems, major passenger ferry operations, and so on, in cooperation with state and local law enforcement. However, the extent to which the additional duties covering other modes of transportation may be taking away from time spent flying on commercial airline flights is unknown. While the Congress has continually pushed for more elaborate security measures in other modes of transportation to more closely parallel what has been done in aviation, particularly following the 2004 Madrid passenger rail bombings and the 2005 London transit bombings, it has also been critical of any perceived gaps in aviation security, including some perceptions that air marshal deployment on commercial airline flights may be inadequate.

One option contemplated to address the level of air marshal coverage of airline flights was to train other federal LEOs to deploy as air marshals on an as-needed basis, providing a surge capability to respond to possible threats of aviation terrorism. To carry out this objective, in December 2003, FAMS was moved by DHS into ICE. According to the DHS, this repositioning of FAMS was intended to provide air marshals with access to broader training opportunities, additional access to intelligence, and improved law enforcement coordination. In addition to providing air marshals with opportunities to rotate into land-based assignment, the DHS also had plans to train immigration and customs officers as federal air marshals, thus increasing their ability to deploy additional air marshals during periods of heightened security concerns for civil aviation.[23] The proposed cross-training initiative would have allowed about 5000 additional trained officers to deploy as air marshals.[24]

This concept of training additional officers to provide a surge capacity if the threat condition warranted the deployment of additional air marshals, however, was never carried out. Rather, in FY2006, the FAMS was formally moved back into the TSA based on the recommendation of the DHS Second Stage Review (2SR), a comprehensive review of the department's organization, operations, and policies ordered by Secretary Michael Chertoff when he assumed leadership of the DHS, replacing the nation's first Secretary of Homeland Security, Tom Ridge, in March 2005. The findings of the 2SR initiative were made public in July 2005. Congress concurred with its recommendation to place the FAMS back inside the TSA, and it accordingly aligned the FAMS budget as a stand-alone component of the TSA in the FY2006 appropriations legislation.

For FY2009, the TSA proposed to merge FAMS with the TSA's Aviation Security program area, a move that could potentially allow for better coordination between airport and in-flight security, and could possibly create new career paths for security screeners seeking a law enforcement career as an air marshal. However, the Congress did not support this proposed merger, citing concerns that it could potentially dilute the effectiveness of the FAMS if airport screening functions took priority over in-flight protection in future budgets. By keeping FAMS as a completely separate functional area for budgetary purposes, it arguably would not have to compete for funding with other aviation security programs to the same extent as it would if it were placed within the Aviation Security program area. As a result of these concerns, FAMS has remained a stand-alone entity within the TSA organization, and it operates much more independently from other elements of the TSA, arguably giving it greater flexibility in carrying out its mission.

AIR MARSHAL OPERATIONAL AND PROCEDURAL ISSUES

In addition to the various controversies regarding FAMS attrition rates and coverage of airline flights, the extent to which TSA policies and procedures impact the air marshals' ability to maintain covert, undercover status has also been a specific area of contention. Former and current air marshals have complained to the media that dress codes, airport check-in and aircraft boarding procedures, and hotel reservation procedures are particular issues of concern that could compromise an air marshal's identity. Air marshals have complained that TSA policies that require male air marshals, which make up more than 90% of the force, to fly in sport coats and ties and maintain strict grooming standards with short cut hair often compromise their covert status. They argue that such strict standards, in an era when airline passengers are often dressed casually, make them stand out among passengers and may threaten their cover.[25] Concerns have also been raised that check-in procedures for air marshals to bypass security screening checkpoints, typically by showing their credentials and being led through checkpoint exit lanes, is often carried out in plain sight of the public, thus potentially compromising air marshal cover.[26] The potential consequences of an air marshal's or air marshal team's cover being compromised are significant because the marshals could be specifically targeted by attackers, and if overpowered, their weapon could be taken and possibly used against them or as a means to gain access to the flight deck.

These concerns came under congressional scrutiny and were the topic of a special investigation by the House Judiciary Committee released in 2006 after two years of probing into the issue following initial media coverage of the potential problems in 2004. The report found that air marshals' dress code, check-in procedures, and requirements to identify themselves to hotel clerks during overnight layovers potentially compromised their anonymity.[27] The report cited two specific incidents in which air marshals' cover was potentially compromised in what was described as possible terrorist probing of airport and commercial airliner security. Since then, changes have been made giving FAMS field offices greater flexibility to set dress codes appropriately for the flight while maintaining a professional image. In some cases, changes have been made to air marshal check-in and preflight procedures to better protect their cover, and the issue has not resurfaced in the media. Nonetheless, various operational aspects of the FAMS have been the source of reoccurring media coverage and could be an area of continued controversy that may be reexamined by policymakers and aviation security specialists in the future.

In December 2003, the DHS announced that, in addition to the deployment of FAMS on domestic flights and on international routes flown by U.S. air carriers, it would require foreign air carriers to carry armed air marshals on certain flights to and from the United States. This came following the receipt of intelligence information that certain foreign air carrier flights originating in Europe may be targeted. Typically, foreign countries would provide their own armed air marshals. However, the DHS indicated that it would assign U.S. air marshals on foreign flights if requested to do so by the foreign country and airline. Many foreign airlines have objected indicating that they would rather cancel flights to the United States when significant threats were identified in lieu of carrying armed air marshals.[28] Objections by foreign countries reflected their policy concerns over introducing weapons in the aviation environment as well as concerns over costs and liability. While some countries, such as Israel and Germany, were reported to be using air marshals already, other countries, such as Great Britain and the Netherlands, subsequently agreed to place air marshals on their aircraft despite opposition from groups representing airline pilots in those nations.[29]

Compared to other law enforcement roles, air marshals, by specific intent, keep a very low profile. This, combined with the effectiveness of other security layers, has meant that, since the 9/11 attacks, air marshals have played much more of a passive deterrent role in protecting airliners, rather than an active role. Nonetheless, in the first two years following September 11, 2001, air marshals responded to over 2000 aviation security incidents, used nonlethal force 16 times, discharged their weapons on three occasions and were involved in 28 arrests or detainments of individuals.[30]

Since the 9/11 attacks, air marshals have only once had to use deadly force to carry out their mission. On December 7, 2005, federal air marshals shot and fatally wounded Rigoberto Alpizar, at MIA, during the reboarding process of an American Airlines flight from Medellín, Colombia with continuing service to Orlando, Florida. Alpizar, who may have suffered from bipolar disorder, reportedly was arguing with his wife and attempted to exit the aircraft as the reboarding was completing. When a flight attendant refused to let him exit, he reportedly threatened that he had a bomb.[31] At this point, he was confronted by the two-person air marshal team on board, who fired at him when he refused to comply with their commands, made continuing threats, and then reached into the bag he was carrying. An investigation by the Miami-Dade State's Attorney's Office found that the air marshals were justified in their use of deadly force in this case.[32] The incident was not linked to terrorism, and it currently remains the only case in which air marshals have fired their weapons in the line of duty since the 9/11 attacks.

The FAMS has been otherwise largely untested in its role of protecting the nation's airlines from future terrorist attacks. Nonetheless, FAMS is considered a vital component of the overall risk-based approach to aviation security and is viewed as a critical element of the layers of in-flight security measures, along with hardened cockpit doors. However, even with a force consisting of thousands of air marshals, FAMS can cover only a relatively small percentage of the total number of the daily domestic and international passenger airline flights. Recognizing that FAMS could not realistically be staffed with sufficient numbers of air marshals to cover all air carrier flights, policymakers in the Administration and in Congress contemplated and debated the rather contentious option of training airline pilots to carry firearms and use deadly force to protect the flight decks of their aircraft from potential future hijacking attempts and other in-flight threats.

ARMED PILOTS AND CREW SECURITY TRAINING

The Homeland Security Act of 2002 (P.L. 107-296) included provisions to arm pilots of passenger aircraft and gives deputized pilots the authority to use force, including lethal force, to defend the flight deck against criminal and terrorist threats. The Act specifies that by February 2003, TSA was to begin administering the training and deputizing of qualified pilots volunteering to participate in the FFDO program. In response to this requirement, TSA developed a prototype program that trained and deputized an initial class of 44 pilots in mid-April 2003, at a cost of $500,000. The TSA was appropriated $8 million (see P.L. 108-7) for the program in FY2003, and has subsequently received $25 million annually to continue the training and deputizing of pilots and conduct advanced self-defense training for airline crews. The FFDO program accounts for the large majority of this annual appropriation. While the FFDO program remains controversial in the eyes of some who have voiced considerable concerns over introducing additional firearms in sterile areas of airports and on board aircraft, these appropriations amounts reflect that the program provides a cost-efficient layer of in-flight security, particularly in comparison with the FAMS, which received an annual appropriation totaling more than $800 million in FY2009. The FFDO program achieves this cost effectiveness by relying on volunteer pilots who receive no compensation or benefits from the federal government for their participation other than the cost of training and equipment.

The statutes establishing the FFDO program specifies that all training, supervision, and equipment needed for the program are to be provided at no expense to the pilots or the air carriers that employ them. However, pilots are not entitled to any compensation for participating in the program. The law also provides liability protection to pilots and the air carriers for use of or failure to use a firearm. Initially, the program was limited to pilots of passenger aircraft, but a provision in the 2003 FAA reauthorization legislation (Vision 100, P.L. 108-176) expanded the program to include pilots of all-cargo aircraft as well as other flight crewmembers, such as flight engineers, in the program.

The TSA began full implementation of the program in July 2003, conducting week-long classes to train FFDO candidates. While training was initially being conducted at Federal Law Enforcement Training Center (FLETC) facilities in Glynco, Georgia and Artesia, New Mexico, all initial training operations for the FFDO program have now moved to the Artesia, New Mexico facility. TSA has the capacity to provide initial training to about 2000 new volunteer pilots annually. Under TSA's implementation plan, pilots must requalify every six months to stay in the program. FFDO participants must also complete recurrent training every five years. To meet these requirements, the TSA has opened sites in Atlantic City, New Jersey, and in Dallas, Texas, in addition to the Artesia, New Mexico site. While the option of using private contract facilities for requalification has been advocated by some, the TSA has not approved any private firearms facilities for this purpose, opting instead to open these two additional facilities to better accommodate pilots who may find it difficult to travel to the remote Artesia, New Mexico site.

Pilots can apply for the program online, but must undergo extensive background checks before being selected to participate. Pilot groups estimate that, in total, about 30,000 pilots may sign up, although initial interest during the first five years of the program has been reported to be much lower. The TSA has indicated that roughly 11% of all eligible flight crewmembers have been trained and deputized as FFDOs at the end of FY2007.[33] Given the Bureau of Labor Statistics estimate of 79,000 pilots and flight engineers working for the airlines,[34] this would place the total number of FFDOs at somewhere around 8500. The TSA expects this number to grow by about 2–2.5% per year through FY2011.

Pilot organizations have accused the TSA of establishing an overly burdensome application and evaluation process and locating the initial training facility in a hard to reach location, which, they argue, has discouraged additional pilots from participating. The TSA has countered that the background checks are necessary and are equivalent to what federal LEOs must undergo. The TSA has also defended their selection of the single training site based on the availability of specialized facilities such as aircraft cabin mockups at the Artesia, New Mexico site, and heavy demand for facilities at the Glynco, Georgia site by other agencies.

LEGISLATIVE BACKGROUND

During the 107th Congress, Representative Don Young and Representative John Mica introduced the Arming Pilots Against Terrorism Act (H.R. 4635, 107th Congress). At the time, the Bush Administration had voiced initial opposition to the concept of arming pilots with lethal weapons. As amended by the House Aviation Subcommittee, the legislative proposal initially considered in the House contained a provision that would have capped participation in the program at 2% of eligible pilots and limited the program to a two-year test period. On July 10, 2002, however, the House approved a floor amendment offered by Representative Peter DeFazio that removed the 2% cap on the number of pilots who could participate in the program and also deleted the two-year sunset provision contained in the bill. In the Senate, Senator Robert Smith introduced the Arming Pilots Against Terrorism and Cabin Defense Act of 2002 (S. 2554, 107th Congress), which contained similar language to the final version of H.R. 4635 (107th Congress) as passed by the House.

On September 4, 2002, Senator Smith offered an amendment to the Senate version of H.R. 5005 (107th Congress), a bill introduced to create the DHS, consisting of provisions to arming pilots similar to those contained in H.R. 4635 (107th Congress). On November 12, 2002, Representative Richard Armey introduced H.R. 5710 (107th Congress) as a new vehicle for establishing the DHS and for other purposes, which contained similar provisions for arming pilots. However, in response to lobbying efforts by the air cargo industry, the language in this legislation limited participation in the program to pilots of passenger air carrier aircraft. On November 19, 2002, the Senate amended H.R. 5005 (107th Congress), incorporating provisions for arming pilots virtually identical to those in H.R. 5710 (107th Congress). The House agreed to the Senate amendment to H.R. 5005 (107th Congress) on November 22, 2002, and it was signed by President Bush on November 25, 2002, becoming P.L. 107-296.

While the original measure limited participation to only pilots flying on passenger airliners, during the first session of the 108th Congress, debate focused on whether pilots of all-cargo aircraft should be included in the FFDO program. Several legislative vehicles were introduced to expand the program to cargo pilots as well as to other flight crewmembers, such as flight engineers. On February 13, 2003, Representative John Mica introduced H.R. 765 (108th Congress), and on March 5, 2003 Senator Jim Bunning introduced S. 516 (108th Congress). Both bills sought to include cargo pilots in the FFDO program, while S. 516 sought to also include other flight crewmembers such as flight engineers. A separate stand-alone bill (S. 1657) introduced by Senator Bunning was passed by the Senate on November 10, 2003. Similar legislation (H.R. 1049 and H.R. 3262) was also introduced in the House. Also, the Air Cargo Security Act (S. 165), passed by the Senate on May 9, 2003, contained a provision that sought to include all-cargo pilots in the FFDO program. An amendment offered by Senator Bunning (S. Amdt. 903 to S. 824) was included in the FAA reauthorization legislation (P.L. 108-176) and was enacted into law on December 12, 2003. This provision expanded the FFDO program to include other flight crewmembers, such as flight engineers, and opened the program to participation by flight crewmembers flying for all-cargo air carriers.

Debate over the issue of arming pilots focused on the benefits, risks, and costs associated with implementing the program. Proponents for arming pilots argued that the potential benefits of deterring or thwarting terrorist and criminal acts against aircraft outweighed the inherent risks associated with arming pilots. Opponents of policy allowing pilots to be armed with lethal weapons, including the airlines and several prominent aviation safety experts, argued that such a program's safety risks and monetary costs outweighed these potential benefits. Key risks cited by critics of the program include

- Added workload and responsibilities associated with participation in the program that may distract pilots from primary flying duties and safety-related functions
- Risks of a firearm discharge to innocent passengers or aircraft structure and systems
- A proliferation of firearms on aircraft and in secured areas of the aviation system that is counter to other security objectives[35]

Many of these concerns raised by critics of the plan to arm pilots were recognized by both Congress and proponents of the plan as key issues to be addressed in implementing the program to arm airline pilots.

FFDO Program Implementation Issues

Implementation issues for the FFDO program included consideration of the standards and guidelines for (1) pilot selection and screening, (2) equipment, (3) training, (4) operational procedures, and (5) costs. To implement the program, the TSA formed a task force to address these issues and developed a plan for implementation of the program. While Congress noted that the TSA's decisions regarding the methods for implementing procedural requirements of the program would be subject to review only for abuse of discretion, there has been continued congressional interest and oversight of the program since its inception in 2003.

A key issue considered during the implementation of the program was the process for selecting and screening volunteer pilots seeking to become FFDOs. The legislation required further assessment to determine whether additional background checks should be required beyond routine background check requirements for pilots and other airline and airport workers. Additional selection and screening criteria were viewed as a tool to help ensure that pilots selected to participate are physically and psychologically capable of carrying out the duties and responsibilities associated with participation in the program and will maintain the standards set forth by the program while serving as FFDOs. Additional background checks and psychological screening measures are used to assess whether a pilot poses a security or safety threat by possessing a firearm on the flight deck or by being trained in the use of lethal force.

Critics of the additional screening requirement, however, point out that pilots already undergo rigorous preemployment evaluations and screening throughout their careers with an air carrier. Captain Stephen Luckey, Chairman of the National Fight Security Committee of the ALPA, International noted that

> Pilots are undoubtedly the most highly scrutinized employees in the work force, submitting to a battery of preemployment evaluations, a flight physical every six months, random drug and alcohol testing, and a criminal history records check, among other formal examinations. Additionally, pilots are constantly interacting with and undergoing de facto monitoring by their airline's management, their peers, FAA personnel, and others.[36]

On the other hand, despite preexisting measures for screening and evaluating pilots, recent examples of confirmed and suspected suicides and sabotage of aircraft by flight crew personnel suggest a potential need for more detailed background checks of pilots wishing to participate in the FFDO program.

Examples of confirmed deliberate acts by flight crew personnel to crash commercial aircraft include an intentional crash of a Japan Airlines DC-8 in 1982, an attempted hostile takeover of a Federal Express DC-10 in 1994 by an off-duty flight engineer who intended to crash the airplane into FedEx headquarters, and the 1999 theft and intentional crash of an Air Botswana ATR-42 into two other Air Botswana aircraft. Additionally, there have been other high profile crashes of passenger air carrier aircraft, such as the 1997 crash of a Silk Air Boeing 737 in Indonesia and the 1999 crash of an EgyptAir Boeing 767 off the coast of Rhode Island, where intentional pilot action was suspected but never conclusively determined. It should, however, be noted that none of these crashes involved flight crews of U.S. flag carriers providing passenger air service.

There is little agreement among experts on whether additional screening measures, including psychiatric evaluation of pilots, would be capable of detecting pilots who may pose a risk by participating in the program. Some argue that current screening and peer monitoring of pilots are insufficient, and detailed psychiatric screening and psychological testing are needed to adequately assess the mental health of pilots.[37] Others argue that many common mental health conditions can be masked during these evaluations. They assert that the costs of implementing such elaborate screening measures may far outweigh the marginal improvement in assessing the mental health of pilots beyond that obtained through the scrutiny pilots already undergo.

Proponents for arming pilots also argued that by having access to the flight deck, a pilot intent on causing harm already possesses the means to do so, and introducing a firearm on the flight deck does little to add to that already existing capability. They argue that, historically, incidents of deliberate acts by pilots to harm the airplane and its occupants are extremely unusual and current background checks, screening, and evaluations of pilots are more than adequate for assessing their fitness to participate in the FFDO program.

Currently, TSA procedures require that pilots applying for the program undergo additional psychological screening, background checks, and a medical examination beyond those already required of airline pilots. The Airline Pilots Security Alliance (APSA), a grassroots organization supporting efforts to arm pilots, has called the TSA screening requirements unacceptable and redundant with many existing FAA and airline screening requirements. However, the TSA asserts that these screening measures are similar to those used in selection of federal LEOs, including federal air marshals, to determine an individual's fitness to carry a firearm and act in a law enforcement capacity, and these investigations are necessary to ensure that participating pilots meet these same high standards.[38] According to TSA, about 6% of the applicants for the program are screened out prior to initial training. About 2% fail to meet the qualifications specified by law, 3% are eliminated through psychological screening, and 1% are disqualified based on information identified by the background check.[39]

The legislation creating the FFDO program also required the TSA to address concerns over the selection of firearms and ammunition for the program, with a specific emphasis on identifying a weapon that would be effective against terrorists but would also pose a minimal risk to the aircraft, aircraft systems, and airline passengers. The legislation specifically called for an analysis to assess the risk of catastrophic failure of an aircraft as a result of the discharge (including an accidental discharge) of a firearm into the avionics, electrical systems, or other sensitive areas of the aircraft.

The selection of firearms and ammunition for use in the FFDO program was regarded as a particularly important consideration. Opponents of arming pilots had argued that a stray bullet could cause serious damage to aircraft systems and structures and jeopardize flight safety. Speaking before the Senate Committee on Commerce, Science, and Transportation, Captain Edward M. Davidson, Director of Flight Safety and QA for Northwest Airlines, cautioned that bullets could pierce flight deck windows creating a potentially catastrophic cockpit decompression, or they could strike flight deck avionics and controls potentially putting at risk numerous safety critical systems.[40] A depressurization of the airplane at altitude would necessitate that the flight crew use supplemental oxygen and complete checklist procedures in response to the depressurization. Similarly, a loss of critical aircraft systems could require a flight crew's immediate attention. Accomplishing required safety-related tasks may prove difficult during a struggle with intruders in the cockpit.

However, in testimony before the House Subcommittee on Aviation, Mr. Ron Hinderberger, Director of Aviation Safety for the Boeing Company stated that "[t]he risk of loss of the aircraft due to a stray round from a handgun is very slight. Boeing commercial service history contains cases of gunfire on board in-service airplanes, all of which landed safely." Hinderberger further noted that "[c]ommercial airplane structure is designed with sufficient strength, redundancy, and damage tolerance that single or even multiple handgun bullet holes would not result in loss of the aircraft. A single bullet hole in the fuselage skin would have little effect on cabin pressurization."[41]

While the official study of risks to the cabin from FFDO firearms remains classified, a growing amount of evidence supporting this conclusion that bullets pose only a slight risk to aviation safety has largely put to rest these concerns. The law, nonetheless, provides for a temporary suspension of the program if the firearm of an FFDO accidentally discharges due to a shortcoming in standards, training, or procedures until the contributing factors are corrected. While there has been one reported case of an accidental discharge of an FFDO weapon in the cockpit while in flight from Denver, Colorado to Charlotte, North Carolina on March 22, 2008,[42] a review of the incident did not lead to any grounding or suspension of the program, suggesting that the incident was not indicative of any specific lapses in the training or operational procedures that warranted a suspension of the program.

Given that FFDO participants are not primarily LEOs, and they receive more limited training, the structure of the FFDO program training was also an issue of particular interest during the initial development and implementation of the program. The law specified that the training program could be administered either by the TSA or by another firearms training facility, either run by a federal agency or by a contract vendor. The advantages of using TSA facilities included better standardization of training for pilots, improved compliance with the standards and guidelines established by the TSA, and better coordination of training and procedures between FFDOs and FAMS with regard to effective coordination and communication in dealing with in-flight situations. However, an initial concern was that TSA training facilities could become overburdened if large numbers of pilots wish to participate in the program. TSA facilities and staff may lack the resources to administer training in a timely manner that meets scheduling constraints of the pilots, especially given that the pilots need to complete this training during their time off.

These concerns led to the consideration of instead using FBI training facilities. In December 2001, the FBI released its proposal for training airline pilots termed the "Cockpit Protection Program." The advantage of this plan was that it was already well defined and included assessments of the facility and staff requirements needed to administer the training. The disadvantage of this program, however, was that it would have removed the training from the direct control of the TSA. Also, there was concern that this arrangement might not offer the opportunity for specific training regarding the coordination of duties and responsibilities between FFDOs and FAMS.

Another federal entity named as a possible provider of training for FFDOs was FLETC, which has facilities in Glynco, Georgia; Charleston, South Carolina; and Artesia, New Mexico. These facilities had the resources to train larger groups of pilots, but like the FBI facilities, there was a concern over the limited oversight by TSA and the lack of opportunity for training on coordination with federal air marshals.

Using contractor facilities and/or contractor staff to administer training to FFDOs were also mentioned as options, but ones that posed several challenges. Extensive oversight of contractor-provided training may have been necessary to ensure that established curriculum and qualifications standards were adequately maintained. If multiple contracts were awarded to train FFDOs, standardization of training across vendors might prove difficult to maintain. One advantage of using contract training for the program, however, might be the reduction of capital investment for facilities and personnel.

After consideration of these alternatives, the option chosen was to base the training at existing FLETC facilities, but have TSA personnel administer and conduct the training. A prototype training program held in April 2003, used FLETC facilities in Glynco, Georgia to train an initial group of 48 pilots. Full implementation of the program began in July 2003 at the Glynco facilities as well as at the facilities in Artesia, New Mexico. In September 2003, the program was moved in its entirety to Artesia, New Mexico facilities because that site has aircraft mockups for training that were not available at Glynco and also because other law enforcement training at Glynco was limiting facilities available for the program there. Some pilot groups, however, complained that the TSA's reliance on a single site, and the remote location of the Artesia, New Mexico facility (269 miles from the nearest major airport in Albuquerque) creates a considerable inconvenience for attending the training.[43]

As the program matured, some in Congress continued to push for the use of private sector sites for conducting FFDO training and requalification.[44] Admiral James Loy, the TSA Administrator at the time, noted that while the initial training was being conducted at federal facilities, as the program evolves "... there very well may be a private sector opportunity ..." to provide the training.[45] More recently, however, the TSA has indicated that it considers initial training of the pilots a federal function, allowing trainees to be appropriately evaluated by TSA personnel before being deputized, but it remains open to the possibility that private firms could provide for recurrent training and requalification of FFDOs. Nonetheless, the TSA has since expanded the federal role by opening evaluation and recurrent training sites in Atlantic City, New Jersey, and in Dallas, Texas, rather than turning these functions over to private training vendors.

The law specifies that FFDO training shall include

- Training to ensure that the FFDO attains a level of proficiency with a firearm comparable to the level of proficiency required of federal air marshals
- Training to ensure that the officer maintains exclusive control over the officer's firearm at all times, including training in defensive maneuvers
- Training to assist the officer in determining when it is appropriate to use the officer's firearm and when it is appropriate to use less-than-lethal force

In designing this training, the TSA was required to establish requirements for training FFDOs based on the training standards applicable to federal air marshals, taking into account the differing roles and responsibilities of FFDOs and FAMS. The law also specifies that FFDOs must requalify at an interval set by the TSA.

Pilot groups, including ALPA and the Allied Pilots Association (APA), pushed for a 48-hour training program. Such a training program was derived from details released in December 2001 regarding the FBI Cockpit Protection Program that proposed a five-day, 48-hour training course in firearms handling, legal aspects, tort law, and policies regarding use of lethal force. The current TSA program similarly consists of a 48-hour curriculum of classroom instruction, firearms training, and tactical drills.

The law establishing the FFDO program does not specify any criteria or guidelines for assessing the effectiveness of the program or the training provided under the program. Given that the primary objective of the program is deterrence of terrorism and criminal acts against the flight deck, the effectiveness of the program, in this regard, is difficult if not impossible to assess. Nonetheless, the effectiveness of certain elements of the program can be assessed. For example, the effectiveness of training can be assessed through evaluation of performance during requalification. Also, effectiveness of the program with regard to risk management can be assessed through analysis of data on incidents of firearms mishandling, accidental discharges, lost and stolen weapons, and so on.

ISSUES REGARDING OPERATIONAL PROCEDURES FOR ARMED PILOTS

The legislation establishing the FFDO program identified storage and transportation of firearms as a key issue to be addressed in establishing the procedural requirements for the program. The legislation specifies that particular attention should be given to storage and transportation of firearms on international flights and when the pilot leaves the airport to remain overnight away from the pilot's base airport. Pilot groups argued for allowing FFDOs to retain the firearm, particularly at the pilot's home base, and further advocate that FFDOs be given the opportunity to train with the firearm to maintain proficiency in its use.[46] Opponents of such a plan argued that pilots carrying weapons, both in airports and to and from work, could be the target of terrorists and criminals seeking to steal their firearms. They also noted that handling the firearm while in transit increases the potential for mishandling of the firearm and accidental discharges.

In February 2003, a TSA task force studying the implementation issues for the FFDO program recommended the use of lock boxes for transporting the firearms, a recommendation that was implemented by the TSA in setting up the program. The TSA requires the firearm to be carried in a secured lock box and only opened inside a secure cockpit. Pilot groups have continued to voice concerns, however, that the use of lock boxes undermines the intent of the legislation which they believe specifies that "... the officer maintains exclusive control over his or her firearm at all times ..."[47] The TSA indicated that its decision was based on the very specific nature of the mission outlined in the legislation, which permits pilots to use their weapons only in defense of the flight deck. The TSA considers the lock box as a means to minimize the risk that the firearms will be used in other situations. However, the APSA remains concerned that the use of lock boxes to transport firearms may make pilots particularly vulnerable targets for thieves seeking to steal their weapons and provides pilots with no means for personal security to protect against this threat.[48]

Another key issue is the credentialing and identity verification of FFDOs as individuals authorized to carry firearms beyond airport screening checkpoints. Adequate methods for preventing forgery of identification and accounting for misplaced or stolen identification are needed to ensure that terrorists and criminals cannot breach security checkpoints by impersonating FFDOs. ATSA mandated the establishment of a uniform system of identification for all state and local law enforcement personnel for use in obtaining permission to carry weapons in aircraft cabins and in obtaining access to a secured area of an airport, if authorized to carry such weapons. Future deployments of systems using biometric technologies may provide enhanced capability to assure positive identification of FFDOs. FFDOs are identified by credentials issued by TSA, but specific procedures for verifying these credentials are considered security-sensitive information.

As previously noted, public identification of FFDOs may have negative consequences for both armed pilots who may be targeted in attempts to seize firearms and for pilots not participating in the program whose flights may be targeted if it is determined that an armed pilot is not on board. Screening of pilots in open view may also compromise specific security procedures to validate the identity of FFDOs. However, alternative arrangements for screening of flight crew may be difficult to implement, particularly at smaller airports where employee and passenger screening are collocated.

The legislation identifies interaction between an FFDO and FAMS on board the aircraft and methods for ensuring that pilots are able to identify LEOs authorized to carry a firearm aboard the aircraft as issues that were required to be addressed in establishing the procedural requirements of the FFDO program. Such coordination is needed to address concerns over concealing the identity of air marshals while allowing sufficient coordination between them and FFDOs. Airlines have procedures in place for identifying armed LEOs and making these individuals known to flight crews. However, these procedures may need to be enhanced and further standardized by the TSA to ensure that flight crews, including FFDOs, can easily recognize armed LEOs on board and coordinate with them as needed.

The legislation also identifies the division of responsibility between pilots in the event of an act of criminal violence or air piracy. The procedures are relevant to instances where either one or more than one member of the flight crew is an FFDO. The issue of coordination and division of responsibility raises questions regarding what amount of training and educational materials regarding the FFDO program should be made available to nonparticipating flight crew and cabin crewmembers. Currently, only very limited information about the program is available to them. While, flight crews and cabin crews already receive initial and recurrent training in FAA mandated crew resource management (CRM) training programs that facilitates coordination of duties and responsibilities, airlines are unlikely to address the subject of division of responsibility when a pilot must perform duties as an FFDO, citing that this is a federal role and not an airline function, and possibly fearing liability issues if such matters are addressed in airline training. Furthermore, there is no requirement in the legislation for training or education of nonparticipating flight crew personnel regarding the program and most details of the program have not been released because of their security-sensitive nature. Thus, it has been largely left up to individual FFDOs to brief nonparticipating flight crew on the coordination of flight duties if the flight deck were attacked. The coordination among multiple flight crewmembers who are deputized as FFDOs is likely much less troublesome as they have undergone the same standard training and thus have a better understanding of the division of responsibilities during an attack.

The legislation specified that procedures for ensuring that the firearm of an FFDO does not leave the cockpit if there is a disturbance in the passenger cabin as an issue to be addressed in establishing the procedural requirements of the program. Current guidelines and procedures prohibit FFDOs from intervening in cabin disturbances. Rather, they are instructed to use their weapons and training only in defense of the flight deck which is consistent with the intent of the law establishing this program. Disturbances in the passenger cabin are left to be handled by flight attendants, federal air marshals, or any other law enforcement personnel on the aircraft. FFDOs and other airline pilots are instructed to use their judgment and any available information they can ascertain from flight attendants and so on to determine the best course of action for diverting the aircraft to a location where ground-based law enforcement can intervene if needed.

Additionally, the legislation specifies procedures for ensuring that the firearm of an FFDO does not leave the cockpit if the pilot leaves the cockpit for personal reasons as an issue to be addressed in establishing the program. Such events may result in a physical separation between the FFDO and his or her firearm since the firearm is to remain in the cockpit at all times in flight. Occasions when the cockpit door is opened and when the flight crew is moving about may be the most risky times with regard to a potential attack. Procedures may be needed to address these various scenarios and mitigate the risks associated with opening the cockpit door and separating an FFDO from his or her firearm in flight. In the future, the use of secondary cockpit barriers, discussed earlier, may provide a solution for allowing FFDOs to maintain positive control of their firearms under most, if not all, times during a flight, including times when they need to leave the flight deck.

SPECIAL CONSIDERATIONS FOR FFDOs

FFDOs are unique among the group of individuals authorized to carry firearms aboard commercial passenger aircraft because their primary duties and responsibilities are not in law enforcement and FFDOs do not have formal law enforcement powers such as arrest powers. FFDOs, in contrast to these other groups, are not formally trained in law enforcement, and their role and authority with respect to carrying firearms is considerably more restricted. Specifically, the FFDO program was established with the specific responsibility to "defend flight decks … against acts of criminal violence or air piracy."[49] The TSA's interpretation of this statute has limited FFDO access to unsecured firearms to only those times when the FFDO is inside a secured cockpit. At all other times, FFDOs are procedurally required to transport their firearms secured in locked boxes.

In the 108th Congress, legislation was introduced seeking to allow FFDOs to carry their firearm on their person outside of the cockpit (see H.R. 4126, 108th Congress). The House-passed version of the IRTPA of 2004 (S. 2845, 108th Congress, as agreed to by the House) included a provision that would have established a pilot program allowing a limited number of FFDOs to carry their weapons on their person outside the cockpit for a one year period, with the option to subsequently allow all FFDOs to carry their weapons outside the cockpit if an equivalent level of safety compared to current practice was demonstrated in the pilot program. However, this provision was not included in the enacted version of the bill. The concept of allowing FFDOs to carry accessible firearms outside the cockpit is not supported by the TSA, and the issue has not since been formally proposed or debated as part of the congressional legislative process.

CONSIDERATION OF LESS-THAN-LETHAL WEAPONS FOR IN-FLIGHT SECURITY

Prior to approving the FFDO program, Congress and the Administration mulled the idea of using less-than-lethal weapons for in-flight security. ATSA directed the National Institute of Justice to assess the suitability of arming pilots with less-than-lethal weapons, such as stun guns. Based on the findings of this study, the TSA may authorize the use of such weapons for flight deck crew. Based on this study, which indicated some potential application for less-than-lethal weapons as part of in-flight security measures, the Homeland Security Act of 2002 (P.L. 107-296) specified that the TSA must respond within 90 days of receiving a request from an air carrier to arm flight crew with less-than-lethal weapons. While several airlines expressed an interest in the concept, and some submitted proposals to the TSA to arm flight crew with less-than-lethal weapons, the TSA has not yet made a final determination regarding the utility and legal ramifications of arming pilots with less-than-lethal weapons.[50] As the FFDO program has continued to increase in size and gain further acceptance, the concept of arming pilots with less-than-lethal weapons has largely been dropped, but nonetheless remains a potential option that has been advocated by some as an alternative approach. Recent cases of deaths resulting from law enforcement use of less-than-lethal weapons, however, raises questions over potential liability if they were to be adopted for in-flight aviation security applications.

SECURITY TRAINING FOR AIRLINE CREWS

Under ATSA, the TSA was directed to develop a mandatory air carrier training program to assist flight crews and flight attendants in dealing with hijack situations. The Homeland Security Act of 2002 (P.L. 107-296) expanded these training requirements to include classroom and hands-on situational training for flight and cabin crews covering various aspects of in-flight security, including recognition of suspicious activity; deterring, subduing and restraining individuals; self-defense; crew communication and coordination; and the psychology of terrorists. Additionally, the Homeland Security Act of 2002 (P.L. 107-296) directed the TSA to conduct a study assessing the benefits and risks of arming flight attendants with nonlethal weapons. Language in the FAA reauthorization legislation (Vision 100, P.L. 108-176) established a mandatory TSA-approved basic security course for flight and cabin crew, administered by the airlines as part of their in-flight security programs, as well as a voluntary advanced course in self-defense training for flight and cabin crew, which is offered by the TSA. While flight and cabin crew do not have to pay a fee for the optional advanced self-defense training program, they are not entitled to compensation for participating.

In FY2007, the TSA began to offer the advanced self-defense training program at airline training facilities, as opposed to a limited number of designated training provider sites, in an effort to increase the opportunities for airline crewmembers to receive this training. The TSA has expressed its intent of continuing to expand the options to increase accessibility to this training. It has also indicated that it is evaluating the option of offering additional course levels to offer more advanced self-defense techniques and specific scenario training.[51]

ARMED LAW ENFORCEMENT ON AIRLINERS

The role of LEOs from various jurisdictions and forces traveling armed on commercial passenger flights presents complex policy and procedural issues for aviation security. With more than 17,000 different federal, state, and local law enforcement agencies throughout the United States, developing uniform standards for identification, training, and procedures for coordinating the handling of in-flight incidents among authorized armed LEOs on aircraft presents a number of unique and complex challenges. LEOs who may be authorized to carry firearms on passenger flight can be divided into two distinct categories: federal LEOs, and state and local LEOs.

HISTORICAL CONTEXT

Regulations pertaining to accessible firearms carriage on commercial passenger aircraft are currently administered by the TSA, but can trace their origins to initial regulation of security in the airline industry first promulgated by the FAA in 1972 and implemented in early 1973. These regulations were expedited in response to the increasingly violent aircraft hijackings of that era, which focused considerable attention on the growing threat of air piracy.

The Nixon Administration and Congress responded to these hijacking incidents by introducing anti-hijacking legislation in the 93rd Congress in 1973. Meanwhile, under an emergency order, the FAA began electronic screening of passengers beginning in January 1973.[52] On January 9 and 10, 1973, the Senate held hearings on the FAA's emergency anti-hijacking regulations and the proposed Anti-Hijacking Act of 1973.[53] In February and March 1973, the House held extensive hearings on the issue of aviation security and the various anti-hijacking bills proposed in the House.[54] Although not a central issue in these hearings, the proposed provisions allowing LEOs and other security personnel designated by the FAA, such as sky marshals, to carry weapons on board commercial passenger flights did raise some concern, particularly among pilots and ALPA. These concerns centered on the qualifications of individuals authorized to carry weapons on board; the coordination between armed LEOs on board; and notification to the pilot-in-command regarding authorized passengers flying armed. The most significant concerns raised centered on the qualifications of armed personnel on board, and in particular, opposition to suggestions that airlines or airports establish their own police forces, although these suggestions were never formally debated or presented as legislative options. Concerns were also raised about jurisdictional issues regarding local LEOs on board and whether armed LEOs on board could be relied on to execute an appropriate action in response to a hijacking incident.

On August 5, 1974, President Nixon signed the Air Transportation Security Act, also known as the Anti-Hijacking Act (P.L. 93-366), into law. With regard to carrying firearms on board aircraft, the law exempted federal, state, and local LEOs acting in official capacities as well as individuals authorized by the FAA, such as sky marshals, from the provisions generally prohibiting firearms to be carried in the cabin of commercial aircraft. The FAA promulgated rules to this effect, which were expanded in their applicability in 1981 to include commuter flights,[55] but have largely remained unchanged since. In 2002, these regulations pertaining to carriage of accessible weapons were reworded and realigned with aviation security functions under the purview of the newly created TSA and can now be found at 49 CFR §1544.219, but have changed little in their purpose or applicability with regard to LEO carriage of accessible firearms on commercial aircraft.

While FAMS and FFDOs travel armed for the primary purpose of enhancing aviation security and are trained for specific aviation security/law enforcement functions, federal, state, and local LEOs traveling armed on board aircraft do not play a specific role in aircraft security. However, some observers maintain that these LEOs can provide an ancillary role in responding to security incidents while in flight. Nevertheless, the primary purpose for allowing armed LEOs other than FAMS and FFDOs on board aircraft is not for aviation security purposes, but rather to carry out other law enforcement functions such as prisoner transport, protective services, undercover surveillance of dangerous individuals, or transiting to an assignment in a ready status.[56]

Since the terrorist attacks of September 11, 2001, consideration of expanding the role of LEOs in aviation security has generally been limited to discussion of whether other LEOs employed by agencies within the DHS should receive specialized training to augment the FAMS and provide a surge capacity of specially trained officers who could perform FAMS functions in the event of an imminent perceived security threat to civil aviation. For this reason, FAMS was realigned with ICE in December 2003, but has now been put back within the TSA since interest in this option has waned, as noted earlier.

While aviation security is not a primary function of any law enforcement agency other than the TSA and FAMS, the U.S. Secret Service, also a component of the DHS, has maintained an information sharing agreement with the FAMS, providing FAMS with information regarding the flight itineraries of its agents. While FAMS may use this information in making flight scheduling decisions and may elect not to assign FAMS to flights where Secret Service agents are on board in some cases, DHS officials point out that Secret Service agents travel on these flights in the course of their normal duties and are not specifically trained, nor assigned, to replace FAMS.[57] Also, the presence of Secret Service agents or other LEOs on board a flight arguably does not appear to satisfy the DHS's statutory obligation to deploy FAMS on all "high-risk" flights.[58]

Federal, State, and Local LEOs Flying Armed

The authority to carry accessible firearms on board commercial passenger aircraft is generally more restrictive for state and local LEOs as compared to federal LEOs. This is attributable, in part, to the greater jurisdictional limitations on state and local LEOs that limit their need to carry accessible weapons on aircraft to a greater degree. While federal LEOs may fly armed under a blanket agency-wide directive or policy statement, state and local law LEOs must demonstrate a specific operational need, certified by their employing agency, to travel armed for each specific flight or travel itinerary that they request to do so. Although the Law Enforcement Officers Safety Act of 2004 (LEOSA; P.L. 108-277) establishes a provision allowing qualified LEOs and retired LEOs to carry certain concealed firearms nationwide, this does not supersede or limit the general restrictions on carrying accessible firearms on board commercial passenger aircraft.[59] Table 8.1 provides a summary of the statutes and regulations regarding the deployment of FAMS on flights; the authority and limitations for pilots participating in the FFDO program; and the authorization, procedures, and restrictions for federal, state, and local LEOs flying with accessible firearms.

TABLE 8.1
Requirements and Procedures for Personnel Authorized to Carry Firearms On board Commercial Passenger Aircraft

	FAMS	FFDOs	Federal LEOs	State and Local LEOs
Authorized individuals	FAMS in on-duty status performing aviation security functions, and FAMS in off-duty status traveling to or from a duty assignment	Volunteer pilots who pass TSA-administered screening complete the TSA training program, and are deputized as FFDOs	Sworn LEOs employed by federal agencies	Sworn LEOs employed directly and in a full-time status by municipal, county, or state government agencies
Required training	Initial and recurrent training as established by the DHS	One week initial training and annual requalification requirements established by the TSA	"Law Enforcement Officers Flying Armed" training program prepared by the TSA Agency provided law enforcement initial and recurrent training	"Law Enforcement Officers Flying Armed" training program prepared by the TSA Agency provided law enforcement initial and recurrent training
Authorization to fly armed	Scheduled passenger and public charter flight operators must carry all on-duty FAMS, and must seat them in the seat requested by the FAMS	Sworn and deputized by the TSA Procedures require that the firearm be transported in a secured case and only be accessible when the FFDO is in a secured cockpit	Agency-wide directive or policy statement governing flying armed	Authorized by employing agency in connection with assigned duties The need to carry an accessible weapon is determined by the LEO's employer based on performing the following operations: – Protective functions – Hazardous surveillance – Official travel to another location where the officer is expected to arrive armed and ready for duty
Notification requirements and procedures	Airlines must restrict identification of FAMS and their seat assignments to those individuals with an operational need to know, such as flight attendants and flight crew	Identification and check-in procedures established by TSA policy	Must notify aircraft operator one hour prior to flight, or as soon as practicable in an emergency situation Must provide credentials that include a full-face photo, signature of authorizing official or an agency seal, and the LEO's signature	In addition to complying with the requirements of a federal LEO, must provide: – A letter, furnished by the LEO's employing agency, authorizing traveling armed on board aircraft – A travel itinerary

continued

TABLE 8.1 (continued)

	FAMS	FFDOs	Federal LEOs	State and Local LEOs
			Must confirm that the LEO has completed the "Law Enforcement Officers Flying Armed" training program Must notify the pilot-in-command and other crewmembers, including personnel responsible for security during the boarding process and other armed LEOs including FAMS Must notify flight crew of subsequent flights and ground security coordinators or designated airline agents if traveling on connecting flights	Same as for federal LEOs
Location of weapon	Not specified	Accessible within cockpit in a location to ensure security and ease of retrieval Locked and secured when not in a secured cockpit environment	If not uniformed, then concealed, either on person or within immediate reach If uniformed, the firearm must be on the LEO Stowage in overhead bin is prohibited Will be contacted by FAMS, if on board, to coordinate seat assignments, response to incidents, and so on	
Restrictions	Dress code and conduct while on duty or traveling to report for duty or to home base following a tour of duty are established by FAMS internal policy Like other armed LEOs, may not be served or consume alcoholic beverages on board or within eight hours prior to flight	Alcohol consumption eight hours prior to and during flight is restricted by statute and regulation covering pilots operating aircraft	May not be served or consume alcoholic beverages on board or within 8 hours prior to flight	Same as for federal LEOs

IDENTITY VERIFICATION PROCEDURES FOR ARMED LEOS

The issue of identifying and authenticating LEOs requesting to travel armed on board commercial passenger aircraft has long been an issue of concern. The IRTPA of 2004 (P.L. 108-458) mandated a uniform LEO travel credential containing a biometric identifier to verify the identity of LEOs seeking to carry an accessible weapon on board. The law specifies that each LEO authorized by the Secretary of Homeland Security to carry a weapon on board commercial passenger aircraft would be issued such identification. However, in practice, the DHS does not authorize individual LEOs, but rather LEOs are authorized by their employing agency, either under an agency-wide directive or policy statement for federal LEOs, or on a case-by-case basis for state and local LEOs. The law, enacted on December 17, 2004, called for issuance of these credentials to begin within six months, but the DHS has not yet finalized the design of the credential, the credentialing process, or the procedures for validating credentials during the airport check-in process.

HANDLING DISRUPTIVE PASSENGERS AND OTHER IN-FLIGHT SECURITY INCIDENTS

Air rage and other disruptive passenger behavior presents a unique security challenge because it places airline crews, particularly cabin crews, as well as passengers, at risk, and also because it can place a burden on security resources. A variety of definitions for air rage have been provided with disruption of cabin crew duties, interference with cabin crew, a compromising of flight safety or the safety of the passengers and crew, or causing damage to the aircraft as being common underlying characteristics of air rage incidents.[60] A 2002 survey found that many cabin crewmembers feel at risk of abuse or violence from passengers, cases of physical violence are perceived as a significant problem, and verbal abuse by passengers is highly prevalent.[61]

It is believed that a wide range of factors may trigger these incidents including alcohol consumption, flight delays, confined conditions, restrictions on smoking, unrealistic service expectations, and so forth. Studies of airline databases suggest that air rage is a problem across all classes of service and is perpetrated by both male and female passengers, although further research is needed to better understand the triggers and causes of air rage incidents among these diverse groups of air travelers. The findings, conclusions, and recommendations stemming from such research could potentially be reflected in training programs for cabin crews to help them better respond to various types of air rage incidents.

Researchers have categorized disruptive passenger behavior and air rage incidents along a continuum of conflict.[62] At the lowest level, disruptive passengers will engage in passive resistance. For example, they will not comply with crewmembers requests, such as requests to extinguish a cigarette or to cease loud, disruptive conversation. At the second level, passengers may exhibit verbal resistance, which may include the use of profanity and insults and may include shouting and yelling. If the situation further escalates, the disruptive passenger may engage in physical aggression including acts such as pushing, shoving, slapping or kicking crewmembers or other passengers, throwing objects, or damaging property. If the situation further escalates, the passenger may exhibit extreme violence that may result in serious injury to another person or damage to aircraft equipment. While incidents rarely begin or escalate to these extremely violent acts, the conflict situation may not necessarily follow a normal pattern of escalation, depending on an individual's propensity to become verbally abusive or violently aggressive. Depending on the individual, the time course of progression may also be quite different. Each situation is unique and can be affected by a wide variety of factors related to the perpetrator as well as the target of his or her aggression, and various environmental conditions or factors. Since perpetrator factors and environmental factors are more difficult to control, much of the effort of research and application has focused on opportunities to better train cabin and flight crews, as well as gate agents and customer service representatives, to mitigate these incidents in a effort to prevent their escalation to air rage and violence against crewmembers and other passengers.

It is important to also note that disruptive passenger incidents may be "staged" by terrorists and others seeking to commit air piracy or carry out other attacks on board the airplane as a means to create a diversion and possibly as a means to compromise cockpit security measures. For example, a terrorist may become verbally and physically abusive with a flight attendant in the hopes that another flight attendant may seek access to the flight deck to apprise the pilots of the situation. Other terrorists may seize this opportunity to attempt to infiltrate the cockpit. While cockpit door procedures have been modified to address such a scenario, both cabin and flight crewmembers must be mindful of the potential for such an attempt whenever assessing and responding to a disruptive passenger event in the cabin. Crew training, including specific role playing scenarios of this sort, can help prepare for the possibility of such an event. Also a terrorist may commit violence against a flight crewmember or another passenger in an attempt to elicit a law enforcement response from a FAMS or an armed LEO on board. Fellow terrorists may lie in wait for the armed individual to identify himself or herself, at which point they may attempt to overpower the individual and seize their firearm to carry out a hijacking. While FAMS routinely train for such scenarios, other LEOs flying armed may not have sufficient training and appropriate situation awareness to respond in the most appropriate manner to an air rage incident that may be staged by a terrorist group. Specific information about such threats included in the computer-based training program for LEOs flying armed may help improve awareness of such possible scenarios; however, more formal training may be beneficial to better prepare armed LEOs who fly on a routine basis and may encounter such a situation.

Air rage incidents and unruly passengers account for approximately two-thirds of in-flight security incidents.[63] These include events such as unruly and disruptive passengers, many of whom are intoxicated, and passengers trying to smoke in the aircraft lavatory. Historically, the other one-third of in-flight security incidents consist of events in which passengers on board were identified as being on a security watch list after the flight departed, suspicious passenger behavior was reported by the cabin crew or a federal air marshal, or the aircraft accidentally transmitted a hijack code to air traffic controllers. The GAO found that responses to these various in-flight security incidents typically involved a four-stage process: identifying the threat and notifying appropriate authorities; sharing pertinent information and collaboratively assessing the severity of the threat; making a decision regarding the in-flight response and carrying out that response; and coordinating and carrying out appropriate law enforcement action upon landing if such action is deemed necessary.[64]

The FAA maintains records on enforcement actions taken in response to unruly passenger incidents. These data show that air rage incidents had been on the rise since the mid-1990s when the FAA began to collect systematic data on these types of incidents. The annual number of reported air rage incidents that resulted in enforcement action from 1995 to 2007 is presented in Figure 8.1. Even after the 9/11 attacks and despite heightened in-flight security measures, the annual number of air rage incidents in 2001–2004 remained at a rate that is almost double what it was in 1995. The comparatively high number of air rage incidents in the years immediately following the 9/11 attacks may be due, in part, to increased tension and fear as a result of heightened security that may cause some individuals to act out against other passengers or against figures of authority such as airline crewmembers or FAMS. Increased numbers of air rage incidents may also reflect growing frustration at delays and hassles, including security-related hassles and flight delays that may aggravate some individuals to the point of acting out in violence or rage. While these factors may all be contributing to the rise in reported air rage incidents to some degree, the statistics may also reflect better reporting as well as heightened efforts on the part of airline cabin crews and the airlines to classify incidents as air rage and request that the FAA, the TSA, and law enforcement agencies intervene as a result of increased security awareness and improved security training to handle such situations being provided to airline crews. Since the data only reflect incidents that resulted in enforcement action, the trend may also be indicative of a growing intolerance for this type of behavior resulting in the FAA, and now the TSA, more readily issuing civil penalties for unruly behavior, in part to serve as a deterrent by making it clear that such incidents will be dealt with harshly. The decline in the number of enforcement actions since 2004 may, therefore, reflect the deterrent effect of imposing strict civil

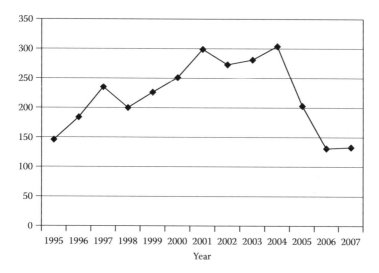

FIGURE 8.1   Unruly passenger incidents (1995–2007). (Data obtained from Federal Aviation Administration.)

penalties on those who exhibit unruly behavior, particularly in high-profile incidents that garner media attention. Airlines can, and do, blacklist individuals based on past in-flight incidents of unruly behavior. However, individual airlines typically do not share such information with other airlines largely over liability concerns. Better tracking of air rage incidents and the individuals who perpetrate these acts remains a specific challenge for policymakers and aviation security specialists. Additionally, ways to reduce and mitigate the occurrence of air rage incidents through airline industry policies and cabin crew training remain as ongoing areas of research and policy analysis.

POSSIBLE TERRORIST PROBING INCIDENTS

The attempted in-flight terrorist acts, such as the attempted shoe bombing of American Airlines flight 63 in December 2001, and terrorist plots, such as the uncovering of plot to bomb trans-Atlantic flights departing London Heathrow Airport in August 2006, provide strong evidence of a continued terrorist interest in attacking airliners. Given this continued terrorist interest in attacking commercial passenger flights, there has been considerable speculation, suspicion, and concern that terrorist operatives may be casing airplanes or conducting "dry runs" on both domestic and international flights.

Potential examples that terrorists may be casing or probing commercial airline flights to spot weaknesses in the layered aviation security system could serve to reify the potential threat. While reports of probing abound, with numerous airline crews reporting incidents of suspicious behavior, substantiating any of these claims has proven difficult. Reportedly, incidents of terrorist probing and other suspicious behavior are reported as often as twice a week.[65] Suspicious activities include things such as passengers videotaping the cockpit area, spending unusually long periods of time in the lavatory, loitering near the front of the airplane, or suddenly rushing to the front of the airplane. These incidents could be foolish pranks, the work of misguided individuals seeking to test the aviation security system, or may actually be perpetrated by terrorist operatives conducting dry runs or probing to find weaknesses in in-flight security measures.

While isolated incidents of suspicious behavior may have explanations other than terrorist probing, specific patterns of incidents could reveal efforts to carry out dry runs and assess in-flight security. For this reason, the TSA and the airlines have implemented various procedures for flight and cabin crews to report suspicious activity on board airliners. However, airline employees have complained that while airline security policies require them to report suspicious activity, these reports often do not get passed along to the TSA.[66] There is concern that, without a consolidated database of all reported security incidents, patterns or trends in the data may be missed and opportunities to "connect the dots" and identify patterns of terrorist probing on commercial airliners might be missed. Notwithstanding these concerns and the potential limitations inherent in current procedures and training for reporting suspicious activity, no solid evidence of terrorist probing on board domestic airliners has been made public since the 9/11 attacks. Nonetheless, anecdotal reports of possible terrorist probes abound.

Perhaps the most widely reported allegation of terrorist probing on board an airline flight in the United States since the 9/11 attacks was the case involving Northwest Airlines flight 327 on June 29, 2004. During the flight from Detroit Metropolitan Wayne County Airport (DTW) in Michigan to LAX, several passengers became alarmed over the suspicious behavior of a group of 13 Middle Eastern men. It was later revealed that the group consisted of 12 Syrian nationals who were part of a musical group, traveling on expired "entertainment" visas along with the musical group's promoter, a lawful permanent resident of the United States who was born in Lebanon.[67] The group's behavior both prior to boarding and in flight was considered suspicious by several passengers, the airplane's flight attendants, as well as by the FAMS team assigned to the flight that kept the group under surveillance. The suspicious behavior included

- Arriving at the gate together, then dispersing and acting like they did not know each other
- Walking up and down the aisles appearing to count passengers
- Rushing to the front of the airplane
- Spending exceedingly long periods of time in the forward lavatory
- Carrying a large bag into the lavatory
- Returning from the lavatory exuding a strong smell similar to toilet bowl chemicals
- Switching seats, congregating in the aisles, and standing when the seatbelt sign was illuminated in preparation for landing
- Making suspicious gestures and hand signals to each other

During the flight, the captain was informed of the situation, and relayed a message that the FAMS on board were requesting a supervisor's assistance upon landing. Upon landing at LAX, the flight was met by FAMS, FBI, TSA, and local law enforcement. When the FBI ran checks of the individuals, it was revealed that the promoter was involved in a similar suspicious behavior incident on board a Frontier Airlines flight on January 28, 2004. Despite the fact that the 12 were traveling on expired artist/entertainer visas, they were released after being questioned at the airport. Two months prior, the FBI had issued a warning that terrorist operatives may be trying to enter the country using these types of visas.[68] Their visas were later extended through July 15, 2004, but this extension was not issued until July 6, 2004, a week after the flight.

While the group left the country on July 14, 2004, the details of Northwest flight 327 was spotlighted in the media after a writer, Annie Jacobsen, posted a story describing her experience on board the flight on WomensWallStreet.com and was interviewed on MSNBC's Scarborough Country. The media attention on the story prompted a full FBI investigation, and later, an investigation by the DHS OIG regarding the handling of the incident. Following its investigation, the DHS OIG recommended improvements for in-flight communication regarding security incidents, better guidance for agency roles and information sharing in responding to in-flight incidents, and better coordination between the FBI and the DHS for conducting postflight investigations.[69] While the DHS acknowledged shortcomings with respect to the manner in which the incident was handled, there has never been a clear determination regarding the motives behind the suspicious activity exhibited by the men on the flight and no one has ever been charged with any crime in connection with the incident.

Since the highly publicized examination of this incident, several airline pilots have stepped forward claiming that they were aware of similar incidents involving suspicious behavior that they believed were examples of terrorist probing. Also some media reports have claimed that some air marshals had concluded, based on available information, that flight 327 was a terrorist probe or dry run. During the investigation of the Northwest flight 327 incident, it was also reported by some media outlets that 9/11 hijacker Mohammed Atta and perhaps others were possibly detected conducting a dry run prior to the 9/11 attacks. Reportedly, the actor James Woods was on board that flight and alerted the pilots that he believed a hijacking was about to take place.[70] However, the incident has never been verified by law enforcement authorities.

Despite these numerous unsubstantiated claims of other dry runs and terrorist probing, there have been no known arrests or detentions of terrorist suspects flying on domestic airliners in connection with these incidents, and furthermore, none have been tied to any actual plot or attempt to carry out hostile actions against a passenger aircraft. While it is impossible to debunk the notion that terrorist probing of airline flights may be going on, it seems improbable that terrorists would continually run the risk of being uncovered conducting dry runs and probes of airport and airline security during a span of over seven years without orchestrating a plot or carrying out an attempt to attack a passenger flight within the United States. Nonetheless, for a policy standpoint, effective methods of tracking and consolidating reported suspicious activity and other security-related incidents of note could serve as an important tool for identifying possible patterns of terrorist probing on board commercial passenger airliners.

RESPONDING TO IN-FLIGHT SECURITY THREATS

Air rage incidents or highly suspicious activity by passengers on board could be grounds for ordering a flight to divert for security reasons and/or a possible military interception of a flight. More frequently, however, military intercepts of commercial passenger jets have been ordered when reviews of passenger manifests indicate that a known or suspected terrorist is on board, or in cases where aircraft are nonresponsive or noncompliant with air traffic control (ATC) instructions and a potential hijacking is, therefore, suspected. Flight intercepts may also be ordered if a flight crew is alerted regarding suspicious behavior on board, if a bomb threat is received, if a suspicious package is found on board, or if there is reason to believe that the airplane has been hijacked.[71]

Under such circumstances, a federal response to an in-flight threat involves elaborate coordination among multiple agencies including the TSA, other components of the DHS, federal law enforcement agencies, and the DOD. In the present day, post-9/11 context, the primary response coordination rests with the TSA, which has established the TSOC to manage and coordinate the interagency response to all types of transportation security incidents, including in-flight security threats.

Under security directives imposed following the 9/11 attacks, air carriers are required to report all incidents and suspicious activity to the TSA so that these events can be monitored by the TSOC. If warranted, the TSA will coordinate a federal response to the reported incident based on available knowledge of the situation. This may range from simply monitoring the flight and remaining in close coordination with airline dispatchers following the flight and communicating with the flight crew, to arranging for law enforcement response to meet the aircraft upon landing, to coordinating an in-flight military intercept and escort of the threatened aircraft, either to the planned destination or to a designated diversion airport.

An important tool utilized by the TSOC and the FAA to monitor and coordinate in-flight responses to potential security threats with interagency and state and local partners is the Domestic Events Network (DEN). The DEN is a continuously monitored (i.e., a 23/7) controlled access, unclassified teleconference line linked in to the FAA, the TSOC, and approximately 60 different state, local, and federal agencies.[72] The DEN has its origins as a conference call established as the terrorist attacks of 9/11 unfolded to coordinate the federal response to the aircraft hijackings. It has remained as an open telecommunication line ever since to broadcast threat-related information, monitor in-flight security situations in real time, and coordinate responsive actions.

In addition, the DOD maintains a classified telecommunications network, called the Defense Red Switch Network (DRSN), for coordinating its response to national security threats. The DRSN is maintained and operated by the Defense Information Systems Agency (DISA) and functions as a secure voice communications and teleconferencing capability for senior military decision makers. With respect to aviation security and responding to in-flight threats aboard commercial passenger airliners, the DRSN may be utilized to coordinate a DOD response, including military intercepts and, potentially, dissemination of orders to shoot down an aircraft threatening national security issued by national command authority.

While the DRSN provides secure telecommunications capability for DOD decision makers, continuous monitoring and defense of U.S. airspace is carried out by the NORAD Command, a joint United States–Canada military component. NORAD headquarters is located at Cheyenne Mountain, Colorado, and its operations are divided into three regions: the Alaska Region (based at Elmendorf AFB, Alaska), the Canadian Region (based at Winnipeg, Manitoba), and the Continental United States Region (based at Tyndall AFB, Florida). The Alaska Region plays a critical role in monitoring and intercepting potential in-flight threats on trans-Pacific flights transiting over Alaska from Asia, while the Canadian Region provides a similar function for trans-Atlantic flights from Europe and also tracks potential airborne security threats in Canadian airspace and along the U.S.–Canada border. These regions are further divided into specific air defense sectors. Within the continental United States, NORAD is divided into three sectors, including the NEADS that was primarily responsible for the coordination of military air defenses on the day of September 11, 2001. Since the 9/11 attacks, the Continental United States Region has taken on a much more significant role in monitoring and responding to potential security threats within U.S. airspace. NORAD uses a network of satellites, ground-based and airborne radar platforms, and fighter aircraft to detect, intercept, and if necessary, engage aerial threats to national security.[73]

Defense operations to protect the sovereign airspace of the United States has been carried out since the 9/11 attacks under an ongoing military operation known as Operation Noble Eagle, which is coordinated through NORAD. Operation Noble Eagle was launched on September 14, 2001, to provide air defenses, including aerial combat patrols over U.S. cities, and to respond to in-flight threats posed by aircraft, including possibly hijacked civilian airliners.

In the most extreme circumstances, the military can assume control of national airspace, air traffic control operations, and/or navigational aids for aviation and order civilian flights from the sky and a shut down of civilian aids to navigation. Prior to the 9/11 attacks, the military had developed a protocol called SCATANA—for Security Control of Air Traffic and Navigation Aids—to direct the immediate landing of nonmilitary flights and shut off navigational aids. These procedures were designed in the 1960s, at the height of the Cold War era, to address the potential threat posed by a possible nuclear strike from beyond the borders of the United States and were intended, primarily, as a means to clear the skies in preparation for responsive military actions, such as scrambling fighter jets to intercept inbound enemy bombers and launching large numbers of U.S. Air Force bombers to carry out retaliatory strikes. Prior to the 9/11 attacks, the plan was never executed. However, on November 9, 1979, a human error at a NORAD facility resulted in the issuance of a nuclear attack warning and, as a result, some FAA controllers were instructed to order aircraft to land immediately.[74]

In 2006, SCATANA was replaced with a more flexible plan for national security air traffic control measures called Emergency Security Control of Air Traffic (ESCAT).[75] ESCAT may be implemented in phases to facilitate a smooth transition from normal air traffic operations to more restrictive aircraft identification and control procedures, and the plan emphasizes minimal interference with normal air traffic operations. The new protocols are designed to recognize and reflect the broad array of potential airborne threats and increase operational flexibility to respond to these diverse threats. ESCAT broadly defines the roles and responsibilities for airspace security and responding to in-flight security threats among the various federal entities including the DHS and the TSA, the FAA, and DOD components. NORAD, along with the U.S. Pacific Command for operations over the Pacific Ocean, has the primary responsibility for establishing the military requirements for ESCAT and for coordinating its implementation. The FAA is responsible for establishing operational plans and directives for air traffic control, and carrying out these plans as necessary, including plans to divert or expeditiously land aircraft according to ESCAT priorities. Within the DHS, the TSA's TSOC serves as the coordinating entity responsible for directing FSDs at airports and field offices to carry out elements of the plan and coordination of aviation security ground forces and FAMS, as necessary. The ESCAT plan requires that a specific priority list be established for handling air traffic and procedures be established for handling the movement of aircraft falling into each of the eight priority list categories identified in the regulations. The regulations call for operational testing of the ESCAT protocols at least once a year.[76]

MITIGATING THE IN-FLIGHT EXPLOSIVES THREAT AND IMPROVING AIRCRAFT SURVIVABILITY

Specific in-flight threats to aircraft survivability include conventional explosives, incendiary devices, directed energy electromagnetic emissions that could interfere with aircraft systems, and shoulder-fired missiles and other standoff weapons that could cause structural, engine, or flight control system damage to an aircraft. Following the bombing of Pan Am flight 103 in December 1988, the FAA, in cooperation with airline manufacturers, has maintained an active research program on aircraft survivability and aircraft hardening, primarily intended to find ways to strengthen aircraft to withstand in-flight explosions. Research initiatives have focused on hardened cargo containers, improved cargo hold fire suppression, and the reduction of fuel flammability. These initiatives have paralleled various safety programs to reduce airliner vulnerabilities to in-flight fires and improve crash survivability.

In January 2007, the FAA proposed specific security-related rulemaking, primarily intended to mitigate the threat of in-flight explosives and incendiary devices, that would require newly certified air carrier aircraft types (i.e., brand new aircraft designs) to have improved fire suppression capabilities in their cargo holds to withstand and suppress a sudden intensive fire from an explosive or incendiary device.[77] Additionally, the proposed rule would require each newly certified aircraft type to include a "least risk bomb location," an accessible location where crewmembers could place a suspected explosive device to minimize the potential for catastrophic damage to the aircraft if the item explodes. The proposal would also require aircraft designers to isolate flight critical systems and maximize separation of systems to minimize the chances that a bomb detonation would render the aircraft unflyable. However, because these proposals would only be applied to newly certified aircraft types, these changes would not have a substantial operational impact on aviation safety and security for several years. It remains unclear whether retrofitting existing air carrier aircraft with these advanced in-flight security technologies and design modifications to improve aircraft survivability would be feasible and cost beneficial.

IN-FLIGHT CHEMICAL AND BIOLOGICAL THREATS

Most in-flight security measures have focused on defending against conventional methods of attack, particularly hijackings, but also possible bombings using IEDs placed on board aircraft or assembled from components inside the passenger cabin during a flight. Possible attacks using chemical and biological agents represent two unconventional forms of attack that have been a growing concern for policymakers and aviation security experts. These methods of attack are unconventional in the sense that there is no historical precedent for them in aviation. However, chemical agents have been used to attack other transportation modes, mass transit systems in particular, and the 2001 anthrax attacks that closely followed the 9/11 attacks serve as a stark example of the potential for a possible attack using a biological weapon.

Several recent events have also raised concerns over the potential to transmit infectious disease from passenger to passenger within the air transportation system. Since large numbers of people use the air transportation system within the United States and along international routes, it provides a unique avenue for the spread of communicable disease. In the late fall of 2002 and the winter of 2003, an outbreak of severe acute respiratory syndrome (SARS), concentrated in China and Southeast Asia, resulted in over 8000 reported infections and almost 800 deaths, a fatality rate of nearly 10%. The rapidity with which infections spread across the globe, from a rural area of China to 37 different countries on five different continents, raised specific concerns over the potential role that global commerce and, in particular, international air travel may play in the rapid spread of infectious disease on a worldwide scale. The SARS outbreak had a significant impact on the airline industry as business travelers cancelled conferences and meetings, and tourists cancelled travel plans, particularly to Asia, but also to Toronto, Canada which was the nexus of North American SARS cases.

The rapid spread of SARS alarmed public health officials over the potential for a worldwide pandemic of influenza or some other infectious virus that could be easily spread by human-to-human transmission. There has been even greater concern over the more deadly H5N1 strain of avian influenza which has had a lethality rate of about 60% among infected humans. While cases have been largely limited to humans who have come in contact with infected poultry, experts worry that if the virus were to mutate to allow human-to-human transmission, a worldwide pandemic could result in millions or tens of millions of deaths. Public health initiatives to protect the traveling public and screen for potentially infected individuals at airports and within the air transportation system may have considerable policy implications for aviation security and agencies that perform aviation security functions such as the TSA. One particular public health function that may be allied with aviation security roles is the risk-based screening for symptoms of infectious disease at airports. Other roles may include in-flight measures to isolate or quarantine sick passengers, and the use of passenger manifests and other travel records to track and mitigate the spread of disease by rapidly identifying and quarantining individuals potentially exposed to infectious disease during a flight.[78]

While high-level policy discussions have focused on various roles that the TSA may play in responding to such a public health crisis, the effectiveness of DHS efforts to assist public health officials in this regard has been questioned as the result of a high-profile incident of lapses in detaining and isolating a known carrier of an infectious disease. In May 2007, a patient from Atlanta, Georgia flew to Paris, France and continued on to destinations in Greece and Italy for his wedding ceremony and honeymoon despite having been diagnosed with a drug-resistant strain of tuberculosis (TB). While in Italy, the Center for Disease Control (CDC) determined that his disease was rarer than originally thought and urged the patient, Atlanta lawyer Andrew Speaker, to turn himself in to Italian authorities. The CDC informed the TSA to place him on the no-fly list to prevent him from boarding a U.S.-bound flight.[79] Speaker instead flew to Prague, Czech Republic and then to Montreal, Canada to avoid being ensnared by the no-fly list. Once in Canada, he rented a car which he drove back into the United States. Although the border agent inspecting Speaker's passport received a lookout warning to isolate and detain him, he allowed Speaker to pass into the country because he did not appear ill.[80] This failure to detain him was viewed as an indication of significant vulnerabilities in frontline screening despite the use of government watch lists to detect and isolate an infected individual. Nonetheless, the use of the no-fly list to prevent airline boardings by infected individuals has been regarded as a potentially effective tool to reduce exposure and the spread of disease.

While the no-fly list could be used in this manner to prevent individuals diagnosed with infectious diseases from boarding an airliner, other tools may be employed to protect against undiagnosed cases, including potential terrorist attacks involving the intentional infection of terrorist operatives, who may travel extensively in an attempt to transmit a deadly disease as much as possible to unsuspecting passengers and others they may come in contact with. Public health screening at airports, particularly at entry control points for international flights may be critical for limiting the spread of infectious disease. These screening measures may consist of rapidly scanning body temperature for either all passengers or those who may appear ill, followed by more detailed health screening and questionnaires for passengers running a fever or exhibiting other symptoms of an infectious disease. Such measures may be of limited benefit, however, in the case of diseases that can be spread by human-to-human contact with individuals who are infected but are not yet exhibiting symptoms of illness.

Infectious diseases may also be spread by terrorists in the form of biological agents, such as inhalation anthrax bacteria spores delivered in a powder or aerosol form. The relatively small, confined space of an airliner cabin, the high density of passengers and crew, and the extended exposure time passengers spend on a flight all introduce unique vulnerabilities to attacks from biological or chemical agents as well as the spread of infectious diseases.[81] On board a commercial airliner, a chemical or biological agent may be released through the aircraft's cabin air system or may be released directly into the cabin. Such an attack could be carried out by someone on board or someone with access to the aircraft prior to flight, such as a baggage handler, a member of an aircraft cleaning crew, a food service worker, or a maintenance worker.

Defensive strategies for protecting airliners against chemical or biological attacks fall into two broad categories: detection-based strategies and proactive steps to reduce the probability and lethality of a possible attack. Detection-based strategies focus on the deployment of various chemical or biological detection systems that can either continuously or periodically monitor cabin air to detect the presence of chemical or biological threats. Such systems must be sensitive enough to detect concentrations of chemical or biological threats to humans while generating low numbers of false alarms that may trigger costly and disruptive responses, including flight diversions, and the possible quarantine and/or decontamination of passengers on board. Ideally, in addition to having high sensitivity for triggering correct detections while minimizing false positives, a detection system would also have a high degree of specificity to be able to provide decision makers and first responders with critical information regarding the nature of the threat detected. While most current generation chemical agent detectors provide general information to identify the presence of a contaminant, they are not capable of identifying the location of the contaminant source. However, researchers are working on precise mathematical models of air cabin air flow and fluid dynamics that may someday allow them to use sensor networks installed on aircraft to pinpoint the source of a possible chemical or biological agent to an area the size of a single airline cabin seat.[82] In addition to these detection-based approaches, operational measures to mitigate the impacts of potential attacks without detecting such an attack may include preventative steps such as continuous filtering of cabin air with particulate filters capable of eliminating fine-sized particles that may pose a threat.

While some progress is being made with respect to detection technologies and preventative measures, in a 2006 report, the NRC expressed concern that, while the U.S. air transportation system remains an attractive target for chemical or biological weapons attacks, no federal agency has been assigned clear responsibility for developing the strategy to defend against such attacks.[83] As a result, formal strategies and approaches for protecting the air transportation system against such threats have not yet been developed, and initiatives to address the various chemical and biological threats to the air transportation system have been relatively limited. While post-9/11 aviation security efforts to combat other in-flight threats, primarily hijackings and bombings, have been extensive, policymakers and aviation security officials continue to face unique challenges to address all potential threats in the in-flight environment, including nonconventional threats from chemical and biological attacks, and even potential threats from terrorist operatives seeking to transmit infectious diseases to other passengers.

REFERENCES

1. U.S. Department of Transportation. *Meeting the Aircraft Security Challenge, Report of the Secretary's Rapid Response Team on Aircraft Security*, October 1, 2001.
2. Federal Aviation Administration. Security Considerations in the Design of the Flightdeck on Transport Category Airplanes; Final Rule. *Federal Register*, *67*(10), pp. 2118–2128. January 15, 2002.
3. U.S. and Foreign Airlines Have Met the U.S. Government's Apr. 9 Deadline for Installing Reinforced Cockpit Doors. *Aviation Week & Space Technology*, *158*(15), p. 18, 2003.

4. Air Line Pilots Association International. *White Paper: Secondary Flight Deck Barriers and Flight Deck Access Procedures, A Call to Action*, Washington, DC, July 2007.

5. Mike M. Ahlers. "Pilots: Cockpits Remain Vulnerable to Terrorist Assault." *CNN*, September 10, 2007.

6. "Pilots Welcome Secondary Cockpit Barrier Legislation." *Air Line Pilot*, November/December 2007, p. 9.

7. Jon Hilkevitch. "Airline is Adding to Cockpit Security: United Installs Steel Barriers." *The Chicago Tribune*, September 1, 2004.

8. "Another Secondary Barrier." *Air Safety Week*, October 25, 2004.

9. "ARINC to Roll Out a Permanent Cockpit Access Security System for Airlines." *ARINC Incorporated*, Annapolis, MD, February 23, 2006.

10. Air Line Pilots Association. *Recommendations of the Air Line Pilots Association, Int'l, for Creating CrewPASS: A Biometric-Based Flight Crew Security Screening System*, Washington, DC. May 2007

11. Federal Aviation Administration. Flightdeck Door Monitoring and Crew Discreet Alerting Systems, Final Rule. *Federal Register, 72*(157), pp. 45629–45636, August 15, 2007.

12. "Suicide Pilot Caused SilkAir Crash." *BBC News*, December 15, 2000.

13. National Commission on Terrorist Attacks Upon the United States. *The 9/11 Commission Report.*

14. See Title 5, U.S. Code, §8335.

15. Brian Friel. "Marshal Draw: As Federal Cops Are Lured to Become Air Marshals, Fewer are Left to Guard People on the Ground." *Government Executive*, August 2002, p. 19.

16. U.S. General Accounting Office. *Federal Air Marshal Service is Addressing Challenges of Its Expanded Mission and Workforce, but Additional Actions Needed.* GAO-04-242, November 2003.

17. Ibid.

18. Alexandra Marks. "Air Marshal Stretched Thin." *The Christian Science Monitor*, December 28, 2005.

19. Brock N. Meeks. "For Air Marshals, Less Equals More." *MSNBC*, September 15, 2004.

20. Drew Griffin, Kathleen Johnston, and Todd Schwarzchild. "Sources: Air Marshals Missing From Almost All Flights." *CNN*, March 25, 2008.

21. Ibid.

22. Jim McTague. "Empty Seats: Where Are The Air Marshals (Review & Preview Follow-Up, A Return Visit to Earlier Stories)." *Barron's*, 13, March 1, 2004.

23. U.S. Department of Homeland Security. *Homeland Security Announces New Initiatives*, Press Release, September 2, 2003.

24. Deborah Charles. "U.S. to Increase Number of Armed Air Marshals." *Reuters*, September 2, 2003.

25. Ricardo Alonso-Zaldivar. "Flight Watchmen: Air Marshals Look to Lower Their Profiles." *The Seattle Times*, June 1, 2004.

26. Larry Sandler. "Security Putting Air Marshals at Risk." *Milwaukee Journal Sentinel*, May 2, 2004.

27. Audrey Hudson. "Probe Finds Air Marshals At Risk." *The Washington Times*, May 20, 2006.

28. Pierre Sparaco and Douglas Barrie. "Marshal Law." *Aviation Week and Space Technology, 160*(2), pp. 35–36, January 12, 2004.

29. "International Response To U.S. Demand for Air Marshals." *Reuters*, March 1, 2004.

30. U.S. General Accounting Office. *Federal Air Marshal Service Is Addressing Challenges of Its Expanded Mission and Workforce, but Additional Actions Needed*, GAO-04-242, November 19, 2003.

31. Tom Frank and Marilyn Adams. "Passenger Shooting Death Still Under Review." *USA Today*, December 8, 2005.

32. Miami-Dade State Attorney's Office. "Office of the State Attorney Eleventh Judicial Circuit Police Shooting Closeout Memo," May 23, 2006.

33. TSA FY2009 justification—Strategic Context.

34. U.S. Department of Labor, Bureau of Labor Statistics. *Occupational Outlook Handbook, 2008–09 Edition, Aircraft Pilots and Flight Engineers.*

35. U.S. General Accounting Office. *Letter to the Honorable Ernest F. Hollings, Subject: Information Concerning the Arming of Commercial Pilots.* GAO-02-822R, June 28, 2002.

36. Statement of Captain Stephen Luckey, Chairman, National Fight Security Committee, Air Line Pilots Association, International Before the Committee on Commerce, Science, and Transportation, U.S. Senate, on Aviation Security, July 25, 2002.

37. See, for example, James N. Butcher. "Assessing Pilots with 'The Wrong Stuff': A Call for Research on Emotional Health Factors in Commercial Aviators." *International Journal of Selection & Assessment, 10*(1–2), 168–184, March 2002.

38. Keith L. Alexander. "Some Pilots Oppose Gun Rules." *The Washington Post*, February 13, 2003, p. A13.

39. Matthew Weinstock. "TSA, Pilots Wage War Of Words Over Gun Program." *Government Exec Daily Briefing*, August 26, 2003.

40. Statement of Captain Edward M. Davidson, Director, Flight Safety and Quality Assurance, Northwest Airlines before the Senate Committee on Commerce, Science and Transportation, July 25, 2002.

41. House Committee on Transportation and Infrastructure, Press Release #253, May 2, 2002.

42. Transportation Security Administration. "TSA Statement on US Airways Flight #1536." *TSA News & Happenings*, March 23, 2008.

43. Brock N. Meeks. "Pilot Gun Training Resumes Amid Flap." *MSNBC News*, July 15, 2003.

44. Hearing of the Aviation Subcommittee of the Senate Commerce, Science and Transportation Committee on Aviation Security and Impacts Associated with the Regulatory and Statutory Requirements of the Aviation and Transportation Security Act (ATSA), Wednesday, February 5, 2003.

45. Ibid.

46. See, for example, Allied Pilots Association, Committee for the Armed Defense of the Cockpit. Report submitted to the National Officers and Board of Directors, Winter Board of Directors Meeting, February 14, 2002. Fort Worth, TX: Author.

47. Air Line Pilots Association. "News Release: ALPA Criticizes Serious Deficiency in TSA Firearms Carriage Recommendation." Release #03.010, February 20, 2003.

48. Sara Kehaulani Goo. "TSA Nearly Ready to Begin Gun Training for Pilots." *The Washington Post*, February 20, 2003, p. A8.

49. 49 USC §44921(a).

50. Sara Kehaulani Goo. "U.S. Nears Decision on Guns in Cockpits: Agency Still Studying Stun Weapons," *The Washington Post*, May 29, 2003, p. E4.

51. See Department of Homeland Security, Transportation Security Administration. *Fiscal Year 2009 Congressional Justification—Aviation Security.*

52. Edmund Preston. *Troubled Passage: The Federal Aviation Administration During the Nixon-Ford Term, 1973–1977.* U.S. Department of Transportation, Federal Aviation Administration, Washington, DC, 1987.

53. Committee on Commerce, United States Senate, *The Administration's Emergency Anti-Hijacking Regulations: Hearings Before the Subcommittee on Aviation of the Committee on Commerce, United States Senate, Ninety-Third Congress, First Session on S. 39*, January 9 and 10, 1973, Serial No. 93-1, U.S. Government Printing Office, Washington, DC, 1973.

54. Committee on Interstate and Foreign Commerce, U.S. House of Representatives, *Anti-Hijacking Act of 1973, Hearing Before the Subcommittee on Transportation and Aeronautics, Committee on Interstate and Foreign Commerce, House of Representatives*, February 27, 28 and March 1, 6–9, 1973, U.S. Government Printing Office, Washington, DC, 1973.

55. See 46 *Federal Register* 3786 et seq., January 15, 1981.

56. See 49 CFR §1544.219.

57. Chris Strohm. "Air Marshal Service Showcases New Command Center." *Government Executive Daily Briefing*, February 24, 2004.

58. See 49 USC §44917(a)(2).

59. See. P.L. 108-277; 44 USC §926B.

60. Lane, Phillip and Robert Bor. "Cabin Crew Experiences and Perceptions of 'Air Rage'," *International Journal of Applied Aviation Studies, 2(2)*, Oklahoma City, OK: FAA Academy, 2002.

61. Ibid.

62. See Angela Dahlberg. *Air Rage: The Underestimated Safety Risk.* Burlington, VT: Ashgate, 2001.

63. U.S. Government Accountability Office. Memorandum to the Honorable John Conyers, Jr., the Honorable Bennie G. Thompson, the Honorable John L. Mica, the Honorable Jerry F. Costello, and the Honorable F. James Sensenbrenner, Jr., Subject: *Aviation Security: Federal Coordination for Responding to In-flight Security Threats Has Matured, but Procedures Can Be Strengthened.* GAO-07-891R, July 31, 2007.

64. Ibid.

65. Alexandra Marks. "Are Terrorists 'Casing' Planes?" *The Christian Science Monitor*, October 7, 2004.

66. Ibid.

67. Department of Homeland Security, Office of Inspector General. *Review of Department's Handling of Suspicious Passengers Aboard Northwest Flight 327*, OIG-06-31, March 2006.

68. "Passengers Describe Flight as a Terrorist Dry Run." *The Washington Times*, April 25, 2005.

69. See note 67.

70. See note 68.

71. See note 63.

72. Ibid.

73. Staff Sgt. Matthew Bates. "NORAD Officials Keep Constant Vigil for Threats to Homeland." *Air Force Print News Today*, July 24, 2008, Air Force News Agency; North American Aerospace Defense Command.

74. The Brookings Institution. "Securing Control of the Skies." *The U.S. Nuclear Weapons Cost Study Project*, Washington, DC: Author, 1998.

75. Department of Defense, Office of the Secretary. "Plan for the Emergency Security Control of Air Traffic (ESCAT), Final Rule." *Federal Register, 71*(203), pp. 61889–61895, October 20, 2006.

76. See 32 CFR Part 245.

77. Federal Aviation Administration. "Security Related Considerations in the Design and Operation of Transport Category Airplanes; Proposed Rule." *Federal Register, 72*(3), pp. 630–639, January 5, 2007.

78. See Transportation Research Board. *Interagency-Aviation Industry Collaboration on Planning for Pandemic Outbreaks (Conference Proceedings 41)*. Washington, DC: Transportation Research Board, 2008.

79. Kevin Duffy and Andy Miller. "CDC Sought To Curb Travel Of TB Patient." *The Atlanta Journal-Constitution*, June 2, 2007.

80. Emily Brown and Jeff Bliss. "Border Agents Failed to Stop Man With Tuberculosis." *Bloomberg News*, May 31, 2008.

81. National Research Council, Committee on Assessment of Security Technologies for Transportation. *Defending the U.S. Air Transportation System Against Chemical and Biological Threats*. Washington, DC: The National Academies Press, 2006.

82. Rachel Ross. "Tracking Down Onboard Contaminants." *MIT Technology Review*, May 31, 2007.

83. Ibid.

9 Commercial Airport Access Controls and Perimeter Security

Airports face many of the same security risks as airliners, including threats posed by terrorist bombings and chemical or biological attacks. Airports also face a particular risk from potential shooting incidents, particularly in public spaces prior to security screening checkpoints. Airline ticket counters and queues at security screening checkpoints are considered especially vulnerable locations to such attacks, as are curbside drop-off and pick-up locations and ground transportation staging areas located in close proximity to airport terminals. Also, possible chemical and biological or radiological and nuclear attacks against airports are seen as a growing threat in the age of global terrorism. Because major commercial airports play a critical role in travel and commerce and handle large volumes of travelers, they are likely to be viewed as highly attractive targets to terrorist groups, particularly among those groups that have historically targeted components of the air transportation system.

Extensive efforts to strengthen in-flight security in response to the 9/11 attacks could result in terrorist groups shifting the focus of their future attack plots from airliners to airports, particularly those portions of airports considered to be comparably "softer" targets. For this reason, many aviation security experts have urged policymakers to assess and implement a variety of options to strengthen the physical security of airport properties through measures such as improved surveillance capabilities; enhanced perimeter security; tighter access controls to aircraft and other critical areas; increased law enforcement presence; and the implementation of effective critical incident response protocols for handling security-related events. Effectively implementing these options requires close coordination between a number of distinct entities, including airport operators, the airlines, a wide assortment of airport tenants, state or local law enforcement with jurisdiction over a given airport property, the TSA, and other federal homeland security and law enforcement agencies. This chapter explores several of the policy issues surrounding various options for strengthening airport security, with an emphasis on enhanced perimeter security and airport access control measures. It also examines the interagency coordination needed to address identified challenges related to these aspects of aviation security and, more broadly, addresses security in the airport environment through a risk-based strategy.

SECURITY RISK IN THE AIRPORT ENVIRONMENT

Security risk in the airport environment can be assessed in terms of threats, vulnerabilities, and potential consequences. As a nexus for air travel, a commercial passenger airport faces a number of security threats, including direct threats to airport facilities and building occupants, as well as threats to aircraft operating at the airport. Figure 9.1 portrays a representative airport layout highlighting significant security threats in the airport environment. These threats include threats within the passenger terminal, both prior to and beyond the security screening checkpoints. The threats also extend to aircraft operating at the airport, and to all-cargo operations and cargo facilities, as well as to GA operations areas and GA aircraft.

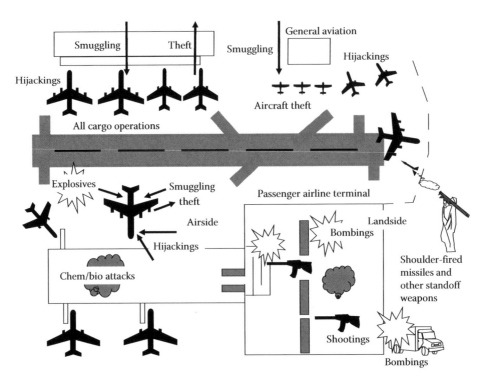

FIGURE 9.1   A typical airport layout showing significant security threats to landside and airside facilities and operations.

Different areas of the airport environment have unique characteristics that are important to consider in evaluating the unique security vulnerabilities of various locations on an airport's property. Airport operators distinguish between the landside of the airport property, consisting of those areas both outside and inside the terminal building that are unsecured and accessible to the general public, and the airside, which consists of various access-controlled, secured, and restricted areas. The landside of the airport has unique vulnerabilities because it is unsecured. Significant threats to landside operations include attacks using conventional explosives, including car and truck bombs, shootings, and attacks involving the dispersal of chemical or biological agents. Like the threat from chemical and biological attacks on board airliners, airport terminals are also vulnerable to these unconventional threats. A "point release" attack of a biological or chemical agent may target a specific area of the terminal where large numbers of people congregate, either on the landside or on the airside of the terminal, such as at ticketing counters, in security checkpoint queues, or in waiting areas near boarding gates. A biological or chemical attack may also target the heating, ventilation, and air conditioning (HVAC) systems to disperse an agent over a broader area of the airport terminal.[1] In addition to chemical or biological attacks, airport terminals may be targeted by conventional explosives or shootings targeting large groups of travelers and are considered particularly vulnerable to these types of attacks. Like attacks using chemical or biological agents, groups of passengers waiting in lines at ticket counters and at security checkpoints may be particularly vulnerable to attack. These areas are particularly vulnerable, not only because they offer attackers opportunities to target large congregations of people, but also because these locations are positioned in publicly accessible areas of the airport terminal prior to checkpoint screening for weapons, explosives, and other threat items.

On the airside of the airport property, aircraft operating within the airport environment are also vulnerable to various threats. Conventional explosives or chemical and biological weapons may be introduced on board an aircraft as air cargo and passenger baggage is loaded or as the aircraft cabin is serviced prior to flight. Other threats to aircraft during these ground operations include smuggling and theft perpetrated by airport and airline workers, such as baggage handlers, or others with access to aircraft and secured areas of airports. For these reasons, background checks and vetting of individuals granted access to secured areas of airports and to aircraft have been a major component of airport security policy and strategy introduced in the 1990s in response to growing concern over the threat of aircraft bombings.

While smuggling and theft remain ongoing security concerns for passenger airline operations, these threats represent considerable concerns for all-cargo operations that are considered in further detail in Chapter 11, which examines air cargo security in depth. To some degree, these threats also exist for GA operations. Smuggling of illegal drugs and contraband using GA aircraft has been a long-standing problem along both the southern and northern borders of the United States, although criminal activity surrounding GA operations has been generally regarded as quite limited. Nonetheless, GA security has long been a particular concern among policymakers, some of which have voiced concerns over possible terrorist thefts or hijackings of large GA aircraft capable of inflicting mass casualties or significant destruction if used to attack large buildings or critical infrastructure facilities. In response to these concerns, there has been considerable policy debate over options for strengthening the security of GA operations and airports, which is discussed in detail in Chapter 12.

With respect to large commercial airports, physical security and access controls to GA operations areas have certainly been policy concerns, but GA has largely been a secondary focus in terms of a commercial passenger airport's overall security strategy and day-to-day security operations. However, policymakers remain concerned that terrorist groups may turn their attention to attempting to exploit perceived weaknesses in GA security because of the considerable efforts that have been undertaken to strengthen the security of commercial passenger operations.

Looking beyond the airport perimeter, the looming threat of a shoulder-fired missile attack has also been a particular concern. The threat posed by shoulder-fired missiles has led airport operators, air traffic specialists, and law enforcement personnel to examine the particular vulnerabilities of flight paths and locations in the vicinity of the airport environment where terrorists may launch an attack. Working with security experts and TSA officials, large airport operators have been exploring various options for improving surveillance and security in these areas to prevent possible attacks. Options for mitigating the risks posed by shoulder-fired missiles are further discussed in Chapter 10.

The third component of the risk equation is the parameter defining the potential consequences or impact of a terrorist attack or security-related incident. With respect to this component of risk, the impact of such an event is largely dependent on the importance of a particular airport in the context of the United States air transportation system. From the perspective of critical infrastructure protection, an attack against a major airport could be far more devastating than an attack against an aircraft, notwithstanding the level of destruction and economic impact resulting from the 9/11 attacks. While an aircraft bombing or similar incident would certainly be catastrophic, a large-scale attack against a major hub airport, like Chicago O'Hare International Airport (ORD) or Hartsfield-Jackson Atlanta International Airport (ATL), could cause wide-scale disruptions to the national air transportation system and could have far-sweeping operational and economic consequences to the airline industry. Reconstituting the aviation system following a large-scale terrorist attack against a major hub airport inside the United States may be particularly challenging and far more difficult than reconstituting aviation operations following an in-flight bombing or some other attack specifically targeting aircraft. Moreover, a large-scale attack against an airport could trigger a long-lasting decline in airline ticket sales if travelers remain fearful that additional attacks may be imminent. Restoring public confidence in air travel may be especially challenging, particularly if an attack were to target publicly accessible portions of the airport environment where implementing effective countermeasures to prevent future attacks may prove to be particularly difficult.

COMMERCIAL AIRPORT SECURITY PROGRAM CONCEPTS

Faced with considerable security risks to airports, airport operators and aviation security officials have examined options to strengthen airport security, largely by building upon airport security program requirements and concepts that were already in place well before the 9/11 attacks. These airport security programs have evolved over many years, with more significant changes coming about in the 1990s amidst the growing concern over aviation security and the threat of terrorist bombings of commercial airliners.

Airport security consists of various physical security measures to protect the airport perimeter, access controls, and surveillance technologies designed to reduce or mitigate the vulnerabilities to these various threats. In addition to physical security measures and security technologies, an integral part of commercial airport security is the law enforcement presence provided primarily by local and state law enforcement entities with jurisdiction over the airport property, as well as security guards and other individuals performing security functions for airport authorities or airport tenant entities. Examples of security-related personnel and positions may include security guards who perform access control and perimeter security patrols under contract arrangements between the airport operator and a private security firm, and airline security officials and security personnel employed by the airlines, freight forwarding companies, or aircraft repair stations with facilities on the airport property. Coordination among this broad array of individuals and entities with shared responsibility for physical security of airport facilities and infrastructure has been an important consideration for airport security managers. Airport security also consists of the various communications and critical incident management needs to effectively respond to security-related incidents that occur on the airport property. A particular emphasis has been placed on critical incident response to threats posed by suspected explosive devices.

Much of the framework for airport security was already in place prior to the 9/11 attacks, and compared to many other aspects of aviation security, commercial airport security policy has undergone much less noticeable changes that are widely regarded as being more evolutionary in nature. This is in considerable contrast to airline passenger and baggage screening security which experienced a dramatic shift in policy with the post-9/11 federalization of the screening workforce. The most significant changes to airport security policy have centered on the strengthening of access controls and credentialing programs for airport workers, including expanded criminal history background check requirements and security threat assessments (STAs) for all workers requiring unescorted and regularly escorted access to aircraft and secured areas. Behind the scenes and largely beyond the scrutiny of policy observers, large commercial airports have invested considerably in security technologies, such as advanced surveillance technologies and access control systems incorporating biometrics, which have seen considerable advancement in the years since the 9/11 attacks. However, this technology investment has largely been done with limited guidance from the TSA and without a unified strategy for airport security technology deployment.

AIRPORT SECURITY TECHNOLOGY INVESTMENT

Several new and emerging technologies are under consideration, and some have been operationally deployed, for application in airport security, ranging from biometric identity authentication and access control systems to a wide array of sensor technologies for perimeter security and surveillance of airport grounds and facilities. Implementation of these technologies, however, has largely been carried out on an airport-by-airport basis with no uniform policy or specific standards. This lack of formal policies and standards and considerable leeway in the regulatory oversight of site security implemented by airport operators allows for flexibility in tailoring security solutions to the unique characteristics of individual airports, but may result in haphazard deployment of security technologies without adequate systems design considerations and without careful evaluation of how each technology contributes to reducing security risk.

In 2004, the GAO found that in the first few years following the 9/11 attacks, airport operators' responses to the lack of formal direction from the TSA varied considerably.[2] While some airport operators indicated that they were awaiting formal technical guidance from the TSA before proceeding with security upgrades, other airport operators had forged forward on their own accord to independently test and deploy various security technologies.

A number of airports had invested in closed circuit cameras, facial recognition software, intrusion detection systems, various biometric access control technologies, and identification and document authentication systems. Some had received grants for these projects through the FAA's AIP. ATSA had specifically instructed the TSA to provide specific financial assistance, as well as technical support, to small and medium-sized airports to aid them in implementing security enhancements. In FY2002, about $560 million in AIP grants was awarded, mostly to small- and medium-sized airports, for security-related projects, such as access control systems, perimeter fencing, and surveillance and fingerprinting equipment. In FY2003, another $491 million was awarded for airport security projects.[3] However, a provision in the 2003 FAA Reauthorization Act (Vision 100; P.L. 108-176) repealed the broad authority to use AIP funds for airport security programs and activities that had been granted under the 1996 FAA Reauthorization Act (P.L. 104-264). This was done in part because the FAA no longer had regulatory oversight over airport security, and also in part over concerns raised by airport operators that the post-9/11 focus on aviation security would potentially take funding away from needed projects to expand capacity and improve safety at airports, which have been widely considered as the primary intended uses of AIP grant money. The Act created a new ASCF, but as noted in Chapter 7, this fund has been exclusively reserved for construction projects to accommodate and streamline explosives detection equipment for screening checked baggage.

While some airports, particularly large airports, had been willing to spend money from non-federal sources, such as income from tenant leases, on security-related projects, such as access control systems and perimeter surveillance technologies, the high cost and general concerns over a haphazard trial-and-error approach to deploying security technologies led most airports to concur that better guidance from the TSA regarding effective security technologies was needed to steer their decisions about procuring and deploying airport security solutions.[4] To avoid haphazard deployment of security technologies at airports and provide general guidance on systems design considerations for security technology acquisition and deployment, the TSA, in coordination with airports and airlines, has since issued a comprehensive set of security guidelines and recommendations for airport planning, design, and construction. These guidelines build upon earlier airport security design guidelines that had been developed and maintained by the FAA's Office of Civil Aviation Security Policy and Planning prior to the 9/11 attacks.[5] The guidelines are a key resource for the design and integration of physical security measures within airport facilities and property. They augment formal federal regulatory requirements for airport security programs and are an integral component of the U.S. strategy for airport security. These airport security design guidelines are discussed in further detail later in this chapter.

AIRPORT SECURITY PROGRAMS

While the TSA maintains primary federal regulatory oversight over the security of airports, the specific operational aspects of airport security rest with each airport operator. These airport operators are responsible for implementing a TSA-approved security program, which is tailored to the unique characteristics of each airport and its facilities. The general regulatory structure and specific security requirements for airport security can be found in the Code of Federal Regulations under Title 49 (Transportation), Part 1542 (Airport Security). An airport security program for commercial passenger airports, as defined in regulation, encompasses all aspects of physical security and surveillance, as well as the airport management of security functions, law enforcement support, and critical incident management. Historically, policy interest in aviation security programs has focused on perimeter security, airport worker credentialing, and access control measures. However, these airport security programs also contain specific details regarding the airport's arrangements with law enforcement agencies having jurisdiction at the airport site, and plans for critical incident response for handling security situations. Law enforcement support and critical incident management have had a growing importance in aviation security policy discussions, not only following the 9/11 attacks but also in response to failures in emergency management response following the devastating hurricanes of 2005 that caused widespread impacts on the Gulf Coast region, and most especially on coastal Louisiana and Mississippi, including significant impacts to airport infrastructure.

Historically, the principal objectives of these airport security programs have been to restrict unauthorized access to aircraft and prevent threat items, such as weapons and bombs, from being placed on aircraft. Recently, however, there has been increasing recognition of the potential threats to airports themselves. A growing public policy issue is the extent to which these airport security programs have been designed to address the wide variety of threats to airport facilities and individuals in these facilities. Airports, and particularly passenger terminals, have been targeted by bombings and shootings. In the current age of global terrorism, threats from chemical, biological, or radiological and nuclear attacks have also become an increasing concern for airport security.

In many regards, major commercial passenger airports in the United States have become the new main streets of America. A large number of individuals transit through these facilities every day. The large volumes of people passing through these airports, the importance of major hub airports to the air transportation network, both within the United States and globally, and a continued terrorist interest in attacking aviation targets make airports themselves highly susceptible to terrorist plots.

While the security threats to airports are considerable, airport operators and the TSA, which is responsible for the oversight of airport security programs throughout the United States, have responded to these persistent threats by strengthening airport security programs based on general security concepts that largely existed prior to the 9/11 terrorist attacks. Elements of these security programs include

- Physical security measures, such as airport perimeter fencing and access control points, to limit and control access to security critical areas
- Surveillance systems for monitoring activity throughout the airport property with a particular emphasis on the airport perimeter, airport terminal areas around aircraft, and other security-sensitive areas
- Identification and access control systems for identifying and validating the credentials of individuals authorized to access secured areas and security-sensitive locations of airport property and facilities
- Employment background checks for vetting those requiring access privileges to restricted areas of airports and aircraft against terrorist watch lists and criminal databases

In addition to these elements of airport security programs, one of the most significant policy issues since the 9/11 attacks has been whether physical screening of all airport workers, as is required for airline passengers, is necessary. While screening procedures for airport workers vary from airport to airport, many airport workers have access to secured areas of airports and aircraft without any requirement that they be physically screened for threat objects. Several policymakers have raised concerns that this constitutes a significant vulnerability that can potentially be exploited by terrorists or criminals to carry weapons or explosives into secured areas of airports, possibly transferring them to other terrorists and criminals boarding aircraft or carrying these prohibited items onto aircraft themselves. On the other hand, screening airport workers is a resource-intensive proposition, and therefore, the adequacy of background checks, random screening, and airport surveillance in lieu of physical screening for all airport workers remain a central policy question, as noted in Chapter 7.

More broadly, a fundamental policy concern is the extent of the so-called "insider" threat posed by airport workers. While, historically, large-scale terrorist attacks have not typically involved insiders, such as airport workers, this appears to be changing. In both the 2006 plot to bomb aircraft departing London Heathrow International Airport for America using liquid explosives and the 2007 plot to attack fuel storage facilities and pipelines at JFK airport in New York, the alleged terrorist groups plotting these attacks each included an individual who either worked at or formerly worked at the airport. In general, insiders are widely considered to pose the most significant threats because of their level of access to secured areas and the knowledge that they may acquire while on the job regarding existing security vulnerabilities and gaps.

Insiders may conduct surveillance and identify airport vulnerabilities, or they may provide material support to carrying out the plot by facilitating the carriage of weapons or explosives into secured areas of the airport. Insiders may also actively engage in executing a terrorist attack, and may exploit positions of trust, such as security-related positions or positions related to airfield operations, to infiltrate secured areas, or to provide unauthorized access to their coconspirators. The threat posed by insiders employed at the airport remains a significant issue for aviation security policy and strategy. At the center of this debate is the goal of striking an appropriate, risk-based balance between providing adequate security measures to prevent or mitigate the consequences of an attack carried out by or with the aid of airport workers on the one hand, and conducting security operations in a manner that does not unduly disrupt ongoing commercial enterprises at the airport or overly burden available security resources on the other.

While airport workers are a specific concern, there are a wide range of security threats to commercial passenger airports involving attack scenarios that may be perpetrated either by airport workers, airlines passengers, or other individuals accessing open public spaces of an airport property or infiltrating restricted access areas. Therefore, it is widely recognized that airport security must be broad in its approach to address the wide array of potential threats and sufficiently flexible to adapt to shifting threats and terrorist tactics.

AIRPORT SECURITY TERMINOLOGY

Understanding the nuances of airport security policy and strategy requires a general understanding of the existing regulatory terminology for describing the various areas of a commercial airport, differentiated on the basis of security considerations and security measures in place. Table 9.1 lists the required elements that commercial passenger airports required to adopt a full security program under TSA regulations must incorporate into that security program. In general, these regulations apply to about 450 airports throughout the United States that have regularly scheduled commercial passenger operations. The specific details of these various security program elements are discussed throughout this chapter. Figure 9.2 provides an overview of the various different operations, facilities, and security designations for areas of the airfield, airport terminal, and other buildings and infrastructure commonly found on commercial airport properties. In general the areas of the commercial passenger airport must be designated for security purposes as openly accessible nonsterile areas, sterile areas of the terminal beyond passenger checkpoint screening, security identification display areas (SIDAs), the air operations area (AOA), or possibly as other secured or restricted areas like GA facilities.

SECURITY DESIGNATIONS WITHIN THE PASSENGER TERMINAL

First, looking inside the passenger terminal, the physical space can be divided into nonsterile and sterile areas. Nonsterile areas are those areas prior to encountering passenger screening checkpoints. These are the publicly accessible areas of the terminal and include passenger pick-up and drop-off locations, ground transportation staging areas, entrances, airline ticket counters, baggage claim areas, and airport lobbies. The sterile area, on the other hand, consists of the physical space

TABLE 9.1
Commercial Airport Security Program Required Elements (Complete Program)

Designated airport security coordinator
Description of the secured areas of the airport
Description of the AOA
Description of the SIDA
Description of the sterile area
CHRC Compliance procedures for individuals seeking unescorted access privileges to SIDA locations
Personnel identification systems
Escort procedures
Challenge procedures
Training for individuals holding security-related positions
Description of law enforcement support
System for maintaining personnel records
Support for TSA screening functions
Contingency plan
Procedures for the distribution, storage, and disposal of sensitive security information (SSI)
Procedures for posting public advisories related to airport security conditions
Incident management procedures
Alternative security procedures in the event of a natural disaster or other emergency situation or unusual condition
Exclusive area agreements (e.g., specifying airline responsibility for security in a specific area of the airport)
Airport tenant security program

beyond passenger screening checkpoints and includes airline gates, passenger waiting areas, retail shops, concession stands, restaurants, and various other facilities located beyond the security screening locations. At larger airports, the sterile areas may also include elaborate ground transportation networks, including subways, trams, monorails, and various other types of passenger movers that transport passengers to and from airline gates and waiting areas.

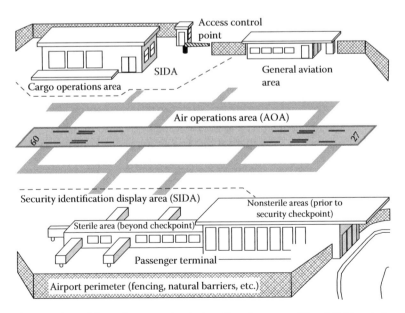

FIGURE 9.2   An overview of the various security designations for areas of the airfield and airport facilities.

Since the 9/11 attacks, access to the sterile areas of passenger terminals has been limited to airport and airline workers, ticketed passengers, and other authorized individuals, such as individuals escorting unaccompanied minors or travelers with disabilities to or from their gates. Individuals dropping off or meeting passengers are otherwise prohibited from the sterile area, largely as a measure to maintain workload at screening checkpoints at reasonable levels, and also to mitigate security risks by restricting sterile area access to only those individuals with a legitimate need for access.

Within the sterile area, all workers must properly display airport-issued identification, and those workers having unescorted access privileges must undergo fingerprint-based CHRCs. Although workers entering the sterile area are required to undergo physical screening or inspection, alternative means of compliance may be used to meet this requirement. For example, airports may grant workers working in a sterile area unescorted SIDA access privileges, described in further detail below, and allow them to enter through SIDA access points and proceed from there into the sterile area thereby bypassing security screening.

Physical screening or inspection of airport workers, if done at all, is not usually performed by TSA screeners at large airports. At small airports, the screening of sterile area workers using passenger screening checkpoints may not substantially increase TSA screener workload, and may provide the most appropriate means of compliance. At large airports, however, TSA staffing is based on passenger volumes, and the additional workload of screening airport employees has not been factored into the TSA's screener staffing models. Consequently, if airport workers are screened at all, this is usually performed by contract screening firms at specially designated employee access points and not by TSA screeners. In many cases, however, airport workers are not routinely screened. Instead, a risk-based approach relying on employee background checks and random screening and inspection is used in lieu of full screening of all airport workers.

SECURITY IDENTIFICATION DISPLAY AREAS

Portions of the terminal, such as baggage handling areas, along with areas on the tarmac around aircraft parked at the gate are restricted access areas referred to as SIDAs. As part of each airport's TSA-approved security program, the airport areas considered SIDAs must be identified and defined, and airports are responsible for posting signage, setting up access controls to SIDAs, issuing employee identification and maintaining credentialing systems to monitor authorized access to SIDA areas, and training airport workers regarding proper security procedures for accessing and working in SIDA locations. In these areas, workers granted unescorted or regularly escorted access must display their airport-issued security identification at all times.

Based on TSA estimates, there are about one million employees who work for the airports, the airlines, vendors, and other companies under contract to these entities that work on-site at about 450 commercial passenger airports throughout the United States. The TSA estimates that about 900,000 of these workers perform some or all of their work in designated SIDA areas. These include a wide assortment of workers including mechanics, catering employees, aircraft cleaning crews, aircraft refuelers, baggage handlers, and air cargo loaders. The remaining workers, about 100,000 in total, work inside the sterile area at concession stands, shops, and restaurants, as well as for contract janitorial service companies and maintenance contractors. Also, since large airports are often continually in the process of completing expansion projects, and renovation of terminals and other facilities, a large number of construction workers also require access to sterile areas, SIDA locations, or areas within the AOA under construction or repair. In addition to construction workers, specialized contract maintenance crews and delivery personnel may require regular escorted access to SIDA and secured areas.[6] Background check requirements for SIDA access and the control and tracking of access credentials have been significant policy issues that are discussed in further detail later on in this chapter.

Cargo operations areas are often found at commercial passenger airports. There are a few airports whose commercial operations involve only all-cargo operations. For example, the airport in

Wilmington, Ohio (ILN) can be characterized as an all-cargo airport. While ILN's operations include numerous large transport category all-cargo aircraft, it has no commercial passenger operations. At some other airports—such as Memphis, Tennessee (MEM), the principal hub for FedEx, and Standiford Field (SDF) in Louisville, Kentucky, the central hub for United Parcel Service (UPS) aviation operations—all-cargo operations make up a majority of the flight operations, but there is still a good amount of passenger traffic. However, more typically, large airports have a busy, active cargo operations area that handle a large amount of freight and express packages, but passenger operations predominate. At smaller airports, such as rural and small city airports that cater primarily to GA traffic, however, cargo operations often predominate among commercial operations. However, these cargo operations typically involve smaller aircraft flying express packages rather than heavy freight operations. At typical large airports, cargo operations are usually geographically isolated from the passenger terminal; however, cargo operations rely considerably on passenger aircraft as well as all-cargo aircraft. The air cargo industry and air cargo security are considered in detail in Chapter 11.

From the perspective of airport security it is notable that up until 2006, cargo operations areas were not considered SIDA locations. Workers operating in and around all-cargo aircraft were not subject to the same background check requirements and credentialing requirements as workers accessing passenger aircraft. However, in 2006, the TSA issued a final rule on air cargo security that, among other things, required that air cargo operations areas be designated as SIDAs and specific security measures be put in place to improve upon the physical security of all-cargo ground operations on airport property.[7]

SECURITY OF DESIGNATED GA AREAS

Besides the passenger terminal and the air cargo operations areas, most large airports also have some form of GA operations that have their own ground support infrastructure. The facilities and infrastructure that support GA activity at commercial airports are typically geographically distinct or separated from the passenger terminal and air cargo operations areas. GA is something of a catch-all phrase that refers to operations other than commercial passenger airlines and large air cargo operators and military flight operations. For most large airports, GA operations consist of private charters, business aircraft, and privately owned aircraft ranging in size from small single-engine aircraft to large corporate jets.

Depending on the size of the commercial airport and its unique characteristics, GA operations may make up a sizable percentage of total flight operations or may be negligible. For example, at John Wayne-Orange County Airport (SNA) in Santa Ana, California, despite having numerous daily passenger airline flights, GA and charter flights make up about 72% of operations and it is not uncommon to see small single-engine aircraft sharing the flight line with large passenger jets.

In this chapter, GA operations are only considered in the context of airport security and access control measures at commercial passenger airports required to have full security programs under TSA regulations. There are also a large number of airports that primarily or solely provide service to GA aircraft, most of which are not subject to federal regulations regarding airport security. The specific security issues related to GA aircraft operating at such airports are considered in depth in Chapter 12.

At commercial passenger airports, ground operations of GA aircraft typically take place is specifically designated locations that are usually separate from the passenger terminal. These GA operations areas are often managed in whole or in part by one or more fixed-base operators (FBOs) that provide hangars, ramp parking spaces, refueling, pilot and passenger lounges, and other services for GA aircraft operators. An FBO is a tenant of the airport property, and as such, would typically implement a TSA-approved tenant security program. This security program would provide details regarding the security responsibilities and requirements of the tenant.

FBOs as tenants providing GA services would likely be required to establish specific security procedures for controlling access to GA aircraft and operations areas and for site security and the use of surveillance technologies. However, unlike the requirements for the complete airport security program encompassing passenger terminal operations, FBOs were not typically required to implement background screening for ramp workers and refuelers and have relied somewhat less on access control technologies and more on observation and reporting of suspicious activity and unauthorized access. Policy advocates for GA have argued that these more limited measures are appropriate and adequate for FBO settings where there are fewer individuals and unauthorized access and other suspicious behavior is, therefore arguably, easier to detect compared to the situation in a crowded passenger terminal environment. Critics of current security practices applied to GA, however, argue that these measures could be easily defeated by criminals or terrorists to gain access to GA aircraft or secured areas of the airport property. In 2009, the TSA issued a security directive seeking to establish background check requirements for individuals accessing GA ramps at commercial passenger airports. This action suggests that the TSA is seeking to strengthen security measures at GA areas of commercial airports, however these steps have been opposed by GA operators who believe they will be overly burdensome, particularly for transient flight crews.

Security of Military Facilities at Commercial Passenger Airports

Some commercial passenger airports also have a military presence, such as an Air National Guard unit, on the field. The military maintains its own physical security measures and access controls for these facilities. While the security measures in place at military installations and restricted military areas of joint use airfields share some common characteristics to security measures for civil aviation, in general, these locations and facilities are comprised almost entirely of highly restricted areas with considerable perimeter protection and surveillance and restricted access protocols and procedures. The specific security measures for military-controlled areas of joint use airfields is not specifically defined in regulatory requirements for civil airport security and is largely beyond the scope of this discussion.

Security of the AOA

At commercial airports, airline flights, all-cargo aircraft, GA aircraft, and any military flight operations share the common AOA. The AOA is the area where active flight operations take place and consists primarily of runways and taxiways and other aircraft movement areas. The AOA includes all parts of the airfield where aircraft and vehicles are under the direction and surveillance of air traffic controllers including ground controllers that direct taxiing aircraft and tower local controllers that control operations on the airport's runways.

Each airport is required to include in its security program specific measures to prevent and detect unauthorized entry, presence, and movement of individuals and ground vehicles in the AOA. Additionally, the airport must put in place signs or other markings to indicate the boundaries of the AOA and warn against unauthorized entry. The airport may, in its security program, designate the entire AOA as a SIDA, in which case all workers would be required to be issued and display SIDA credentials when inside the AOA. All workers accessing the AOA must receive security awareness training on detecting and reporting suspicious activity.

The Airport Perimeter

The entire airport is surrounded by a perimeter that defines the boundaries of the airport property. Typically, to control access to the airport, significant portions of the airport perimeter are fenced. Under most security programs for large commercial passenger airports, a contiguous fence, with controlled entry access points, is required along the entire length of the airport perimeter. However, at large airports, the perimeter is often several linear miles long making the task of perimeter surveillance and security to deter, detect, and respond to potential intrusion attempts or unauthorized access a particular challenge. Also, water or other geographic barriers on the border or within the perimeter of an airport property can pose unique vulnerabilities and add additional complexities to conducting perimeter surveillance and patrols. Considerable attention has been given since the 9/11 attacks to more closely monitor the airport perimeter and develop improved capabilities to detect and interdict possible intrusion attempts.

Airport Contractor and Vendor Security Programs

In addition to the master aviation security program for a commercial passenger airport, ATSA also requires airport vendors that have direct access to the airfield and aircraft, such as airline catering services and refuelers, to develop and implement security programs. These vendor security programs must be consistent with the overall airport security program which is applicable to these vendors and their employees.

AIRPORT SECURITY RISK CATEGORIES

Among airports that have regularly scheduled commercial passenger operations, the TSA, and the FAA before it, has found it useful to categorize airports based upon security risk characteristics. Under the scheme that has been implemented, commercial passenger airports, of which there are about 450 across the United States, have been placed into one of five airport security categories (Figure 9.3). The primary risk determinant for assigning an airport to a security risk category is the volume of airline passengers. The busiest airports are designated as Category X airports for security purposes. The 26 busiest airports in the United States are Category X airports. In addition to these 26, DCA has also been placed into Category X because of its close proximity to critical government facilities in Washington, DC, even though it would not otherwise meet the criteria for inclusion in Category X based solely on the volume of airline passengers it handles.

The remaining airports fall into Categories I through IV, arranged according to passenger activity levels. The top 82 airports make up Category X and Category I, and these airports collectively account for more than 80% of all passenger activity across the United States. Airports falling into security categories II through IV are, consequently relatively small in size and have relatively low levels of commercial passenger activity. However, each of these airports is unique, and some have high levels of military operations or GA activity, as noted previously.

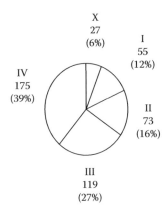

FIGURE 9.3 The distribution of commercial passenger airports in the United States among the five airport security risk categories (Category X, I, II, III, and IV) as of April, 2006. (Data obtained from U.S. Government Accountability Office. *Aviation Security: TSA's Staffing Allocation Model Is Useful for Allocating Staff among Airports, but Its Assumptions Should Be Systematically Reassessed.* February 2007, GAO-07-299, p. 10.)

While each airport has unique characteristics that are important to consider in the context of airport security, from a policy perspective, it has been useful to distinguish these airports according to the five security categories to establish priorities for resource allocation and staffing. TSA policies, and FAA policies prior to the 9/11 attacks, have given priority to security operations at the busiest airports, particularly Category X airports. From the perspective of a risk-based strategy, this approach can serve to direct security resources to where the perceived threat is the greatest: at large airports. So, while this approach may leave smaller airports more vulnerable to attack, the comparatively low threat to these locations, and more limited consequences of a possible attack at these locations to the broader air transportation system, suggests that this strategy of focusing security resources and funding priorities on the largest airports is intended to minimize risk across the entire aviation system.

These policies, however, pose something of a dilemma with respect to security screening of passengers and baggage, because the entire aviation security screening system in the United States typically operates as a single point entry system. That is, passengers and their baggage are typically only screened once, usually at their airport of origin. Therefore, terrorists seeking to attack aircraft to carry out a hijacking, bombing, or on board dispersal of a chemical or biological agent, may attempt to exploit this situation by originating at a smaller to mid-sized airport, which may have more limited screening resources and lack the latest screening technologies because of priority given to major airports.

EVALUATING AIRPORT COMPLIANCE WITH SECURITY REQUIREMENTS

At the airport level, the TSA FSD assigned to the airport is ultimately responsible for monitoring compliance with security regulations incorporated into an airport's security program. The FSD arranges periodic compliance inspections to evaluate airport security programs and adherence to federal regulations. In initial evaluations of the compliance process, the GAO noted that the TSA had adopted a cooperative process of evaluating airports largely based on the premise that voluntary and collaborative compliance to identify and correct deficiencies would be more effective than the use of enforcement actions and penalties.[8] The approach is intended to identify root causes of security problems, develop remedies in the context of a cooperative work environment involving the TSA and the airport, while resorting to enforcement actions only for the most serious compliance failures. For years, aviation safety experts have extolled the potential value of applying such an approach to airport and airline safety oversight, and the same principals may prove beneficial in the oversight of compliance with security functions. The process solicits inputs from the airport operators and law enforcement officials to identify and target key threats, vulnerabilities, and critical assets. The local FSD is ultimately responsible, however, for determining the scope and emphasis of the inspections process and for managing the local TSA inspections staff. In its 2004 audit, the GAO found that, in general, airports had high compliance rates with security requirements as determined by TSA compliance audits and inspections.[9]

This high level of compliance is in stark contrast to the numerous deficiencies in airport security identified prior to the 9/11 attacks. For example, in a 1999 audit of airport security, the DOT OIG successfully penetrated secure areas of airports on 68% of its attempts (117 out of 173 attempts) by piggybacking on employees with access cards, and passing through unguarded and unsecured doors on foot, or driving through unmanned vehicle access gates. Once the inspectors had penetrated the secured areas, they went unchallenged and were able to board 117 passenger airliners.[10] Based on its observations, the DOT OIG recommended that the FAA

- Work with airports and airlines to strengthen access control requirements
- Implement comprehensive initial and recurrent security training programs for airport employees
- Establish requirements for programs to foster and reward compliance with access control requirements and discourage and penalize noncompliance

- Adequately inspect and test for compliance with access control requirements, and impose penalties or take other appropriate enforcement actions in response to findings of noncompliance
- Accurately report and improve the database of security compliance audits and use it to identify systemic problems and allocate resources
- Fully implement a quality control program to ensure that annual airport assessments are adequately performed and accurately reported
- Require airports and airlines to strengthen access controls to secured areas and aircraft[11]

Since the 9/11 attacks, addressing these recommendations has been among the many priorities for strengthening airport and aviation security, and the GAO's initial indications of high compliance rates with access control and perimeter security requirements suggest that considerable improvements have been made. In addition to these periodic compliance audits, TSA headquarters relies on its red team testing methods, discussed in Chapter 7, not only to test passenger and baggage screening performance, but also to assess airport compliance with access control requirements and the effectiveness of access control measures. Much as the DOT OIG teams did, the TSA red teams periodically assess the effectiveness of challenge programs and antipiggybacking procedures, physical security in secured areas, and perimeter security and surveillance capabilities at airports throughout the United States.

AIRPORT PHYSICAL SECURITY AND SECURITY TECHNOLOGIES

Airports are required to establish access control and worker identification systems for controlling access to secured areas. While such systems are more costly to implement at larger airports because of the larger number of employees and the larger physical size and number of access points throughout the airport, a large airport's system may be more cost effective because it may more fully utilize the core information technology (IT) equipment and systems network capabilities. In contrast, a small airport may have to make a sizable IT investment to support a comparatively smaller database of employees and a much smaller number of access control points. Similarly, surveillance systems may be more costly, but more efficient at larger airports; however, monitoring these systems is often labor intensive. Large airports may spend tens or even hundreds of millions of dollars on comprehensive perimeter security and airport-wide surveillance systems. Implementing these security measures is often much more costly and logistically complex at larger airports, although these entities may have the advantages of their size and scale in gaining certain efficiencies in implementing their security programs.

AIRPORT PERIMETER SECURITY AND ACCESS CONTROL MEASURES

Under ATSA, all individuals, goods, property, vehicles, and other equipment seeking access to secure areas at an airport must be screened and inspected in a manner that assures at least the same level of protection as screening passengers and their baggage. Additionally, ATSA requires employment investigations and background checks of individuals having access to aircraft and secured areas of an airport. ATSA also requires that all vendors with direct access to the airfield and aircraft have a security program in place. A detailed list of the specific perimeter security and access control requirements mandated under ATSA are presented in Table 9.2. Presently, background checks serve as the principal means of security for workers with access to airside operations areas, airport terminal concessions, and so on. Workers who pass these background checks are issued identification badges that they must wear inside any SIDA to which they are authorized unescorted access.

While airport workers with SIDA access privileges must undergo standardized background checks that include CHRCs and checks against the consolidated terrorist database, each airport is responsible for implementing its own worker credentialing and access control systems. These systems vary from airport to airport but generally rely on card readers at access control points and identification display requirements.

TABLE 9.2

Requirements for Perimeter Security, Access Controls, and Airport Worker Security Specified in the ATSA (P.L. 107-71)

Assess and test compliance with access control requirements on an ongoing basis and provide annual reports on the level of compliance

Assess the effectiveness of penalties and in ensuring airport compliance with security procedures

Implement other enforcement actions as appropriate when airports are found to not be in compliance with security requirements

Recommend to airport operators commercially available measures or procedures to prevent unauthorized access, including a review of emerging technologies and a deployment strategy for available technologies at all Category X airports

Establish a pilot program at 20 or more airports evaluation to evaluate technologies, including biometrics, for access controls and security operations

Develop a plan to provide technical support and financial assistance to small- and medium-sized airports for enhancing security

Perform criminal history background checks of all existing employees and applicants for positions requiring unescorted access or routinely have escorted access to secured areas

Require airports and airlines to develop security awareness training for employees

Require vendors with direct access to the airfield and aircraft to develop TSA-approved security programs

Require screening or inspection of all persons, vehicles, equipment, goods, and property entering secured areas of commercial passenger airports

Airport perimeters are typically protected by various man-made barriers, most typically chain-linked fencing, or natural barriers, such as bodies of water, cliffs, or other unique topographical features. Historically, security patrols along these perimeters have served as a primary means to detect intrusion attempts, and perimeter security patrols remain an integral part of airport security functions. Recently, however, there has been increased interest in setting up video and electronic surveillance capabilities to monitor these perimeter defenses to detect potential intrusion attempts.

SURVEILLANCE TECHNOLOGIES

A number of technologies exist for airport surveillance. While remote video surveillance is an ubiquitous form of perimeter security, a wide variety of sensor options exist for perimeter intrusion detection systems that may rely on a combination of video cameras tied into automated intrusion detection algorithms, motion sensors, infrared imaging sensors, and even capabilities to tie into airport ground surveillance radar systems used primarily to monitor airplane movements on the airport's runways and taxiways. In all of these cases, false alarm rates are a significant consideration, as wildlife in the vicinity of the airport perimeter can often trigger intrusion alarms. This may be especially true at airports located near prairies and wooded areas, as well as airports located near bodies of water that may attract large flocks of migratory birds and other animals. In such instances, intrusion detection systems may be of limited utility if they are not sensitive enough to distinguish between possible human intruders and wildlife activity since the detection criteria for such systems may otherwise have to be set at considerably high levels to avoid large a number of false alarms generated by wildlife activity. False alarm rates are likely to be a significant consideration for airport planners and designers contemplating the purchase and installation of perimeter intrusion detection systems.

For surveillance of the airport terminal, other airport buildings and infrastructure, and the airfield, airports have historically relied on closed-circuit television (CCTV) cameras, but are increasingly turning to other technologies including infrared sensors and thermal imaging cameras; advanced computer vision technologies for analyzing scenes from security cameras; ground surveillance radar to track movements on the airfield; tracking capabilities to monitor vehicles on the airfield; and various sensor integration solutions to integrate this information, improve situation awareness, and aid security personnel in detecting possible threats in the airport environment.

INFRARED SENSORS AND THERMAL IMAGING CAMERAS

Thermal imaging is fast becoming the technology of choice for conducting perimeter surveillance and detecting unauthorized movement in restricted areas among several major airports throughout the world.[12] Key advantages of thermal imaging are its considerable range capabilities—up to 9 miles for some high-end cameras—and its proven reliability and performance. Thermal imaging solutions can be expensive, however. While thermal imaging cameras having short-range capability may cost a few thousand dollars, long-range thermal imaging cameras can cost over $100,000 a piece.[13] Short-range infrared cameras can be positioned strategically along perimeter fences, while long-range cameras may be needed in remote areas of the airfield to monitor for potential unauthorized access and movement.

COMPUTER VISION TECHNOLOGIES

Historically, monitoring surveillance cameras and other sensors has been carried out by human operators at a remote monitoring facility. The use of human observers poses all sorts of human factors challenges. Potential threats may be missed due to inattention, distraction, fatigue, lack of adequate staffing, or failures to adequately consider limitations in human perception and performance capabilities in the design of these remote monitoring facilities.

Computer vision algorithms can be used to automatically detect motion, track, and identify possible intrusions or unauthorized activity in the airfield, or in airport facilities. Another example of computer vision algorithms being applied to airport security challenges is the use of reverse flow detection to spot possible attempts to circumvent security by entering through exit lanes to sterile areas and other secured areas of airports. By continually analyzing the motion in scenes taken from surveillance cameras at exit lanes, computer vision algorithms can provide alerts when reverse motion, possibly indicating a person trying to enter through the exit and bypass security screening, is detected. These alerts can prompt security personnel to analyze the scene and determine whether a possible threat exists. Computer vision technologies may aid in the detection of suspicious activity within airport property; however, adopting computer vision solutions should incorporate human factors design considerations to ensure that these technologies complement the work of security personnel and provide a demonstrable benefit in the context of the larger perimeter surveillance and access control systems in place at the airport.

GROUND SURVEILLANCE RADAR

In the airfield environment, security solutions may be able to exploit the information provided by airport ground surveillance radar that has now been deployed at most of the major airports across the United States. Ground surveillance radars, such as the Airport Surface Detection Equipment, Model X (ASDE-X) is primarily intended as a tool for air traffic controllers to monitor ground movements of aircraft and airport vehicles to prevent possible runway incursions or collisions. Some security solutions have been looking to tap into the raw ground surveillance radar data to help detect unauthorized individuals or vehicles in the AOA.[14]

GROUND VEHICLE TRACKING

Tracking of authorized ground vehicles operating on airport property, using various tracking technologies, such as RFID tags or GPS trackers, has been advocated by some as a means to provide situation awareness to security personnel regarding authorized vehicles and vehicle movements in the airport environment. A key advantage of having positive tracking and identification of authorized ground vehicles is that it can help detect unauthorized vehicles that are not positively identified as well as suspicious activity or movement patterns of authorized vehicles.

SENSOR INTEGRATION

With the large number of candidate surveillance technologies and capabilities that may be incorporated into a security monitoring system for a given airport, the amount of data collected by security cameras and sensors may become overwhelming for human operators charged with the task of monitoring conditions and detecting potential security threats.

Some level of multisensor integration capability is often needed to assimilate the data collected from these various surveillance platforms. As an example, computer vision algorithms, discussed above, can aid in highlighting or conveying information about potential threats rather than relying solely on human observers to extract this information from the visual scene presented on remote monitors. Higher levels of sensor integration may pool and compare data from multiple cameras or sensors, possibly using computer vision technology, to synthesize or fuse data and present aggregated information to security personnel. For example, computer algorithms can pool computer vision analyses of scenes from multiple cameras and provide a likelihood estimate or probability that a threat, such as an intrusion along the airport perimeter, has been detected. Such information can be used to alert security personnel to examine camera imagery to assess the threat or to deploy security personnel to a specific airport site to investigate and possibly interdict suspected intruders.

PATROLLING THE AIRFIELD AND THE AIRPORT PERIMETER

Frequent patrols of airport property, particularly along the perimeter, can also serve as an effective means to detect and interdict possible intrusion attempts and can serve as an effective deterrent to unauthorized access and activity, crime, and possible terrorist acts. This function is usually carried out by airport security personnel or contract security firms. To some extent, airport law enforcement agencies also participate in patrolling airport properties and airport perimeters.

In addition to security and law enforcement patrols, some airports have adopted unique approaches to patrolling their perimeters and airfield property for suspicious activity. For example, at Houston George H.W. Bush Intercontinental Airport (IAH) in Texas, large portions of the airfield property are patrolled by volunteers on horseback. These patrols address the challenge posed by the fact that about 3000 acres of the airports vast 11,000 acre property are heavily wooded. The IAH Airport Rangers Equestrian Volunteer Program, which was created in December 2003, requires applicants to undergo background checks in order to participate in the program. Volunteers approved for the program are issued access identification allowing them to enter certain remote areas of the airport property. The volunteers get access to an extensive network of trails and prairies within the airport perimeter for riding, and are given special instructions for reporting any suspicious activity. All volunteer riders are required to carry cell phones with them so that they can promptly notify airport security or law enforcement regarding anything suspicious. The airport, in cooperation with the volunteers, has posted markings and signage along many of the trails and distributes trail maps to riders to assist in providing geographic references when reporting suspicious activity.

As another example, at Boston Logan International Airport (BOS) in Massachusetts, the airport operator, Massport, has enlisted the help of local clam diggers and fisherman who work near the shores of the airport to help spot suspicious activity. The airfield at BOS is largely surrounded by water, posing unique security challenges. Following the 9/11 attacks, the airport authority sought to restrict access to the waters around the airport, making most of the best clamming areas around the airport's secured areas off limits to clammers. Responding to criticism from the clammers that the security restrictions were significantly impacting their livelihood, Massport altered its security approach, allowing some clammers back into these otherwise restricted areas and enlisting them to aid in airport perimeter security efforts. Massport now allows clammers to work in otherwise restricted waters around the airport after undergoing a background criminal history check. Once cleared, the clammers registered in the program are issued identification badges and reflective vests to wear. Since the clammers are intimately familiar with the waters around BOS and the people that clam and fish in the area, they are particularly well suited for spotting anything out of the ordinary, they argue. Like the Airport Rangers at IAH, the clammers at BOS are required to carry cell phones, and they are given contact numbers for Massport security operations to report anything suspicious. The TSA has viewed the program as a positive initiative and has tested the use of cell phones equipped with GPS receivers and voice recognition software to improve the communication capabilities between the clammers and airport security personnel.[15] Like the Airport Ranger program at IAH, the program has been widely regarded as a successful example of community involvement in homeland security efforts.

SECURITY AWARENESS TRAINING

Provisions in ATSA require airport operators to conduct security awareness training for certain workers, such as ground crews, gate and ticket agents, and workers with unescorted SIDA access privileges. However, there is no specific security training requirement for workers whose functions are limited to the sterile area. Also, several airport officials have raised concerns over the lack of recurrent training requirements for airport workers.[16]

Nonetheless, some airports have developed their own security awareness training programs for workers not covered under mandated security training programs. For example, BOS has developed a training program called Logan Watch designed to provide information on how to identify and report suspicious activities. As discussed in further detail in Chapter 12, the Aircraft Owner's and Pilots Association (AOPA), in cooperation with the TSA, has developed a similar program, called Airport Watch, for GA airports, where security training is not required for many workers and individuals having access to the airfield.

While there is no direct evidence that these efforts for including a wide array of airport workers and the community in airport security has detected or prevented any terrorist acts, most security experts believe that these initiatives can be effective deterrents. Terrorist may be less likely to attempt intrusions, test security, or conduct surveillance if they know that their actions may be monitored and reported. In comparison with the various technology solutions for surveillance, these initiatives provide relatively low-cost options to augment available security measures. However, while these various programs are seemingly beneficial deterrents, they cannot be relied upon as primary means for monitoring airport perimeters, facilities, and properties at commercial airports.

LAW ENFORCEMENT SUPPORT

Airport security relies heavily on state and local law enforcement having jurisdiction and law enforcement powers throughout the airport property, including the terminal building and other facilities, to provide a law enforcement presence and support security functions including support for checkpoint screening functions; responding to suspicious behavior and security-related incidents; conducting patrols of airport facilities; deploying explosives detection canine units; and responding to suspicious packages and bomb threats with explosives ordinance detection and removal teams. By policy, state and local law enforcement have taken on a broad role in airport security which is largely a reflection of the fact that they have retained broad law enforcement powers and jurisdiction over much of the airport property, whereas the federal role in aviation security operations is more specifically limited to carrying out screening functions and providing security and law enforcement on board aircraft from the time an aircraft's doors are secured for departure until they are reopened upon arrival. Since state and local law enforcement shoulder a considerable amount of the responsibility for law enforcement activity in the airport environment, the TSA has worked closely with airport operators and responsible law enforcement entities to provide resources and support and to establish cooperative working relationships to complement federal screening functions and TSA's regulatory oversight responsibilities. Two specific ways in which the TSA has worked collaboratively with state and local law enforcement to enhance their capabilities and provide necessary resources to ensure continued law enforcement support of airport and aviation security functions are through the explosives detection canine team program and through law enforcement reimbursable agreements for checkpoint screening law enforcement support.

EXPLOSIVES DETECTION CANINE TEAMS

Since the 9/11 attacks, the TSA has significantly expanded the deployment of explosives detection canine teams to major airports throughout the United States. While the explosive detection canine program, originally operated by the FAA, has been in existence since the early 1970s, it has expanded considerably in recent years. The original program consisted of 40 canine teams deployed to 20 airports in 1973. The program was significantly expanded in 1998 based on recommendations made by the Gore Commission on aviation safety and security stemming from the work of the ASAC' Baseline Working Group. In response to these recommendations, Congress allocated additional funding for the specific purpose of deploying more canine teams and expanding the program to additional airports. The program was subsequently expanded to 87 canine teams positioned at 27 airports throughout the United States. Following the 9/11 attacks and in response to the persisting threat posed by explosives, additional funding and support for the explosives detection canine team program has been reflected in homeland security budgets over the past several years. As a result, the program has seen increased funding and has continued to expand over the past several years. The total number of canine units now exceeds 600 teams that have been deployed to most large- and medium-sized commercial passenger airports.

Each canine explosives detection team consists of a dog that has undergone extensive training to sniff out explosives, and a dog handler. The dog handlers are not employed by the TSA or the federal government, but rather are employees of state and local law enforcement agencies with jurisdiction over the airport property. The TSA trains the dogs and the dog handlers through a cooperative arrangement with the DOD Military Working Dog School located at Lackland AFB in San Antonio, Texas. Once fully trained there and deployed to their respective airport, the TSA provides partial reimbursement for the cost of the canine teams through reimbursable agreements with participating state and local law enforcement agencies. The TSA partially covers the costs for care of the dogs, handler salaries, and other miscellaneous expenses. Participating airports and law enforcement agencies are required to commit to maintaining at least three TSA-certified canine teams in order to provide around-the-clock incident response, and are required to utilize the teams at least 80% of the time in the airport environment.[17]

LAW ENFORCEMENT REIMBURSABLE AGREEMENTS

Immediately following the 9/11 attacks, President Bush called upon the National Guard to deploy to the nation's passenger airports to provide a security presence at screening checkpoints. Rather than creating a federal law enforcement role at airport checkpoints, The National Guard presence was replaced by relying on state and local law enforcement presence at checkpoints to meet the ATSA mandate requiring the deployment of law enforcement personnel at each airport screening location. The TSA's interpretation of that mandate was subsequently relaxed, under so-called flexible response authorities. Under the changes made pursuant to this flexible response interpretation, LEOs were no longer required to stand duty at screening checkpoints, but were allowed to patrol the terminal area and perform other law enforcement duties, so long as they could respond in a timely fashion in response to a security breach or some other security incident at a screening checkpoint.

While the flexible response authorities allowed airport LEOs to conduct other duties not directly tied to the federal mandate for law enforcement support at passenger screening checkpoints, concerns remained over the fiscal impact on state and local law enforcement agencies to meet this mandate. To partially offset the cost to state and local law enforcement and airport operators to meet the mandate for law enforcement presence and support at screening checkpoints, the TSA has established reimbursable agreements for law enforcement support. Through these reimbursable agreements, the TSA partially reimburses state and local agencies for law enforcement hours worked to meet the statutory requirements for law enforcement support at screening checkpoints. Although ATSA allows for the establishment of a federal law enforcement role at commercial passenger airport checkpoints, this option has not been pursued, and law enforcement support at screening checkpoints has largely been delegated by agreement to state and local law enforcement agencies having broader jurisdiction and law enforcement powers across the entire airport property.

In FY2007, the TSA reimbursed state and local law enforcement for over two million work hours. In FY2008, the TSA reimbursed state and local law enforcement agencies deployed at 271 airports a total of about $68 million, and significantly expanded the program to include about 343 airports, encompassing about 75% of all commercial passenger airports required to meet the mandate for law enforcement support at screening checkpoints. In FY2009, the TSA plans to spend about $79 million on reimbursable agreements and salaries for Assistant Federal Security Director (AFSD) for law enforcement positions at airports that coordinate the TSA's security operations with law enforcement agencies assigned to the airport.

ACCESS CONTROL MEASURES

Commercial passenger airports must implement airport access control and identification systems as part of their TSA-approved security program. While these identification systems are airport-specific and not universal, they must address TSA requirements regarding information content of identification credentials; accountability for identification cards; procedures for controlling and restricting access; a challenge program to determine the authority of any individual not displaying proper identification; and procedures for escorting individuals without unescorted access privileges.

Access control points must be secured through either posted security guards or through the use of electronically controlled locks,[18] including combination cipher locks or access card readers. Posted security guards or card reader systems are generally considered superior because they can provide a specific record or log of authorized accesses that may be useful to detect suspicious patterns or identify suspects in the event that a crime or an act of terrorism is committed.

Additionally, airports must implement challenge programs and require that airport employees with SIDA access are instructed to look for proper identification, challenge anyone not displaying proper identification, and prevent the practice of piggybacking, or following someone through a controlled access point without using proper access certification procedures, such as swiping or properly displaying their own identification badge. Despite the requirement for these challenge programs and related employee training, elaborate and expensive access control systems can be easily defeated and rendered ineffective by the careless actions of employees who do not follow proper antipiggybacking and challenge procedures. Consequently, some airports have implemented challenge reward programs, in which airport workers are given small rewards for challenging unauthorized individuals or reporting suspicious activity.

BACKGROUND CHECK REQUIREMENTS

Security background checks for certain airport workers are required at all commercial passenger airports and air cargo facilities. In 2006, these requirements were expanded to include areas where cargo is loaded and unloaded from large all-cargo aircraft and cargo handlers working in all-cargo operations as well as workers having access to passenger airline operations.[19] These requirements include the completion of fingerprint-based CHRCs of airport workers with unescorted and regularly escorted access to secured areas and aircraft. In addition to the CHRC requirements for airport workers, certain passenger airline employees with access to the flight deck, checked passenger baggage, and air cargo must also undergo background checks. Similarly, since 2006, workers with access to large all-cargo aircraft and cargo operations areas must also undergo CHRCs and STAs.

Flight crews of large all-cargo aircraft and charter aircraft weighing more than 12,500 pounds must also pass CHRCs. A list of criminal convictions within the past 10 years that would disqualify an individual from obtaining SIDA access privileges is provided in Table 9.3. With the approval of the TSA, some airports have implemented more rigorous background check requirements for certain employees, looking back and verifying information for the past 20 years.[20]

TABLE 9.3
Disqualifying Criminal Offenses as Defined in Statute for Airport Workers and Other Aviation Positions Required to Undergo CHRCs

Aviation-Specific Crimes

Forgery of certificates, false marking of aircraft, and other aircraft registration violation, 49 U.S.C. 46306

Interference with air navigation, 49 U.S.C. 46308

Aircraft piracy, 49 U.S.C. 46502

Interference with flight crewmembers or flight attendants, 49 U.S.C. 46504

Commission of certain crimes aboard aircraft in flight, 49 U.S.C. 46506

Carrying a weapon or explosive aboard aircraft, 49 U.S.C. 46505

Aircraft piracy outside the special aircraft jurisdiction of the United States, 49 U.S.C. 46502(b)

Unlawful entry into an aircraft or airport area that serves air carriers or foreign air carriers contrary to established security requirements, 49 U.S.C. 46314

Destruction of an aircraft or aircraft facility, 18 U.S.C. 32

Violence at international airports, 18 U.S.C. 37

Transportation-Related Crimes

Improper transportation of a hazardous material, 49 U.S.C. 46312

Lighting violations involving transporting controlled substances, 49 U.S.C. 46315

General Crimes

Conveying false information and threats, 49 U.S.C. 46507

Murder

Assault with intent to murder

Espionage

Sedition

Kidnapping or hostage taking

Treason

Rape or aggravated sexual abuse

Unlawful possession, use, sale, distribution, or manufacture of an explosive or weapon

Extortion

Armed or felony unarmed robbery

Distribution of, or intent to distribute, a controlled substance

Felony arson

Felony involving a threat

Felony willful destruction of property

Felony importation or manufacture of a controlled substance

Felony burglary

Felony theft

Felony dishonesty, fraud, or misrepresentation

Felony possession or distribution of stolen property

Felony aggravated assault

Felony bribery

Felony illegal possession of a controlled substance punishable by a maximum term of imprisonment of more than one year

Conspiracy or attempt to commit any of the criminal acts listed above

The TSA also performs STAs to conduct checks of airport workers seeking SIDA access against government-maintained terrorist watch lists, mainly the TSDB. Under the STA procedures, employers are required to authenticate individuals using two forms of acceptable identification and provide the TSA with the individual's detailed personal information for conducting the threat assessment. Workers cannot be granted unescorted access privileges until the TSA issues a determination that they do not pose a threat to national security, transportation security, or a threat of terrorism.

While STAs are a relatively new requirement, fingerprint-based CHRCs of airport workers having or seeking unescorted or regularly escorted SIDA access at airports have been required since January 31, 1996.[21] In October 2001, in response to the terrorist attacks of September 11, 2001, the FAA announced that every current employee or applicant holding or seeking about 900,000 nationwide positions with unescorted SIDA access would have to undergo a fingerprint-based CHRC, even if they previously had completed one. ATSA contained similar statutory provisions requiring new employment investigations and fingerprint-based CHRCs of those employees having SIDA access. With the passage of ATSA, oversight of this background check process was transferred from the FAA to the newly formed TSA. The extensive requirements to process a high volume of background checks for existing airport employees required the TSA to swiftly implement a streamlined process for handling background check applications.

By December 2002, the TSA had completed CHRCs and TSA watch list checks of all existing and newly hired airport workers having unescorted assess privileges to secured areas of airports. About 900,000 workers nationwide were covered under this requirement. In late 2002, the TSA also required all workers who perform duties in the sterile area of passenger terminals to also undergo CHRCs and watch list checks. The background checks on an additional 100,000 workers covered under this requirement were completed by April 2004. In 2006, when air cargo operations areas were required to be designated as SIDAs, an additional 50,000 air cargo workers were required to undergo CHRCs and STAs, as were about 51,000 off-airport employees working for freight forwarding companies. While these large waves of processing workers for background checks have now been completed, according to the TSA, about 1100 new applicants for unescorted SIDA access positions continue to be vetted each week.[22]

Soon after the 9/11 attacks, federal law enforcement agencies, including the Immigration and Naturalization Service (INS) and the FBI, in coordination with U.S. Attorneys' offices, the DOT OIG, the Social Security Administration, and the FAA, carried out an extensive investigation of airport workers called Operation Tarmac. The investigation identified over 4200 airport workers who had falsified information to gain unescorted access to secured and sensitive areas of airports. In some cases, individuals who had falsified information had subsequently passed background checks, pointing out that the background check process is not entirely foolproof, lacked sufficient mechanisms and safeguards for identity authentication, and was susceptible to false negative results or Type II errors (i.e., reporting that an individual did not have a criminal past when, in fact, he or she did). While background checks have not always proven fully successful at detecting individuals who potentially pose a threat to aviation based on their criminal past or a suspected connection to terrorist groups, background checks remain a central component of airport security strategy. The process is well defined and, in the years since the 9/11 attacks, it has been considerably streamlined to accommodate the continual demand for background checks of new applicants and recurring threat assessments of airport workers against available government terrorism databases.

TRANSPORTATION SECURITY CLEARINGHOUSE

ATSA required a new background check for all airport employees who were required to have passed a background check when they were initially hired. The Act also expanded the requirement for those employees requiring background checks to include, in addition to employees granted unescorted SIDA access, those employees having routine escorted access to SIDA areas. At the time, routine background check for newly hired airport employees typically took about 52 days to process.

Because this slow process would not be capable of meeting the large influx of background checks required to be processed under this mandate, a streamlined process for submitting background check paperwork and fingerprint records for checks against criminal, and now terrorist, databases, was needed. This need led to the creation of the TSC.

On November 26, 2001, recognizing the need for a uniform, streamlined system for processing the large volume of CHRC fingerprints and records, the FAA entered into an agreement with the AAAE, a trade organization representing airports throughout the United States. That agreement established the Aviation Security Clearinghouse, which later became known as the TSC, to facilitate fingerprint-based CHRC processing. While the Transportation Security Clearinghouse is sometimes referred to in the aviation industry as the TSC, it is important to note that this is not a component of the FBI's Terrorist Screening Center discussed in Chapter 6, which also goes by the acronym TSC. The TSC is a private entity created by the AAAE that processes fingerprint-based CHRC applications on behalf of participating airports, and other aviation and transportation industry entities that utilize its services for processing these applications.

The TSC became fully operational on January 1, 2002.[23] The clearinghouse was largely a product of the acute need for a centralized means for processing fingerprint-based CHRCs following the mandate for background checks of all current workers with SIDA access after the terrorist attacks of September 11, 2001. However, the genesis for this project can be tied to a provision in the Airport Security Improvement Act of 2000 (P.L. 106-528) calling on the FAA to transform its electronic fingerprint transmission pilot project into an aviation industry-wide system within two years, which would have been by November 22, 2002.[24] The ongoing collaboration between the FAA and AAAE on this project allowed them to quickly respond to the acute demand for processing a large number of fingerprint-based CHRCs in the aftermath of the 9/11 terrorist attacks.

The TSC is owned and operated on a not-for-profit basis by AAAE and serves as a centralized processing center and liaison between airports and airlines and federal agencies (TSA and FBI) responsible for performing the fingerprint-based CHRCs and as a repository for maintaining CHRC data and results.[25] Functionally, airports transmit required background information and fingerprint submissions in either paper or electronic format to the TSC. The clearinghouse compiles these records into a standard electronic format and performs quality control on the records before transmitting them to the TSA. The TSA's Office of TTAC oversees the TSC and the fingerprint-based CHRC process for airport workers.

The TSA, in turn, transmits the data to the FBI, which performs fingerprint-based CHRCs against criminal records databases and returns the results through the TSA's secure fingerprint results distribution website. Under separate regulations, individual airports are required to maintain credentialing systems and access control methods for credentialing cleared workers with unescorted access privileges and controlling access to designated SIDA areas.[26]

According to AAAE, the TSC has reduced processing times for background checks from the 52 days average prior to its creation to a current average of four hours, "with many checks occurring in a matter of minutes."[27] The TSC system utilizes a high-speed secure network for fingerprint and background records transmission to the TSA, which can be transmitted from over 400 enrollment centers, including centers overseas. In addition to airport worker background checks, the TSC also processes background checks for GA flight crews; armed security officers required to be on board GA flights into DCA; commercial charter pilots; foreign applicants to flight schools in the United States; and contract airport screeners at airports that have opted for private screening companies instead of TSA screeners. The TSC has also recently been selected by the TSA to facilitate background checks for applicants for TSA screener jobs.

According to a fact sheet released by AAAE, since its inception, the TSC has reduced the processing time for fingerprint-based background checks for airport workers from 52 days to four hours.[28] The fact sheet further noted that many checks are processed in a matter of minutes. The AAAE also credits the TSC with reducing error rates for fingerprint transmissions to 2%, compared to an average government error rate of 8%.

Further, the AAAE notes that the TSC has kept processing costs relatively low. At the time the fact sheet was released, the fee per applicant was $29, of which $22 went to the FBI to offset its costs. The AAAE contrasts this with the fee of about $100 to vet HAZMAT truckers. According to the TSA FY2008 Budget Congressional Justification, the total applicant fee for HAZMAT drivers is $94 in states that utilize the TSA's contractor for processing applications with $22 of that amount offsetting the FBI's costs and $34 offsetting the TSA's program costs.

SECURITY THREAT ASSESSMENTS

The TSA conducts name-based STAs concurrent with the FBI's CHRC check. The name-based STA vets individuals against approximately 10 databases, including the TSDB and the FBI's NCIC and Interstate Identification Index (the III or Triple I), that maintain records of those with known or suspected ties to terrorism, suspicious immigration and identity theft activity, and criminal wants and warrants. Since September 2005, the TSA has been vetting airport employees against these databases on a continuous basis. Under this process, each time a new name is added to any of the databases, the names of all individuals with SIDA access at commercial passenger airports are checked against this new information.[29] At present, however, there is no requirement for recurrent or periodic fingerprint-based CHRCs for airport employees who are continuously employed by an airport or airline in a position that required a background check.[30]

REGULATIONS PERTAINING TO AIRPORT BADGES AND IDENTIFICATION SYSTEMS

The TSA does not directly issue security credentials or badges for airport workers, but has broad authority to oversee and regulate the security systems and procedures for credentialing airport workers, which is carried out on an airport-by-airport basis. Most specifically, 49 CFR §1542.211, titled "Identification Systems," describes the specific regulatory requirements for airports to administer their airport worker identification systems. These regulations specify that each airport must establish procedures for displaying identification as well as specific procedures for accountability and control of identification media. Specific procedural requirements for control of employee identification badges include retrieving expired identification and surrendering badges when individuals no longer have access authority; methods for reporting lost or stolen identification; measures to secure unissued identification media stocks and supplies; and annual audits of the identification system to insure integrity and accountability of all identification media.

Such safeguards have proven necessary as, historically, individuals have exploited their airport access credentials to bypass existing security measures in airport terminals to carry out crimes, including aircraft hijackings and sabotage. In a particularly tragic example, on December 7, 1987, a PSA regional jet crashed near San Luis Obispo, California killing all 43 people on board.[31] Investigation revealed that a disgruntled former USAir employee, recently fired for alleged theft, used his employee identification, which had not been returned, to bypass airport security at LAX with a loaded handgun. At altitude, he shot his former supervisor who was a passenger on the airplane. He then entered the flight deck, shot the two pilots, and then shot himself after putting the airplane into a crash dive. At the time, airline employees were allowed to bypass airport security checkpoints, and it remains the case that many airline and airport workers are not routinely screened for threat objects before passing into secured areas of airports.

At many airports today, employees with unescorted access privileges to SIDAs may access secured areas and aircraft without being subject to physical screening. Specific screening procedures for airport workers vary from airport to airport and are part of the airport's TSA security program, which is considered security sensitive. Collecting airport access credentials from terminated employees remains a problem to this day. However, a provision in the FY2008 Omnibus Appropriations Act (P.L. 110-161) establishes civil penalties for airport contractors and vendors that fail to collect access credentials and notify the airport of employee terminations within 24 hours.

The regulations also stipulate that airports are to issue only one credential to each airport worker authorized to have such a credential. The regulations also require that airports implement procedures regarding the issuance and control of temporary identification, procedures for escorting individuals required to be escorted, and implement a required challenge program to ensure that employees properly display identification cards and verify the identity of those accessing areas where identification must be displayed. The TSA has oversight responsibility for ensuring that airports develop and satisfactorily implement these regulatory requirements. In this capacity, the TSA will review, approve, and assess each airport's identification system and related identification control procedures detailed in the airport's security program.

Federal regulations also specify that each airport's security program must outline procedures for revalidating or reissuing identification cards if either a certain portion or all of the issued, unexpired identification cards are lost, stolen, or otherwise unaccounted for. For example, if an annual audit of an airport's identification system reveals that the portion of unaccounted for identification credentials exceeds a trigger threshold, then the airport would be required, under its TSA-approved security program, to either go through a process of revalidating all identification cards or issuing new identification cards.

BIOMETRIC TECHNOLOGIES FOR CREDENTIALING AND ACCESS CONTROLS

ATSA specifies that airports may deploy biometrics or other identity verification technologies to authenticate employees and law enforcement personnel seeking to access airport secured areas.

ATSA called for the TSA to explore the use of biometrics and other identification technologies for credentialing transport workers and the use of biometrics for airport access controls. It specifically called for the TSA to establish pilot programs at no fewer than 20 airports to test and evaluate new and emerging technology for providing access control and other security protections for closed or secure areas of the airports, including biometrics or other technologies.

However, unlike the Transportation Worker Identification Credential (TWIC) program being implemented at seaports across the United States, there is no effort underway to standardize, harmonize, or consolidate airport-issued identification under a single system, like TWIC. Each airport is expected to maintain its own credentialing and identification system for airport workers, which may or may not incorporate biometrics. Despite considerable interest among policymakers to incorporate biometrics into airport access control systems and despite several mature technologies for reliably enrolling, storing, and verifying biometric data, the application of biometrics to airport identification and access control systems has, thus far, been quite limited.

Commonly available biometrics technologies include systems that rely on fingerprint and iris scan recognition. While the use of fingerprints for identification purposes has a long history in law enforcement and security applications, there is now considerable interest in the more recent application of identifying individuals based on the patterns of the iris, the colored membrane around the pupil of the eye. According to biometrics experts, some potential advantages of iris recognition compared to fingerprint-based systems are that the patterns of the eye are less likely to change over time, and performance evaluations of iris recognition systems have demonstrated very low false acceptance rates or Type II errors, but somewhat higher false rejection rates or Type I errors.[32]

Low false acceptance rates are considered an important feature of biometric systems to prevent potential unauthorized access; however, high false rejection rates can create operational hassles and impede routine operations in an airport setting. Therefore, striking an appropriate balance between false acceptance rates and false rejections is a critical consideration for systems design and decisions regarding whether or not to acquire and deploy biometric systems for airport access control applications. In practice, both fingerprint and iris scan biometric access control and identity verification systems have been deployed in operational settings, including airports, receiving overall favorable performance and operational effectiveness. Besides iris and fingerprint recognition systems, various other biometrics, such as facial recognition, hand geometry, retinal scans, and voice recognition, have all been explored, but either do not have the same degree of accuracy and reliability as field-deployed technologies or have not been fully evaluated in operational settings.

Access control systems and identity verification are typically well suited to applications of biometrics because they involve a one-to-one matching, that is matching a single scan to a single database record. A more challenging problem for biometrics, however, is the one-to-many type of matching often done in law enforcement. For example matching one unknown latent fingerprint left at a crime scene to a database containing very large numbers of fingerprint records of known offenders maintained for law enforcement purposes can be a difficult task that may yield a high number of false matches.

Regardless of the choice of biometric technologies, the use of biometrics raises a number of policy issues regarding data protection and privacy rights. Data protection is a major issue, because a potential breach of databases containing biometrics could significantly compromise site security, and could also lead to identity theft. Data protection issues aside, other privacy concerns associated with biometrics in general fall into the broader issue of potential abuses or misuse of tracking information that can be derived from access control systems, although these concerns also exist for other types of identification card readers that do not include biometrics. In general, there is concern that such systems could be used for purposes other than security, for example, to monitor employee abuse of break periods or possibly to track employee association or affiliation with others by monitoring movement patterns. However, employees generally acknowledge consent to monitoring of their activities as a condition of employment, and therefore specific rights to privacy that may be more broadly regarded as policy concerns in the context of biometric identification for the public at large have been less of an issue for workplace applications.

In the context of airport security, it should be noted that biometrics, like other forms of access credentialing, are not foolproof. Access control systems can potentially be compromised by computer hacking, by insiders who provide aid and assistance to allow unauthorized individuals to gain access to restricted areas, by theft or the use of force to gain access using an employee's credentials, or through social engineering to gain access or compromise system security by deceiving employees with access or knowledge of system security measures.

PLANNING, DESIGN, AND CONSTRUCTION GUIDELINES
FOR COMMERCIAL AIRPORT SECURITY

In June 2006, the TSA issued significantly revised guidelines and recommendations for security aspects of airport planning, design, and construction, building upon guidelines originally issued by the FAA and last revised in June 2001. The revised guidelines issued by the TSA provide a framework for strengthening physical security and surveillance capabilities at airports, while providing flexibility for airports to tailor security solutions to their own specifics requirements and design considerations.

Stemming from recommendations made by the President's Committee on Aviation Safety and Security following the bombing of Pan Am flight 103 in 1988, the Aviation Security Improvement Act of 1990 (P.L. 101-604) directed the FAA, in cooperation with the aviation industry, to develop guidelines for airport design and construction to enhance the security aspects of airports. The FAA developed a series of recommended security guidelines in 1993 to meet that mandate and, for the first time, formally address security design considerations in the airport environment. However, the initial guidelines were geared toward new construction and major airport renovations. Recognizing that many airports and airport terminals in the United States had been originally built prior to the considerable expansion of security requirements and considerations that evolved throughout the 1990s, the FAA issued revised guidelines in June 2001, broadening the scope to consider the integration of new security and surveillance technologies into existing airport environments.

In June 2006, the TSA issued a revision to the airport security design guidelines, encompassing design consideration of new procedures, new security technologies, and new and emerging terrorist threats identified as part of the intensive focus on aviation security following the 9/11 attacks. The guidelines provide guidance and recommendations regarding airport layout, accommodations for security screening of passengers and baggage, physical security measures, surveillance technologies, access control systems, communications, and emergency management and response. The guidelines can be applied to new airport construction, airport expansion projects, and existing airports seeking to incorporate and accommodate new aviation security technologies and procedures. While the primary focus of the guidelines is commercial passenger airports, the broad recommendations provided in it may provide useful suggestions and information for major all-cargo airports, as well as GA airports, particularly large GA airports in major metropolitan areas.

Key security concerns and concepts that the recommendations focus on include

- Access controls to the AOA, SIDAs, and secured areas
- The flow of passengers, airport workers, and other authorized individuals between the landside of the airport and the airside of the airport
- The physical separation of security areas and the use of signage to identify security areas and inform individuals regarding security procedures
- Physical protection of vulnerable areas and assets
- Protection of people, aircraft, and property
- Blast mitigation measures and explosives ordnance disposal (EOD) and threat containment capabilities
- Space allocation for checked baggage screening and passenger screening checkpoints

The security guidelines emphasize the potential changing nature of security measures in response to shifting threats, noting that consideration should be given during airport design to ensure efficient implementation of temporary security enhancements, considering the potential impacts of various contingency measures and emergency plans. For example, design considerations may need to consider additional space requirements for additional screening procedures or for expanding screening checkpoint queues in anticipation that, during certain times of heightened alert, additional security screening requirements may be put in place that may require the temporary use of additional screening equipment, and may result in longer than usual processing of passengers through screening checkpoints.

LANDSIDE SECURITY CONSIDERATIONS

The landside of the airport consists of that portion of the airport property where the general public has unrestricted access. Because of the open nature of airport landside property and facilities, these areas are exposed to unique vulnerabilities. At large airports, landside facilities may consist of parking garages, drive-up, drop-off, and pick-up locations where vehicles may stand in close proximity to airport terminals, and various public transportation facilities, such as bus, rail, and mass transit stations providing multimodal transportation links between the airport and the communities that it serves. At large airports, landside facilities may even include on-site hotels and other facilities that may accommodate a large number of individuals.

Ground transportation staging areas, that accommodate taxi stands, pick-up and drop-off locations for airport shuttles, and pick-up and drop-off locations for private vehicles present unique security challenges, as do parking lots and parking garages located in close proximity to the airport terminal. Parking garages and drive-up locations near the terminal are particularly vulnerable to attacks from explosives-laden vehicles. At drive-up locations, strict enforcement of wait time limitations and prompt investigation and removal of unattended vehicles is necessary not only to mitigate potential threats, but also to facilitate ongoing surveillance operations that may be hindered by congestion and high densities of vehicles and persons in these areas. Besides surveillance, targeted and random screening of vehicles may provide additional options to reduce landside vulnerabilities to conventional explosives threats.

Mass transit systems and other intermodal transportation facilities located in the landside portion of the airport property, along with publicly accessible airport lobbies may also be vulnerable to explosives attacks, but may be especially vulnerable to shootings and also to possible chemical or biological attacks. As is the case with most publicly accessible facilities, the primary defense against such attacks consists of a combination of security and law enforcement presence and surveillance monitoring capabilities to detect suspicious activity.

CRIME PREVENTION STRATEGIES

While the primary focus of airport security policy in the age of global terrorism has focused on reducing vulnerabilities to potential terrorist attack scenarios, airport operators must also be concerned with creating a safe environment for air travelers and cargo operations that effectively mitigates the risk of criminal activity. This is typically approached through various airport design characteristics, incorporation of surveillance capabilities that take into consideration vulnerabilities to crime and patterns of criminal activity, and physical presence of law enforcement and security to deter and prevent crime. While stepped up law enforcement and security presence at airports in response to the heightened terrorist threat may deter criminals, a security emphasis on the terrorist threat may, on the contrary, fail to adequately consider the potential for criminal activity.

Historically, criminal activity has been a problem for major airports, as might be expected given the large volume of individuals who pass through these facilities on a daily basis. Vandalism and theft are particular concerns for landside portions of the airport, such as baggage claim areas and parking lots. Design considerations, such as lighting and open space designs may deter criminal activity in these locations. However, crime has also been a problem in secured areas at some airports. Theft rings have been uncovered at several major airports, often involving airport workers and airline baggage handlers who have stolen from checked baggage and cargo shipments. Smuggling has also sometimes been a problem, with various airport workers abusing their access privileges to sneak drugs, firearms, and other contraband on board aircraft or to receive deliveries of drugs and contraband hidden aboard inbound international flights. Concerns over these types of criminal activity have been addressed primarily through regulatory requirements for mandatory criminal history background checks of airport workers.

COUNTERMEASURES FOR CHEMICAL AND BIOLOGICAL THREATS

As with in-flight security, while airport security has primarily focused on defending against conventional methods of attack, such as bombings and shootings, possible attacks using biological or chemical agents are a growing policy concern. Efforts to mitigate the threat posed by such attacks in the airport environment have focused primarily on detection-based approaches using chemical and biological agent detection systems. Chemical detection systems have been widely applied for various security applications and can provide relatively rapid detection and verification of the presence of a chemical agent. While chemical sensors can rapidly detect threats, chemical agents can be fast acting, thereby requiring relatively rapid response decisions and actions to contain an attack or mitigate the impact of an attack using a chemical agent. Biological agent detectors, on the other hand, may require considerably longer dwell times to collect sufficient samples, and may take several hours to analyze and verify the presence of a possible biological threat. In contrast to chemical agents however, biological agents are usually much slower acting, having their effect on exposed individuals over a time course of hours or days, rather than minutes, although this is not always the case.

The different time course associated with chemical and biological attacks suggests two different approaches to applying countermeasures. Both, however, would generally involve containment and isolation of the threat source once identified. Additionally, steps can be taken to minimize the spread of an agent, for example, by shutting down HVAC systems and restricting airflow, and by closing down and sealing off areas to contain the agent. While the response to chemical attacks would seek to immediately remove individuals from the threat, and decontaminate and treat them as soon as possible, the key to effectively responding to biological attacks, on the other hand, may rely on the timely positive identification and quarantine of exposed individuals to limit further spread of an agent through human-to-human contact.

The open spaces of airports and the large number of travelers passing through these spaces make it difficult to apply proactive countermeasures to mitigate a possible chemical or biological attack. Some options that have been suggested include designing air-handling systems in airport terminals to minimize drafts that could disperse chemical or biological agents; designing HVAC systems so that they can be rapidly shut down in the case of a suspected attack; and ensuring that critical space, such as air traffic control towers, and emergency situation rooms within the airport terminal have access to independent supplies of clean air and are maintained at a higher pressure than surrounding locations to restrict the flow of potentially contaminated air into these facilities.[33] Continuous air treatment using high-efficiency particulate air (HEPA) filters has also been suggested, and in some cases, making particulate masks available to individuals may help reduce exposure. Masks and self-contained breathing apparatus certified for chemical and biological threats and protective clothing for emergency responders, and appropriate training in the use of this equipment for suspected chemical and biological attacks, are critical for minimizing exposure risks among emergency responders, including LEOs assigned to the airport and airport rescue and firefighting (ARFF) personnel.

DETECTING RADIOLOGICAL AND NUCLEAR THREATS IN THE AIRPORT ENVIRONMENT

In addition to the threats from possible chemical and biological agent attacks, there has been growing concern over potential terrorist radiation and nuclear threats in the airport environment and growing interest in assessing technologies and procedures to screen for these threats. Thus far, the main focus of these efforts has been the screening of inbound international air cargo shipments, although the DHS DNDO is also looking to test radiation/nuclear detection and identification systems for scanning commercial aviation passengers and their baggage in an international terminal environment.[34] While much of the current focus on radiation and nuclear detection capability is aimed at preventing terrorists from carrying such materials into the United States, initiatives to screen for these materials have broad implications for airport security. Airport security plans may need to specifically address how to respond to alarms indicating positive detections of radiological or nuclear material. The screening process may also make airports, and major international airports in particular, more vulnerable to radiological or nuclear attacks. While terrorists attempting to sneak such materials into the United States may ideally wish to attack a major urban center, they may alternatively carry out an attack at an international airport of arrival if their device is detected or if they believe that it is about to be detected.

CRITICAL INCIDENT MANAGEMENT AND RESPONSE

By regulation, each commercial passenger airport must establish procedures for evaluating and responding to bomb threats, threats of other forms of sabotage, possible hijacking incidents that occur on the airport property or in response to hijacked airplanes requesting to land at the airport, and all sorts of other possible security-related situations or other critical incidents. More broadly, airports must be capable of effectively responding to a wide range of security and safety incidents, including terrorist acts as well as aircraft accidents and natural and man-made disasters. Each commercial passenger airport is required to develop an FAA-approved Airport Emergency Plan specifically designed to minimize the possibility and extent of personal injury and property damage at an airport in the event of a critical incident.[35]

Additionally, airport operators are required to take specific actions under the general framework established by the NIMS for responding to either natural disasters or terrorist attacks. The NIMS derives from Homeland Security Presidential Directive 5 (HSPD-5) entitled the Management of Domestic Incidents.[36] This directive charges the DHS with implementing the nationwide incident management program, which is overseen by the FEMA. The HSPD-5 initiatives coincided with the integration of FEMA into the DHS under its Emergency Preparedness and Response Directorate. The NIMS provides a structure for critical incident management that includes an incident command system (ICS), a multiagency coordination (MAC) system, and public information systems for structuring command and management functions and disseminating information, as well as resource management capabilities for identifying and accessing resources necessary to establish readiness, response, and recovery capabilities.

For first responders, including local law enforcement on an airport facility, ARFF crews, on-site emergency medical personnel, and local community first responders who may respond to airport incidents, there are specific requirements for interoperable communications and processes for effective information management, incident command structure, and resource management. At the airport level, considerations are also given to continuity of operations and various contingency plans in response to various critical incident threat scenarios.

As noted previously, airports face a number of terrorist threats including possible shootings, bombings, or attacks using chemical, biological, radiological, or nuclear weapons. Responding to potential terrorist incidents involving such threats will require considerable coordination and cooperation among various airport and community elements including state, local, and federal law enforcement agencies and ARFF personnel; community first responders; airport and airline security personnel; the TSA, including the airport's FSD; and other on-site DHS components, possibly including CBP and FEMA. New and emerging security threats may pose unique challenges for airport critical incident management and response. Chemical, biological, radiological, or nuclear attacks at an airport would create a complex coordination effort for the airport and the surrounding community, because the nature of such attacks may significantly limit first responder access to the impacted site.

Increasingly, critical incident responders are using simulations and exercises to review and improve critical incident response plans, better define necessary resources, and hone the skills of responders and incident commanders. Research has shown that responders and, in particular, incident commanders are more likely to make better decisions and respond more effectively when exposed to a wide array of incidents, through real-world experience as well as simulations and exercises. By increasing the effectiveness of critical incident training, airport officials and responders may be better prepared to manage critical incidents and effectively implement the airport emergency plan and incident management systems and concepts in the event of a terrorist incident. Effective critical incident response may result in better containment of a security incident, minimizing potential loss of life, injuries, property damage, and disruption to airport and airfield operations. While comparatively little public policy attention has been devoted to airport critical incident management and response, these functions are clearly a vital component of an airport's overall security program.

REFERENCES

1. National Research Council. National Research Council, Committee on Assessment of Security Technologies for Transportation. *Defending the U.S. Air Transportation System against Chemical and Biological Threats.*
2. U.S. General Accounting Office. *Aviation Security: Further Steps Needed to Strengthen the Security of Commercial Airport Perimeters and Access Controls.* GAO-04-728, June 2007.
3. Ibid.
4. Ibid.

5. Transportation Security Administration, *Recommended Security Guidelines for Airport Planning, Design and Construction*, Revised June 15, 2006.

6. See note 2.

7. U.S. Department of Homeland Security, Transportation Security Administration. *Air Cargo Strategic Plan.* November 13, 2003; Department of Homeland Security, Transportation Security Administration. "Air Cargo Security Requirements, Final Rule." *Federal Register, 71*(102), pp. 30477–30517, May 26, 2006; 49 CFR 1544.239.

8. See note 2.

9. Ibid.

10. U.S. Department of Transportation, Office of Inspector General. *Report on Audit of Airport Access Control, Federal Aviation Administration.* Report Number AV-2000-017, November 18, 1999.

11. Ibid.

12. Jerome Greer Chandler. "Fruition or Frustration?" *Air Transport World*, December 2007, pp. 29–32.

13. Ibid.

14. Robert Poole. "New Technology for Airport Perimeter Security." *Airport Policy and Security Newsletter*, Issue 41, January 2009. Los Angeles, CA: The Reason Foundation.

15. "Security Solutions from State Police to Clammers." *Centerlines: Special Report Boston Logan's New Terminal A*, 2005, p. 11. Washington, DC: Airports Council International-North America (ACI-NA).

16. See note 2.

17. Transportation Security Administration. *National Explosives Detection Canine Team, Program History.*

18. Testimony of Robert Jamison, Deputy Administrator, Transportation Security Administration, Before the U.S. House of Representatives, Committee on Government Reform, Subcommittee on Federal Workforce and Agency Organization, April 4, 2006.

19. TSA Air cargo final rule.

20. Testimony of Greg Principato, President, Airports Council International-North America, before the Committee on Transportation Security and Infrastructure Protection, Committee on Homeland Security, U.S. House of Representatives, Hearing on Airport Security: The Necessary Improvements to Secure Americas' Airports, April 19, 2007.

21. See 14 CFR §107.31, January 1, 2001 edition.

22. See note 18.

23. American Association of Airport Executives. "AAAE To Process Background Checks." Airport Report, January 1, 2002.

24. Ref. 49 U.S.C. §44936 note.

25. American Association of Airport Executives. *AAAE and the Transportation Security Clearinghouse.* September 18, 2007. Alexandria, Virginia.

26. See 49 CFR, §1542.203 and §1542.205.

27. See note 25.

28. See note 25.

29. See note 18.

30. U.S. Government Accountability Office. *Transportation Security: DHS Efforts to Eliminate Redundant Background Check Investigations.* GAO-07-756, April 2007.

31. National Transportation Safety Board. Accident Brief, NTSB Identification: DCA88MA008.

32. See C. Wilson, A. R. Hicklin, H. Korves, B. Ulery, M. Zoepfl, M. Bone, P. Grother, R. J. Michaels, S. Otto, and C. Watson. *Fingerprint Vendor Technology Evaluation 2003: Summary of Results and Analysis Report.* National Institute of Standards and Technology (NIST) Internal Report 7123, June 2004; Elaine M. Newton and P. Jonathon Phillips. *Meta-Analysis of Third-Party Evaluations of Iris Recognition.* National Institute of Standards and Technology, NISTIR 7440, August 2007.

33. See note 1. Washington, DC: The National Academies Press, 2006.

34. Department of Homeland Security, Office of the Chief Procurement Officer. *Passenger and Baggage Radiation Nuclear Detection.* Federal Business Opportunities, December 11, 2008.

35. See Title 14 CFR §139.325.

36. George W. Bush. *Homeland Security Presidential Directive/HSPD-5 Subject: Management of Domestic Incidents.* Office of the Press Secretary, The White House, February 28, 2003.

10 Mitigating the Threat of Shoulder-Fired Missiles and Other Standoff Weapons

There is a general consensus among aviation security experts that civil aircraft, and commercial airliners in particular, face a persistent threat from terrorist attacks using shoulder-fired missiles or other standoff weapons. The threat of aircraft shootings from standoff weapons is complex and has been a significant focus of policy discussions because no single solution to mitigating the threat has been identified. Policies and strategies for combatting the threat posed by these weapons have centered on a multilayered approach involving

* Weapons nonproliferation initiatives
* Efforts to reduce existing weapons stockpiles
* Counterterrorism initiatives to disrupt transfers of these weapons to terrorist groups
* Programs to improve security and reduce vulnerabilities around airports
* Technology development programs to adapt aircraft-based and ground-based missile countermeasures to protect aircraft, airport terminal areas, and approach and departure corridors

While policy discussions regarding the threat of aircraft shootings have focused almost exclusively on possible terrorist attacks using shoulder-fired missiles, some in the aviation industry have raised concerns that attacks using less sophisticated standoff weapons, such as unguided rocket-propelled grenades (RPGs) and large-caliber munitions, are also a considerable threat to civil airliners. Nonetheless, shoulder-fired missiles are widely regarded as the most capable weapons in terrorist hands for downing a commercial airliner and thus remain at the center of policy discussions regarding the threat of aircraft shootings.

Although the threat of aircraft shootings has historically been limited to overseas operations and largely confined to civil aviation operations in war-torn regions of the world, there is growing concern among some aviation security and counterterrorism experts that there is an emerging worldwide threat to civil aircraft from shoulder-fired weapons and perhaps other standoff weapons. While this terrorist threat in the current context of the global war on terrorism is considered greatest in regions of the world where Islamic extremists and other terrorist groups have more of an unfettered presence—such as in the Middle East, in the horn of Africa, in other areas of Africa plagued by political unrest, in Afghanistan and Pakistan, and in regions of southeast Asia—the potential for shoulder-fired missile attacks or attacks using other standoff weapons against civilian airliners in western countries and in the U.S. homeland is likely increasing and cannot be disregarded. Rather, many aviation security experts have speculated that, in the post-9/11 environment, increased security measures at airports may logically lead terrorists to contemplate such attacks, allowing them to target aircraft, passenger airliners in particular, from far beyond the airport perimeter and its associated security enhancements.

While the threat posed by shoulder-fired missiles and other standoff weapons is certainly a credible threat, it poses a dilemma for policymakers for a variety of reasons. First, although terrorists are known to possess these weapons, actual attacks using them against civilian aircraft have been relatively rare. The failed attack against an Israeli charter airliner in November 2002 in Mombasa, Kenya stands out as a singular incident in recent history in which a large civilian jet was fired upon by such weapons in a conflict-free area. So, while the general threat of a terrorist attack using such a weapon is credible given known terrorist possession of these weapons, past experience suggests that the level of threat may be much lower than one would expect based on proliferation data alone. On the contrary, some experts argue that the threat of attack from shoulder-fired missiles and other standoff weapons may be growing as post-9/11 security measures become more effective against other methods of attack, primarily hijackings and bombings. For example, a study by the RAND Corporation published in 2005 concluded that "... given the measures being taken to preclude 9/11-style attacks, the use of [shoulder-fired missiles] will unavoidably become more attractive to terrorists."[1] While it is considered likely that terrorists have a desire to carry out attacks against civilian aircraft using shoulder-fired missiles and other standoff weapons, attacks of this kind have not been attempted against U.S. aircraft to date, and no credible intelligence has been reported to the public that al Qaeda or other terrorist groups may be planning such attacks. Nonetheless, terrorist organizations like al Qaeda frequently highlight their possession of such weapons in casting their public image for propaganda and recruiting purposes. These images lead many experts to conclude that, given the opportunity, terrorists would seek to carry out attacks using these types of weapons, and the most likely target for such an attack would be a passenger airliner.

Second, while historical attacks have been relatively small in number, civilian aircraft remain quite vulnerable to an attack from these types of weapons. They fly at relatively low altitudes within range of shoulder-fired weapons for extended distances during takeoff and departure and approach to landing. Commercial aircraft, unlike military aircraft, presently carry no special countermeasures to thwart a missile attack. Also, large commercial aircraft are not agile or maneuverable enough to effectively evade a missile attack. Based on this, one may conclude that commercial airliners are especially vulnerable to attack. While it may be true that commercial airliners are vulnerable to being hit by a shoulder-fired missile or other standoff weapon, aircraft manufacturers and aircraft survivability experts point out that they may not be as susceptible to being brought down by such an attack. Commercial airliners are large in size and have redundant systems allowing them to be flown to an emergency landing after such an attack, and damage from these weapons, whose warheads are relatively small, is usually isolated. Historical data of such attacks actually suggest that the odds of a commercial airliner surviving a hit from a shoulder-fired missile attack are relatively good. While the flight crew's actions to save a crippled DHL cargo airliner that was struck in a widely publicized shoulder-fired missile attack in Iraq in November 2003 was an exemplary demonstration of proficient airmanship and effective teamwork to save a crippled aircraft, it demonstrates that appropriate training and proper execution of emergency flight procedures for handling aircraft shooting scenarios may be quite effective in increasing the likelihood of surviving such an attack.

However, the third consideration in the dilemma over policy approaches to address the threat of aircraft shootings centers on the final element of the risk equation: the consequence of an attack, whether it be a successful attack or not. With regard to consequence, even if commercial aircraft are likely to survive such an attack, it may be extremely difficult to convince the traveling public of this and to restore confidence in air travel even if one unsuccessful attempt to down a passenger airliner using such a weapon were carried out in the United States. The decline in passenger traffic from such an incident could cause lasting economic damage to passenger air carriers. A successful attack would undoubtedly be devastating to the airline industry and could have lasting, widespread economic impacts. Some speculate that the consequences of a successful shoulder-fired missile attack against a civilian airliner within the United States could potentially have a longer lasting and more damaging impact on the airline industry than the terrorist attacks of September 11, 2001. The reason being that, unlike the swift action taken by policymakers to strengthen passenger security to regain the confidence of the flying public after the 9/11 attacks, there may be no simple "quick fix" to effectively mitigate the risk of additional aircraft shootings and reassure the public that it is safe to fly again. Even if highly effective countermeasures could be quickly installed on commercial aircraft, the public may curtail their flying considerably out of fear that they still could be shot at, even though the likelihood of actually being hit if fired upon may have been effectively reduced to being a highly unlikely outcome.

This brings up a fourth element in the policy dilemma over combatting threats to aircraft from shoulder-fired missiles and other standoff weapons: the cost of mitigating the threat. Missiles countermeasures being contemplated for installation on commercial airplanes may be extremely expensive to procure and maintain on a large-scale basis, with lifecycle costs to deploy and maintain these systems across the entire U.S. air carrier fleet expected to be in the tens of billions of dollars over a projected 10-year system lifespan.[2] Even at this relatively high cost, not all threats could be mitigated as countermeasures being contemplated would protect only against IR-guided weapons, and will not be capable of protecting against unguided standoff weapons or shoulder-fired missiles that use other technologies for homing in on a targeted aircraft. Therefore, many have advocated a multipronged or multilayered policy approach to mitigating the threat of aircraft shootings, rather than pursuing high-cost single approaches to address a subset of this more general threat, albeit one widely considered the most formidable and widely proliferated of these weapons—the IR-guided missile.

In the following discussion, the threat posed by standoff weapons, especially shoulder-fired-guided surface-to-air missiles, is explored in further detail. This is followed by a brief examination of the vulnerability of large civil transport aircraft and a discussion of the potential consequences of a standoff attack against such aircraft. Current policy and strategy for protecting against such an attack is subsequently discussed in the multilayered risk framework examining nonproliferation initiatives, counterterrorism strategies, and aviation security approaches including enhanced surveillance measures at airports and possible deployment of aircraft-based and ground-based countermeasures.

THE PROLIFERATION OF SHOULDER-FIRED WEAPONS AND THE TERRORIST THREAT THEY POSE

Shoulder-fired missiles with guidance systems and other MANPADS—a military term to describe portable guided missile systems that include shoulder-fired missiles as well as similar weapons that can be mounted on a stand or a vehicle—were initially developed in the late 1950s, and the first operational model, the U.S.-made Redeye, entered service in the early 1960s. MANPADS are produced in about 17 different countries, including the United States, and are typically about 5–6 feet in length and weigh about 35–40 pounds. A sketch of a typical shoulder-fired MANPADS is presented in Figure 10.1. The small size and easy portability of these systems make them especially

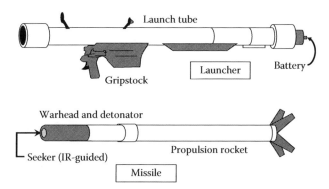

FIGURE 10.1   Sketch of a typical shoulder-fired MANPADS launcher and missile.

difficult to detect and defend against from the standpoint of airport and aircraft security and counterterrorism operations.

MANPADS were first used extensively in the Vietnam era, by both sides in the conflict, to provide military ground force protection from aircraft attacks. Historically, these weapons have been used successfully by militaries around the world and also by insurgents and terrorist groups. They have been demonstrated to be a lethal threat against aircraft in several military conflicts over the past 40 years including the Arab–Israeli Wars, Vietnam, the Iran–Iraq War, in the Falklands, and in the Balkans Conflict in the 1990s. They have also been used by various factions and insurgent groups in Nicaragua, Yemen, Angola, Uganda, and in Chad and Libya. Insurgent use of MANPADS have also posed a continuing menace to United States and allied forces in Iraq. At present, MANPADS are believed to be widely available to terrorist groups throughout the world at relatively low cost through a variety of sources. They are widely regarded by weapons experts as formidable weapons, particularly against transport aircraft and helicopters.

Over the past 40 years, approximately 20 countries have engaged in manufacturing MANPADS and a wide assortment of systems exist. It is estimated that over one million of these systems have been produced.[3] Available estimates of the current worldwide MANPADS inventory vary considerably, ranging from an estimated 350,000 to 500,000 missiles.[4] A listing of several common MANPADS is provided in Table 10.1. This list is by no means comprehensive as several countries, including China, North Korea, Egypt, Pakistan, and Iran, produce an assortment of MANPADS variants based on the listed Russian, French, and U.S. designs.[5] Russian SA-7 missiles are the most widely proliferated with 56 countries known to be in possession, while U.S.-made Stingers have been acquired by 20 other countries besides the United States. Second generation Russian models, including SA-14 and SA-16 variants, have been exported to numerous countries, and newer, more capable SA-18 systems have also been exported to a smaller number of countries.[6] Perhaps the most

TABLE 10.1
The Evolution of Common MANPADS Systems and Their Characteristics and Capabilities

System	Country of Original Manufacture	Maximum Effective Altitude (Feet)	Type	Year Introduced
Redeye	USA	<10,000	First generation IR	1967
SA-7A	USSR	<10,000	First generation IR	1968
SA-7B	USSR	10,000–15,000	First generation IR	1972
Blowpipe	U.K.	<10,000	Command line of site	1975
RBS-70 Mk I	Sweden	<10,000	Laser beam rider	1977
SA-14	USSR	15,000–20,000	Second generation IR	1978
Stinger	USA	15,000–20,000	Second generation IR	1981
SA-16	USSR	20,000–25,000	Second generation IR	1981
SA-18	USSR	20,000–25,000	Third generation IR	1984
Javelin	U.K.	<10,000	Command line of site	1984
Stinger POST	USA	15,000–20,000	Third generation IR	1986
RBS-70 Mk II	Sweden	20,000–25,000	Laser beam rider	1988
Mistral	France	20,000–25,000	Cruciform array IR	1989
Stinger RMP Block I	USA	15,000–20,000	Third generation IR	1990
Starburst	U.K.	<10,000	Command line of site	1990
RBS-90	Sweden	15,000–20,000	Laser beam rider	1991
SA-18 (IGLA)	Russia	20,000–25,000	Third generation IR	1994
Starstreak	U.K.	15,000–20,000	Laser beam rider	1993
Keiko II	Japan	10,000–15,000	Focal plane array IR	1995
Stinger RMP Block II	USA	25,000–30,000	Focal plane array IR	1996

troubling trend in the current context is the Iranian production of two variants based on Chinese knockoffs of the Russian SA-16, the Misagh-1 and the Misagh-2 MANPADS. Given Iran's designation as a state sponsor of terrorism and its support of Hezbollah in Lebanon and Shia insurgents in Iraq, state transfer of these weapons either directly or indirectly into terrorist and insurgent hands is a looming threat to both military operations and civil aviation, particularly in the Middle East. Recent civil unrest in Pakistan may also raise concerns that weapons produced for the Pakistani military could potentially fall into the hands of terrorist groups, including al Qaeda.

As indicated in Table 10.1, there are a number of different types of MANPADS primarily classified into three general categories based on their method for detecting and engaging targets. These three general categories include command line-of-sight (CLOS) systems, laser beam riders, and IR-guided missiles. IR-guided MANPADS are by far the most common and have been greatly improved over the last 40 years.

IR-Guided MANPADS

IR-guided MANPADS have sensor or seeker elements that sense and track energy in specific portions of the IR spectral band emitted by target aircraft. IR guidance systems are designed to home in on a heat source on an aircraft, and the missile is typically detonated in or near the heat source to disable the aircraft, typically by impact detonator fuses. For aircraft, the predominant IR energy source is the hot jet engine and its trailing exhaust plume. However, radiant heat reflected off the aircraft's skin also generates a smaller amount of IR energy that can be detected by these weapon guidance systems, particularly among more recently introduced MANPADS. IR-guided MANPADS employ passive weapon guidance systems, meaning that they do not emit any signals to detect a heat source. This makes them more difficult to detect by targeted aircraft employing missile warning and missile countermeasure systems.

The first MANPADS deployed in the 1960s used IR guidance systems. These early MANPADS, introduced in the 1960s and early 1970s, such as the U.S. Redeye, early versions of the Soviet SA-7, and the Chinese HN-5 (a reverse-engineered knockoff of the SA-7), are considered "tail chase" or rear aspect weapons because their seekers can only effectively acquire and engage a jet aircraft from behind, after it has passed the missile's firing position. In this flight profile, the aircraft's engines are fully exposed to the missile's seeker and provide a sufficient thermal signature from the hot engine exhaust for the missile to track to. These first generation IR missiles are highly susceptible to interference from a variety of other heat sources, including the sun and flares dispensed by military aircraft to confuse IR guidance systems, which renders them far less effective than more recent IR-guided MANPADS that use more advanced seeker technologies.

Second generation IR missiles—such as early versions of the U.S. Stinger, the Soviet SA-14, and the Chinese FN-6—use improved coolants to lower the temperature of the seeker thereby enabling the seeker to filter out most interfering background IR sources. This greatly improves the signal to background noise ratio when targeting aircraft thus allowing head-on and side engagement profiles giving these weapons all-aspect capability, that is, the capability to effectively fire on a target aircraft from any angle or aspect. These missiles also employ some basic antispoofing capabilities allowing them to reject the IR signatures of flares—a common countermeasure used to confuse IR missiles—that might be deployed by targeted aircraft. Some of these systems also have backup target detection modes such as the ultraviolet (UV) mode found on the Stinger variant with Passive Optical Seeker Technique (Stinger POST).[7]

More advanced third generation IR MANPADS, such as the Russian SA-18, and the U.S.-made Stinger with Reprogrammable Microprocessor (Stinger RMP), use single or multiple detectors to produce a multiband IR image of the target and also have the advanced capability to recognize and reject flares dispensed from targeted aircraft.[8]

The latest MANPADS incorporate more advanced focal plane array guidance systems, allowing a more detailed IR image of the target to be used to steer the missile, and other advanced sensor systems that will permit engagement at greater ranges.[9] The U.S.-made Stinger RMP Block II and the Japanese Keiko II MANPADS employ this technology, while the European-made Mistral employs a cruciform or cross-shaped targeting array rather than a full two-dimensional focal plane array. Some regard these systems, particularly those that utilize full focal plane array imaging of the target, as fourth generation IR systems. These fourth generation systems employ the most advanced seeker technology that can engage targets at greater ranges and are highly resistant to IR counter-measures, including some laser-based IR countermeasures that are being considered as possible options for mitigating the MANPADS threat to both military transport aircraft and the commercial airline fleet in the United States.

CLOS MANPADS

While IR-guided MANPADS are by far the most widely proliferated, systems produced in the United Kingdom have primarily relied instead on CLOS guidance systems. CLOS MANPADS rely on the missile operator to visually acquire the target using a magnified optical sight and guide or steer the missile toward the target during the missile's flight using radio signals to relay guidance commands from the launch site. One of the benefits of such a missile is that it typically cannot be spoofed by standard aircraft-mounted countermeasure systems like flares and newer laser-based directed countermeasures that are designed primarily to defeat IR-guided missiles. The major draw-back of CLOS MANPADS, however, is that they require highly trained and skilled operators. Reportedly, the Afghan mujahadeen were rather disappointed with the performance of Blowpipe CLOS MANPADS supplied to them by the United Kingdom for use during the Soviet–Afghan War in the 1980s because they proved to be too difficult to operate and highly inaccurate, particularly when employed against fast-moving jet aircraft.[10] Given these considerations, many experts believe that CLOS missiles are not as ideally suited for terrorist use as IR missiles, which are often referred to as "fire and forget" missiles because of their comparative ease of use.

Later versions of CLOS missiles, particularly the United Kingdom's Javelin missiles, use a solid-state television camera in lieu of the optical tracker to make the gunner's task easier, potentially quelling some concerns over the difficulty of training operators to use these weapons effectively. CLOS MANPADS like the Blowpipe and the Javelin are relatively impervious to commonly deplo-yed countermeasures used to spoof small missiles that largely assume an IR-guided threat. However, these CLOS weapons may be defeated by radio-frequency jamming that disrupts the guidance transmissions between the launch site and the missile during the missile's flight. The newer Starburst MANPADS, introduced in 1990 and deployed during the 1991 Gulf War, uses a laser data link transmission system in place of the radio-frequency guidance systems of earlier models, and is thus much more difficult to jam. More recently, systems developed in the United Kingdom have switched to laser-guided systems, referred to as laser beam riders, which were first developed and deployed by the Swedish military in the late 1970s.

Laser Beam Rider MANPADS

Laser beam rider MANPADS use lasers to guide the missiles to their intended target. The missile literally flies along a laser beam path typically controlled by the weapon system operator, and strikes the aircraft where the missile operator or gunner aims the laser. These beam-riding missiles cannot be spoofed by current countermeasure systems deployed on military and civilian aircraft, including flares and laser-based IR countermeasures and cannot be jammed by radio-frequency jammers. Missiles such as Sweden's RBS-70, the first weapon of this kind, and the more recently developed Starstreak, produced in the United Kingdom, can engage aircraft from all aspects. However, these weapons require the operator to continuously track the targeted aircraft, either by using a joystick or by maneuvering the firing pod, to keep the laser beam directed at the target. Because there are no data links from the ground to the missile, the missile cannot be effectively jammed after it is launched. Future beam-riding MANPADS may require the operator to designate the target only initially, providing automated guidance control to keep the laser beam on target while the missile is in flight. While laser beam rider MANPADS require relatively extensive training and skill to operate, weapons experts consider these missiles a significant threat in the hands of terrorists due to the missiles' resistance to most conventional countermeasures in use today. However, because laser beam rider weapons have not been as widely proliferated as IR-guided MANPADS, they have been generally regarded as less of a concern and have not garnered the specific attention of policymakers and aviation security strategists in the U.S. government. Perhaps also because there are no readily adaptable military countermeasure technologies that can potentially be deployed in the civil aviation environment to mitigate the risk posed by laser beam rider MANPADS, policies and strategies to mitigate the MANPADS threat to civil aviation have not paid particular attention to the specific threat posed by missiles with these types of guidance systems. However, in policy debate, it is important to note that the various countermeasures under consideration for mitigating the MANPADS threat are not designed to be effective against all types of MANPADS and are not considered to be capable of thwarting attacks using either laser beam rider or CLOS MANPADS.

TERRORIST ACQUISITION AND POSSESSION OF MANPADS

Of the half million or so MANPADS proliferated throughout the world, the number of MANPADS in terrorists hands is estimated to be anywhere from 5000 to 150,000.[11] These widely varying numbers are indicative of the lack of good tracking and intelligence on proliferation of these weapons as well as the relative lack of arms controls for the transfer of these weapons that existed up until a few years ago. At present, the continuing threat that state sponsors of terrorism are either directly or indirectly supplying insurgents and terrorist groups with MANPADS in unknown quantities raises both greater uncertainty as well as greater concern over the number of these weapons that may be in the hands of terrorists. While a precise breakdown of the specific MANPADS in terrorist hands has not been compiled, most experts agree that the vast majority are IR guided. Most experts believe that the most commonly proliferated shoulder-fired missiles in terrorist hands are likely SA-7s and SA-7 derivatives and knockoffs. It is known that about 750 Stingers were delivered to Afghanistan during the Soviet invasion and occupation and have been credited with about 100 shootdowns of Soviet aircraft. The Afghan mujahadeen are believed to have still had in their possession hundreds of these Stinger MANPADS at the conclusion of the conflict, although most of these systems are now reaching the upper limits of their shelf life and may no longer be reliable.

There are a variety of means that terrorist organizations use to obtain shoulder-fired missiles and other weapons capable of downing a large commercial passenger airplane. These methods include theft, the black market, international organized crime rings, arms dealers, and transfers from states willing to supply these weapons to terrorists. Depending on the model, MANPADS can be purchased on the black market anywhere from a few hundred dollars for older models to about a quarter million dollars for newer, more capable models. Typical black market cost of MANPADS range between $5000 and $30,000 per unit.[12] Often, the only verification that a terrorist group has acquired such weapons is following an attack, when it becomes apparent that such a weapon had been used after the fact.[13] Relatively large numbers of these missiles are believed to be available to terrorists and insurgent groups. For example, coalition forces in Afghanistan had captured more than 5000 shoulder-fired missiles from the Taliban and al Qaeda.[14] Some of these included U.S. Stinger missiles supplied to the Afghan mujahadeen in the 1980s. In Iraq, it is believed that as many as 4000–5000 shoulder-fired missiles may be available to insurgents.[15] On the African continent, the region where most attacks against civilian aircraft using these missiles have occurred, large quantities of Russian-supplied MANPADS that were provided during periods of civil wars and uprisings in various African nations are believed to still exist.[16] It is also believed that large stockpiles of MANPADS and other standoff weapons supplied during the conflict in the 1990s still exist in the Balkans, although cooperative efforts with the U.S. State Department in recent years have resulted in the destruction of large numbers of these weapons.[17] Unclassified estimates suggest that between 25 and 30 nonstate groups are in possession of MANPADS. However, specific estimates regarding the number of these weapons in the hands of these various terrorist and nonstate groups is largely undocumented in publicly available sources.

OTHER STANDOFF WEAPONS

While the policy focus in the United States has been dominated by the terrorist threat to civil aviation posed by MANPADS, and particularly the threat of IR-guided MANPADS, other highly proliferated standoff weapons may also pose a considerable threat to civilian aircraft. These weapons include high-caliber firearms, rocket-propelled antiarmor and antipersonnel munitions—such as variants of the U.S.-made bazooka and the Russian-made RPG-7—as well as more sophisticated wire-guided and laser-guided antitank and antiarmor mortars and missiles.[18] These weapons could potentially be used in an attack against an airborne aircraft, but far more likely, could be used in an attack against an aircraft on the ground or an attack against aviation infrastructure including airport terminals as well as air traffic control and navigational facilities. While such weapons may not be as capable in terms of range and precision as remotely guided MANPADS for attacking aircraft in flight, the fact that these weapons are readily available from a wide range of sources and are relatively inexpensive may make them particularly attractive to terrorist groups, especially those that may be contemplating a large-scale attack or multiple attacks against ground-based targets in the airport environment.

Attacks using such weapons have been carried out before and are still regarded as a formidable terrorist threat. For example, during a campaign of terror in January 1975, members of the Black September terrorist organization, led by the notorious terrorist leader Carlos the Jackal, targeted two El Al aircraft in separate attacks at Paris Orly airport using RPGs and bazookas. Four days after a failed attempt at shooting an El Al jet preparing for takeoff with an RPG-7, a second attempt at shooting an El Al aircraft also failed, leading to a gunfight with security forces and a hostage standoff in the Orly passenger terminal. More recent attacks, however, have more typically targeted airport terminals rather than aircraft. The terrorist threat to parked and taxiing aircraft from these weapons is still a considerable concern, particularly in volatile regions of the world where terrorists may have a greater capacity to carry out such an attack. A lesser threat to airplanes on approach to landing and during takeoff and climb-out using such weapons also exists. In March 2007, for example, an Ilyushin IL-76 four-engine transport jet was reportedly hit and extensively damaged by an RPG-7 while on approach to Mogadishu, Somalia.[19] Mitigation efforts to counter such attacks include nonproliferation initiatives, counterterrorism efforts to detect and prevent the planning and execution of such attacks, and increased airport perimeter security measures to detect and thwart such an attack. Therefore, these initiatives are largely regarded as complimentary to the ongoing efforts to address the larger perceived threat posed by more capable MANPADS, which can target civil aircraft from much greater standoff distances and attack aircraft in flight far beyond the airport perimeter as well as in the immediate vicinity of an airport like these shorter-range standoff weapons.

THE VULNERABILITY OF COMMERCIAL AIRLINERS

Although terrorist attacks against airliners using MANPADS or other standoff weapons have been relatively small in number, experts generally agree that they are vulnerable to a potential attack of this type. These aircraft operate at lower altitudes, within range of MANPADS in particular, well beyond airport boundaries making them vulnerable to attack. More considerable debate, however, exists regarding how susceptible these aircraft may be to being destroyed as the result of a MANPADS attack. While historic incidents involving commercial airliners suggest that the chances of surviving such an attack are better than one might expect, military experience suggests that shoulder-fired missiles are a formidable threat to military transports similar in characteristics to civilian airliners. Military data indicate that numerous transport airplane losses over the years have been attributed to MANPADS, and IR-guided missiles including MANPADS and larger-sized surface-to-air missiles represent the greatest threat to transport aircraft, historically accounting for 63% of all U.S. military transport aircraft losses due to enemy fire.[20]

THE VULNERABILITY OF TYPICAL COMMERCIAL FLIGHT OPERATIONS

MANPADS generally have a target detection range of about six miles and an engagement range of about four miles, so aircraft flying at 20,000 feet (3.8 miles) above the ground or higher are relatively safe. Most experts, however, consider aircraft departures and approach and landings as the most vulnerable phases of flight to the threat of MANPADS engagement. Figure 10.2 portrays flight profiles for landing and departing aircraft that are typical of the type of approach to landing and departure altitude profiles flown into and out of many major airports within the United States. These profiles have been established based on consideration of aircraft climb performance, aircraft altitude separation requirements, and additional procedural considerations to facilitate traffic flow and maintain air traffic controller and pilot workloads at reasonable levels. Unlike military flight procedures, security considerations regarding the threat posed by MANPADS and other surface-to-air weapons have not been considered a factor in establishing flight patterns and altitude profiles for landing and departing aircraft at commercial airports.

Based on analysis of currently proliferated MANPADS and past experience with MANPADS, large transport aircraft operating below 10,000 are generally regarded as being highly vulnerable to attack. At very low altitudes, close to the airport, aircraft might be somewhat less vulnerable, particularly to IR-guided MANPADS, because of background clutter that can confuse the weapon's guidance system and minimum engagement distances needed to accurately home in on a target. At these ranges, however, it is notable that other standoff weapons such as RPGs are maximally effective and may pose a considerable threat. In the range between 500–10,000 feet or so, MANPADS are maximally effective and transport aircraft are consequently most vulnerable at these altitudes. From 10,000 to about 15,000 feet, earlier generation IR systems in particular become less effective, and from 15,000 to about 20,000 feet only newer generations of IR-guided and laser beam rider MANPADS can sufficiently maintain their effectiveness.

Commercial jets and other civil aircraft such as business jets are considered most vulnerable from about 500–10,000 feet. Of the documented historical incidents involving successful strikes

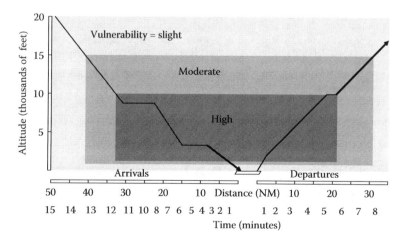

FIGURE 10.2 Typical approach and departure profiles for commercial jets leave them vulnerable to MANPADS attacks for 50 miles or more from the airport.

against large civilian airliners, all are believed to have occurred in this approximate range of altitudes, with most occurring at or near 8000 feet. From 10,000 to 15,000 feet above the ground, aircraft are still moderately vulnerable to MANPADS attacks, and from 15,000 to about 20,000 feet aircraft are still slightly vulnerable, although most systems capable of remaining highly effective at these altitudes are newer generation systems that are not believed to be as widely proliferated among terrorist and insurgent groups.

As previously noted, when operating at these lower altitudes, commercial jets are generally not agile or maneuverable enough to evade fast-moving missiles—many of which rapidly accelerate to about twice the speed of sound (Mach 2) after being fired—even if provided with adequate missile detection and warning capabilities found on military aircraft. Therefore, training flight crews in evasive maneuvers would not likely be effective and presents considerable risks. There is considerable concern that defensive maneuvering of large transport category airplanes could result in a loss of control or structural failure.[21] Consequently, most observers concur that evasive maneuvering is not a viable option for mitigating the risk of missile attacks.

Airline pilots already receive considerable simulator training on handling engine failures during critical phases of flight such as takeoffs and landings. Pilots also receive some training on loss of flight control systems and other aircraft controllability situations. Such training may prepare flight crews to some degree to handle possible loss of engine power or loss of flight control effectiveness resulting from a missile strike or other standoff weapon attack. However, specific simulator exercises using missile attack scenarios may be beneficial by preparing pilots for such an event and preparing them to fly and land a damaged aircraft. As discussed, modern airliners are built with various redundancies and failure protections built into their avionics and flight control systems. Consequently, a standoff weapon's attack that does not cause a catastrophic structural failure would likely be survivable if the flight crew is properly trained to handle such a scenario.

THE SURVIVABILITY OF CIVILIAN TRANSPORT AIRCRAFT

The structural survivability of passenger jets following missile strikes is largely unknown, although the Air Force is engaged in ongoing research to evaluate the vulnerability of large transport aircraft structures and to test the vulnerability of large jet engines to shoulder-fired missiles.[22] In general, the probability of an aircraft being destroyed by a missile attack [the probability of a kill or $p(K)$ in military parlance] is the conditional probability of a catastrophic loss of the aircraft given a missile strike or hit against the aircraft. While a weapon's accuracy, reliability, and lethality are all factors in this outcome, the survivability characteristics of the targeted aircraft are also important considerations. While commercial airliners are not designed with the threat of possible missile attacks specifically in mind, various safety design considerations, such as protecting and separating hydraulic systems, providing redundancies in avionics and flight control systems, designing engines to prevent uncontained failures that can damage other systems and aircraft structures, and protecting fuel tanks from ruptures and explosions, may improve the chances that an aircraft will be able to withstand a missile attack.

It is expected, however, that further hardening aircraft structures, beyond these incremental safety improvements to newly manufactured aircraft, will be a challenging problem. Most IR guidance systems seek hot engine exhaust and are believed to most likely detonate at or near an aircraft engine. Since most jet airliners have wing-mounted engines, further hardening of surrounding aircraft structure will likely be extremely difficult, particularly with regard to modifying existing aircraft. However, many aircraft survivability experts believe that taking additional steps to improve aircraft survivability, such as isolating critical systems like redundant hydraulic lines and flight control linkages, improving fire suppression and containment capabilities, and reducing fuel tank flammability, could prevent catastrophic failures cascading from the initial missile strike.[23]

One possible technology to improve aircraft survivability under consideration is a Propulsion-Controlled Aircraft Technology (PCA) system that has been under development and testing by

NASA since the early 1990s. This technology allows flight crews to more effectively maneuver a damaged aircraft whose flight control systems have become inoperative or unreliable, either because of a systems malfunction or accidental damage or due to damage from an event such as a standoff weapons attack. ALPA believes that "PCA systems could significantly enhance the ability of an aircraft to survive any type of standoff weapons attack, not just shoulder-launched missiles."[24] Another technology that could potentially improve aircraft survivability following a MANPADS or standoff weapons attack is fuel-tank inerting systems that the FAA is now pursuing as a means to reduce the chances of an accidental explosion in center fuel tanks. These systems pump inert gases, typically nitrogen, into the fuel tank to replace oxygen and greatly reduce the flammability and explosive potential of a tank's fuel/air mixture. Further application of inerting systems in wing tanks as well as tanks in the center fuselage may also reduce the vulnerability of aircraft to fuel-fed fires and explosions triggered by missile strikes or other standoff attacks.

Options for further improving safety can potentially be integrated into new aircraft designs, and some technologies, like center fuel-tank inerting systems, are already being incorporated into newly manufactured aircraft. Retrofitting existing aircraft with such systems, however, has involved a slower approach through the regulatory process, carefully examining economic impacts and cost and benefits as well as the merits of the specific technologies. Installing fuel-tank inerting in center wing tanks, for example, is being phased-in among the existing air carrier fleet over several years, and retrofitting wing tanks on existing aircraft is not part of this requirement. Therefore, such initiatives are not likely to have any near-term impact on reducing the MANPADS threat to the existing commercial airline fleet. Other options for retrofitting existing air carrier jets with damage tolerant structures and systems will require extensive testing and many are likely to be regarded as either technically infeasible or not economically practical. Initial indications suggest that aircraft hardening and structural redesign, if feasible, will likely be very costly and could take many years to implement. Therefore, improving aircraft survivability has not been a central focus of the U.S. policy and strategy for mitigating the MANPADS threat to commercial airliners. Nonetheless, a review of historical incidents involving MANPADS attacks against civil aircraft suggests that among large transport aircraft, their large size and already-incorporated safety design considerations have likely had some positive effect in reducing the odds that a missile strike will bring down an aircraft, at least compared to MANPADS encounters involving smaller, lighter aircraft.

CIVILIAN AVIATION ENCOUNTERS WITH SHOULDER-FIRED MISSILES

Estimates vary, but the most widely reported statistics on civilian aircraft experience with MANPADS indicate that, over the past three decades, 36 aircraft have come under attack from these weapons. Of those 36, 24 aircraft were shot down resulting in more than 500 deaths.[25] While these statistics have been frequently cited, at least one report has suggested that these figures may significantly overstate the actual number of civilian-use aircraft that have been attacked by MANPADS.[26] That report instead concluded that only about a dozen civil-registered airplanes have been shot down during this time period and further notes that some of these aircraft were operating as military transports when they were shot down. On the contrary, available statistics may underestimate the total number of civilian encounters with shoulder-fired missiles because some aircraft shootings may have been attributed to other causes for various reasons and are not included in these statistics. Also, it is possible that some failed attempts to shoot down civilian airliners have either gone undetected or unreported. For many incidents considered to be shoulder-fired missile attacks against civilian aircraft, there is insufficient information to make a conclusive determination if the aircraft, in fact, came under fire. In some instances, while it is widely acknowledged that the incident was a shooting, there has been no conclusive determination regarding the weapon used. For example, in some instances of aircraft shootings there are discrepancies among accounts of the event, with some reports indicating that the aircraft was brought down by a shoulder-fired missile and others claiming that antiaircraft artillery was used. Also, in many instances, there are questions as to whether the flight operation was strictly for a civilian use or may have been for military or dual use (civilian/military) purposes. Therefore, there is no universal agreement as to which incidents should be included in the tally of civilian aviation encounters with shoulder-fired missiles.

Since most documented incidents involving shoulder-fired missile attacks against civilian aircraft have occurred in conflict zones, these attacks typically have not been formally classified as terrorist acts or politically motivated attacks.[27] Most of these historical examples, therefore, do not provide any particular insight into the political motivation behind shooting attacks carried out against civilian aircraft in the current context of the global war on terrorism and the global terror threat, nor can they offer any estimates of the potential economic and socio-political consequences of such an attack to the United States and its allies in the war against terrorism. An examination of these historic incidents, however, can provide some unique insights into the possible outcomes of such an attack that may help in understanding aircraft vulnerability to attack and aircraft survivability if such a terrorist attack were attempted.

Based on the commonly cited statistic of 24 aircraft destroyed out of 36 attacks over the past three decades, the odds of surviving an attack do not seem particularly encouraging. Based on these findings, the odds of surviving an attack may be estimated to be only about 33%. However, it is important to note that these incidents include a wide variety of aircraft types including small piston-engine propeller airplanes, turboprop airplanes, helicopters, and business jets, as well as a comparatively smaller subset of attacks against large jet airliners.

Since the policy focus in the United States has been aimed at addressing ways to reduce the MANPADS threat to large commercial passenger aircraft, it is particularly useful to examine past incidents involving these types of aircraft and weapons in order to gain further insight regarding the specific vulnerabilities to such attacks among these types of aircraft. Six suspected incidents involving MANPADS attacks against large western-built transport category jets have been identified over the past three decades. These incidents are listed in Table 10.2. Whether all of these incidents

TABLE 10.2
Reported Shoulder-Fired Missile Attacks Against Large Western-Built Civilian Turbojet Aircraft (1978–2007)

Date	Location	Aircraft	Operator	Outcome (Credibility of Report)
11/08/1983	Angola	Boeing 737	Angolan Airlines (TAAG)	Catastrophic:130 fatalities of 130 people on board (unconfirmed)
02/09/1984	Angola	Boeing 737	Angolan Airlines (TAAG)	Hull Loss: Aircraft overran runway on landing after being struck by a missile at 8000 feet during climb-out. No fatalities with 130 on board (unconfirmed, possible bomb on board)
09/21/1984	Afghanistan	DC-10	Ariana Afghan Airlines	Substantial Damage: Aircraft was damaged by the missile, including damage to two hydraulic systems, but landed without further damage. No fatalities (confirmed)
10/10/1998	Democratic Republic of Congo	Boeing 727	Congo Airlines	Catastrophic: 41 fatalities of 41 people on board (probable but unconfirmed)
11/28/2002	Kenya	Boeing 757	Arkia Israeli Airlines	Miss: Two SA-7s were fired at the aircraft during climb-out, but missed. No fatalities (confirmed)
11/22/2003	Iraq	Airbus A300	DHL Cargo	Hull Loss: Aircraft wing struck by a missile while departing from Baghdad. Aircraft suffered a complete loss of hydraulic power and departed the runway during an emergency landing (confirmed)

were in fact attacks using shoulder-fired missiles is still a matter of considerable debate as conclusive evidence supporting such a finding is lacking for several of these incidents.

Of these six encounters identified, there was a wide range of outcomes. Only two of the six shootings resulted in catastrophic losses of the airplanes killing all on board, neither of which has been conclusively determined to have been the result of a MANPADS attack. In three other incidents, the airplanes received significant damage but no one was killed. Finally, in the widely reported November 2002 attempt to shoot down an Israeli charter jet in Mombasa, Kenya, the aircraft was fired upon by two missiles but was not hit.

In the first instance, the official findings by Angolan authorities attributed the November 8, 1983, crash of a TAAG Angolan Airlines Boeing 737 to a technical problem with the airplane, but UNITA rebels in the area claimed to have shot down the aircraft with a surface-to-air missile.[28] All 130 people on board were killed, potentially making this the deadliest single incident involving a shoulder-fired missile attack against a civilian aircraft. However, investigation of the incident failed to produce any conclusive evidence of missile or gunfire damage on any of the aircraft wreckage. Therefore, this incident is generally regarded as an unconfirmed but reported MANPADS attack against a large, western-built transport category airplane. Based on the report issued by the Angolan government, the crash is still officially regarded as an accident caused by a mechanical failure.

In the February 9, 1984, incident involving a TAAG Angolan Airlines Boeing 737, the airplane was reportedly struck by a missile at an altitude of 8000 feet during climb-out. The crew attempted an emergency landing at Huambo, Angola, but was unable to extend the flaps because of damage to the airplane's hydraulic systems. Consequently, the crew was unable to slow the airplane sufficiently before landing and overran the runway by almost 600 feet. The airplane was a total loss but no one was killed.[29] Investigators found evidence leading them to suspect that a bomb detonated in the forward hold, rather than a missile, was responsible for the damage observed. However, press accounts reporting that the aircraft was struck by an SA-7 fired by UNITA guerillas have led some to conclude that this incident was, in fact, a shoulder-fired missile attack.[30] This conclusion, however, was not supported by available investigative findings and therefore is considered unconfirmed.

In the September 21, 1984, incident, an Ariana Afghan Airlines DC-10 was struck causing damage to two of the airplane's three hydraulic systems. While some sources defined this incident as a shoulder-fired missile attack,[31] another account indicated that the DC-10 was hit by "explosive bullets."[32] This, however, is generally regarded as a confirmed incident of a MANPADS attack against a large western-built civilian transport aircraft based on investigative findings.

The most recent suspected catastrophic loss of a large civilian air transport aircraft from a suspected MANPADS attack was the October 10, 1998, downing of a Congo Airlines Boeing 727 near Kindu, Democratic Republic of Congo. The aircraft was reportedly shot down by a missile, possibly an SA-7, that struck one of the airplane's engines. Tutsi rebels took responsibility for the alleged shooting, claiming that they believed the airplane to be carrying military supplies. The final call from the airplane captain indicated that the aircraft had been hit by a missile and had an engine fire. It was reported that a missile struck the airplane's rear engine. The ensuing crash killed all 41 persons on board. While this incident has never been confirmed as a MANPADS attack by conclusive investigative evidence, the circumstances lend considerable credibility to the conclusion that this aircraft was hit by a surface-to-air missile, and therefore this crash is widely regarded as a probable but unconfirmed MANPADS attack.

The most recent MANPADS incident involving a passenger jet was the November 28, 2002, attempted shootdown of an Israeli-registered Boeing 757 aircraft operated by Arkia Israeli Airlines. Two SA-7 missiles were fired at the airplane while it was departing from Mombasa, Kenya, but both missiles missed. While the threat of shoulder-fired missiles has long been recognized by aviation security experts, this incident focused the attention of many in the U.S. Congress and the Bush Administration on this threat and options to mitigate it. Unlike the prior attacks on jet airliners that occurred in war-torn areas and conflict zones, the Mombasa attack was clearly a politically motivated attack, believed to have been carried out by terrorists with links to al Qaeda.[33] That fact, coupled with already heightened concerns over aviation security in the aftermath of the September 11, 2001, terrorist attacks, elevated policy concerns over the shoulder-fired missile threat to commercial airliners within the United States as well as overseas. The issue has since been a major area of focus for homeland security policy considerations.

Amid this heightened concern over the MANPADS threat to commercial aircraft, a DHL cargo airplane was struck by a missile on November 22, 2003, while departing Baghdad International Airport in Iraq. The aircraft's left wing was struck outboard from the engine. Damage from the missile severed the airplane's hydraulic lines. However, the flight crew was able to return to the airport and land by applying differential thrust on the two engines to maneuver the airplane and operating manual cranks to lower the landing gear. The aircraft, an Airbus A300-B4, departed the runway on landing causing additional damage, including extensive engine damage from ingesting sand and debris.[34] While no one was killed or injured, the airplane was determined to be a total loss.

In addition to these large western-built jet airliners that have come under attack, two Soviet-made Tupolev passenger jets were reportedly shot down by shoulder-fired missiles in two separate incidents, one on September 21, 1993, and the other on the following day, September 22, 1993. Both incidents involved aircraft operated by Transair Georgia and occurred in the Georgian city of Sukhumi during a period of intense fighting between Abkhazian separatists and ethnic Georgians. In the September 21, 1993, attack, the Tupolev Tu-134A airplane—which is similar in design to a DC-9—reportedly crashed into the Black Sea while on its final approach to the Sukhumi airport killing all 27 on board. In the September 22, 1993, the aircraft—a Tupolev Tu-154B, which is similar to a Boeing 727—was reported to have been shot down by a shoulder-fired missile while taking off from the same airport. In that incident, it was reported that 106 of the 132 on board were killed.

Although only a relatively small number of large transport aircraft are believed to have come under attack from MANPADS over the past 30 years, policymakers and aviation security experts still consider the risk of a future MANPADS attack against a large commercial aircraft to be quite significant, not only because the terrorist threat of such an attack exists and is perceived to be growing and airliners remain quite vulnerable because of their inherent operational and design characteristics, but also because of the potentially high severity of consequence assigned to scenarios involving missile attacks against commercial airliners as illustrated by the accounts of the two reported attacks in Soviet Georgia. While these two incidents occurred in the context of a brutal civil conflict, if a similar scenario were to occur in the context of the current threat of global terrorism, it could have the same devastating consequences in terms of loss of life and destruction of aircraft, but additionally such an event could have significant implications to both the United States and worldwide airline industry and the broader global economy.

ASSESSING THE POTENTIAL CONSEQUENCES OF A STANDOFF ATTACK

It has been estimated that the direct economic cost of a catastrophic loss of an airplane from a MANPADS strike or an attack using some other standoff weapon would range somewhere from about $500 million to $1 billion per aircraft, depending on the size of aircraft and the number of passengers lost in such an attack. Beyond these direct costs associated with the actual destruction of property and loss of life, an attack could have a considerable impact on the airline industry and the broader economy. However, the scope and duration of such an impact is difficult to gauge, and it is extremely difficult to provide a monetary estimate of the economic impact from such an attack.

Possible responses to an aircraft shooting could be to cancel certain flights, shut down certain airports, or shut down the NAS entirely. For example, if a shootdown of an airplane occurred at an overseas destination, policymakers in the United States may decide to cancel flights to and from that destination until security could be adequately improved or the threat conditions diminished. The FAA has taken such action in the case of Somalia where it has imposed restrictions against flights below 20,000 feet in Somali airspace because of the threat posed by standoff weapons attacks following multiple incidents in Mogadishu, Somalia.[35] However, if an aircraft shooting incident—whether successful or not—were to occur within the United States, policymakers may face a difficult decision whether to close the airport where the incident occurred, close certain airports (such as the largest U.S. airports), or shut down the NAS in its entirety, as was done in response to the terrorist attacks on September 11, 2001. While there are numerous possible scenarios for how the United States may respond to an attack, with regard to shutting down the entire airspace system, an analysis by the RAND Corporation in 2005 concluded that the cost to the airline industry of doing so would be about $460 million to $490 million per day, based on a combination of lost profits and unavoidable expenditures incurred by the airlines during the shutdown period.[36]

In addition to any losses realized by the airlines as the result of a temporary shutdown, it can be anticipated that the airlines would experience a subsequent period of reduced passenger loads and could also face significantly higher insurance premiums. Based on passenger load reductions following the 9/11 attacks, the RAND Corporation estimated that a week-long shutdown would lead to a 10–15% reduction in passenger loads for the subsequent two weeks. In the aftermath of the 9/11 attacks, passenger loads were still 8% lower one year later. Based on these observations, the RAND Corporation estimated that taking steps to avoid an attack that would seriously affect airline passengers' confidence for six months would have a value of $12 billion, while that value would increase to $50 billion if the impact on passengers' confidence were expected to last for a year and a half.[37] A study carried out by the University of Southern California's Center for Risk and Economic Analysis of Terrorist Events (CREATE) was predicated on projected economic losses from a MANPADS attack against civilian airliners in the United States of either $50 billion or $100 billion, but the researchers went on to conclude that economic losses stemming from a coordinated, multiple attack scenario could be as great as $250 billion.[38] Other studies have placed the total economic impact from an attack to be somewhere between $40 billion and $400 billion. While these figures are highly speculative, few experts would disagree that the likely impact on the airline industry and the broader economy from a successful standoff weapons attack against a commercial airliner in the United States would run into tens of billions of dollars. The psychological impact of a standoff attack against an airliner, even an unsuccessful one, could have lasting consequences on individuals' decisions to fly in the future.[39] This could potentially cause a long-lasting and significant economic hardship on the airline industry that could spread more broadly to other industries including, in particular, the travel and tourism industry and the aerospace industry. Effects on the broader economy are widely acknowledged and could be substantial but are even more speculative.

Strategies for responding in the event of an attack, reconstituting civil aviation infrastructure and operations in the United States following a possible attack, and restoring public confidence in aviation security following a successful standoff attack, or even an unsuccessful attempt, however, have not been a particular focus of U.S. policy and strategy to date. Considering the potential severity of consequences stemming from such an event, this may be a particular issue for future policy debate and strategic planning. Issues such as whether and to what extent the NAS would be shut down or transferred to military control following such an event and what specific actions would be taken to allow flight operations to resume, restoring air travel and air commerce following an attack, have not been fully addressed in open policy debate. The adequacy of existing strategies and plans is therefore largely unknown, but is critically important to the aviation industry.

Policies and strategies adopted by the U.S. government to date have principally focused instead on preventing a standoff attack against aviation assets through a variety of approaches including nonproliferation initiatives, counterterrorism strategies, and some limited efforts at improved aviation security. Further, initiatives to mitigate the outcome or severity of consequences of an attack using various countermeasures are being pursued through research and development efforts aimed largely at adopting existing and emerging aircraft-based and ground-based military countermeasures technologies for application in the civil aviation domain. These approaches are discussed in detail below.

U.S. POLICY AND STRATEGIC APPROACHES

Most aviation security and counterterrorism experts believe that no single solution exists to effectively mitigate the threat to airliners posed by the wide assortment of standoff weapons that are available to terrorist groups. Instead, most generally agree that a risk-based, layered approach involving an assortment of options for preventing terrorist acquisition of these weapons, disrupting terrorists activities during their planning and preparation for carrying out a standoff attack, reducing the risk of such an attack through enhanced airport and flight operational security measures, and exploring ways to mitigate the likelihood or severity of such an attack offers the best opportunity to mitigate the risk to the flying public posed by MANPADS and other standoff weapons to acceptable levels. Contrary to some popularly held misconceptions, the research, development, and testing of aircraft-based countermeasures to spoof IR-guided MANPADS is not the only course of action being pursued by the U.S. government, although it has been the most widely discussed and debated. While this initiative is a high-profile and technically complex program, this is only one element of a broader, more comprehensive strategy for mitigating the terrorist threat posed by various standoff weapons capable of causing mass casualties and significant economic damage if used in a terrorist attack against aviation.

Developing a multilayered approach to protecting passenger airliners and other aviation assets from potential terrorist shootings and stopping the proliferation of shoulder-fired missiles and other standoff weapons to state sponsors of terrorism and nonstate groups throughout the world has been an ongoing initiative widely supported throughout the U.S. federal government, and reflected in statutes enacted, policies adopted, and strategies pursued since the 9/11 terrorist attacks. As part of this policy approach, however, particular attention has been given to the threat posed by IR-guided shoulder-fired missiles. The U.S. strategy for addressing the threat is consistent with a multilayered approach to mitigating risk, as shown in Figure 10.3. The various elements of this multilayered strategy approach are discussed in further detail below.

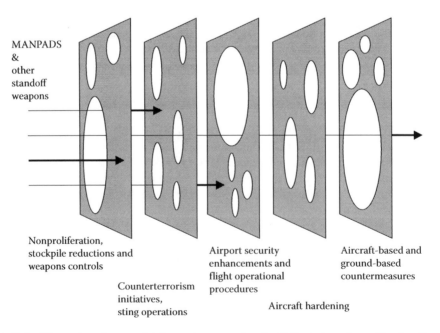

MANPADS & other standoff weapons

Nonproliferation, stockpile reductions and weapons controls

Counterterrorism initiatives, sting operations

Airport security enhancements and flight operational procedures

Aircraft hardening

Aircraft-based and ground-based countermeasures

FIGURE 10.3 The various layers of defense that comprise the U.S. strategy for mitigating the risks of standoff attacks against civil aircraft.

NONPROLIFERATION AND WEAPONS REDUCTION INITIATIVES

Since the 9/11 hijackings and the failed attempt to down the Israeli charter jet in Mombasa, Kenya using shoulder-fired missiles, the United States has pursued through diplomatic channels various agreements and arrangements with other nations to limit further proliferation of standoff weapons, particularly MANPADS. Additionally, both the U.S. Department of State and the DOD have spearheaded initiatives to both prevent further weapons proliferation and reduce existing stockpiles of MANPADS and other standoff weapons that could wind up in the hands of terrorists. These efforts, however, are complicated by the fact that the legal transfer of such weapons is not governed by a formal international treaty. The Wassenaar Arrangement is the principal multinational agreement that addresses shoulder-fired missiles sales. However, provisions in that arrangement governing sales of such weapons were only formally adopted by the 33 participating countries relatively recently, in December 2000, after these weapons had already been widely proliferated for many years with few restrictions or capabilities to track their whereabouts. Faced with the looming threat posed by these weapons in the current context of the global war on terrorism, the United States and other nations have endeavored to tighten controls on sales and transfers of these types of weapons. In December 2003, the Wassenaar Arrangement adopted strengthened guidelines over the control of MANPADS stockpiles and the sale and transfer of these weapons. Additionally, in 2003, the Bush Administration was able to obtain commitments from 21 Asian and Pacific Rim countries belonging to the Asia Pacific Economic Group (APEC) to "adopt strict domestic export controls on MANPADS; secure stockpiles; regulate MANPADS production, transfer, and brokering; ban transfers to nonstate end users; and exchange information to support these efforts."[40]

Similarly, the Group of Eight (G-8) countries have given increased emphasis to multilateral efforts to reduce the proliferation of and risk from MANPADS in terrorist hands. At the 2003 G-8 summit, member countries agreed to promote adoption of Wassenaar Arrangement's strengthened MANPADS export guidelines by other countries that were not signatories to the Wassenaar Arrangement. The G-8 countries also agreed to implement the following initiatives to prevent terrorist acquisition of MANPADS:

- Providing assistance and technical expertise for the collection, secure stockpile management, and destruction of surplus MANPADS
- Adopting strict national export controls on MANPADS and MANPADS components
- Ensuring strong national regulation of MANPADS production, transfer, and brokering
- Banning transfers of MANPADS to nonstate users and limiting exports to foreign governments or authorized agents of those governments
- Exchanging information on uncooperative countries and entities
- Examining the feasibility of developing MANPADS performance or launch control features that preclude their unauthorized use
- Encouraging action in the ICAO Aviation Security (AVSEC) Working Group regarding the MANPADS threat to civil aviation

The ICAO, a United Nations Specialized Agency, has also increased efforts to limit the proliferation of MANPADS. ICAO has proposed that all 188 member countries adopt the MANPADS export guidelines set forth in the Wassenaar Arrangement and develop a standardized approach for controlling MANPADS.

In step with Bush Administration initiatives, Congress included a provision in the IRTPA of 2004 (P.L. 108-458) directing the President to urgently pursue international treaties to limit the availability, transfer, and proliferation of MANPADS worldwide. The Act further directs the President to continue to pursue international arrangements for the destruction of excess, obsolete, and illicit MANPADS stockpiles worldwide. The Act also requires the Secretary of State to provide the Congress with annual briefings on the status of these efforts.

The U.S. State Department has engaged in a number of bilateral and multilateral initiatives to reduce the number of shoulder-fired SAMs that could conceivably fall into the hands of terrorists.[41] Through its Small Arms/Light Weapons Destruction Program, the State Department is working with countries and regions where there is a combination of excess MANPADS and other high-caliber standoff weapons, poor weapons inventory control, and a risk of proliferation to terrorists and insurgent groups. The State Department has assisted several countries account for and destroy surplus weapons and develop adequate security and accountability measures for those weapons that they retain in their inventories.

Considerable progress on these initiatives has been reported over the last few years. Notably, the United States and Russia, the largest producers of MANPADS, have agreed to facilitate destruction of obsolete MANPADS and engage in continued cooperative efforts to reduce further proliferation of these weapons.[42] The United States has also worked with its NATO partners to reduce MANPADS stockpiles. On February 18, 2005, the NATO Partnership for Peace Trust Fund Project was established to help the Ukraine destroy its stockpiles of excess munitions, including MANPADS. Other countries, such as Serbia, Bosnia-Herzegovina, Cambodia, Nicaragua, and Liberia have pledged to destroy excess MANPADS in their possession, and State Department tracking of these initiatives suggests that considerable progress is being made.

Since 2001, the United States has spent more than $10 million annually supporting weapons reduction initiatives in 25 countries in Asia, Africa, South America, the Middle East, and in several former Soviet block countries. The State Department has reported that, as of July 2007, a total of more than 21,000 MANPADS had been destroyed worldwide along with more than one million small arms/light weapons and 90 million pieces of assorted ammunition as a result of these U.S.-supported initiatives.[43] When countries have balked at implementing their pledges, economic and diplomatic pressures have been applied. For example, in 2005, the United States threatened to withhold military aid to Nicaragua unless it destroyed approximately 1000 SA-7 MANPADS.[44] Additionally, the U.S. military has initiated purchase or "buy back" programs, offering monetary incentives for MANPADS turned over to authorities in Iraq and Afghanistan, thereby reducing their availability to insurgents and terrorist groups.

Despite the success of these programs, the U.S. GAO, in an audit conducted in 2004, found that the State Department needed to implement a more formalized strategy for working within the context of multilateral forums to monitor the efforts of other countries in fulfilling their commitments to reduce MANPADS proliferation.[45] The GAO study also found that the DOD lacked adequate processes to track the proliferation of Stinger missiles sold overseas, and recommended that a DOD-wide database be established and standardized procedures be implemented for tracking and inspecting the worldwide Stinger inventory. Efforts are underway to implement these recommendations, and Congress has looked favorably on and has provided increased funding to expand ongoing State Department programs to control proliferation of MANPADS and small arms and reduce stockpiles of these weapons worldwide.

In addition to nonproliferation initiatives and efforts to reduce existing weapons stockpiles, design features for standoff weapon systems could implement various safeguards to prevent unauthorized use. Permissive action links (PALs)—microchip-based cryptographic "trigger locks"—are one example of a technology that could be incorporated in future shoulder-fired missile designs and may be considered as retrofit options for some existing systems. Some in Congress have shown interest in exploring the use of PALs for Stinger MANPADS. However, a lack of implementation suggests that there may be some resistance on the part of the Army, which may be concerned that installing PALs could complicate legitimate weapons use and drive up systems costs. In any case, technologies to prevent unauthorized weapons use are not likely to have near-term impacts on reducing the standoff weapons threat to civil aviation, given that existing weapons without such safeguards are still widely proliferated.

COUNTERTERRORISM STRATEGIES AND TACTICS

Besides limiting the spread or proliferation of standoff weapons systems, reducing stockpiles of these weapons, and making them harder for insurgents and terrorists to obtain and use, counterterrorism operations can serve a critical role in uncovering terrorist plots to carry out standoff weapons attacks and preemptively preventing terrorists from either acquiring or using these kinds of weapons in such an attack. Counterterrorism approaches may include infiltrating the black market, organized crime syndicates, or terrorist groups, or setting up "sting" operations to target and disrupt illegal sales and transfers of such weapons.

In the current context of combatting global terrorism, there have been a number of criminal investigations and sting operations that have unveiled black market and organized crime networks willing to arrange for the illegal import and sale of MANPADS and other standoff weapons that could potentially be used to attack civilian aircraft within the United States. Of particular note, an FBI-led sting investigation that began in 2001 and culminated in August 2003—which was carried out in cooperation with the Russian Federal Security Service (FSB)—nabbed three individuals who aided in arranging for the illegal sale and import to the United States of shoulder-fired missiles from Russia. The arms dealer at the center of the investigation, Hemant Lakhani, was convicted of arranging an initial deal to pay Russian agents $70,000 for one SA-18 for delivery to a cooperating witness in the United States. He was led to believe that this was a sample shipment, and a much larger order for 50 missiles would be placed in the future if he was able to successfully broker the deal and deliver the sample weapon as promised. He arranged to have the sample weapon—which was actually an inert unit supplied by Russian agents—shipped to the United States under a manifest listing it as medical equipment. Lakhani, who expressed praise for bin Laden and the 9/11 attacks, was told that the weapon was being acquired to be used in an attack against a commercial airliner.[46]

Another sting operation, during the summer of 2004, nabbed two leaders of an Albany, NY mosque, one of whom was suspected of having ties to terrorist camps in Iraq, for attempting to launder money for a cooperating individual posing as a Pakistani arms dealer.[47] The two were told that the money was obtained from the sale of a RPG that was to be used to attack a Pakistani ambassador at the Pakistani consulate near the United Nations building in New York City. In another counterterrorism operation in 2004, a group of individuals in the United States connected with the Tamil Tigers (Liberation Tigers of Tamil Eclam or LTTE), a designated terrorist organization based in northern Sri Lanka, were arrested on allegations that they sought to acquire SA-18 shoulder-fired missiles, truck-mounted missile launchers, automatic rifles, and other assorted weapons to support the Tamil Tigers in their escalating conflict with the Sri Lankan military.[48] Also, in 2005, as part of a larger investigation of illegal smuggling, drug trafficking, and counterfeiting called "Operation Smoking Dragon," indictments were brought against two individuals for arranging to illegally import several Chinese-made QW-2 shoulder-fired missiles from Asia. According to the DOJ, the individuals planned to bribe customs officials in other countries to make the deal seem as if it was a legal arms transfer from one country to another, but the weapons would instead be shipped to the United States in sea-land containers under a manifest listing them as civilian equipment, such as machine components.[49] The link between weapons smuggling and other racketeering and organized crime activity unveiled in this case strongly suggests that elements of organized crime operating domestically with established international ties could facilitate terrorist access to weapons within the United States that could be used in a standoff attack against civilian aircraft. This risk highlights a continued need for counterterrorism initiatives to detect and deter attempts by terrorist groups to acquire standoff weapons. In recognition of these concerns, counterterrorism initiatives are likely to remain a key element of U.S. policy and strategy for preventing a terrorist attack of this kind.

AIRPORT SECURITY MEASURES

While a variety of airport security measures can be implemented to mitigate the risks posed by standoff weapons acquired by terrorist groups that are not detected by counterterrorism efforts, these initiatives are likely to be limited in their effectiveness, particularly against MANPADS whose effective range allow for attacks to be launched many miles away from an airport. A variety of airport security enhancements are being implemented as part of the overall U.S. strategy for mitigating the standoff weapons threat to civil aviation. One of the most expedient measures to mitigate the risk of standoff weapons is to heighten security, surveillance, and patrols in the vicinity of airports served by air carriers. The difficulty with implementing these security measures is that the approach and departure corridors where aircraft operate within range of MANPADS extend for several miles beyond airport perimeters. Therefore, while heightening security in the immediate vicinity of an airport may reduce the threat from some short-range standoff weapons, these measures cannot effectively mitigate the threat from MANPADS during the entire portion of flight while airliners are vulnerable to attack.

Nonetheless, using threat and vulnerability assessments, airport and airspace managers can work with security forces to determine those locations beyond the airport perimeter that have high threat potential and where aircraft are most vulnerable to attack. Using this information, security forces can concentrate patrols and surveillance in these high-risk areas. Airport security managers will likely need to work closely with local law enforcement to coordinate efforts for patrolling these high-risk areas. The IRTPA of 2004 (P.L. 108-458) formally required the DHS to assess the vulnerability of aircraft to MANPADS attacks and develop plans for securing airports and aircraft from this threat. The DHS has completed vulnerability assessments of major U.S. airports and has worked with foreign countries to assess vulnerabilities of major international airports serviced by U.S. airlines. Based on these assessments, security forces and local law enforcement can step up patrols and increase surveillance in those areas around airports and under flight corridors considered to be highly vulnerable sites from which a standoff attack could be launched. In addition to security and policing efforts around airports, public education and "neighborhood watch"-type programs in areas around airports and other locations regarded as high-risk areas for aircraft shootings may be effective tools for mitigating the threat. The Air Force has instituted a program of this type, called the "Eagle Eye Program" that might serve as a model for broader application, perhaps to train airport workers or civilians living near airports to recognize potential terrorist activity and how to effectively report their observations to authorities.[50]

In addition to these ground-based security and surveillance initiatives put in place around airports, aerial patrols using sensor and imaging technology, such as forward-looking infrared (FLIR), may also be an effective tool for detecting terrorists lurking underneath flight paths. However, use of aerial patrols may significantly impact normal flight schedules and operations, particularly at the nation's larger airports. While the DHS is exploring the use of unmanned aircraft as missile countermeasure platforms to provide protection in terminal airspace around major airports, an initiative discussed in further detail below, unmanned aircraft may also be well suited as sensor platforms for surveilling wide areas around airports and along low-altitude flight corridors to detect potential threats. Nonetheless, the size of area to be surveilled and the limited availability of human resources to respond to and investigate potential threats detected will likely be significant limiting factors in effectively mitigating the threat of standoff weapons, particularly MANPADS, in the airport and terminal airspace environment. For this reason, a variety of aircraft-based and ground-based countermeasures are being explored as options to specifically address the threats posed by IR-guided MANPADS. Additionally, modifications to flight operational procedures to reduce the vulnerability of airliners to standoff attacks may provide additional options for reducing the risks to civil aviation posed by these weapons.

FLIGHT OPERATIONAL PROCEDURES

Another option to reduce the vulnerability to standoff weapons attacks may be to alter air traffic and flight operational procedures to minimize the amount of time airliners are vulnerable to shoulder-fired missile launches and to make flight patterns less predictable. Current arrival procedures rely on gradual descents along well-defined and publicly known approach courses that place airplanes within range of shoulder-fired missiles as far away as 50 miles from the airport.[51] Similarly, departing aircraft with heavy fuel loads operating at high engine power, usually along predefined and published departure routes, may be particularly vulnerable and can be targeted up to 30 miles away or more from the airport before they climb above the effective range of MANPADS.[52]

Military aircraft often use spiral descents from high altitude directly above the airfield when operating in hostile areas to limit their exposure to hostile fire. Using spiral descents may be a limited option for mitigating the terrorist threat from MANPADS around civilian airports. Using these maneuvers could limit approach and descent patterns to a smaller perimeter around the airfield where security patrols may be able to somewhat more effectively deter terrorist attacks. While spiral approaches may be implemented on a limited basis, for example in international high-risk areas, wide-scale use of spiral patterns at domestic airports would likely require extensive restructuring of airspace and air traffic procedures. This technique may present safety concerns by greatly increasing air traffic controller workload and requiring pilots to make potentially difficult turning maneuvers at low altitude. The use of spiral patterns could also reduce passenger comfort and confidence in flight safety. Also, this technique would not mitigate the risk to departing aircraft, which are generally considered to be the most vulnerable to missile attacks.

Another technique used by military aircraft, particularly fighter jets, to reduce vulnerability on departure is to make steep, rapid climb-outs above the effective range of surface-to-air missiles over a short distance. Like spiral descents, such a technique has limited application for civilian jet airliners. A typical climb gradient for these aircraft is between 400–500 feet per mile, which means that they remain in range of shoulder-fired missiles for about 40–50 miles after departure. Even if an airplane were to double its climb rate, which would probably be close to the maximum practically achievable climb rate for most jet airliners, the distance traveled before safely climbing above the range of shoulder-fired missiles would still be 20 miles or more. Climbing out at such a steep rate could pose a risk to the aircraft since it may not provide an adequate margin of safety if an engine were to fail during climb-out. Also, such steep climb angles would likely be perceived as objectionable by many passengers.

Another option that may be considered is to vary approach and departure patterns. Regularly varying approach and departure patterns in nonpredicable ways may make it more difficult for terrorists to set up a shoulder-fired missile under a known flight corridor and may increase the likelihood that they would be detected by ground surveillance, local law enforcement, or civilians reporting suspicious activities while trying to locate a suitable launch site. One challenge to implementing this technique is that aviation radio frequencies are not protected, and terrorists might gather intelligence regarding changing flight patterns. Also, flight tracking data are available in near-real-time from Internet sources and may be exploited by terrorists to gain information about aircraft position and flight track. Nonetheless, this approach could be a deterrent by making overflights of particular locations less predictable. Limitations to this approach include disruption of normal air traffic flow, which may result in delays, increased air traffic controller workload, and possible interference with noise mitigation procedures. Varying air traffic patterns may nonetheless be a viable mitigation technique, particularly at airports with low to moderate traffic and for approach and departure patterns that overfly sparsely populated areas. Also, maximizing the use of over-water approach and departure procedures, when available, coupled with measures to limit or restrict access to and increase patrols of waters under these flight paths has also been suggested as a mitigation alternative.[53]

Other suggested changes to air traffic procedures include the increased use of nighttime flights and minimal use of aircraft lighting. However, this approach is likely to be opposed by the airlines and passengers since there is little demand for night flights in many domestic markets. Furthermore, minimizing the use of aircraft lighting raises safety concerns for aircraft collision avoidance. While the airspace system within the United States includes good radar coverage in the vicinity of airports and airliners are required to have collision avoidance systems, the last line of protection against midair collisions is the flight crew's ability to see and avoid other aircraft. Therefore, increased use of night flights and minimizing aircraft lighting is not thought to be a particularly viable mitigation option.

Additionally, flight restrictions and other operational limitations may be imposed to reduce the risk to U.S.-registered aircraft operating in hostile territories and other areas where a high risk or clear and present danger of aircraft shootings is known to exist. For example, on April 5, 2007, the FAA imposed restrictions against flight operations below 20,000 feet (flight level FL200) within the territory and airspace of Somalia.[54] This action was taken in response to two suspected aircraft shooting incidents near Mogadishu, Somalia in March 2007. In the first incident, on March 9, 2007, an Ilyushin IL-76 large four-engine transport jet supporting deployment of Ugandan peace-keeping forces was stuck, probably by an RPG, and heavily damaged but landed with no serious injuries or loss of life. Then, on March 23, 2007, another IL-76—one that had dropped off engineers and parts to repair the airplane damaged in the previous incident—crashed on takeoff, possibly the result of either an RPG or possibly a MANPADS strike. The FAA determined, based on these attacks, that it is neither safe nor in the national security interests of the United States for U.S.-registered aircraft and operators to overfly Somalia at altitudes where they could be vulnerable to shootings from MANPADS and other standoff weapons.

While such restrictions could protect aircraft by eliminating or reducing exposure to areas where a clear and present danger of aircraft shootings exists, applying such measures on a broad scale could significantly impact air commerce and the operations of certain U.S. companies, such as air cargo operators that support peace-keeping and reconstruction efforts in hostile areas. For such operators, in addition to applying some of the above-mentioned flight operational procedures and practices to reduce the vulnerability to attack, options to install aircraft-based countermeasures to protect against IR-guided missiles in particular may be considered. The use of these systems, now deployed on several military transport aircraft, is also being explored by U.S. policymakers in terms of their potential application for protecting passenger airliners operating on both international and domestic routes. Some aircraft-based IR-countermeasure systems have received FAA approval for use on civilian aircraft and thus could be installed on U.S. flag aircraft, including aircraft operating in high-threat areas. While the FAA has certified a limited number of such systems as being safe for civilian use, the effectiveness, reliability, acquisition costs and operational benefits of deploying such systems on civilian airliners is currently a matter of considerable interest for the DHS and Congress.

AIRCRAFT-BASED PROTECTIONS AND COUNTERMEASURES

While military transport aircraft employ a variety of countermeasures to mitigate the threat posed by IR-guided missiles, including smaller shoulder-fired missiles, the use of IR-countermeasures on commercial aircraft has been quite limited, and generally speaking, commercial passenger airliners are not equipped with such systems. A notable exception is in Israel, where a number of El Al aircraft were initially equipped with deployable flares in 2004, but are now being fitted with laser-based IR countermeasure systems.[55] In the United States, however, flares have generally been regarded as being too hazardous for airline operations, and initiatives have focused instead on exploring the feasibility of adapting military lamp-based and laser-based IR countermeasures for use on commercial airliners. Proposals to deploy various aircraft-based countermeasures on civilian airliners, however, have raised considerable policy debate in the United States regarding the effectiveness of such an approach, the cost deploying and sustaining such systems, their potential impact on flight safety, possible environmental constraints on their use, and the fear that their deployment may promote perceptions that flying is not safe.

Besides flares, lamp-based IR countermeasure systems have been in use for about three decades and operate by broadcasting radiant energy in the IR spectrum to jam or confuse a MANPADS' IR guidance system. Used extensively on military helicopters and transport aircraft over the past 25 years, this technology has also had some limited use in countermeasure systems deployed on civilian aircraft. For example, the FAA-certified MATADOR™ IRCM system, developed by BAE Systems, has been installed on a wide variety of transport jet aircraft, including numerous VIP and head-of-state aircraft throughout the world. Gulfstream Aerospace Corporation offers the system as a tailcone-mounted option or retrofit for some of its high-end business jets.[56] Given recent attention to the MANPADS threat to civil aircraft, particularly those operating in hostile or less secure areas of the world, interest in such systems has increased considerably in recent years, despite the system's cost and weight.[57] A potential low-cost, light-weight alternative, called the Tactical Integrated Illumination Countermeasure (TIICM) is currently being developed and tested by Flight Safety Technologies, Inc. The TIICM system employs an array of Halogen-Sapphire heat lamps that replace an aircraft's anticollision lights. Illumination of these lamps is sequenced to create an IR pattern mimicking a turning aircraft, causing a heat-seeking missile to veer off target. Both the DHS and the Air Force have expressed an interest in this technology, which may be able to provide always-on protection to a wide range of aircraft for a fraction of the cost of other countermeasure systems currently in operational use and under development.

Presently, however, new technological advances in laser-based directed infrared countermeasure (DIRCM) systems, have been the central focus of U.S. policy and strategy for protecting large military transport aircraft as well as exploring the feasibility, cost, and potential benefits of adapting such systems for use on civilian passenger aircraft. Unlike flares and lamp-based systems that are designed to create a broad field of IR energy to confuse the missile seeker and can be used either preemptively or reactively in coordination with a missile approach warning system (MAWS) capable of detecting MANPADS launches, DIRCM systems are always used in response to a suspected launch signaled by their MAWS component. Consequently, MAWS performance in detecting and pinpointing the flight path of a suspected incoming missile is a critical factor in system performance. Figure 10.4 illustrates how laser-based DIRCM systems equipped with MAWS capability can detect, declare, track, and jam or confuse the guidance system of an inbound MANPADS missile. With recent advances in MAWS detection and tracking capabilities combined with the capability of the laser-based DIRCM to quickly acquire and direct laser energy at the missile seeker, this has proven to be quite a promising technology for both military and civilian aircraft application. In the civilian environment, however, false alarms in the MAWS component remain a considerable concern because, unlike in the military domain where aircraft are expected to come under fire, any MAWS alarms or activations of a DIRCM system on a civilian aircraft will likely involve activation of various security measures to protect other aircraft while the alert is investigated. In extreme

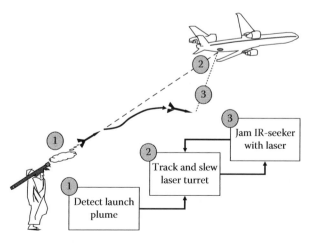

FIGURE 10.4 The detection, tracking, and jamming of an IR-guided MANPADS using a system consisting of a MAWS integrated with an aircraft-based laser-based DIRCM system.

circumstances, this could involve ground stoppages and aircraft diversions which could result in considerable costs to the airlines, particularly if large numbers of false alarms were generated by these systems. In addition to these considerations, a variety of factors including cost, weight, reliability, and system effectiveness remain key factors in determining whether DIRCM systems can or should be adapted for use on civilian jets, particularly passenger airliners.

Homeland Security Counter-MANPADS Systems Development and Testing

In 2003, during the 108th Congress, largely in response to the attempted shooting of the Israeli charter Boeing 757 in Mombasa, Kenya, Representative Steve Israel and Senator Barbara Boxer introduced broad-sweeping legislation that sought to require all airliners to be equipped with missile defense systems.[58] While Congress did not act upon these legislative proposals, it did agree to language included in a conference report accompanying the Emergency Wartime Supplemental Appropriations Act of 2003 (P.L. 108-11; H. Rept. 108-76) directing the DHS Under Secretary for S&T to prepare a program plan for developing such missile protection systems for commercial aircraft. This program, which became widely known as the DHS Counter-MANPADS or C-MANPADS program, was funded in subsequent appropriations legislation and involved a comprehensive research, development, and testing program run by the C-MANPADS Special Program Office (SPO) within the DHS S&T Directorate. The program was specifically focused on adapting military-based aircraft IR countermeasure systems for use on large civilian transport jets. The DHS established the system development program in a manner that would apply existing technologies from the military environment to the commercial airline environment rather than developing new technologies thereby leveraging military investment and experience in C-MANPADS technology in order to identify a technical solution that could be deployed in the civil aviation environment in a much faster time frame, assuming that such a system could be tailored to meet the operational needs and requirements of civilian flight operations.

Phase I of the DHS C-MANPADS program, which was completed in July 2004, consisted of an intensive 6-month effort to assess proposed solutions based on threat mitigation capabilities, system costs, airframe and avionics integration, and FAA certification issues. Three contractor teams led by Northrop Grumman, BAE Systems, and United Airlines were awarded $2 million each to develop detailed systems descriptions and analysis of economic, manufacturing, maintenance, systems safety, and operational effectiveness issues for applying their systems in the commercial aircraft environment.

Following a DHS-led review of each contractor team's Phase I work and their proposals for Phase II, on August 25, 2004, DHS awarded $45 million to BAE Systems and Northrop Grumman to carry out Phase II of development.[59] Both BAE Systems and Northrop Grumman have also developed DIRCM systems for the U.S. military giving them particular expertise in developing this technology. Critics, however, have argued that by selecting two DIRCM systems for continued development under this program, the DHS was essentially offering the airlines the potential of "two flavors of vanilla,"[60] meaning that the focus of the technology development was too narrowly focused on this particular technology at the potential cost of failing to adequately consider other countermeasures options for further development and testing. The United Airlines-led team, which was not selected for Phase II, had instead proposed a system that would have used expendable flare decoys to divert incoming missiles.[61] According to DHS officials, two primary reasons why the United Airlines-led team was not selected were that there were safety issues on the flight line for the expendable pyrotechnic decoys and that there were issues with the system concerning false alarms.[62]

Phase II of the C-MANPADS program consisted of an 18-month prototype development and evaluation based on existing military technology adapted for civilian use. Both contractors developed prototype systems that rely on laser-based DIRCM systems to protect commercial aircraft from IR-guided MANPADS attacks. The BAE Systems team, which also included American Airlines and Honeywell, and the Northrop Grumman team, which included Federal Express and Northwest Airlines, developed prototypes that were tested on commercial aircraft. The Northrop Grumman prototype system, called Guardian, and the BAE Systems prototype, dubbed JetEye, have both undergone extensive airborne testing on wide-body airliners to determine their effectiveness and have received FAA certification, indicating that they are safe for operational flying. Although, it will ultimately be up to the DHS, not the FAA, to make a determination regarding the system performance and potential security benefit of deploying these systems on civilian passenger jets.

A third phase of the DHS C-MANPADS program for commercial aircraft was funded in FY2006 appropriations with the intent of gaining further experience installing and testing the systems on a broader array of commercial aircraft types and improve the robustness of the systems under operational conditions encountered in the commercial aviation environment. This phase also included the delivery and installation of preproduction equipment on commercially operated aircraft by U.S. cargo carriers similar to those aircraft designated for use in the DOD's Civil Reserve Air Fleet (CRAF). CRAF aircraft must stand ready for and engage in transporting U.S. military troops and supplies under contract agreements that the airlines enter into with the DOD and often fly into hostile areas like Iraq and Afghanistan.

To foster competition, Phase III funding was allocated to both Northrop Grumman and BAE Systems to install test systems on a variety of aircraft types and obtain certification for use on additional aircraft types. The components of Phase III included live-fire testing, improving system reliability to meet performance specifications for commercial airline applications, adding ground notification alerting capabilities, and developing security features to safeguard sensitive military technology in units installed on aircraft that travel internationally or are exported to foreign countries.

Policy Considerations for Aircraft-Based Countermeasures Deployment

Besides identifying which countermeasure systems may be best suited for use in airline operations, a key policy question is whether these aircraft-based countermeasures, if determined to be effective and cost beneficial, should be widely deployed among passenger aircraft, or should be deployed in more limited quantities to only those aircraft believed to be at greatest risk. For example, several proposals have sought to equip a limited number of commercial airliners that are part of the military's CRAF used for transporting troops and supplies to hostile areas like Iraq. Other proposals have been offered to equip only those aircraft flying overseas, or more specifically those flying to high-risk destinations; however, the airlines have voiced concerns that targeted deployment of countermeasure systems in this fashion could limit their ability to interchange aircraft equipment for scheduling or maintenance needs if functioning C-MANPADS systems were to be required for dispatching aircraft to certain destinations.

According to FAA projections of the U.S. commercial aviation turbojet fleet, more than 6000 U.S.-registered passenger jet aircraft will be in service in 2010, including more than 3500 large narrow-body airplanes, more than 600 large wide bodies, and almost 2000 regional jets. Additionally, there will be about 1000 large all-cargo jets deployed in U.S. air carrier operations. Estimates on equipping some or all of the air carrier jet fleet with IR countermeasures vary because of assumptions regarding the type and design of system selected and the overall number to be procured. A comprehensive and widely cited analysis by the RAND Corporation found that, in addition to initial purchase and installation costs of about $11 billion, it would cost about $2.1 billion annually in terms of both direct and indirect or incidental costs to maintain and sustain aircraft-based IR countermeasures on a fleet of 6800 passenger jets over a projected 10-year system lifespan.[63] This translates to a per aircraft acquisition cost of slightly more than $1.6 million, and an annual cost per aircraft cost of about $310,000 for operations and sustainment (O&S), which amounts to about $440 per flight, assuming each aircraft makes about 700 flights annually, a typical ballpark number for the airline industry. While various estimates of the cost of acquiring and installing IR countermeasures on commercial aircraft range between $1 million and $3 million per aircraft, the DHS has set a target price of $1 million per aircraft for acquisition and installation of IR countermeasures based on purchases of such systems in 1000 unit blocks.[64]

While both acquisition and operational costs that are considerably lower than the original RAND Corporation estimates are now believed to be achievable, the O&S costs for deploying aircraft-based countermeasures on civilian airliners are nonetheless estimated to be quite substantial. While the DHS originally sought to keep O&S costs below $300 per flight, it has set a new target of $350 per flight. These relatively high annual O&S costs—estimated to be in the range of $250,000 to $300,000 per aircraft—has raised considerable concern among both commercial airplane manufacturers and airlines over the use of aircraft-based C-MANPADS systems, leading some to question whether alternative technologies or approaches should be explored in more detail.

The DHS has also set a lofty target for aircraft-based IR countermeasure system reliability that seeks to achieve a mean time before failure (MTBF) of 3000 hours or more, commensurate with heavy maintenance schedules typical in the airline industry. Military IR countermeasure systems upon which the civilian systems being tested are based on demonstrated MTBF values of the order of 300–400 hours, values not considered acceptable for deployment in airline operations, raising concern that systems reliability may have difficulty meeting expectations for deployment in a commercial air carrier environment.[65]

Another issue for installing IR countermeasures on passenger jets is the logistics of equipping the fleet and the potential indirect costs associated with taking airplanes out of service to accomplish these installations. Besides maintenance considerations, equipping with IR countermeasures could also increase the airline's operating costs by increasing aircraft weight and drag to some extent and thus increasing fuel consumption. With rising fuel prices and fuel costs making up greater portions of airline operating costs, this may become a more critical consideration with regard to potential impact on the airlines. Because cost, logistics, system performance, and derived security benefit remain considerable concerns, there has been a hesitation among policymakers to move forward with deploying aircraft-based DIRCM countermeasures on civilian airliners, despite the potential promise of this technology. The DHS C-MANPADS program has, nonetheless, served an important role in maturing this technology and adapting it for civilian use so that it is certified and ready for deployment as needed, pending specific policy decisions regarding their use. Thus far, however, it appears that these decisions would first come from U.S. government officials, as financially strapped U.S. air carriers have generally viewed the option of equipping aircraft with certified C-MANPADS systems on their own accord as being far too complex and costly.

UNMANNED ESCORTS PROVIDING IR-COUNTERMEASURE PROTECTION

Faced with the large costs and complexities of equipping large numbers of passenger jets with DIRCM systems, another concept being explored is the use of DIRCM-equipped escorts and patrol aircraft, including possibly unmanned aircraft, that can roam the skies around airports, including approach and departure paths, and provide protection against IR-guided missiles for proximate aircraft. This has sometimes been referred to as the E-DIRCM or Escort-DIRCM concept. While the concept appears to be promising, at least in theory, several operational performance and logistics issues need to be worked out before the concept can be considered viable. Some limited testing has been carried out to assess how close in proximity the escort must be to the aircraft it is protecting in order to provide sufficient protection. The results of such testing can be used to determine the number of escort aircraft that may be needed to provide protection where it is considered needed. Based on analysis and subsequent policy setting, DIRCM-equipped escorts may provide an alternative to equipping large numbers of commercial jets with DIRCM systems, by providing protection around the nation's busiest airports and other high-vulnerability locations.

In the near-term, it is most likely that any DIRCM-equipped escorts would be manned aircraft, largely because too many safety considerations still need to be worked out before unmanned aircraft can be commingled with commercial jets in busy airspace, which is where the escort concept would have the most likely benefit. Nonetheless, there appear to be some distinct advantages to using unmanned aircraft systems as DIRCM-equipped escorts in the future, primarily because many high-endurance unmanned platforms are capable of remaining on duty for long periods of time at comparatively lower costs than manned aircraft. The DHS appears to be pursuing this option under a program concept called "Project Chloe," designed to protect airspace around airports using the Global Hawk UAV platform.[66]

GROUND-BASED COUNTERMEASURES

In addition to aircraft-based C-MANPADS systems, ground-based countermeasures deployed at or near airports have also been suggested as a possible option for mitigating the threat posed by MANPADS. Ground-based missile countermeasures could potentially take many forms. For example, dispensing flares in the vicinity of airports remains an option, one that Israel used during periods of heightened tension in the 1980s. However, flammability risk, potential annoyance to airport neighbors, and the creation of a public perception that flares are needed because of a heightened threat to civil aviation security make ground-based flares, like aircraft-based flares, an unlikely choice from a policy perspective. Ground-based missile interceptors offer another option for protecting airports and airport approach and departure paths. In the past, missile interceptors have involved the use of antimissile missiles to intercept and destroy missile threats. For example, the Raytheon HUMRAAM system—which consists of an AMRAAM missile launcher mounted on a military vehicle—may be capable of intercepting MANPADS missiles and offers the flexibility of a mobile platform, which could allow for specific placement of these defenses based on specific intelligence regarding MANPADS threats or vulnerability assessments at airports. The prospect of potentially engaging and destroying a missile in congested terminal airspace near an airport and possibly over a densely populated area, however, does raise considerable concerns over risk.

More recently, technology advances in directed energy weapons have introduced the possibility that directed ground-based lasers capable of destroying launched missiles or electromagnetic pulse jammers that can confuse missile guidance systems could be deployed to intercept and jam missile guidance systems in the event of a MANPADS launch. For example, Northrop Grumman has proposed a system for deployment at airports and military airbases called HORNET, for Hazardous Ordnance Engagement Toolkit. HORNET is based on Northrop Grumman's Tactical High Energy Laser (THEL) system. The THEL system consists of a ground-based high-energy chemical laser that, unlike the DIRCM laser which just confuses the missile guidance system, is capable of destroying a launched missile. The THEL has successfully intercepted and destroyed rockets and artillery shells in tests.[67] The THEL concept has also been configured in a mobile platform, the MTHEL for mobile-THEL, in which the system components, including the laser, the tracking system, and chemical fuel for the laser are loaded and transported by a tractor-trailer truck. The HORNET concept proposed by Northrop Grumman would use the MTHEL mobile platform concept to position and reposition these defenses as needed based on runway configuration and other operational considerations. Because the HORNET and MTHEL engages and destroys the threat rather than simply confusing the guidance system, it has the potential of being effective against a broader array of standoff weapons, not just MANPADS. However, the effectiveness of these systems against various weapons is still being evaluated in live-fire testing. As previously noted, the THEL was successfully demonstrated against rockets and artillery rounds suggesting that such systems can be effectively deployed against smaller munitions of the type that might be launched by terrorists seeking to quickly launch an attack and flee. However, because the high-energy laser, like antimissile missiles, destroys its target, it too raises some concerns regarding possible damage or destruction of civilian aircraft in a friendly fire accident or potential damage and loss of life on the ground, even though these may be remote possibilities.

In addition to the ground-based high-energy laser concept, the defense industry is also exploring and promoting the potential deployment of microwave-based countermeasures. These systems consist of ground-based antennas capable of emitting a microwave pulse intended to defeat a terrorist missile by "jamming" or confusing its electronic systems. For example, Raytheon has developed a system called Vigilant Eagle which was designed as an airfield protection system for both military airbases and, potentially, civilian airports. The Vigilant Eagle system is designed specifically to defend against MANPADS by using a ground-based array of missile warning sensors to detect a MANPADS launch near an airfield coupled with a high-powered microwave (HPM) amplifier transmitter (HAT)—a billboard-sized array of microwave antennas—that directionally beams a tailored waveform at the launched missile to confuse its guidance system. Like the MTHEL system, Raytheon envisions that the Vigilant Eagle system could also be deployed as a mobile platform allowing for positioning and reconfiguration of the protection envelope to address specific threat intelligence or vulnerability assessments for an airbase or airport. In addition to these efforts, the DOD has been sponsoring research to improve the development of ground-based electro-optical sensor grids to reduce costs and improve launch detection and warning capabilities around airbases, focusing particularly on improving launch detection in cluttered urban environments. Improved sensor capabilities may benefit a wide variety of ground-based countermeasure systems including concepts like HORNET and Vigilant Eagle.

Ground-based systems offer policymakers with additional options for protecting aircraft from MANPADS threats, and potentially from threats posed by other standoff weapons. Raytheon estimates, for example, that deploying Vigilant Eagle at the 30 busiest airports in the United States, which handle about 70% of all passenger airline traffic, would cost between $1 and $2 billion, a price tag that may make such an approach less expensive than aircraft-based DIRCM systems.[68] A lingering concern with this approach, however, is that aircraft often remain vulnerable beyond the range that ground-based systems can protect them, and may be most vulnerable when operating overseas, particularly in countries and regions that do not have effective aviation security and counterterrorism measures in place. To protect aircraft operating overseas, particularly in high-risk areas, aircraft-based DIRCM may be considered in conjunction with domestic deployment of ground-based countermeasures. Current proposals, for example, seek to equip limited numbers of CRAF aircraft with DIRCM systems. However, with regard to protecting aircraft and airspace in the homeland, a variety of ground-based options in addition to E-DIRCM approaches, using either manned or unmanned aerial platforms, offer possible alternatives that policymakers may consider for protecting airliners against shoulder-fired missiles and other standoff weapons threats.

REFERENCES

1. Chow, James; James Chiesa, Paul Dreyer, Mel Eisman, Theodore W. Karasik, Joel Kvitky, Sherrill Lingel, David Ochmanek, and Chad Shirley. *Protecting Commercial Aviation against the Shoulder-Fired Missile Threat.* Santa Monica, CA: The RAND Corporation, 2005.
2. Ibid.
3. "The MANPADS Menace: Combating the Threat to Global Aviation from Man-Portable Air Defense Systems." *Fact Sheet.* Bureau of Political-Military Affairs. U.S. Department of State. September 20, 2005.
4. "Mombasa Attack Highlights Increasing MANPADs Threat," *Jane's Intelligence Review,* February 2003, p. 28; Gusinov, Timothy. "Portable Weapons May Become the Next Weapon of Choice for Terrorists," *Washington Diplomat,* January 2003, p. 2; Withington, Thomas. "Terrorism: Stung by Stingers," *Bulletin of the Atomic Scientists,* May–June 2003, p. 1.
5. Shaffer, Marvin B. "The Missile Threat to Civil Aviation," In Paul Wilkinson and Brian M. Jenkins (Eds), *Aviation Terrorism and Security,* pp. 70–82. Portland, OR: Frank Cass, 1999.
6. Ibid.
7. Schaffer, Marvin B. "Concerns about Terrorists with Manportable SAMS," *RAND Corporation Reports,* October 1993, p. 2.
8. Ibid.
9. "Raytheon Electronic Systems FIM-92 Stinger Low-Altitude Surface-to-Air Missile System Family," *Jane's Defence,* October 13, 2000, p. 3.
10. Gusinov, Timothy. "Portable Weapons May Become the Next Weapon of Choice for Terrorists," *Washington Diplomat,* January 2003, p. 2.

11. Soyoung Ho. "Plane Threat," *Washington Monthly*, April 2003, p. 2; "Mombasa Attack Highlights Increasing MANPADs Threat," p. 28.

12. Organization of American States, Inter-American Committee Against Terrorism (CICTE). *MANPADS: A Threat to Civil Aviation*. Presented by the Delegation of the United States at the Third Meeting of National Points of Contact of CICTE, Washington, DC, February 16, 2005.

13. Thomas B. Hunter. "The Proliferation of MANPADS," *Jane's*, November 28, 2002, p. 1.

14. "SAMs-The New Air Security Threat," *Travel Insider*, December 12, 2002, p. 6.

15. "Shoulder-Fired Missiles Not too Hard to Find," *Associated Press*, August 17, 2003.

16. Ibid.

17. U.S. Department of State. "Department of State's MANPADS Threat Reduction Efforts."

18. See O'sullivan, T. *External Terrorist Threats to Civilian Airliners: A Summary Risk Analysis of MANPADS, Other Ballistic Weapons Risk, Future Threats, and Possible Countermeasures Policies*, Center for Risk and Economic Analysis of Terrorism Events, University of Southern California, Los Angeles, CA, April 14, 2005. CREATE Report #05-009.

19. Federal Aviation Administration. "Prohibition Against Certain Flights Within the Territory and Airspace of Somalia, Final Rule," *Federal Register, 72*(65), pp. 16710–16712, April 5, 2007.

20. Anthony R. Grieco. "Missile Warning—A Must for IRCM," Presented at *Electronic Warfare 2004*, DefenceIQ, 28–29 September 2004, London.

21. See Dave Carbaugh, John Cashman, Mike Carriker, Doug Forsythe, Tom Melody, Larry Rockliff, and William Wainwright. "Aerodynamic Principles of Large-Airplane Upsets," *FAST Special: Airbus Technical Digest*, June 1998 (Also published in Boeing Aero No. 3).

22. Robert Wall. "Research Accelerates Into Hardening Aircraft Against MANPADS Strikes," *Aviation Week & Space Technology*, August 23, 2004, p. 59.

23. See Bill Sweetman. "The Enemy down Below," *Air Transport World*, September 2003, pp. 34–36.

24. Air Line Pilots Association. *Position of the Air Line Pilots Association, Int'l on Man-Portable Air Defense Systems (MANPADS) Countermeasures*. Washington, DC: Air Line Pilots Association, Int'l, February 2006, p. 6.

25. See, for example, Phillip O'Connor. "Planes are easy targets for portable missiles," *Saint Louis Post-Dispatch*, June 1, 2003, p. A1; Association of Old Crows. "AOC Position Statement: 'Missile Defense Systems for the American Commercial Airline Fleet,'" Revised August 15, 2003, Alexandria, VA.

26. See note 23.

27. See Federal Aviation Administration.*Criminal Acts Against Civil Aviation* (1996–2000 Editions).

28. See http://aviation-safety.net/

29. See http://www.b737.org.uk/accident_reports.htm.

30. Schaffer, Marvin B. "Concerns About Terrorists With Manportable SAMS."

31. Ibid.; Bill Sweetman. "The Enemy Down Below."

32. See note 28.

33. Bill Sweetman, "The Enemy Down Below."

34. David Hughes and Michael A. Dornheim. "No Flight Controls," *Aviation Week & Space Technology*, December 8, 2003, pp. 42–43.

35. See note 19.

36. See note 1.

37. Ibid.

38. von Winterfeldt, Detlof, and O'sullivan, Terrence M. "Should We Protect Commercial Airplanes Against Surface-to-Air Missile Attacks by Terrorists? *Decision Analysis, 3*(2), 63–75, June 2006.

39. O'sullivan, T. *External Terrorist Threats to Civilian Airliners: A Summary Risk Analysis of MANPADS, Other Ballistic Weapons Risk, Future Threats, and Possible Countermeasures Policies.*

40. "New APEC Initiatives on Counterterrorism," Fact Sheet from the Office of the Press Secretary, the White House, Bangkok, Thailand, October 21, 2003.

41. See note 17.

42. Ibid.

43. U.S. Department of State. *Update on U.S. Efforts to Destroy Excess Small Arms/Light Weapons Worldwide.* Office of the Spokesman Fact Sheet, Washington, DC, July 9, 2007.

44. Pablo Bachelet. "U.S. Withholds Aid Over Missing Weapons," *Miami Herald*, March 22, 2005.

45. U.S. General Accounting Office. *Nonproliferation: Further Improvements Needed in U.S. Efforts to Counter Threats from Man-Portable Air Defense Systems*, May 2004, GAO-04-519.

46. U.S. District Court, District of New Jersey. Criminal Complaint, United States v. Hemant Lakhan, August 11, 2003.

47. U.S. Department of Justice, U.S. Attorney Glenn T. Suddaby, Northern District of New York, *Two Sentenced to Serve 15 Years in Prison for Terrorism Offense*, Albany, NY, March 8, 2007.

48. U.S. Department of Justice, U.S. Attorney Roslynn R. Mauskopf, Eastern District of New York, *Eight Defendants Arrested by the FBI and Charged With Conspiring to Provide Material Support and Resources to A Foreign Terrorist Organization and Related Offenses*, Brooklyn, NY, August 21, 2006.

49. U.S. Department of Justice, Debra Wong Yang, U.S. Attorney for the Central District of California. *Press Release: "Smoking Dragon" Undercover Investigation Results in New Indictment Alleging Scheme to Smuggle Surface-to-Air Missiles Into United States*, Los Angeles, CA, November 9, 2005.

50. 2nd Lt. Ashley Conner. "Eagle Eyes in Action," *Air Force Print News*, September 14, 2005.

51. See note 30.

52. Robert Wall and David A. Fulghum. "Israel to Protect Airliners; U.S. on the Fence," *Aviation Week & Space Technology*, December 9, 2002, p. 26.

53. See note 30.

54. Federal Aviation Administration. "Prohibition Against Certain Flights Within the Territory and Airspace of Somalia."

55. "Israeli Airliners To Replace Flares With Laser-Based Anti-Missile System," *World Tribune*, October 16, 2007.

56. GlobalSecurity.org. *AN/ALQ-204 Matador Infrared Countermeasure (IRCM)*; BAE Systems. *BAE Systems MATADOR™ Infrared System Certification a First for BAE Systems.*

57. Kim Rosenlof. "Countering Threats: Securing Business Aircraft," *Avionics Magazine*, October 1, 2005.

58. See H.R. 580 and S. 311 (108th Congress).

59. "BAE, Northrop Grumman Tapped for Counter MANPADS Development, Prototypes," *Defense Daily*, August 26, 2004.

60. Meenan, John, Executive Vice President and Chief Operating Officer, Air Transport Association, Speaking at *Commercial Aviation, The Threat from Shoulder-Fired Missiles and Potential Counter-Measures: An Update*, Washington, DC: The Heritage Foundation, December 9, 2005.

61. See note 59.

62. Ibid.

63. See note 1.

64. Phillips, Zack. "A Shot in The Dark," *Government Executive*, June 15, 2007, pp. 18–20.

65. McKenna, Ed. "Counter MANPADS Live-Fire Finale?" *Avionics Magazine*, July 2007, pp. 26–29.

66. Ibid.

67. Marc Selinger. "Laser to Target Large-Caliber Rockets for First Time, U.S. Army Says," *Aerospace Daily & Defense Report*, April 19, 2004.

68. Wagner, Breanne. "DHS Expands Search for Anti-Missile Technology," *National Defense*, March 2007.

11 Air Cargo Security

The air cargo system is a complex, multifaceted system responsible for moving a vast amount of freight, express packages, and mail carried aboard passenger and all-cargo aircraft. The air cargo system consists of a large, complex distribution network linking manufacturers and shippers to freight forwarders and then on to airport sorting and cargo handling facilities where shipments are loaded and unloaded from aircraft (Figure 11.1). Business and consumer demand for the fast and efficient shipment of goods has fueled rapid growth in the air cargo industry over the past 25 years.

In FY2006, about 10.5 million tons of freight cargo were shipped by air within the United States, and another 8.5 million tons were shipped on international flights to and from the United States on both passenger and all-cargo aircraft. In addition to this, over half a million tons of mail were carried on aircraft, roughly 460,000 tons on domestic flights and 140,000 tons on international flights to and from the United States. The weight of freight and mail carried aboard domestic and international flights between 2003 and 2006 is shown in Figure 11.2.

Since 1980, the growth in freight mileage for air cargo, measured in terms of ton-miles transported on an annual basis, has far outpaced growth in any other transportation mode.[1] It is forecast that domestic air cargo shipments, expressed in terms of revenue ton miles (RTMs), will continue their historic growth trends and increase another 58% by FY2020 compared to FY2006 levels. Internationally, cargo shipments have seen steady growth over the past few years and are anticipated to increase 135% by FY2020 compared to FY2006 levels. The volume of air cargo shipments since FY1999 and the forecast volume of air cargo through 2020 are shown in Figure 11.3.

Air cargo shipments also make up a significant percent of the total value of cargo shipments. In 2002, while air freight movements accounted for only about 0.3% of total domestic freight shipments by weight, these shipments accounted for 4.3% of the total value of freight shipped within the United States.[2] In terms of global trade, air cargo accounted for 25.3% of the value of goods shipped to and from the United States, surpassed only by maritime shipping, which accounted for 43.5% of the import/export value of cargo in 2005.[3] However, by weight, nearly 78% of imports and exports travel by water, compared to just 0.4% by air. These statistics highlight the fact that international air cargo plays a major role in the transport of high-value, time-sensitive, light-weight imports and exports. Such items include consumer electronics, electronic components for industry and manufacturing, flowers, and other high-value perishable foods and goods, to name a few examples. The speed of delivery afforded by air cargo support just-in-time demand for such goods in the global marketplace, allowing far-away manufacturing and distribution sites to rapidly deliver items to businesses and end-customers worldwide. These unique characteristic of the air cargo industry are important considerations for policymakers in addressing air cargo security requirements in a manner that will not unduly impede the flow of commerce that travels by air, particularly as the size and complexity of the air cargo system continues to grow and become more diverse.

SECURITY RISKS POSED BY AIR CARGO

Since September 11, 2001, a variety of air cargo security measures have been put in place or are under consideration. The primary purpose of these security measures is to mitigate (1) the potential risks associated with the contents of cargo placed on passenger as well as all-cargo aircraft and (2) the risks associated with individuals given a high level of access to aircraft to carry out cargo operations. While no specific attacks or terrorist plots exploiting air cargo have been publicly disclosed

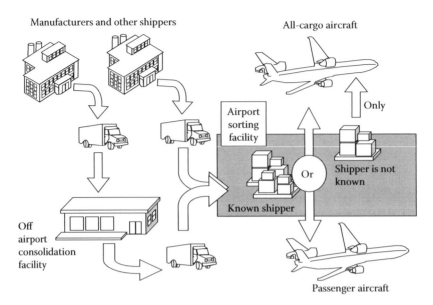

FIGURE 11.1   The air cargo system, showing the use of "known shipper" verification processes for allowing cargo to travel on passenger airliners.

since the 9/11 terrorist attacks, there is a general concern among some policymakers and aviation security experts that heightened security at airport terminals and a focus on passenger and baggage screening could lead terrorists to consider exploiting weaknesses in air cargo security as a possible means to attack aviation targets.

Air cargo has long been regarded as aviation's soft underbelly, undoubtedly a reflection of the relatively open environment that had existed until recently, in which crimes such as smuggling and theft are believed to have been widespread. Potential security risks associated with air cargo shipments and operations include the possible introduction of explosives and incendiary devices in cargo placed aboard aircraft; shipment of undeclared or undetected hazardous materials aboard aircraft; cargo crime including theft and smuggling; and aircraft hijackings and sabotage by individuals with access to aircraft. The security risks associated with air cargo are believed to be considerably different for passenger airline operations, where the greatest perceived threat is the introduction of

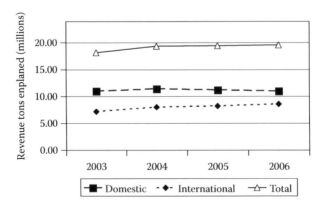

FIGURE 11.2   Total weight of freight and mail shipments carried annually on domestic and international routes (2003–2006). Data obtained from Bureau of Transportation Statistics, *Air Carrier Data*.

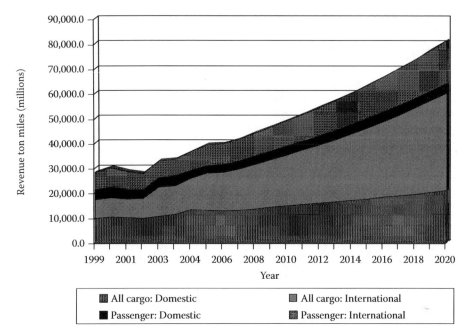

FIGURE 11.3 Historic volume (1999–2007) and projected growth (2008–2020) of air cargo RTMs flown by passenger airlines and all-cargo aircraft on domestic and international routes. *Note:* An RTM is one ton of cargo carried one air mile. Data obtained from Federal Aviation Administration, *FAA Aerospace Forecasts Fiscal Years 2005–2016, 2006–2017,* and *2007–2020.*

an explosive device through an air cargo shipment, and all-cargo operations, where the greatest perceived threat is considered to be the potential hijacking of a large all-cargo aircraft to carry out a suicide attack against a ground target. Additionally, the air cargo system may be exploited by terrorists as a means of conveyance for terrorist weapons, including weapons of mass destruction such as chemical agents, biological agents, radioactive material, or nuclear devices.

EXPLOSIVES AND INCENDIARY DEVICES

Undetected explosive or incendiary devices placed in air cargo are potential threats to aircraft, particularly passenger aircraft that carry cargo consignments. Experts have warned that air cargo may be a potential target for terrorists because screening and inspection of air cargo has historically not been as extensive as required screening of passengers and checked baggage. For this reason, Congress has pushed the TSA to increase screening and inspections of air cargo, and recently mandated 100% screening of all cargo placed on passenger aircraft by August 2010 (see P.L. 110-53).

However, some aviation security and counterterrorism experts regard placing explosives in air cargo as a less appealing option to terrorists because typically a specific flight cannot be targeted without the assistance of an individual with access to aircraft. Furthermore, experts generally believe that all-cargo aircraft are less appealing targets to terrorists because a bombing attack against an all-cargo aircraft is not likely to result in mass casualties and generate the degree of public and media attention that a bombing of a commercial passenger aircraft would have.

Aircraft bombings remain a considerable concern, although recent aircraft bombings and bombing plots have not specifically involved the introduction of a bomb placed in air cargo. Rather, at present, the specific aviation security focus has been in response to attempts to carry onboard or assemble IEDs in the passenger cabin. Particularly, the December 22, 2001, attempted shoe bombing aboard an American Airlines Boeing 767 on a trans-Atlantic Paris to Miami flight, the August 2004 bombings of two passenger airliners in Russia, and the foiled plot to bomb U.S.-bound airliners from the United Kingdom in August 2006 have heightened concerns over the threat of terrorist bombings to passenger aircraft.

Historically, bombings of U.S. airliners have been relatively rare and have mostly involved bombs placed in either the aircraft passenger cabin or checked passenger baggage. The most notable event involving detonation of an explosive device transported as cargo aboard an airliner in the United States was the November 15, 1979, explosion aboard an American Airlines Boeing 727 that was able to make a successful emergency landing at Dulles Airport in Virginia. This event, while tied to an individual terrorist but not a terrorist organization, did not intend to target the aircraft. Rather, investigation revealed that the device was contained in a parcel shipped by U.S. mail that the FBI linked to convicted "Unabomber," Theodore Kaczynski.[4]

While there are no identifiable historical bombing incidents involving the use of the air cargo system to specifically target passenger airliners, heightened screening of passengers, baggage, and aircraft may make cargo a more attractive means for terrorists to place explosive devices aboard aircraft in the future. However, some terrorism experts believe that placing explosives or incendiary devices in cargo may not be particularly appealing to terrorists, because it would be difficult to target specific flights without the cooperation of individuals with access to aircraft such as cargo workers. Thus, increased efforts to perform background checks of workers with access to aircraft and increased physical security around air cargo operations have been a key emphasis of security initiatives to mitigate the potential threat of explosives and incendiary devices introduced by air cargo. In 2006, the TSA finalized rules requiring fingerprint-based CHRCs and terrorist screening of individuals working in cargo operations areas, and workers at freight forwarding companies that handle the routing of air cargo, as had been previously required of workers with unescorted access to ramps and other restricted areas in and around passenger terminals.

Additionally, the use of hardened cargo containers capable of withstanding internal bomb blasts has been evaluated. Deployment of these containers may provide an additional layer of security to mitigate the risks of explosives and incendiary devices by improving the chances that an aircraft can survive a bombing. The 9/11 Commission specifically recommended the deployment of at least one hardened cargo container in each passenger aircraft to mitigate the potentially catastrophic consequences of a bomb carried in air cargo or in checked baggage placed in aircraft cargo holds.[5] Under a provision in the IRTPA of 2004 (P.L. 108-458), a pilot program was established to evaluate this concept. A provision in the Implementing the 9/11 Commission Recommendations Act of 2007 (P.L. 110-53) directed the TSA to provide an evaluation of the pilot program and, based on its findings, implemented a program to pay for, provide, and maintain blast-resistant cargo containers for use by air carriers on a risk-managed basis.

HAZARDOUS MATERIALS

Despite increased FAA and DOT oversight and enforcement efforts, undeclared and undetected shipments of hazardous materials continue to pose a significant safety problem for air carriers. Hazardous materials or dangerous goods include explosives, gases, flammable liquids and solids, oxidizers and organic peroxides, toxic materials and infectious substances, radioactive materials, corrosive materials, and other miscellaneous dangerous goods (e.g., asbestos). Most explosives and gases are prohibited aboard aircraft; however many properly handled hazardous materials are permitted aboard passenger and all-cargo aircraft within specified quantity limitations.[6]

Risks are introduced when hazardous materials are not declared leading to the potential transport of prohibited materials by air or improper handling of hazardous goods during loading and while in transit. The dangers of undetected and improperly handled hazardous materials in air cargo shipments were highlighted by the May 11, 1996 crash of a ValuJet DC-9 in the Florida Everglades. The NTSB determined that improperly carried oxygen generators ignited an intense fire in one of the airplanes' cargo holds leading to the crash and issued several safety recommendations for improving the handling and tracking of hazardous materials to prevent improper carriage aboard passenger aircraft.[7]

While safety concerns regarding hazardous cargo shipments aboard passenger aircraft are a particular concern, preventing unauthorized shipments of hazardous materials is a challenge for all-cargo aircraft operators as well. About 75% of hazardous materials shipped by aircraft are carried aboard all-cargo aircraft, while the remaining 25% is shipped on passenger aircraft.[8] Enhanced air cargo security measures may also improve air cargo safety by increasing the detection of undeclared hazardous materials through screening and inspections of cargo shipments and related paperwork.

CARGO CRIME

Cargo crimes include the theft of goods transported as cargo, and the shipment and smuggling of contraband, counterfeit, and pirated goods through the cargo distribution network. It has been estimated that direct losses due to cargo theft across all transportation modes total between $15 billion and $30 billion annually in the United States.[9] The large range in this estimate reflects the fact that cargo theft and other cargo crimes have not historically been a specific designated crime category, and therefore reliable statistics on cargo theft are not available. A provision in the USA PATRIOT Improvement and Reauthorization Act (P.L. 109-177), however, required the Department of Justice to establish a separate category for cargo theft in the Uniform Crime Reporting System. The Act also refines relevant statutes and increases criminal penalties for cargo theft and stowaways.

The large estimated level of cargo theft and other cargo crimes is indicative of potential weaknesses in cargo security, including air cargo security. Specific weaknesses in air cargo security have been highlighted in several high-profile investigations of cargo theft. For example, major cargo and baggage theft rings have been uncovered at JFK International Airport in New York, Logan International Airport in Boston, and at Miami International Airport in Florida.[10] In addition to theft, smuggling has also been a problem for air cargo security. Smuggling of contraband, counterfeit, and pirated goods undermines legal markets and reduces government tax and tariff revenues. Smuggling operations are often linked to organized crime and may provide support for terrorist activities. A large portion of cargo crime is committed either by cargo workers or with the assistance of cargo workers. Therefore, increased security measures such as conducting more stringent or more frequent background checks of cargo workers and enhancing physical security of cargo operations areas are likely to reduce cargo crimes and improve the capability to detect criminal activity in air cargo operations. A review of transportation security needs for combatting cargo crime identified six key issues regarding cargo security:

- A lack of effective cargo theft reporting systems
- Weaknesses in current transportation crime laws and prosecution
- A lack of understanding regarding the nature of cargo crime by governments and industry
- Inadequate support for cargo theft task forces
- A need to improve local law enforcement expertise on cargo theft
- The need for more effective cargo security technology including cargo tracking systems, tamper-evident and tamper-resistant seals, high-speed screening devices, and the integration of security technology into supply chain management systems[11]

While some of these issues may be addressed through the Department of Justice's approach to meeting the mandate for uniformly reporting cargo crimes, concerns over the adequacy of law enforcement approaches to combatting cargo crime and the implementation of cargo security technologies remain. Addressing these issues specific to cargo crime may also improve overall cargo security and could deter terrorist threats to cargo shipments. While these recommendations are directed toward cargo crime issues in all modes of transportation, they may be particularly applicable to air cargo security where other security concerns such as explosive and incendiary device detection, hazardous materials detection, and deterring hijackings and sabotage may also be addressed through the implementation of tighter controls to deter cargo crime.

AIRCRAFT HIJACKING AND SABOTAGE

Individuals with access to aircraft may pose a risk of potential hijackings and aircraft sabotage. While instances of hijackings by individuals with access to aircraft have been extremely rare, a particularly dramatic hijacking attempt by an individual with access to cargo aircraft and cargo operations facilities occurred on April 7, 1994.[12] An off-duty Federal Express flight engineer attempted to hijack a FedEx DC-10 aircraft and crash it into the company's Memphis, Tennessee headquarters. At the time there was no requirement or company procedure to screen or inspect personnel with access to cargo aircraft or their baggage. The flight crew thwarted the hijacker's attempt to take over the airplane by force and made a successful emergency landing in Memphis despite serious injuries to all three flight crew members.

Under regulations issued in 2006, all-cargo operators must take steps to prevent unauthorized individuals from accessing aircraft and to ensure that crew members and individuals carried aboard large all-cargo aircraft are prevented or deterred from carrying weapons, explosives, or other destructive items on board aircraft.[13] However, physical screening of all cargo workers in a manner similar to passenger screening procedures is not required and is generally considered as being too costly, complex, and inflexible to meet the dynamic characteristics of air cargo operations. Some experts, however, remain concerned that individuals with access to cargo operations areas could introduce weapons and stowaway on board all-cargo aircraft as a method of hijacking a large transport aircraft that could be used in a suicide attack against a ground target.

Acts of sabotage not involving explosives or incendiary devices, such as tampering with, disabling, or destroying flight-critical systems and aircraft components, carried out by individuals with access to aircraft and cargo operations, are also a potential risk. Although this is not generally considered a significant threat because of the level of knowledge needed to sabotage flight-critical systems, the degree of redundancy of these systems on modern transport category airplanes, and the existing capabilities to detect sabotage attempts through preflight inspections, and maintenance checks. While numerous cases of sabotage by disgruntled employees have been documented, these incidents of aircraft tampering have typically been discovered during preflight inspections resulting in aircraft groundings and delays and costly repairs, but have not resulted in catastrophes. Such incidents have not been linked to terrorism.

AIRMAIL CONSIGNMENTS

The transport of U.S. mail aboard aircraft introduces unique security challenges to prevent illegal hazardous material shipments and the introduction of explosive and incendiary devices. Inspecting first class, priority, and express mail prior to shipment by air is difficult because the United States Postal Service (USPS) regard these items as private materials protected by the Fourth Amendment against search.[14] The USPS had implemented a screening process to prevent unauthorized shipments of hazardous substances that relies on customer screening by postal clerks who are trained to question individuals shipping packages weighing more than one pound by air. Following the 9/11 terrorist attacks, however, mail weighing more than one pound was prohibited from being carried aboard passenger aircraft. As seen in Figure 11.4, there has been a precipitous decline in mail shipments by passenger airlines as a result of this restriction. While all-cargo air carriers have increased their mail carriage to some degree in response, most of the mail once carried aboard passenger aircraft is now being transported by other transportation modes.

Items weighing less than one pound are not subject to any inquiry and can be deposited in mailboxes thereby precluding any questioning or screening of the sender. While these mail items may be shipped on passenger aircraft, only a relatively small percentage of U.S. mail is shipped by air. About 5–7.5% of all domestic mail shipments, regardless of weight, are transported by either passenger or all-cargo aircraft, and the amount of mail transported on aircraft has declined considerably since the prohibitions following the 9/11 terrorist attacks were put in place. Passenger air carriers have been pushing to have these restrictions lifted because of a significant loss of revenue

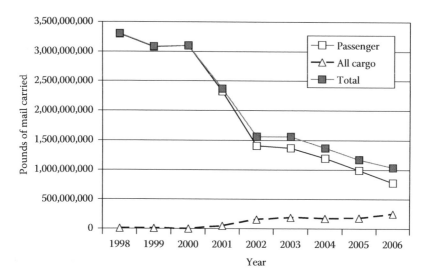

FIGURE 11.4 The decline in domestic airmail carried following post-9/11 restrictions. (Data obtained from Bureau of Transportation Statistics, *Air Carrier Data*.)

from U.S. mail shipments. Federal Express is currently the largest carrier of U.S. mail and its all-cargo operations account for about half of the total volume of U.S. mail shipments by air.[15]

In 1997, the Gore Commission had recommended that the Postal Service obtain authorization from customers shipping mail weighing more than one pound allowing screening of shipments using EDSs, and if necessary, seek appropriate legislation to accomplish this.[16] However, this recommendation has never been implemented, and physical inspection of mail shipments is still generally prohibited.

Canine teams, which have been advocated by industry for increased use in screening and inspecting air freight, have provided the only means approved by the TSA for screening mail weighing more than one pound that is put on passenger aircraft under a pilot program conducted at 11 airports.[17] Despite indications that the pilot program has worked well, the TSA has not announced any plans to expand the use of canine teams for the specific purpose of screening airmail.

Assuring the safety and security of U.S. mail transported by aircraft, and preventing the introduction of explosives or incendiaries in mail shipped by aircraft while maintaining privacy rights of postal patrons, remains an important issue in the larger debate over air cargo security, although experts do not expect any significant changes to the restrictions on mail greater than one pound anytime soon. Following the events 9/11 attacks, and the Postal Service anthrax incidents, the Technology Subcommittee of the President's Commission on the USPS recommended that the USPS, in coordination with the DHS, should explore technologies and procedures for utilizing unique sender identification on all mail.[18] While such procedures may provide a means of prescreening all mail shipped by air, including packages weighing less than one pound, they introduce considerable concerns over the privacy of citizens using the U.S. mail system. Despite considerable policy discussion of implementing unique sender identification, and possibly mail tracking technologies as well, in the aftermath of the 2001 anthrax attacks, implementing these capabilities for all types of mail presents considerable legal and logistic challenges that are yet to be resolved.

SCREENING VERSUS PHYSICAL INSPECTION OF CARGO SHIPMENTS

Given the sheer volume of cargo that must be expediently processed and loaded on aircraft, it has been generally argued that physical screening of all air cargo using explosives detection technologies, as is now required of checked passenger baggage, is likely to present significant logistic and operational challenges. Since the 9/11 attacks and the passage of ATSA, considerable progress has been made to increase the amount of cargo placed on passenger airliners that is subject to physical inspection, as opposed to screening techniques that rely solely on shipping documents or other records regarding what is known about a shipper, the documented contents of the package, supply chain security practices, or other indicators of risk. For this reason it is critical to distinguish between the term physical inspection and the broader term of screening. While screening may involve physical inspection, in the context of air cargo security measures, it has also been understood to more broadly refer to a variety of methods, such as known shipper programs and other risk-based targeting or profiling systems to differentiate high-risk cargo from lower-risk cargo. For example, for several years following the 9/11 attacks, the use of known shipper programs, involving a process for determining whether a piece of cargo was shipped by a known source with a trusted business relationship with the freight forwarder or airline, has been regarded as a screening technique for determining whether a cargo shipment can be placed on a passenger airliner. By regulation, only cargo from known shippers can be placed on passenger airplanes.

Amid continued pressure from Congress to increase the amount of cargo that undergoes physical inspection, the DHS has invested in several research and development initiatives to adapt explosives screening technologies for use in the air cargo environment. The results of these efforts are best described as a slow evolution of increasing physical inspections of air cargo shipments placed on passenger aircraft since 2002, coupled with some promising opportunities to further increase cargo inspections and screening through an array of various techniques and technologies. This is in contrast to baggage screening, which relies predominantly on a single technology, EDS, as was required under ATSA.

Since 2007, there has been an intense focus on developing and tailoring technologies and procedures for screening and inspecting air cargo to meet a mandate in the Implementing Recommendations of the 9/11 Commission Act of 2007 (P.L. 110-53) that requires 100% screening of all cargo placed on passenger aircraft by August 2010, with an interim requirement of screening 50% of such cargo by February 2009. Unlike baggage screening operations that are, for the most part, conducted by TSA personnel, cargo inspections and screening operations are typically conducted by employees of the airlines, freight forwarders, and sometimes shippers, with the TSA being responsible for oversight of these functions. In 2004, the IRTPA of 2004 (P.L. 108-458) required the TSA to pursue screening technologies and enhance security procedures to improve the inspection, screening, and tracking of air cargo on passenger aircraft as recommended by the 9/11 Commission. Since then, implementing increased oversight and inspections of air cargo operations coupled with more stringent regulations for air cargo carriers and freight forwarders has been a high priority for the TSA.

Congressional appropriators have provided increased funding for inspections, screening, and tracking of air cargo, and for research, development, and pilot testing of various explosives screening techniques and technologies to increase the amount of air cargo that undergoes physical inspection. While the TSA does not divulge the percentage of cargo that undergoes physical inspection, language in the FY2005 Homeland Security Appropriations Act (P.L. 108-334) called for at least tripling the amount of cargo placed on passenger aircraft that was inspected at that time. FY2006 appropriations language (P.L. 109-90) directed the TSA to take all possible measures—including the certification, procurement, and deployment of screening systems—to inspect and screen air cargo on passenger aircraft and increase the percentage of cargo inspected beyond the level mandated in the FY2005 appropriations measure. FY2007 appropriations language (P.L. 109-295) directed the TSA to work with industry stakeholders to develop standards and protocols to increase the use of explosives detection equipment for screening air cargo. The FY2008 Omnibus Appropriations Act (P.L. 110-161) directed the DHS to research, develop, and procure new technologies to screen and inspect air cargo loaded on passenger aircraft and utilize existing checked baggage explosives detection equipment and screeners to the greatest extent practicable to screen air cargo until dedicated air cargo screening technologies can be developed and deployed. The Act requires the DHS to work with air carriers and airports to ensure that the screening of cargo carried on passenger aircraft continually increases and requires the DHS to submit quarterly reports detailing the incremental progress being made toward achieving the mandated 100% screening of cargo placed on passenger aircraft.

The mandate for 100% screening contained in P.L. 110-53 requires inspection of all air cargo placed on passenger aircraft in a manner that provides a level of security equivalent to the screening of passenger checked baggage. The legislative language specifically defines screening in this context to mean a physical examination or the use of other nonintrusive methods to assess whether a particular cargo shipment poses a threat to transportation security. The Act identifies specific methods of screening that would be acceptable in meeting this requirement, including the use of x-ray systems, EDS, ETD, TSA-certified explosives detection canine teams, and physical searches conducted in conjunction with manifest verifications. Additional methods may be approved by the TSA. However, the provision specifically prohibits the use of cargo documents and known shipper verification by themselves as being acceptable screening methods. In other words, the provision clarifies that the screening of cargo is to involve some sort of inspection process that cannot be met solely by a record's verification of shipment contents or shipper status. The TSA is required to promulgate regulations to meet these requirements, and it must provide justification for any exemptions made to these air cargo screening requirements. Also, the GAO, the investigative arm of the U.S. Congress, would be required to assess the methods used by the TSA in granting, modifying, or eliminating any exemptions to these requirements. The measure was generally opposed by various stakeholders in the air cargo industry who believe that its requirements are overly burdensome and costly.[19]

SECURITY IN THE ALL-CARGO ENVIRONMENT

While the primary policy focus of legislation to date has been on cargo carried aboard passenger aircraft, air cargo security also presents a challenge for all-cargo operators. Some concern remains that heightened security measures for passenger airline operations may make all-cargo aircraft a more attractive target to terrorists. However, unlike passenger operations where the threat from explosives introduced in air cargo represents the greatest perceived risk; the greatest perceived risk associated with all-cargo operations arises from the potential threat that an individual or individuals with access to aircraft may hijack a large transport category all-cargo aircraft to carry out a suicide attack against a ground target. Looking beyond aviation security, there is also a broader risk that terrorists may attempt to ship weapons, including possible weapons of mass destruction, into and within the United States using the global cargo distribution network. For example, various law enforcement and counterterrorism operations have shown how illegal sales and shipments of various weapons, such as shoulder-fired missiles, may be facilitated by falsified shipping documents allowing such items to potentially wind up in international and domestic air cargo shipments. Homeland security policies and strategies may need to further consider the potential risks that all-cargo operations, as well as passenger airline cargo operations, may be exploited to facilitate the movement of terrorist weapons, including not only conventional weapons like shoulder-fired missiles, but also possibly various weapons of mass destruction including chemical and biological agents, radioactive material, and nuclear weapons.

The largest all-cargo operators in the United States include FedEx, UPS, Atlas Air, Polar Air Cargo, Kallita Air, ABX Air, Evergreen International Airlines, Gemini Air Cargo, and World Airways.[20] In addition, some airlines with passenger service, such as Northwest Airlines and United, also have fleets of all-cargo aircraft. Figure 11.5 shows the distribution of air freight shipments among passenger and all-cargo aircraft. In recent years, only about 10% of domestic air freight has been carried aboard passenger aircraft within the United States. Ninety percent is carried aboard all-cargo aircraft. In international operations, passenger aircraft have played a bigger role, carrying roughly one-third of air freight shipments to and from the United States; however, most international air freight is carried by all-cargo aircraft.

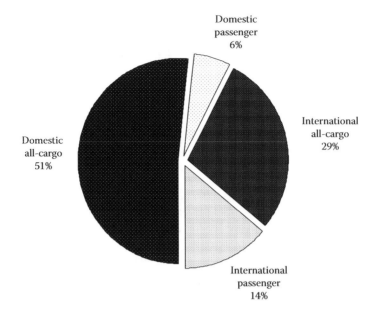

FIGURE 11.5 Distribution of freight cargo on passenger and all-cargo aircraft along domestic and international routes (2003–2006). (Data obtained from Bureau of Transportation Statistics, *Air Carrier Data*.)

While passenger airlines continue to play an important role in carrying air freight, the percentage of air cargo carried on passenger aircraft has continued to drop since September 11, 2001. Industry analysts expect that there will likely be a further decline in the proportion of freight carried on passenger aircraft as a result of new federal requirements to achieve 100% screening of all cargo placed on passenger aircraft by August 2010. This may have a greater impact on international air cargo operations that have historically relied more heavily on the use of passenger aircraft. Experts note, however, that if effective security measures are not implemented and a bomb carried as air cargo were to take down an passenger airliner lawmakers and regulators may respond by imposing significant restrictions on air cargo placed aboard passenger aircraft, possibly banning cargo on passenger aircraft altogether.[21] Regardless of whether passenger air cargo is specifically targeted or not, the long-term outlook points to a continued shift toward increased reliance on all-cargo aircraft, both domestically and in international operations.

As mentioned previously, heightened security measures on passenger aircraft since September 11, 2001, could make all-cargo aircraft more attractive to terrorists seeking to hijack large airplanes. Currently, federal air marshals are not deployed on all-cargo aircraft, and cargo airplanes are not required to have hardened cockpit doors so long as alterative TSA-approved security measures are implemented to control access to aircraft and the flight deck while an airplane is on the ground.

ARMING ALL-CARGO PILOTS

For this reason, arming all-cargo pilots with firearms and training these pilots to use these firearms to defend the flight deck against attack has been viewed as the primary in-flight security measure for protecting large all-cargo aircraft against the potential threat of suicide hijackers. The 2003 FAA Reauthorization Act, Vision 100 (P.L. 108-176), expanded the FFDO program to include pilots of all-cargo aircraft. This program trains and deputizes pilots to carry firearms to protect the flight deck against a possible terrorist hijacking attempt. While the TSA has indicated that more than 10% of airline pilots have been deputized as FFDOs, data on specific numbers and percentages of all-cargo pilots participating in the program are regarded as security-sensitive information.

Proponents for including all-cargo pilots in the program point out that some all-cargo aircraft lack hardened cockpit doors, and cargo flights lack federal air marshals and passengers that may assist in thwarting a hijacking attempt.[22] They also point out that physical security and access control to cargo operations areas and all-cargo aircraft had not been held to the same standard as passenger airline operations prior to the implementation of tougher regulations for air cargo security. Proponents for arming all-cargo pilots also point out that the lack of screening of individuals and property at air cargo facilities could offer the opportunity for terrorists plotting to hijack an aircraft to board an all-cargo aircraft as stowaways and seize the cockpit in flight. All-cargo aircraft include more than 1000 transport category jet airplanes, of which about half are wide-body jets similar to those used in the September 11, 2001 terrorist attacks.[23] Proponents for arming all-cargo pilots contend that the provision in Vision 100 that includes cargo pilots in the FFDO program mitigates the risk of a hijacking aboard all-cargo aircraft.

Cargo airlines, on the other hand, had generally opposed allowing their pilots to join the FFDO program. Air carriers, in general, have been hesitant about the program because of liability concerns even though specific liability protections were extended to the airlines and pilot participants when the FFDO program was established under the Homeland Security Act of 2002 (P.L. 107-296). Others opposed to arming pilots have raised concerns over the introduction of firearms on board an aircraft and in the sterile areas of airports. This appears to be somewhat less of a concern in the all-cargo environment where it would be less likely that a firearm could be lost or stolen.

CARGO INSPECTION METHODS AND TECHNOLOGIES

Screening and inspection of air cargo may be an effective means for detecting explosives, incendiary devices, and hazardous materials in air cargo. ATSA (P.L. 107–71) requires the screening of all property, including mail and cargo, carried aboard passenger aircraft in the United States. ATSA also specified that, as soon as practicable, a system must be implemented to screen, inspect, or otherwise ensure the security of all cargo transported in all-cargo aircraft. However, the GAO noted that the TSA lacked specific long-term goals and performance targets for cargo security.[24] In response, the TSA has developed an air cargo security strategic plan and has proposed comprehensive regulations designed to enhance air cargo security. The TSA's strategy centers on risk-based assessments and targeted physical screening of cargo based on risk as well as increased random inspections of shipments.

While ATSA established such a requirement, it is important to note that this has not been interpreted to require physical screening or inspection of cargo shipments carried aboard passenger aircraft. Rather, in implementing the security procedures for cargo carried aboard passenger airplanes, the TSA has relied extensively on the use of "known shipper" programs to prevent the shipment of cargo from unknown sources aboard passenger aircraft. Initially, air carriers and freight forwarders maintained their own lists of shippers that had established known and trustworthy business relationships to screen shipments placed on passenger aircraft. However, under rules finalized in 2006, airlines and freight forwarders must now use an industry-wide database of known shippers to clear shipments before they can be placed on passenger aircraft. However, some Members of Congress have expressed continued concern over applying targeted risk-based screening to cargo shipments placed on passenger aircraft. Through appropriations legislation, Congress has continually pressed the TSA to increase the percentage of cargo carried on passenger aircraft that is inspected, and has directed the DHS to invest in the research, development, and deployment of explosives screening technologies tailored for air cargo. As previously noted, the Implementing the 9/11 Commission Recommendations Act of 2007 (P.L. 110-53) establishes specific requirements and a timetable for implementing 100% physical screening or inspection of air cargo carried aboard passenger aircraft.

Current aviation security regulations require each passenger aircraft operator and indirect air carrier to develop a security program for acceptance and screening of cargo to prevent or deter the carriage of unauthorized explosives or incendiaries. An indirect air carrier refers to an entity, such as a freight forwarder, that engages indirectly in the air transportation of property on passenger aircraft. The volume of air cargo handled and the distributed nature of the air cargo system presents significant challenges for screening and inspecting air cargo. Presently, in the United States, about 50 air carriers transport air cargo on passenger aircraft handling cargo from nearly two million shippers per day.[25] About 80% of these shippers use freight forwarders who operate about 10,000 facilities across the country.[26] Since the air cargo industry has contended that 100% screening of all air cargo is not a practical solution with currently available technology, up until now security programs have relied primarily on prescreening of cargo to identify shipments for targeted physical screening and inspection. The TSA has adopted a risk-based strategy that relies heavily on the known shipper process. The TSA had planned to include other factors in its cargo risk assessment through the use of a freight assessment system that it has been developing, based in part on CBP's targeting methods. However, given the new mandate for achieving 100% physical screening of passenger air cargo, the future plans for the risk-based freight assessment system seem somewhat uncertain. Nonetheless, risk-based approaches remain a cornerstone of the TSA approach to air cargo security, and more broadly aviation security in general.

The TSA is currently working toward implementing its Air Cargo Strategic Plan, which was released in November 2003.[27] In keeping with the risk-based approach of implementing air cargo security measures typified in the known shipper concept, the core elements of this plan consist of improving shipper and supply chain security through improved vetting of shippers and freight forwarders, enhancing cargo prescreening processes, developing and deploying appropriate screening technologies to conduct targeted air cargo inspections, and implementing appropriate facility security measures. In addition to the known shipper system, the TSA is also developing a more comprehensive targeting tool for air cargo, known as the "Freight Assessment System." While few details of this system have been publicly disclosed, the TSA had indicated that it expected to fully deploy this system sometime in 2008, but as previously noted, the mandate for 100% screening of passenger air cargo has altered these plans.[28]

KNOWN SHIPPER APPROACH

The principal means for prescreening or profiling cargo in the United States has been through the use of air carrier and freight forwarder "known shipper" programs. In May 2006, the TSA issued a final rule establishing an industry-wide KSD or KSDB for vetting all shipments placed on passenger aircraft.[29] Previously, some air carriers and indirect air carriers had voluntarily participated in a system using a central database of known shippers to vet cargo destined for passenger aircraft as required under ATSA. Other air carriers and freight forwarders relied on internal databases and security protocols approved by TSA for determining whether shipments bound for a passenger airplane come from known sources and that shippers have adequate security measures in place to protect the integrity of those shipments.

Known shipper programs were created to establish procedures for differentiating trusted shippers, known to a freight forwarder or air carrier through prior business dealings, from unknown shippers who have conducted limited or no prior business with a freight forwarder or air carrier. Using this system, packages from unknown shippers can then be identified for additional screening and inspection. Currently, shipments from unknown sources are prohibited from passenger aircraft. Additionally, air carriers and freight forwarders must refuse to transport any cargo from shippers, including known shippers, that refuse to give consent for searching and inspecting the cargo. ATSA provides for use of known shipper programs as an alternate means for ensuring the security of cargo carried aboard passenger aircraft in lieu of screening of property by federal government employees prior to aircraft boarding.

The development of known shipper programs was prompted by industry experts and Congress in the mid-1990s who recognized that increased controls over air cargo shipments were needed to better ensure air cargo safety and security. Key concerns included the need for increased compliance with guidelines for the shipment of hazardous materials and the need to deter terrorists from using cargo as a means to place explosives or incendiary devices on aircraft. In addition, congressional hearings on the 1996 ValuJet accident concluded that air cargo safety could only be achieved through a comprehensive inspection program encompassing all components of the air cargo network.[30]

In December 1996, the FAA's ASAC Security Baseline Working Group issued a series of recommendations that formed the basis for FAA's effort to strengthen air cargo safety and security. Recommendations issued by the working group regarding air cargo security included tightening the definition of a "known shipper"; using profiles to review the shipments of known shippers and apply additional security measures; and exploring technologies to develop a profile to be applied to cargo shipments. The Gore Commission urged the adoption of the recommendations made by the FAA's Baseline Working Group regarding the profiling of "known" and "unknown" shippers.[31] As part of FAA's efforts in air cargo safety and security, a "known shipper" program was subsequently established, outlining procedures for freight forwarders and air carriers to review the security practices of known frequent customers and establish a cargo security plan for handling cargo from known and unknown shippers. With the passage of ATSA, oversight of cargo security measures was transferred from the FAA to the TSA. The TSA has continued to rely on known shipper programs as a principle means for prescreening air cargo.

A review of aviation security after the September 11, 2001 terrorist attacks by the DOT Office of the Inspector General drew attention to the vulnerabilities of air cargo and questioned the overall effectiveness of the known shipper program.[32] In congressional testimony following the terrorist attacks of September 11, 2001, DOT Inspector General, Kenneth Mead, referenced a 1998 report by the DOT Office of the Inspector General documenting a high rate of noncompliance with hazardous materials regulations and cargo security requirements across the air cargo industry and a lack of industry oversight to ensure that security procedures were carried out by cargo workers.[33] Several loopholes have been noted, including the relative ease of obtaining known shipper status, and the relative ease with which someone could pose as a known shipper by falsifying or counterfeiting shipping documents used to identify the source as a known shipper.[34]

Two central issues regarding the post-9/11 implementation of known shipper programs have been the adequacy of procedures for auditing and monitoring known shippers and consideration of the potential need for a consolidated database of known shippers, as has now been created. Critics of known shipper programs have argued that relatively little investigation of known shippers is required to demonstrate that these shippers are trustworthy and have adequate security measures in place to ensure the integrity of their shipments.[35] Freight forwarders and air carriers have also questioned why extensive background checks and established relations with a particular customer are required to establish that the customer is a known shipper when that customer is already considered a known shipper to another air carrier or freight forwarder. Therefore, some had identified a need for a standardized, centralized database of known shippers, as has now been created by the TSA. To address these concerns, the TSA initially instituted an industry-wide pilot program database of known shippers. This initiative poised the TSA to address congressional interest in establishing an industry-wide KSDB that was included in language passed by the Senate during the 108th Congress (see S. 165, S. 2845 as passed by the Senate). The Administration's subsequent initiatives regarding regulatory action to require an industry-wide KSDB led Congress to ultimately drop the Senate-passed provision in the Intelligence Reform Act of 2004 (P.L. 108-458) that would have established a statutory requirement for establishing a standardized industry-wide known shipper program and database. Congress instead settled on including language calling for the TSA to finalize its rulemaking on air cargo security, including the proposed establishment of the industry-wide KSDB, by September 2005. Those rules were not finalized until May 2006, but has now been implemented, including the provision to establish an industry-wide KSDB. The CBO estimates that it will cost about $10 million per year to maintain the industry-wide database of known shippers.[36]

The TSA initially implemented an industry-wide KSDB, which was replaced by a more comprehensive Known Shipper Management System (KSMS) in October 2007. All freight forwarders must
now vet information provided by shippers they do business with through this system, which provides an Internet-based query tool for ascertaining known shipper status. Under this system, the
TSA has taken on a more active role in assessing supply chain security and granting known shipper
status, addressing criticisms regarding the conflicting roles of freight forwarders in assessing the
security of their customers. In transitioning to this new system, the TSA also created a requirement
that each pick-up location obtain independent known shipper status, rather than granting known
shipper status for entire corporations or shipping entities based on the billing address for shipments.
The requirements and goals of the program, however, remain unchanged and all shipments from
unknown sources are prohibited from being placed on passenger aircraft. While the TSA has taken
these additional steps to strengthen the known shipper program, the air cargo industry has raised
concerns that the additional requirements for TSA certification of all shipping sites creates additional burdens that can significantly slow the shipping process, a significant concern for an industry
whose markets depend on the speed of delivery services.

PHYSICAL SCREENING AND INSPECTION

Another issue for air cargo security is the adequacy of cargo inspection procedures and oversight of
cargo inspections at air carrier and freight forwarder facilities. The debate over explosives screening
of cargo has been around for more than 10 years, but was significantly intensified following the 9/11
attacks. In 1997, the Gore Commission recommended that unaccompanied express packages shipped
on commercial passenger aircraft should be subject to examination by EDSs.[37] Following the 9/11
attacks, ATSA established a requirement for screening and inspection of all individuals, goods,
property, vehicles, and other equipment entering a secured area of a passenger airport. This requirement mandated the same level of protection as passenger and baggage screening, but did not explicitly require the use of any specific screening technologies or techniques.

With regard to all-cargo aircraft, ATSA mandated that a system to screen, inspect, or otherwise
ensure the security of all-cargo aircraft be established as soon as practicable, but set no specific
deadlines or time frame for compliance. Current regulations specify that aircraft operators must use
the procedures, facilities, and equipment described in their security program to prevent or deter the
carriage of unauthorized explosives or incendiaries in cargo on board a passenger aircraft and
inspect cargo shipments for such devices before it is loaded onto passenger aircraft. Aircraft operators must establish controls over cargo shipments, in accordance with their security program, that
prevent the carriage of unauthorized explosive or incendiary devices aboard passenger aircraft and
access by unauthorized individuals. Further, aircraft operators must refuse to transport any cargo
presented by a shipper that refuses to consent to a search and inspection of their shipment.[38]

The Homeland Security Appropriations Act of 2005 (P.L. 108-334) called for tripling the amount
of cargo placed on passenger airplanes that is screened or inspected; however, the absolute number
or percentage of cargo subject to inspection is considered security sensitive. FY2006 appropriations
language (P.L. 109-90) directed the TSA to take all possible measures—including the certification,
procurement, and deployment of screening systems—to inspect and screen air cargo on passenger
aircraft and increase the percentage of cargo inspected beyond the level mandated in the FY2005
appropriations measure. Further, FY2007 appropriations language (P.L. 109-295) directed the TSA
to work with industry stakeholders to develop standards and protocols to increase the use of explosives detection equipment for screening air cargo. Similarly, the FY2008 Omnibus Appropriations
Act (P.L. 110-161) directed the DHS to research, develop, and procure new technologies to screen
air cargo, and in the interim utilize checked baggage explosives detection equipment to the maximum extent practicable to screen air cargo placed on passenger aircraft.

While the TSA has taken steps to increase physical inspections of cargo carried aboard passenger
aircraft, 100% screening of all cargo placed on passenger aircraft remains a challenge. In August

2007, the Implementing the 9/11 Commission Recommendations Act of 2007 (P.L. 110-53) was enacted. Air cargo screening was a contentious issue during its legislative debate. In the end, the Act included a provision requiring 100% physical screening and inspection of all cargo placed on passenger aircraft by August 2010, with an interim requirement to screen 50% of such cargo by February 2009. The Act identifies specific methods of screening that would be acceptable in meeting this requirement, including the use of x-ray systems, EDSs, ETD, TSA-certified explosives detection canine teams, and physical searches conducted in conjunction with manifest verifications. Additional methods may be approved by the TSA. However, the provision specifically prohibits the use of cargo documents and known shipper verification by themselves as being acceptable screening methods. Language in the FY2008 Omnibus Appropriations Act requires the TSA to continually increase the percent of passenger air cargo that is screened and provide Congress with quarterly updates on the progress being made toward achieving 100% screening of all cargo placed on passenger aircraft. In January 2008, the Chairman of the House Committee on Homeland Security Bennie Thompson and Representative Ed Markey requested a GAO review of the TSA's approach and progress toward meeting the mandate for 100% screening of passenger air cargo, citing concerns that Congress has limited information regarding the TSA's implementation plans.[39]

During congressional debate, air cargo industry stakeholders voiced considerable opposition to requiring 100% screening of passenger air cargo, urging Congress instead to "... focus on realistic solutions based on a framework that identifies and prioritizes risks, works methodically to apply effective and practical security programs, and makes optimal use of federal and industry resources."[40] The industry has continually advocated for a risk-based screening system for cargo placed on passenger airlines that incorporates threat assessment and targeting capabilities, provides incentives for shippers to strengthen supply chain security measures, and focuses increased inspections on cargo determined to be of elevated risk through risk assessment and targeting capabilities. This roughly parallels the TSA's strategic plan for air cargo security, which focuses on risk-based targeted screening of cargo. The industry has specifically recommended increased use of canine explosives detection teams; enhanced supply chain security; enhanced targeting of shipments based on the CBP experience with its ATS; expanded use of ETD technology for targeted screening; and accelerated research and development of technologies that can more efficiently inspect elevated risk cargo.[41]

A significant ongoing challenge regarding cargo inspection is the feasibility of implementing inspection procedures that offer adequate assurances for security without unduly affecting cargo shipment schedules and processes. However, many in the air cargo industry have expressed continued concerns that current technology does not offer a readily available, affordable solution for scanning cargo containers or bulk cargo in an expeditious manner that would not unduly affect the schedule of air cargo operations. Also, scanning or inspecting individual packages is considered infeasible by many experts due to the volume of cargo handled and the schedule demands of the air cargo business. Therefore, many industry experts have maintained that the most practical solution, using available technology, is the application of physical screening and inspections on selected shipments and the use of cargo profiling procedures, including the known shipper and indirect air carrier vetting programs, coupled with canine explosives detection teams to identify shipments that may require additional screening and inspection. Alternatively, the TSA has been pursuing options for conducting the screening at earlier stages along the supply chain, coupled with strengthened supply chain security measures through its Certified Cargo Screening Program (CCSP) designed to meet the mandate for 100% screening of cargo placed on commercial passenger aircraft. The CCSP would place a much larger burden on shippers, freight forwarders, and cargo consolidators raising considerable concerns over what the impact on operating costs and logistics to these entities will be.

The DHS Science and Technology Directorate, in coordination with the TSA, initiated an air cargo screening pilot program at three airports—San Francisco International Airport (SFO), Seattle-Tacoma International (SEA) in FY2006, and Cincinnati/Northern Kentucky International (CVG) in FY2007—to test technologies and procedures for cargo screening.[42] The tests examined a combination of x-ray, EDSs, and ETD screening technologies to determine the best fit for effectively screening air cargo and optimizing the flow and speed of cargo screening. It is anticipated that the results of these pilot tests will be provided to the TSA in FY2009 to aid in decisions regarding the technology approach to be taken to meet the 100% cargo screening mandate, along with guidance regarding the best insertion point for selected technologies in the supply chain to optimize security and efficiency. Additional research will focus on capabilities to better detect, and also to disable, IEDs in cargo.

CANINE EXPLOSIVES DETECTION TEAMS

Since the ability to screen and inspect cargo may be limited to some degree by available technology, flight schedules, and cargo processing demands, alternative measures for screening and inspection at cargo handling facilities have been suggested. The use of canine explosives detection teams has long been suggested as a possible means to screen cargo for explosives. In 1997, the Gore Commission recommended a significant expansion of the use of bomb-sniffing dogs. Similarly, as Congress began looking at options for addressing concerns over explosives placed in air cargo in 2003, former TSA head, Admiral James Loy, testified that increased use of canine teams may be an effective means for increasing inspections of cargo and mail.[43] Canine teams may offer a viable alternative means for screening air cargo at a relatively low cost. As previously noted, air cargo industry stakeholders are presently advocating the increased use of explosives detection canine teams as an integral part of a risk-based approach to air cargo targeting and screening. However, some believe that adequate assurances regarding the security of cargo placed upon passenger aircraft cannot be provided without 100% physical screening predominantly relying on explosives detection technology, as is currently required for all checked baggage.

Supplemental appropriations provided in FY2007 (see P.L. 110-28) provided a total of $80 million for air cargo, to be expended through FY2008, to carry out a variety of air cargo security initiatives including increasing the number of canine teams in the National Explosives Detection Canine Program by at least 170 new teams. All totaled, this will bring the number of TSA canine teams covering all transportation modes to about 600. A large percentage of these teams are involved in passenger air cargo screening activities, and air cargo screening activities comprise more than 25% of the work performed by these teams.

The TSA is working with the DHS Science and Technology Directorate to study training techniques and operational procedures to improve canine detection capabilities in the air cargo environment. One technology being examined is Remote Air Sampling Canine Olfaction (RASCO) sensors, which can provide a concentrated sample from a container for a canine to inspect, and has been used extensively in Europe.[44] The DHS project plans to expand this concept to include chemical sensors carried on jackets worn by the canine that will be capable of transmitting data to remote monitoring stations. This appears to address a provision in the FY2007 supplemental appropriations language directing the TSA to "pursue canine screening methods utilized internationally that focus on air samples."[45]

CARGO SCREENING TECHNOLOGY

In response to the 9/11 Commission recommendation that the TSA intensify its efforts to identify, track, and appropriately screen potentially dangerous cargo, the IRTPA of 2004 (P.L. 108-458) directed the TSA to develop technologies for this purpose and authorized $100 million annually in FY2005 through FY2007 for the research, development, and deployment of enhanced air cargo security technology. The Act also established a competitive grant program to foster the development of advanced air cargo security technology.

Appropriations for research and development of technologies specifically tailored for air cargo security thereafter increased significantly, totaling $55 million in FY2004 and $75 million for FY2005. In FY2006, TSA research and development functions were realigned into the Department of Homeland Security's Science and Technology Directorate and research and development funding for air cargo was scaled back to $30 million, and specifically designated for conducting three cargo screening pilot programs testing different concepts of operation. In FY2007, the aviation security research and development functions were realigned within the TSA and appropriated a total of $92 million. The appropriations measure did not specify what portion of this would be allocated to air cargo-related research and development, but did urge the TSA to work with industry stakeholders to develop standards and protocols to increase the use of explosives detection equipment for screening air cargo.

Various technologies are under consideration for enhancing the security of air cargo operations. Tamper-evident and tamper-resistant packaging and container seals may offer a relatively low-cost means of protecting cargo integrity during shipping and handling. Cargo screening technology using x-rays, including x-ray backscatter systems, chemical element sensing ETD systems, CT scan-based EDS, or possibly neutron beams or other techniques, such as millimeter wave imaging systems, may offer various means to screen cargo prior to placement aboard aircraft. Newer technologies under consideration for screening passengers at screening checkpoints including x-ray backscatter and millimeter wave imaging technologies have the capability to penetrate various cargo container materials, and thus may also be adaptable for use in air cargo screening. In addition to these technological approaches, several experts and TSA officials have been advocating and pursuing an increased use of canine teams for screening cargo and mail. The main drawback to any of these screening techniques is that the screening process takes time and may significantly impact cargo delivery schedules. Another concern regarding these technologies is the cost associated with acquisition, operation, and maintenance of screening systems.

X-Ray Screening

The most common systems currently available for large-scale screening of cargo shipments utilize x-ray technology. These systems rely on well-understood transmission and newer backscatter x-ray techniques to probe cargo containers. Many of these systems utilize low-dose x-ray sources that emit narrow x-ray beams, thus virtually eliminating the need for shielding. These devices are compact and light weight, allowing them to be mounted on moving platforms that can scan over containers.[46] X-ray devices are becoming more common at major ports of entry, border crossings, and airports overseas as post-9/11 security concerns are spurring increased development and deployment of these devices. The systems are also being utilized to screen for drugs and other contraband as well as explosives in cargo shipments.

In addition to traditional transmission x-ray systems, x-ray backscatter technology, which measures the scatter or reflections of the x-ray beam, is also under consideration. The x-ray backscatter technology tends to do a much better job of differentiating organic materials because different chemical elements in these materials scatter the x-ray in quite different patterns. This makes x-ray backscatter a well-suited technology for detecting organic explosives in either solid or liquid form. However, like traditional x-ray technology, current x-ray backscatter systems are extremely labor intensive and require considerable staffing and training requirements because these systems require human operators to control the system and interpret the backscatter images. Automated threat detection capabilities and computer-aided threat identification capabilities are just emerging for x-ray systems, but may offer future options for automated threat detection in the air cargo environment.

One of the most significant operational challenges in using x-ray screening devices, whether traditional x-ray systems or newer x-ray backscatter technologies, is the performance of the human operator. A variety of human factors considerations contribute to the operator's ability to detect threat objects when viewing x-ray images. These include the monotony of the task, fatigue, time pressure, the adequacy of training, and working conditions. These human factors are important to consider in fielding x-ray screening systems to ensure high detection rates of threat objects while minimizing false alarm rates that would unnecessarily slow the cargo inspection and handling process.

Technologies such as TIP that superimpose stored images of threat objects on x-ray scans can help keep operators alert. These technologies may be effective tools for training and performance monitoring and may be adopted for use in the air cargo environment. Additional technologies, such as computer-aided threat detection algorithms for highlighting potential threat objects, may also be considered to aid human observers.

EXPLOSIVE DETECTION SYSTEMS

Currently, EDS technologies are being used extensively in the aviation security environment, particularly in response to the mandate in ATSA requiring screening of all checked passenger baggage by electronic explosives screening technologies. The TSA has gained considerable experience with the large-scale deployment and use of EDS equipment to meet the mandate for full explosives detection screening of checked passenger bags. Many of the lessons learned by TSA from this experience will be useful for assessing the technical and operational challenges of applying large-scale EDS screening initiatives for air cargo operations. Efforts are also underway at TSA to improve the performance of EDS equipment and reduce its cost. However, air cargo operations are likely to present some of their own unique challenges for implementing large-scale EDS screening of freight, express packages, and mail. Some of the potential operational challenges associated with effectively fielding existing EDS equipment for screening air cargo include

- The limited size of objects that can be placed in EDS machines, which would require objects to be screened before being placed in containers or on pallets
- The distributed nature of the air cargo system often involves loading containers at remote sites, and EDS screening at these remote sites may leave the system vulnerable to the possible introduction of explosives or incendiary devices at points along the supply chain beyond the screening site
- Reported high false alarm rates of current generation EDS systems may lead to high levels of secondary screening and detailed inspections that could impact the ability to meet the schedule demands of cargo operations
- The processing rate of EDS equipment may require the purchase of large numbers of EDS machines and investment in the research and development of alternative technologies, thus increasing program costs, to minimize the impact on cargo operations scheduling and meet desired security program goals, although the throughput of EDS equipment has markedly improved over the last few years

CHEMICAL TRACE DETECTION SYSTEMS

Chemical trace detection systems, referred to commonly as ETD devices, are being widely used as secondary screening tools for passenger carry-on and checked baggage. Items identified for closer scrutiny by initial screening methods or selected at random may undergo further examination using these systems. These systems use a variety of technical principles to analyze the chemical composition of sample residue wiped from suspect articles. These systems compare the chemical composition of such a sample to the signature of known explosive materials and signal an alarm to the operator if the probability of a match exceeds a specified threshold.

The use of chemical trace detection systems is now common practice in the screening of checked and carry-on bags. It has been reported that TSA is considering expanding the use of chemical trace detection systems for screening cargo carried aboard passenger aircraft.[47] However, screening procedures using these systems are very labor intensive and time consuming. Like the manner in which this technology is used to perform secondary screening of checked and carry-on bags, chemical trace detection may be employed in air cargo operations to perform detailed screening of suspicious packages identified through KSDBs, or can be used for detailed secondary screening in conjunction with primary screening performed by x-ray and EDS systems similar to procedures currently in use for checked baggage screening. Random screening of cargo using chemical trace detection systems as a primary screening method is unlikely to be effective given the very low percentage of cargo that could be screened using this technique without significantly impacting cargo operations schedules. However, using chemical trace detection systems in conjunction with canine teams as a secondary screening tool appears to provide a possible option for increasing the proportion of cargo that can be effectively screened in a time-efficient manner.

Neutron Beam Technologies

Another potential class of technologies for screening air cargo is based on neutron beams. These systems use a pulsed neutron generator to probe an object, initiating several low energy nuclear reactions with the chemical elements comprising the object. Detectors can then measure the nuclear signature of the transmitted neutrons and/or the gamma-rays emitted from the reactions. Since neutrons and gamma-rays have the ability to penetrate through various materials to large depths in a nonintrusive manner, neutron-based technologies may have advantages for cargo screening, and some of these technologies are currently being operationally evaluated for use in contraband and explosives detection.[48] However, the GAO noted that currently available neutron-based technologies cost about $10 million per machine and require about one hour per container for screening, thus making this option very expensive and time consuming.[49]

In addition to the cost and time factors associated with neutron beam technologies, the NRC has raised considerable doubts about performance capabilities for screening the full spectrum of cargo containers or pallets for explosives.[50] The NRC also expressed potential safety concerns over the use of radiation-producing particle accelerators and expressed concerns over the practicality of using this technology in the aviation environment because of the size and weight of the equipment.

In 1999, the NRC advised the FAA against further funding for research, development, and deployment of a neutron-based explosives detection technology known as pulsed fast/thermal neutron spectroscopy (PFTNS) for primary screening of carry-on baggage, checked baggage, or cargo citing low current explosive threat levels and inadequate performance. In 2002, the NRC concluded that another neutron-based technique, pulsed fast neutron analysis (PFNA), is not ready for airport deployment or testing. However, the NRC conceded that PFNA has greater potential for screening containerized cargo than any other technology currently under consideration at the time of their analysis.[51] Since this analysis, however, interest in neutron beam screening technologies has largely taken a back seat to EDS and ETD technologies, as well as other potential screening technologies, including x-ray backscatter and millimeter wave imaging systems. Because the perceived threat of explosives has increased since September 11, 2001, neutron-based detection technology continues to be mentioned as a possible means for screening air cargo. However, wide-scale deployment of this technology for air cargo security in the near-term seems unlikely.

Millimeter Wave Imaging Systems

Millimeter wave screening technology refers to a wide array of screening devices capable of creating highly detailed images by measuring the reflections of ultrahigh frequency (i.e., in the 30–300 giga-Hertz frequency range) waves emitted by the system that are capable of passing through barriers that normally preclude visual inspection. Millimeter wave imaging systems are capable of penetrating many shipping container materials, and therefore potentially have a broad array of homeland security applications, including the screening of air cargo. While the TSA has been field testing millimeter wave imaging systems for passenger screening that are capable of penetrating clothing to detect concealed weapons and explosives, interest in the use of millimeter wave imaging systems for air cargo screening has been more limited at this point. Nonetheless, commercial products using millimeter wave imaging are currently available for application in standoff scanning of a wide variety of objects, including cargo, from a distance of several meters.[52] While images from multiple angles are typically required to get a complete picture of a container's contents, currently available millimeter wave imaging systems are capable of generating relatively high-detail images of items held inside a cargo container. However, like x-ray screening technologies, millimeter wave imaging systems are labor intensive, and can be expensive to operate, because they require trained operators to interpret the images generated by the system and identify potential threats for further examination. While interest in millimeter wave technology for air cargo screening has thus far been somewhat limited, interest in this technology may be intensified by new screening requirements and searches for efficient technologies to meet the mandate for 100% screening of cargo placed on passenger airliners.

COST OF CARGO SCREENING AND INSPECTION

The costs of air cargo security options are significant to both the Federal government and the air cargo industry. Furthermore, the indirect costs of air cargo security on air cargo operations may pose significant long-term challenges. On the other hand, the potential costs of a terrorist attack, both in terms of the loss of life and property and the long-term economic impacts would also be significant but are difficult to predict and quantify. An ongoing debate tied to air cargo appropriations and oversight of aviation security is the amount of physical screening and inspection of air cargo that is needed and achievable and whether risk-based prescreening tools can provide an adequate means to ensure the security of air cargo by identifying at-risk cargo for targeted physical inspections. Besides the logistic complexities of inspecting large amounts, or 100%, of cargo on passenger flights, many are concerned that the cost of doing so may impose a significant burden on the aviation and air cargo industries.

While federal expenditures on air cargo security measures have been growing over the past two years, these efforts represent a relatively small element (about 2%) of TSA's overall operating budget for aviation security. These expenditures could continue to grow, however, if additional technology and resources are devoted to the tracking and screening of cargo shipments. In contrast to passenger and baggage screening, which are, with few exceptions, the operational responsibility of the TSA, under the current scheme, much of the cost of inspection and screening of cargo is borne by the airlines and shippers, while TSA only maintains oversight responsibility. As previously noted, to meet the mandate of 100% inspections of air cargo, the TSA estimates a cost of more than $650 million in the first year of implementation, and a total cost of roughly $3.6 billion over 10 years, while the CBO estimates these costs to total $3.5 billion over six years, $250 million in the first year and $650 million for the next five years.[53]

POTENTIAL IMPACTS ON PASSENGER AIRLINES AND FREIGHT FORWARDERS

While P.L. 110-53 included the mandate for 100% cargo screening, it did not include any provisions to establish new taxes, air cargo security fees, or identify any other new revenue sources to pay for this mandate. During legislative debate, House majority leadership has indicated that it would not propose new deficit spending to pay for cargo screening, and that "… airlines would be expected to pay for air cargo inspections."[54] Under such a scheme, it would be most likely that physical screening of air cargo would become an air carrier responsibility with TSA oversight to insure regulatory compliance. Under such an arrangement, airlines, freight forwarders, consolidators, and shippers would incur the direct costs for meeting the 100% screening requirements. However, more recently, both House Homeland Security Chairman Bennie Thompson and House Transportation and Infrastructure Committee Chairman Jerry Costello made statements indicating that cargo screening should be a government responsibility and that it was the intent of the legislation to have federal employees carrying out the cargo screening required under this mandate.[55]

The Act, however, does not specify who is to conduct the screening, and the TSA has interpreted the language to allow airlines, freight forwarders and consolidators, or even possibly shippers and manufacturers to conduct the screening so long as they can assure the security of the shipment through the supply chain until it is loaded onto an aircraft.[56] The TSA maintains that this is the only viable means for meeting the mandate, as the TSA does not currently have the resources to screen the volume of cargo placed on passenger aircraft, and such an inflexible approach would slow the flow of air cargo. The TSA remains confident that, so long as a flexible approach is permitted, it will meet the August 2010 deadline for 100% screening, noting that at several smaller airports the requirement is already being met.[57] Under such an approach, it is likely that much of the operational costs associated with cargo screening and inspection will be borne by industry, including airlines, freight forwarders, and shippers. The extent to which these screening costs can be absorbed by passing them along to shippers and consumers may be a particular issue of interest, particularly as airlines continue to deal with other rising costs, especially increased fuel costs.

Besides the impact of direct costs for screening, passenger airlines may be competitively disadvantaged compared to all-cargo airlines if these new mandates are implemented. Industry stakeholders have expressed concerns that additional security screening requirements could slow shipments on passenger aircraft, and certain routes may no longer be profitable if cargo revenues are reduced or eliminated as a result of new screening requirements.[58] Given that profit margins for most passenger airlines are relatively small, and most large passenger airlines have failed to achieve any consistent profitability in recent years, the additional burden of both direct and indirect costs associated with a mandate to screen all cargo placed on passenger aircraft may present particular fiscal challenges to the airlines. While estimated cargo revenues of about $4.7 billion[59] annually make up only about 5% of total industry-wide operating revenues among passenger air carriers, these additional revenues can make the difference between profit or loss in an industry that has seen net losses averaging 3.8% of total revenue during the period from 2003 to 2005 and saw a profit margin of just 1.9% in 2006, the first profitable year for the industry since 2000, when it similarly realized a 1.9% profit margin.[60]

POTENTIAL IMPACTS ON MANUFACTURERS AND OTHER SHIPPERS

Another possible concern over the increased cost of cargo security associated with screening operations and other security enhancements is the potential that these actions will result in increased shipment costs for manufactured goods, particularly costs related to the distribution of time-critical parts. If unit shipping costs rise enough because of security-related costs and fees, it is possible that domestic manufacturing and assembly costs will not be able to remain competitive in a global market. For example, if the costs of shipping time-critical parts from Asia for final assembly in the United States rise because of security-related costs, it may become cost advantageous to manufacture the entire product overseas or within the United States. In the long term, this could result in a possible loss of manufacturing jobs in the United States, or in some cases, relocation of certain manufacturing facilities to the United States to eliminate dependence on air cargo. For this reason, the economic implications of any proposal to impose security-related fees on air cargo or impose costly security requirements on air cargo operators and shippers will likely need to be carefully evaluated to avoid or minimize any unintended impacts on manufacturers and their suppliers.

HARDENED BLAST-RESISTANT CARGO CONTAINERS

In addition to cargo screening technology, hardened cargo container technology is being considered as a means to mitigate the threat of an explosion or fire caused by a bomb or incendiary device that makes its way onto an aircraft undetected. The 9/11 Commission formally recommended the deployment of at least one hardened cargo container on every passenger aircraft that also hauls cargo to carry suspicious cargo. The IRTPA of 2004 (P.L. 108-248) required the TSA to establish a pilot program to explore the feasibility of this concept and authorizes the use of incentives to airlines to offset added fuel, maintenance, and other operational costs associated with using hardened cargo containers in an effort to encourage voluntary participation in the pilot program. The Act authorized $2 million for the pilot program. A provision in the Implementing the 9/11 Commission Recommendations Act of 2007 (P.L. 110-53) directed the TSA to provide an evaluation of the pilot program and, based on its findings, implement a program to pay for, provide, and maintain blast-resistant cargo containers for use by air carriers on a risk-managed basis.

This concept of deploying hardened cargo containers has been a topic of ongoing research for some time. Following the December 21, 1988 bombing of Pan Am flight 103 over Lockerbie, Scotland, the British Air Accident Investigation Branch recommended that regulatory authorities and airplane manufacturers study methods to mitigate the effects of in-flight explosions.[61] During the 1990s, the FAA had an active research program on blast-resistant containers, airworthiness, ground handling, and blast resistance of hardened containers. The program is now overseen by the DHS's Transportation Security Laboratory in Atlantic City, New Jersey. These containers, or hardened unit-loading devices (HULDs), are seen as a potential means for mitigating the threat of explosives placed aboard passenger aircraft in either checked baggage or cargo. These containers must withhold an explosive blast of a specified magnitude without any rupturing or fragment penetration of the container wall or the aircraft structure, and must contain and "self-extinguish" any postblast in order to meet the FAA-established test criteria.[62]

However, the increased weight of these containers can have significant operational impacts on airlines by increasing fuel costs and decreasing payload capacity for carrying revenue passengers and cargo. Challenges associated with deploying hardened cargo containers include

- Increased weight affecting aircraft range and payload capacity
- Increased procurement cost for hardened containers
- Potentially higher maintenance costs for hardened container materials
- Potential reduction in cargo volume (in addition to reduced payload weight) due to thicker container walls
- Possible design specifications, such as door hinging and positioning, that are not compatible with current airline baggage and cargo loading procedures and operations facilities[63]

The NRC estimated that the per unit cost for acquiring hardened cargo containers would be about $10,000, and recommended that the FAA continue efforts to operationally test HULDs and establish more rigorous protocol for certifying HULDs, but should not deploy them unless deemed to be a necessary security measure based on the assessments of cost, operational, and deployment studies by FAA and other stakeholders.

The NRC panel also recommended further economic assessment of their proposed deployment plan for fielding one HULD per wide-body aircraft. The NRC panel also noted that research and development on the use of HULDs on narrow-body aircraft was lagging far behind the work done on wide-body aircraft and recommended an increased emphasis on research in this area to assess the operational effectiveness of HULDs in narrow-body aircraft before any further recommendations could be made. The NRC panel estimated that the cost of deploying enough HULDs for airlines to carry at least one HULD per passenger flight would require an industry-wide procurement cost of $125 million, and would create an annual industry-wide economic impact of $11 million in increased fuel burn and reduced payload revenue.[64]

Given the recent increase in aviation jet fuel costs, the economic impact would likely be considerably higher than the NRC originally estimated in 1999. Recognizing the continued concerns over the cost and weight associated with currently available blast-resistant container technology, the DHS has proposed a new research program in FY2009 to examine the potential of adapting composite container material development efforts for use in air cargo to provide tamper detection and intrusion resistance with possible blast-resistant capabilities.

The recommendation made by the 9/11 Commission also called for the deployment of at least one hardened cargo container on every passenger aircraft for carrying any suspect cargo.[65] This recommendation implies that a cargo prescreening or risk evaluation process such as a known shipper program or the proposed freight assessment system would be used to determine what cargo should be loaded into the hardened container. Presently, ATSA requires shipments from unknown sources to travel on all-cargo aircraft. One strategic objective of the TSA's Air Cargo Strategic Plan is to develop a means for identifying elevated risk cargo through prescreening.[66] Such a tool would likely be needed to assess risk and determine what cargo should be placed in a hardened container. Besides the need for a prescreening process, the use of hardened cargo containers is likely to be opposed by the airline industry because of the direct costs of acquiring these units as well as the increased operational cost associated with increased fuel burn and lost payload capacity. The benefits of using hardened cargo containers would likely be highly dependent on the security of the prescreening process and its ability to detect high-risk cargo since the benefits of a hardened container would largely be negated if the prescreening process could be circumvented by terrorists. A key policy issue that is likely to emerge as the feasibility of hardened cargo containers is further evaluated is the potential implications of allowing suspicious cargo to travel on passenger aircraft even if this cargo is secured in hardened cargo containers. In other words, policymakers may debate what the risks and benefits of loading suspicious cargo on passenger airplanes in hardened cargo containers are as compared to the alternative of offloading this suspicious cargo to all-cargo aircraft.

In any case, under a plan in which only one hardened cargo container is deployed per aircraft, it is likely that only a relatively small fraction of available cargo space will be reinforced. For example, a Boeing 747-400 passenger jet is capable of holding up to 13 full-width, or 26 half-width containers.[67] Thus, providing just one full-sized hardened cargo container for a 747-400 would provide reinforcement for less than 10% of the available cargo storage area. While a greater percentage of available cargo space on smaller jets could be protected by hardened containers, any policy regarding the use of just one hardened container per aircraft will likely need to carefully evaluate the criteria and methods for vetting cargo to determine what cargo should be designated for carriage inside these hardened cargo containers.

TECHNOLOGIES FOR EFFECTIVELY SECURING THE SUPPLY CHAIN

In addition to the various screening technologies under consideration, other technology initiatives are being pursued to strengthen security along the supply chain. These measures have application to all modes of conveyance where their primary intent is to reduce the vulnerability to cargo crime; however, in the aviation mode, the primary threat that these initiatives are designed to mitigate is the threat of explosives. Supply chain security technologies include various kinds of tamper-evident and tamper-resistant container seals and packaging, and tracking technologies including RFID tags. In addition to these means of tracking and securing shipments as they travel along the supply chain, other technologies, such as biometric access control technologies, are designed to prevent unauthorized access to cargo shipments at points along the supply chain.

TAMPER-EVIDENT AND TAMPER-RESISTANT SEALS

Various technologies exist for sealing cargo shipments and cargo containers to prevent tampering. Relatively low-cost solutions such as tamper-evident tapes that provide visual indications of tampering are readily available and could easily be implemented during packaging. Such technology could be used in combination with "known shipper" protocols to insure that known shippers provide sufficient security in their packaging facilities and to deter tampering and theft during shipping and handling. Tamper-evident tape can identify cargo during inspection processes for further screening and inspection to safeguard against the introduction of explosives and incendiary devices. Tamper-evident tape may also be an effective tool to deter cargo crime, including cargo theft and the introduction of contraband, counterfeit, and pirated goods during shipment.

At cargo handling facilities, tamper-evident seals and locks can be utilized on cargo containers to prevent theft and the introduction of contraband or threat objects into air cargo shipments. Electronic seals may serve as an additional deterrent to terrorist and criminal activity by providing more immediate detection of tampering. Electronic seals have alarms, some triggered by fiber optic cable loops, that activate a transmitted signal when tampered with.[68] Electronic seals cost about $2500 per unit, but are reusable. However, the utility of electronic seals in air cargo operations has been questioned by some experts because currently available electronic seals have a limited transmission range, which may make detecting and identifying seals that have been tampered with difficult. In addition, there is some concern that they may interfere with aircraft electronic systems.[69]

In addition to tamper-evident and tamper-resistant seals, technologies to better track cargo shipments are being considered to maintain better control and tracking of cargo shipments along the supply chain. Both GPS and RFID technologies are seen as emerging technologies for improving the tracking of air cargo in the supply chain.

ACCESS CONTROL AND BIOMETRIC SCREENING TECHNOLOGY

Provisions of ATSA gave the TSA authority to use biometric technology to verify the identity of employees entering the secured areas of airports and directed the TSA to review the effectiveness of biometrics systems currently used by airports. Available biometric technologies such as fingerprint, retinal scan, and facial pattern recognition are being tested and implemented as part of a variety of transportation security programs, including the TWIC smart cards and readers for access controls at seaports and the Registered Traveler program for airline passengers who voluntarily provide detailed background information in exchange for expedited processing through airport screening checkpoints.

The IRTPA of 2004 (P.L. 108-458) contains extensive provisions requiring the TSA to develop specific guidance for the use of biometric or other technologies for airport access control systems. The guidance is to include comprehensive technical and operating system requirements and performance standards for the use of biometric identifier technology in airport access control systems; a list of products and vendors meeting these specifications; specific procedures for implementing biometric identifier systems; and a discussion of best practices for incorporating biometric identifier technologies into airport access control systems. The Act also provided authorization for $20 million for the research and development of advanced biometric technology applications for aviation security. Pilot studies have been conducted to examine methods for incorporating biometrics into airport access control systems. Given the proposed regulatory changes to enhance access controls to all-cargo facilities and improve existing access controls around passenger aircraft, it is likely that the implementation of biometric identifier technology will play an increasingly important role in air cargo security policy.

PHYSICAL SECURITY OF AIR CARGO FACILITIES

Air cargo facilities present unique challenges for physical security. The large physical size of these facilities and relatively continuous high-volume cargo operations introduce numerous individuals, vehicles, and shipments into secured access areas around aircraft. Key issues regarding physical security of these air cargo facilities include the adequacy of

- Inspections and oversight of air cargo facilities to ensure compliance with aviation security regulations and procedures established in the approved security programs of air carriers and freight forwarders

- Training for air cargo personnel with regard to security procedures and guidelines
- Access control requirements for personnel with access to air cargo facilities and aircraft

These issues are presently being addressed through air cargo security regulations issued by the TSA in May 2006 that are currently being implemented at air carrier and freight forwarder operations and logistics facilities[70]

INSPECTION AND OVERSIGHT OF AIR CARGO FACILITIES

Current regulations specify that all air carriers and freight forwarders must allow the TSA to conduct inspections and to review and copy records in order to determine compliance with applicable laws and regulations pertaining to aviation security. The Homeland Security Appropriations Act for FY2005 provided the TSA with $40 million to hire an additional 100 inspectors to carry out oversight and enforcement activities related to air cargo security. The TSA has responded by launching focused inspections of air cargo operations and conducting monthly "blitz" audits or "(strikes" of selected air cargo facilities. In FY2006, Congress again provided the TSA with a $10 million set aside to hire 100 more air cargo inspectors and for travel related to carrying out regulatory oversight and inspections of air cargo shipping and handling facilities, but the TSA has been slow to obligate these funds for air cargo security. For FY2007, appropriations report language directed the TSA to hire additional permanent staff to enhance TSA's analytic air cargo security capabilities.[71] In addition, an FY2007 supplemental appropriation (see P.L. 110-28) totaling $80 million was provided for air cargo security activities, including the hiring of an additional 150 compliance inspectors and cargo vulnerability assessments at the nation's busiest airports (i.e., Category X airports). Similarly, increased funding for air cargo security in FY2008 appropriations was provided for hiring additional air cargo inspectors and reducing reliance on contractors to carry out regulatory compliance activities related to air cargo security.

Increased oversight of air cargo facilities is likely to be highly dependent on the continued availability of resources and funding. The effectiveness of this oversight will also likely be highly dependent on the adequacy of available tools and procedures to track needed corrective actions and ensure compliance among air carriers and freight forwarders.

SECURITY TRAINING FOR AIR CARGO PERSONNEL

Currently, air cargo handlers are not required to receive any specific or formal training on security procedures or identification of suspicious activities. However, air cargo handlers may be considered the front line in protecting against security threats by adhering to procedures that would mitigate physical security breaches at cargo operations facilities, by increasing their awareness of suspicious activities, and by following proper procedures for reporting their observations. Security training for cargo workers may focus on security procedures for ensuring cargo integrity, protecting facilities, reporting suspicious activities, and so on. Under the TSA regulations imposed in 2006, workers for all-cargo carriers and for indirect air carriers with security-related duties—such as carrying out security inspections of shipments—are now required to receive specific training on the company's security program and their individual security-related responsibilities under that program. Similar training is already required of workers for passenger airlines that are assigned security-related duties.

INCREASED CONTROL OVER ACCESS TO AIRCRAFT AND CARGO FACILITIES

Under ATSA, TSA was directed to work with airport operators to strengthen access control points in secured areas and was authorized to use biometric screening procedures to positively identify individuals with access to secure airport areas. ATSA contains provisions for TSA oversight of secured-area access control to assess and enforce compliance with access control requirements. These requirements include screening and inspection of individuals, goods, property, vehicles, and other equipment seeking to access secure airport areas. Background checks for individuals having access to passenger aircraft are required and vendors with direct access to airfields where passenger operations take place are required to have a TSA-approved security program in place. Presently, background checks and displayed identification serve as the principal means for screening airport workers including cargo handlers.

There has been growing concern over the adequacy of these procedures for screening and monitoring airport workers. One particular concern is the integrity of airport worker credentials and the potential that unauthorized individuals could gain access to secure areas of the airport using stolen or fraudulent identification. The TSA has begun to implement a universal biometric TWIC for the nation's seaports. Biometric technology has received considerable attention from Congress as a means to authenticate individuals, particularly airport workers, and improve access controls to secured areas of airports. While it is not expected that the TSA will incorporate airports into the TWIC program, at least anytime soon, it has been moving forward in developing specific guidelines for airports to incorporate biometrics into their airport credentialing and access control systems.

In addition to ongoing concerns over access controls around passenger aircraft, access control and monitoring of workers at all-cargo facilities remains a significant challenge. Regulations promulgated in 2006 establish an all-cargo security program detailing the physical security measures for air cargo operations areas, cargo placed aboard all-cargo aircraft, and background checks and screening of individuals having access to all-cargo aircraft on the ground or in flight. In addition, these new air cargo security rules require airports to designate cargo operations areas, including areas where all-cargo aircraft are loaded and unloaded, as SIDAs. This effectively elevates the required security measures for these cargo handling areas and requires that workers with unescorted access to these areas be vetted through fingerprint-based CHRCs and STAs, as has been required for workers having access to secured areas around passenger aircraft for some time.

REFERENCES

1. Bureau of Transportation Statistics. *Freight in America: A New National Picture*, January, 2006. Washington, DC: U.S. Department of Transportation.
2. Bureau of Transportation Statistics. *Pocket Guide to Transportation*, 2006. Washington, DC: U.S. Department of Transportation.
3. Bureau of Transportation Statistics. *Pocket Guide to Transportation*, 2007.
4. Affidavit of Assistant Special Agent in Charge, Terry D. Turchie, before the U.S. District Court, District of Montana, April 3, 1996.
5. Ibid.
6. U.S. General Accounting Office. *Aviation Safety: Undeclared Air Shipments of Dangerous Goods and DOT's Enforcement Approach.* GAO-03-22, January 2003.
7. National Transportation Safety Board. *Aircraft Accident Report: In-Flight Fire and Impact with Terrain, ValuJet Airlines, Flight 592, DC-9-32, N904VJ*, Everglades, Near Miami, Florida, May 11, 1996, AAR-97/06.
8. See note 6.
9. Federal Bureau of Investigation. "Cargo Theft's High Cost: Thieves Stealing Billions Annually." Washington, DC, July 21, 2006.
10. U.S. General Accounting Office. Ibid.; Department of Transportation, Office of the Inspector General. *Press Release: Six MIA Airport Employees Indicted for Stealing from Checked Passenger Bags.* December 11, 2002.
11. Ed Badolato. "Cargo Security: High-Tech Protection, High-Tech Threats." *TR News*, 211, November–December 2000, pp. 14–17.
12. Dave Hirschman. *Hijacked: The True Story of the Heroes of Flight 705.* New York: William Morrow & Co, 1997.

13. See 49 CFR §1544.202.
14. U.S. General Accounting Office. *Aviation Security: Federal Action Needed to Strengthen Domestic Air Cargo Security*, October 2005, GAO-06-76.
15. "Northwest to drop U.S. mail; Canceled domestic routes to cost 250 ground jobs." *Detroit Free Press*, September 5, 2003.
16. White House Commission on Aviation Safety and Security. *Final Report to President Clinton.* Vice President Al Gore, Chairman. February 12, 1997. Washington, DC: The White House.
17. U.S. Department of Homeland Security, Transportation Security Administration. "TSA Canine Teams Screen U.S. Mail for Explosives—Pilot Program to Expand to Airports across the Country." Press Release 03-34, May 29, 2003.
18. President's Commission on the United States Postal Service. *Final Recommendations of the Technology Challenges and Opportunities Subcommittee.* Washington, DC: United States Department of the Treasury (http://www.ustreas.gov/offices/domesticfinance/usps/).
19. "House To Consider Bill Today Requiring Additional Cargo Screening." *Transportation Weekly*, January 9, 2007, p. 7.
20. "The World's Top 50 Cargo Airlines." *Air Cargo World*, September 2006, pp. 22–26.
21. Michael Fabey. "Cargo's Security Scare." *Traffic World*, December 17, 2007, p. 29.
22. See Statement of Captain Duane Woerth, President, Air Line Pilots Association, International. *The Status of the Federal Flight Deck Officer Program,* before the Subcommittee on Aviation, Committee on Transportation and Infrastructure, U.S. House of Representatives. Washington, DC, May 8, 2003.
23. Federal Aviation Administration. *FAA Aerospace Forecast Fiscal Years 2003–2014.*
24. U.S. General Accounting Office. *Post-September 11th Initiatives and Long-Term Challenges.* Statement of Gerald L. Dillingham, Testimony before the National Commission on Terrorist Attacks upon the United States, April 1, 2003, GAO-03-616T; see note 14.
25. See S. Rept. 108-38.
26. U.S. General Accounting Office. *Aviation Security.*
27. U.S. Department of Homeland Security, Transportation Security Administration. *Air Cargo Strategic Plan.* November 13, 2003; Department of Homeland Security, Transportation Security Administration, "Air Cargo Security Requirements, Final Rule," *Federal Register, 71*(102), pp. 30477–30517, May 26, 2006; 49 CFR 1544.239.
28. Executive Office of the President of the United States, Office of Management and Budget, *Program Assessment, Transportation Security Administration: Air Cargo Security Programs.* Washington, DC.
29. Department of Homeland Security, Transportation Security Administration. "Air Cargo Security Requirements; Proposed Rule." *Federal Register, 69*(217), 65258–65291, 2004.
30. Department of Transportation, Office of the Inspector General. *Aviation Security: Federal Aviation Administration*, Report No. AV-1998-134, May 27, 1998.
31. See note 16.
32. Ken Leiser. "Gaps in air cargo security may offer terrorism openings." *AEROTECH News and Review*, June 21, 2002, p. B2.
33. Statement of the Honorable Kenneth M. Mead, Inspector General U.S. Department of Transportation. "Action Needed to Improve Aviation Security." Before the Committee on Governmental Affairs and the Subcommittee on Oversight of Government Management, Restructuring and the District of Columbia, United States Senate, September 25, 2001.
34. Greg Schneider. "Terror Risk Cited for Cargo Carried on Passenger Jets; 2 Reports List Security Gaps." *The Washington Post*, June 10, 2002.
35. See note 32.
36. See S. Rept. 108-38. *Air Cargo Security Improvement Act: Report of the Committee on Commerce, Science, and Transportation on S. 165.* United States Senate, April 11, 2003.
37. White House Commission on Aviation Safety and Security. Op. cit.
38. See Title 49, Code of Federal Regulations, Chapter XII, Part 1544.205.
39. Bennie G. Thompson and Edward J. Markey. Letter to the Honorable David M. Walker, Comptroller General of the United States, January 29, 2008.
40. Air Carrier Association of America, Airforwarders Association, Air Transport Association, Cargo Network Services Corporation (CNS), High Tech Shippers Coalition, International Warehouse Logistics Association, National Air Carrier Association (NACA), National Customs Brokers and Forwarders Association of America, Inc., National Fisheries Institute, Regional Airline Association, Society of American Florists, and the U.S. Chamber of Commerce, *Letter to the Honorable Daniel Inouye and the Honorable Ted Stevens*, January 8, 2007, p. 1.

41. Ibid.
42. Department of Homeland Security, Office of the Press Secretary. "Aircraft Cargo Screening Program to Begin at Cincinnati/Northern Kentucky Airport." March 26, 2007; David Hughes. "Airports Conducting Air Cargo Screening Trials." *Aviation Daily*, May 7, 2007.
43. Statement of Admiral James M. Loy, Administrator, Transportation Security Administration, before the Senate Committee on Commerce, Science, and Transportation, on Oversight of Transportation Security, September 9, 2003.
44. Wickens, B. "Remote Air Sampling for Canine Olfaction," *IEEE 35th International Carnahan Conference on Security Technology*, October 2001, pp. 100–102.
45. P.L. 110-28, 121 Stat. 141.
46. David S. De Moulpied and David Waters. "Cargo Screening Techniques Become More Widely Accepted." *Port Technology International*, *10*, 127–129, 1999.
47. See note 34.
48. G. Vourvopoulos and P.C. Womble. "Pulsed Fast/Thermal Neutron Analysis: A Technique for Explosives Detection." *TALANTA*, *54*, 459–468, 2001.
49. See note 14.
50. National Research Council. *The Practicality of Pulsed Fast Neutron Transmission Spectroscopy for Aviation Security.* NMAB-482-6. Washington, DC: National Academy Press, 1999.
51. National Research Council. *Assessment of the Practicality of Pulsed Fast Neutron Analysis for Aviation Security.* Washington, DC: National Academy Press, 2002.
52. By Calvin Biesecker. "Rapiscan To Market Brijot's Stand-Off Millimeter Wave Body Scanner," *Defense Daily*, October 31, 2007.
53. Jeff Bliss. "Air-Cargo Screening 'A Disaster Waiting to Happen,' Critics Say," *Bloomberg.com*, November 29, 2005.
54. Chris Strohm. "Democrats Look to Industry to Pay for Cargo," *Government Executive Daily Briefing*, January 9, 2007.
55. Del Quentin Weber. "Democrats, TSA Scuffle on Who Inspects Cargo." *The Washington Post*, September 8, 2007, p. D1.
56. Ibid.
57. "TSA Says It Will Adhere to Cargo Screening Deadlines." *World Trade*, *20*(12), December 2007, p. 10.
58. Thomas Frank. "Bill Would Order All Air Cargo Screened," *USA Today*, January 8, 2007.
59. Air Transport Association, *ATA Issue Brief: Air Cargo Security—The Airlines View*, Washington, DC: Air Transport Association.
60. CRS analysis of airline industry economic data presented in Air Transport Association, *Smart Skies: A Blueprint for the Future, 2007 Economic Report*, Washington, DC: Air Transport Association.
61. United Kingdom Air Accidents Investigation Branch. Op. cit.
62. National Research Council. *Assessment of Technologies Deployed to Improve Aviation Security: First Report*. Publication NMAB-482-5. Washington, DC: National Academy Press, 1999.
63. Ibid.
64. Ibid.
65. National Commission on Terrorist Attacks upon the United States. *The 9/11 Commission Report.*
66. U.S. Department of Homeland Security, Transportation Security Administration. *Air Cargo Strategic Plan.*
67. Boeing Commercial Airplanes. *747-400 Airplane Characteristics for Airport Handling.* D6-58326-1, December 2002.
68. "Electronic Cargo Security Seals." *Frontline Solutions, 3*(6), 42, June 2002.
69. U.S. General Accounting Office. *Aviation Security.*
70. Department of Homeland Security, Transportation Security Administration, "Air Cargo Security Requirements, Final Rule," *Federal Register, 71*(102), pp. 30477–30517, May 26, 2006; 49 CFR 1544.239.
71. See H. Rept. 109-699.

12 Security for GA Operations and Airports

When the term GA is mentioned, the image most likely to be conjured is one of a small single-engine airplane droning over America's farmland on a tranquil summer's day. In the post-9/11 context, this pastoral image of GA has been tarnished to a degree by knowledge that the 9/11 hijackers trained in small GA aircraft in the United States and amid lingering concerns that GA aircraft could be used to carry out a future terrorist attack. While some recent high-profile breaches of GA security have pointed to persisting vulnerabilities, and limited intelligence information may suggest a possible terrorist "fixation on using aircraft to attack U.S. interests."[1] GA aircraft vary considerably with regard to the risks they pose. The security risk posed by a small single-engine airplane operating in rural settings is intuitively quite different than the risk characteristics of large business jets operating in and near major metropolitan areas. Most experts agree that an adaptive, risk-based approach to securing GA aircraft and airports that takes into account the unique characteristics of the various distinct components of GA is needed to assure that security needs are adequately met and balanced with economic and operational considerations of the GA industry.[2]

Policymakers have received mixed signals about the relative risk posed by GA. While the 9/11 Commission asserted that "[m]ajor vulnerabilities still exist in ... general aviation security,"[3] the Commission did not further elaborate on the nature of those vulnerabilities nor did it make specific recommendations pertaining to GA security. The FAA has noted that "[w]hile the DHS has no specific information that terrorist groups are currently planning to use GA aircraft to perpetrate attacks against the United States, it remains concerned that (in light of completed and ongoing security enhancements for commercial aircraft and airports) terrorists may turn to GA as an alternative method for conducting operations."[4] In other words, while GA aircraft and airports may not be optimally suited for terrorist objectives, the hardening of commercial operations may make them an attractive alternative to terrorists seeking to identify and exploit vulnerabilities in aviation security. In this context, GA airports and aircraft are viewed as comparatively soft targets that may be exploited by terrorists because of known weaknesses and vulnerabilities. This view focuses primarily on the vulnerability of GA and does not systematically assess risk with regard to the interaction between these vulnerabilities, the threat posed by GA aircraft, and the potential consequences of a terrorist attack using GA aircraft.

In fact, there is considerable debate over the threat element of the risk equation for GA operations. While GA advocates argue that the threat is minimal, some policymakers and security experts have expressed concern that, to the contrary, GA may pose a significant security threat. Part of the difficulty in resolving this debate is the diversity of operations and aircraft types that make up GA, making a single threat assessment for all sectors of the GA industry arguably inappropriate. To put the threat into context, the following discussion provides an overview of the variety of aircraft types, flight operations, and airport characteristics that make up GA. This discussion is followed by an analysis of the existing vulnerabilities in GA security, the terrorist threat posed by GA aircraft, the potential consequences of an attack using various GA aircraft, and how these elements factor into a risk-based assessment of GA security. Based on this analysis, possible approaches and ongoing initiatives to enhance GA security are discussed.

WHAT IS GA?

GA is a catch-all term that encompasses about 54% of all civil aviation activity within the United States, measured in terms of total airport flight operations.[5] Therefore, it is often easier to frame GA in terms of what it is not rather than what it is. In this context, GA refers to most aviation operations not conducted by scheduled passenger airlines, large air cargo operators, or the military. To add to the confusion, commercial charter operations are grouped in with GA and nonrevenue flights, such as maintenance test flights and repositioning flights conducted by passenger and cargo airlines, are usually operated under regulations often regarded as "GA" flight rules. Thus, virtually all flight activity outside the scope of scheduled passenger or cargo air carrier flights and military and government operations may be considered GA. This encompasses a wide variety of aircraft types and flight operations. Table 12.1 shows the distribution of aircraft and flight operations formally categorized as GA.

GA FLIGHT OPERATIONS

As indicated in Table 12.1, recreational flying in personal aircraft (personal flying) and flight instruction, the typical activities one might expect to see at a small to mid-sized GA airport, make up about half of all GA operations and cover about 79% of all aircraft in the total GA fleet. Business and corporate flying, in a wide variety of airplanes and helicopters, make up about one-quarter of all GA operations and slightly less than one-quarter of all GA aircraft. On-demand charter services, referred to as air taxi services, along with air tours and chartered sightseeing flights are also considered GA operations, and these activities combined account for about 13% of all GA operations. In addition to these major categories, there are a wide variety of additional GA operations—such as, aerial advertising (e.g., banner towing and skywriting); aerial application (e.g., crop dusting); aerial observation and other work (e.g., aerial photography, aerial mapping and data collection, traffic reporting, and search and rescue); and medical services (e.g., air ambulance and medical evacuation)—that account for the remaining 17% of all GA operations.

TABLE 12.1
U.S. GA Fleet and Activity (2005 Data)

Category	Number of Aircraft	Percent of GA Fleet	Hours Flown (Millions)	Percent of Operations
Personal	151,400	67.5	9.3	34.4
Business	25,500	11.4	3.2	11.9
Instructional	13,400	6.0	3.6	13.3
Corporate	10,600	4.7	3.1	11.5
Air taxi/charter	6900	3.1	2.9	10.7
Aerial observation	4700	2.1	1.3	4.8
Aerial application	3500	1.6	1.0	3.7
Medical services	1400	0.6	0.7	2.6
Sightseeing	900	0.4	0.2	0.7
Aerial other	800	0.4	0.1	0.4
Other work	700	0.3	0.2	0.7
Air tours	600	0.3	0.4	1.5
External load	200	0.1	0.1	0.4
Unspecified	3800	1.7	0.9	3.3
Total	224,400	100.0	27.0	100.0

Source: Compiled from Department of Homeland Security, Transportation Security Administration, *Fiscal Year 2008 Congressional Justification* and *Fiscal Year 2009 Congressional Justification.*

GA AIRCRAFT

GA encompasses a wide spectrum of aircraft types specifically suited for the broad array of GA operations. Registered GA aircraft in the United States—numbering slightly more than 220,000—range in size and purpose from very light sport aircraft, with maximum takeoff weights of less than 1320 pounds used strictly for recreational flying, to very large business jets, weighing more than 100,000 pounds and used for long-range transcontinental and international travel. The composition of the current GA fleet along with total hours flown in each aircraft category is shown in Figure 12.1. Single-engine piston aircraft make up the large bulk of the fleet (66%). The large majority of these aircraft are comparably small in size, most weighing less than 5000 pounds maximum takeoff weight including payload. Experimental aircraft, mostly small home-built airplanes, make up an additional 11% of the current fleet. Thus, while GA is quite diverse, the typical image of a GA aircraft as a small, light, single-engine airplane is an accurate portrayal of the large majority of GA aircraft, accounting for slightly more than three-quarters of all GA aircraft.

Although turbojet aircraft are a fast-growing segment of the GA fleet, they comprise only about 4% of the current GA fleet, and this is not expected to change much over the next decade. Nonetheless, the growth in the turbojet fleet has important implications for GA security as these heavier, faster, and more capable aircraft become more and more prevalent. While the number of GA pistons and turboprop aircraft are expected to remain essentially flat for the foreseeable future, the numbers of GA turbojets is forecast to grow at a brisk pace of 4.1% per year over the next 10 years. By 2018, it is expected that there will be about 18,000 GA turbojets in service in the United States compared to slightly more than 10,000 in 2005. Turbojet flight activity is expected to grow at an even faster rate of 9.4% annually through 2020. Turbojet flight activity is expected to make up about 31% of all flight hours flown by GA aircraft in 2020, more than double the 14% of the total GA flight hours flown in turbojets in 2005. By 2020, total turbine operations—which include turbojets, turboprops,

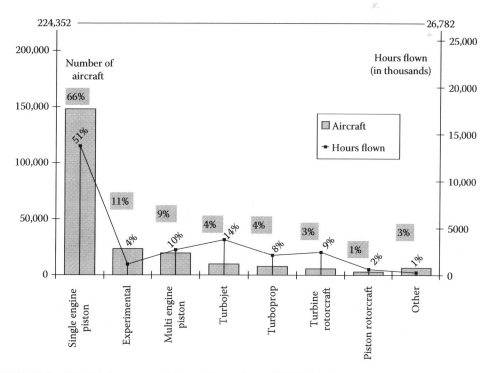

FIGURE 12.1 U.S. GA fleet composition and hours flown (2005 FAA data).

and turbine rotorcraft—are expected to make up 48% of all GA flight activity compared to about 31% in 2005.

While the number of GA turbojets is expected to increase dramatically over the next 10 years, it is important to bear in mind that small, single-engine aircraft will continue to make up a large majority of the GA fleet through 2020. The FAA expects that through 2020, propeller-driven single-engine airplanes, two-seat light sport aircraft, and small home-built experimental airplanes will continue to make up more than 73% of the GA fleet, spurred by projected growth in the fledgling light sport aircraft category. Security experts recognize that both the threats and vulnerabilities of these smaller aircraft are significantly different from the threats and vulnerabilities of medium and large-sized GA turbojets and turboprops. Another segment of the GA industry is helicopters (rotorcraft), which make up only about 4% of the total GA fleet but are involved in several diverse and unique flight operations that introduce their own distinct set of security threats and vulnerabilities. The diversity of GA aircraft types and operations flown suggests that a one-size-fits-all approach to security is not practical—a tenet that both the GA industry and the TSA generally agree on.[6]

GA Airports

Like GA flight operations and aircraft types, GA airports also vary significantly in their size and purpose. They range from unpaved private airstrips with runways less than 2000 feet in length located in remote, unpopulated areas to busy GA reliever airports situated in major metropolitan areas and converted military airbases with runways of sufficient length to handle the largest of jets.

In the United States, there are more than 19,000 total landing facilities including both public- and private-use facilities. Out of these, only about 450 airports serve regularly scheduled commercial passenger flights. The remainder consists of a wide variety of GA airports, heliports, and seaplane bases. Of these, almost 5000 are public use, of which about 3500 have paved runways. A large number of private-use airports—more than 4500 out of about 14,000 total airports—also have paved runways. About 3500 public-use GA airports and another 1000 private-use landing facilities have lighted runways for night operations.[7] The FAA's National Plan of Integrated Airport Systems (NPIAS)—a compilation of those airports eligible for federal AIP funding because they are considered vital to the nation's aviation infrastructure—includes 274 GA reliever airports that primarily serve GA operations in major metropolitan areas, plus slightly more than 2500 additional GA airports—many located in rural communities—that serve as critical links to the NAS. Only these airports are specifically eligible for federal AIP funds to implement security enhancements such as hangars to secure aircraft or improved perimeter fencing.

Airports that exclusively serve GA vary widely in terms of their proximity to densely populated areas, their levels of activity, and the types of operations conducted. To illustrate, consider Peachtree–Dekalb County Airport (PDK), a busy GA reliever located near Atlanta, Georgia. According to the FAA, PDK experiences an average of 639 operations per day, 64% by transient GA aircraft. In 2006, PDK ranked 22nd among the busiest GA airports in the United States.[8] While PDK has an air traffic control tower, even at this relatively busy airport, the tower closes during late night and early morning hours. Almost 600 aircraft are based on the field including 56 jets and 13 helicopters. Contrast this with Red Stewart Airfield (40I) in Waynesville, Ohio—a 2400 foot long grass strip located roughly midway between Dayton and Cincinnati. The airport—considered an "uncontrolled field" because it has no operating control tower—sees less than 50 operations per day. The airport is home to only 42 aircraft—40 small single-engine airplanes and two gliders—that account for most (89%) of the flight activity at the airport.

While airports such as Red Stewart Airfield do not appear to pose any particular security risk, security concerns may be raised about similarly sized airports that are located near critical assets. Consider, for example, Potomac Airfield (VKX) in Friendly, Maryland, which is located about 12 miles south-southeast of Washington, DC. The airport houses about 80 based aircraft, almost all of which are small single-engine airplanes, and sees only about 33 aircraft operations per day. However, because of its close proximity to critical national security assets in Washington, DC, background checks are required for all pilots operating to and from the airport, and special aircraft identification and tracking procedures have been established to closely monitor flight activity at the airport. Thus, location in relation to major national security assets and other potential terrorist targets is a key factor in determining appropriate security measures for GA airports. Implementing measures like this at large numbers of small GA airports would be extremely costly, and it would not be possible to implement such measures effectively on a large scale, given currently available resources.

Most security experts agree that applying identical or inflexible security measures at GA airports that vary so widely in their characteristics is likely to yield an unsatisfactory solution that could either overburden small airport operators or fail to mitigate potential vulnerabilities unique to specific airports or specific types of flight operations. Therefore, a risk-based strategy, implementing security measures tailored to the unique characteristics and vulnerabilities of specific airports, is generally thought to be preferable and has been advocated by aviation security experts and representatives from the GA industry.[9]

THE ECONOMIC IMPACT OF GA

According to the FAA, GA directly generated $13.7 billion and 178,000 jobs in 2000 and its overall economic impact was $40.7 billion (roughly 0.4% of the gross domestic product) and 511,000 jobs.[10] As noted by the FAA, GA provides "on-the-spot efficient and direct aviation services to many medium and small-sized communities that commercial aviation cannot or will not provide."[11] GA also plays an increasingly important role in training pilots and mechanics to serve the airline industry. Additionally, GA operations provide wide-ranging capabilities critical to our economy such as emergency medical services, overnight package delivery to small and mid-sized communities, helicopter transport to support oil drilling in offshore and remote locations, and the aerial application of pesticides to support agriculture, to name a few.

The potential economic impact of security measures for GA could be quite significant. Since the terrorist attacks of September 11, 2001, GA airport operators and the industry have largely relied on their own initiatives and resources to implement security enhancements. These efforts have been somewhat limited because large-scale security enhancements to protect GA assets across the country are expected to be rather substantial. In addition to the terrorist threat, the GA industry has a vested interest in implementing security measures to adequately secure and protect airplanes from theft and vandalism. An article in a GA trade publication noted that while the intent of tightening GA security has largely been seen as a means to prevent terrorism, "... a more immediate benefit could be a stronger bottom line for GA."[12]

The ASAC Working Group on GA Airport Security—an industry group assembled to assist the TSA in developing security guidelines for GA airports—concluded that "... a flexible, common-sense approach to general aviation airport security is mandatory if the industry is to retain its economic vitality and prosper."[13] Securing GA operations without incurring large costs and without imposing burdensome restrictions on legitimate GA operators is likely to remain a significant challenge for policymakers.

THE SECURITY CHALLENGE POSED BY GA

GA security poses significant challenges for policymakers and security experts because GA is highly diverse, geographically dispersed, and relatively open compared to commercial airports servicing passenger airlines and other protected infrastructure such as nuclear reactors and chemical plants. The security threat is not so much to GA assets themselves, but rather, from terrorists seeking to exploit GA assets to attack critical infrastructure or high-profile targets. Nonetheless, some GA assets could themselves become terrorist targets. For example, some corporate aviation operators have expressed concern that aircraft carrying high-profile business leaders and executives, such as presidents of major U.S. corporations, could be targeted, particularly when operating overseas in volatile areas and in regions of the world where security concerns exist. Nonetheless, the primary threat identified regarding GA, both overseas and within the United States, is the concern that aircraft may be used by terrorists to launch an attack against critical facilities or infrastructure.

A secondary threat is that terrorists may infiltrate or otherwise exploit GA to gain knowledge and/or access to the airspace system in the United States. It is known that some of the 9/11 hijackers trained in small GA airplanes in the United States before carrying out their attack using commercial jets. Consequently, following 9/11, there was a specific focus, from both a law enforcement and a policy perspective, on the security of flight schools within the United States and the vetting of foreign students seeking flight training at these schools. ATSA (P.L. 107-71) originally called on the DOJ to implement a program to conduct background checks of all alien applicants seeking flight training in the United States in aircraft weighing more than 12,500 pounds and mandated security training for flight school employees. Vision 100 (P.L. 108-176) placed the responsibility for these flight school background checks in the hands of the TSA and expanded the program to include a notification requirement when foreign students initiate training in lighter aircraft weighing less than 12,500 pounds. These measures were enacted in direct response to the perceived threat that terrorists may infiltrate flight schools in order to gain operating knowledge of aircraft and the NAS.

Since September 11, 2001, policies and approaches for protecting GA aircraft and airports from being exploited in terrorist attacks have focused on providing general guidelines and establishing cooperative arrangements between the GA industry and the TSA for carrying out security enhancements without imposing a rigorous statutory or regulatory framework. The GA industry has argued that inflexible statutory or regulatory measures could impose unnecessary burdens on certain sectors of the GA industry and could be extremely costly to carry out effectively. Legislative actions addressing GA security have focused primarily on the vetting of foreign flight school applicants, GA pilots, and more recently, prospective charter and lease customers. In addition, regulatory actions have been taken to establish airspace restrictions and protections, mostly around the nation's capital, and to implement statutory mandates for vetting certain individuals with access to GA airports and aircraft.

Physical security of GA airports and aircraft has largely been left to aircraft owners and pilots, airport operators, and local authorities. While aircraft owners and pilots have generally favored this approach to avoid potentially restrictive federal security regulations, it has created a perceived burden on airport operators and local authorities to identify and address security needs at the airport level. The TSA has issued guidelines, largely based on industry recommendations, but the federal involvement in terms of both regulatory activity and funding for GA security initiatives has been relatively limited. This approach has led the media and some policymakers and security experts to voice concerns over what they perceive to be persisting vulnerabilities at some GA airports.

SECURITY VULNERABILITIES

Some media reports have raised significant concerns over what has been described as "practically nonexistent" security at many small GA airports.[14] GA advocates have countered that small GA aircraft do not pose a significant threat and point out that many GA airports have taken reasonable steps, largely on their own initiative, to enhance security.[15] However, security concerns remain and a few high-profile incidents pointing to vulnerabilities in GA security have attracted considerable attention and raised concerns among some policymakers and security experts.

In the first of these high-profile incidents following the terrorist attacks of September 11, 2001, a student pilot intentionally crashed a small single-engine airplane into a skyscraper in downtown Tampa, Florida on January 5, 2002. The pilot, described as a troubled youth, reportedly had expressed support for Osama bin Laden and the 9/11 terrorist attacks, but acted alone and had no known ties to any terrorist groups.[16] More recently, on July 22, 2005, a small ultralight crashed near the German parliament building and Chancellor's office in Berlin in what was described by German air traffic control officials as a suspected suicide.[17] The crash prompted German officials to establish a no-fly zone over central Berlin and again raised concerns in the United States over protecting key assets from possible attacks using GA aircraft as this incident occurred just over two months after a high-profile breach of the protected airspace around Washington, DC, by an unauthorized single-engine airplane that prompted evacuations of the White House and the U.S. Capitol.[18] Previously, on June 9, 2004, a miscommunication between air traffic controllers and airspace security monitors in the Washington, DC area resulted in the evacuation of the Capitol and a near shootdown of an airplane transporting Kentucky Governor Ernie Fletcher to the state funeral for President Ronald Reagan.[19] The event sparked congressional hearings delving into the adequacy of airspace defenses and the coordination of airspace protection in the Washington, DC area.

On October 11, 2006, the accidental crash of a small single-engine plane, piloted by New York Yankees pitcher Corey Lidle, into a New York City high rise condominium killing Lidle and his flight instructor and severely injuring one building occupant, renewed post-9/11 concerns over the safety and security of GA flights operated in closed proximity to major population centers. Following the crash, the FAA took action by restricting aircraft access to the East River corridor, a narrow wedge of airspace between Manhattan and Brooklyn where GA flights had been permitted at low altitudes, on the grounds of safety rather than for security reasons. However, following the crash, some policymakers resounded their calls for enhanced security measures, such as GA flight restrictions, in the vicinity of New York City.[20]

While these various incidents have received significant attention given the focus on aviation security following the attacks of September 11, 2001, GA aircraft have been used maliciously in earlier incidents. Most notably, in the early morning of September 12, 1994, a suicidal individual with a history of mental illness, reportedly despondent over personal and business problems, intentionally crashed a stolen small single-engine airplane on the south lawn of the White House.[21] While the airplane was completely destroyed and the perpetrator was killed in the crash, property damage was minimal and the incident posed no threat to those in the White House.

Although these security incidents involving GA aircraft have attracted substantial media interest, such events are relatively rare. While they identify real vulnerabilities in GA security, GA advocates caution that they should be properly viewed in the broader context of risk assessment which fully takes into account the security threat and potential consequences to critical infrastructure posed by these aircraft as well as the nature and scope of specific vulnerabilities. First, while each of these cases highlights a potential security risk posed by GA aircraft, it is important to note that in each of these cases, damage caused by the aircraft was relatively limited and no injuries or deaths to persons on the ground occurred. In other words, these events provide anecdotal evidence supporting the position of GA advocates that the severity of consequences element of the risk equation is comparatively quite small, at least for the small, single-engine prop planes that make up most of the GA fleet. Second, while the incidents in Tampa and Berlin and the 1994 White House incident point to a legitimate concern over suicidal pilots, an examination of NTSB aviation accident data, spanning from 1962 to 2007, found that determined or suspected suicides using GA aircraft have been extremely rare, occurring at a rate of less than two incidents per year.[22] Perhaps more notably, none of these incidents resulted in any deaths of persons on the ground.

In addition to intentional crashes of GA aircraft, aircraft thefts provide additional indications that GA operations may be vulnerable to exploitation by terrorists seeking access to aircraft to carry out attacks against critical infrastructure or other high-profile targets. Two widely reported thefts of GA aircraft in 2005 raised concerns among several policymakers because they were viewed as indicators of the kinds of vulnerabilities in GA operations that could be exploited by terrorists. For example, in an incident that occurred on June 22, 2005, a 20-year-old Connecticut man allegedly stole an aircraft from a Danbury, Connecticut flight school and took two teenage accomplices on a late night "drunken, three-hour joyride" before landing on a taxiway at the Westchester County, New York airport.[23] Later that year, on October 9, 2005, a 22-year-old Georgia man stole a Cessna

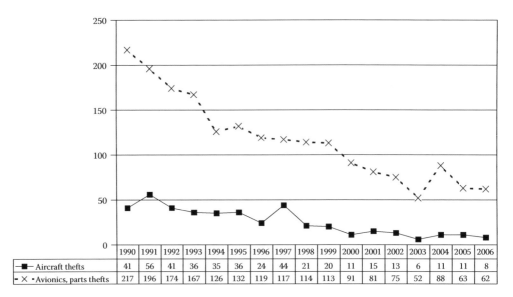

	1990	1991	1992	1993	1994	1995	1996	1997	1998	1999	2000	2001	2002	2003	2004	2005	2006
▬■▬ Aircraft thefts	41	56	41	36	35	36	24	44	21	20	11	15	13	6	11	11	8
▬ ✕ ▪ Avionics, parts thefts	217	196	174	167	126	132	119	117	114	113	91	81	75	52	88	63	62

FIGURE 12.2 Annual number of GA aircraft thefts and thefts of avionics and parts from aircraft in the United States (1990–2006). (Data obtained from Aviation Crime Prevention Institute, Inc., www.acpi.org.)

Citation VII business jet—one that he had served as a copilot on but was not qualified or authorized to fly on his own—from the St. Augustine, Florida airport. The individual took his friends on a late night joyride of more than 300 miles, landing the jet at its base airport, Gwinnett County (Georgia)–Briscoe Field airport near Atlanta.[24] This incident raised considerable security concerns, as the jet was flown in close proximity to several Florida and Georgia cities and nuclear power facilities without raising any suspicion because aircraft operating below 18,000 feet, regardless of size or capability, typically are not required to file flight plans or establish communications with air traffic controllers when operating under VFRs. While thefts of jet aircraft are extremely rare, in another incident that occurred on December 15, 1997, an individual with falsified FAA credentials stole a Lear Jet from the Fort Lauderdale Executive airport in Florida and piloted the airplane to Nicaragua to use the plane for charter flight operations.[25]

Like suspected suicides using aircraft, thefts of small GA aircraft are relatively rare, and thefts of jet aircraft are practically unheard of. Statistics from the Aviation Crime Prevention Institute, Inc. indicate that thefts of GA aircraft have declined considerably since 2000, compared to incidents of GA aircraft theft during the 1990s (Figure 12.2). While airplane thefts may be rare and these data suggest that steps to prevent aircraft thefts are working, high-profile thefts, like the cases cited above, provide some anecdotal evidence that individuals with knowledge of GA airports and aircraft could exploit existing security vulnerabilities to gain access to aircraft relatively easily, despite the increased security awareness at GA airports since the 9/11 attacks.

THE TERRORIST THREAT

While none of the events discussed above has been linked to terrorism, some limited intelligence information that has been made public suggests a continued terrorist interest in using GA aircraft to carry out attacks both domestically and overseas. For example, a crop duster pilot in Florida identified 9/11 suicide hijacker Mohammed Atta as an individual who had approached him in early 2001 inquiring about the purchase and operation of crop duster aircraft.[26] Similarly, U.S. authorities presented evidence that Zacharias Moussaoui—who was arrested prior to the 9/11 attacks after raising suspicions surrounding his desire to train in large aircraft simulators and pleaded guilty to conspiring with the 9/11 hijackers—made similar inquiries about starting a crop-dusting company while living in Norman, Oklahoma. Evidence was also presented that Moussaoui was in possession of a computer disk containing information regarding the aerial application of pesticides.[27] This evidence raised concerns at the CIA that al Qaeda has "considered using aircraft to disseminate [biological warfare] agents."[28]

The CIA also suggested that, in initially planning the 9/11 attacks, one of Osama bin Laden's associates proposed that the WTC be targeted by small aircraft packed with explosives, but bin Laden himself altered the plan to use large commercial jets instead.[29] If true, this suggests that terrorists engaged in some deliberative process of weighing the pros and cons of using small GA aircraft as compared to commercial airlines in planning the 9/11 attacks. While al Qaeda favored commercial aircraft in carrying out its attack on September 11, 2001, in the post-9/11 environment, heightened security measures at commercial airports could make GA assets considerably more attractive to terrorists than in the past. While it is unlikely that small GA aircraft packed with conventional explosives could cause the amount of destruction inflicted on September 11, 2001, large jet aircraft in the GA fleet or smaller aircraft carrying chemical, biological, radiological, or nuclear (CBRN) weapons may pose a more formidable threat.

Although no publically available intelligence on terrorist operations since September 11, 2001, has indicated any specific threat involving GA aircraft domestically, evidence indicates that al Qaeda has maintained a continued interest in using small aircraft to attack U.S. interests overseas. For example, on April 29, 2003, Pakistani authorities apprehended Waleed bin Attash (a.k.a., Khallad or Tawfiq bin Attash)—the suspected mastermind of the U.S.S. Cole bombing and a known associate of the 9/11 hijackers—along with five other suspected al Qaeda operatives in Karachi, Pakistan. Soon after the arrests, authorities uncovered a plot by this group to crash a small, explosives-laden airplane into the U.S. Consulate office in Karachi.[30] The DHS subsequently issued a security advisory indicating that al Qaeda was planning to use GA aircraft to attack warships in the Persian Gulf as well as the U.S. Consulate in Karachi, Pakistan. While the advisory characterized these threats as a demonstrated "fixation" on using aircraft in attacks against U.S. assets, it was strongly criticized by GA interests for being overly alarmist in its tone and overstating the potential threat posed by small GA aircraft.[31]

POTENTIAL CONSEQUENCES OF AN ATTACK USING GA AIRCRAFT

The potential consequences of an attack using GA aircraft are dependent on the intended target and the method of attack. Methods of attacking ground targets may include using aircraft by themselves as WMDs or using them to carry a payload of conventional explosives, or a payload of chemical, biological, or radiological materials, or as a platform to detonate a nuclear device. In these cases, the intended target is presumed to be a target of national security significance, a densely populated area, or a large outdoor congregation of people, such as at a major sporting event or outdoor concert. In addition to these methods of attack and potential targets, the potential that terrorists might use GA aircraft to attack nuclear power facilities to attempt to cause an environmental release of nuclear material has also been cited by some as an additional security concern.

SUICIDE ATTACKS AND CONVENTIONAL EXPLOSIVES

In examining the security risk posed by aircraft that could be utilized in suicide attacks or as launch platforms for conventional explosives, the potential severity of consequences is largely a function of aircraft weight, payload capacity (including fuel capacity), and speed. GA advocacy groups point out that most GA aircraft are capable of carrying less payload than a typical light car. For example, both the Cessna 172 and Piper Warrior—very popular single-engine aircraft—have maximum take-off weights of less than 2500 pounds and useful payloads (including fuel and occupants) of less than 1000 pounds. In contrast, the truck bomb used in the April 19, 1995, Oklahoma City bombing was believed to have contained about 5000 pounds of improvised explosives and the truck bomb involved in the February 26, 1993, bombing at the WTC in New York City was believed to contain a 1300 pound device. While these events involved unusually large explosive devices, typical light GA aircraft would only be able to carry a device a small fraction of this size. Thus, at least with regard to being used as a platform for a conventional explosives attack, the threat posed by light GA aircraft is relatively small compared to trucks that have significantly larger payload capacities.

However, as ground-based security measures such as setbacks, barriers, and access controls are implemented around critical infrastructure, terrorists may view GA aircraft as a possible means to circumvent these defenses. While many forms of ground transportation, especially trucks, can accommodate significantly larger payloads than almost all GA aircraft, some observers fear that aircraft may be used in a terrorist attack because they cannot be as easily thwarted by blockades, barriers, or other physical security measures. Nonetheless, executing an attack that involves loading a GA aircraft with a large quantity of explosives may be difficult without raising some suspicion at the airport, at least domestically, where airport operators and pilots have been instructed to be vigilant for such unusual activities.

CHEMICAL, BIOLOGICAL, RADIOLOGICAL, AND NUCLEAR THREATS

While the threat posed by light GA aircraft carrying conventional explosives is limited by the size and speed of these aircraft, some experts argue that small aircraft may pose a significant threat if used as a platform to launch a CBRN attack over a densely populated area. In these cases, payload capacity and speed may not be regarded as significant components of the risk equation and may have less of an influence in predicting the potential severity of an attack. Rather, with regard to the CBRN threat, the most significant element associated with small GA aircraft appears to be their unique capability to fly at relatively low altitudes and low speeds above densely populated areas and large congregations of people on the ground. In fact, the slow speed of these smaller aircraft and the ease at which doors and windows on nonpressurized airplanes and helicopters can be opened in flight may actually pose a greater potential for launching chemical and biological attacks of consequence compared to larger, faster aircraft. Agricultural aircraft used for spraying crops with pesticides and fertilizers pose a unique threat as a platform for a biological or chemical attack because they are specifically designed for aerial dispersal and could be exploited by terrorists for this specific purpose.

However, the chemical and biological threat using GA aircraft may not be as ominous as some casual observers may fear. First, many of these chemical agents must be released in rather high concentrations. Some, such as cyanides, may only be effective on a large scale if dispensed in an enclosed area, therefore greatly limiting the threat of aerial dispersion.[32] While other chemical agents—such as caustic mustard agents and military nerve agents—may be effective in open air settings, the limited payload of small GA aircraft may limit the scope of an aerial attack using such agents. Second, aerial dispersion of either a chemical or biological agent over populated areas or large congregations of individuals is likely to be easily detected. If a suspected release of a chemical or biological agent is promptly reported, a timely public health response could significantly limit the impact of such an attack. In general, experts believe that if any chemical or biological attack were to occur—whether using a small airplane or some other methods to attack—it would likely be on a small scale physically, but nonetheless, it may have a large psychological impact on the population.

The greatest threat of an aircraft-launched chemical or biological attack appears to be to large, open air assemblies such as major outdoor sporting events and concerts. In fact, one of several homeland security planning scenarios—developed by the White House HSC in partnership with the DHS—describes the potential effects of an adversary using a light aircraft to spray a chemical blister agent into a packed college football stadium holding 100,000 people.[33] The scenario's predicted impact includes 70,000 hospitalizations due to exposure, including many permanent impairments, and 150 deaths. The report, however, notes that expedient decontamination could reduce injuries by one half. This likely represents a worst case scenario in which an extremely large assembly of people could potentially be targeted. Even in densely populated areas, this degree of impact from an aerial attack not specifically targeting a large outdoor assembly is unlikely because it might be expected that many individuals would be indoors or adequately protected by buildings and other structures. Nonetheless, while such an attack may be limited in terms of its physical impact, it may cause widespread fear and panic.

By comparison, the threat from radiological and nuclear devices appears to be much greater in terms of the potential for mass casualties and physical destruction. A small-scale explosive radiological dispersal device—a so-called "dirty-bomb"—could easily fit inside a suitcase or a backpack,[34] and a pilot carrying such a device onto a small GA airplane may not arouse any particular suspicion at an airport. However, the threat posed by such devices is not unique to GA aircraft as these devices could reach their intended target by other means, including being carried in a small car or even being carried by a pedestrian. Most experts concede that, once in the hands of terrorists, it may be difficult to stop an attack with a radiological or nuclear device because many options are available to deliver the weapon to its intended target. One particularly troublesome vector for a nuclear attack would be the use of a GA aircraft that originates outside the United States. While the DHS launched an initiative at the end of 2007 requiring customs officials to screen all inbound GA aircraft for nuclear or radiological threats upon landing in the United States, the possibility that terrorists may fly a nuclear weapon or radiological dispersal device directly to a target on a flight originating outside the United States remains a particular concern because such a scenario offers no real opportunity for detection.

NUCLEAR POWER FACILITIES AS POTENTIAL TARGETS

Concerns have also been raised over the potential threat that an aircraft attack may pose to a nuclear power plant, a chemical plant, or other potentially vulnerable infrastructure where a terrorist attack could inflict widespread damage and mass casualties. A review of security measures at nuclear reactors prepared by the office of U.S. Representative Ed Markey from Massachusetts identified several perceived vulnerabilities at nuclear reactor sites suggesting that these facilities may be vulnerable to 9/11-style attacks using GA aircraft. Based on information provided by the Nuclear Regulatory Commission, Representative Markey's office issued a report on nuclear reactor security that included an assessment of the vulnerability of these facilities to an attack by aircraft.[35] The report noted that while 21 out of 103 reactors in the United States are located within five miles of an airport, 96% of U.S. nuclear reactors did not factor the impact from even a small aircraft into their design. Four reactors were evaluated during their design to consider impacts from aircraft weighing up to 12,500 pounds which would include most GA aircraft except for business jets and large twin-engine aircraft. Three Mile Island in Pennsylvania was cited as the only facility where portions were designed to withstand the impact of large airliners in addition to smaller aircraft. In contrast, the report noted that some European countries, including Switzerland and Germany in particular, incorporate safety features such as reinforced concrete walls and spatial separation of critical safety systems to withstand the crash of certain types of military and commercial aircraft.

Other examinations of the potential threat to nuclear facilities from aircraft have focused on perceived vulnerabilities of spent-fuel pools used to cool expended nuclear fuel. However, power companies maintain that a study modeling the impact of an aircraft crash into a spent-fuel pool wall concluded that while such a scenario could crush or crack the wall, it would not likely cause a release of radiation.[36]

A report prepared for the AOPA by Robert Jefferson, a nuclear reactor safety consultant, concluded that the threat to nuclear reactors from small GA aircraft is "practically non-existent" and "… it is unlikely that a terrorist would choose a light general aviation vehicle to threaten a nuclear power plant."[37] Jefferson's analysis concluded that even the impact of a large airliner would, in all likelihood, be unable to penetrate the outer containment vessel and argued that the analysis referenced by Representative Markey significantly overstates the risk potential and "… overlooks the fact that by their very design, nuclear power plants are inherently resistant to [airborne attacks]."[38] The report also concluded that the proximity of nuclear reactors to GA airports does not increase the exposure of these facilities to terrorist threats.

Although the specific threat posed to nuclear facilities by GA aircraft remains a contentious issue, the FAA has kept in force restrictions on circling, loitering, or otherwise flying in a suspicious manner around nuclear facilities. Arguably, these measures would provide little deterrent against a well-planned terrorist attack. However, they highlight the continued concern over possible airborne threats to nuclear facilities, whatever the true risk may be. More elaborate measures to protect nuclear facilities, such as implementing antiaircraft defense capabilities around nuclear facilities, are wrought with operational and policy complexities including high costs, questionable effectiveness, and a potentially high risk of shooting down an errant GA aircraft whose pilot meant no harm.

THE RISK PICTURE FOR GA AIRCRAFT

While light GA aircraft appear to pose a relatively limited risk by themselves in terms of physically damaging critical infrastructure, larger GA aircraft pose a potentially more formidable risk. Due to the size and speed of some of these aircraft, particularly mid-sized and large business jets, they could inflict significant damage to buildings and critical infrastructure if used in a suicide attack. These aircraft have significantly larger payload and fuel capacities—factors that determine an airplane's so-called "throw weight"—that would have a direct bearing on the degree of physical damage they could cause to buildings and infrastructure. Thus, in terms of both assessing risk and identifying options for mitigating the security risk posed by GA, the distinction between small GA aircraft that make up the large majority of the fleet and larger business jets has important implications. While small aircraft appear to pose a greater risk as possible platforms for chemical or biological attacks, large business jets appear to pose more of a risk from being exploited in a suicide attack scenario similar to the 9/11 attacks using commercial airliners. Because various types of GA aircraft and operations pose distinct security risks, risk mitigation strategies arguably should be tailored to some degree to address the specific threats, vulnerabilities, and potential consequences of an attack involving different sectors of the GA industry.

OPTIONS FOR MITIGATING GA SECURITY RISKS

A variety of options exist for mitigating security risks posed by GA aircraft and flight operations, many of which have been implemented or are currently under development or consideration. Approaches have focused on traditional security techniques to improve access controls and surveillance around GA facilities and better protect aircraft against theft and unauthorized use. Additional initiatives include procedures for vetting individuals that are granted authorized access to aircraft and aviation facilities, and procedures for checking passenger names against terrorist databases. Another approach for enhancing GA security centers on law enforcement and homeland security response to suspicious activities and improved intelligence tracking of such incidents to identify patterns indicative of possible terrorist activity. Also, in terms of adopting a layered security system to augment measures put in place at airports, airspace restrictions and defenses have been implemented in certain areas, such as around Washington, DC, to protect high-profile sites and critical infrastructure from the threat of aerial attacks.

Cost, in terms of direct implementation and oversight costs as well as the indirect costs related to disruption of air commerce and restricted access to airports and airspace, has been an important issue raised in debate over the utility and feasibility of implementing various options to enhance GA security. For example, implementing broadly applied security requirements for all GA airports may impose significant cost challenges, particularly to small, rural airports where the need for such measures may be questionable. Also, airspace restrictions tend to be highly contentious because they have a direct economic impact on GA activity, and they are viewed by some experts as being of questionable value in preventing a terrorist attack unless coupled with elaborate air defense capabilities. Deploying air defense capabilities on a large scale to protect against possible aircraft attacks carries a relatively high cost and involves extensive commitments of resources and collaboration between the FAA, the DHS, and the DOD. The costs and benefits associated with various mitigation options can be analyzed in a risk analysis framework—examining the threat and vulnerability of specific sectors of the GA industry as well as the potential consequences of various attack scenarios exploiting GA—to better understand the tradeoffs between various options.

Security Risk Assessments

Because of the diversity of GA airports, aircraft, and flight operations, and the varied threats and vulnerabilities posed by different sectors of the GA industry, a logical starting point in mitigating security risk would be to perform systematic risk analyses examining specific components of GA. Congress has called for such assessments. Specifically, the FY2006 Department of Homeland Security Appropriations Act (P.L. 109-90) required the DHS to examine the vulnerability of high-risk areas and facilities to possible attack from GA aircraft. Subsequent legislation has focused on assessing risk at GA airports. The Implementing the 9/11 Commission Recommendations Act (P.L. 110-53), enacted in August 2007, included a requirement for the TSA to develop and implement a standardized threat and vulnerability assessment program for GA airports, and implement that assessment program "on a risk-managed basis" at GA airports.

Experts acknowledge that various security threats and vulnerabilities to GA exist. An analysis of GA security by ICAO concluded that "[t]he challenge of designing general aviation security measures focuses on the need to thoroughly define the threat. Before security standards can be developed, there must be a clear picture of the problem."[39] Using the risk analysis framework, the relative effectiveness of mitigation options can be evaluated in terms of how specific security enhancements might address specific threats and reduce existing vulnerabilities to such threats. Examining security strategies in the risk analysis framework can help define how resources can be best allocated in a manner that will mitigate threats based on their likelihood and their potential consequences. The anticipated risk reduction can then be compared to expected costs in an attempt to determine the most cost-effective strategies for enhancing GA security.

One challenge in developing a set of criteria for evaluating risk is the diversity of GA airports. In many respects, the characteristics of GA airports are much more diverse than those of commercial passenger airports. The TSA has provided, as part of its security guidelines for GA airports, an airport characteristics measurement tool.[40] The self-assessment tool scores airports on a scale ranging from 0 to 64, based on a variety of factors, including their proximity to metropolitan areas and sensitive sites; surrounding airspace; the number of based aircraft; runway lengths; the numbers and types of flight operations; and the presence of maintenance, repair, and overhaul (MRO) facilities. Based on the scoring, airports will fall within one of four bands, and the TSA has provided suggested security enhancements for each of the four bands.

Suggestions for airports in all four bands include erecting security signage, establishing documented security procedures, urging operators to adopt procedures for positive passenger/baggage matching and securing aircraft, implementing a community watch program, and designating security contacts. For airports that score in the second band, the TSA recommends in addition to these measures, establishing agreements for law enforcement support, creating a designated security committee, and establishing sign-in/sign-out methods for tracking transient aircraft and pilots. For airports scoring in the third band, operators should also consider implementation of access control systems, enhanced security lighting, identification systems for airport personnel and vehicles, and security challenge procedures for detecting unauthorized access. Finally, for airports scoring in the highest band using this self-assessment tool, the TSA suggests possible enhancements to perimeter fencing, expanded use of secured hangar facilities to protect aircraft, and consideration of CCTV surveillance and/or intrusion detection systems. While these are useful suggestions, the process is relatively generic and does not consider site-specific factors. It thus provides only a rudimentary risk assessment tool and process for GA airport operators.

More detailed security risk assessments can be carried out at the airport level or, for some larger operators, such as large corporate and fractional-ownership fleets, at the operator level. Among state initiatives aimed at improving GA security at the airport level, several aviation security experts and members of the GA community have praised the Commonwealth of Virginia's approach. The Virginia Department of Aviation, relying on an advisory committee on aviation security comprised of various stakeholders, developed a voluntary program for GA airports that provides incentives for capital investment to those airports that complete security "self-audits" on annual basis and undergo Virginia State Police security audits every three years. The audits focus on access controls, maintenance and upkeep of security aspects of the airport property, and surveillance capabilities and weaknesses at the airport. Key strengths of the program highlighted by its supporters include the fact that it is a voluntary, incentive-based program, that it is proactive in its approach, and that it fosters a cooperative partnership between airports and law enforcement that may prove beneficial in responding to security incidents at the airport.[41] Various other states, such as Massachusetts and Ohio, either mandate that all GA airports carry out security audits and/or develop a formal security plan or require such actions for an airport to be eligible for state funding.[42]

As previously noted, in 2007, the Implementing the 9/11 Commission Recommendations Act (P.L. 110-53) included a provision requiring the TSA to develop and implement a standardized threat and vulnerability assessment program for GA airports, and implement that assessment program "on a risk-managed basis" at GA airports. Additionally, the law requires the TSA to complete a feasibility study to assess the concept of providing grants to GA airport operators for security enhancements based on a risk-managed approach. If deemed feasible, the bill authorizes the implementation of such a grant program.

Based on detailed risk analyses, cost-effective security programs that address the specific degree and nature of risk at specific airports can be designed and implemented. Various combinations of security measures are available and can be tailored for airport-specific or operator-specific security plans. These include various approaches to: surveillance and monitoring; airport access controls; and physical security measures to protect aircraft. These specific security systems implemented by airports and operators may be augmented by broader initiatives such as the vetting of GA pilots and airport workers at the federal level, and establishing specific procedures and defenses to protect airspace near critical locations. In the following discussion, these various approaches and the challenges associated with applying them to GA security are discussed in further detail.

SURVEILLANCE AND MONITORING

Surveillance and monitoring of GA operations present significant challenges. Of the 5286 public-use landing facilities in the United States, only about 500 have operating control towers and most of these are located at airports with regularly scheduled commercial service. Only the busiest airports that cater exclusively to GA aircraft have operating control towers. These airports usually are geographically large and congested making surveillance for security purposes from the tower difficult. What is more, even at the limited number of GA airports with operating control towers, most towers are not operated on a continuous basis and close during late night and early morning hours. Further, even during times of operation, the security role of staffed control towers is unclear. During operating hours, controllers remain busy performing air traffic separation and control functions, making it difficult for them to spot unusual activity or detect unauthorized aircraft usage unless suspicions are raised by unusual requests, improper phraseology, or procedural violations. Therefore, the mere presence of an operating control tower appears to provide little additional security to a GA airfield.

Smaller GA airports, most of which do not have operating control towers, are usually not attended by airport management or FBOs on the field 24 hours a day. Depending on the frequency of traffic, an airport may be attended only during daylight hours, or sometimes during limited evening hours. Aircraft may still use many of these airports during late night and early morning hours as runway lights can be controlled from the cockpit using on-board radios. Airport access controls and surveil-lance during these unattended hours present a unique challenge to airport operators. On the one hand, accessibility is important to meet the needs of air commerce by allowing operations such as late night arrivals and departures for business trips and overnight cargo delivery to small communities. Furthermore, maintaining airport accessibility at night serves a critical safety function providing alternate landing sites if an airplane is required to deviate for weather or mechanical reasons. Providing for airport access for these purposes, including access for transient aircraft, must be incorporated into security plans and programs for GA airports, adding additional complexity to implementing effective security measures.

Full-time on-site security personnel are a costly option for many small airports. Remote sensing and surveillance using cameras and motion sensors, for example, may offer a somewhat more cost-effective alternative, but requires close coordination with local security forces and law enforcement to respond to suspected threats or security breaches. Uncertainty and high false alarm rates in detection systems can drive up costs associated with security response and can lead to complacency that may limit the effectiveness of these systems. However, these remotely monitored security sys-tems provide an alternative to security monitoring for many airport sites where full-time on-site security personnel is cost prohibitive. At least one vendor provides tailored security packages that integrate alarms, cameras, entry and access controls, fencing, lighting, motion detectors, and acous-tic sensors in a system specifically tailored for the GA airport environment.[43] Several vendors now offer customized security sensor integration and remote monitoring capabilities that can be deployed in a GA airport environment. A key element of these types of integrated security systems is their monitoring capabilities, including remote Internet-based monitoring of cameras and other intrusion detection devices and the capability to tie into local law enforcement networks for coordinated response. However, these integrated systems can be quite costly to install, maintain, and operate. Consequently, the GA community, in coordination with the TSA, has applied a long-established, low-cost approach to security and surveillance in residential neighborhoods—the neighborhood watch concept—to GA airports throughout the United States.

THE AIRPORT WATCH PROGRAM

To enhance surveillance at airports, the TSA, in cooperation with the AOPA and the National Response Center, launched an airport watch program at GA airports in December, 2002. The Airport Watch program is similar to a neighborhood watch program and relies on the cooperation and participation of pilots, airport tenants, and airport workers to observe and report suspicious activity. Educational and training materials have been made available to these individuals to increase their awareness regarding potentially suspicious activity, and a hotline—1-866-GA-SECURE—has been set up to log reports of suspicious activity. Under this program, instructional materials advise observers to call local law enforcement using 911 if they believe the situation potentially poses an immediate threat.

Since its inception, the Airport Watch program has been credited with alerting authorities to suspicious activities at GA airports on several occasions. For example, the AOPA cited one peculiar incident as a demonstration of the effectiveness of the airport watch concept. In August 2004, two men of "Middle Eastern appearance" presented themselves at an airport near St. Louis offering cash to charter a helicopter and presenting driver's licenses from two different states as identification. The charter operator also noted that the men were driving a vehicle registered in a third state and observed the men removing "odd shaped luggage" from that vehicle in preparation for the flight. Based on these observations, the charter operator stalled the suspicious individuals and notified the FBI and local law enforcement who responded and arrested the two individuals. The suspicious individuals turned out to be reporters on an assignment to demonstrate how easily terrorists could hijack a helicopter.[44] The AOPA noted several other successes of the Airport Watch program including the capture of a suspected con man in Kansas who attempted to rent aircraft at several facilities, and several cases of suspicious inquiries regarding aircraft rentals, charter flights, flight instruction, and use of hangar storage space. These incidents all resulted in responses by federal law enforcement authorities, although none have been specifically linked to terrorism.

Despite the benefits and successes of the Airport Watch program, which have been achieved at a relatively low cost, there are several challenges to implementing a successful watch program. A major limitation of the Airport Watch program is that it may be difficult—especially for untrained observers—to distinguish suspicious behavior from normal activities. Past terrorist attacks have indicated that terrorists are likely to use methods that avoid arousing suspicion. In essence, terrorists have hidden in plain sight in the past, and may be likely to do so in the future. Suspicious terrorist activities may not appear out of the ordinary to the casual observer. While convicted terrorist Zacharias Moussaoui's peculiar inquiries about flying large jet aircraft and his obvious lack of qualifications to seek such training did raise suspicions at the flight school where he sought advanced jet training, terrorist behavior patterns are likely to be much more subtle. None of the 9/11 terrorist pilots nor Moussaoui attracted similar attention during their initial training in small GA aircraft. The all too obvious example of a clandestine rendezvous where cargo is loaded from a vehicle onto a small aircraft at a remote area of the airport is likely to be regarded by terrorists as too likely to arouse suspicion. Rather, terrorists may try to blend in as well as possible. For example, a pilot loading a small single-engine airplane with dangerous chemicals or biological agents on the ramp may look no different than a pilot loading his personal effects on board for a weekend getaway to casual observers. While single incidents like this typically arouse little suspicion, aggregate behavior that might appear somewhat odd or suspicious could collectively signal possible terrorist or criminal activity. TSA training for employees at flight schools and FBOs as well as educational materials developed by the AOPA for the Airport Watch program delve into these various nuances of suspicious activity, and provide appropriate courses of action for documenting and providing notification of such activity.

Such training is an important part of these kinds of programs to minimize potential undesired consequences of high false alarm rates and possible racial and ethnic profiling by well-intentioned pilots and airport tenants. High false alarm rates could place a strain on local law enforcement, especially in rural areas and small communities where law enforcement support is limited. Also, security personnel and local law enforcement may become complacent if a large number of false alarms are reported at local airports. Without training and informational material, there is also a greater potential for possible racial and ethnic profiling in reporting suspicious activity. Besides the potential for falsely targeting individuals in certain racial and ethnic groups, there is also the danger that, conversely, untrained observers may not notice suspicious behavior patterns exhibited by other individuals. For example, would the individuals in the St. Louis incident cited by AOPA have raised similar suspicions if they were not of "Middle Eastern appearance"? Intelligence sources suspect that al Qaeda is seeking to recruit non-Middle Eastern individuals for the very reason that they may be less likely to raise suspicions. More specific guidance and training for airport workers, tenants, and pilots could improve the effectiveness of the Airport Watch program and other surveillance operations. Other limitations to these types of programs are that the response time of local law enforcement is often slow, and local law enforcement—especially in small, rural communities— may not be adequately integrated with homeland security systems to receive a timely notification when an incident is reported, although observers are specifically instructed to dial 911 if they believe the situation poses an immediate threat.

APPLYING BEHAVIORAL PATTERN RECOGNITION TECHNIQUES IN THE GA ENVIRONMENT

A possible solution to overcome some of these limitations involves the implementation of training in behavioral pattern recognition techniques. As described in a commentary on GA security, behavioral pattern recognition was highlighted as being "... designed to maximize detection while minimizing, if not eliminating, issues of civil liberties."[45] Behavioral pattern recognition—which is in use at airports worldwide and has been highlighted in numerous profiles of Israel's El Al airlines' preboarding security screening—examines deviations from normative behavioral patterns. In addition to the TSA's widespread use of behavior pattern recognition at commercial passenger airports in recent years, it has been suggested that behavioral pattern recognition could also be applied in the GA environment. This could be done by providing specific training to maintenance and line workers, for example, making them an integral part of an airport's security network rather than having a small number of employees responsible for security.

One challenge in effectively using behavioral pattern recognition techniques is that single events may not stand out, but aggregate samples of slightly unusual activity may provide telltale signs of preparations for launching a terrorist attack. However, assimilating and correctly interpreting this data remains a significant challenge. For this reason, a "reporting tree" is recommended for guiding decisions about responding to suspicious behavioral patterns.[46] The "reporting tree" concept is integrated into the TSA's security training for flight schools, which is a required security training element for flight school employees. A reporting tree might include notifying a supervisor, such as a chief flight instructor or flight school manager, about strange inquires or behaviors exhibited by a student pilot, and escalating this information up the reporting tree to law enforcement or federal officials only if the behavior is repeatedly demonstrated and, in aggregate, raises enough concern to warrant further action. In this manner, the Airport Watch program, in coordination with specific training and guidance in techniques such as behavioral pattern recognition and the use of reporting trees, has the potential to contribute to the intelligence gathering function at a relatively low cost by enlisting the support of a broad segment of the GA community.

AIRPORT ACCESS CONTROLS

Controlling access to GA airports is a significant challenge for many reasons. First, as already discussed, few GA airports are continuously attended or monitored, and doing so is likely to be costly and resource intensive. Second, GA airports support a wide variety of operations and consequently must provide extensive access to airports, aircraft, and facilities to support and sustain these varied operations, including late night cargo operations, training flights, and maintaining adequate numbers of landing facilities that are continuously available for safety in the case of diversions due to weather or mechanical difficulties.

Providing airport access for transient operators also presents a unique security challenge for GA airports, especially during hours when the facility is not attended. However, restricting airports from transient access has significant consequences both for air commerce and for safety. For example, restricting access after hours may impede air commerce and business, especially in remote areas that rely significantly on the presence of a GA airport. Professionals who use GA aircraft to conduct business in these areas may be reluctant to do so if they run the risk of being denied access to the airport because of a late running business meeting that extends beyond the operating hours of the airport, for example. Also, for safety reasons, sufficient numbers of GA airports need to remain accessible, at least for landing aircraft, to provide suitable alternate airports in case of emergency or diversion due to weather.

Allowing airport access during nonattended hours, however, poses significant security challenges. Access control measures must adequately accommodate transient users or the airport runs the risk of becoming inaccessible to certain users. Various options exist for providing both local and transient operators with adequate access to the flight line. For example, at airports implementing access controls to aircraft storage and operations areas, keypad locks can be installed to control access to flight lines. Codes could be provided to transient operators in case they need to access aircraft after hours and could be changed frequently to prevent unauthorized access. Alternatively, more sophisticated access controls can be implemented using key code or card reader systems where transient operators are provided with codes or cards that expire and cannot be used after a certain period.

Display of identification badges in aircraft operations areas may also improve security by identifying those individuals with authorized access. This can alert observers and security personnel to possible unauthorized access. TSA security guidelines for GA airports suggest that airport identification credentials include features such as a photograph showing a full face image, the holder's full name, the airport name, employer information, a unique identification number, the scope of access and movement privileges through easily interpretable means such as color-coding, and a clear expiration date.[47] These guidelines parallel regulatory requirement for commercial passenger airports and air cargo operations areas.

Pilots, for whom access privileges at multiple airports are needed, require a standardized identification that is easily recognizable at all airport facilities. Presently, FAA certificates do not contain photographs of the certificate holder. Older paper certificates, which are being phased out, could be easily forged, especially with the sophistication of consumer printers now available. However, current regulations require pilots to carry government-issued photo identification, such as a driver's license, and present that identification along with their pilot credentials upon the request of a LEO or federal official. This, however, would not allow for easy detection of someone with phony pilot credentials, so long as those credentials matched information on the individual's identification. ATSA (P.L. 107-71) directed the FAA to study ways to improve pilots' licenses such as including photos. In response, the FAA has taken steps to make newly issued pilot certificates more tamper-resistant and more difficult to forge. The IRTPA of 2004 (P.L. 108-458, Sec. 4022) required the FAA to begin issuing improved pilot certificates that include a photograph of the holder and have the capability to accommodate a digital photograph, a biometric identifier, and any other unique identifiers that the FAA may determine to be necessary. While specific plans for issuance of the new pilot certificates with photographs have not yet been announced by the FAA, statutory language provides for the use of designees such as designated pilot medical examiners to issue these new licenses in an effort to "minimize the burdens on pilots."[48] Advocates for GA pilots have pushed for the use of designated aviation medical examiners for issuance of the new certificates, noting that forcing pilots, particularly pilots in rural areas, to travel to an FAA Flight Standards District Office (FSDO) would be, in their opinion, an unacceptable burden.[49]

While these new pilot credentials must include the capability to store biometric information, the use of biometrics for identification purposes and access controls in the GA environment introduces many complex technical and policy questions. Implementing biometric access controls at GA airports may be feasible in some cases, but presents significant challenges because of the possible need to obtain and encode biometric information for transient operators as well as those local tenants, pilots, operators, and airport workers who are authorized to have unescorted access to the flight line. While biometrics have distinct advantages in terms of logging and tracking access to restricted areas, privacy issues, cost, and logistics may make them difficult to implement effectively in the GA airport environment. However, biometrics may play a more significant role at the GA operator level of security where they could be implemented to control access to operator facilities such as aircraft storage and maintenance hangars. Biometrics may also be used on more limited sets of individuals and integrated into identification card access systems for local aircraft owners, operators, pilots, and airport workers. Doing so may allow security efforts to focus more directly on those individuals at an airport that pose more of an unknown threat, such as charter passengers not known to their flight crews and other airport visitors.

BACKGROUND CHECKS AND VETTING

Because GA airports must maintain a level of reasonable accessibility, surveillance, access controls, and physical security measures to protect aircraft and facilities must be designed to accommodate a diverse set of legitimate airfield uses. For this reason, implementing access controls and physical security on par with commercial passenger airports is likely to be unrealistic. However, conducting background checks and vetting individuals who routinely access GA airports is seen as a possible technique for assessing potential threats and also as a possible means to focus security resources on conducting surveillance and limiting access to aircraft for airport visitors and others who are of an unknown risk.

Vetting of transportation workers and others who routinely access transportation facilities has been a cornerstone of several statutorily mandated projects related to transportation security. For example, the TSA is required to conduct background checks of workers at commercial passenger airports, and the TSA has several ongoing projects, such as the TWIC program, focused initially on seaport workers, and various airport access control pilot studies, that are attempting to integrate background checks and vetting with the use of biometric access credentials. While it may be some time before these biometric technologies will be mature enough and available at a low enough cost to be considered for application in the GA environment, there are already several statutory requirements for vetting GA pilots, pilot applicants, and more recently, prospective aircraft charter and lease customers.

VETTING OF INDIVIDUALS SEEKING FLIGHT TRAINING

The most widely known of these GA vetting activities is the TSA's alien flight training rule, which requires the TSA to conduct background investigations of non-U.S. applicants seeking flight training in the United States for aircraft weighing more than 12,500 pounds and requires flight schools or flight instructors to notify the TSA whenever a non-U.S. applicant wishes to initiate flight training in smaller aircraft weighing less than 12,500 pounds.[50] U.S. citizens seeking any type of flight training, including proficiency checks and periodic flight reviews by flight instructors, must present a valid birth certificate and a government-issued photo identification, such as a driver's license or passport, to demonstrate that they are not subject to these background check requirements.

In response to law enforcement and intelligence information revealing that the 9/11 hijackers and accomplice Zacharias Moussaoui received flight training in the United States and amid concerns that foreign terrorists could further infiltrate flight schools in the United States, ATSA (P.L. 107-71) initially placed the DOJ in charge of conducting fingerprint-based record checks for alien flight school applicants seeking training to fly aircraft weighing more than 12,500 pounds. Under Vision 100 (P.L. 108-176), this responsibility was moved to the TSA, the process was streamlined to limit the impact of the process on legitimate flight training activities, and reporting requirements were expanded to include a notification requirement whenever foreign flight school applicants initiate flight training in the United States in smaller aircraft weighing less than 12,500 pounds.

CHECKING FAA RECORDS ON PILOTS AND OTHERS AGAINST
CRIMINAL AND TERRORIST DATABASES

A lesser known component of TSA's efforts to vet pilots (whether they are GA pilots, charter pilots, or airline pilots), aircraft mechanics, and dispatchers is the use of threat assessments to screen holders of and applicants for FAA certificates, ratings, or authorizations. Rules pertaining to the STAs for FAA certificate holders and applicants were promulgated on January 24, 2003.[51] Under these rules, the TSA notifies the FAA whenever an FAA certificate holder or applicant who is not a citizen of the United States is determined to present a security threat. The FAA, in turn, will deny, suspend, or revoke the individual's FAA certificate as appropriate. While a parallel rule was initially issued to carry out STAs for U.S. citizens holding or applying for FAA certifications, this measure was criticized because it lacked adequate safeguards for redress. Critics argued that the rule gave the TSA significant power over the issuance of pilot certificates and other aviation credentials without any oversight or redress process for the TSA to demonstrate the specific evidence or basis for its decisions and actions.[52] In response to these concerns, Vision 100 (P.L. 108-176, Sec. 601) mandated the TSA to establish a redress and remedy process entitling U.S. citizens subject to certificate action on the basis of a STA to a formal redress hearing before an administrative law judge and an appeals process before a panel convened by the Transportation Security Oversight Board. While the DHS has established a central office for handling redress cases, the TSA has not yet issued revised rulemaking to conform with the statutory requirements set forth in Vision 100, and therefore, existing regulations to enforce FAA certificate actions on the basis of STAs no longer apply to U.S. citizens.[53]

In 2009, however, the TSA issued a security directive requiring that certain FAA certificate holders and other GA workers undergo STAs and CHRCs to obtain access credentials in order to access GA ramps and operations areas at commercial passenger airports. It has been reported that, despite the fact that TSA cannot prompt certificate actions solely on the basis of STAs, FAA databases of pilots, mechanics, and other certificate holders are routinely culled to identify any individuals with known or suspected links to terrorism.[54] The new security directive also appears to provide a means for the TSA to deny access to GA operations areas of commercial airports when FAA certificate holders are considered to pose a security threat on the basis of STAs and CHRCs.

BACKGROUND CHECK REQUIREMENTS FOR CHARTER OPERATORS

Regulations require fingerprint-based CHRCs for charter pilots who fly aircraft weighing more than 12,500 pounds. These pilots undergo the same fingerprint-based CHRC required of airline pilots and employees with unescorted access to aircraft and restricted areas of commercial passenger airports and are subject to the same list of disqualifying criminal offenses. While charter pilots must pass these background checks in order to fly larger aircraft in charter flight operations, other GA pilots—who make up the majority of the almost 600,000 active pilots in the United States—are not required to submit to any formal background screening or checks, unless as previously noted they require access to GA operations areas at commercial passenger airports. Some critics of background checks and vetting maintain that they are costly and unnecessary intrusions into the privacy of citizens. On a pragmatic level, some question whether background checks for GA are needed at all, particularly at small, rural airports where pilots, ramp workers, and others who frequent the airport are largely known to each other. Nevertheless, background checks and other vetting activities have been looked upon favorably by many policymakers as a core component of a layered security system and could be further expanded in their application to GA airports and operators.

VETTING OF CHARTER AND AIRCRAFT LEASE CUSTOMERS

One area where background checks and STAs are being incorporated into GA operations is for the vetting of prospective charter and lease customers. Under statutory provisions set forth in the IRTPA of 2004 (P.L. 108-458, Sec. 4012), the TSA is charged with the task of setting up a mechanism for charter and aircraft lease operators to voluntarily submit the names of prospective clients seeking access to aircraft weighing more than 12,500 pounds for screening against the consolidated terrorist watch list. Aircraft operators may deny individuals access to aircraft if their name is found to match watch list records. While the legislative language limited the applicability of this vetting procedure to aircraft weighing more than 12,500 pounds, the feasibility of extending this capability to charters and leases of smaller aircraft and renter pilots, based on the initial experience with larger aircraft, was debated during consideration of this legislation. While terrorist database screening of prospective charter and lease customers as legislated is voluntary, policymakers may also consider whether mandatory screening of aircraft charter and lease customers is warranted.

TRACKING AIRCRAFT SALES

Besides prospective charter and lease customers, the screening of prospective aircraft purchasers can serve as an important deterrent to prevent terrorists or organizations that support terrorism from acquiring aircraft that could be used in a terrorist attack. Under Department of the Treasury regulations, promulgated to meet requirements of the USA PATRIOT Act (P.L. 107-56), aircraft sales must comply with various information sharing, reporting, and records keeping requirements aimed at identifying suspicious transactions and preventing money laundering. However, because many other large-scale financial transactions such as the sale of houses, boats, and cars must be similarly reported, the volume of transactions may make it difficult to quickly identify suspicious aircraft transactions. The main intent of these regulations is to spot potential attempts to launder illegal funds in support of terrorist or criminal activities, and therefore the regulations are not specifically designed to vet purchasers of GA aircraft against terrorist watch lists. The capability to detect aircraft sales to suspected terrorists or their associates and vet aircraft purchasers against terrorist watch lists under these reporting requirements remains unclear.

PHYSICAL SECURITY MEASURES FOR AIRPORTS

Other than surveillance, access controls, and background checks, there are a variety of other options for enhancing the general physical security of airport facilities. One of the most obvious of these measures is erecting physical barriers, such as chain-link perimeter fencing, around security-sensitive locations on the airfield. While most GA airports have some fencing, relatively few have a completely fenced perimeter. Enclosing an entire airport perimeter would typically require miles of fencing, even for a relatively small field. One survey of GA airports found that the amount of fenced perimeter ranges from less than 10% to 100%, with most airports having more than 40% of their perimeter fenced.[55] The TSA cautions that while physical barriers such as fencing, walls, electronic boundaries, and even natural barriers can protect airport areas from unauthorized access, these methods by themselves will not prevent determined intruders from gaining access. The TSA further notes that excessive spending on extensive perimeter enhancements may actually be detrimental to an airport's overall security posture to the extent that these efforts take away from opportunities to improve upon other aspects of security.[56] Besides fencing, protective lighting can often serve as an effective deterrent against theft, vandalism, unauthorized access, and other illegal activity at night.

While various combinations of physical barriers and lighting may deter unauthorized access at airports, the TSA notes that storing aircraft in hangars is one of the most effective methods of securing GA aircraft. However, at many GA airports, hangar space is in short supply and the demand for hangars makes them very costly, especially for some small, privately owned aircraft.

In October 2008, the TSA proposed to require certain GA airports to adopt formal security programs. Specifically, the TSA proposed requirements that GA reliever airports, that relieve congestion from major commercial airports, and GA airports that regularly serve scheduled commuter flights and public charter operations must adopt formal, TSA-approved security programs. Under the proposal, these airports would be required to designate an airport security coordinator, establish procedures for law enforcement support and incident management, implement training programs for law enforcement personnel assigned to the airport, establish procedures for informing the public regarding airport security matters through public advisories, and establish a system for maintaining security-related records of law enforcement response to incidents that occur at the airport.[57]

PHYSICAL SECURITY MEASURES FOR AIRCRAFT

While surveillance, access controls, and physical security measures at airports can provide effective deterrents, these measures may be costly and challenging to implement at many GA airports, especially smaller airports. Measures to physically secure aircraft can be viewed either as an additional layer of security to prevent theft and unauthorized access to aircraft at airports with extensive surveillance and access controls or as a primary means of security at some airports with more limited security capabilities.

Physical security measures for aircraft may include cabin and ignition locks, which may already exist for certain aircraft, as well as supplemental immobilizing devices such as propeller, throttle, control surface, and tie-down locks. The TSA's *Security Guidelines for General Aviation Airports* recommends storing aircraft in locked hangars, consistently using aircraft door locks, using keyed ignitions when appropriate, and not leaving keys in aircraft as some basic steps to secure GA aircraft. The guidelines also recommend using an auxiliary lock such as commercially available propeller, throttle, or tie-down locks to further protect GA aircraft. The TSA suggests that "[p]ilots should employ multiple methods of securing their aircraft to make it as difficult as possible for an unauthorized person to gain access to it."[58]

While building or renting secured hangar space may be cost prohibitive to many light aircraft owners, locks and other security devices may provide a common-sense, cost-effective means to reduce the vulnerability of GA aircraft to theft. Given that aircraft are high-value assets, locks may offer a relatively low-cost means to reduce vulnerability. Purchasing and installing secondary locks could benefit aircraft owners and operators by providing added protection against theft and unauthorized access.

In the absence of explicit federal standards or requirements, some states have taken initiatives to require specific actions for securing GA aircraft. New Jersey, for example, has implemented a statewide "two-lock rule" requiring any aircraft parked or stored at a GA facility within the state for more than 24 hours to either secure the aircraft with two distinct locking devices or disable the aircraft in a manner to prevent theft or illegal use.[59] Propeller locks and throttle locks may provide relatively low cost, relatively effective deterrents to unauthorized use and theft of aircraft.

SECURING AGRICULTURAL AVIATION OPERATIONS

The specific intelligence and law enforcement evidence pointing to al Qaeda's interest in cropdusting aircraft in the months leading up to 9/11 suggests that the agricultural sector of GA should be particularly alert to suspicious activities. Because agricultural aviation operations largely take place in rural environments, away from highly populated areas, increased awareness of this threat coupled with operators increasing their vigilance and taking steps to secure their aircraft may serve as an adequate deterrent. However, the unique capabilities of aircraft, both airplanes and helicopters, used in aerial application operations make them specifically attractive to terrorists. For this reason, the TSA recommended to operators of agricultural aircraft that they use multiple security devices—such as throttle and control locks, propeller locks, and hidden ignition switches—to secure aircraft, store aircraft in hangars with electronic security systems and steel doors, and when hangars are not available, park heavy equipment in a manner to prevent the movement of aircraft.[60] The National Agricultural Aviation Association has provided additional guidance to operators of agricultural aircraft advising them to secure pesticide storage areas; implement procedures for the shipping and receiving of chemicals; secure facilities and limit access; post security signs; improve lighting of storage areas; secure fences and gates; conduct security inspections to check for signs of intrusion or tampering; maintain logs to track visitor access to facilities; coordinate with local law enforcement and fire departments; and develop site security plans as required to comply with hazardous materials (HAZMAT) regulations.[61]

FLIGHT SCHOOL SECURITY

Besides agricultural aircraft operations, another sector of GA flying that has raised security concerns has been flight schools. Flight schools have been spotlighted, in large part, because of intense media coverage of the apparent relative ease that some of the 9/11 hijackers were able to obtain flight training in the United States, and the reported lack of safeguards to prevent incidents like the intentional crash of a small single-engine airplane into a downtown Tampa, Florida building piloted by a student pilot who stole the aircraft while conducting an unsupervised preflight inspection.[62]

To address lingering concerns over flight school security, Vision 100 (P.L. 108-176) required specific flight school security awareness training for all flight school employees. To meet this statutory requirement, the TSA has developed a standardized computer-based flight school security awareness training program, although flight schools have the option of developing their own security training program that must obtain TSA approval. New hires must receive initial security awareness training within 60 days of employment, and employees must complete recurrent training in security awareness on an annual basis. The training indoctrinates flight school employees on fundamentals of security awareness, security practices, and appropriate responses to suspicious events. In addition to the statutory requirement for security awareness training, the TSA has issued several recommendations for flight schools in its security guidelines for GA airports. These recommendations largely focus on increasing surveillance and supervision of students and renter pilots and better controlling access to aircraft and aircraft keys. For example, it is recommended that students conducting unsupervised pre-flight inspections only be given keys to unlock the aircraft and not ignition keys. Other steps that may be taken by flight schools to improve security include employment background checks and screening of prospective employees, particularly prospective flight instructors and maintenance personnel; establishment of formal written security procedures for employees and customers; display of identification by employees; and various access controls and surveillance measures for the flight line.

SECURITY PRACTICES FOR BUSINESS AND CHARTER AVIATION

In addition to agricultural aviation and flight schools, another sector of GA with unique security needs is business aviation. Larger, faster business jets introduce unique security concerns because of their size and speed as well as their relatively high value and, in some instances, the prominence of passengers carried on board these aircraft. While business jets make up a relatively small percentage of GA aircraft, their larger size, heavier payload, and faster speed introduce unique risks. Chartered business jets and turboprops also pose unique security risks because, unlike corporate or privately owned aircraft, charter companies and flight crews often do not know their passengers.

In coordination with the TSA, the National Business Aviation Association (NBAA) has implemented a program promoting aviation security best practices among business aircraft operators. The program focuses on various facets of operator security including identifying security roles within an operator's organization; providing security training to flight department personnel; establishing sound physical security measures to control access to facilities and aircraft; issuing photo identifications for crewmembers; conducting preflight security inspections of aircraft; matching baggage to passengers; maintaining positive control of baggage; and developing and keeping up-to-date site-specific security and emergency response plans.

The TSA Access Certificate Program

Based in part on the NBAA's initiatives regarding aviation security best practices, the TSA initiated a pilot program, called the TSA Access Certificate or TSAAC program, for business aircraft operators in the spring of 2003. The TSAAC program was initially offered to operators based at Teterboro Airport (TEB) in New Jersey, and was later expanded to include operators at Westchester County Airport (HPN) in New York, and Morristown Airport (MMU) in New Jersey. While the specifics of the TSAAC program are regarded as security-sensitive information, the program generally requires operators to implement security procedures similar to the operational security measures required for charter aircraft operators who fly aircraft weighing more than 12,500 pounds. Elements of the program include various physical security measures for aircraft, vetting of customers and other visitors, control of passengers and baggage, access controls for the flight line and aircraft operations areas, and the utilization of threat intelligence. From 2003 until 2006, aircraft operators approved under TSAAC were allowed to enter the United States from all foreign destinations, whereas nonparticipating aircraft had been restricted to enter into U.S. airspace from only a limited number of "portal" countries. These restrictions were rescinded in August 2006 for aircraft weighing less than 45,500 kg (roughly 100,000 pounds), effectively eliminating the incentive for TSAAC participation. As a result, there is presently no clear need to expand the TSAAC program. The NBAA, however, remains hopeful that the security standards developed under TSAAC can be applied in a manner that would provide additional benefits to participants and create incentives for applying security best practices among business jet operators.[63]

Security Measures for Charter Operations

While corporate and privately owned aircraft primarily deal with passengers known to the pilots and operators, passenger charter aircraft present unique security challenges because customers are sometimes unknown or unfamiliar. Charter aircraft weighing more than 12,500 pounds maximum takeoff weight must adhere to specific security regulations referred to as the twelve-five security program in reference to the aircraft weight criteria. Twelve-five security program requirements include passenger identification checks, fingerprint-based CHRCs for flight crewmembers, application of specific bomb and hijacking notification procedures and requirements, and implementation of a TSA-approved operator security program. Each operator must designate a security coordinator within the organization, provide training and information to employees with security-related duties, and have procedures in place to coordinate with law enforcement entities responding to security threats. Although cockpit doors are not required for twelve-five operations, if an aircraft has a cockpit door, procedures must be in place to restrict access to the flight deck.

In addition to these requirements of the twelve-five security program, operators of passenger charter flights in aircraft weighing more than 45,500 kg (roughly 100,300 pounds) maximum gross weight or an aircraft with 61 or more passenger seats must implement additional security measures laid out in the TSA's Private Charter Standard Security Program (PCSSP), including a requirement for physical screening of passengers and accessible baggage. Also, regardless of aircraft weight, if a passenger-carrying charter flight loads or unloads passengers at a designated sterile area of a commercial airport (i.e., beyond the security screening checkpoint), that operation must also adopt the private charter security program. The private charter program prohibits passengers from carrying weapons, explosives, and incendiary devices, and requires that metal detectors and x-ray systems used in the screening of charter passengers meet standards established by the TSA. However, physical screening of passengers can be conducted by TSA-approved private screeners and is not typically carried out by federal screeners unless arrangements are made to enplane and deplane from the sterile area of commercial airports. Private charter operators of these larger aircraft must establish procedures to prevent unauthorized access to aircraft and other access-controlled areas as specified in the operator's security program and must carry out a security inspection of aircraft whenever access control measures, such as posted security guards or adequate access controls to aircraft, are not maintained. In addition to flight crewmembers, other employees of private charter operating large aircraft who have unescorted access to aircraft and secured areas must submit to fingerprint-based CHRCs, and security coordinators and crewmembers must complete annual recurrent security training.

While the twelve-five and private charter security programs specifically apply to charter operations, the TSA requires GA operators authorized to enplane or deplane into the sterile area of commercial passenger airports to conduct TSA-approved physical screening of passengers, flight crewmembers, and their carry-on items. While these regulations are in place to make allowances for certain GA operations that might be permitted to enplane and deplane at sterile airport areas while preventing the introduction of weapons, explosives, or incendiary devices into the commercial passenger aircraft environment, corporate and privately owned GA aircraft are rarely granted access to sterile areas. Also, while the required adoption of a twelve-five security program is only required of charter operators, regulations stipulate that GA operators of aircraft weighing more than 12,500 pounds maximum takeoff weight could be required to conduct preflight security searches and screen passengers, crewmembers, and carry-on items before boarding in accordance with security procedures approved by TSA if notified to do so by the TSA. While these security measures have never been implemented, they could become effective upon notification to operators through means such as the NOTAM system or the issuance of a security directive and may be required, for example, upon receipt of specific, credible intelligence suggesting a terrorist plot to hijack business jets.

SECURITY MEASURES FOR LARGE PRIVATE AND CORPORATE AIRCRAFT

There has been considerable debate over options to expand the security measures implemented for charter operations to flight operations of other large GA aircraft, primarily large privately owned and corporate jets and jets operated as part of fractional-ownership fleets. While security experts have remained concerned over the potential damage that can be done by larger aircraft, weighing more than 12,500 pounds, GA advocates have argued that extensive security measures similar to those applied for charter operations are not necessary because passengers are typically well known to pilots and aircraft operators and do not pose a security threat. Despite these arguments, the TSA has proposed to implement a variety of security measures for operators of all large GA aircraft, weighing more than 12,500 pounds, including privately owned, fractionally owned, and corporate aircraft. The proposed security measures include

- Fingerprint-based CHRCs for all flight crewmembers
- Terrorist watch list checks of all passengers
- Security inspections of aircraft for unauthorized property or persons on board
- Completion of security compliance audits every two years[64]

In addition, operators of aircraft weighing more than 45,500 kg would be required to screen passengers and their accessible property.

VETTING AND TRACKING GA FLIGHTS AT THE U.S. BORDERS

Close monitoring of GA flights arriving in the United States from foreign destinations is a significant challenge as well as a significant concern. According to CBP, almost 400 private aircraft enter the United States on international flights made by private aircraft every day. Almost 500,000 people, including both passengers and crew, enter the United States on board private aircraft annually.[65] Private aircraft crossings of the expansive land and water borders of the United States pose a persistent threat of narcotics and human smuggling. In the post-9/11 context, concerns have been raised that terrorists may infiltrate the U.S. borders using GA aircraft to transport operatives and weapons, including possible WMDs. There is also concern that terrorists could launch a 9/11-style suicide attack using large GA aircraft flights that originate outside of U.S. borders to attack ground targets.

CBP regulations for private aircraft entering the United States were largely designed to counter cross-border narcotics trafficking. Regulations require advance notification to CBP one hour prior to an inbound border crossing. Aircraft entering U.S. airspace are required to file a flight plan, establish radio communication with air traffic controllers, and must be assigned a unique "squawk" code to identify their radar blip to air traffic controllers and others that may be monitoring airspace for security purposes. Aircraft transiting from Mexico or other countries in Central and South America must fly to the first designated airport of entry nearest to their border crossing point to clear customs prior to continuing their flight, unless they receive a waiver from this requirement. Aircraft entering from other countries, including Canada, however, may proceed to any designated airport of entry.

A provision of the Implementing the 9/11 Commission Recommendations Act of 2007 (P.L. 110-53) required CBP to develop a system under which all GA aircraft entering U.S. airspace must submit passenger information as part of the advance notification to check against appropriate government databases. This information can be vetted against terrorist watch lists and FAA aircraft and pilot registry databases to detect any anomalies that may be indicators of increased risk associated with a specific flight. CBP published a final rule to fulfill these notification requirements on November 18, 2008, which went into effect on May 18, 2009.[66] In addition to meeting the mandated requirements for vetting inbound international flights, the rule also requires advanced notice and departure manifests to be transmitted one hour prior to outbound international flights.

Besides the vetting of flight crews and passengers on inbound international flights by GA aircraft, tracking those aircraft is also an issue of considerable concern. Tracking flights along the northern border has been a particular challenge because it lacks the extensive low-altitude radar coverage that is available along the southern border in some locations. Drug smuggling along the northern border has been a persistent problem, including smuggling activity using small GA aircraft that can operate into and out of remote landing strips without detection. There is some concern that terrorists could use similar tactics to transport weapons, including WMDs, and operatives across

U.S. borders without being detected. While CBP Air and Marine (A&M) Branch aircraft patrol the northern border and interdict suspicious flights, monitoring of flight activity, particularly low-altitude flight activity along the northern border remains a significant challenge. The DHS aviation operations capabilities along the northern border are more limited in size and scope than those along the southern border, particularly along the U.S.-Mexico land border.

In addition to manned flights to patrol both the southern and northern borders, CBP initiated unmanned aerial vehicle (UAV) patrols along the southern border in 2004, and is expanding southern border UAV operations and initiating UAV patrols along the northern border. These unmanned systems are viewed as having high endurance capability, meaning that they can stay airborne for extended periods of time, thus significantly augmenting the surveillance capabilities of existing ground radar and manned aircraft patrols of the U.S. borders.[67] The AOPA, however, has raised considerable objections and safety concerns over the DHS utilization of unmanned aircraft, noting that airspace restrictions to keep GA flights away from UAV operations cause inconvenience to GA operators and may impact safety, particularly in and near mountainous areas where small aircraft may be forced to operate over rugged terrain to avoid restricted airspace.[68]

AIRSPACE RESTRICTIONS

Aviation security measures addressing GA flight operations have focused extensively on imposing flight restrictions over various potential terrorist targets. These security-related airspace restrictions have been highly contentious because they have a direct impact on air commerce and the freedom of movement by air; the potential for airspace violations has significant repercussions for both professional and private pilots; and surveillance, airspace protection, and enforcement of airspace restrictions can be costly and resource intensive. The effectiveness of some of these airspace restrictions has also been questioned by the GA community and aviation security experts.

AIRSPACE RESTRICTIONS AROUND WASHINGTON, DC

While a variety of low-altitude flight restrictions have been in place for many years around sensitive locations for reasons of national security, the number and scope of these restrictions have expanded significantly since the terrorist attacks of September 11, 2001. The most comprehensive of these restricted areas is the airspace around Washington, DC, which consists of a flight restricted zone (FRZ), 15 nautical miles in radius, and a larger 30-mile radius—referred to as the Washington, DC ADIZ—where flights must adhere to specific flight plans and air traffic communications and surveillance requirements.

The airspace in the National Capital Region (NCR) around Washington, DC has been placed under close surveillance and special flight restrictions primarily affecting GA aircraft ever since September 11, 2001. Previously, the airspace around Washington, DC was relatively open and accessible to GA as well as commercial aircraft. While the airspace directly above some sensitive locations—like the White House and the Capitol—was then and still is prohibited airspace (i.e., generally off-limits to all civil aircraft), this comprised a relatively small portion of the total airspace in the NCR. Before September 11, 2001, GA aircraft were routinely permitted to operate over Washington, DC, and the surrounding area so long as these prohibited areas were avoided and applicable air traffic procedures were followed. DCA, which is located in close proximity to downtown Washington, DC, and key federal facilities, was open and accessible to most GA aircraft. However, following the 9/11 attacks, airspace restrictions in the Washington, DC region have gone through several significant changes affecting GA operations to address heightened security concerns.

THE FLIGHT RESTRICTED ZONE

As flight operations resumed following the terrorist attacks of September 11, 2001, a no-fly zone—25 nautical miles in radius, extending from the surface to 18,000 feet—around Washington, DC, was established. All civil airports within this area, including DCA remained closed to both the airlines and GA traffic. Commercial flights gradually resumed at DCA starting in early October 2001, and limited GA operations were permitted in the airspace within the 18–25-nautical-mile ring around DCA. In December 2001, the size of the restricted airspace around Washington, DC was reduced to roughly a 15-nautical-mile radius, the dimensions that continue to exist today for the area known as the FRZ. The FRZ extends from the surface up to 18,000 feet. GA flights are generally prohibited from operating within the FRZ except for certain charter and corporate jet operations at DCA and limited activity at three small GA airports located within the FRZ.

GA Access to DCA

Procedures allowing certain GA operations to resume at the DCA were mandated under Vision 100 (P.L. 108-176). Because DCA is in such close proximity to Washington, DC, it had generally been off-limits to GA operators for almost four years following the terrorist attacks of September 11, 2001. However, on August 18, 2005, DCA reopened to GA operators on a very limited basis under an interim final rule detailing extensive security requirements for GA operators to gain access to the airport.[69] These security requirements are collectively referred to as the DCA Access Standard Security Program (DASSP).

Operators wishing to fly to and from DCA under the DASSP must implement TSA-approved security programs for securing access to aircraft; have their flight crews cleared by background checks; submit passenger and crewmember names for vetting against terrorist watch lists; submit to physical screening of passengers, crewmembers, and baggage; transit into DCA from a small number of designated gateway airports; and post armed security officers on board each flight to and from DCA. Operators must reimburse the TSA for the direct costs associated with these security measures which in effect makes access to DCA cost prohibitive for most GA operators. As currently implemented, the security provisions for access to DCA are designed primarily to accommodate larger charter operators and high-end corporate aircraft. The program is not currently available to privately owned aircraft, but the TSA indicated that the program may be expanded in the future.

The Maryland Three Airports

In February 2002, the ban on GA operations in the FRZ was eased somewhat, permitting the three GA airports located within its boundaries—referred to as the Maryland three or sometimes the DC-three airports—to reopen on a limited basis.[70] Potomac Airfield, Washington Executive Airport/ Hyde Field, and College Park Airport were permitted to resume operations of based aircraft whose pilots were vetted through background checks and must follow strict security protocols for flight operations. In February 2005, FRZ restrictions were further relaxed allowing transient aircraft to fly to and from these airports provided that their pilots had passed background checks, received special training, and adhered to specific security procedures. The reopening of these airports has been a politically sensitive issue. Both Washington Executive and Potomac airports are operated by small business entities that have been significantly impacted by the flight restrictions, while College Park Airport—established in 1909 as a site for the Wright brothers to train military aviators—is considered the world's oldest continuously operated airport.

The Washington, DC, ADIZ

In February 2003, additional steps were taken to secure the skies above Washington, DC, by establishing an outer area, beyond the FRZ, where GA flights must operate under close surveillance and in constant two-way radio contact with air traffic controllers. This area is known as the Washington, DC ADIZ and its existence has been highly controversial because of the operational requirements it imposes on GA aircraft.

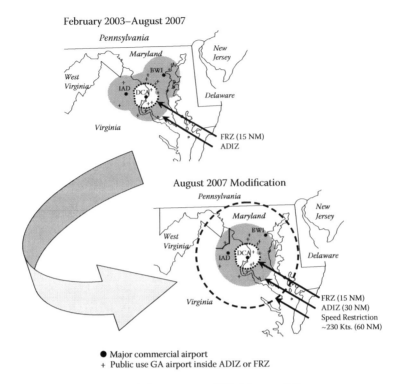

February 2003–August 2007

August 2007 Modification

● Major commercial airport
+ Public use GA airport inside ADIZ or FRZ

FIGURE 12.3   Changes to the restricted airspace around Washington, DC.

The term ADIZ has long been in place and refers to any area of airspace where the identification, location, and control of aircraft are required in the interest of national security. Prior to September 11, 2001, this term generally referred to buffer zones around coastal waters and international borders of the United States. Since September 11, 2001, however, the ADIZ concept has been expanded to include zones within the United States such as in the vicinity of Washington, DC.

The Washington, DC ADIZ came into existence not immediately following September 11, 2001, as many mistakenly assume, but rather as part of Operation Liberty Shield, an operation launched by the DHS to enhance homeland security during the build up toward the war in Iraq. The Washington, DC ADIZ was established as a temporary flight restriction (TFR), and a similar ADIZ was established around New York City for brief period during the winter and spring of 2003. A smaller-scale restricted area was also put in place over downtown Chicago during that time. The temporary restrictions in New York and Chicago have since been rescinded, but the Washington, DC ADIZ has remained in place. Largely in response to criticism that the special procedural requirements for flying inside the DC ADIZ were overly burdensome to operators, including some whose flight paths brought them no closer than 50 miles away from Washington, DC landmarks, the size of the ADIZ was reduced in size to a 30-mile ring around DCA in August 2007 (Figure 12.3).

Prior to this resizing of the ADIZ, the area covered by the ADIZ consisted of the 30-nautical-mile ring around DCA *plus* the additional airspace extending for 20 nautical miles around both Dulles International (IAD) and BWI airports. During that time, the ADIZ has a lateral extent—not including the FRZ which it completely encapsulates—of more than 3000 square nautical miles. As a result of the August 2007 change made by the FAA, the size of the ADIZ was reduced to an area roughly 2000 square miles in size. Thus, the area included in the ADIZ was reduced by roughly one-third as a result of this change. Like the FRZ, the ADIZ extends from the surface to 18,000 feet, and this has remained unchanged.

Along with this reduction in the size of the ADIZ the FAA implemented a new speed restriction around Washington, DC, limiting aircraft operating below 18,000 feet within 60 nautical miles of DCA to speeds below 230 knots. The rationale for this being that faster moving aircraft would offer less time to prepare and launch defensive measures to prevent a possible terrorist attack using aircraft. By imposing a speed restriction, airspace security monitors could more rapidly identify fast-moving threats and initiate a defensive response. The GA community has not voiced any particular opposition to this measure, in large part, because few GA aircraft are even capable of speeds greater than the 230 knot limit.

While the ADIZ was initially established as a TFR, and remained so from 2003 until February 2009, the FAA made the ADIZ airspace configuration and special procedures implemented in August 2007 permanent effective February 19, 2009.[71] When the FAA had proposed to make the ADIZ in its prior form permanent in August 2005, it was barraged by more than 20,000 public comments, almost all opposing the plan. The AOPA, in particular, had strongly opposed making the ADIZ permanent, contending that the ADIZ confuses both pilots and controllers, diverts controller's attention from their primary aircraft separation duties, causes considerable departure delays for GA flights, and confines training flights to limited airspace creating a potential safety hazard.[72] The AOPA also asserted that flight activity at airports within the ADIZ had decreased by about 30–50% since the ADIZ was put in place, and fuel sales at area airports have declined by as much as 45%.[73] Implementing ADIZ procedures also involves a sizable federal investment, costing about $11 million annually for additional air traffic controllers and equipment to monitor flights in the ADIZ, according to FAA estimates.[74] The AOPA has consequently voiced concern that "[i]f the ADIZ is not eliminated or modified, it will permanently jeopardize the economic viability of general aviation operations in the Washington, DC area."[75] Critics of the ADIZ have viewed the reduction in its size as a positive step toward reducing the operational burden associated with the special flight procedures required to operate inside the ADIZ, although the AOPA and others maintain that the ADIZ should be completely eliminated and replaced with less burdensome measures that can provide an equivalent level of security.

SECURITY-RELATED FLIGHT RESTRICTIONS THROUGHOUT THE UNITED STATES

Other than the airspace restrictions around Washington, DC, various security-related flight restrictions have been put in place to protect national security interests and ostensibly to protect potential high-profile terrorist targets from aerial attacks. At various times since September 11, 2001, flight restrictions have been imposed to protect airspace around major U.S. cities and other potential terrorist targets. For example, during the build up toward the war in Iraq in early 2003, additional airspace restrictions were put in place around New York City, Chicago, and Disney theme parks in addition to establishing the ADIZ around Washington, DC to augment the FRZ that had already been put in place following the terrorist attacks of September 11, 2001. Flight restrictions around major cities besides Washington, DC were lifted, but have been reinstated for brief periods during times when the national security threat level has been elevated or when special events warranted the establishment of TFRs. However, the flight restrictions around Disney theme parks have continuously remained in effect and are now mandated in statute. In addition to these restrictions, the Consolidated Appropriations Act of 2004 (P.L. 108-199, Sec. 521) established permanent flight restrictions over stadiums and motor speedways during Major League Baseball (MLB) games, National Football League (NFL) and National Collegiate Athletic Association (NCAA) division I football games, and major auto racing events. These flight restrictions establish a 3-nautical-mile flight-restricted area around the effected facility extending from the surface to 3000 feet. GA aircraft are generally prohibited from this airspace, but exceptions may be made for flight operations directly related to the sporting event, broadcast coverage of the sporting event, or to provide safety and security for the event. Exceptions may also be made in cases where the venue is in close proximity to an airport, in which case aircraft may enter into the restricted area if necessary to land or takeoff from the airport using standard air traffic procedures. These restrictions have been criticized by some because they are selective in the events that are covered by the statutory mandate and therefore do not encompass all large-scale outdoor assemblies. The restrictions have also been criticized because the relatively small size of restricted airspace, while often interfering with flight operations, is considered by many to provide an inadequate perimeter for establishing adequate airspace protections to the sites they are intended to protect.

AIRSPACE RESTRICTIONS FOR PRESIDENTIAL VISITS

In addition to the stadium and theme park overflight rules, the temporary flight restricted areas put in place around sites visited by the President of the United States are particularly troublesome for many pilots. Unlike the stadium and Disney theme park areas that encompass a relatively small footprint and a fixed location, the flight restrictions put in place for presidential visits encompass a much wider area and are put in place all across the United States, often with little advance notice. The area of these restrictions has grown from a 3-nautical-mile radius extending 3000 feet in altitude before 9/11, to a 30-nautical-mile radius reaching up to 18,000 feet in altitude. Typically, during a presidential visit, GA flights are completely prohibited within 10 nautical miles of the designated site. Between 10 and 30 nautical miles from the designated site, flights below 18,000 feet must be on active flight plans and in constant communication with air traffic controllers.

The fact that these airspace restrictions to protect the President are often put in place with little advance notice has the potential of catching pilots off guard. Because these presidential movement TFRs change dynamically with the President's schedule, pilots can be easily misinformed or confused about the specific location of the restricted airspace and the effective times of the restrictions, which usually includes a block of time around the President's expected presence but can change on short notice. Also, these restrictions are often defined in terms that may not be meaningful to GA pilots whose aircraft may lack the navigational capability to identify the boundaries of restricted areas. The FAA and user groups such as AOPA have worked to increase pilot awareness regarding the movements of the President and provide pilots with up-to-date information regarding presidential movement TFRs including graphical depictions of affected airspace. Nevertheless, identifying these airspace boundaries continues to be a challenge, particularly to pilots flying primarily by visual means and relying on landmarks on the ground to avoid airspace incursions. The AOPA and other GA advocacy groups have questioned the need for restrictions over such a wide area and have lobbied to keep the impacts of these security measures on airspace accessibility to a minimum.[76]

POLICY ISSUES REGARDING AIRSPACE RESTRICTIONS

Besides these specific objections to security-related flight restrictions, many aviation interests and homeland security specialists have raised broader policy questions about the effectiveness of these various airspace restrictions and special operating procedures, noting that enforcing airspace restrictions is costly and resource intensive and providing protection to defend sites against aerial attacks is an even greater challenge. The resource requirements and associated costs for monitoring restricted airspace and providing airspace protection around critical sites raise policy questions regarding the appropriate balancing of these measures with efforts to address other homeland security threats, and the effect of these measures on air commerce and the freedom of movement by air. Ongoing policy debate regarding the implementation of airspace restrictions, particularly those in place around Washington, DC, is focused on ensuring that surveillance and monitoring of restrictive airspace is carried out in an effective manner that provides tangible security benefits, and on curbing inadvertent airspace violations that make the task of protecting airspace around critical location all the more difficult. Additionally, policymakers and homeland security strategists continue to grapple with the complexities of implementing effective defensive capabilities to protect critical assets within restricted airspace from hostile acts using aircraft while offering reasonable assurances that these defenses are not inadvertently deployed against nonhostile aircraft and have a minimal chance of causing harm to individuals and property on the ground.

EFFECTIVE SURVEILLANCE AND MONITORING OF RESTRICTED AIRSPACE

Surveillance and monitoring capabilities present a significant challenge for protecting airspace. This is, in part, because detailed information on specific GA aircraft is not provided to air traffic controllers and airspace monitors unless the aircraft is transmitting a unique identifying code to air traffic radar sites. Under the current radar system, providing GA aircraft with unique identifiers and tracking all GA aircraft could, at times, prove overwhelming for air traffic controllers. Under present day air traffic control procedures, pilots submits flight plans receive unique identifier codes to transmit, and make radio calls to air traffic controllers to establish "radar contact" allowing controllers to identify and track a specific flight. Under normal circumstances in clear weather, many flights never file a flight plan nor contact air traffic controllers because they are not required to do so. But, to operate inside certain restricted airspace like the Washington, DC ADIZ, pilots must follow the aforementioned procedures for filing flight plans, transmitting unique identifying transponder codes, and communicating with air traffic controllers, procedures that are often workload intensive for both pilots and controllers. Technologies may provide a solution that could ease pilot and controller workload associated with these transactions. For example, Mode S transponders are capable of automatically relaying detailed aircraft identifier information to air traffic radars, but most small GA aircraft do not have this technology and it is expensive to install. Similarly, emerging technology called ADS-B can transmit detailed aircraft information to ground stations and other aircraft, but this new technology is only beginning to become available and surveillance capability is not yet available in all parts of the United States. While ADS-B shows significant promise for improving safety as well as security, it will be some time before all GA aircraft are equipped with ADS-B transmitting equipment. The FAA is proposing that all aircraft be equipped with such equipment by 2020.

In the meantime, surveillance of GA aircraft must rely on current radar capabilities, involving close coordination between pilots and air traffic controllers. This imposes additional workload on both pilots and controllers. This increased workload has a direct bearing on FAA resources. For example, the FAA estimates that maintaining the ADIZ around Washington, DC costs about $11 million per year, mostly linked to increased labor costs associated with processing flight plans and providing air traffic services to aircraft operating under VFR that would otherwise present little or no impact on the air traffic control system.

CURBING AIRSPACE VIOLATIONS

Curtailing frequent inadvertent airspace violations by unauthorized aircraft that complicate surveillance and defense efforts is an ongoing challenge. According to NCR Command Center statistics, there were almost 3500 airspace incursions between January 27, 2003, when the center first opened, and July 17, 2005—a rate of almost four incidents per day. On 655 of these occasions, government or military aircraft were deployed or diverted to intercept the intruding aircraft. Based on this experience, about one in every five or six incursions requires an intercept, and this occurs about five times a week. However, all but one of these incidents was inadvertent. In three high-profile incidents, all inadvertent, the U.S. Capitol was evacuated, raising concerns over the adequacy of airspace protections among lawmakers.

Curbing inadvertent violations is likely to become increasingly important with increased GA flight activity at DCA and the three Maryland airports within the FRZ, making the task of surveillance and tactical response all the more critical. Pilot training is likely to be an important tool for mitigating these inadvertent airspace violations. In fact, significant efforts have been made by user groups such as the AOPA, in coordination with the FAA, to increase pilot awareness and understanding of the airspace restrictions and provide training materials via the Internet to pilots regarding security-related flight procedures, including training on operating in the Washington, DC ADIZ airspace.

Besides information and training, additional measures to improve in-flight situational awareness may help curtail inadvertent airspace violations. Available technologies may provide GA pilots with improved positional awareness to avoid airspace violations. For example, global positioning satellite moving map displays can provide pilots with precise navigation capabilities. These systems are now widely available for use in GA aircraft and could be programmed to include features to raise situational awareness regarding airspace restrictions and requirements.

A more controversial option under consideration is stiffer penalties and stepped-up enforcement for airspace violations. User groups oppose additional punitive actions beyond those already available to the FAA and point out that the threat of a shootdown is already a strong enough deterrent for pilots to take heed.

AIRSPACE PROTECTION AND HOMELAND DEFENSE

Besides the resources and costs associated with monitoring flights, the capability to establish formidable airspace protections in restricted airspace is a central issue for homeland security. The effectiveness of airspace protections and interagency coordination in providing homeland security and defense is at the crux of the policy debate over effective airspace security. This is because airspace restrictions by themselves are not particularly useful tools unless a coordinated response to protect critical assets within those protected areas is effective. Merely relying on enforcement tools is not likely to be of significant benefit because terrorists are likely to care little that they are violating airspace restrictions in carrying out an attack.

The NORAD Command's Operation Noble Eagle is charged with the task of interdicting aircraft believed to pose a national security risk. Since September 11, 2001, fighter jets have scrambled to respond to almost 2000 domestic air security events.[77] While these incidents include some escorts of passenger airliners because of security incidents or suspected terrorists on board, the large majority of these interdictions involved intercepts of small GA aircraft that strayed into restricted or prohibited airspace. In the environment of heightened security since the 9/11 attacks, the FAA, NORAD, and aviation user groups such as the AOPA and the NBAA have made extensive efforts to heighten pilots' awareness regarding airspace restrictions and proper procedures to follow if intercepted by DHS, law enforcement, or military aircraft.

Despite these intensified efforts to protect major metropolitan areas and critical sites from aerial attacks, it has been reported that military officials have concluded that stopping a 9/11-style attack would be difficult unless fighter jets were already airborne.[78] Maintaining a constant airborne defense capability, however, would be extremely costly and resource intensive. Ground-to-air missiles have been deployed around Washington, DC, but are largely seen as a measure of last resort for protecting a limited number of key locations against an aerial attack, whether that attack may involve GA aircraft or commercial airliners.[79]

Because of the continuing challenges in providing effective national airspace defenses, the adequacy of airspace protection initiatives will likely depend on close cooperation and coordination between the FAA, the DHS, and the DOD as well as effective command and control within each of these organizations. Presently, event response is coordinated through the FAA's DEN, a continuously operated unclassified network for sharing critical incident information regarding aircraft deviations and violations of security restricted airspace, and the TSA's TSOC, the central hub for exchanging information regarding aviation threats located in Herndon, Virginia. The function of these facilities is to provide a shared situational awareness of aviation threats including, but not limited to, threats posed by GA aircraft. Besides the TSA, NORAD, and the FAA, other key agencies involved in airspace surveillance and protection include the Coast Guard and CBP, which provide air interdiction and situation response within the DHS, as well as the FBI. These agencies also coordinate with federal, state, and local law enforcement to integrate threat response.

Coordinated threat response was observed in the May 11, 2005 event where an errant small private airplane penetrated deep into the FRZ around Washington, DC. The coordinated response to this threat included deployment of fighter jets, helicopters from the USCG, and federal and state law enforcement assets to interdict and intercept the aircraft. While the response to this perceived threat was by most accounts well coordinated, concerns have been raised that response to a more formidable threat, such as a faster moving aircraft attempting to evade airspace protections and defenses, may be much more difficult to interdict and may require a carefully orchestrated response involving close coordination between responsible agencies. These agencies have been continually assessing and refining their airspace monitoring and threat response capabilities. Policymakers and government officials are also seeking ways to improve interagency coordination of response to airborne threats, including threats posed by GA aircraft. In the course of these deliberations, advocacy groups for GA, such as the AOPA and NBAA, have been urging policymakers to carefully assess the various measures taken to protect critical assets from aerial attacks to ensure that they do not unduly burden GA operators or compromise flight safety. Striking an appropriate balance between effective security measures for GA flight activity and unencumbered access to the NAS for all users, including the wide array of GA aircraft operations and aircraft, remains an ongoing and complex challenge.

REFERENCES

1. Associated Press. "U.S. Uncovers Al-Qaida Plot in Pakistan; The Terrorist Group Allegedly Planned to Fly an Airplane into the American Consulate." *Telegraph-Herald* (Dubuque, Iowa), May 3, 2003, p. A7.
2. Report of the Aviation Security Advisory Committee Working Group on General Aviation Airport Security, October 1, 2003; and Transportation Security Administration. *Security Guidelines for General Aviation Airports.* Information Publication A-001, May 2004.
3. National Commission on Terrorist Attacks upon the United States. *The 9/11 Commission Report.* New York: W.W. Norton & Co., p. 391.
4. Federal Aviation Administration. "Washington, DC Metropolitan Area Special Flight Rules Area; Proposed Rule." *Federal Register, 70*(149), p. 43251, August 4, 2005.
5. Calculations Based on Federal Aviation Administration. *FAA Aerospace Forecasts—Fiscal Years 2007–2020.* March 2007.
6. See note 2.
7. Federal Aviation Administration. *Administrator's Fact Book,* April 2007.
8. General Aviation Manufacturers Association. *General Aviation Statistical Databook 2006.* Washington, DC, Updated February 12, 2007.
9. Report of the Aviation Security Advisory Committee Working Group on General Aviation Airport Security, and Transportation Security Administration. *Security Guidelines for General Aviation Airports.*
10. Federal Aviation Administration. *FAA Aerospace Forecasts, Fiscal Years 2005–2016.*
11. See note 10, p. V-1.
12. Robert Ross. "Keeping GA Safe and Secure." *Professional Pilot,* September 2005, p. 70.
13. Report of the Aviation Security Advisory Committee Working Group on General Aviation Airport Security. Oct. 1, 2003. Department of Homeland Security, Transportation Security Administration, p. 3.
14. See, for example, Jim Hoffer. "Security Practically Nonexistent at Many Small Airports." *WABC TV-New York Eyewitness News,* February 5, 2004.
15. Aircraft Owners and Pilots Association. *General Aviation and Homeland Security: A Security Brief by the Aircraft Owners and Pilots Association.* Frederick, MD, January 23, 2004.
16. Vickie Chachere. "Police: Student pilot who crashed Cessna into Florida building inspired by bin Laden." *Associated Press Newswires,* January 7, 2002.
17. David McHugh. "Small Plane Crashes Near German Parliament." *Associated Press Newswires,* July 22, 2005.
18. Hugh Williamson. "Ban on Small Aircraft Flying over Berlin." *Financial Times* (London), July 25, 2005.

19. Spencer S. Hsu. "Plane That Caused Capitol Evacuation Nearly Shot Down." *The Washington Post*, July 8, 2004, p. A1.

20. Carol Eisenberg. "FAA Bans Fixed-Wing Planes from East River." *Newsday*, October 14, 2006.

21. The White House Office of the Press Secretary. Press Briefing by Ron Noble, Under Secretary of the Treasury for Enforcement and Carl Meyer, Special Agent, United States Secret Service. September 12, 1994. Robert Pear. "Crash at the White House: The Pilot." *The New York Times*, September 13, 1994, p. 20.

22. See NTSB *Aviation Accident Database and Synopses* from 1962–2004. Available at http://www.ntsb.gov/ntsb/query.asp.

23. Richard Liebson. "1 Held in Drunken Joy Ride in Cessna." *The Journal News* (White Plains, NY), June 23, 2005, p. 1A.

24. Mike Morris. "Bufurd Man, 22, Accused of Stealing Jet." *The Atlanta Journal-Constitution*, October 12, 2005.

25. U.S. Department of Justice. Marcos Daniel Jiménez, United States District Attorney for the Southern District of Florida. "Defendant Sentenced for Transporting Stolen Lear Jet and Possession of False Identification Documents." Press Release, Miami, FL, January 5, 2005,.

26. Statement for the Record of Robert S. Mueller III, Director, Federal Bureau of Investigation, Before the Joint Intelligence Committee Investigation into September 11, U.S. Congress, June 18, 2002.

27. United States of America v. Zacharias Moussaoui (Defendant). Indictment. In the U.S. District Court for the Eastern District of Virginia, Alexandria Division. December 2001 Term.

28. U.S. Central Intelligence Agency. *Terrorist CBRN: Materials and Effects.*

29. U.S. Central Intelligence Agency. Unclassified Version of Director of Central Intelligence George J. Tenet's Testimony before the Joint Inquiry into Terrorist Attacks against the United States, June 18, 2002.

30. See note 1.

31. Ibid.

32. U.S. Central Intelligence Agency. *Terrorist CBRN.*

33. White House Homeland Security Council, David Howe, Senior Director for Response and Planning. *Planning Scenarios: Executive Summaries*, Version 2.0, July 2004.

34. See note 32.

35. Staff Summary of Responses by the Nuclear Regulatory Commission to Correspondence from Rep. Edward J. Markey (D-MA), Member, Energy and Commerce Committee, U.S. House of Representatives. *Security Gap: A Hard Look At the Soft Spots in Our Civilian Nuclear Reactor Security*, March 25, 2002.

36. Gary Stoller. "Nuclear Plants near Airports May Be at Risk." *USA Today*, June 10, 2003.

37. Robert M. Jefferson. *Nuclear Safety: General Aviation Is Not a Threat*, p. 1 and 4. Available from Aircraft Owners and Pilots Association, Frederick, MD, May 16, 2002.

38. Ibid, p. 1.

39. Donald Spurston. "Security Requirement for GA Operations Should be Based on Threat Assessment." *ICAO Journal, 8*, 18, 2002.

40. Transportation Security Administration. *Security Guidelines for General Aviation Airports.* Information Publication A-001, May 2004.

41. Craig Williams. *General Aviation Safety and Security Practices: A Synthesis of Airport Practice.* Airport Cooperative Research Program, ACRP, Synthesis 3, Washington, DC: Transportation Research Board of the National Academies, 2007.

42. Ibid.

43. Robert Ross. "Keeping GA Safe."

44. Aircraft Owners and Pilots Association. *Proof AOPA Airport Watch Concept Works.* Frederick, MD: AOPA, August 12, 2004.

45. Robert Olislagers. "General Aviation Security: The Ups & Downs of Threat Management." *Airport Magazine*, May/June 2005. pp. 59–61.

46. Ibid.

47. Transportation Security Administration. *Security Guidelines for General Aviation Airports.*

48. P.L. 108-458, Sec. 4022.

49. Aircraft Owners and Pilots Association. *Pilot ID Process Needs to be Convenient, Inexpensive, AOPA Reminds the FAA.* Frederick, MD: AOPA, July 8, 2005.

50. Title 49, U.S.C. §44939; Title 49 Code of Federal Regulation, Part 1552.

51. Transportation Security Administration. "Threat Assessment Regarding Citizens of the United States and Alien Holders Who Hold or Apply for FAA Certificates; Final Rules." *Federal Register, 68*(16), pp. 3756–3769, January 24, 2003.

52. See, for example, Llewellyn King. "Adm. Loy, You Know Better: Rescind This Rule." *White House Weekly,* 24(10), 1–2, March 11, 2003.

53. Transportation Security Administration. Memorandum to the Dockets from Pamela Hamilton, Director of Aviation Initiatives Regarding TSA Rulemaking Docket No. TSA-2002-13732 and TSA Rulemaking Docket No. TSA-2002-13733. March 16, 2004.

54. Aircraft Owners and Pilots Association. *GA Security: GA Pilots Are Not a Threat.* Available at www.gaservingamerica.org/GA-Pilots-Security.htm.

55. Craig Williams. *General Aviation Safety and Security Practices.*

56. See note 47.

57. Department of Homeland Security, Transportation Security Administration. "Large Aircraft Security Program, Other Aircraft Operator Security Program, and Airport Operator Security Program; Proposed Rule." *Federal Register,* 73(211), pp. 64790–64855, October 30, 2008.

58. See note 47, p. 10.

59. U.S. Government Accountability Office. *General Aviation Security: Increased Federal Oversight Is Needed, but Continued Partnership with the Private Sector Is Critical to Long-Term Success.* GAO-05-144, November 2004.

60. See note 47.

61. Regulatory Consultants, Inc. "Secure Your Operation Today." *Agricultural Aviation,* July/August 2005, 17–18.

62. Jean Heller and Alicia Caldwell. "Flight Schools: Breach of Trust Difficult to Prevent." *St. Petersburg Times,* January 8, 2002.

63. National Business Aviation Association. *TSA Access Certificate (TSAAC).* Washington, DC: National Business Aviation Association, Inc., Updated February 22, 2007.

64. See note 57.

65. Department of Homeland Security, Bureau of Customs and Border Protection. "Advance Information on Private Aircraft Arriving and Departing the United States; Proposed Rule." *Federal Register,* 72(180), pp. 53394–53406.

66. Department of Homeland Security, Bureau of Customs and Border Protection, "Advance Information on Private Aircraft Arriving and Departing the United States (Final Rule)," *Federal Register,* 73(223), 68295–68313, November 18, 2008.

67. Michael J. Pitts, Director, UAS Program Office, U.S. Customs and Border Protection, *Office of Customs and Border Protection Air and Marine,* Presented at FAA UAS Tech Conference, January 2007, Arlington, VA.

68. Aircraft Owners and Pilots Association. *AOPA Alerts Congress to UAV Threat to GA Operations.* Frederick, MD, March 29, 2006.

69. Transportation Security Administration. "Ronald Reagan Washington National Airport: Enhanced Security Procedures for Certain Operations; Interim Final Rule." *Federal Register,* 70(137), pp. 41586–41603, July 19, 2005.

70. Federal Aviation Administration. "Enhanced Security Procedures for Operations at Certain Airports in the Washington, DC Metropolitan Area Special Flight Rules Area; Final Rule." *Federal Register,* 67(33), pp. 7538–7545, February 10, 2005.

71. Department of Transportation, Federal Aviation Administration. "Washington, DC Metropolitan Area Special Flight Rules Area." *Federal Register,* 73(242), pp. 76195–76215, December 16, 2008.

72. Aircraft Owners and Pilots Association. *Air Traffic Services Brief: Security Officials Want Washington, D.C. Air Defense Identification Zone (ADIZ) to Be Made Permanent.* Frederick, MD, Updated Wednesday, August 29, 2007.

73. Ibid.

74. Federal Aviation Administration. "Washington, DC Metropolitan Area Special Flight Rules."

75. Aircraft Owners and Pilots Association. *Air Traffic Services Brief.*

76. See, for example, Aircraft Owners and Pilots Association. *Members of Congress Join AOPA Outcry Over Presidential Movement TFRs.* Frederick, MD; May 16, 2003.

77. First Air Force. *Operation Noble Eagle: Defending America's Skies.* Tyndall Air Force Base, FL.

78. Associated Press. "Intercept Tests Show U.S. Air Vulnerability." January 15, 2004.

79. Statement by the Honorable Paul McHale, Assistant Secretary of Defense for Homeland Defense before the Committee on Government Reform, United States House of Representatives, July 21, 2005.

Index

3-1-1 for carry-ons, 210, 224
4R-TOSE framework, 155, 156
9/11 attacks and ensuing policy debate, 41, 49–50
    al Qaeda, rising threat of, 43–45
    Aviation and Transportation Security Act (ATSA),
        59–62
    Bojinka plot, 42–43
    Century of Aviation Reauthorization Act of 2003,
        64–66
    congressional response, 55–59
    DOT rapid response teams, 51–55
    Homeland Security Act of 2002, 62–64
    plans, 45–48
    preattack phase, 48–49
    precursors to 9/11 attacks, 42
    tactical response, 50–51
9/11 Commission, 161, 336, 348, 353, 355
    aviation security policy, impact on, 69–70
    aviation security-related recommendations of, 70–75
9/11 Public Discourse Project, 69–70

A

A Layered Security System, 70
AAAE. *See* American Association of Airport Executives
Abu Nidal Organization, 22
Access control measures, 284–285, 290
ACLU. *See* American Civil Liberties Union, 198,
        216–217, 227
Active failures, 143
Adaptive systems approaches, to aviation security,
        156–158
ADASP. *See* Aviation Direct Access Screening Program
ADIS. *See* Arrival and Departure Information System
ADIZ. *See* Air Defense Identification Zone
ADS-B. *See* Automated Dependent Surveillance-
        Broadcast
Advance Passenger Information System (APIS), 121, 172,
        174, 175–176, 177, 178, 179, 181, 182, 183
Advanced technology (AT) x-ray systems, 195, 202,
        203–204, 214, 218
Aerial suicides, 22–23
AFSD. *See* Assistant Federal Security Director
AGCC. *See* Aviation Government Coordinating Council
Agricultural aviation operations, 382
Air and Marine (A&M) Branch aircraft, 386
Air Botswana ATR-42, 249
Air cargo facilities
    inspection and oversight, 357
    physical security, 356–357
Air cargo handlers, security training for, 357
Air cargo regulations, 77–78
Air cargo screening, 347
Air Cargo Security Act, 248
Air Cargo Strategic Plan, 344

Air cargo system, 333
    air cargo personnel, security training for, 357
    aircraft and cargo facilities, access control, 357–358
    all-cargo environment, security in, 341
        arming all-cargo pilots, 342–343
        cargo inspection methods and technologies,
            343–344
        known shipper approach, 344–346
    canine explosives detection teams, 348
    cargo screening and inspection, cost of, 352
        hardened blast-resistant cargo containers, 353–355
        manufacturers and shippers, potential impacts
            on, 353
        passenger airlines and freight forwarders,
            potential impacts on, 352–353
    cargo screening technology, 348
        chemical trace detection systems, 350–351
        explosive detection systems (EDS), 350
        millimeter wave imaging systems, 351–352
        neutron beam technologies, 351
        x-ray screening, 349–350
    inspection and oversight, 357
    physical screening and inspection, 346–348
    physical security, 356–357
    screening versus physical inspection of cargo
        shipments, 339–341
    security risks, 333
        aircraft hijacking and sabotage, 338
        airmail consignments, 338–339
        cargo crime, 337
        explosives and incendiary devices, 335–336
        hazardous materials, 336–337
    shipments, 333
    supply chain security technologies, 355
        access control and biometric screening
            technology, 356
        tamper-evident and tamper-resistant seals,
            355–356
    threats involving hostile exploitation of, 106–107
Air carriers, 176
Air Defense Identification Zone (ADIZ), 66
Air Domain Surveillance and Intelligence Integration
        Plan
    to achieve capability, essential elements, 121–123
    considerations and assumptions, 120–121
    guiding principles, 120
Air France Boeing 747 bombing, 20
Air France flight, hijacking of 8969, 46
Air India Boeing 747 bombing, 1, 20
Air India flight 182 bombing, 20
Air Line Pilots Association (ALPA), 54, 237, 252, 313
Air National Guard unit, 281
Air operation area (AOA), 273, 274, 275
    security of, 281
Air rage, 259–261

Air taxi services, 362
Air traffic control (ATC), 263
Air Transportation Security Act, 14, 256
Airbus A300-B4, 316
Aircraft
    bombings, 24–25
        looming menace, 15–18
        threat of, 45
    and cargo facilities
        access control, 357–358
    hijacking and sabotage, 338
    lighting, 323
    physical security measures for, 381–382
    surveillance, future systems for, 240
    survivability, improving, 265
    thefts, 367
    threats, 45, 104–105
Aircraft-based countermeasures deployment, policy
        considerations for, 327–328
Aircraft-based protections and countermeasures,
        324–328
    aircraft-based countermeasures deployment, policy
        considerations for, 327–328
    Homeland Security Counter-MANPADS systems
        development and testing, 326–327
Aircraft Owner's and Pilots Association (AOPA), 288,
        375, 389
Aircraft Sabotage Act of 1984, 20
Aircraft Security Rapid Response Team, conclusions and
        recommendations of, 53–55
Airfield and airport perimeter, 287–288
Airline crews, screening and vetting of, 221–222
Airline in-flight security measures, 235–236
    aircraft surveillance, future systems for, 240
    aircraft survivability, improving, 265
    armed law enforcement on airliners, 255
        federal, state, and local LEOs flying armed,
            256–258
        historical context, 255–256
        identity verification procedures for armed LEOs,
            259
    armed pilots and crew security training, 246–247
        airline crews, 254–255
        FFDO
            program implementation issues, 248–252
            special considerations, 254
            legislative background, 247–248
            operational procedures for armed pilots issues,
                252–254
    Federal Air Marshal Service, 241
        force size and flight coverage controversies,
            242–245
        operational and procedural issues, 245–246
        post-9/11 air marshal hiring and training, 241–242
    flight deck access procedures, 238–239
    handling disruptive passengers and other in-flight
        security incidents, 259–261
    hardened cockpit doors, 236–237
    in-flight chemical and biological threats, 265–267
    in-flight explosives threat, mitigating, 265
    in-flight security threats, responding to, 263–265
    less-than-lethal weapons for in-flight security
        consideration, 254
    possible terrorist probing incidents, 261–263

    secondary flight deck barriers, 237–238
    uninterruptable aircraft transponders, 239–240
    video surveillance of the airliner cabin and improved
        cabin–cockpit communications, 239
Airline passenger prescreening and terrorist watch lists,
        166
    aviation workers and general aviation passengers,
        prescreening of, 179–180
    CAPPS II development effort, 171–172
    computer-assisted passenger prescreening system,
        167–168
    international air travelers and shipments, risk-based
        targeting of, 176–177
    international airports of entry, immigration controls
        at, 177–179
    international passengers, prescreening of, 175–176
    no-fly and automatic selectee lists, 169–171
    pre-9/11 passenger prescreening initiatives, 167
    Secure Flight
        system development, 172–174, 175
        terrorist watch list checks, 174–175
Airline passenger traffic growth, 194, 204–206. *See also*
        under passenger screening
Airline Pilots Security Alliance (APSA), 249–250
Airmail consignments, 338–339
Airplane thefts, 368
Airport access controls, 377–378
Airport badges and identification systems
    regulations pertaining to, 294–295
Airport compliance with security requirements,
        evaluation of, 283–284
Airport contractor and vendor security programs, 282
Airport environment, security risk in, 271–273
Airport perimeter, 281–282
    security and access control measures, 284–285
Airport physical security and security technologies, 284
Airport Rangers Equestrian Volunteer Program, 287
Airport security, 277, 278
    airport contractor and vendor security programs, 282
    airport perimeter, 281–282
    AOA, security of, 281
    commercial passenger airports, military facilities
        at, 281
    designated GA areas, security of, 280–281
    measures, 321–322
    physical security measures for, 381
    risk categories, 282–283
    security designations within passenger terminal,
        277–279
    security identification display areas, 279–280
    technology investment, 274–275
Airport Security and Improvement Act of 2000, 37, 293
Airport security programs, 275–277
Airport Security Rapid Response Team, conclusions and
        recommendations of, 52–53
Airport Surface Detection Equipment, Model X
        (ASDE-X), 286
Airport terminals
    space constraints at, 194–195
Airport watch program, 288, 375–376
Airport workers
    "insider" threat posed by, 277
    screening procedures for, 219–221, 276
Airspace protection and homeland defense, 392–393

Airspace restrictions, 386
    policy issues regarding, 390
        airspace protection and homeland defense, 392–393
        curbing airspace violations, 391–392
        effective surveillance and monitoring of restricted
            airspace, 391
    for presidential visits, 390
    around Washington, DC, 386
        flight restricted zone, 386–387
        GA access to DCA, 387
        Maryland three airports, 387
        Washington, DC ADIZ, 387–389
Airspace violations, curtailing, 391–392
Al Qaeda, 44, 45, 48, 82
    post 9/11 ambitions, 84–86
Al Zawahiri, Ayman, 44, 85
Alaska Region, 264
All-cargo aircraft, 248
All-cargo environment, security in, 341
    arming all-cargo pilots, 342–343
    cargo inspection methods and technologies, 343–344
    known shipper approach, 344–346
Allied Pilots Association (APA), 252
ALPA. See Air Line Pilots Association
Alpizar, Rigoberto, 246
American Airlines, 246, 326
American Airlines Boeing 727 bombing, 16
American Airlines Boeing 767, 335
American Airlines flight 11, 49
American Airlines flight 63, 83, 84, 261
American Airlines flight 77, 49
American Association of Airport Executives (AAAE), 37,
    56, 293–294
American Civil Liberties Union (ACLU), 170, 198,
    216–217, 227
American Recovery and Reinvestment Act of 2009, 197
AND logic structure, 188
Anthrax attacks, 83
Anti-Hijacking Act of 1973, 255
Anti-Hijacking Act. See Air Transportation Security Act
AOA. See Air operation area
AOPA. See Aircraft Owner's and Pilots Association
APA. See Allied Pilots Association
APEC. See Asia Pacific Economic Group
APIS. See Advance Passenger Information System
A-prime (A′), system sensitivity computation, 152–153
Ariana Afghan Airlines DC-10, 315
ARINC, Inc., 221, 238
Arkia Israeli Airlines, 315
Armed Islamic Group, 46
Armed law enforcement on airliners, 255
    federal, state, and local LEOs flying armed, 256–258
    historical context, 255–256
    identity verification procedures for armed LEOs, 259
Armed pilots and crew security training, 246–247
    airline crews, 254–255
    FFDO
        program implementation issues, 248–252
        special considerations, 254
    legislative background. 247–248
    operational procedures for armed pilots issues,
        252–254
Armed pilots issues, operational procedures for, 252–254
Armey, Richard, 248

Arming all-cargo pilots, 342–343
Arming Pilots Against Terrorism Act, 62, 247
Arming Pilots Against Terrorism and Cabin Defense Act
    of 2002, 247
Arrival and Departure Information System (ADIS), 178
ASAC. See Aviation Security Advisory Committee
ASCF. See Aviation Security Capital Fund
Asia Pacific Economic Group (APEC), 319
ASIF. See Aviation Security Infrastructure Fee
Assistant Federal Security Director (AFSD), 290
Association of Professional Flight Attendants, 239
ATC. See Air traffic control
ATS. See Automated Targeting System
ATSA. See Aviation and Transportation Security Act
Atta, Mohammed, 263, 368
Attack consequences, as risk parameter, 133, 134, 135
Attash, Waleed bin, 369
Austrian Airlines Caravelle bombing, 17
Automated Biometric Information System (IDENT), 178
Automated carry-on bag EDS, 214
Automated Dependent Surveillance-Broadcast (ADS-B),
    240–241
Automated Targeting System (ATS), 165, 167, 176–177
Automatic selectee list, 169–171
    use of, 166
Aviation and Transportation Security Act (ATSA), 59–62,
    70, 74, 163, 169, 228, 236, 238, 239, 240, 241,
    243, 254, 290, 295, 343, 346, 355, 357–358, 366
Aviation Crime Prevention Institute, Inc., 368
Aviation Direct Access Screening Program (ADASP), 220
Aviation Government Coordinating Council (AGCC), 126
Aviation mode, tracking terrorist travel in, 164–166
Aviation Operational Threat Response Plan, 123–125
    considerations and assumptions, 124
    guiding principles, 124
    operations, concept of, 125
Aviation Screening Assessment Program, 199
Aviation Sector Coordinating Council, 126
Aviation security, 99
    exploiting intelligence information to strengthen, 185
    FAA and, 100–101
    issues for consideration, 127
        comprehensive and robust, 129–130
        proactive or reactive approach, 129
        strategy align with budgetary and resource
            allocation processes, 130–131
        system sustainability, 128
        validity of underlying risk assumptions, 127–128
    mode-specific plans, 115
        Air Domain Surveillance and Intelligence
            Integration Plan, 120–123
        Aviation Operational Threat Response Plan,
            123–125
        Aviation Transportation System Security Plan,
            116–120
        Domestic Outreach Plan, 126–127
        International Aviation Threat Reduction Plan, 123
        International Outreach Plan, 123
    National Aviation Security Policy, 102–104
    post-9/11 actions, 101–102
    pre-9/11 approaches, 100–101
    risk-based framework, 106–109
    strategy, actions, 110–113
        to assure continuity of operations, 112–113

Aviation security, 99 (*Continued*)
    domain awareness, maximize, 110
    fostering international cooperation, 112
    layered security, 110–112
    to promote a safe, efficient and secure aviation
        transportation system, 112
    strategy, objectives, 109
    strategy, roles and responsibilities, 113–115
    threats, 104
        aircraft, 104–105
        to aviation infrastructure, 105–106
        involving hostile exploitation of air cargo, 106
Aviation Security Act, 59
Aviation Security Advisory Committee (ASAC), 73, 223
    Baseline Working Group, 289
    Security Baseline Working Group, 345
    Working Group, 365
Aviation Security Capital Fund (ASCF), 64–65, 73, 81,
    223, 224
Aviation Security Clearinghouse, 293
Aviation Security Improvements Act of 1990, 29–30, 296
Aviation Security Infrastructure Fee (ASIF), 59, 60
Aviation security operations, federal role expansion in,
    56–57
Aviation Security program area, 245
Aviation security screening
    applications for, 218–219
    checkpoint technologies, 213–219
    human performance, effect of, 197–198
    impacts of privacy on, 198–199
    policy considerations for, 193–197
        airline passenger traffic growth, 194
        explosives detection at passenger checkpoints,
            improving, 195
        in-line EDS integration, 196
        projected costs and funding issues, 196–197
        screening efficiency and passenger wait times, 194
        space constraints at airports, 194–195
        technology and human factors needs, strategic
            planning for addressing, 196
Aviation security-related legislation and regulatory
    action, 82
Aviation targets, 84, 85
Aviation Transportation System Security Plan
    goals and requirements, 117
        aviation infrastructure protection, 118–120
        passenger, employee, and crew security assurance,
            117
        threat object detection and interdiction, 117–118
    guiding principles, 116–117
Aviation workers and general aviation passengers,
    prescreening of, 179–180

B

BAE Systems, 325, 326, 327
Baggage, options for reducing, 224–225
Baggage screening, 193
    carry-on, 203–204
    checked, 222–223
        firearms in, 225–226
    equipment for, 94
    funding for, 196, 197
    optimization, 223–224

Baggage Screening Investment Study, 223
BAO. *See* Bomb appraisal officers
BASS. *See* Behavior Assessment Screening System
Bazookas, 310
BDOs. *See* Behavioral Detection Officers
Behavior Assessment Screening System (BASS), 226
Behavioral Detection Officers (BDOs), 186, 188–189, 194,
    226, 227, 229
Behavioral pattern recognition, in GA environment,
    376–377
Bin Laden, Osama, 43–45, 46, 366–367
Biological/chemical attack, 272
Biometric technology
    and access control, 295–296, 356
Black Diamond lane, 207
Blind Sheikh, 42
Blowpipe, 306, 308
BLSs. *See* Bottle liquid scanners
Blue Square lane, 207
Boeing 247 bombing, 16
Boeing 707 bombing, 17
Boeing 737 bombing, 20
Boeing 747-400 passenger jet, 355
Boeing Corporation, 139
Bomb appraisal officers (BAOs), 226, 227, 229
Border and Transportation Security Policy Coordination
    Committee, 103
Boston Logan International Airport, 220, 287, 288
Bottle liquid scanners (BLSs), 195, 214, 215–216
British Air Accident Investigation Branch, 354
Bunning, Jim, 248
Bureau of Labor Statistics, 247
Bush Administration, 79, 247
Business and charter aviation, security practices
    for, 383
    charter operations, security measures for, 383–384
    large private and corporate aircraft, security measures
        for, 384–385
    TSA access certificate program, 383
BWI Airport, 212

C

Cabin–cockpit communications, 239
Cable News Network (CNN) investigative report (2008),
    243, 244
Canadian Pacific Airlines DC-3 bombing, 16
Canadian Region, 264
Canine explosives detection teams, 348
Canine teams, 339
Cannon, Howard, 13
CAPPS systems. *See* Computer-Assisted Passenger
        Prescreening Systems
CAPS systems. *See* Computer-Assisted Passenger
        Screening system
Card reader systems, 290
Cargo airlines, 343
Cargo crimes, 337
Cargo inspection methods and technologies, 343–344
Cargo screening and inspection, cost of, 352
    hardened blast-resistant cargo containers, 353–355
    manufacturers and shippers, potential impacts on, 353
    passenger airlines and freight forwarders, potential
        impacts on, 352–353

Cargo screening technology, 77–78, 348
    chemical trace detection systems, 350–351
    explosive detection systems (EDS), 350
    millimeter wave imaging systems, 351–352
    neutron beam technologies, 351
    x-ray screening, 349–350
Cargo security, 73–74
Carlos the Jackal, 310
Carry-on baggage screening, 203–204. *See also* baggage
        screening
CASS system. *See* Cockpit Access Security System
Cast and prosthesis scanners, 195, 214
Castro, Fidel, 2–3
Castro, Raúl, 2
CBP, 163, 176
    Data Center, 176
CBRN. *See* Chemical, biological, radiological, and
        nuclear
CCSP. *See* Certified Cargo Screening Program
Center for Disease Control, 266
Center for Risk and Economic Analysis of Terrorist
        Events (CREATE), 317
Central Intelligence Agency (CIA), 21, 26, 28, 45, 46, 47,
        49, 185, 369
Century of Aviation Reauthorization Act of 2003, 64–66
Certified Cargo Screening Program (CCSP), 347
Cessna 172, 369
Cessna Citation VII business jet, 367–368
Chance diagonal, 151
Charter aircraft, 384
Charter and aircraft lease customers, vetting of, 380
Charter operations
    background checks for, 380
    security measures for, 383–384
Checkpoint Evolution, 211–213
    design of, 212
Checkpoint Security Screening Fund, 195, 213–214
Chemical, biological, radiological, and nuclear (CBRN)
    attacks, 133
    threats, 370–371
        countermeasures for, 298–299
    weapons, 369
Chemical trace detection systems, 350–351
Chertoff, Michael, 244
Chinese FN-6, 307
Chinese HN-5, 307
CIA. *See* Central Intelligence Agency
Cincinnati/Northern Kentucky International, 347
Civil Reserve Air Fleet, 327
Civilian aviation encounters, with shoulder-fired missiles,
        313–316
Civilian transport aircraft, survivability of, 312–313
Clear Identity Pass RT program, 208
Clear®, 208
Clinton, Bill, 32, 34, 35, 37
CLOS MANPADS, 308
C-MANPADS program, 326
Cockpit Access Security System (CASS), 221, 238–239
Cockpit Protection Program, 251
College Park Airport, 387
Combat air patrol (a CAP), 50
Commercial airliners, vulnerability of, 310
    civilian aviation encounters, with shoulder-fired
        missiles, 313–316

civilian transport aircraft, survivability of, 312–313
commercial flight operations, 311–312
Commercial airport access controls and perimeter
        security, 271
    access control measures, 290
    airfield and airport perimeter, patrolling, 287–288
    airport compliance with security requirements,
        evaluation of, 283–284
    airport perimeter security and access control
        measures, 284–285
    airport physical security and security technologies,
        284
    airport security, 277, 278
        airport contractor and vendor security programs,
            282
        airport perimeter, 281–282
        AOA, security of, 281
        commercial passenger airports, military facilities
            at, 281
        designated GA areas, security of, 280–281
        security designations within passenger terminal,
            277–279
        security identification display areas, 279–280
    airport security programs, 275–277
    airport security risk categories, 282–283
    airport security technology investment, 274–275
    background check requirements, 290
        airport badges and identification systems,
            regulations pertaining to, 294–295
        security threat assessments, 294
        Transportation Security Clearinghouse, 292–294
    commercial airport security, planning, design, and
        construction guidelines for, 296
        chemical and biological threats, countermeasures
            for, 298–299
        crime prevention strategies, 298
        detecting radiological and nuclear threats in
            airport environment, 299
        landside security considerations, 297–298
    commercial airport security program, 274
    credentialing and access controls, biometric
        technologies for, 295–296
    critical incident management and response, 299–300
    law enforcement support, 288
        explosives detection canine teams, 289
        law enforcement reimbursable agreements,
            289–290
    security awareness training, 288
    security risk, in airport environment, 271–273
    surveillance technologies, 285
        computer vision technologies, 286
        ground surveillance radar, 286
        ground vehicle tracking, 286
        infrared sensors and thermal imaging cameras,
            286
        sensor integration, 287
Commercial airport security, 274
    planning, design, and construction guidelines for, 296
        chemical and biological threats, countermeasures
            for, 298–299
        crime prevention strategies, 298
        landside security considerations, 297–298
        radiological and nuclear threats in airport
            environment, detecting, 299

Commercial flight operations, vulnerability of, 311–312
Commercial passenger airports, military facilities at, 281
Committee on Assessment of Security Technologies for
        Transportation, 187
Communications intelligence, 160
Computer-Assisted Passenger Prescreening System
        (CAPPS), 33, 70–71, 167–168, 189
Computer-Assisted Passenger Prescreening System II
        (CAPPS II), 65, 166
    development effort, 171–172
Computer-Assisted Passenger Screening (CAPS) system,
        46, 167
Computer vision technologies, 286
Congo Airlines Boeing 727, 315
Congressional Budget Office (CBO), 223
Congressional policy concerns, lingering, 78–80
Congressional response to 9/11 attacks, 55–56
    aviation security operations, federal role expansion in,
        56–57
    post-9/11 debate over federalizing passenger
        screening, 57–59
Consequences of attack, mitigating, 155–156
    adaptive systems approaches to aviation security,
        156–158
Consolidated Appropriations Act (2004), 389
Consolidated Appropriations Resolution, 237
Continental Airlines Boeing 707, 7, 16
Continental United States Region, 264
Continuing terrorist threats, 82–83
    Al-Qaeda's post 9/11 ambitions, 84–86
    post-anthrax attacks, 83
    shoe bombing of American Airlines flight 63, 83–84
Cooper, D. B., 7
Cost of aviation protection, 91–96
Costello, Jerry, 352
Countermissile technologies, 79
Counterterrorism
    strategies and tactics, 321
Covert testing, 199–202
CREATE. See Center for Risk and Economic Analysis of
        Terrorist Events
Credentialing and access controls, biometric technologies
        for, 295–296
Crew resource management, 253
CrewPASS, 221–222
Crime prevention strategies, 298
Critical incident management and response, 299–300
Critical infrastructure and key resources, 107
Crop duster aircraft, 368
CT-based scanners, 218–219
Cuba
    bilateral agreement on hijackings, 9
    hijackings in, 2–3
Current Intelligence and Assessments Division (CI&A),
        163, 164

D

Data fusion, in aviation environment
    data logic and current data fusion practices, 187–188
    meaning, 186
    ongoing initiatives, for improving data fusion
        practices, 189–190
    parametric data fusion networks, 188–189

Data logic and current data fusion practices, 187–188
Davidson, Captain Edward M., 250
Dawson's Field hijackings, 4, 50
DCA Access Standard Security Program, 387
DCA, GA access to, 387
Deadly diseases, 266–267
Decision data fusion, 187–188
DeFazio, Peter, 247
Defense Information Systems Agency, 264
Defense Red Switch Network, 263–264
Delta Airlines flight, 220
DEN. See Domestic Events Network
Denver International Airport, 207
Department of Defense (DOD), 263–264, 319
Department of Homeland Security (DHS), 241, 243, 244,
        245, 256, 259, 266
    DHS C-MANPADS program, 326, 328
    Office of Appeals and Redress, 183
    Science and Technology Directorate, 347, 348
    Second Stage Review (2SR), 244
    Traveler Redress Inquiry Program (DHS TRIP),
        183–184, 185
    Transportation Security Laboratory, 354
Department of Homeland Security, Office of Inspector
        General (DHS OIG), 198, 200, 201, 262
Department of Justice (DOJ), 321, 366
Department of Transportation (DOT), 63
    DOT OIG recommendations, 283–284
    Rapid Response Team on Airport Security, 208, 224
Depressurization of airplane, 250
Detection-based strategies, 267
Detection criteria and system errors, security risks,
        149–150
Detroit Metropolitan Wayne County Airport, 262
DHL cargo airplane, 316
DHS. See Department of Homeland Security
Dillingham, Gerald, 36
Directed infrared countermeasure systems, 325
"Dirty-bomb", 371
DISA. See Defense Information Systems Agency
Disruptive passenger behavior, 259–261
DOD. See Department of Defense
DOJ. See Department of Justice
Domestic Events Network, 263
Domestic Outreach Plan, 126–127
DOT. See Department of Transportation
Double-door system, 237
d-prime (d'), system sensitivity computation, 151–152
DRSN. See Defense Red Switch Network
Dry runs, 261, 263

E

Eagle Eye Program, 322
EBSVERA. See Enhanced Border Security and Visa
        Reform Act
E-DIRCM, 328
EDS. See Explosive detection systems
EgyptAir Boeing 767, 249
EgyptAir flight 990, 47
Egyptian Islamic Jihad, 44
El Al airlines, 24, 237, 310
El Al Boeing 707, 3, 17
Electronic Baggage Screening Program, 223

Electronic intelligence (ELINT), 160
Electronic System for Travel Authorization (ESTA)
    system, 178–179
ELINT. *See* Electronic intelligence
Emergency Security Control of Air Traffic (ESCAT),
    264–265
Emergency Wartime Supplemental Appropriations Act of
    2003, 326
Enhanced Border Security and Visa Reform Act
    (EBSVERA), 176, 178
ESCAT. *See* Emergency Security Control of Air Traffic
ESTA system. *See* Electronic System for Travel
    Authorization system
ETD. *See* Explosives trace detection
Exit tracking, 178
Explosive detection systems (EDS), 148, 149, 195, 197,
    222, 350
    automated carry-on bag EDS, 214
    for carry-on screening applications, 195
    in-line integration, 196, 197, 223
Explosives and incendiary devices, 335–336
Explosives detection at passenger checkpoints,
    improving, 195
Explosives detection canine teams, 289
Explosives detection, on passengers, 71–72
Explosives trace detection (ETD) portal systems, 72, 151,
    350
    machines, 215, 222
    technologies, 215
    walk-through, 195, 214, 216
Explosives trace portals (ETPs), 195

F

FAA Reauthorization Act of 1996, 34–35, 167
FAA Reauthorization Act of 2003, 275, 342
False alarm rates, 285
False negatives, 149, 181, 182
False positives, 148, 149
FAMS. *See* Federal Air Marshal Service
Fatwa, 44
FBI
    Cockpit Protection Program, 252
    Terrorist Screening Center, 293
Federal Air Marshal Service (FAMS), 61–62, 77, 241
    force size and flight coverage controversies, 242–245
    operational and procedural issues, 245–246
    post-9/11 air marshal hiring and training, 241–242
    statutes and regulations regarding the deployment of,
        on flights, 257–258
Federal Aviation Administration (FAA), 2, 168, 236, 237,
    238, 239, 240, 260, 265, 296, 354, 365
    action against escalating violence
    behavioral profiling techniques, 8
    Civil Aviation Security Strategic Plan, 100
    projections, 327
    Reauthorization Act, 34–35, 167, 275, 342
    records on pilots, against criminal and terrorist
        databases, 379–380
    screening system, 8, 9
        multidisciplinary task force, 10
Federal Aviation Authorization Act of 1996, 56, 57
Federal Express, 326, 339
Federal Express DC-10, 23, 249, 338

Federal Flight Deck Officer (FFDO) program, 62, 65, 95,
    246–247, 342
    implementation issues, 248–252
    special considerations, 254
Federal Information Surveillance Act, 48
Federal law enforcement agencies, 263
Federal Law Enforcement Training Center (FLETC),
    247, 251
Federal role expansion, in aviation security operations,
    56–57
Federal security directors, 62
Federal Security Service, 321
Federal spending on aviation security-
    related activities, 93
FFDO program. *See* Federal Flight Deck Officer program
Fido PaxPoint, 215
Fighter jets, 323
Fixed-base operators, 280–281
FLETC. *See* Federal Law Enforcement Training Center
Fletcher, Ernie, 367
Flight deck access procedures, 238–239
Flight operational procedures, 322–324
Flight restricted zone (FRZ), 386–387
Flight Safety Technologies, Inc., 325
Flight school security, 382–383
Flight Standards District Office (FSDO), 378
Flynn, Cathal, 47
Fort Dix military installation, 89
Fort Lauderdale Executive airport, 368
Forward-looking infrared (FLIR) technology, 322
Freight Assessment System, 344
Frontier Airlines Boeing 737 hijacking, 7–8
FRZ. *See* Flight restricted zone
Fuel-tank inserting systems, 313
Funding for Security Support, 214
FY2002, 275
FY2003, 244, 275
FY2003 Appropriations, 236
FY2003 Emergency Wartime Supplemental
    Appropriations Act, 236
FY2005 Homeland Security Appropriations Act, 340, 357
FY2006 appropriations language, 340, 346, 357
FY2006 Department of Homeland Security
    Appropriations Act, 373
FY2007 appropriations language, 340, 346, 357
FY2008 Omnibus Appropriations Act, 294, 340, 346, 347
FY2009, 81, 244
FY2028, 81

G

GA (General Aviation) aircraft, 363–364
    potential consequences of attack using, 369
        chemical, biological, radiological, and nuclear
            (CBRN) threats, 370–371
        nuclear power facilities, as potential targets,
            371–372
        risk picture for, 372
        suicide attacks and conventional explosives,
            369–370
GA airports, 141, 361–365
GA areas, security of, 280–281
GA flight operations, 362
    at U.S. borders, vetting and tracking, 385–386

GA operations and airports, security for, 41, 66, 361
  aircraft, physical security measures for, 381–382
  airport access controls, 377–378
  airports, physical security measures for, 381
  airspace restrictions
    policy issues regarding, 390–393
    for presidential visits, 390
  airspace restrictions, 386
    around Washington, DC, 386
  background checks and vetting, 378
    background checks, for charter operators, 380
    charter and aircraft lease customers, vetting
      of, 380
    FAA records on pilots, against criminal and
      terrorist databases, 379–380
    tracking aircraft sales, 380–381
    vetting of individuals seeking flight training, 379
  business and charter aviation, security practices
      for, 383
    charter operations, security measures for,
      383–384
    large private and corporate aircraft, security
      measures for, 384–385
    TSA access certificate program, 383
  flight school security, 382–383
  GA aircraft, potential consequences of attack
      using, 369
    chemical, biological, radiological, and nuclear
      threats, 370–371
    nuclear power facilities as potential targets,
      371–372
    risk picture for GA aircraft, 372
    suicide attacks and conventional explosives,
      369–370
  mitigating security risks, options for, 372
    airport watch program, 375–376
    behavioral pattern recognition techniques, in GA
      environment, 376–377
    security risk assessments, 373–374
    surveillance and monitoring, 374–375
  securing agricultural aviation operations, 382
  security vulnerabilities, 366–368
  security-related flight restrictions, throughout United
      States, 389–390
  terrorist threat, 368–369
  vetting and tracking GA flights at U.S. borders,
      385–386
GA security risks, 372
  airport watch program, 375–376
  behavioral pattern recognition techniques, in GA
      environment, 376–377
  security risk assessments, 373–374
  surveillance and monitoring, 374–375
Game theory, 140
GAO. See Government Accountability Office
"Garbage in, garbage out" phenomenon, 140
GE, 209
General aviation. See GA entries
Glasgow International Airport, 106
  attack at, 87–88
Global Hawk UAV platform, 329
Global terror threat, intelligence reforms in response to,
      161–163

Gore Commission, 168, 339, 345, 346, 348
  impact on aviation security, 35
  recommendations on aviation security, 32–34
Government Accountability Office (GAO), 65, 172,
      200–201, 229, 242, 260, 275, 283, 341, 343, 351
  screener detection of threat objects, recommendations
      for, 201
Green Circle lane, 207
Ground-based countermeasures, 329–330
Ground surveillance radar, 286
Ground vehicle tracking, 286
Gulfstream Aerospace Corporation, 325

H

H5N1 strain of avian influenza, 266
Hadayet, Hesham Mohamed, 85
Hague Convention, 6
Hahneman, Frederick, 8
Hamadei, Mohammed Ali, 21–22
Hamilton, Lee, 69
Hand wands, 195
Handling disruptive passengers and other in-flight
      security incidents, 259–261
Hanjour, Hani, 48
Hansen, Michael Lynn, 8
Hardened blast-resistant cargo containers, 353–355
Hardened cargo container, deploying, 74
Hardened cockpit doors, 236–237
Hardened unit-loading devices, 354
Hartsfield-Jackson Atlanta International Airport, 273
Hazardous materials, 336–337
Heathrow Airport, 210
Heating, ventilation, and air conditioning systems, 272
Hezbollah, 82, 88
Hijacking contagion, 6–8
Hinderberger, Ron, 250
"Hits," SDT, 148, 149
Homegrown terrorists threats, in United States, 88–90
Homeland Security Act of 2002, 61, 62–64, 228–229,
      239, 246, 254, 343
Homeland Security Appropriations Act (2005), 346
Homeland Security Council, 103
Homeland Security Counter-MANPADS systems
      development and testing, 326–327
Homeland Security Presidential Directive 5 (HSPD-5),
      300
Homeland Security Presidential Directive 6 (HSPD-6),
      161, 162
Homeland Security Presidential Directive 16 (HSPD-16),
      102
Honeywell, 326
HORNET (Hazardous Ordnance Engagement Toolkit),
      329, 330
House Appropriations Committee, 223
House Aviation Subcommittee, 247
House Judiciary Committee, 245
HSPD. See Homeland Security Presidential Directive
Human intelligence (HUMINT), 159, 160
Human performance effect, on aviation security
      screening, 197–198
HUMINT. See Human intelligence
Hydrogen peroxide-based explosives, 87

I

ICAO. *See* International Civil Aviation Organization
ICE. *See* Immigration and Customs Enforcement
ICx Technologies, 215
IDENT system, 178
Identification Systems, 294
IED. *See* Improvised explosive devices
IID. *See* Improvised incendiary device
Ilyushin IL-76, 310, 324
Image stripping, 203
Imagery intelligence (IMINT), 159
IMINT. *See* Imagery intelligence
Immigration and Customs Enforcement (ICE), 256
Implementing the 9/11 Commission Recommendations
        Act (2007), 178, 183, 195, 196, 197, 213,
        221, 223, 230, 336, 340, 343, 347, 354, 373,
        374, 385
Improvised explosive devices (IED), 71, 196, 199,
        201, 203
Improvised incendiary device (IID), 201
Indirect air carrier, 344
Infectious diseases, 266–267
In-flight chemical and biological threats, 265–267
In-flight explosives threat, mitigating, 265–267
In-flight security
    improving, 53
    incidents, 260
    threats, responding to, 263–265
Infrared sensors, 286
Infrastructure, threats to aviation
In-line baggage screening systems, 73, 76
Instrument flight rules, 51
Intelligence and counterterrorism information, 159
    airline passenger prescreening and terrorist watch
        lists, 166
        aviation workers and general aviation passengers,
            prescreening of, 179–180
        CAPPS II development effort, 171–172
        computer-assisted passenger prescreening system,
            167–168
        international air travelers and shipments,
            risk-based targeting of, 176–177
        international airports of entry, immigration
            controls at, 177–179
        international passengers, prescreening
            of, 175–176
        no-fly and automatic selectee lists, 169–171
        pre-9/11 passenger prescreening initiatives, 167
        Secure Flight system development, 172–174, 175
        Secure Flight terrorist watch list checks,
            operational implementation of, 174–175
    data fusion, in aviation environment, 186
        data logic and current data fusion practices,
            187–188
        ongoing initiatives, for improving data fusion
            practices, 189–190
        parametric data fusion networks, 188–189
    identification of terrorist networks, 185–186
    intelligence gathering and analysis, overview of,
        159–161
    intelligence reforms, in response to global terror
        threat, 161–163

        passenger prescreening and terrorist watch list
            checks, policy issues related to, 180
            accuracy and reliability, of terrorist databases, 180
            false positive matches and failures to detect
                terrorist threats, 181–183
            passenger redress procedures, 183–185
        to strengthen aviation security, 185
        tracking terrorist travel, in aviation mode, 164–166
        transportation security intelligence, TSA's role in,
            163–164
Intelligence gathering and analysis, overview of, 159–161
Intelligence Reform Act of 2004, 345
Intelligence reforms, in response to global terror threat,
        161–163
Intelligence Watch and Outreach Division, 163, 164
Intentional violations, 143
Interagency Border Inspection System, 176
Intercontinental Airport, 287
International air travelers and shipments, risk-based
        targeting of, 176–177
International airports of entry, immigration controls at,
        177–179
International Aviation Threat Reduction Plan, 123
International Civil Aviation Organization (ICAO), 5–6,
        319, 373
International Outreach Plan, 123
International passengers, prescreening of, 175–176
International Security and Development Cooperation Act
        of 1985, 23
IR-countermeasure protection, 328–329
IR-guided MANPADS, 307–308
IRTPA of 2004. *See* National Intelligence Reform and
        Terrorism Prevention Act of 2004
Islamic Army Shura, 44
Israel, Steve, 237
Israeli charter Boeing 757, 326
Israeli-registered Boeing 757 aircraft, 315

J

Jackson-Evers International Airport
Jacobsen, Annie, 262
Japan Airlines DC-8, 249
Javelin missiles, 306, 308
Jefferson, Robert, 371
Jet aircraft, thefts of, 368
JetEye, 327
Jihadization, 89
John F. Kennedy International Airport, 88, 209,
        277, 337
John Wayne-Orange County Airport, 280

K

Kean, Tom, 69
Keiko II, 306
Kennedy, Edward, 171
Khaled, Leila, 3
Known shipper database, 78
Known Shipper Management System, 346
Known shipper programs, 343, 344–346
Korean Airlines Boeing 707 bombing, 24
Korean Airlines flight 858, 211

L

L3 PassPort, 209
Lackawanna Six terrorist cell, 89
Lakhani, Hemant, 321
Landside security considerations, 297–298
Langely F-16s, 50
Large business jets vs. small GA aircraft, 372
Large private and corporate aircraft, security measures
    for, 384–385
Laser beam rider MANPADS, 308–309
Latent conditions, 143–144
Law enforcement availability pay, 241
Law Enforcement Officers Safety Act of 2004, 256
Law enforcement reimbursable agreements, 289–290
Law enforcement support, 288
    explosives detection canine teams, 289
    law enforcement reimbursable agreements, 289–290
LAX shootings, 85
Lear Jet, 368
Lehman, John, 71
LEOs, with arms in aircraft, 253, 255–256
    identity verification procedures for, 259
Less-than-lethal weapons, for in-flight security
    consideration, 254
Letters of intent, 73
    use of, 65
Lewis, John, 171
Liberal criterion, in signal detection, 150
Lidle, Corey, 367
Liquids
    checkpoint procedures for, 210–211
    public criticism over liquids ban, 211
Logan International Airport, 337
Logan Watch, 288
London Heathrow International Airport, 277
London transit bombings (2005), 244
Long War, 90, 91
Loy, James, 63, 251, 348
LTTE. *See* Tamil Tigers
Luckey, Captain Stephen, 249

M

Madrid passenger rail bombings (2004), 244
Magaw, John, 63
Magnetometers, 195, 213
Makkawi, Mohammed Ibrahim, 85
Manila air plot, 43
MANPADS. *See* Man-portable Air Defense Systems
Man-portable Air Defense Systems (MANPADSs),
    77, 306
    terrorist acquisition and possession, 309–310
Manufacturers and shippers, potential impacts on, 353
Marchi, Richard, 56
Markey, Ed, 78, 347, 371
Maryland three airports, 387
MASINT. *See* Measurement and signature intelligence
Massport, 287
MATADOR™ IRCM system, 325
McCoy, Richard Floyd, Jr, 7
Mead, Kenneth, 345
Measurement and signature intelligence (MASINT), 159
Merit System Protection Board, 231

Metal detectors, 150
Miami International Airport, 337
Mica, John, 247, 248
Middle Eastern terrorist organization, hijackings by, 3–4
Military aircraft, 323
Millimeter wave imaging systems, 217, 218, 219,
    351–352
Mineta, Norman Y., 51, 63
Minneapolis-St. Paul International Airport, 227
Misagh-1, 307
Misagh-2, 307
Missile approach warning system, 325
Missiles, 306
Mistral, 306
Mohammed, Khalid Sheikh, 42, 43, 44–45, 84–85
Monte Carlo simulation methods, 139
Montreal Convention of 1971, 6
Morristown Airport, 383
Moussaoui, Zacharias, 48, 368, 369
Mubarak, Hosni, 44

N

Nairobi bombing, 1
Nash equilibrium, 55
National Agricultural Aviation Association, 382
National Airlines DC-6 bombing, 16
National Aviation Security Policy, 102–104
National Business Aviation Association, 383
National Capital Region (NCR), 386, 391
National Counterterrorism Center (NCTC), 161
    primary functions, 162
National Crime Information Center (NCIC) database, 178
National Explosives Detection Canine Program, 348
National Guard C-130, 50
National Incident Management System (NIMS), 300
National Infrastructure Protection Plan, 106
National Institute of Justice, 254
National Intelligence Reform and Terrorism Prevention
    Act (IRTPA) of 2004, 75–77, 179, 223, 259,
    322, 336, 340, 353–354, 356
National Plan of Integrated Airport Systems, 364
National Research Council (NRC) Committee, 74, 187,
    189, 267, 351, 354
National Response Center, 375
National Response Framework (NRF), 124
National Response Plan. *See* National Response
    Framework (NRF)
National Security Agency, 161
National Security Presidential Directive 47, 102
National Strategy for Aviation Security, 104
National Strategy for Homeland Security, 102
National Targeting Center (NTC), 164, 177
National Transportation Safety Board (NTSB), 17,
    240, 336
NATO Partnership for Peace Trust Fund Project, 320
NCIC database. *See* National Crime Information Center
NCR. *See* National Capital Region
NCTC. National Counterterrorism Center
Neutron beam technologies, 351
Newark Liberty airport, 209
Nighttime flights, 323
NIMS. *See* National Incident Management System
Nixon Administration, 255

Nixon administration, 4–5
  screening of passengers, 13
  Senate-passed bill, 14
  Anti-hijacking Act of 1974, 14
Nixon, Richard M., 256
No-fly lists, 167, 169–171, 266
Nonproliferation and weapons reduction initiatives, 319–320
Nonsterile areas, 277
NORAD. *See* North American Aerospace Defense
North American Aerospace Defense (NORAD), 50, 241, 264
  Northeast Air Defense Sector (NEADS), 50, 264
  Operation Noble Eagle, 392
Northrop Grumman, 326–327, 329
Northwest Airlines, 168, 326, 327, 262–263
Northwest Orient Airlines Boeing 727, 7
NRC Committee. *See* National Research Council Committee
NTC. *See* National Targeting Center
NTSB. *See* National Transportation Safety Board
Nuclear power facilities, as potential targets, 371–372
Nuclear Regulatory Commission, 371

O

Occupational Safety and Health Administration, 218
Office of Civil Rights, 198
Office of Internal Affairs and Program Review, 199
Office of Occupational Safety, Health, and Environment, 231
Office of Security Operations, 200
Office of Special Counsel, 231
O'Hare Airport, 273
Oklahoma City bombing, 1, 369
Open source intelligence (OSINT), 159, 161
Operation Bojinka, 43
Operation Liberty Shield, 388
Operation Noble Eagle, 264
Operation Smoking Dragon, 321
Operation Tarmac, 292
OR logic structure, 188
Orlando International Airport, 209
Orly airport, 310
OSINT. *See* Open source intelligence
Otis Air Force Base, 50
Overseas terrorist hijackings
  international response, 5–6
  U.S. response, 4–5

P

Pacific Southwest 737 hijacking, 9
Pacific Southwest Airlines, 22–23
Pan Am flight 73 hijacking, 22
Pan Am flight 103, 25–26, 100, 167, 169, 183, 265, 296, 354
Pan Am in-flight bombing, 2
Parametric data fusion networks, 188–189
Parker, Istaique, 43
Passenger airlines and freight forwarders, potential impacts on, 352–353
Passenger prescreening, enhancing, 70–71
Passenger prescreening and terrorist watch list checks, policy issues related to, 180

accuracy and reliability, of terrorist databases, 180
false positive matches and failures to detect terrorist threats, 181–183
passenger redress procedures, 183–185
Passenger redress procedures, 183–185
Passenger screening, 193
  airline passenger traffic growth, 194
  checkpoint efficiency of
    checkpoint inefficiencies, potential security risks of, 206
    for liquids, 210–211
    passenger education and information materials, 211
    passenger wait times, 204–206
    queuing practices and procedures, 206–207
    RT pilot program, 206, 207–209
    self-select screening lane initiative, 207
    streamlining procedures, 209–210
  explosives detection at passenger checkpoints, improving, 195
  funding for, 196–197
  screening efficiency and passenger wait times, 194
Pat-down screening, 198–199
PCA system. *See* Propulsion-Controlled Aircraft Technology
Peachtree–Dekalb County Airport, 364
Pearl, Daniel, 84
Pentaerythritol tetra-nitrate, 84
Performance and Accountability Standards System, 230
Performance Management Information System, 198
Permissive action links, 320
PFLP. *See* Popular Front for the Liberation of Palestine
Philippine Airlines flight 434, 43, 211
Philippines, terrorist attacks in, 42
Physical screening and inspection, 346–348
Physical space, 277
Pilot organizations, and TSA, 247
Pilot program, 336
Pilot training, 391
Pilots, screening and peer monitoring, 249
Piper Warrior, 369
Point release attack, 272
Policy debates, 41
Policy refinement, in response to evolving terrorist threats, 69
  9/11 Commission
    aviation security-related recommendations of, 70–75
    impacts of, 69–70
  asymmetric threat, 90–91
  aviation protection, cost of, 91–96
  congressional policy concerns, lingering, 78–80
  continuing threats, 82–83
    Al-Qaeda's post 9/11 ambitions, 84–86
    post-9/11 anthrax attacks, 83
    shoe bombing of American Airlines flight 63, 83–84
  evolving terrorist threats, 86–88
  homegrown terrorists threats, in United States, 88–90
  National Intelligence Reform and Terrorism Prevention Act (IRTPA) of 2004, 75–77
  recommendations of 9/11 Commission Act of 2007, implementing, 80–82
  TSA regulations, to strengthen air cargo security, 77–78

Popular Front for the Liberation of Palestine (PFLP), 3, 4
Positive passenger bag match procedures, 25
Possible terrorist probing incidents, 261–263
Post-9/11 anthrax attacks, 83
Post-9/11 debate over federalizing passenger screening, 57–59
Posted security guards, 290
Potomac Airfield, 364, 387
Power circuitry for electric-powered avionics and equipment, 240
Pre-9/11 passenger prescreening initiatives, 167
Precursors to 9/11 attacks, 42
    Al Qaeda, rising threat of, 43–45
    Bojinka plot, 42–43
President's Commission on Aviation Security and Terrorism, 26–29
Primary surveillance radar, 240
Private charter program, 384
Private Charter Standard Security Program, 384
Proactive steps to reduce possible attacks, 267
Professional Flight Attendants Association, 239
Project Chloe, 329
Propulsion-Controlled Aircraft Technology (PCA) system, 312–313
Provisional Irish Republican Army, 90, 91
Public health initiatives, 266
Pulsed fast neutron analysis, 351
Pulsed fast/thermal neutron spectroscopy, 351

Q

QW-2 shoulder-fired missiles, 321

R

R4 framework of resilience, 155
Radicalization incubators, 89
Radiological and nuclear threats, in airport environment, 299
Rahman, Sheikh Omar Adbel, 42
RAND Corporation, 304, 317, 328
Rapid Response Teams, 51–55
    on Aircraft Security, recommendations of, 235
Rapidity, 155, 156
Raytheon HUMRAAM system, 329
RBS-70 missile, 308
RBS-70 Mk I, 306
RBS-70 Mk II, 306
RBS-90, 306
Reagan, Ronald, 367
Reason, James, 142, 143, 144
Receiver Operating Characteristic (ROC) function, 150, 151
Red Stewart Airfield, 364
Red team testing, 199
Redundancy, 155, 156
Registered Traveler (RT) program, 52
Reid, Richard Colvin, 83–84
Remote Air Sampling Canine Olfaction sensors, 348
Reporting tree, 377
Research, development, test, and evaluation (RDT&E) program, 79
Resilience, 155
Resourcefulness, 155, 156

Ressam, Ahmed, 47
Ridge, Tom, 244
Risk-based priorities, for transportation assets protection, 74–75
Risk Management Assessment Tool, 139
Risk of catastrophic failure of aircraft, 250
Risks. *See* Security risks, evaluation and management
RMAT. *See* Risk Management Assessment Tool
Robust security, 91
Robustness, 155, 156
ROC function. *See* Receiver Operating Characteristic
Rocket-propelled grenades (RPGs), 303, 310
Rome, 86
RPGs. *See* Rocket-propelled grenades
RT pilot program, 206, 207–209
Russian SA-18, 307

S

SA-14, 306
SA-16, 306
SA-18 (IGLA), 306, 321
SA-7A, 306
SA-7B, 306
SABRE 4000, 215
Salt Lake City, Utah, Airport, 207
San Francisco International Airport, 208, 347
SARS. *See* Severe acute respiratory syndrome
SCATANA (Security Control of Air Traffic and Navigation Aids), 264
Screener attrition
    involuntary attrition, 228
    voluntary attrition, 228
Screener retention, 227–231
    hiring standards, 228–229
    salaries, benefits, and career advancement initiatives, 230
    TSA staffing needs, 229–230
    whistleblower protections, 231
    workplace injuries, reducing, 230–231
Screener Training Exercises and Assessments (STEA). *See* Aviation Screening Assessment Program
Screener workforce issues, 226–227
    TSO's, broadcasting roles for, 226–227
Screening checkpoints, 72–73
Screening Passengers by Observation Techniques program, 226
Screening versus physical inspection, of cargo shipments, 339–341
SDT. *See* Signal detection theory
Seattle-Tacoma International, 347
Secondary flight deck barriers, 237–238
Secret Service agents, 256
Secretary of Homeland Security, 259
Secure Flight, 65, 163, 166, 171, 172, 173
    decision criteria, 182
    passenger prescreening system, 175
    system development, 172–174, 175
    system sensitivity, 182
    terrorist watch list checks
        operational implementation, 174–175
Secure Flight Passenger Data, 173
Secure Transportation for America Act, 58–59
Security awareness training, 288

Security background checks
    airport badges and identification systems, regulations
        pertaining to, 294–295
    security threat assessments, 294
    Transportation Security Clearinghouse, 292–294
Security challenges, 157–158
Security Control of Air Traffic and Navigation Aids. *See*
        SCATANA
Security designations within passenger terminal, 277–279
Security Guidelines for General Aviation Airports, 381
Security identification display areas, 279–280
Security layers, 144–146
Security measures, impact on air transportation system
        efficiency, assessment, 153–155
Security-related flight restrictions, throughout United
        States, 389–390
Security risks, evaluation and management
    complex models of risk in the aviation security
        domain, approaches for developing, 139–141
    consequences of attack, mitigating, 155–156
        adaptive systems approaches to aviation security,
            156–158
    mitigating, 141–142
    mitigation measures and security systems
        effectiveness, evaluation of, 146–147
        detection criteria and system errors, 149–150
        SDT, 147–149
        system sensitivity, 150–153
    monetary risk, 137–138
    multilayered approach to aviation security, 142–146
    risk assessment methods, 133–135
    risk-based framework to determine a risk valuation
        and assess costs and benefits, 135–139
    risk matrix, 134
    security measures, impact on air transportation
        system efficiency, 153–155
Security risks, posed by air cargo, 333
    aircraft hijacking and sabotage, 338
    airmail consignments, 338–339
    cargo crime, 337
    explosives and incendiary devices, 335–336
    hazardous materials, 336–337
Security system sensitivity, 150–153
Security threat assessments, 294
Security vulnerabilities, 366–368
Self-select screening lane initiative, 207
SENSIT, 219
Sensor data fusion, 189–190
Sensor integration, 287
Severe acute respiratory syndrome (SARS), 266
Shoe bombing (attempt) of American Airlines flight 63,
        83–84
Shoe scanners, 195, 209, 214
Shoulder-fired missiles and standoff weapons, mitigating
        threat of, 303
    against large western-built civilian turbojet aircraft, 314
    commercial airliners, vulnerability of, 310
        civilian aviation encounters, with shoulder-fired
            missiles, 313–316
        civilian transport aircraft, survivability of, 312–313
        commercial flight operations, 311–312
    ground-based countermeasures, 329–330
    standoff weapons attack, potential consequences of,
        316–317

    terrorist threat and shoulder-fired weapons,
        proliferation of, 305
    CLOS MANPADS, 308
    IR-guided MANPADS, 307–308
    laser beam rider MANPADS, 308–309
    MANPADS, terrorist acquisition and possession
        of, 309–310
    standoff weapons, 310
    U.S. policy and strategic approaches, 318
        aircraft-based protections and countermeasures,
            324–328
        airport security measures, 321–322
        counterterrorism strategies and tactics, 321
        flight operational procedures, 322–324
        nonproliferation and weapons reduction
            initiatives, 319–320
        unmanned escorts providing IR-countermeasure
            protection, 328–329
Signal detection theory (SDT), 147–149
Signal intelligence (SIGINT), 159–160
SIGNIT. *See* Signal intelligence
SilkAir Boeing 737, 240, 249
Single-engine airplane, 363
Single-engine piston aircraft, 363
Sky Marshal Program, 241
Small Arms/Light Weapons Destruction Program, 320
Small GA aircraft vs. large business jets, 372
Smith, Robert, 247
Social contagion, 6–7
Southern Airways DC-9 hijacking, 9
Southwest Airlines, 222
Soviet SA-14, 307
Speaker, Andrew, 266
Spiral descents, 323
Standoff weapons, 310
    potential consequences, 316–317
Starburst, 306, 308
Starstreak, 306, 308
Sterile area, 277–278, 279
Stinger, 306
Stinger POST, 306
Stinger RMP Block I, 306
Stinger RMP Block II, 306
Stinger variant with Passive Optical Seeker Technique
        (Stinger POST), 307
Stinger with Reprogrammable Microprocessor (Stinger
        RMP), 307
Sudan, 44
Suicide aircraft hijacking, 46–47
Suicide attacks and conventional explosives, 369–370
Supply chain security technologies, 355
    access control and biometric screening technology,
        356
    tamper-evident tape, 355–356
    tamper-resistant seals, 356
Surveillance and monitoring
    of GA operations, 374–375
    of restricted airspace, 391
Surveillance technologies, 285
    computer vision technologies, 286
    ground surveillance radar, 286
    ground vehicle tracking, 286
    infrared sensors and thermal imaging cameras, 286
    sensor integration, 287

Suspicious behavior/activities, 261–262, 263
Suspicious Incident Reports (SIRs), 164
Swiss cheese metaphor, 142–144
Swissair Convair 990 bombing, 17

T

TAAG Angolan Airlines Boeing 737, 315
Tactical High Energy Laser system, 329
Tactical Integrated Illumination Countermeasure, 325
Tamil Tigers, 321
Tamper-evident tape, 355–356
Tamper-resistant seals, 356
Tax credit bond program, 223, 224
TB. *See* Tuberculosis
TECS. *See* Treasury Enforcement Communications
        System
Temporary flight restriction, 388
Terrorist databases, accuracy and reliability of, 180
Terrorist Identities Datamart Environment, 162
Terrorist incidents
    and aviation security-related legislation and
        regulatory action, 82
Terrorist networks
    intelligence information for identification, 185–186
Terrorist Screening Center, 162
Terrorist Screening Database (TSDB), 162, 163
Terrorist threat and shoulder-fired weapons, proliferation
        of, 305
    CLOS MANPADS, 308
    IR-guided MANPADS, 307–308
    laser beam rider MANPADS, 308–309
    MANPADS, terrorist acquisition and possession of,
        309–310
    standoff weapons, 310
Terrorist Threat Integration Center (TTIC), 161–162
Terrorist threat, 368–369
    false positive matches and failures for detection,
        181–183
Terrorist travel in aviation mode, tracking, 164–166
Teterboro Airport, 383
Thermal imaging cameras, 286
Thompson, Bennie, 347, 352
Threat image projection (TIP), 72, 202–203
Threats, 104
    aircraft, 104–105
    to aviation infrastructure, 105–106
    involving hostile exploitation of air cargo, 106
    as risk parameter, 133, 134, 135, 141, 145
TIP. *See* Threat image projection
TIP-Ready x-ray (TRX), 202
TOPOFF 2 project, 140
TOSE, R4 framework of resilience, 155, 156
Total Information Awareness program, 166
Tracking aircraft sales, 380–381
Transair Georgia, 316
Transponders, 239–240
Transportation Intelligence Analysis Division, 163, 164
Transportation Intelligence Gazette, 164
Transportation Sector Network Management, 164
Transportation Sector Specific Plan (TSSP), 106–108
Transportation Security Administration (TSA), 74, 139,
        141, 163, 169–170, 187, 237, 238, 241, 242,
        243, 244, 246, 247, 249–252, 263, 290,
        296–297, 341, 344, 346–347, 353, 373

access certificate program, 383
Air Cargo Strategic Plan, 355
aviation security-related budget activities,
        appropriations for, 94
aviation security screening, policy recommendations
        for, 193–197
aviation security spending, 92–96
Checkpoint Evolution design, 211–213
checkpoint procedures for liquids, 210–211
checkpoint screening operations, 201, 204–211
covert testing, 199–202
federal screeners, 61
mandatory air carrier training program, 254–255
Office of Civil Rights, 198
Office of Intelligence (OI), 113–114
Office of Internal Affairs and Program Review, 199
Office of Investigations (TSA-OI), 163, 169, 199,
        200–201
Office of Security Operations, 200–201
Performance Management Information System, 198
regulations, to strengthen air cargo security, 77–78
role in transportation security intelligence, 163–164
RT pilot program, 207–209
staffing needs, 229–230
strategic roles and responsibilities, 113–115
threat image projection, 202–203
workforce, 65
Transportation Security Clearinghouse (TSC), 37, 180,
        292–294
Transportation security intelligence, TSA's role in,
        163–164
Transportation Security laboratory, 216
Transportation Security Officers (TSOs), 79
    broadcasting roles for, 226–227
Transportation Security Operations Center (TSOC), 164,
        263, 265
Transportation Security Oversight Board, 60, 379
Transportation Worker Identification Credential program,
        295
Treasury Enforcement Communications System, 178
Triacetone triper-oxide, 84
Trigger locks, 320
Truck bomb, 369
True negatives, 149
True positives, 149
TSA. *See* Transport Security Administration
TSAAC program. *See* Transport Security Administration,
        access certificate program
TSC. *See* Transportation Security Clearinghouse
TSDB. *See* Terrorist Screening Database
TSO. *See* Transportation Security Officers
TSOC. *See* Transportation Security Operations Center
TSSP. *See* Transportation Sector Specific Plan
TTIC. *See* Terrorist Threat Integration Center
Tuberculosis (TB), 266
Tunnel of truth, 216
Tupolev passenger jets, 316
Tupolev Tu-134A airplane, 316
Tupolev Tu-154B, 316
Turbojet aircraft, 363
TWA flight 800, 100, 167
TWA flight 847, 21–22
Twelve-five security program, 384
Type I errors, 149, 181, 182, 183
Type II errors, 149, 181, 182

U

UAV patrols. *See* Unmanned aerial vehicle patrols
UK airplanes bombing plot, 87–88
Uniform Crime Reporting System, 337
Uninterruptable aircraft transponders, 239
United Airlines, 237
United Airlines DC-6 bombing, 16
United Airlines flight 93, 49
United Airlines flight 175, 49
United States, homegrown terrorists threats in, 88–90
Unmanned aerial vehicle (UAV) patrols, 386
U.S. airliners, bombings of, 336
U.S. aviation security policy, pre 9/11 threats
   aircraft bombing, looming menace, 15–18
   aviation terrorism, significance, 1–2
   failure of imagination and adequate preparation,
      1990s, 30
      Airport Security and Improvement Act of 2000, 37
      FAA Reauthorization Act of 1996, 34–35
      Gore Commission impact on aviation security, 35
      Gore Commission recommendations on aviation
         security, 32–34
      hijackings as forgotten threat, 37
      lingering concerns and persisting vulnerabilities,
         35–37
      scrutiny of FAA aviation safety, 31
   global terrorism, late 1960s and early 1970s, 2
      aviation security roles and responsibilities, debate
         over, 12–15
      Dawson's Field hijackings, 4
      escalating violence and FAA action, 8–10
      hijacking contagion, 6–8
      Middle Eastern terrorist organization, hijackings
         by, 3–4
      overseas hijackings, U.S. response, 4–5
      passenger screening, debate over, 10–12
      terrorist hijackings, international response, 5–6
   shifting threats, 1980s, 18
      aerial suicides and airplanes as missiles, 22–23
      aircraft bombings, escalating threat, 24–25
      Aviation Security Improvements Act of 1990, 29–30
      escalating violence and terrorist animosity, 22
      international aviation security, U.S. initiatives,
         23–24
      Pan Am flight 103 bombing, 25–26
      President's Commission on Aviation Security and
         Terrorism, 26–29
      TWA flight 847 hijacking, 21–22
U.S. Commercial Aviation Partnership (USCAP), 139
U.S. Customs Service, 63, 176
U.S. Department of State, 319, 320
U.S. GA fleet and activity, 362
U.S. policy and strategic approaches, for mitigating
      threat, 318
   aircraft-based protections and countermeasures,
      324–328
   airport security measures, 321–322
   counterterrorism strategies and tactics, 321
   flight operational procedures, 322–324
   nonproliferation and weapons reduction initiatives,
      319–320
   unmanned escorts providing IR-countermeasure
      protection, 328–329
U.S. Postal Service (USPS), 338

U.S. Redeye, 307
U.S. Stinger, 307
U.S. Visitor and Immigrant Status Indicator Technology
      (US-VISIT) program, 178, 209
USA PATRIOT Improvement and Reauthorization Act, 337
USCAP. *See* United States Commercial Aviation
      Partnership
USPS. *See* U.S. Postal Service
USS Cole, 46, 48
USS The Sullivans, attack against, 47
US-VISIT. *See* U.S. Visitor and Immigrant Status
      Indicator Technology program

V

ValuJet accident (1996), 345
ValuJet DC-9, 336
ValuJet flight 592, 100
Verified Identity Pass, Inc., 208, 209
VFR. *See* Visual flight rules
Video surveillance of the airliner cabin, 239
Vienna, 86
Vigilant Eagle system, 330
VIPR team. *See* Visual Intermodal Prevention and
      Response teams
Virginia Department of Aviation, 374
Visa Waiver Program (VWP), 177, 209
Vision 100, 64–66, 70, 73, 342, 343, 366, 379, 382
Visual flight rules (VFR), 51
Visual Intermodal Prevention and Response (VIPR)
      teams, 244
Vulnerability, as risk parameter, 133, 134, 135, 140, 145
VWP. *See* Visa Waiver Program

W

Walk-through ETD portals, 195, 214, 216
Walk-through metal detectors (WTMDs), 213
Washington Executive Airport/Hyde Field, 387
Washington, DC
   ADIZ, 387–389
   airspace restrictions around, 386–387
Wassenaar Arrangement, 319
Watch lists, 166
WBI. *See* Whole body imaging
Weekly Field Intelligence Summary (WFIS), 164
WFIS. *See* Weekly Field Intelligence Summary
"What-if" analyses, 139
Whole body imaging (WBI) systems, 72, 195, 199, 202,
      214, 216–217, 229
Woods, James, 263
Workplace injuries, reducing, 230–231
World Trade Center (WTC), 1, 42
WTC. *See* World Trade Center
WTDMs. *See* Walk-through metal detectors

X

X-ray backscatter systems, 217–218, 349
X-ray screening, 349–350

Y

Young, Don, 171, 247
Yousef, Ramzi, 42, 43